PALO ALTO

ALSO BY MALCOLM HARRIS

Kids These Days: Human Capital and the Making of Millennials

Shit Is Fucked Up and Bullshit: History Since the End of History

PALO ALTO

A HISTORY of CALIFORNIA, CAPITALISM, and THE WORLD

MALCOLM HARRIS

Little, Brown and Company

New York • Boston • London

Little, Brown and Company
Hachette Book Group
1290 Avenue of the Americas, New York, NY 10104
littlebrown.com

First Edition: February 2023

Little, Brown and Company is a division of Hachette Book Group, Inc. The Little, Brown name and logo are trademarks of Hachette Book Group, Inc.

The publisher is not responsible for websites (or their content) that are not owned by the publisher.

The Hachette Speakers Bureau provides a wide range of authors for speaking events. To find out more, go to hachettespeakersbureau.com or call (866) 376-6591.

Excerpt on page 289 from Bob Kaufman's "Caryl Chessman (Reel I, II, III, IV)" originally published in *Golden Sardine* by Coffee House Press. Reprinted with permission.

ISBN 9780316592031
LCCN 2022936529

10 9 8 7 6 5 4 3 2 1

LSC-C

For my father

Contents

Section V
2000–2020

I should be very much pleased if you could find me something good (meaty) on economic conditions in California, of course at my expense. California is very important for me because nowhere else has the upheaval most shamelessly caused by capitalist centralization taken place with such speed.

—*Karl Marx, letter to*
Friedrich Adolph Sorge,
November 5, 1880

PALO
ALTO

Carleton E. Watkins, *El Palo Alto Tree* (ca. 1878)
Guy Miller Archives, Palo Alto Historical Association

Introduction

Palo Alto is nice. The weather is temperate; the people are educated, rich, healthy, innovative. Remnants of a hippie counterculture synthesized with high technology and big finance to produce the spiritually and materially ambitious heart of Silicon Valley. In some circles the small city—population near 70,000, as of this writing—has acquired the mythical reputation of a postmodern El Dorado, where money flows by the billions from the investors on Sand Hill Road to hundreds of garages where scrappy coders are changing the way we do everything, from driving around to eating food. On per-capita terms, the Valley ranks with the planet's wealthiest spots: Qatar, Macao, Luxembourg. A few people seem convinced that Palo Alto is in fact the center of the world.

Leland and Jane Lathrop Stanford gave the town its reason to be and its name, but they weren't the first to colonize the area and they didn't invent the words *palo alto*, which mean "tall tree" in Spanish and refer to a particular specimen. El Palo Alto is a sequoia that got its name from a governor of California—or, rather, the Californias. The Spanish expedition of Gaspar de Portolá was the first European group to reach the San Francisco Bay area, and many of the names they assigned to the natural features remain. (A quarter-millennium or so later, nearby Portola Valley is the richest town per capita in the richest country in the world.) For five days in November of 1769, the expedition camped under a towering tree near what is now San Francisquito Creek. El Palo Alto, now over one thousand years old, still stands, a straight mile shot from Palo Alto High School, right down the train tracks.

Today's settlers find the schools a bigger draw than the foliage. For parents hoping to give their children the best chance at a successful life, the Palo Alto Unified School District is choice. In a society where skills and education are supposed to make the difference, it's hard to make a better tuition-free bet than PAUSD. Even more than the hot job market and the Silicon Valley stock options, the school system is what has driven the median home price up near $3 million at the time of this writing.

I was born in Santa Cruz, California, but my mother and father met in Palo Alto, as a research assistant and a temp typist respectively. They moved our family back to town in 1996, and I spent the second half of my childhood on quiet culs-de-sac in the very nice place. My life felt traditionally United States suburban, a lot like what I saw on TV. But every now and then something else shone through the figurative fence posts at the edge of town. There were signs that, if Palo Alto was normal, it was *too* normal, *weirdly* normal.

I attended Ohlone Elementary — named for what we were told was the tribe that used to live on the Peninsula — and one day in fourth grade we had a substitute teacher. Most of the adults in my life were pretty stable as far as I could tell; I wasn't used to their behaving unpredictably. Maybe that's why I was so spooked that day when, instead of following the regularly scheduled curriculum, the substitute sat us down on the carpet and tried to tell us something important. "You live in a bubble," she said, her voice strained and urgent. "The rest of the world isn't like this. Do you know that?" Two dozen wide-eyed children looked back at her. We did not know that.

I don't recall a lot of specific days from that age, but this one stuck with me. Apparently some of my classmates told their parents about the unscheduled bubble lecture because when he returned, our regular teacher apologized to us for what happened and reassured us that the bad substitute wouldn't be back, that the district had blacklisted her. If that was supposed to make us disregard what we heard, it had the opposite effect on me.

As I grew up, Palo Alto gradually offered its own explanation for why things were the way they were — why some people had big houses and others didn't, why some people lived here and everyone else didn't: They deserved it. Hard work and talent allowed some people to change the world single-handedly, and they earned whatever they got. Sometimes this message was literally written on the walls — like the stories about Hewlett and Packard in the Stanford engineering building, printed on a permanent informational display near a water fountain I frequented as a teenager — but it was also the town's implicit underlying ideology from its founding. We all got the message.

The suicides started in 2002. That year, a Palo Alto High freshman stepped in front of the Caltrain, the same locomotive line on which Leland Stanford built the town. Thirteen months later, one of his classmates ended his life the same way. Both picked the Churchill Avenue crossing, right near the school. In 2009, four more students between the ages of thirteen and seventeen killed themselves at the Meadow Drive crossing near their school, Gunn High. Another string of Palo Alto teenagers died by train in 2014 and 2015. These deaths were well publicized, particularly as a social-scientific example of the rare "double cluster" of suicidality, as if it were an unusual astrological phenomenon. The *Atlantic* magazine ran a cover story on the "Silicon Valley Suicides," and no investigation of self-destructive teens was complete without a reference to Palo Alto.[1] One thing the coverage missed was that the official tally undercounts the victims by at least half because it excludes young people who killed themselves after graduation, even when they returned to the tracks to do it. The community experienced not two clusters but a constant flow of tragic deaths in the twenty-first century. It continues: a month before I finished this manuscript, a twenty-two-year-old Gunn High graduate ended his life on the tracks.

As kids, when we talked about the place where we lived, my brother, sister, and I used to make morbid jokes about Sunnydale, the fictional California setting for the TV show *Buffy the Vampire Slayer*, where perfect weather conceals the portal to hell under the high school. As I got older, I began to think of the idea earnestly. We have a word for idyllic towns where the youth suicide rate is three times as high as it's supposed to be: *haunted*. Palo Alto is haunted.

When I say haunted, I don't mean haunted in the ghost sense, not exactly, or at least not necessarily. We use the word all the time without referring to actual phantoms. We can be haunted by a loss or a traumatic event or even by that dumb thing we said that one time. Haunting happens when a past action won't go away, won't stay past. But the word usually refers to a relation between the living and the dead: There's an imbalance between the realms, something stuck where it isn't supposed to be. Haunting is homologous with theft, which also involves things being where they shouldn't, but we're not talking about a stolen wallet; it takes more than that to disturb hell. What haunts are the kinds of large historical crimes that, once committed, can never truly be set right.

The simplest imbalance between the living and the dead is just that: We're still here and they're not. When it comes to my classmates, the division feels arbitrary. Some of those who died were depressive, some weren't—a description of the living as well. Anything you could say about them you could say about us, too, except the one. That has haunted me, and I have struggled to find a way to approach it as a writer. There is a whole pile of journalistic investigations of the Palo Alto suicides, as well as a long Centers for Disease Control report, and I've found them uniformly unsatisfying in a way that suggests a problem with the medium rather than the reporters. I have no interest in writing a suburban California survival memoir, either, and I write about myself like a bad bowler anyway, always headed straight for the gutters of historical context rather than for the pins of personal revelation.

One thing I learned about in Palo Alto was C. Wright Mills's concept of the sociological imagination, which he describes as a tool people can use to "understand what is happening in themselves as minute points of the intersections of biography and history within society."[2] Much like the sociological imagination, a haunting pulls together biography and history on the social field. Haunting connects the haunted to unseen lineages of historical responsibility. The cursed painting looted in the Holocaust, the construction project that disturbs an Indian burial ground, the pollution that awakens a swamp monster: These are social crimes from which some suffer and others profit. Hauntings are a reversal: The profiteers are made to suffer. At its best, superstition reminds us not to take advantage of others, even if nobody will ever see us doing it. The violations are embedded, written in the world. Something knows. But the revenge targeting is rarely quick or exact, and in our haunting narratives, when a curse comes alive, it's often those nearest to the loot who end up paying. It's the inheritors, the unsuspecting couple who buys an old house, or the violator's descendants, the children, those who were meant to cleanse the ill-gotten fortune with their innocence and carry it into the future, their naiveté an element of the crime.

"The children of California shall be our children," Leland Stanford told his wife, Jane, when they decided to build Palo Alto. It's a grandiose claim, but as applied to me it's not as inaccurate as I'd prefer. History doesn't stay put: It works itself under your skin in fragments like shrapnel; it steals into your bloodstream like an infection. I'm a product of my environment, and I'm shot through with its symptoms. If that experience is to be useful rather than obfuscating, then it's as a place to start, a set of intersections between biography and history.

With some sociological imagination, in the following five sections I'm going to focus my attention back up the historical tracks, the line that happened into what Mills would call my biography and spun my particular life into being. I'm not a character worth naming in that history, and the reader will be spared my childhood recollections from here on. Rather, I understand myself as a result of something the town founders called the Palo Alto System. It's that haunted system I pull apart in this book, a system that has become centrally important to the present era no matter where you look.

Palo Alto is a bubble. I do know that now, but it's an important bubble for the twentieth century, and a thorough accounting of the town's role explains a lot about California, the United States, and the capitalist world, where it has found itself elevated to the status of promised land. That story fills the following pages.

Section I

1850–1900

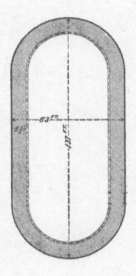

DIAGRAM A—COVERED TRAINING-PAD-
DOCK—DISTANCE AROUND CENTER
OF DRIVE 313 FEET.

Diagram of Palo Alto "kindergarten track," in Charles Marvin,
Training the Trotting Horse (1890)

To Whom Time Is Money

The Uneventful Conquest of Alta California — Gold
Rush — West Coast Genocide — The New Almaden
Mine — Immigrant Agriculture — Bank of America

To speak of the Ohlone is to speak of the broken link between the Bay Area's indigenous people and the Bay Area itself. Disease — rather than extermination campaigns, death by labor, or environmental destruction — killed half of the approximately 300,000 Alta California Indians during the Spanish and Mexican periods, beginning in 1769 and 1821 respectively. It's worth noting that these populations were not uniquely vulnerable to the spread of intercontinental disease in the nineteenth century, which killed millions of people all around the world. I mention this not to soften the cruelty of Spanish colonization but rather to make clear that there was no natural tendency toward the elimination of the California Indians. But when the United States showed up, the rules changed.

Unlike the Armenian genocide or the Nazi Holocaust, the California genocide was a bottom-up, settler-led process. And yet unlike the eastern states, California was a project of a United States federal government. The resulting synthesis of grassroots action and national planning expanded the country at a speed the world had not seen before. California settlers didn't negotiate. "Government officials apparently preferred to kill California Indians rather than make peace or honor treaties," writes Benjamin Madley in *An American Genocide: The United States and the California Indian Catastrophe, 1846–1873*, his blow-by-blow reconstruction of the state's eliminationist program.[1] Historians like Madley are still trying to reconstruct the massacres: Militias guarded water sources and tried to force every Indian onto rancherias, where they were enslaved. Settlers slaughtered the members of indigenous communities by the hundreds, and the federal government as well as the new state of California paid them to do it. There was no single Ohlone tribe; anthropologists used the term to refer to the dozens of small, distinct regional groups that occupied the South Bay when white settlers broke the mutualistic relationship of belonging between humans and the rest of the ecology. As California became California, settlers forced the Ohlone to become the Ohlone.

The adventurer John C. Frémont was a perfect synthesis of U.S. federal authority and U.S. "just some guys." On the one hand, he was a commissioned officer in the federal army and the son-in-law of Thomas Hart Benton, who had been a senator from the state of Missouri for as long as there had been a state of Missouri; on the other hand, he was a topographer by trade and an adventurer by vocation, accustomed to making decisions far away from and out of communication with his bosses. This was a useful combination for the federal authorities at the time, and in 1845 the expansionist president James K. Polk sent him on a military expedition to survey the Rockies and the Sierra Nevadas, conveniently located in poorly defended Mexican territory. Frémont got the message, from Polk and from the manifest-destiny-inspired Benton, and he took his handful of soldiers through the mountains to the Pacific. Along the way, Frémont stirred up nationalist sentiment among Anglo settlers in Alta California, implying (but not declaring) that he was there to help them break the territory away from Mexico and deliver it to the United States as their countrymen had recently done with the Lone Star Republic, which he was. Resentful of answering in any fashion to the absentee Mexican government and worried about the legitimacy of their land claims (which varied), the settlers were already primed to revolt.

Frémont's entrepreneurial insurrectionism paid off, and in the summer of 1846, a few dozen Anglo dudes rode on the pueblo of Sonoma from Napa Valley, bloodlessly seized the ex-Spanish installations, and took Colonel Mariano Vallejo prisoner. Out of a Chilean flour sack and some scraps of flannel the men made a flag, adding a single star alluding to the breakaway republic's statehood aspirations. Without much else to occupy them, they drew "something that they called a Bear" onto the flag with berry juice and hoisted the banner over the empty Sonoma Barracks.[2] Then, with no one to fight, they waited, drank, and assigned themselves titles. Ten days later Frémont arrived, took command, and rode south with 120 or so men looking for Mexicans. The American military gang spent the spring practicing on California Indians, massacring unknown hundreds in repeated acts of wanton brutality. Mexico didn't present the same opportunity, and Frémont's troops (now informed that, in fact, Mexico and the United States had been at war since April) occupied the old coastal military infrastructure almost entirely without shooting, which was lucky because they didn't have much gunpowder left. The number of Frémont's combined volunteer and uniformed army forces never topped 500, and the U.S. Navy sailed into Los Angeles unopposed. The federal government was prepared to renounce Frémont if things went badly, as they had renounced William Walker when his tiny 1853 invasion of Baja California and Sonora failed. But in more sparsely colonized Alta California everything worked out, and even a court-martial resulting from Frémont's semi-rogue campaign didn't stop him from getting elected the state's first U.S. senator.

The short-lived Bear Flag Republic was now a United States territory, but the title was no long-term guarantee. Greater Mexico proved far too unwieldy for Spanish colonial occupation, and independent Mexico suffered from the same problem. The country not only lost Alta California, New Mexico, and Texas to conquest in the north, it was also fighting a losing war with Maya insurgents in the Yucatán, to the south. California was isolated from the rest of the United States, much farther from the White House than it was from Mexico City. Frémont felt safe massacring unarmed indigenous groups in 1846, but the Anglo settlers were vastly outnumbered, and the tables could turn fast—never mind the European powers and wildcards like Russia and the Chinese. In the West, the United States was out on a limb.

What the United States needed was for a bunch of people to go to California and stay there, anchor the territory, and ready it for statehood. The problem was that there were not a whole lot of reasons for settlers to try it. The sea routes around the Cape of Good Hope or down to British Nicaragua and up the West Coast after an overland trek were long, dangerous, and expensive; the Oregon Trail across the continent was even worse. When they got to the California territory, settlers found unsurpassed natural beauty and unbelievable biodiversity, but the pecuniary prospects—the only thing that could lure them in large numbers—were not all that great at first. There was plenty of land but no one was especially enthusiastic about working it for profit. Indians comprised the vast majority of laborers (as they comprised the vast majority of the population), but their connection to the land always left them an exit if the contracted terms were insufficiently remunerative. Wages tended to be high, which allowed Indians to labor on their own seasonal terms, supplementing traditional subsistence practices with paid work and maintaining independence from white employers. And though some Anglos kept workers under conditions we can uncontroversially describe as involuntary servitude, and some southern Anglo immigrants held on to their black slaves regardless of if not in defiance of the law, Frémont was a Free Soiler and the slave trade was banned in the territory. The United States could not rely on slave dealers to profitably colonize the West Coast the way they had Texas. California had plenty of land, but there was a lot of space between the western states and the Pacific coast and ambitious settlers didn't have to go all the way out there to get started. For Europeans and Anglo-Americans to want to go settle in California before 1848, they had to be a bit weird.

One of those weirdos was John Sutter. Born Johann, the Swiss merchant ditched his wife, children, and debts in Europe to seek his fortune in the West. His circuitous route indicates just how far Alta California was from Anglo territory: Sutter only arrived in the Bay after traveling through New Mexico, Vancouver, and Hawaii. Yerba Buena (now San Francisco) was the final stop, and he stuck around there, traveling up the river and establishing a fort and farm complex after talking the Mexican governor into a land grant of just under 50,000 acres. Sutter invited American settlers, establishing them as an overseer caste above the Indians who made up the majority of workers on the wheat ranch. He named the complex New Helvetia, and reports describe it as on par with southern plantations in its horrors. Sutter enslaved hundreds of Miwok, Nisenan Maidu, and "missionized" Ohlone Indians during harvest time.[3] Although whites were racially outnumbered between 100 to one and 1,000 to one in the region, Sutter relied on brutality as well as racial division to secure his place, importing native workers from Hawaii and South Asia. Still, he suffered from the same problems as the Spanish settlers did: California Indians were on their own land, where they could provide for themselves just fine. For some Indians, white people who didn't guard their horses well enough became another natural resource.

Anglo settlers denigrated Alta California Indians, and in particular Ohlone communities, as "diggers" who lacked accumulative agriculture practices. Although they did use digging sticks to pry up edible bulbs, Bay Area Indians enjoyed an outstandingly diverse diet based on seasonal community rotation. Nomadic in the sense of not having permanent constructed dwellings, the Ohlone moved in response to abundance rather than scarcity, and individual communities maintained small, consistent territories. Natural cycles of ripening and spawning dictated short periods of intense hunting and collecting labor, followed by longer periods of social luxury. To European settlers who had no idea what was going on, the natives seemed lazy. But California Indian life was exceedingly complicated, rooted in the qualities of many different plants and particular flocks and herds. That map of specificity included one of the densest concentrations of human linguistic and cultural diversity scholars have ever been able to reconstruct anywhere in world history. If California Indian life appeared too easy to Europeans it's because the former could rely on thousands of years of enduring knowledge about their environment.

The settlers, by contrast—especially socially isolated settlers like Johann Sutter, who was half on the run from creditors—didn't know anything about where they were. To combat Indian specificity, they wielded the scientific power of white genericity: one day like the next, one bushel of wheat like the next, one bowl of gruel like the next, one worker like the next, and (most important) one gold dollar like the next. Historian Albert L. Hurtado describes the impact of Sutter on the region, in particular the bell he used to summon Indians to work:

> Sutter's bell heralded the arrival of a modern sense of time in the Sacramento Valley...Now, for at least part of their lives, some Indians were wedded to a concept that proclaimed that time was limited and that it had economic value. The clang of Sutter's bell announced that time was money, that it marched onward, and that it waited for no man, including Indians in the 1840s. Necessarily, the arrival of the modern sense of time coincided with the establishment of market agriculture, which in turn was linked with an international economic network.[4]

When Sutter couldn't entice enough workers on the right terms with wages or credit he used force, but harvest was only one season, and it was more efficient to let the majority of workers feed themselves off the land most of the year. There weren't nearly enough whites (or sufficient demand for year-round wage labor) to institute total rule by the bell. That all changed when Sutter built a sawmill on the American River, a precursor to the city he wanted to build on his land. In 1848, a carpenter he employed named James Marshall brought Sutter some rocks he'd found in a drainage ditch. Marshall was pretty sure it was gold, and try as they might, the two of them couldn't disprove it. When word got around, Sutter's workers quit to go looking for nuggets. And when word got to San Francisco, the river was soon awash in what came to be called forty-niners.

The gold strike on the American River wasn't the first sign that there was precious ore in the region. For example, a Mexican soldier named Andres Castillero acquired a land grant to an ancient cinnabar (mercury ore) mine in the South Bay in 1846, though the grant became difficult to enforce soon after. But nuggets of gold that you could pluck off the ground was a whole different ball game. Gold was money, *the* universal equivalent, good for buying basically anything anywhere you could buy things, which at the time was more of the world every day. The allure to opportunistic settlers was unmatchable: *There was money on the ground.* Men (and the settler population was almost all men) dropped what they were doing and headed for the gold fields. Boats stacked up abandoned in the harbor as crews disappeared up the river. Settlers hiked down from the Oregon Territory up north. No boss made as good an offer as California's waterways did in the early days of the gold rush. Using pans with ridges patterned on Indian baskets, the miners filtered rivers and streams, dragging gold-flecked sediment through their hands. As it turned out, the world center of cultural and biological diversity was also full of generic gold, and whites couldn't get enough.

The forty-niners destroyed the Alta California Indian lifeworld in a different and much more comprehensive manner than the Spanish and Mexican settlers did. Unlike the ranchers, the surface miners needed little capital for overhead, and they had incentive to spread quickly. With their complex societies Indians lived off the land efficiently, communing abundantly in small territories for countless generations. Gold mining is much the opposite, single-mindedly exhausting territory and moving on to the next as fast as possible, extracting and piling inorganic nonreplenishing nuggets and dust until it seems like it might be easier to get it somewhere else. Instead of cycling with the seasons, mining moved linearly, exponentially, cumulatively. There is no such thing as enough gold. The forty-niners disregarded the Mexican land grants, which the United States promised to respect according to the treaty between the two countries, pushing the descendants of Spanish colonists off the good spots. Claim jumping was par for the course for streambed "placer" miners, and the first jumped claims belonged to the Indians. As violent whites crowded them off their land, California's indigenous peoples lost the basis for their shared existence; in their place, white men found a basis for their own.

Gold rushers were not really settlers — at least most of them didn't think of themselves that way. They were there to stack up gold and go back or onward, rich. Even after the state's inaugural constitution — itself a rogue affair — and California's quick incorporation as a "free" state to balance Texas in the Compromise of 1850, the men weren't coming to stay, and their behavior reflected that. Greed and opportunism were an unstable basis for a society, but a war of all against all wasn't good for business, either. If you spent your time jumping claims, you never got any gold. In the frontier camps, miners formed crude protocols for collective governance. Immortalized in Charles Howard Shinn's 1885 account, *Mining Camps: A Study in American Frontier Government*, these temporary associations of free men settled property disputes and kept retaliatory violence between the guys under control. But this was Anglo-Californian self-government, and that hardly described the mass of miners. Gold was nearly universal, and people came in large numbers from anywhere they could: French adventurers, Chinese fortune seekers, experienced miners up from Chile and the northern Mexican region of Sonora. "Difficulties with such foreigners were inevitable," Shinn writes, "and they only served to weld the Americans into a closer union."[5] Excluding foreigners and Indians from gold claims became a raison d'être for the miner councils and then for the Golden State government itself.

From the beginning, the state of California was a whiteness cartel, defining national belonging in relation to territorial access. In 1850, the state passed the Foreign Miners' Tax Act, assessing a monthly rent for access to the land, putting everyone else at a comparative disadvantage. It wasn't a bad deal for, say, French miners, who could (for a fee) secure claims that in former days the Anglos might have simply bullied them off of, but the protections didn't apply universally. The state's civil and criminal procedural codes excluded testimony from Indians and black people in cases involving white people. The testimony

ban ensured that nonwhites could not protect themselves from white predation—that they had no claim a white man was bound to respect. In 1853,
George Hall appealed his conviction for the murder of miner Ling Sing to the
California Supreme Court, and the judges ruled for Hall, concurring in a ruling full of bizarre race science that the Chinese were also ineligible to testify
against whites because to allow them to do so opened the door to full civic
equality.[6] The result was that California's whites were legally permitted to kill
nonwhites as long as no other whites complained. Mining-camp governance
and the state it birthed didn't simply quell violence: It stoked it, focused it, and
organized it along racial lines.

With the state endorsing white supremacy by statute, American miners
turned their attacks on the Indians into a national mission. In the decades following the gold rush, these settlers murdered and plundered on their country's
behalf, organizing themselves into Indian-hunting militias that demanded
payment from the state, which in turn demanded reimbursement from the
feds. The synthesis between national power and grassroots initiative was similar to the one that drove the Bear Flag Revolt and Frémont's campaign, now
with the additional state layer. The first civilian governor of California, Peter
Burnett, explained in his 1851 state of the state address that "the white man,
to whom time is money, and who labors hard all day to create the comforts
of life, cannot sit up all night to watch his property; and after being robbed a
few times, he becomes desperate, and resolves upon a war of extermination."[7]
He provided direct support for the genocidal project with an 1855 law that
assessed an annual 25-cent tax on all fighting-age white men who didn't join
a militia, a tax the legislature doubled the next year. The big giveaway, however, was federal: The 1855 Bounty Land Act offered 160 acres to any soldier
or militia member who fought for two weeks or more. Predictably, California
militias embarked on rinky-dink expeditions against unarmed Indians, killing a few at a time and confiscating land. With these land grants, settlers saw a
future in California, and they advanced inland and north, driving an increasing number of tribal communities from territory that the militiamen then
received in payment. The Bounty Land Act was a prelude to the 1862 Homestead Act, which offered the same 160 acres to settlers who spent five years
improving the land, drawing an equivalence with two weeks of Indian killing.
And the federal government sent hundreds of thousands of dollars to the state

to pay California's "war debt," thanks to the support of Louisiana senator (and future Confederate secretary of state) Judah P. Benjamin. It was a particularly American mode of legalized conquest, plot by plot.

On the stolen land, miners planted wheat, barley, and oats—not as valuable as gold, though similarly generic—but the population wasn't set up for a plantation economy. To become gentlemen farmers the settlers needed laborers, and there weren't many around. As a result, even displaced Indians (who comprised the majority of potential wage workers) commanded high pay. The Anglos came to the same conclusion as the Swiss psychopath Johann Sutter did: forced labor, enslavement. While free workers commanded at least a dollar a day, farmers could buy Indian captives from labor contractors for not much more than a month's wages. While black slaves in the South sold for upwards of $1,000 each, planters could get kidnapped California Indians for under $100 per person. White women were nearly absent from the coast, and white men enslaved Indian women and children for domestic labor, including sex. Militia campaigns drove Indians off their land into Anglo homes and fields. Slavery was illegal, but so was Indian testimony, and in the early 1860s, California slave raiding peaked, which along with technological improvements in mining and wheat agriculture finally drove down the price of Indian wage labor. By 1870, scarcely twenty years since the initial rush, California's settlers had destroyed 80 percent of the California Indians by one estimate, bringing the population from 150,000 down to 30,000—"quite possibly the most extreme demographic disaster of all time," in the words of historian Roxanne Dunbar-Ortiz.[8] Commenting on the public abuse of one young Indian farm laborer who was dragged behind a horse in Mendocino County in 1865, a Sacramento reporter scoffed about the supposed ban on forced labor: "So much for slavery in California."[9]

Move Fast and Break Things

As Albert Hurtado notes, California Indians were not alone in being pushed off their land into a harsh new historical epoch in the second half of the nineteenth century. Settler colonialists seized and enclosed agricultural lands around the world, forcing peasant and indigenous communities into capitalist work, whether waged, enslaved, or (most prevalent) somewhere desperate in between. "The age of empire was dead; that of free traders, economists, and calculators had succeeded," wrote economist Eric Williams of Atlantic plantation slavery's collapse. Beginning in the 1840s, "the whole world...became a British colony."[10] The London-led imperial core optimized its overseas territories for genericity and export, undermining subsistence systems, and as a result millions of people died of starvation from Ireland to India. Starving the peasants into the factories is the classic narrative of proletarianization, the creation story of the industrial working class. California didn't have the factories of a Manchester, UK; a Lyon, France; or a Lowell, Massachusetts, but the state took on a factory orientation toward what it did have, which was gold and land. Unlike so much of the world, California did not see capitalist economics evolve step-by-step out of feudal property relations. Capital hit California like a meteor, alien tendrils surging from the crash site.

It didn't take long for the forty-niners to exhaust the placer mines. In the absence of accumulative economies, gold didn't have much to offer California Indians — some communities ceremonially destroyed people's possessions with them when they died because those items were thought to have died spiritually with their specific owners. Much of Ohlone material culture, like the reed huts and canoes they remade every year, was intentionally disposable. By contrast, the gold miners were linked to a burgeoning global financial system, and they fed a bottomless pit of demand as fast as they could. But soon the system of distributed independent miners, with their iron pans, small claims, and murder militias, could no longer pull out gold at the same awe-inspiring rate. It was time for the capitalists to take over. The initial model for California gold mining didn't have much to do with blowing bedrock; instead, miners used water to wash sediment, letting the exceptionally heavy gold fall to the bottom of their collecting pans. The genius engineers of genericity figured out that, in order to get their yield up, there were two things they could do: more and faster.

First, miners upgraded from the pans to rockers, essentially big narrow pans made out of lumber with a filtered hopper on top to catch large stones. The men set the boxes up on an incline, piled sediment in the hopper, and washed it downhill through the trough with a bucket of water, rocking the hopper frame to get the water washing the rocks and dirt into the filter, then the wooden channel, then over a series of riffles that caught the dense gold.

One miner could operate a rocker by himself, and without a constant flow of water. The Long Tom was a step up, a giant rocker 10 or 20 feet long whose operation required several men at a time as well as a constant natural flow of water. California Chinese miners could find secure employment in these jobs if they were willing to forgo the potential upsides of independence, and racist laws made them cheaper to hire than Anglos. From there, investors scaled the model, combining boxes into channels hundreds of feet long and diverting natural waterways into their sluice boxes. A little mercury at the bottom helped collect the tiny bit of gold "flour." The more efficient the model, the more investment capital was required—for research into claims, for engineers and construction, for expensive field provisions, and for employees. (More capital also meant more mercury flushed into the regional water system.) The frontier community of free white gold miners with nothing but the clothes on their backs disintegrated as specialists such as engineers and managers took over operations on behalf of clean-handed investors.

The sluice box channels were water-powered, but hydraulic mining, or hydrolicking, used the fluid element in a different way: Instead of digging up sediment to wash, hydrolickers used pressurized water to do the digging for them, intensifying their work by orders of magnitude. Using metal pipes and then canvas hoses (followed by leather, rubber, and hybrid models), California mining engineers washed away whole hillsides looking for golden veins. It was brand new technology, relying on ironworks that could forge the necessary high-pressure nozzles and connectors, and it was incredibly destructive. That was the idea, to drag as much of the land as possible over some riffles as fast as possible, to unearth the earth. Hydrolickers carved away whole mining-camp villages, washing their own geological legs out from under them. No problem; they could move on. But they were a menace to anyone who wanted to settle in California for the long term, including farmers and other property owners who didn't appreciate all the sediment washing into their land. The complaints reached a fever pitch and in 1884, California federal district court judge Lorenzo Sawyer—a friend of the railroad—banned hydrolicking as a public nuisance.[11] There was still some gold to be had in California, particularly now in hard-rock mining, but the water-powered rush of '49 was definitely over. At least in California.

The rush called into being a new creature: the California engineer, master of water, stone, and labor. These frontier scientists were a superior, more evolved form of the panner, still entrepreneurial (and often motivated by an equity share in the project rather than a wage) but also dependable and often college-educated. California exported these men to English-speaking colonies, from the Hawaiian Islands to British-occupied India and Palestine to South Africa and Australia to foreign-owned mines in South America and East Asia. There they replicated their Golden State experience, turning the water against the land and subordinating the nonwhite laboring populations. California's cowboy scientists helped transform the colonies for commodity agriculture and the societies for white capitalist rule, increasing the profitability and therefore the plausibility of colonial projects. As Jessica Teisch observes in her book *Engineering Nature: Water, Development, and the Global Spread of American Environmental Expertise*, the "California model" was so adaptable because it reformatted the relationships between capital, labor, and the environment according to a generic formula: Anglos rule; all natives are Indians; all land and water is just gold waiting to happen. Geopolitics took on the character of the gold rush, as European colonial powers engaged in competitive scrambles for colonial territory in sub-Saharan Africa and China.

California engineers became the heralds of proletarianization around the world, the shock troops of global enclosure, drawing the lines that so many others were forced to follow. In their packs they carried very particular ideas gleaned from the Golden State about how society should be arranged. "Engineers played a central role in inventing and implementing racialized labor practices in the British colonies, similar to practices that had developed to ensure White supremacy in the multiethnic American West," writes Jeffrey Michael Bartos in his study of transnational gold extraction around the turn of the twentieth century. These practices included "different pay scales and job assignments based on race, a callous disregard for the health [of] nonwhite miners, importing scab labor, and leveraging perceived racial differences to suppress the wages paid to all of the miners who worked the ore seams."[12] The Wild West was the model for a new world, an integrated sphere of value and labor flows arranged according to white power and generic accumulation. If European leaders came to see the rest of the earth as their private juice box, then California's engineers were on the ground aiming the straw.

Though it was a planetary phenomenon, there is perhaps no better example of proletarianization than the burgeoning Santa Clara County, growing up around the old Santa Clara mission, in particular the pueblo of San Jose. In the middle of its South Bay territory, the Spanish mission disintegrated the traditional Ohlone "tribelets" and the general lifeworld. Yet there remained a significant minority population of Ohlone in Santa Clara County into the early 1850s, and with the Mexican majority they centered around the ancient San Jose mercury mine. The colonists named it for Spain's richest mercury-ore mine, suggesting that they had a hint how profitable New Almaden would be. Unable to get to his claim during the war, the Mexican grantee leased it to the British import-export firm Barron, Forbes & Company, which successfully exploited the reserves. In the years following the war, "no other California locale of comparable importance to Mexican Americans experienced such an immediate change" as San Jose and the Santa Clara Valley, writes historian Stephen Pitti.[13] The prewar immigrant population increased by nearly 25 times by 1860, from around 150 to over 3,500, contemporaneous with a breathtaking demographic collapse for Santa Clara County Indians, from 450 in 1852 to only 29. For almost all Mexicans, becoming Mexican-American meant losing your land, because U.S. authorities invalidated Mexican land claims in contravention of the Treaty of Guadalupe Hidalgo. Only 26 Mexican-Americans could still call themselves professionally landed in California at the end of the decade. This process of racial expropriation culminated in 1863, when the United States Supreme Court invalidated Andres Castillero's claim to the New Almaden mine and turned it over to the Quicksilver Mining Company of New York.[14]

New Almaden collected proletarianized Mexicans like mercury at the bottom of a gold pan, concentrating California's largest Spanish-speaking population in San Jose. The mine offered more industrial jobs than any other enterprise in the state, and hundreds of Chicanos found themselves employed underground, a new racialized low-wage workforce. By 1860, 55 percent of Mexican-American men in San Jose were laborers. "No Californio or Mexicano resident entered a professional position in the county [of Santa Clara] between 1860 and 1900," writes Pitti in *The Devil in Silicon Valley: Northern California, Race, and Mexican Americans*.[15] Between the Ohlone (who held a default claim predating enclosure) and Mexican landowners, at the end of the 1850s there were fewer than 60 people left in Santa Clara County with a pre-Anglo claim to land. The rest had to work.

When the Quicksilver Mining Company took over at New Almaden, workers quickly realized they faced a new, worse order. The American owners took a holistic orientation toward the workers, extending the mine's control over their lives. Quicksilver instituted a company store, monopolizing commerce in "Spanishtown" and jacking up prices for new, inferior goods. The owners claimed title to everything on company land, including the homes workers built for themselves and even the firewood they were accustomed to harvesting for use and sale.* Quicksilver banned independent peddlers, merchants, and water carriers, as well as Mexican-run taverns and restaurants. In their place, a company saloon served expensive rotgut. The new mine owners changed the compensation metric to one they controlled and started paying monthly instead of biweekly like the Brits had. Real wages fell, and workers ended up in perpetual debt, borrowing to pay for essentials such as food and funerals. By 1865, New Almaden's Mexican laborers had had enough of U.S. capitalism, and at least 600 of them (along with some white coworkers) halted production and issued a set of reform demands. The Quicksilver company petitioned the genocidal state militia, which in turn petitioned the Northern California regiment of the Union Army, which, having finished defeating slavery, came to San Jose to intimidate the state's largest Mexican-American community back into the mine. What had been a relative haven for the state's Spanish-speaking population during the war and gold rush years became a trap. As much as anywhere this was the birthplace of the Mexican proletariat, forged in contrast and service to the new white owners of California.

The San Jose mercury mine provided the setting for a century of stories about post-'49 California pioneer life.[16] In the mid-1870s, the New Almaden superintendent, Arthur Foote, brought his talented and educated wife out from New York to join him in the Bay and then on a series of engineering assignments throughout the West. Mary Hallock Foote was an artist with a command of the written word, and without too much expected of her in a community devoid of married white women, she became a correspondent for

---

* The criminalization of "wood theft" was a symptom of proletarianization around the world during this period. Restriction of the poor's traditional access to firewood in the 1840s inspired one 25-year-old magazine writer in the German Rhineland to begin formulating a concept of a ruling class that collaborated to exploit the emerging mass of workers. See Daniel Bensaïd, *The Dispossessed: Karl Marx's Debates on Wood Theft & the Right of the Poor* (University of Minnesota Press, 2021).

publications back home, writing and illustrating stories from New Almaden for *Scribner's*. Her first piece, "A California Mining Camp," published in 1878, tells of an exotic land with a camp of energetic white workers living segregated from and geographically above a village of Mexicans with their "dark-eyed women" who look at you with a "grave stare like that of a child" and whiskey-drenched men who repeat to Foote their single phrase: "No possible, Señora!"[17] As to why she doesn't see any elderly Mexicans, Foote concludes that they must be a "feeble race," which helps explain why they seem to exist to serve her. (There are no Indians in Foote's account, only Mexican proletarians with brown skin and dark hair.) The Chinese, too, are servants by nature ("A Mexican brought our wood—of course a Chinaman chopped it"), and she records their "profane and hardened baby-talk." She figured herself as a white lady castaway in a land populated by races of childlike servants, and the country's magazine readers ate it up. The Footes also served as the models for the noble Susan and Oliver Ward in Wallace Stegner's 1971 historical novel *Angle of Repose*, which turned the Mexican and Chinese workers at New Almaden into background scenery for a rugged settler romance based on Mary's real-life letters, winning Stegner the Pulitzer Prize and delivering Foote's settler colonialist perspective to new generations of readers.

At New Almaden we can see the steps in the proletarianization dance: the alienation of indigenous and peasant populations from the land, the formal establishment of white racial rule, scientific management continually optimizing for maximum profits, looming soldiers. It all adds up to a laboring class with no legal way to reproduce their lives except to sell themselves hour by hour to an employer, on the employer's terms.* Anglo-American settlers found

---

* A few became bandits, though not particularly "social" ones in the famous Robin Hood terminology of historian Eric Hobsbawm; Chinese immigrants made good targets since they lacked the law's protection. (John Boessenecker, "California Bandidos: Social Bandits or Sociopaths?" *Southern California Quarterly* vol. 80, no. 4 [Winter 1998], 419–34.) The most famous of these brigands was Joaquin Murieta, a legendary Sonoran forty-niner who turned to banditry after being violently dispossessed of his claim by Anglos. Murieta is the subject of John Rollin Ridge's 1854 *Life and Adventures of Joaquín Murieta*, California's first novel and the source material for the character Zorro, who was recharacterized as the do-good costumed son of a wealthy landowner and rechronologized in California's Spanish colonial or Mexican periods, obscuring the story's anti-imperial origin and Ridge's perspective as a Cherokee man born in the 1820s. John Rollin Ridge, *The Life and Adventures of Joaquín Murieta* (Penguin Classics, 2018).

themselves correspondingly enfranchised, whether squatting on land until the government recognized their claims or getting grants legitimately by joining a militia gang and murdering Indians on the state's behalf. California's agriculture was ranch-based, with amber waves of grain and large herds of cattle, so there was no significant yeoman tradition. Instead, California smallholders saw their titles as speculative investments that they could sell or rent to planters and other capitalists, less territory than an increasingly valuable entry in the expanding U.S. property register. After the Homestead Act, for example, mill owners encouraged their employees to register timber claims and then lease them to the company. That didn't always work out so great for the small speculators, as I'll explain in the following chapter, but they weren't wrong about the land's potential value. It soon came to outshine even the gold.

All the Way to the Bank

After paying out to the easterners and Europeans who helped finance the rush of '49, the relatively small California capitalists were looking for new opportunities. They found a big one in Nevada with the Comstock Lode's first hit, in 1859, an exploding sequence of silver bonanzas to end all silver bonanzas that helped codify the membership of the West Coast aristocracy and its important institutions. What few cattle operations were left over from the Mexican period failed frequently in the 1860s in the face of natural disasters and falling prices, which aided the squatters and their U.S. government in efforts to transfer land claims to the Anglos. Wheat boomed, along with oats to power the horses and other draft animals who dragged the farm equipment. Santa Clara Valley farmers could rely on natural aquifers, which allowed them to skip the costly irrigation systems that much of the rest of the state required. Lucky for California's remaining planters, there was still some money on the West Coast—after all, the state's big industry was money mining. The Bank of California opened in 1864 as the nation's first commercial bank, successfully investing deposits in Comstock silver claims and reinvesting in California agriculture. The state now had a new capitalist class to mirror its new working class, and they doubled down on commodity crops, plowing mining money into monoculture (mostly grains, but also wine grapes) and triggering boom-and-bust cycles. By the end of the 1860s, California agriculture topped gold in terms of both employment and output value. In only 20 years the gold rush had started, finished, and transitioned the state to a new economic foundation.

When it came to agriculture, California held a competitive advantage over the rest of the country—money, which financed scale and mechanization, pioneering factorylike efficiency in the fields. The state had twice as much machinery and equipment (by value) per farm as the national average and three times as many draft animals.[18] As a result, individual holdings were more than three times as large. This was industrial agriculture, and it was new to the world, but it was also the only kind California's Anglo capitalists knew. Having shaken off the Mexican feudal bonds—never all that tight in Alta California to begin with—the state's planters and engineers trained a techno-scientific maximizing gaze on the land. It was the same look that had turned the manual gold panner into the mountain-crushing hydrolicker in a few short years, and it had a similar effect in the days of wheat, encouraging land speculation, claim jumping, and the redirection of water for short-term gain.

As they did during the gold rush, the state's advanced engineers looked to invent and develop new technologies as part of their plan to increase efficiency. "Because it had an agrarian capitalist order from the outset, California farmers could be pulled along rapidly by the booming market demand of the state and exports to the rest of the country," concludes Richard A. Walker in *The Conquest of Bread: 150 Years of Agribusiness in California*, "and it could be pushed along by remarkable innovations coming from irrigation engineers, machinists, and plant scientists."[19] Among those innovations Walker lists new and improved plant and animal breeds; locally produced farm machinery like new plows, harvesters, and later the caterpillar tractor tread; irrigation tools like concrete dams and water pumps; and the first enclosed chicken hutch and cattle feedlot. In-state manufacturers had an edge, at least until the transcontinental railroad was completed, in 1869, and California's ironworks absorbed its share of agricultural capital.

Still, monoculture for the world market was a wobbly economic foundation, and financialization was a double-edged sword. A run on the Bank of California in 1875 wiped out its deposits, and the firm's founder, William C. Ralston, one of San Francisco's most distinguished businessmen, went for a one-way swim into the bay. The wheat boom inspired planters across the Midwest and Canada and as far away as India, Russia, and Australia, and following

California's mechanized path they flooded the planet, transforming humanity's diet. Commodity wheat was such a successful model that it undermined itself as cash crops colonized agricultural land around the world. Trading land that provided subsistence food for land that grew gold was a no-brainer for capitalist landowners, but it was a brittle system for feeding people. Facing an alienation from their traditional lands similar to what California Indians encountered, indigenous peoples and peasants starved as foreign landowners shipped the wheat they grew to hungry Europe. In the closing decades of the century, "[t]he new, globally integrated grain trade…ensured that climate shocks and corresponding harvest shortfalls were translated into price shocks that crossed the continents with the speed of a telegraph," writes historian Mike Davis. "A futures 'corner' in Chicago or a drought in the Punjab could now starve (or enrich) people thousands of miles away."[20] Wheat weakened the landscape, and California became both increasingly prone to floods and vulnerable to dry weather. Unpredictable returns pulled the rug out from under a whole cohort of small West Coast Anglo settlers. Luckily for the state, California wasn't a monoculture; it was still one of the most diverse places in the world.

Other than grains and grain-fed animals, California's biggest gold rush–era agricultural crops were grapes and apples, partly because the best way to get gold miners to eat fruit was to squeeze it into alcohol. The global demand in the 1860s for wine spiked following the Great French Wine Blight, caused by the inadvertent importation of the grape phylloxera aphid from North America to France after intercontinental commerce accelerated in the 1860s and mining capitalists reinvested capital in the cash crop of the moment. As a result, even after French scientists repaired the massive damage, mining colonies from the nineteenth century still provide the world with some of its best wine: South Africa, Australia, Chile, Argentina, and, of course, California. Locally, the demand for wine and cider was higher than the demand for fresh fruits and vegetables, especially among Anglo-Americans and Mexican-Americans, who were used to diets high in grains and meat. Anglo farmers grew subsistence plots with root vegetables and cabbage, but among the miners, only the Chinese were accustomed to a diet that featured fresh produce, and Chinese immigrant communities placed a premium on familiar dishes — a reasonable choice considering the nutritional deficiencies endemic to colonial foodways. Chinese shippers imported boatloads of preserved foodstuffs for the comparatively well-paid Gold Mountain expat community, and some left the mines to grow produce for local (and then regional) consumption. White miners didn't fight their Chinese counterparts for agricultural space the way they booted them off gold claims. Left alone in the culinary labor-market niche, California Chinese found employment as cooks, both in the mining districts and in the fast-growing cities.

The railroad (as I'll explain in the following chapter) absorbed more Chinese laborers in the 1860s than California had to offer and as a consequence supercharged the trans-Pacific labor contractors. Increasing the supply of Chinese workers increased the demand for Chinese food, and the new cohort of California Chinese gardener-peddlers found they could make a decent, reliable living on relatively small plots, and without the risk or trouble of the gold business. The gardening work was much more labor-intensive than industrial wheat farming, but the produce sold for a lot more, and the cultivators could vend their products themselves locally or in the surrounding region, vertically integrating their operations and cutting out the middlemen and the speculators. Until the introduction of refrigerated train cars at the end of the 1880s, these perishable goods mostly fed California, not Europe or other nodes on the global market. It's also worth noting that small, internally diverse plots made for a much stronger food system and a more resilient income stream for the growers. They came to be called truck farms—show up early to a farmer's market and you'll know why—and scholars apply the term retrospectively to what were more accurately called cart farms and even bucket farms. Much to the consternation of some white customers, Anglo-Americans were not eager to compete with the Chinese, who were working with a deeper body of agricultural knowledge. As a result, the California Chinese grew crops for the vegetably distinct Anglo market as well.

In Santa Clara County, mercury capital of the West Coast and ground zero for the wheat boom, planter capitalists started to figure out that the most efficient way they could use their land was to lease it to Chinese agriculturalists, finance whatever equipment they needed, and get out of the way. In 1860, the county census counted 22 full-time residents of Chinese extraction; in 1870, Santa Clara had over 500 full-time Chinese farm workers and another 500 who helped with the harvest, half of them in strawberries.[21] But whereas in other areas the California Chinese sought out land to rent on a fixed basis, in Santa Clara County the agricultural landowners "appear to have been instrumental in bringing Chinese into the area," concludes Sucheng Chan in *This Bittersweet Soil: The Chinese in California Agriculture, 1860–1910*, her study of the Chinese role in California agriculture in the post-gold-rush era.[22] These men leased land on a partnership or sharecropping basis, depending on how you looked at it. That is, the owners provided operational financing and split the proceeds with the farmers and, later, the Chinese labor contractors who provided a layer of distance between the two. Berries—strawberries predominantly, but also raspberries, blackberries, and gooseberries—became a Santa Clara County specialty, and literally 100 percent of the industry's workers were Chinese, from the introduction of the crops, in the 1860s, through the 1880 census. As you'll read in the following chapter, that was a temporary peak of the California Chinese population, after which white capital and labor came together to ban further competition.

The workers were all Chinese but the landowners were white, and the contracts between the two increased in complexity. Landowners dictated what grew where, if not how, as well as the type of person to be employed, if not who specifically (vetoing the "quarrelsome or lazy or incompetent"). It was a complicated dance between capital and labor that rarely took the straightforward form of wage work, at least at first. "Chinese agriculturalists in California followed a reverse sequence," writes Chan. "Only some two decades after they began to grow crops as owner-operators and tenants did many of their members become agricultural laborers."[23] She describes this "reverse mobility path" as a kind of proletarianization, a proletarianization in which Anglos *induced* Chinese farmers in the 1860s to manage the land, rescuing the wheat-ravaged state, and then snatched control back, along with the increased rate of profit the Chinese delivered. Spurred by the Comstock Lode, interest rates fell, and more owners were prepared to behave like investors rather than mere landlords. And with the Central Pacific Railroad's link to the Midwest completed in 1869, more whites were on their way, even if they weren't quite white yet.

A link to the Midwest was a link to the East and, just as important, a link to Europe. Once the pipes were connected, European immigrants began to flow west fast—from the starved, colonized island of Ireland, from proletarianized France and the Swiss cantons, from the Portuguese Azores Islands, and from the newly formed nations of Germany and Italy. WASP Americans looked down on the newcomers, while the Mediterraneans in particular were not thrilled with the Atlantic end of the North American climate. Many set off for the West, where the old-stock Anglo-Americans were fewer and farther between and the weather was more like that of home. There they encountered a very different mobility path from the one imposed on Indians, Chicanos, and the California Chinese as well as on arriving Japanese, Filipinos, Punjabis, and some black migrants from the American South. This inequality — a product of discrimination at the individual, social, and legal levels — dried to whiteness in the California sun decades before the U.S. federal government codified it in immigration law.

When this wave of European immigrants arrived in the Golden State, most of the gold already belonged to someone else. Instead of slugging it out with the Anglo hydrolickers or the Chicano mercury miners, they took up the intensive agriculture model pioneered by the California Chinese. Like the Chinese and unlike the Anglo forty-niners, these Europeans were familiar with fruits, vegetables, and the cultivation thereof. The Portuguese Azoreans, for example, settled almost entirely in the Bay Area, where they took up truck farming for fruits and vegetables, as well as the operation of small chicken coops and dairies. "They would work for wages for a while, then rent land, and then finally buy land," writes one historian, describing the familiar white-immigrant mobility narrative as the Bay Area Azoreans encountered it.[24, 25] It was a workable plan, and thousands of Azoreans moved to the area in the 1860s and '70s, edging Chinese truck farmers into seasonal wage labor.*

The most successful group of proto-white Catholic European immigrants in early U.S. Alta California were the Irish, whose infamous famine and one of their failed uprisings lined up perfectly with the gold strike. With the precise structure of the West Coast racial order still up in the air, the Hibernians found fewer barriers to social advancement there than they found in other American destinations. In San Francisco in particular, Irish immigrants assumed an important role in municipal organization from the beginning of Anglo rule. Quick on their heels were the Swiss-Italians, who took to the familiar climate and established the region as the capital of the nation's wine

---

* This competition was not purely zero-sum. For example, the Azoreans took up dairy farming, an agricultural industry that had not much interested the California Chinese.

industry before expanding into other roles in the intensive agriculture sector. One of those Swiss-Italians was Theo Medici, who put his name on two big signs on the 22-room Swiss Hotel he owned on Market Street in San Jose, next to a giant flag logo familiar from the army knives. In 1869, Medici rented the hotel to another Italian-speaking immigrant, the forty-niner Luigi Giannini, whose California adventure netted him enough gold to go back to Italy, find a wife, and persuade her to join him on this new move.[26] The hotel did well enough to support three children, and Giannini followed the class mobility path to a deed on a 40-acre farm, where he took a big stumble. Accounts differ regarding who killed Luigi—whether it was an angry workman to whom he owed $1 or an eccentric neighbor who owed him the buck—but somebody stabbed him to death over a pittance. Yet even death couldn't arrest the Giannini family's progress. Watching his father bleed out was Luigi's eldest son, Amadeo.

Virginia Giannini was now a twenty-two-year-old widow with three sons, which made her a catch on the Alta California Italian marriage market. She wed Lorenzo Scatena, who was significantly younger than her ex but climbing a similar path up the class ladder. He seems to have been a decent person, and he treated Virginia's young sons well. Rather than a landowner like Luigi, Scatena became a produce middleman, filling his cart with fruits and veggies at the wharf in the morning and bringing the load downtown to distribute among small retailers in San Jose. His stepson Amadeo joined Lorenzo in the cart and displayed an aptitude for business. Amadeo studied the subject (in what passed for a semester of college in California) as a young teenager and then joined his stepfather's growing distribution concern. Tall and big, first for his age and then simply in general, Amadeo established relationships with farmers up and down the state, mailing cold-call letters. He encouraged Lorenzo to make small loans to the farmers they worked with and to use the company's knowledge of the urban market to nudge them toward profitable planting decisions. The more Scatena and company behaved like investors, the more they turned truck farmers into specialized suppliers, which allowed them to scale up their plots. By the age of nineteen, Amadeo was a partner in the business, and by the age of twenty-one he owned half of it in his own name. Strutting around San Francisco's seaside Italian neighborhood of North Beach, the young, handsome, and increasingly prosperous businessman attracted the interest of Clorinda Cuneo, the heir to a bunch of North Beach real estate and a share of the neighborhood's sole small bank. They married (both at the age of twenty-two), and in fewer than 10 years Amadeo built the Scatena business up to the point where he could sell his half to some employees for $100,000 (a few million dollars in 2022 money) and retire. When his father-in-law died the next year, Amadeo took his seat on the bank's board of directors.

Amadeo Giannini was a capitalist organizer from his first days, always partnering with new associates and figuring out profitable ways to meet their needs. He helped centralize intensive produce production, and by putting himself and his family in the middle he learned how much money there was to be made from financing the suburban truck-farm archipelago. Now a dynamic young banker, he took his energy into his new field. Amadeo wanted to loan money to the North Beach Italians the way local Irish and German banks loaned money to their ethnic communities. He wanted to transform the bank into an urban institution that would finance the block-by-block growth of San Francisco and the rest of the Bay Area, not just speculate on big mine projects and distant wheat fields. Amadeo saw a whole city full of Amadeos ready to burst forth, and he knew they were a good investment. But most of the bank board didn't agree, so he quit and called his friend James Fagan—the banker for Scatena and company, known as Giacomo to Amadeo—and asked him how to start a bank. With a group of ambitious Italians (plus the Irish consigliere Fagan), they formed the Bank of Italy. Giannini's determination set their organization apart. When the 1906 earthquake and the subsequent fire burned down San Francisco's financial center, Amadeo took a bag of gold and a plank of wood and set up a teller window on the docks. It didn't matter that the displayed wharf reserves were only 10 percent of deposits on the book; like a jealous husband reassured by the mere presence of his wife's car in the driveway, bank customers saw the sack of gold, and instead of pulling their money out, they put more in.[27] Stacking gold in the teller window where customers can see it became the standard Giannini move for warding off doubt in the event of crisis.

Watching his dad get stabbed to death over a dollar—one detail where the accounts agree is that the boy saw it happen—couldn't stop the young man from becoming a professional lender; there were much bigger forces at play. Banking was supposed to be a dull job, but Giannini wasn't a dull guy, and neither were the young Italian hustlers he hired. While the existing players sat in their offices waiting for the money to walk in the door, the Bank of Italy pursued every Italian dollar in the state of California, and not only as deposits. They encouraged clients to buy into the bank, reserving shares to sell to working-class depositors. Giannini eliminated minimum deposit requirements, bought advertising wherever he could, and sponsored community events. He brought customer service to California banking, and in 1909, when the state officially legalized branch banking, with its satellite storefronts, the Bank of Italy turned Italian communities throughout the state into financial outposts. Soon they probably did have an actual majority of the California Italians' deposits, and some branches (including the one in San Diego) claimed to hold 100 percent of the deposits in their localities. By getting regular people's money in the bank and lending it out, Giannini made the savings of the Italian working class available to capitalists at his discretion, accelerating the state's growth and tying its fortunes to the bank. He turned the Bank of Italy into the state's largest farmer, accumulating mortgages on around 10 percent of California farms. Giannini then compelled farmers to behave like businessmen, requiring standardized record keeping from his borrowers. If you wanted the good interest rate, you had to modernize in ways that made the good interest rate possible. And since rationalized farming was more efficient, farms that didn't borrow from Giannini still had to change in order to keep up with the ones that did.

Giannini was an uncommonly talented banker. He turned the maximizing gaze that Santa Clara County was so good at developing onto money itself. Part of what made him so successful was better information: A roving squad of bank detectives assembled a file of typed three-by-five cards at the San Francisco headquarters, one for each California Italian, listing basic information as well as subjective assessments related to creditworthiness. Making good loans meant the Bank of Italy could make more loans and on better terms than its competitors, and Giannini put nearly everything the bank had back to work. He invested in farms of course, but he also invested in housing developments and the extremely early motion picture industry, putting $500 into a San Francisco cornershop nickelodeon in 1909 and spotting $250,000 ten years later for Charlie Chaplin's debut, *The Kid*.[28] Crucially, Giannini also bought other banks, which had high rates of failure during the era, and converted them into branches. This was a way to circumvent the state supervisors who, concerned about what the chairman called Giannini's "weird mosaic" of bank offices, stopped issuing him new charters.[29]

Amadeo single-handedly inspired the creation of the California League of Independent Bankers, who all vowed not to sell out to the finance prodigy. The group's president told a congressional committee investigating branch banking that the Bank of Italy had tried to trigger a failure at a small California bank that refused to sell, buying up tens of thousands of dollars in deposits and then withdrawing them when they figured the institution's reserves were at its lowest.[30] But no one could argue with the numbers: The Bank of Italy loaned money more cheaply than the other banks did. Who would want to regulate that away? One retrospective study found that Giannini's aggressive expansion strengthened California's bank system because he forced not just his branches but also his competitors to be more efficient, just as he nudged the truck-farm industry into rationalizing first as a distributor with Lorenzo Scatena and then as a mortgage lender.[31] The Bank of Italy was like a constant stress test on its competitors, and the state's banks performed better than average during the Depression in part thanks to Giannini.

In the 1920s, the Bank of Italy pursued a conscious ethnic diversification strategy, hiring multilingual bankers to work with the region's many other (non-Italian) immigrant communities and pursuing them with a similar zeal. At the end of the decade, they had the most California Chinese deposits of any bank in San Francisco. The banker, who was using the distinguished moniker A.P., for Amadeo Pietro, named his first son for his kind and generous stepfather Lorenzo, but in a nod to their new homeland he anglicized the name to Lawrence. A.P. picked a new name for his bank, too, one befitting his role in the changed society: Bank of America.

A.P. Giannini was an exemplar of the national melting pot. "Before Giannini I was a dago," one North Beach customer told a reporter in an oft-cited quotation from 1928. "Now, I am an American."[32] Giannini's role was much more than representational, and he worked with his friend and fellow successful assimilant Joseph Kennedy to finance the presidential election of assimilator in chief Franklin Delano Roosevelt. The change from the Bank of Italy to the Bank of America stands for a whole slew of national, racial, and financial transitions underway at the close of the nineteenth century. In one lifetime, in a single county, the Italians (and more) became white and the

Chinese didn't. Indians became Mexican workers, and California's Indian land became not just the United States of America but the *Bank* of America. California's white dictatorship literally prepared the ground for capitalism; settlers turned the ecological abundance that supported a dense collage of indigenous communities into the farms that capitalized Giannini's "weird mosaic" of bank branches. Anglo-American West Coast history is so brief that there is no California fortune we can't trace back through these original expropriations of land and labor. It takes work *not* to see it.

The point of this story isn't that Amadeo Giannini was a bad man because he profited from stolen land. If we're weighing hearts, his doesn't seem to have been so bad unless you were a complacent banker, a forgivable antagonistic tendency if ever there was one. The point isn't even that Johann Sutter and John Frémont were bad men because they stole and enslaved, though they were and it's worth saying so. The point is that the series of plagues visited upon California in the second half of the nineteenth century took the form of men, and we can see the character of the tendencies that shaped the state (and in turn, the world) reflected in the men seized by them.

The gold rush turned Sutter's bell with its generic, money days into a hegemonic order, but order needs actors and Anglo California needed these men, or men like them. Gold called out to the settlers from Sutter's bell, begging them to find the shining flakes and kill anyone who got in the way, to do it more and faster and on a bigger scale until there was more gold to be made in some other way. The state's farms and cities and banks called out for discipline, for an ambitious outsider unbeholden to the finance elite to whip everyone into rational shape. Amadeo Pietro Giannini filled the bill, but if after watching his father bleed out in front of him he had instead dedicated his life to stitching wounds, California would have found another such outsider.

The impersonal force that animates this chapter, this book, this state, this country, this period of world history isn't fate or human nature; it's capitalism. That's the name we've given to the particular system of domination and production in which landowners, on their own behalf, proletarianize the working class into being. It's a predictable system with consistent, lawlike tendencies. As Karl Marx suspected at the time, California has a privileged place in that story, which it seems to me is the only way to explain why what the Ohlone called "the brink of the world" became, within a few decades, ground zero for exciting new banking practices and white racial formation.

What interests me is not so much the personal qualities of the men and women in this history but how capitalism has made use of them. To think about life this way is not to surrender to predetermination; only by understanding how we're made use of can we start to distinguish our selves from our situations. How can you know what you want or feel or think—who you *are*—if you don't know which way history's marionette strings are tugging? In the following pages you'll meet characters who find ways to tug back, who pit themselves against the way things are and come to personify the system's self-destructive countertendencies. People aren't puppets, and to pull a person is to create the conditions for rebellion. Maybe we're more like butterflies, pinned live and wriggling onto history's collage.

If, as I have been convinced, the point of life and the meaning of freedom is to make something with what the world makes of you, then it's necessary to locate those places where history reaches through your self and sticks you to the board. I began this project with the fact that the railroad that brought the mass of capitalist white settlers to California is the same railroad my classmates used to kill themselves. The man who built that railroad called himself Leland Stanford.

The Combine

Leland Stanford and the Rise of the Shopkeepers — The
Southern Pacific Railroad — Octopus — Rebirth of a
Nation — The World Market

If there's anything today's historians agree about when it comes to Amasa Leland Stanford, it's that he was a relatively unexceptional guy blessed with extraordinary timing. He was born in the spring of 1824 in Albany, New York, to parents who ran the Bull's Head tavern, one of a number of such establishments near a toll road his grandfather helped build. When young Amasa Leland was one year old, he watched the completion of the Erie Canal right down the road. The canal connected New York State (and thereby New York City) to frontier settlements in the Midwest via a navigable waterway that ran through the western part of the state. It made New York City the premier commercial port of North America's East Coast, surpassing Boston and Philadelphia. For the Stanford family, the canal was a godsend. With an international business artery passing through their backyard, the toll-road rest stop built by Lyman Stanford, Leland's grandfather, grew more prosperous in his son Josiah's hands. Amasa Leland was the fourth of seven sons, and his parents could afford to keep their daydreaming boy in full-time education much longer than was typical at the time, even though he failed to distinguish himself academically. (If there was one thing Leland, the large son of a second-generation barman, could do, it was drink.)

Born at the edge of a commercial frontier, Leland was a restless young man, moving from mediocre school to mediocre school, performing in accordance with his surroundings. Leland liked reading more than he liked working, and he didn't like reading all that much. He decided on a career in law, perhaps with a quick transition to politics, a professional path forever beloved by ambitious slackers. A politician needs a good name, and so Leland dropped the biblical Hebrew Amasa, which, fittingly, means "burden." The frontier had lower standards than New York did, so he took the law books his father bought him and in 1848 moved to Port Washington, Wisconsin. After an apprenticeship, he opened his own law office, which suffered from his total lack of German-language proficiency, given that German immigrants formed the bulk of the settler population. A run for district attorney on the progressive Whig line flopped. In 1850 he briefly returned to Albany to marry Jane Lathrop, a merchant's daughter from his hometown milieu. Back in Port Washington, Leland's office burned down, taking with it his law books and legal career, such as it was. Leland's life to that point—he was in his mid-twenties—was a total loss. Despite the cosmic luck of being born alongside the Erie Canal, he'd squandered the little he put together. What he did have left was family, including four surviving brothers. He (scandalously) deposited his new wife back home, and set out to join the rest of the Stanford boys in California. With his family's support, he took the ritziest of the three routes west: a ship down to British-occupied Nicaragua, an overland trek, and another boat up the continent's flank.

Josiah Jr., Leland's eldest brother, was a forty-niner, and he discovered faster than others that for most men like him there was more money to be made by selling shovels than by digging with them. By the time Leland made it out to California, his brothers had set up a modest but respectable commercial concern, centered on a shop in Sacramento. Last to arrive, Leland was sent to the barest frontier mining sites, where life was hard, margins were high, and men paid their tabs in gold (or credit backed by mining claims, which was also gold). As part of his brothers' network, he bought goods on credit at wholesale prices, and he finally started to find the success into which he seemed determined to stumble. In Michigan City, a chaotic outpost of hydraulic mining full of hungry young men, the thirty-year-old lawyer-merchant could pass for a distinguished citizen. He rolled his trading gains into ownership of a tavern (the Empire Saloon) and got himself elected a frontier justice of the peace. He sold whiskey and ruled over the small town of miners, at least when it came to minor disputes. The medium-size fish found himself enlarged by the small pond, and in 1855 he went east to collect his wife. Promoted within the family, Leland took over the Sacramento store. That was good timing, too: Ownership of the land ringing Michigan City consolidated under the Big Gun Mine, and the proprietors dug so deep that in 1858 the whole town's earthen foundation started slipping, cracking walls and rendering it totally unsafe for habitation the next year.[1] *Après moi le déluge.*

Leland moved to a bigger pond with the Sacramento store, and there he swam with bigger fish. The brothers Stanford weren't the only ones who saw the reliable profit opportunities in selling scarce dry goods and hardware to miners with more gold than sense. But the surface-mining claims were quickly tapped out, and so were the price-unconscious independent miners bidding nuggets for jeans and eggs. Leland moved the shop and switched to groceries. At the new location he found himself in the company of three other like-minded shopkeepers: Charles Crocker, Mark Hopkins, and Collis Huntington. The four, who soon began to refer to themselves by the ominous collective name the Associates, were ambitious, physically large, and politically "progressive." The first two qualities were common among leading California settlers in the years preceding the Civil War, but the last was not. That made the start-up Republican Party another small pond for Leland Stanford, and he kept running for office, losing, and moving up the ladder. After winning the nomination in an ill-fated run for governor in 1859, he was the leading figure in the state Republican Party, and a solid choice to become the Associates' front man. In addition, the Stanford store took over a failed gold mine from some debtors, only to see it turn around under a hired manager. Leland gave up drink, fitting in with the abstemious Associates, and people had no reason not to assume he was the original brains behind the Stanford Brothers store rather than the little brother who showed up late. By the end of the 1850s, he could look in the mirror and see something like the man he wanted to be. He passed for a person of substance in California, and as he reflected on his short life, he could see that the trajectory was going great; Leland had become a guy to bet on.

Events threatened to overtake the Associates. Capital-intensive mining and agriculture made employees out of the settlers on behalf of eastern and European capital, and you just couldn't charge these workers the same prices. Wages declined, headed in the wrong direction as far as independent retailers were concerned. Men like the Associates had made good, but they were very petty businessmen on the economy's national and increasingly international scale. They were like the luckiest of surface miners: financed to make a move in the burgeoning region but overmatched by agents who represented larger economic forces. A relatively common disaster like a fire or flood could wipe them out, as such things did other men in their position. The Associates had to find a niche from which they could grow. When the country elected Republican Abraham Lincoln to the presidency, Leland, as California's reigning GOP gubernatorial nominee, found himself among the president's senior West Coast advisers at a time of national crisis. And he had a business proposal for Honest Abe.

In 1859, *New-York Tribune* founding editor and leading Republican Horace Greeley made the tough overland trek through Yosemite to California. Published the following year, his account *An Overland Journey from New York to San Francisco in the Summer of 1859* pitched the West to eager readers in the East. "If you come to California at all, come to stay," he writes, "and nowhere else will you find a little money more desirable than here. Even one thousand dollars, well applied, may, with resolute industry and frugality, place you soon on the high road to independence."[2] Greeley especially hoped more women would make the trip, to even out the gender ratio and provide the domestic basis for permanent U.S. settlement. The book concludes with a full-throated call for a transcontinental railroad, financed via the inexhaustible promise of unsettled lands near the tracks. Lincoln's Republican Party supported the idea, as did a group of southern Democrats led by Mississippi senator Jefferson Davis. The 1854 Gadsden Purchase of a small slice of territory in northern Mexico cleared the way for a transcontinental route south of the forbidding Sierra Nevada mountain range. But the railroad question was also a slavery question, and both the southern planter class and the northern industrial class knew that a southern route would extend the institution to the coast, turning California into another Texas slaver paradise and throwing off the country's fragile political balance. The railroad languished in a Washington stalemate, a question for a united nation that did not exist in practice. When the South seceded, the balance question was suddenly moot and the northern route could proceed unopposed. There was just one problem: The mountains were still there.

The Sierra Nevadas were a thoroughly forbidding natural barrier, and with no clear way through, existing railroad capitalists wanted no part of a northern route, even though the speculative upside was obviously massive. That's why, when a railroad engineer from Troy, New York, named Theodore Judah went around telling people that he found a way to get through the Sierras, no one took him very seriously. That is, until he met a handful of guys in Sacramento. The Associates invested just under $20,000 to form a company to execute Judah's plan, "a considerable sum for storekeepers, but a pittance for a California railroad," in the words of historian Richard White.[3] They figured if the whole transcontinental thing didn't work out they could pivot the project to a toll road, like the one Lyman Stanford built in Albany back in the day. But their real play was political. Infrastructure of this scale required Washington's support—specifically its credit—and they were in an unusually good place to secure it. Leland sold the Stanford Brothers store to go East for a spell and advise the new president about whom to trust in California. When he returned to Sacramento, the Associates had two jobs waiting for him: that of 1861 gubernatorial nominee and that of president of the Central Pacific Railroad. This time, with a three-way race and the Democrats split nearly evenly between Unionist and pro-slavery Chivalry Democratic candidates, Leland won with a solid plurality. Not even a decade in the state, the slacker Stanford was now an important industrialist and governor to boot. For lucky men of the right type, that's how things went in California.

Leland served only one term as governor, from 1861 to 1863, and without particular distinction—the rest of the region was busy, with civil wars in China, Mexico, the temporarily Disunited States, and incipiently in Japan. But Stanford never gave up the title and the prestige that came with it, going by "Governor" for the rest of his life. President of the railroad was in some ways the more important job, and it was the one he held longer, though the two gigs surely complemented each other. Who better for president than the Governor? The 1862 Pacific Railway Act chartered the Union Pacific to build west from the Missouri River (ultimately from Omaha, Nebraska) and authorized the Central Pacific to lay tracks east until the two met somewhere in the middle. The transcontinental line linked the West Coast to existing networks in the East rather than forming a whole new single rail across North America, as the name implies. Even with federal support, financiers kept their distance from the Central Pacific, and the effort stalled out after putting together only 11 miles of tracks. Collis P. Huntington—the uncontested shrewdest of the bunch—went to Washington and lobbied for an increase in government subsidies and incentives, winning the Pacific Railway Act of 1864. From there the road was easier, and by jumping ahead to flatter land in Nevada, the Central Pacific was able to secure the financing it needed to complete the (by then deceased) Theodore Judah's plan and blow through the Sierras. The Associates connected their California and Nevada tracks, and by the end of the spring of 1869, they prepared to link with the Union Pacific in Ogden, Utah.

If there had been a contest among the four Associates regarding who contributed the least, Leland Stanford would have been the dominant competitor. But the Governor liked the limelight, and he made a good mascot. Given the amount of financial chicanery going on not so far behind the scenes, the others may have made a considered decision to let the big oaf stand in front for the proverbial cameras. On May 10, 1869, he used a hammer of silver to tap in the transcontinental's symbolic final stake (made of gold, immediately replaced), and people poured into the streets to celebrate the new nation, which now rolled effortlessly from sea to shining sea. San Francisco, Chicago, St. Louis, New Orleans, New York, Boston, and Philadelphia all got the news at the same time because the transcontinental link was more than just a railway. The workers strung telegraph lines as they went, and May 10 also established the country as a single media environment. The circuit connected with a hammer blow and a single message lit up the nation: "Done!" Cities had fun triggering their own responses, such as a 100-gun salute in New York City, and a gong in Buffalo. Chicagoans paraded impromptu, while Philadelphians dutifully answered fire bells that they were relieved to discover were celebratory. The next morning the first passenger car passed from the Union Pacific to the Central Pacific tracks, and the inaugural batch of imported tea departed for the East, linking West Coast international trade to the nation's financial centers via rail. This was more branding than anything else—goods from the East were just as easy to send to New York by boat, especially with the Suez Canal up and running—but the settler nation celebrated nonetheless.

The shopkeepers from Sacramento proved the railroad industry wrong, and they got rich doing it. Now everyone else wanted in on the game too, and money from around the world poured into speculative new lines. Sketchy stocks floated on international markets as newly global capital stretched its railroad limbs. The track was built, the subsidies harvested, and the Associates' job was finished, but a new task rose in front of them. Failing to sell the Central Pacific off in its entirety (a move they attempted at various times throughout the building process), the men found themselves railroad *operators*. The transcontinental link reduced the cost of travel from the frontier to the coast dramatically, from an eventful $225–500 stagecoach ride to a sub-$50 "emigrant" bench seat or $112 for first class. Kids under three rode free.[4] Between ferrying settlers inspired by Horace Greeley's "Go West, young man!" and dragging the rocks out of new mines, the Associates filled their cars, and the world's systems accelerated rapidly. Freight rates dropped, and information raced ahead thanks to speedier mail delivery and instant telegraph connections. A year after the golden spike, a passenger could telegraph his wife at home in Boston from the train and receive an answer before getting 50 miles farther down the line. The Associates were shopkeepers no more. They had become founding fathers of the West, and they had one more grand strike of luck to come.

In 1873, the global financial system that had emerged in the previous decade entered its first crisis. Newly united Germany moved to the gold standard, and the United States followed, pressing the price of silver down and triggering a gut check for the world's financiers and promoters. It was a crisis of confidence: The ostensible basis for speculative investments in the railroad system and its weedlike expansion in the West was the revenue these systems planned to generate down the line, and because those equations were based on hype rather than solid math, a crisis of confidence cut right to the core of the business model. A drop in silver prices hurt the value of silver-mine claims, which in turn called the viability of railroads into question. Were they absolutely sure these lines were worth building after all? Eighty-nine railroads defaulted on payments as banks called in loans only to discover that there was no there there, leading to over 100 bank failures.[5] Like Tinker Bell and Santa Claus, these speculative roads disappeared when the investors stopped believing, and their stock certificates turned back into plain paper. Investment capital, realizing it had wandered too far afield and into danger, retreated for safety, and the money that flowed to enterprises so freely in the transcontinental wake dried up. But every crisis is someone's opportunity, and in this case that someone was the Associates.

The difference between the Central Pacific cabal and all the other fly-by-night railroad concerns that collapsed in the panic was not that the Sacramento shopkeepers were financially scrupulous. They were at least as overleveraged as their peers; their books were obvious bullshit; and they had taken advantage of the exact same scams that felled the Union Pacific's directors the year before, in the Crédit Mobilier scandal. Rather, the difference was that they persuaded their bankers to persuade *their* bankers to play it cool. With the interested parties denying anything was amiss, the Associates were in place to snatch up failed lines at a discount. For capitalists at the end of the nineteenth century, it paid — as it has ever since — to have several corporate shells to switch between, just in case. They funneled money into the construction of their Southern Pacific line, another Associates-controlled railroad that subsumed the Central, earning the budding monopoly the nickname the Combine.

But corporate costume changes didn't fool the public. Railroads by their nature depended on politicians, and the Associates became expert bribery artists, spending millions in cash and stock to make sure they got their way. The men stood for corruption itself. Their western transportation monopoly developed a stranglehold on economic and political life in California, and it came to represent the strange new species of corporation in the popular mind. An 1882 cartoon in the *San Francisco Wasp* by G. Frederick Keller titled "The Curse of California" depicted the Southern Pacific empire as a giant grinning octopus, and dangling in its tentacles were the state's industries: timber, communications, wine, mining, large commodity farmers, fruit growers, stage coach lines, and wheat exporters. All depended on the railroad, and there was only the one option. Glaring out from the octopus's right eye was the unmistakable face of Leland Stanford. The image of a network of choking tentacles resonated, and other cartoonists used the octopus to represent their own regional monopolists, but the writer Frank Norris forever connected the sea creature and the Associates with his 1901 novel, *The Octopus*.

Can I Stop It?

No novel from the period has captured the particular intrasettler conflict that structured California in more detail than Norris's. *The Octopus* is a fictionalized version of the 1880 events at Mussel Slough, an irrigation ditch in California's wheatful Central Valley that became a flash point in the fight between homesteaders and the railroad. Theoretically, the groups' interests were aligned. The railroad made homesteading possible, both by reducing the costs of the trip out and by connecting the small farms to the global economy. Railroads depended on settlers to build the farms and towns that made railroads to the middle of nowhere worth owning. Based on these codependencies, the Combine made an offer to restless men in the East: Come homestead on railroad-owned land now, and later the railroad will sell it to you based on its surveyed *unimproved* value, around $2.50 an acre. The agreement allowed farmers who lacked the capital or credit to secure their own land to build equity as homesteaders by locking in the original price. That way they could develop the land into wheat fields without worrying about the railroad coming in and taking advantage of their hard work. When it was time to buy the land, the farmers who were so inclined could turn around and sell it for four or five times what they'd paid for it and make a quick profit, just like the capitalist speculators did. In effect, the Combine contracted land speculation to homesteaders, promising to cut them in on the huge rewards in exchange for an advance in sweat.

When it came time for the farmers to buy, however, the railroad forgot the deal. The land was clearly worth more than the $2.50 or so an acre the farmers wanted to pay: Look at the beautiful wheat farms! For the Combine, it was a convenient misunderstanding; the promise on a promotional pamphlet (if, that is, anyone could dig up an original one as evidence) wasn't an enforceable contract, and they weren't about to sell land at a fraction of its value. For the homesteaders it was a disaster, retroactively transforming them from yeomen to serfs. The settlers filed suit, but the judge was Lorenzo Sawyer, author of the hydrolicking ban, friend to big land speculators, bought and paid for by the Combine. Sawyer ruled that the homesteaders were squatters, and they were welcome to buy their own farms at market price or get out. The homesteaders of Mussel Slough picked option three. Led by Confederate veterans still smarting from their Civil War loss, the settlers dug in, and as agents tried to evict them, they started shooting. When the dust settled, seven men were dead. The public blamed the Combine and its front man, Leland Stanford, who led compromise negotiations before running off to Europe in advance of the bloodshed. It didn't look good, but the Associates didn't rely on looking good to make their money. They could depend on their strangleholds, and there were enough tentacles to go around.

Norris's book endures as a touchstone, and his evocative description of the Southern Pacific—"the galloping terror of steam and steel, with its single eye, Cyclopean, red, shooting from horizon to horizon, symbol of a vast power, huge and terrible; the leviathan with tentacles of steel, to oppose which meant to be ground to instant destruction beneath the clashing wheels"—alone keeps *The Octopus* in rotation. But the most important insight in the novel comes toward the end, when the protagonist, a writer named Presley (Norris's stand-in), ends up alone with Shelgrim—Norris's amalgamation of the Associates into one railroad baron. The scene is almost surreal: On a whim, Presley goes to Shelgrim's office, where he suddenly finds himself with an audience. Stunned to discover the oligarch familiar with his socialist poem "The Toilers," Presley isn't sure what to say now that he's behind the curtain. Their dialogue is worth quoting at length:

"I suppose you believe I am a grand old rascal."

"I believe," answered Presley, "I am persuaded——" He hesitated, searching for his words.

"Believe this, young man," exclaimed Shelgrim, laying a thick powerful forefinger on the table to emphasise his words, "try to believe this—to begin with—THAT RAILROADS BUILD THEMSELVES. Where there is a demand sooner or later there will be a supply. Mr. Derrick, does he grow his wheat? The Wheat grows itself. What does he count for? Does he supply the force? What do I count for? Do I build the Railroad? You are dealing with forces, young man, when you speak of Wheat and the Railroads, not with men. There is the Wheat, the supply. It must be carried to feed the People. There is the demand. The Wheat is one force, the Railroad, another, and there is the law that governs them—supply and demand. Men have only little to do in the whole business. Complications may arise, conditions that bear hard on the individual—crush him maybe—BUT THE WHEAT WILL BE CARRIED TO FEED THE PEOPLE as inevitably as it will grow. If you want to fasten the blame of the affair at Los Muertos on any one person, you will make a mistake. Blame conditions, not men."

"But—but," faltered Presley, "you are the head, you control the road."

"You are a very young man. Control the *Road*! Can I stop it? I can go into bankruptcy if you like. But otherwise if I run my road, as a business proposition, I can do nothing. I can NOT control it. It is a force born out of certain conditions, and I—no man—can stop it or control it. Can your Mr. Derrick stop the Wheat growing? He can burn his crop, or he can give it away, or sell it for a cent a bushel—just as I could go into bankruptcy—but otherwise his Wheat must grow. Can any one stop the Wheat? Well, then no more can I stop the Road."[6]

The scene recalls the finale of L. Frank Baum's *The Wonderful Wizard of Oz* (released the year before *The Octopus*), in which Dorothy discovers that the sorcerer is no more than a man. Except here we have a man who's discovered to be less and more than that at the same time. Shelgrim presents himself as a bundle of social forces, the embodiment of impersonal currents—and he is, but not of the currents he claims. Because it wasn't demand for wheat that built the speculative railroad lines. Supply and demand determine commodity prices—though not nearly so directly as we've been led to believe—and if someone orders a loaf of bread, you can't tell the hungry customer to hold on while you build a railroad, a farm, a mill, and a bakery. Capital and capitalists built the lines, under logic much closer to "If you build it they will come" (or even "There's a sucker born every minute") than to "Give the people what they want." As Richard White explains in his book *Railroaded: The Transcontinentals and the Making of America*, many if not *all* of the railroads were nonsensical from a consumer supply-and-demand perspective. The impersonal drive animating those big men in suits wasn't the people's hunger for bread; it was capital's hunger for profit.

Back in the 1860s, Lincoln's tenuous national government needed a railroad that built itself the way Shelgrim talked about, but demand wouldn't get it done. As Theodore Judah found out, the strong value of the transcontinental proposition wasn't initially clear to investors. That's what allowed the relatively modest Associates to step up. But how did they get the money? Recall that their combined investment was less than $20,000. The feds offered monetary awards per mile, but they needed a funding mechanism adequate to the project. The country needed a way to access some portion of the immense value stored in the West in advance in order to pay for the expansion in the first place. Speculation is a lever big enough to move mountains, and through financial alchemy as powerful as any magic the world had yet seen, the Associates and their friends in the government turned the vast landscape of the West into the ultimate speculative commodity: real estate. How they did it is magisterially simple: Since having a train line through it immediately multiplied the land's value, the federal government could be conservative and still trade half of it for a railroad and come out on top financially. Land on either side of the proposed line was divided into a checkerboard, with alternating plots deeded to the Central Pacific. The Associates ended up with a territory larger than the state of Maryland. Now they weren't just selling shares in the railroad; they were selling shares in the West itself. And there was nothing more valuable than that.

The scent of profit wafted from gold country all over the world, long after the easy gold itself was gone. Bankers from New York, Paris, Frankfurt, and especially London wanted the high, quick returns that California represented, but they weren't about to move to the frontier.* They needed a way to set their money to work in the West without having to follow it themselves. The world's capital was increasingly liquid, searching out opportunities far from home. New forms of financial engineering allowed the Associates to feather a nest for capitalists, providing a space for them to "work on the railroad" from the comfort of their studies. Bond financing was the simple way: The railroad issues promissory notes backed by the government land grants, then capitalists buy the bonds and enjoy a solid rate of return as the West is won. Or, as was becoming the style, financiers could buy up batches of railroad bonds and turn them around to retail investors for a quick profit. Once you start speculating, it's easy to add new layers—you just need another buyer. European investors had spent an estimated $243 million on American railroad securities by 1870 (over half a trillion dollars in 2022 money).[7] These pieces of paper had issued values, but they were also worth whatever someone was willing to pay; the

---

* Among the rich Europeans to invest in western railroads via Continental bankers was author Marcel Proust, who captured his demimonde of Parisian speculators for posterity. In the sixth book of Proust's series, his narrator laments that, having sought out high-reward investments to keep his mistress Albertine in style, "the wisest judgments of the previous generation had been proved unwise by this generation," as his stocks slid and funds dwindled. Vincent Kaufmann, *Post Scripts: The Writer's Workshop* (Harvard University Press, 1994), 81–2; Marcel Proust, *In Search of Lost Time Volume V: The Captive & The Fugitive* (Modern Library Classics, 1999), 866.

spark across the gap between those two numbers ignited fuel in the belly of the Central Pacific.

Railroad bonds allowed capitalists around the world to wet their beaks on settlement in the West, and the railroads absorbed "close to half of all private investment during the last two decades of the nineteenth century and opened up outlets for a great deal more," according to economist Pauls Baran and Sweezy, making the frontiers the roads opened "the greatest external stimulus in capitalist history."[8] But the bonds only offered fixed interest rates. Bond speculators could flip them to others (if they were lucky), but the nature of the instrument made for limited returns. Those promised returns were stronger than what capital could expect to find in savings accounts or government securities, but the point of investing in exotic railroads wasn't to hit your head on limits; the point was to exceed them. Financiers wanted a way to access the potentially unlimited western gains they read about. Like the forty-niners who chased easy, transformative wealth, speculators were looking to get their hands on yields that weren't yoked to the magnitude of the investment, all without having to do any actual work. Here again is the real impersonal demanding force that built the West—not hunger for bread but hunger for increased profits. Of course they could buy businesses, or invest in founding their own firms the way the Associates themselves had, but ownership was so restrictive. Converted to productive capital, money ceased to be liquid; it was tied up in machinery and other concrete assets. To make the best use of the opportunities to finance settlement in the fourth quarter of the nineteenth century—in California in particular, but also throughout the colonized world—capital needed a middle road between a bonded loan and a partnership, an instrument with the tradable liquidity of the former and the speculative upside of the latter. The answer was the joint-stock corporation.

In his 1910 book, *Finance Capital: A Study of the Latest Phase of Capitalist Development*, the economist Rudolf Hilferding gives an outstanding account of the market transformations that occurred during this period, and he singles out the financing of the American railway system as the "peak of perfection" when it came to the technique. For investors, buying stock in a company offered the Goldilocks solution to the bonds-versus-partnership problem. Investors in stock could get access to speculative increase via dividends (interest-type payments based on profits rather than invested capital) and by reselling their stock on the market when the price went up. For the railroad operators, it was a great deal. By selling up to half their stakes, the principals in a joint-stock corporation could double their effective capital without losing control. (If you have $1 million invested in your company, it's worth $1 million. If you sell half of the company for $1 million, then your company has $2 million.) But it was even better than that, because a high level of firm capitalization could attract and serve as collateral for loans. (Now you have $4 million.) And if you create subsidiary companies, you can issue whole new blocks of stock for those, too. "The amount of capital necessary to ensure control of a corporation is usually less than half," writes Hilferding, "amounting to a third or a quarter, or even less."[9] If Richard White's account of the Associates is correct, it was *much* less than 25 percent: They came to control hundreds of millions of dollars in capital with an initial collective investment of less than $20,000. Through these stock instruments, shop owners used other people's money to puff themselves up into monopoly men.

Theoretically, the joint-stock model works out for everyone. Investors are rewarded with a higher rate of return than they can get from mere interest. The founders are rewarded not only with an infusion of capital (which, unfortunately, dilutes their ownership stake) but also with what Hilferding calls promoter's profit. Since the profits from a productive firm tend to be higher than interest rates—after all, people don't invest in a business if they can expect a bigger return just by loaning their money to a bank or government—the promoter can split the difference into two parts, returning one to the stockholder as a dividend and keeping the other. Of course the promoter gets dividends too, as a stockholder. The model allowed owners to align the interests of some workers with their own via employee stock grants, which made managers and engineers as eager for speculative opportunities as capitalists and reduced labor costs until revenue showed up, if it ever did. If the whole project went bust then the workers were out of luck, losing their work and time the way investors lost money.

As long as you were willing to overlook the uncompensated expropriation of the land around the railroad tracks by the U.S. authorities—and everyone involved in the financing certainly was—a joint-stock transcontinental railroad sounds like a good deal all around. Global capital gets to be of productive use, profiting both professional financiers and the Atlantic's lounging bourgeois investors. Enterprising small California capitalists elevated themselves, compensated appropriately for their assumed risk and filling the vacuum where, after the collapse of the cattle barons, a new Anglo West Coast aristocracy was required. Visionary workers such as Theodore Judah could make a class leap, too, if everything worked out, which made California a strong draw for the ambitious, clever young men whom the railroad required. Everyone wins but the Indians, a United States settlement motto.

But financial innovation offered many opportunities for actors up and down the model to cut corners and mark cards, none more than the Associates. The stock system meant that investors were induced to buy pieces of paper of no fixed worth, based only on their confidence; that was a recipe for fraud. Everyone wanted something for nothing, but only some of them could get it. The unlucky counterparties were stuck with the reverse: nothing for something.

Selling bogus stock to retail suckers was the lowest level of securities scamming, and there were plenty more opportunities as one scaled the corporate ladder. Accountants and managers skimmed funds directly, engineering the complicated financial statements in their own interests, reasonably sure no one else could tell what they were doing. And even if the higher-ups did find out, they wouldn't want to shake the confidence of their stockholders by making a big deal out of it. Besides, it was the higher-ups who were engaged in the bigger frauds. They created their own supplier firms and gave themselves lucrative no-bid contracts. New investors allowed them to pay dividends to the old investors without producing real profits, pyramid-style. Owners moved value between subsidiary firms at will, generating gains and losses when and where they wanted them and nowhere else. The Associates mastered these techniques and more, making themselves outstandingly wealthy. And yet they were ready to turn out a silk pocket on command, pleading poverty with top hat in hand. They didn't make money from the railroad; they made sure of that. Instead they made their fortunes on the sketchy subsidiaries: the Contract and Finance Company overcharging for supplies, the Western Development Company and Pacific Improvement Company using land grants to speculate on California's new towns.

Perhaps the most egregious con the Associates played was a switcheroo with the Central and Southern Pacific. Since they directed both but owned much more of the Southern outright, they had the Central lend its line to the

Southern, leaving no dividend payment worth mentioning for the Central shareholders, the bulk of whom were in London. Eventually the frustrated British shareholders deployed as their representative Sir Charles Rivers Wilson, the former government director of the Suez Canal Company and railroad finance expert. He negotiated a settlement with Huntington on behalf of the Central Pacific's stockholders, proving that British bondholders could protect themselves in the American West.*

They were caught with their hands in the cookie jar, but the Associates did not drop the pretense of their good character. When the *Economist* described the scam and called the Southern Pacific "virtually Mr. Huntington in what may be termed a corporate form," Huntington couldn't let it stand. He wrote a letter to the editor, claiming that he "intended to deal fairly with all people having dealings with the company, and I believe I have done so."[10] This set off a firestorm in the financial press, including a point-by-point detailing of the Associates' various scams over the previous two decades printed in the *Investors' Review*: "It may almost be said that all known operations of the Pacific railroad management in this State are saturated with fraud and dishonesty which recur at every turn of their proceedings."[11] The editor of *California Banker's Magazine*, in a bit of melodramatic excess, went even further, blaming the *Economist* for selling the stock to London's investors in the first place.[12] The besuited Associates were paragons of the new perfidy, and they were booed from across the ocean.

The *Economist* was wrong, however, to see the Southern Pacific as Huntington in "a corporate form." It's precisely the error the poet Presley makes in *The Octopus*, mistaking the railroad for a representation of the oligarch Shelgrim when the reverse was closer to the truth. *You are dealing with forces, young man, when you speak of Wheat and the Railroads, not with men.* The railroads came to stand for capitalism's impersonal forces writ large: fast, loud, disruptive, dangerous, encased in metal. Legally, too, the Combine became its own person. When California rewrote the state constitution at the end of the 1870s, delegates included a provision that revoked the mortgage tax deduction for the

---

* The Associates were playing a dangerous game; when Mexico left bondholders hanging in 1861, France invaded, overthrew the government, and occupied the country. The handpicked Emperor Maximilian ran the country in the interests of foreign capital until his defeat and execution in 1867.

railroad, since it was a corporation rather than a human being. The Combine refused to pay, and the state and two counties sued for their money. Aggregating the three cases, the justices of the Supreme Court agreed in 1886's *Santa Clara County v. Southern Pacific Railroad Company* that corporations were entitled to avail themselves of the young Fourteenth Amendment and its equal protection clause.[13] They ruled for the Combine and established the doctrine of corporate personhood. Long before Santa Clara County stood for Silicon Valley, *Santa Clara County* meant that companies are people, too, and the United States endowed its scams with civil rights. The case itself, of course, was part of the game. Representing California on the Supreme Court was Stephen J. Field, appointed by Lincoln on the recommendation of the state's governor: Leland Stanford.

It's no surprise, then, that the settlers of California took the rebel side when the shooting started. After the conflagration at Mussel Slough, locals celebrated the surviving "squatters," and they served their short jail sentences in relative luxury. The only people who could be fooled by the Associates' thin ruse of public interest were perhaps their own children. And yet these criminals dominated the state. In a time and place of street duels and hangman's justice, why didn't the scammed settlers of California march up to the Associates' big famous mansions on San Francisco's Nob (as in nabob) Hill and tear the octopus limb from human limb?

They almost did.

Nation Time

The problem with a railroad that built itself was that it didn't. No matter how good the incentives, the Combine needed men to lay track, and those men needed to be paid. It wasn't like the Associates' previous shopkeeping business: Labor costs were a serious problem once they started building national infrastructure. They needed a reliable workforce that moved as fast as their ambitions. Speed was essential, since they were racing the Union Pacific to the flatlands, where the miles were easier and the government incentives hung lower. But the whole lure of California for the people who could become the workers the Central Pacific needed was the chance to overcome their station, to get lucky. There was only so lucky anyone could get doing dangerous backbreaking labor for $1 a day on the moving frontier; the forty-niner gold-mining wages that pulled them to the coast were ten times that.

The largest group of Alta California's wage workers were indigenous, but it was that connection to the land that made them less than reliable from the capitalist's point of view. Indian railroad work was seasonal; the men used limited wage labor to supplement traditional subsistence practices. Given the choice between sovereign community life and sex-segregated work 12 or more hours a day on the white settlers' tracks, it's not a particularly tough call. The chance for the former narrowed as settlers destroyed indigenous lifeworlds that had survived and adapted through Spanish-Mexican occupation, but California Indians were still far from dependent on the Central Pacific. Racing against Midwest capital, the Associates needed workers who were reliant on them, workers who ran on the company's schedule rather than on a seasonal calendar. They needed men who were estranged from the land. Anyone else demanded an arm and a leg for the work the Associates were trying to get done.

The initial solution to the Central Pacific's labor problem was the mass of Irish immigrants who came West for gold only to find the surface exhausted and the jobs controlled by well-capitalized bosses. Unlike Indian workers, the Irish didn't have families to see or provide for, and they didn't have homes to return to when conditions got too lousy. In theory, they were stuck. The reality was a little different. Central Pacific engineer L. M. Clement told the Pacific Railway Commission that these workers were "indifferent, independent, and their labor high-priced."[14] When the Comstock Lode hit in 1859, mining wages shot up again, to $4 and more per day according to Clement. Railroad workers walked off the job and into the mines.

The relationship between white immigrants and the land was closer than the Associates might have imagined: They were settlers, establishing a domain on behalf of the United States. Though they didn't realize it, the railroad men already depended on these Irish settlers in another sense—as the front lines of white domination. In exchange for that work, the settler-colonial powers of Alta California already implicitly deeded the entire territory to them as white men. It was, in a meaningful sense, their land now, and for most of them the land had more to offer than the railroad. White settlers could be tricked into scams that promised speculative payouts in line with their skin privilege—as they were at Mussel Slough—but there was nothing very promising about working on the railroad all the livelong day.

Building the Central Pacific through the Sierras as quickly as possible required men who were vulnerable in a way that neither the indigenous peoples nor the conquering white Americans were. That's where the Chinese came in. Substantial numbers of Chinese men came to California with the gold strike for the same reason most white men did: to get some, get rich, and leave.* Compared to the eastern settlers, who had to take two ships and travel across Central America, if they were lucky—or take the overland route through many different sovereign territories, if they weren't—coastal Chinese workers had the more direct route there. But when Alta California became part of the United States, the region joined a white-supremacist slave power. The nation's wealth was based on the expropriation of Indians, Africans, and now Mexicans, but the racists had plenty left in the tank. U.S. California's white settlers used formal race laws and informal intimidation to kick Chinese miners off any valuable claims. They were stuck paying more for worse territory, only to lose it if a white man took notice. Since the courts refused to hear the testimony of "Celestials"—China was the "Heavenly Kingdom"—the Chinese could not rely on the protection of the law, which marked them as vulnerable to predation by everyone else, including Mexican bandits and especially the Chinese firms that shipped workers to California. And to the Central Pacific.

The prevailing story is that when Charles Crocker suggested contracting Chinese workers to build the railroad, his associates told him it couldn't be done, that the Chinese weren't biologically fit for such work, to which Crocker replied with some version of "Well, they built the Great Wall, didn't they?" What's more, they were organized by labor contractors who were ready and able to supply work like any other kind of commodity. The lead contractor for

---

* California was only one location for coastal Chinese emigrants during the period. Others went to Caribbean plantations, where they formed a new indentured agricultural workforce, and some later traveled, as we'll see, to the mines of South Africa. Most, however, ventured to colonial territories in Southeast Asia: the Dutch East Indies, British Malaya, and French Indochina. "While many of these immigrants remained poor," writes Sebastian Strangio, "a significant number flourished under colonial rule, slotting into roles as tax collectors and economic middlemen between the European authorities and native populations." Sebastian Strangio, *In the Dragon's Shadow: Southeast Asia in the Chinese Century* (Yale University Press, 2022), 26.

the Central Pacific was a man named Hung Wah, an enterprising guy who got his start supplying employees for low-wage hydrolicking mine work. At his peak he was responsible for a quarter of the railroad's workers—over 900 men—and handled tens of thousands of dollars' worth of wages a month.[15] Instead of paying individual workers, the Associates could pay Hung Wah, and however he did it, he supplied them at an average cost to the railroad of $1 a day, one-third cheaper than what white men demanded for the same work. What's more, the Chinese railroad workers did have plenty of germane experience, and their techniques, including the lowering of men in baskets down mountain faces, helped speed the Central Pacific's construction. Chinese workers also handled explosives, including the new, highly unstable nitroglycerine, when whites wouldn't, until Alfred Nobel's licensing demands proved too costly.

The Associates lucked into some of the world's most efficient construction crews; challenged by Europe's celebrated miners to a public contest, the California Chinese cleaned their Cornish clocks.[16] Over the course of construction wages increased—and the railroad paid better than work to be had in the politically and economically unstable Chinese coastal districts of Fujian and Guangdong, where they sailed from—but there were strong sticks to go with the carrot incentives. In San Francisco, informal and formal restrictions pushed the Chinese into low-wage domestic jobs such as cooking and laundering, replacing unpaid women, of whom there weren't enough to go around on the frontier. And when the Central Pacific's Chinese workers did strike in the summer of 1867 for a raise and an eight-hour day, it was the labor contractors who settled it, and without direct concessions from the Associates. The record implies that contractors withheld the men's food and supplies. Still, we can imagine that compared to the chaotic violence of life in a frontier town without the law's protection, the railroad's scheduled exploitation could have been a sensible choice.

Many hundreds of Chinese workers died, occasionally gruesomely, building the Central Pacific, and it was their hard work more than any white engineer's plan or shopkeeper's capital that made the transcontinental path through the Sierra Nevadas possible. But by the time the tracks were ready to kiss in Utah, the Associates were shuffling Chinese workers to the back. Leland Stanford commissioned the painter Thomas Hill to memorialize the moment of the transcontinental accomplishment, and Hill's oil painting *The Driving of the Last Spike* became the moment's iconic representation. Front and center is Leland in his penguin suit, leaning on a hammer as workers ready the ceremonial spike. Hill included some of the people who weren't there—such as Theodore Judah, deceased—and omitted others, most notably all the Chinese laborers. Not even Hung Wah, who could surely take as much credit as any white man for the road's completion on such favorable terms to the Central Pacific, made the cut. (Hill did include a couple of visibly distressed Indians in the foreground, which is perhaps part of why Leland refused to purchase the painting as promised.) Chinese workers could build the railroad, but the country it linked didn't belong to them. California's settlers made that clear.

When the transcontinental line concluded, the Chinese railroad workers entered a depressed California economy, where wages declined as immigration increased. "That national connection brought many migrants from the east coast to San Francisco, and as well as manufactured goods from eastern factories to the west coast, creating pressure on the high prices and high wages that had previously flourished in a market of scarcity," writes historian Mae Ngai. "Far from delivering untold wealth and development to the Pacific coast, the railroad brought joblessness and poverty—the long tail of the national depression of 1873–77."[17] Notable among those immigrants were defeated Confederate rebels, and the racist militants hadn't undergone any postwar ideological reeducation. The boom era of settlement, when men who made it to the coast could count on low supply and high demand for whatever it was they wanted to do or sell, was over. Now the state's economic life reorganized under capitalist auspices, and settlers became workers.

California's manufacturers also suffered as a result of the state's new umbilical cord to the national market: Stuck competing with more developed industry in the East, the young sector struggled to keep labor costs down. White trade unions succeeded in metal work, shipbuilding, and construction, which, as Alexander Saxton points out in *The Indispensable Enemy: Labor and the Anti-Chinese Movement in California*, are all industries that require large numbers of men working together in the open. That wasn't the case with the new commodity manufacturers; an undergarment factory could fit in a Chinatown basement. All you had to do was teach one person the technique and contract him to round up the rest of the labor, providing capital as needed.

Chinese contract workers were as appealing to these small-scale manufacturers as they were to the Central Pacific. The contractors transformed labor into just one more resource for capitalists, one they could turn on and off like a faucet.

In industries such as cigars and shoes, only producers so small that they couldn't afford the outlays for Chinese contract labor still used white workers, who lacked the numbers to form an effective trade union. Instead, organized white workers in these sectors played on race hate to get customers to pay more for white-produced goods, which they tagged with (white) labels. This wasn't so much trade union activity—which might have involved trying to *increase* Chinese wages—as cartel behavior. As the scholar Iyko Day writes, "In the rapidly industrializing context of nineteenth-century railroad building and mining,...the Chinese body stood for the *devaluation* of white labor"[18] (emphasis Day's). Chinese workers came to represent a whole set of social forces that portended badly for white settlers who expected less competition in the West, which spurred especially fierce racial conflict in those industries—such as clothing, shoes, and cigars—that were entering mass production and national distribution in a process that was displacing artisans. In the white-settler mind, the Chinese workers were another tool that capitalists were using to speed up work and lower wages. The capitalists thought much the same.

As the nineteenth century closed, California's white labor movement increasingly shifted toward racial exclusion as its central operating principle. Instead of trade unions, the settlers had "anti-coolie clubs." The Workingmen's Party of California emerged from this milieu, cobbling together socialist rhetoric, trade union demands like an eight-hour day, and anti-Chinese racism. They were the ones who, in the midst of the 1877 unemployment crisis, marched up to Leland Stanford's mansion and threatened him. But their front man, Denis Kearney, was better at being a racist than a labor leader. "I will give the Central Pacific just three months to discharge their Chinamen," he railed, "and if that is not done, Stanford and his crowd will have to take the consequences."[19] However, it was easier for the Workingmen to impose consequences on Chinese workers than on white bosses: Stanford simply had Kearney arrested. Still, the Workingmen posed a threat to the Democrat-Republican duopoly, and with the railroad built, Chinese wages rising relative to white, and a surplus of "American" immigrants (who were more likely German or Irish), California's capitalists no longer had the same need for Asian work. Besides, Chinese workers were starting to become Chinese businessmen and farm owners, competing with white capital in addition to white labor. The only things that separated labor contractors from the capitalists were money and race, and the contractors were making money. This was a dangerous place for the California Chinese to be, for it was the "vigilance committees" organized by Republican businessmen that helped keep white rioting in check. (These committees weren't the only thing: Though settlers [and indeed, on occasion, indigenous residents] victimized individual Chinese, "the ghetto itself was armed," Saxton writes of Chinatown.)[20] As long as Republican officials extended the most basic protection of the law to their Chinese business partners, Chinatown could defend itself.* But the balance was tenuous, and white-settler plans for "abatement by force"—ethnic cleansing—were ghastly.

The "Chinese question" found its answer at the national level, in the debate over a California-led plan for Chinese exclusion. In reconstructing the United States, California was emerging as the regional swing vote, just as the state's enfranchised settlers became single-issue voters. The transcontinental railroad solidified the state's membership in the Union, which was far from a given considering how often the territory had changed hands in the previous few decades as well as its continual political instability and foreign interference in Mexico, not to mention the temporary sundering of the United States itself. California's Unionist majority helped repair that split, cutting off the Confederacy's western tendency. But Unionist didn't necessarily mean faithfully devoted to principles of abolition democracy and the spirit of the slave revolution. The race-based exclusion of Chinese from the country flew in the face of Reconstruction and the black-led attempt to create a pluralist, racially equal nation. But that seeming contradiction was no contradiction at all for California's white Jacksonians, because they maintained a consistent position in favor of free white labor and free white labor only. As for the regionally aligned party duopoly, California's vote swung against the South during the war, but it could swing back. Federal civil rights legislation meant to force the ex-Confederate states to integrate also applied to settler California's relations with the Chinese,

---

* Arson attacks failed due to the unusual durability of Chinatown relative to the rest of the city.

which left the southern and western delegations looking for a solution to their linked nonwhite labor problems. If former slaves and their children were able to escape not just their commodity status but also their working role in the regional economy, southern planters threatened to bring in Chinese laborers to replace them, just as planters had in the West Indies. That would blow the exclusion plan out of the water, which gave California an incentive to compromise with the South. These two racist blocs came to an agreement that permanently set the direction of the modern American project: They agreed to cede the South to the Confederate redeemers and exclude the Chinese.

The Chinese Exclusion Act, which closed the door to immigration from the territory, passed in 1882, after a couple of years of ironing out the details conveniently gave employers some time to figure out their labor situations. The Burlingame Treaty with China prevented Congress from banning Chinese immigration, so the act set a ten-year clock (after which the restriction was renewed). Over the following decades, the California and federal governments tightened restrictions on Chinese people living in the United States, excluding them from naturalized citizenship and even barring them from land ownership. These legal restrictions made assimilation into an integrated society along the same path as white immigrants impossible. The 1882 legislation also served as a signal to racist vigilantes in the West, who were already organized to varying degrees. In September of 1885, a settler pogrom in Rock Springs, Wyoming, killed 28 Chinese Union Pacific Railroad workers and triggered anti-Asian riots across the region. Not content with halting the flow of immigrants and now implicitly blessed by Congress, these civic vigilantes put their abatement plans into action. To a point, it worked: By the end of the century, the U.S. Chinese population fell by nearly a third, from 133,000 before the Exclusion Act down to 90,000, a direct consequence of the ethnic-cleansing campaign.[21]

—◇—

The transcontinental United States of America was a new nation. Where parochial standards endured—in timekeeping, for example, or in the gauge of the railroad track—the transcontinental line hammered them to uniformity. It secured the country's continental borders, and they haven't come up for much serious debate since. Chinese railroad workers made the country that in turn made the twentieth century, and that nation, never so friendly in the first place, turned on them hard. It's no use speculating on the various moments that seem contingent in retrospect. This story is not a product of men's choices, a series of psychic coin flips that results in the world as it is, one piece of fruit among many on a branching tree of equally probable outcomes. With the advent of the integrated world system, in which the transcontinental line was, along with the Suez Canal, a decisive link, investment flows determined the shape of what was to come. Capital's ravenous hunger for higher returns carved a new physical and social geography out of the earth. It figuratively flattened space, blowing holes in some mountains as well. But contrary to some progressive expectations, it failed to dissolve barriers between peoples. Instead it formalized new ones. Capitalists used racial segregation to generate wage differentials, and legal, economic, social, and civic exclusion fell together in a dialectical tumble, each determining and determined by the others.

Around the world, the new model of railroad colonialism, as scholar Manu Karuka labels it, held to a common pattern: "territorial expansion through financial logics and corporate organization, using unfree imported laborers, blending the economic and military functions of the state, materializing in construction projects across the colonized world."[22] Once in play, these elements repeatedly yielded the same reaction. Capital flows obey systematic laws the way objects in motion obey theirs: predictably, inexorably. Confronted with a runaway train, men could get out of the way, get run over, or, if they were among the lucky few, get on board and find out where the tracks went.

What, then, of the shopkeepers? What of Leland Stanford? Norris's railroad-baron composite, Shelgrim, urged readers (and writers) to think of the world's transformation at the end of the nineteenth century in terms of forces rather than men, and indeed that explains how a man as insubstantial as Stanford could come to occupy such an important historical place. With the silver hammer handed him he blessed the accomplished fact of the transcontinental railroad and labored not much more. "He has never made any money but has had a good deal made for him and knows no more of its value when he gets it than he does of the way in which it was obtained," Stanford's associate Huntington wrote of the man.[23] But in this way, the Governor is more representative of his milieu than the smarter, harder-working Huntington. Neither of them laid anything but a symbolic track between California and the East.

They hardly even enriched their shareholders. Instead, they had a good deal of money made for them. Such was the role of the Great Man under global capitalism.

"That such and such a man and precisely that man arises at that particular time in that given country is of course pure accident. But cut him out and there will be a demand for a substitute, and this substitute will be found, good or bad," Friedrich Engels wrote in an 1894 letter. "[That] if a Napoleon had been lacking, another would have filled the place, is proved by the fact that the man has always been found as soon as he became necessary: Caesar, Augustus, Cromwell, etc."[24] Necessity, he says, appears in the form of accidents, which appear in the form of men. Leo Tolstoy comes to similar conclusions inspired by the same Corsican in *War and Peace* ("History, that is, the unconscious, swarmlike life of mankind, uses every moment of a king's life as an instrument for its purposes"), and Fyodor Dostoevsky dispatches him as a "pseudo great man" in *The Brothers Karamazov*. It's entirely possible that after Napoleon has faded from the history books—as inevitable as it seems unimaginable at the moment of this writing—he will remain in literature, standing in these stories for all the world's crowned accidents. Leland Stanford's stature contrasted less with his accomplishments than the *empereur*'s did, but the Governor's character seems to have been so unexceptional that his frame fooled few. No matter: The money was in his accounts, the land in his name.

In Stanford, the new system coughed up another man to stand for the larger forces pulling his strings. Though he was but a happy monkey dancing for history's organ grinder, the West was so dear to the world market, the mass of value involved so gigantic, that the size of his small share surpassed even his fantastic appetite for luxuries. What's a mortal man to do when he accumulates more than he can consume in a lifetime? The remainder is called a legacy, and Leland Stanford named his legacy Leland Stanford Jr. And he named it Palo Alto.

Blood That Trots Young

Horse Power — The Palo Alto System — Edward
Muybridge and the First Movie — Leland Stanford Jr. —
Founding Stanford University

Toward the end of the 1870s, the Stanfords started decreasing the amount of time they spent in their luxurious Nob Hill mansion. Not even two decades into the rush San Francisco had become a rowdy metropolis, the biggest city on the West Coast and gaining on the East, in no small part thanks to Stanford and the railroad. The city's growth came at the people's expense, as industry corralled pioneers into jobs. Capital-intensive gold mining was consolidated, with nothing on the surface left to pan, and by 1870 there were more Californians working on farms than in mines.[1] Completion of the railroad brought more competition, for laborers and for the smaller West Coast manufacturers and merchants that employed them. A transcontinental link undermined the advantages that motivated most forty-niners to set out on the perilous journey in the first place — and so soon, before they could enjoy their rewards too much or recoup the risk-cost of their adventure. Unemployment in San Francisco exceeded one in five, in a city where women's unpaid labor (which insulates men from the pitiless market) was in short supply.[2]

The railroad stood for capital in California, the Combine stood for the railroad, and Leland Stanford stood for the Combine. It was an easy and incredibly well-remunerated gig — he didn't have to do a whole lot more than the standing — but one consequence is that a lot of people hated him and his family. The white labor cartels held him personally responsible for the importation of Chinese workers and the resulting speed-up and attack on wages. If an individual could be responsible for all that, Stanford was as good a choice as any.

The top of the hill in one of the city's biggest houses sounds like a nice place to live depending on your taste, but one potential drawback is that everyone knows where to find you. The location of the Stanford home was no mystery, and protesters made it a frequent target. Early that decade, the whole world saw what happened when an urban elite got too comfortable with the people's complaints: The radical workers of Paris, France, took control of the city and declared the Commune. Journalist James Ayers recalled a different French insurrection when, during a visit to the Nob Hill estate, Stanford showed off a gadrooned Sèvres vase, once a present from Marie Antoinette to the Marquis de Villette. He told his guest to just ignore the interrupting cries from the workers outside the window. "Was there, I asked myself, a fatality attending the ownership of that vase?" Ayers wrote in his memoir. "I said to myself that were I Stanford, I would look upon that beautiful work of art as a 'hoodoo' and neutralize whatever evil spell it might possess by donating it to some institution where its power for good or evil would expend itself, not on an individual, but on the general Public."[3] The Stanfords' ruling-class spiritualism didn't help them see what was obvious to everyone else: Their ill-gotten wealth tempted fate.

The Central Pacific wasn't about to capitulate to the sandlot crowd. Instead, Stanford gathered his family—which now included Leland Jr., born in 1868—and servants and got out of town. Like other prominent robber barons of the day, the Stanfords "sought security in a country estate," as Kenneth T. Jackson put it in his classic study, *Crabgrass Frontier: The Suburbanization of the United States*, providing a model for elites looking to dodge racial strife a century later.[4] In 1876, they bought a 650-acre farm, called Mayfield Grange, in Santa Clara County off the train tracks south of the city. No fan of the contemporary Grange Movement of organized farmers, Stanford renamed the area for a big tree next to the tracks: Palo Alto. In Palo Alto the Stanfords could keep any worker who didn't work for them at a distance, something that wasn't possible in San Francisco. Compared to the perch in Nob Hill, exposed to the howling winds of class conflict, the South Bay ranch was placid, a grassy pseudo-feudal expanse of lords and servants.

Concurrent with Thomas Hill's aforementioned railroad commission, Stanford asked the painter to reflect on the estate's majesty, which he did in *Palo Alto Spring*. The extended Stanford family reposes around a well-manicured lawn, children playing croquet beneath the trees' shade, a bit of sky peeking out above a house of undefined large proportions. Leland Sr. sits, his left arm leaning on the back of his son's chair. The family is bracketed by two black attendants in gray suits, bearing beverage trays and angled away from the viewer. As he did in his more famous painting of the railroad's completion, Hill seems to have included a lonely Indian in *Palo Alto Spring*, standing in the background across a road, between the family and their house. In the foreground, at Jane Stanford's feet, is a bearskin, its dead face the painting's most alive. The rug's yellow eye reproaches the viewer as two overdressed young girls sit on its splayed back. Leland escaped the Workingmen's shouts, but the curse followed his family to Palo Alto. The Stanfords didn't seem to notice the painting's implications, and Hill's work remains on view in the memorial collection.

Away from the Associates, Stanford came into his own in Palo Alto. Never all that interested in railroads (or really anything in particular), he finally found something worth his time: horses. The *nouveau riche* hobby of breeding racehorses captured his attention in a way that other business didn't. What with the care Stanford lavished on Leland Jr. and the trotters, his partners among the Associates despaired of getting him to fulfill even his official duties, never mind add any value to their common enterprise. By that time he had plenty of cash secured, and the Stanfords invested it in land and luxuries. The ranch became the Palo Alto Stock Farm, a place where Stanford could see to the rearing and training of his horses (as well as his son). He poured money into the farm, hiring dozens of workers to equip the stables, including his elite chief trainer, Charles Marvin. The project grew massive, and he kept acquiring land to expand his now beloved Palo Alto tract. By the end of the 1880s, the stock farm boasted nearly 800 horses and a staff of 150 spread over 11,000 acres, the largest and finest institution of its kind in the world. Shipping horses back and forth to the West Coast from the farms of Kentucky and the markets of New York might have been a prohibitive expense for most, but not for Stanford the railroad man. He had a custom railcar built for his fine equine cargo.

Leland Stanford was not content to own horses, nor was he content to own the fastest horses in all the land. He saw himself as engaged in a serious scientific campaign regarding the improved performance of the laboring animal—hippology, or equine engineering. For Stanford the capitalist, the horses were productive biological machines, and in races he could analyze their output according to simple, univocal metrics. The trotters he raised raced with carriages behind them, restrained below a gallop to simulate a horse at work, not play. Within these restrictions, faster horses were better horses, and if he could master the production of better horses, then he could improve the country's capital stock. Stanford figured that if through the application of scientific methods he could build a program that would raise the value of the average horse by $100, that would be worth $1.3 billion to a country with 13 million horses (over $30 billion in 2022 money).[5] Stronger, more durable horses led faster carriages and bigger plows for longer, which reduced the costs of production and increased social circulation in unimaginable ways. Horses were the dominant mode of local transportation (especially during the still-dreaded "last mile" stage of delivery). They were the military's most important weapon and the chief source of agricultural power. The country was deeply dependent on them, as demonstrated when a wave of equine influenza in the winter of 1872–73 infected roughly 100 percent of its horses, killing more than 1 percent and temporarily debilitating the rest. The Great Epizootic ground eastern cities to a halt, stopping the horse-powered Delaware, Hudson, and Erie Canals in addition to virtually all local transport.[6] New York City streetcar operators had to drag the cars themselves, and much of Boston burned down when sick horses were left too tired to pull fire engines.[7]

Though the inventions that replaced draft animals were soon to arrive, the tractor didn't get there in time to lead the agricultural development of the West. The number of farm-based horses in the United States tripled to over 25 million in the following decades, before falling even faster in the 1920s, '30s, and '40s.[8] In 1910, the peak of the pre-tractor era, horses and mules constituted two-thirds of farm implements and machinery by value—$2.6 billion of the $3.9 billion in national "crop-growing capital."[9] Never mind what the animals cost in daily upkeep. Around the turn of the century, finding ways to reduce horse costs was a pressing question for business, particularly in California, a rising agricultural power. The state's growers used larger and more advanced machinery to get better yields than the rest of the country, and perhaps counterintuitively, late nineteenth-century mechanization meant high horse intensity. Horses were the engines of the West, and by 1870, recall, the state's farms already had three times as many draft animals per farm as the national average.[10] Ultimately that's what the Palo Alto Stock Farm was all about.

More valuable than any single horse, any thousand horses, were the insights into natural efficiency the farm developed. The "13 million horses × $100" calculation is the kind of disruption math that twenty-first-century start-ups use to persuade venture capitalists to sink millions into protean projects, but Leland only had to convince himself it was worth his money, which he seems to have had no problem doing. Bringing industrial techniques, goals, and capital to the production of animals, Stanford's farm was the prototype for what the scholar Phillip Thurtle calls the laboratories of speed, with their limitless resources, firm-style employment bureaucracies, (pseudo)scientific breeding methods, and focus on a single product.[11] This was not an animal farm in any classic sense; it was an experimental engine factory, churning out high-performance horse flesh by the ton. Since they sold horses for their genetics — the blood more valuable than the muscle — the Palo Alto Stock Farm was really in the business of intellectual property.

Horse breeders were at the vanguard of genetics, tracing lineages back over many generations and pricing studs for their genetic material. Winning a race was nice, but the real prize went to the horse who could produce winners by the cupful. The industry was well-convinced about the significant role of hereditary traits in the development of racing champions, but this (correct) fundamental understanding wasn't necessarily incompatible with (incorrect) community folk knowledge. As the paragon of a new ruling class that prided itself on overturning ossified assumptions, Leland Stanford was sure that despite being a newcomer to the sport, he knew more than the rest of the breeders and trainers did. He was a man of science, with no undue regard for the way things had been done in the past, and he had the money to go at it however he wanted. Stanford bought the untested stallion Electioneer (against professional advice, the story goes) as part of his first batch of breeders; the horse became the greatest of all time, "the sire...of more young record-breakers than any horse in the world."[12]

The prevailing wisdom was that the best trotters were pure-blooded, the product of a trotting stallion and a trotting mare. Crossbreeding with the galloping Thoroughbreds was thought to produce willful colts that were unable to maintain a trot. Stanford was unconvinced, and Electioneer bred promiscuously.[13] Old hands had to eat their words when the Palo Alto Stock Farm produced both pure and mixed champions, though they tended to credit the extraordinary "brain-controlling power" in Electioneer's genes rather than any breakthrough in the science. Soon, Stanford's colts were selling for extraordinary prices, setting a record in 1892 when he sold the two-year-old champion Arion to breeder J. Malcolm Forbes for $125,000 — over $2 million in 2022 money. Stanford and his money changed the industry, and the brand-new Palo Alto Stock Farm quickly became the world headquarters for hippology, equine engineering, or whatever the newspapers wanted to call what it was he was doing.

By applying capitalist rationality to trotter production, Stanford's Palo Alto horse factory transformed more than just breeding practices. Before Stanford entered the field, trotters were the domain of small-market investors and horsemen guided by instinct. One reason is that true aristocrats considered the sport déclassé, but another was the life cycle of a performance trotter. Training began in earnest around the third year, and horses didn't mature until age seven or eight, which meant owners had to feed and shelter them that whole time, even if they *and* their offspring turned out to be mediocre racers. And since the real money was in breeders, a trotter only acquired substantial value when its spawn (its "get") turned out to be fast, too, forcing a lot of patience from investors. It wasn't a great business unless you liked horses for their own sake. This would not do for Leland, and he and Charles Marvin went about changing the way horses were raised, trained, and sold. By summer of 1889, Palo Alto's trotters set new world records for yearlings, two-year-olds, three-year-olds, and four-year-olds, a staggering triumph that the sport's leading thinkers were forced to acknowledge. Electioneer's surprisingly strong blood helped, they all agreed, but a good initial stud wasn't enough to succeed the way Palo Alto had. How did they do it?

Capital's exigencies dictated that Palo Alto shorten the horse production cycle. That meant training the animals to trot younger rather than letting colts learn to walk before they run. Instead of optimizing for adult speed, they optimized for *visible potential*. Drawing inspiration from the young children's education movement, which had recently spread from Germany to the United States, Stanford built a shrunken "kindergarten" track where colts as young as five months learned to maintain a strong trot.* Its small size allowed two

---

* This in turn inspired local educational reformers. Kate Douglas Wiggin cited the Stock Farm in her book *Children's Rights*: "Look at Senator Stanford's famous Palo Alto Stock Farm. Each colt born into that favored community is placed in a class of twelve. These

trainers with long whips to stand near the oval's foci and control the whole track, guiding their charges toward excellence by snap. At this point the competitive selection process begins, and a youngster with a lot of promise gets "all the work he can safely stand," a dedication of significant expense. Based on the Palo Alto Stock Farm understanding that potential reveals future performance, resources were apportioned for horse development according to colt speed. Stanford opposed jogging, preferring to build the animals' maximum sprint and worry about distance later. "We aim to first develop the speed, and after that to condition the horse to carry it," wrote Marvin in his guide to the method.[14] By deriving (or generating) information about his colts' characters early, Stanford flipped the whole industry's incentive structure. "The business of breeding has now reached a point where few feel able to wait six or seven years for the get of their stallion to bring prestige to the farm," wrote racing expert Leslie Macleod about Stanford's impact in his review of the Palo Alto equine factory, "and hence he buys the blood that trots young." The blood that trots young is exactly what Stanford's farm was designed to showcase, and by revealing and embracing those market incentives he forced others to follow his lead.

There were consequences. "When you get several yearlings to trot quarters in 0:40, and two-year-olds to show you a 2:20 gait, you must not be surprised if some tendon snaps," conceded Macleod. "Some good material has without a doubt been spoiled."[15] No reward without risk, but in Palo Alto they interpreted these failures as inevitable. In their genetic-determinist view, training could only reveal and realize the underlying immutable potential—a view that was good for sales, because genes are much easier to reproduce off-site than the capital-intensive training is. Based on this flawed premise, they figured that if you're going to fail, you might as well do that fast, too. "If he goes wrong at two years old he will be a cheaper failure than if he goes wrong at ten years old," wrote Marvin. "If a stallion has not the power to make a great sire, and his get have not the capacity and quality to make good performers, the

---

twelve colts are cared for and taught by four or five trained teachers. . . . The end is supposed to justify the means. But when the creatures to be trained are human beings, and when the end to be reached is not race-horses, but merely citizens, we employ a very different process of reasoning." Kate Douglas Wiggin, *Children's Rights: A Book of Nursery Logic* (Gay and Bird, 1892), 194–95. She founded the first free kindergarten west of the Rockies in San Francisco in 1878, and the movement quickly attracted Jane Stanford's support.

quicker the owner and trainer find it out the better."[16] Better to snap a year-ling's tendon than feed him to age five just to see it snap then. If performance was destiny, then there could be no accidents in colt training, just early information, and early information was money saved.

The stock farm's regimen of capitalist rationality and the exclusive focus on potential and speculative value was called the Palo Alto System and it worked. Horse-driven chariots were a literally ancient technology, studied for millennia, and the Palo Alto System transformed their production in just a decade. All a man needed to improve the world was an uncompromising dedication to profit and the capital to realize the necessary scale. Stanford had both, and he created Palo Alto to house them. The twin whips of science—data and control—sped money around its circuit like colts around the *kindergarten* track, accumulating valuable mass with every lap.

Unsupported Transit

Perhaps if horses still dragged the country's artillery, plows, and delivery vans, we would remember the Palo Alto Stock Farm for the animals. But Leland Stanford's semiconscious drive for the age of invention's constellation of intangibles (information, control, speed, efficiency, value, and profit) yielded something better than horses: pictures of horses. The Governor's farm was a scientific project from the outset, part of a larger atmosphere in which ambitious thinkers began applying the tools of systematic observation to the world's mysteries, and one of those mysteries concerned horses and their gait. Unsupported transit was the name of the controversial theory that horses lifted all four of their legs off the ground at the same time, flinging themselves through the air. Scholar Étienne-Jules Marey explored the question at the Collège de France with the use of what was in effect a mini seismograph—an apparatus that automatically recorded footfalls with scratches on pieces of paper. The evidence was clear: Horses fly. The experiment captured Stanford's imagination, and he wondered if the mythical unsupported transit could be frozen by camera, arrested in place for analysis. The Governor could certainly afford to find out. And if it could be done, there was one man in Alta California to make it happen.

Edward Muybridge was going by the *nom de bouton* Helios, his brand logo a camera with wings, and quite a brand it was. A notoriously irascible man—later attributed in part to a traumatic brain injury from an 1860 carriage accident—Muybridge preferred to work alone, which was difficult to do as a nineteenth-century photographer since portraiture, with its emphasis on customer service, was the bulk of the business. Still, there was plenty worth seeing in the West besides wannabe genteel white people, and Muybridge decided he was the man to capture the rest. With no small effort he converted a covered wagon into a mobile darkroom and set off from San Francisco. In 1867 he went to Yosemite Valley just as the majestic site was beginning to acquire a reputation for its scenery and natural features. He was contracted to take photos for a guidebook to the valley, and he brought a large-format camera for the book pictures as well as a stereoscope to get some of the faux-3D images popular with consumers to sell on the side. He settled his gaze on Yosemite's sublime vistas and brought them home in slices for sale. The book was a hit. Unlike commission-dependent portraitists, Muybridge was an entertainer, and he enjoyed being both artist and subject. A later Yosemite self-portrait shows him dangling his legs from a sheer rock cliff, thousands of feet off the ground, like a social media influencer.

The Governor first hired Helios in 1872 to document his Sacramento mansion and many fine possessions, applying new technology to the classic form. Though by then Muybridge had a policy against taking boring photos inside people's houses, other people didn't have houses like Stanford's, and Stanford was a good friend to make in California, so Helios made an exception. The photos show the ornate home mostly empty, and only a few of the plates contain images of the residents. Muybridge makes it look elegant and cavernous, the kind of pictures you might take to advertise a wedding venue for rent. He also took photos of Leland's two-horse carriage at rest, headed in some by the trainer Charles Wooster and in others by family coachman James Vickers.[17] These were the self-congratulatory collectibles of a wealthy man—nothing scientific about them, but already there were more photos of the horses than of Leland Jr. Later in the year, when the Governor thought to use his resources to improve on Marey's unsupported-transit work, he reached out to Muybridge with the idea of capturing the champion trotting horse Occident in motion. Even Helios thought it was a stretch, but Stanford paid his bills without looking too hard at the numbers, and he was adamant.

They set up at the Sacramento race track near the first Stanford base of operations, before a move to continue the experiments at the new Bay District Track in San Francisco. A white sheet background provided maximum contrast in the California sun. Muybridge replicated human vision with a dual-lens system, informed by his experience with the stereoscope. To capture Occident midstride, he needed a very fast shutter, an apparatus that could blink faster than an eye to isolate an instant of time at a level below human perception. Ever the inventor, Helios used another new technology: the rubber band. French aviation engineer Alphonse Pénaud had recently begun using twisted rubber bands to power model propeller planes, which made for a cool kid's toy in 1871. The Lelands Stanford were noted collectors of new mechanical toys, and it's distinctly possible that that's where Muybridge got the idea to use the exotic item.*[18] Muybridge's rubber-band shutter system caught the horse with enough detail to confirm Marey's findings, but the picture apparently wasn't worth saving, though a printmaker published a commercial lithograph based on the result, with all four of Occident's legs in the air.[19]

The Governor hired Muybridge again in 1876 to shoot his new Palo Alto estate, apparently not begrudging Helios the murder and child abandonment that characterized the intermission in their working relationship.† These

---

* By coincidence, Pénaud was a collaborator of Marey's. They built a mechanical bird toy together, and Pénaud encouraged the horse researcher to use photos to really solve the unsupported-transit question, as Stanford and Muybridge were busy doing. No one financed Pénaud's designs for a full-size propeller plane—all the money was in hot-air balloons—and he killed himself in 1880 at the age of thirty. Marey's "photochronographic gun" debuted in 1882, shot 12 frames per second, and was a proximate inspiration for the Lumière Brothers' cinematograph. See Alison McMahan, *Alice Guy Blaché: Lost Visionary of the Cinema* (London: Continuum, 2002), 5–6.

† In the spring of 1873, Muybridge left his young wife, Flora, in Frisco and headed north for the craggy Lava Beds of the Klamath Reservation where the U.S. Army had driven the Tule Lake Modoc. The group continued to disobey orders to leave their land for good, and when the army refused a compromise that would have left them on the Klamath territory, Modoc leader Kientpoos had no room left to negotiate. The shooting lasted nearly two months, and the campaign is most notable for the ferocity of Modoc resistance, the death of General Edward Canby, and Muybridge's photographs. His cave picture presents a forbidding black void in the earth where the Modocs made their last stand, a final nook of unconquered California. When the army finally triumphed in June, they shipped the 150 surviving Modocs to Oklahoma on Stanford's Central Pacific. The campaign solidified U.S. control of Alta California and Muybridge's reputation as the country's premier adventure photographer. Though his personal attempts at land speculation failed, the settler-artist Muybridge gained directly from Indian dispossession. Meanwhile, San Francisco theater critic and leading municipal

pictures are much like the Sacramento ones, but the technology had improved to better display the baroque opulence: marble columns, expansive rugs, intricate moldings that threaten to overwhelm the visual field. Now Stanford was ready to give the horse pictures another try, this time with increased resources. Muybridge figured that more shots improved the chances of a direct hit, so Stanford financed the purchase of a dozen cameras and lenses. He also enlisted the Central Pacific's Oakland office to help design the trigger mechanism, and the railroad sent a young engineer named John Isaacs.

Technology had advanced rapidly since Stanford and Muybridge's first attempt, and the team could now work with electric circuits. The CPR engineers built an electromagnetic trigger for a rubber-band shutter. As the carriage wheel passed over exposed wires, the horse took its own picture. Next they designed a machine that echoed the hand-crank mechanism of the Gatling gun, metal pins completing circuits to the dozen cameras, tracking the horse as the spiked cylinder rotated. They captured motion in pictures one camera at a time, all before Thomas Edison got to the lightbulb. Leland Jr. served as a riding subject and as he got older he took up photography himself, imitating

---

cad Harry Larkyns became the first man to cuckold a photographer deployed by the U.S. Army. Flora Muybridge was only twenty-two years old—twenty years younger than her absent husband—and alone in the big city, where young women remained exceptionally rare. She fell hard for Larkyns, and when Muybridge arrived home in late 1873 to a pregnant Flora, he managed to suppress the implications in his mind, if not among San Francisco's gossips. But in the fall of 1874, confronted with an unfamiliar photo of baby Florado Muybridge, Edward turned it over to see the words "Little Harry" in Flora's handwriting. Helios boarded a ferry boat, connected to a North Bay train, and finally hailed a buggy to get him to the seducer's door in Calistoga. He knocked, and when Larkyns answered, Muybridge dropped some quip about Flora and fatally shot the man. Facing a slam-dunk capital murder trial in California, where the penalty was hanging, Helios hired a strong legal team with the implied assistance of his sometimes-patron Leland Stanford. The lawyers argued a mix of temporary insanity and justification: Muybridge's discovery had driven him out of his mind with fury, as it would have so driven any red-blooded nineteenth-century man in the West. Though there were hardly grounds in the criminal code, the all-male jury acquitted, deciding the theater critic had been asking for it. Flora divorced Muybridge and filed for alimony. Helios got a gig in Central America and split town, leaving his ex-wife and child destitute in a boarding house. Flora quickly succumbed to grief and illness, and died before her twenty-fifth birthday. When Edward returned to discover his ex-wife deceased and his son in a Catholic orphanage, he rescued Florado, only to re-abandon him at a Protestant orphanage. Florado Helios Muybridge died in 1944 after being hit by a car in Sacramento. Beyond his name and lifespan, his grave is inscribed only "Son of Photographer Eadweard James Muybridge." Hayden Bennett, "A Review of Florado Helios Muybridge's Tombstone," *The Believer*, April 27, 2018.

the master in his backyard. Leland Sr. spent as much time as he could in Palo Alto near the horses and the photography, and he seems to have enjoyed a close, admiring relationship with his son, unusual for the time (and perhaps any time). Their collective project made history, and the Stanford-Muybridge horse photos remain iconic, coming to represent abstract phenomena such as technology and movement itself.

By the summer of 1878, Muybridge was ready to show off his photos to the press. He was a sort of expert at showing off, and he performed his motion photography like a stage magician for the crowd, taking the photographs, disappearing into his trackside darkroom, and emerging with the horse frozen in instants, shrunken onto small glass rectangles.[20] The reporters went nuts, tripping over one another to tell the world about the accomplishment before someone else did. Muybridge used a flame-powered slide projector to show the photos to San Francisco's fashionable audiences, no doubt gratifying his patron as well. *Scientific American* published engravings of the Palo Alto photos in October of 1878, and *La Nature* republished some to a Paris readership in December. All of a sudden Muybridge was more than an artist, a showman, and an infamous murderer: He was an internationally renowned scientist. Stanford signed off on another dozen cameras, and Muybridge extended his ambitions, collecting more four-legged animals and a troupe of athletes down from the city to perform feats of strength for the lenses, the cameras capturing their every muscled curve.

When audiences saw Muybridge's motion studies, the sophisticated among them quickly realized the implications. For 50 years inventors and entertainers used the retina's afterimage effect to generate the illusion of motion. A series of minimally different drawings interspersed with the black of a shutter and spun around a center axis yielded cartoon couples who danced or animals that jumped around. The most popular format was the zoetrope, which mounted images vertically around the inside of a small spinning drum with viewing slits in the sides, allowing a crowd to gather around a table and watch. When *Scientific American* published the Palo Alto engravings, they suggested that readers cut them out and paste them into their home displays to watch the horse in action.

Muybridge had a better idea, and in 1879 he started experimenting with his own scope—a zoetrope combined with a slide projector, an apparatus that could entertain whole rooms at a time. He taped his horse shards in order around the edge of a glass disk and spun it in front of the gas-jet flame. The images blurred until he added a black shutter wheel with light slits, something that Pénaud hinted early in the decade might be necessary for rapid photography. All put together, Muybridge had the first movie projector. He gave it the ungainly name zoopraxiscope, making him the world's only zoopraxographer. In January of 1880, he gave the first of his many zoopraxographic performances, at the Stanford mansion in San Francisco for Leland and a select group of friends. The age of movies began in California, not in Hollywood but in the Bay.

Up until this point, the two titanic egos—Helios and the Governor—had maintained a productive tension, one that was based on incompatible ideas about their relationship. To Muybridge, the two were partners, Stanford providing the capital and the impetus, the photographer bringing the expertise and the technical labor. To Stanford, though, Muybridge was an especially skilled employee, hired the way future Silicon Valley tycoons hired expert sailors to pilot their racing yachts. Stanford paid Muybridge's (extensive) bills, but he never compensated the photographer directly. When the Governor finally cut him a check for a measly $2,000, it marked a break between the two, collapsing Muybridge's hopes into disappointment.[21] While Helios toured Europe, received as the scientist-artist-maestro he now believed himself to be, Stanford hired a writer to put together a book of the Muybridge photographs, but without any credit to the man himself—Stanford mentioned him once in the introduction as just another hired hand.

Audiences were surprised to find the inventor they believed responsible for the images mostly unfeatured in the book's account, and some suggested he must be claiming undue credit, a swindler. Muybridge was outraged, and he used his touring revenue to fund Palo Alto's first intellectual property lawsuit: *Muybridge v. Stanford*.[22] The judge dismissed the case. Helios was broke, unemployed, and exiled from Bay Area high society. He resumed his motion experiments in Philadelphia at the University of Pennsylvania, where his photographic studies of naked women—sometimes crawling on the ground, sometimes kissing each other on the mouth—raised eyebrows.

Muybridge, framer of landscapes, has kept most historians focused on the tree of his photos rather than the forest of the Palo Alto Stock Farm. Society's progressive lurches require proper names to inhabit as well as flesh-and-blood limbs, and Muybridge was an inveterate namer, giving himself Helios and zoopraxiscope, but also changing the spelling of his own name, leaving scholars unsure how to refer to the man even as they knew they had to. (I have opted for the simplest spelling.) Stanford enjoyed naming things, too, and he had plenty of opportunities as a pioneer politician/land baron. The namers get named because we have to explain where the names for things come from, and the namers often name things after themselves and one another. These promoters leave their fingerprints on the civilizational timeline, using the portraits of themselves they commission to illustrate our collective past. That was the relatively tame to-do Stanford and Muybridge began with: the self-aggrandizing images the rich always seem to generate. Novelty is the cousin of scarcity, and wealthy patrons are frequently the first to embrace new representational techniques. Who else is going to pay for experiments such as the motion studies? And yet both men quickly found themselves swept up by larger systematic currents, their tasks transformed into vast unbounded projects related to production and circulation, money and speed.

Unlike past generations of court painters, Muybridge could sell reproductions of his work to the general public, or at least a class that claimed to represent the general public. Stanford paid him in exposure and equipment, financing the photographer's commercial image line. It was a unique opportunity for a self-branding expert like Helios, allowing him to tour on the horsepower of the special pictures, selling slices of the horse in motion the way he sold slices of the park, the unsupported equines representing the technovisual frontier the way a waterfall represents the natural frontier — a "substitute horizon" in the words of French philosopher Paul Virilio.[23] Stanford's investment in the multiple-camera apparatus allowed Muybridge to shoot the way no other photographer could, and he made the most out of it.

The zoopraxiscope was less a scientific step than a commercial one, bringing the entertainment of a moving zoetrope to the room-size audience of a "magic lantern" slide projector, inventing the movie for the movie theater. Rather than relying on a single unreliable patron, Muybridge could harvest his fees from a whole class of customers, one ticket or photo set at a time. Not lords or barons or even capitalists like Stanford, these consumers couldn't afford to employ their own artists and technicians, but they could and did pay for their share of an evening projector show or a photo reproduction. Discontented with the conditions of home portraiture and the classic role of the court artist, with its high-intensity customer-service labor, Muybridge made images that entertained a more popular audience instead.

Stanford's money came from the Combine and the Combine's money came from bonds sold against the federal government's land grants and the speculative promise of the conquered West. The Yosemite photos allowed everyone to see through Muybridge's white eyes as they settled on majestic virgin territory. His photos of Central America pitched those far-off lands to investors, the seafaring gate to California turned into the southern tip of the U.S. commercial empire. Muybridge's photo sets were homesteads on the technovisual frontier, affordable pieces for the destined people, advertisements for everything the state had to offer. Bits of Palo Alto circulated around the Western world, entering the bloodstream of the emerging global bourgeoisie.

Leland Stanford saw himself as Muybridge's boss rather than partner, and not without cause. The horse-in-motion photos were one small part of the Palo Alto Stock Farm's equine engineering project, and considering what went into the apparatus it's fair to say the photographer was only one small part of the horse-in-motion photos. They were, after all, Stanford's horses and cameras. Trotting horses were the established purview of competitive local elites, but Leland Sr. couldn't keep his money from transforming the whole industry. The Governor wasn't seasoned with generations of folk knowledge about horses; instead he had a whole world's capital coursing through his veins. The 1870s saw European money—vacuumed up from colonies around the world with the help of California engineers—follow railroad speculators all the way to the West Coast. Value seemed to fling itself by the millions across long distances, across oceans, gathering in municipal centers and popping up wherever it could expect to find higher profits. Unsupported transit.

Capital began organizing at national and global levels in earnest. What was left of Congress in 1863 passed the National Bank Act, and that decade yielded lasting finance names such as Morgan and Goldman. In 1870, some of newly unified Germany's bankers joined to form Deutsche Bank, which quickly opened international offices to cash in on higher returns abroad. The Rothschilds had had agents in Alta California since before U.S. conquest, but the London branch of the banking family formed a close new relationship with the state's mining capitalists in the latter part of the decade.[24] California allowed foreign banks to set up local branches, and in 1875 the Hongkong and Shanghai Banking Corporation (HSBC) took the state up on the offer, followed by the Yokohama Specie Bank in 1899, along with a number of London-, Paris-, and Canada-based banks.[25] Worldwide investment flows drove invention toward profitable ends, fueling major technological efficiencies and advances in all aspects of life, which in turn spurred new colonial interventions. The midcentury invention of vulcanized rubber and the resulting European demand pushed explorers up the Amazon basin to open the latex-filled veins of South America, and into the African Congo for analogous reasons. European finance capital completed the Suez Canal and headed on to Panama. Stocks and bonds could move mountains and wrangle electrons.

Leland Stanford was but a historical vector, albeit a robust, capacious one, and he puffed up like a balloon, coat buttons pulled taut with pressure. Anything in his orbit tended to bulge the same way, from his vineyard (the world's biggest) to his wife's jewels (among the world's gaudiest).[26] As a man, he was notably unexceptional; as an embodiment of historical forces, he couldn't own horses without transforming them into the world's fastest. The scientific principles of control, measurement, and deliberate change opened a road to modernity, and capital was the draft mule that pulled the whole world down that path, California first. Here is where the twentieth century's fortunes were made, and so much of that demand flowed in one way or another through the body of Governor Leland Stanford. Like a financial King Midas, he turned everything he touched into an international speculative concern. Everything could be made more.

And his son, Leland Jr. What would be made of him?

The School of Sorrow

The second Leland was first among California's organic Anglo-American gentry. He was born Leland DeWitt Stanford in Sacramento in 1868, the only child to Leland Sr. and Jane, who was nearing forty after two decades of childless marriage. At a time when American parents were not necessarily expected to know all their children's names, the Stanfords treasured their son. Years before the Palo Alto System was established, they took a concerted interest in

Leland DeWitt's education and development. Growing up between the family mansions and the stock-farm lands, the boy played with servants and the children of servants. As a son of nearly peerless wealth, he was taught noblesse oblige. The suburban move sheltered the boy from the Workingmen, and one of the many privileges he inherited was an idealistic picture of his father, who appeared generous and grand to his son despite his consensus reputation among the public and indeed his own friends and acquaintances. In 1882, the teenage Leland insisted on dropping DeWitt from his name and adding Jr. as a tribute to his dear papa. He was shaped not so much in the Governor's image but in his *imago*, his idealized self, the character he played in industry propaganda, the one his business partners chuckled at in private. Whereas Leland Sr. contracted out his childhood woodchopping at a profit, Leland Jr. laid Palo Alto railroad track to build his own character. Leland Stanford Jr. was the Leland Stanford that Leland Stanford Sr. liked to imagine himself to be.

In the final quarter of the nineteenth century, the Western middle and upper classes began to think of children as occupying their own developmental category. Previously split into the reasonless gremlin time of toddlerhood and the family-owned labor of adolescence, the notion of childhood expanded with the need for workers skilled in book learning. The number of children per family shrank as adolescents and teenagers shifted from asset to liability in the domestic ledger.[27] The Stanfords were an extreme example, with their single child and outlying wealth. Leland Jr. grew up a spoiled child at the dawn of the age of spoiled children — Frances Hodgson Burnett's serialized novel *Little Lord Fauntleroy* about a golden-hearted boy aristocrat was a transatlantic sensation in the mid-1880s, for example, inspiring the frilly-shirt-and-curls look. As a natural consequence of his wealth, Leland Sr. exposed his son to serious concerns at a young age. Recall that Leland Jr. participated in the Muybridge photos, and he rode his pony at the world-class stock farm. His toys were mechanical wonders, especially the functional and rideable quarter-scale train built by company engineers, which ran a quarter-mile loop between the house and the stables.[28] His childhood playroom featured a telegraph and telephone. Now interest in giant machinery is considered typical in children, but Leland Jr., as the adored son of a railroad tycoon, had unparalleled opportunities. From the Sacramento railroad workshop to the New York Central Railroad station, from the mechanical exhibitions at the Agricultural Hall in London to the massive silk factories of Lyon: Leland Jr. held a backstage pass to it all. The world's first commercial cable car went up the hill to his house. Intellectually precocious, he sketched designs for his own industrial inventions: smokestacks and train-car couplings.

The Stanfords kept their son unusually close as he got older. He frequently joined them for dinner with national and global dignitaries, and he even accompanied his parents on their trips abroad. It was normal for Western elites to send their young adult men on an acculturating cruise around the continent, but as scholar Karen Sánchez-Eppler notes, "The notion that such travel should be undertaken by an 11-year-old boy and his parents was a decidedly American adaptation, and in a sense really an invention of the new California millionaires."[29] It's hard to imagine a child with more opportunity to see the world under conditions of luxury than Leland Stanford Jr., who rode the railroad across the country in his mother's arms and accompanied his parents as far east as Constantinople as a teenager. From his travels he took souvenirs, and he added them to the Indian artifacts he dug up as a child in Palo Alto to create a repository of antiquities. Children, like certain birds, are wont to assemble small collections out of their treasured objects, but as with everything else in the Stanford family, the money ensured that Leland Jr. approached his collecting in a serious way. He was inspired by the great museums he visited with his parents: the Louvre, the Vatican, the Berlin Museum, the British Museum, the Metropolitan Museum. Not many young boys had access to items of museum quality, but Leland Jr. did, acquired from Paris shops, where he chatted with the antiquarians in fluent French, and from British archaeological sites in Greece. His inaugural European piece was a bit of mosaic purloined on a visit to Pompeii. He planned his own museum for the West Coast public in the grand continental style.

At his parents' side, Leland Jr. was more than privileged. He toured the Ottoman sultan's treasury, writing to a girlfriend back home about "diamonds literally by the bushel, and one emerald as large as your hand, bowls full of emeralds, rubies and pearls, and carpets of gold covered with precious stones as close as they could be laid on."[30] They sipped coffee on diamond-studded gold saucers with a side of preserved rose petals. In Venice, the Stanfords hired a boatload of singers to serenade their gondola through the canals for three nights in a row. In Vienna, they went to the opera and ballet and dined with

Alphonso Taft, United States minister to Austria-Hungary and father of the future president. In Bordeaux, Leland Jr. inspected Baron Rothschild's Château Lafite, which his father hoped to replicate in Northern California. He was blessed, and not merely in a figurative sense: Pope Leo XIII put his hands on the boy's head during a private audience with him and Jane in Rome. Leland's young life was a whirlwind of peak experiences, an itinerary so rich that even the description is hard to take. Only a boy, he was familiar with so many of the world's most powerful men, prepared to take his place among them. In a way, considering that his parents always made room for him at the table, he already had.

On his second trip to Europe, he posed for a portrait by Léon-Joseph-Florentin Bonnat in Paris. A professor at the École des Beaux-Arts, Bonnat was among the world's best-regarded painters, and his *Leland Stanford Jr.* is a paragon of young aristocratic masculinity. The boy stands in front of a tree on a seaside cliff in his three-piece suit, chest out, gold watch chain dipping across his vest, left thumb hooked into his jacket pocket, a hat dangling by the brim from his other four fingers. There's some baby fat left on his cheeks, but his body is long and proportioned like a man's, and he leans a cane on his right hip. He wears the same impassive poker face that drove his father's business associates up a wall. Pride radiates from his shoulders. His tutor, Herbert Charles Nash, referred to a poem by Longfellow: "Some must follow, and some command, / Though all are made of clay." Leland Jr., he recalled, was one who must command.[31] The boy was the future embodied, a natural leader for the first generation of children in Anglo-ruled California, and he knew it. He was fifteen years old.

And then he was dead. Maybe it was the unusual cold in Athens—he had frolicked in the deep snow at the Parthenon—but somewhere between Greece and Italy Leland Jr. fell ill. His parents moved him to Florence for the climate on doctor's orders, and he fell into a fevered delirium for weeks. On March 13, 1884, two months before his sixteenth birthday, the Stanfords' only child died. Losing a child was not an unusual experience for nineteenth-century parents, but Jane and Leland didn't have any to spare. They had all their eggs in the one beautiful basket, and without warning the handle snapped. "Our darling boy went to heaven this morning at half-past seven o'clock after three weeks' sickness from typhoid fever," they messaged home, and the condolences poured in immediately, from government officials, from royalty, from their friends, from strangers.[32] The Stanfords were public figures, one way or another, and their tragedy was public, too. The English poet Elizabeth Ayton Godwin sent lines from her collection *Songs for the Weary*: "I sat in the school of sorrow, / The Master was teaching there, / But my eyes were dim with weeping / And my heart was full of care."[33] Leland Sr. completely broke down, according to Jane's secretary, which must have been something to behold, the bulky bearded railroad titan reduced to a pile of grief. His son's child-size train rusted in the Palo Alto yard.

The Stanfords were sophisticated modern thinkers of the late nineteenth century, which means they thought they could talk to ghosts. Jane found refuge in the Christian spiritualism that animated many of the letters and telegrams sent their way, and she prayed in an increasingly instrumental way, straining to contact her boy in the afterlife, the "better place" where she needed to know he was spending eternity. Bereaved, the couple made another trip around the globe. They consulted the world's most acclaimed mediums, including Leland's brother Thomas Welton Stanford, who moved from California to Melbourne, Australia, where he became a successful sewing machine distributor as well as a leading mystic, credited as the father of the Australian séance. It's not clear whether the Stanfords reached their son in the hereafter—from the records it seems that she believed more than he did, and that her belief may have been overstated as well by backbiting contemporaries eager to portray her as emotionally overwhelmed—but when they arrived home their purpose was clear, and they set about founding Leland Stanford Junior University.

Leland Sr. and Jane were renewed by their mission, and they went east to visit the country's great private colleges for inspiration. They tried to recruit Columbia president Nicholas Murray Butler to run the school, apparently after the presidents of MIT and Cornell turned them down. Stanford offered Butler a $20,000 salary, more than five times his Columbia pay and over half a million dollars in 2022 money, but he was refused. No respectable Ivy League academic was about to exile himself to California. The East Coast scholar-administrators thought no amount of money could sprout a world-class university in the intellectual wasteland of California. But Leland Stanford knew that the right amount of money could do anything.

"The children of California shall be our children," Stanford announced on behalf of the couple. "It is our hope to found a university where all may have a chance to secure an education such as we intended our son to have." The boy's name was now an invitation to the promising young settlers of the Golden State. It helped that the Stanfords already owned enough land to create the nation's largest university campus, a designation the school maintains at the time of this writing. Palo Alto was a beautiful place to live, but it wasn't San Francisco, where the state's culture was concentrated. Leland, however, wasn't looking to build a library for eggheads and philosophers. He wanted the school that bore his name to teach useful arts, among which he included cobblery, printing, carving, telegraphy, and stenography, "no less but rather more than the arts of music and painting and sculpture."[34] It was to be a school of laborers, and free tuition would allow the children of all classes to attend. How much this curriculum shared in common with Leland Jr.'s real-life educational experience of hanging out with the most powerful people in the world is up for debate, but the boy did do some wood carving.

Jane was more interested in realizing her son's plans for a great artifact collection. She planned and built the world's largest privately held museum, based on the sketches Leland Jr. made before his death. Among the relics was a set of pottery that had been unearthed in Cyprus and acquired by the Met; when curators realized they had duplicates they sold them to Governor Stanford, who gave them to his son. The museum held items of contemporary importance as well, such as a collection of objects from the 1871 Paris Commune, including rifle balls and bits of bread—Leland Jr. had turned three while the City of Light was under worker occupation. In one room was the boy's original group of collectibles, "exactly as he left them in 1882."[35] The grieving mother's plan was to leave it that way forever, the most magnificent shrine to a son's death in almost 2,000 years.

To design the campus, the Stanfords brought Frederick Law Olmsted back to Northern California. The godfather of U.S. landscape architecture, Olmsted's Central and Prospect Parks in New York are among the country's most iconic green spaces, and he drew up UC Berkeley's original master plan, too. Though his plan for Golden Gate Park was too progressive—San Francisco's oligarchs preferred something in the northern European rather than the Mediterranean mode Olmsted felt was more appropriate—he was the natural choice for the Stanfords, who liked his Mission revival concept.[36] They laid the campus cornerstone in 1887, but between trouble attracting faculty and Jane's outsize memorial-construction ambitions, the school's first class of students didn't arrive until the fall of 1891. Leland Sr. spent much of the interim period in Washington, DC, having had himself selected to the U.S. Senate by the state legislature in 1884, undermining the Combine's plan and further alienating his associates. Still, in the name of the son, the massive project advanced.

Between the stock farm's famous Palo Alto System and Muybridge's famous photographs, the small rural town was already at the forefront of capitalist technology when the Leland Stanford Junior University foundation went into the dirt. The original board of trustees helped solidify the relationship. It included a number of regional capitalist families — representatives of the Crocker and Hopkins clans (no Huntington, however); Irving M. Scott of Union Iron Works; and Henry L. Dodge of the grocer Dodges, among others — as well as a number of politicians and jurists, including Lorenzo Sawyer, former chief justice of the California Supreme Court and author of the famous Sawyer decision, which ended hydrolicking in the state, and U.S. Supreme Court justice Stephen J. Field, who ruled on *Santa Clara County v. Southern Pacific*.[37] They were, of course, Leland's friends. If Palo Alto was pastoral when Leland first bought his ranch, it was becoming something more.

"We only stand on the margin of the great sea of possibilities," the first issue of *Santa Clara County, California*, a quarterly published by the San Jose Board of Trade, announced in 1887. "That there is within our limits opportunities for the investment of unlimited capital can be realized by the dullest comprehension.... Those who have capital, and want it to increase, can find ample opportunity here." Buying and working an orchard or vineyard could make you comfortable, but "just at this particular time, the most profitable investment is in real estate."[38] As the article went on to explain, the chief value in the beautiful lands of Santa Clara County was that comparatively few eastern capitalists had heard about them yet. If you invested now, at prices one-tenth what they were in Los Angeles, you could count on a quick return as the word got out. "Capital will be doubled, trebled and quadrupled, in two years, by investment in Santa Clara County lands at present prices."[39] The university's trustees might have been tempted, but the founding documents were explicit: its 8,000 or so acres could never be sold.

"Remember that life is, above all, practical," the Governor told the "pioneer class" of LSJU on opening day. "You are here to fit yourselves for a useful career…"[40] Here was the Stanford child reborn, split into 559 fragments. Too late perhaps, but as James Ayers wrote of the cursed Marie Antoinette vase, the Stanfords donated their fortune "to some institution where its power for good or evil would expend itself, not on an individual, but on the general Public." A nonprofit bobbing in a sea of financial speculation, Stanford University was private interest inflated to a public cause, and whatever the Governor's founding intentions were, it became a clubhouse for organized capital. Stanford University was much more like the Palo Alto Stock Farm than its founders planned. The spirit of Leland Stanford Jr. animated those young men and women, his blessings, privileges, and curses diluted and sprayed over hundreds of people by the crop duster of education. For good or evil.

Section II

1900–1945

Shimada Sekko, illustration for "Mitgard Serpent," in
David Starr Jordan, *Eric's Book of Beasts* (1912)

Local Ghosts

Battle for LSJU — The Almost Certain Murder
of **** ******* ******** ***** ***** ****** —
Earthquake — Federal Telegraph

Leland Stanford Sr. died within two years of his speech to the pioneer class, his body laid to rest alongside that of his son in the grand family mausoleum on campus in Palo Alto, guarded by sphinxes. With both Lelands in the crypts, Jane Lathrop Stanford inherited control of the university as well as responsibility for her husband's finances, a tangle of obligations so complex that the feds put an immediate hold on the will. The attorney general of the United States filed suit against the Stanford estate, seeking the repayment of government loans made to the Central Pacific. The widow had little control over the funds, which were earmarked for the university anyway, and she sought to leave the railroad business entirely. But it wasn't a good time for the old Southern Pacific gang to buy her out. Highly leveraged (as always) and fighting off creditors (as always), Huntington and company didn't have the cash for Stanford's quarter share, and at the time it wasn't clear what kind of unmortgaged assets there were left for the company to sell. If she forced a sale, it could pop the whole bubble. The university held its breath while the federal government froze $15 million (over a quarter of a billion dollars at the time of this writing) in promised funds.

Jane Stanford did her best to keep the school going. She attempted to sell her jewel collection, though in the recession that closed the nineteenth century she couldn't find any takers.[1] Even after the Supreme Court ruled in Stanford's favor and turned over the money, Jane kept liquidating to ensure that the school was on a firm footing. She sold the famous horses out of the barn and eventually her jewels, too. The widow's total commitment and political connections established the university more than her husband's lofty promises ever did. In 1901, she secured a property-tax exemption for the school's 8,000-plus acres by state constitutional referendum, a canny move successfully mimicked by other universities and later by regular property owners.

Yet, despite Jane's follow-through at a time when others advised that she give up the university, Stanford's president and nonhereditary heir, David Starr Jordan, had some quibbles. The widow led the school as a person accountable to no one, which was her prerogative as founder and funder. Jordan beseeched her for more money so that he could offer raises to faculty sufficient to entice the country's best scientists to the West Coast, but the widow was more concerned with monumental architecture—recall that she was building the world's largest private museum in the small rural outpost. The Stanford Memorial Church paid glorious stained-glass tribute to the school's namesake, but it didn't do much to develop the campus's academic reputation. When Jordan suggested improving the school's engineering department to match an MIT or Cornell, the founder scoffed, telling her president to cool it. "Let me say, even at the cost of repeating myself, I intend to keep just where we are at present as far as the payroll and other expenditures of money are concerned," she wrote him in December of 1899.[2] But when it came to subjects that captured Jane's interest, like spiritualism and philosophy, there were more funds available. In a 1905 letter, JLS recounted an argument with Jordan over faculty salaries: Frustrated at her promise to pay philosopher William James $5,000 to get him west from Harvard for a year, Jordan fumed that he couldn't offer loyal scientists whom *he* deemed brilliant their deserved salary advances. "Dr. Jordan," she told him, "there is only one Prof. James."[3] The widow Stanford complained that the president was overpaying used-up instructors in botany and entomology, subjects close to Jordan's heart.[4]

Their fight wasn't just about capital expenditures versus faculty, as it is sometimes described; it was also about two different views of the university and even two different versions of truth and reality. On one side was the mystic Jane, cultivator of the "soul germ" within the West's brightest young men (and up to 500 of its young women, as an early rule had it), devoted to the memory of her son above all. Campus rumor had it that her devotion crossed into madness, with continued attempts to contact Leland Jr. in the afterlife. In fact, it doesn't seem that Jane's interest in the supernatural was any deeper than was common among the credulous rich of the era, though, and through it all she maintained a fundamentally Christian orientation. Still, Jane's opponents in the Stanford administration leaned on the stereotype of the grief-addled mother when they sought to explain her spending priorities, which included the scientific study of ghosts via parapsychology and tributes to ghosts via memorial architecture. But grief-addled or not, Jane's hold on the school's purse was strong. She had allies as well, including her brother-in-law Thomas Welton Stanford, the wealthy Australian sewing machine distributor turned séance master who was one of the school's leading early donors.

On the other side was David Starr Jordan, an ichthyologist and school administrator committed above all to the genetic future of the white race. He appreciated the Stanfords' largesse and shared their inspiration when it came to higher education in the West, but micromanagement at the budget-line level from an old woman with no academic training aggravated the man of science. Jordan worked to manage the widow, but he struggled with the school's founding spiritualism. In his short foreword to the 1917 volume *Experiments in Psychical Research at Leland Stanford Junior University*, Jordan tried to fit the work of the Welton Stanford–funded experiments into his larger empirical project: "That the phenomena in this field are peculiarly baffling affords no ground for discouragement. By the methods of precision they are reducible to scientific order, and we may be sure that in this field as in any other we can safely follow wherever Truth shall lead. Genuine knowledge can never run counter to sound principles in human life."[5] The text included a long series of studies from Stanford's early decades on subjects like "the feeling of being stared at" and "local ghosts," to which Jordan was able to give his strained endorsement because they were almost all inconclusive.* Despite the aggravation, Jordan had good reason to stick around, JLS having no direct heir but the school. If he could outlast her he would find himself in a unique position in American academia as the head of a well-capitalized young institution — its first and only president, designated by the deceased founders. As long as she

---

* In his history of psychical research at Stanford, the philosopher Frederick C. Dommeyer writes that the unusually negative results gave rise to suspicions "that Stanford University administrators and the Department of Psychology were engaged in a conspiracy against psychical science." Whether such a conspiracy was necessary to obtain those results, Jordan did redirect Welton Stanford's endowment from psychical research to psychological research. Frederick C. Dommeyer, "Psychical Research at Stanford University," *Journal of Parapsychology* 39, no. 3 (September 1975).

didn't blow the whole founding grant on memorial antiquities, big buildings, and philosophers first.

The university's two leaders maintained their delicate *pas de deux* for years, but a couple of conflicts pushed them toward a breaking point. The more famous of the two is the Edward A. Ross controversy. A sociologist at a time when the discipline was still finding its footing, Ross was (like Jordan) a former professor at Indiana University, a partisan in the struggle for racial "hygiene," and a believer in the western frontier. He described California's archetypal white settler as a "restless, striving, doing Aryan, with his personal ambition, his lust for power, his longing to wreak himself, his willingness to turn the world upside down to get the fame, or the fortune, or the woman, he wants."[6] Ross was also a provocateur. At a public meeting in 1900, he railed against the importation of Japanese workers, saying, "Should the worst come to the worst, it would be better for us if we were to turn our guns upon every vessel bringing Japanese to our shores rather than permit them to land."[7] Ross was a professional white populist, and when Jordan fired him (at JLS's prompting), he called it a violation of academic freedom. To dismiss a tenured instructor because of a controversial statement was an attack on scholarship, and the furor went national, damaging the young school's reputation. Jordan did his best to avoid responsibility, and he blamed the Stanford widow instead. The national press turned against Stanford the school and Jane Lathrop Stanford the woman. Ross sympathizers formed the American Association of University Professors, which remains one of the profession's central organizations over a century later.[8]

Frustrated by the public perception of the Ross case and (correctly) fearful that Jordan was blaming her, JLS published a pamphlet in 1903 clarifying her position on free speech (pro) and revealing Jordan's private statements to her in which he characterized Ross as a "consummate fool" and "dime-store villain," lending credence to her claim that Ross was dismissed for cause.[9] Jordan's toadying was bad enough, but the pamphlet revealed him as a backbiter, willing to throw his friend and recruit under the wheels of the Southern Pacific, then lie about it. (And according to Ross, Jordan was the one who suggested that he make the explosive comment about Japanese boats in the first place.) Ross, who landed on his feet, took the Stanford revelations with good humor. "It will not hurt me but it will hurt Jordan terribly," he gossiped with barely suppressed glee to Lester Ward, with whom he soon helped form the American Sociological Association. "The letters he wrote to her throughout the episode show him to be so cringing, shifty and mendacious that I don't see how he can ever regain his influence on the Pacific Coast. Some of my friends who have read the address think Mrs. Stanford's motive in giving out the whole correspondence is to make it impossible for Jordan to remain. Otherwise her action is inexplicable."[10] She hit Jordan where it hurt, in his reputation among men.

By the summer of 1904, both Jordan and JLS were waiting for the other: she for his resignation, he for her death. In October, Jane Stanford met with her faculty confidant, the head of the German department, Julius Goebel, about the university's deficiencies. She no longer trusted the president, and Goebel told her what she wanted to hear: There was too much emphasis on the sciences, not enough on the humanities. They should bring a big-name philosopher over from Harvard, or even from Germany. The two also discussed the case of Charles Henry Gilbert, an Indiana-trained zoologist and one of Jordan's favorites. Professor Gilbert was formally accused of a pattern of improper conduct toward a young woman who worked at the library. When Jordan found out, he flew into a rage and threatened the informer, a young man who worked at the library, saying that unless he left the state of California immediately, Jordan would have him incarcerated "in the insane asylum for sexual perversity"—a serious threat from a powerful man like the Stanford president.[11] The whistleblowing librarian left; Gilbert stayed. In fact, he was one of the professors to whom Jordan suggested Jane give the $5,000 she had earmarked for William James. Jane confessed to Goebel that (as Edward Ross's friends perceived) she expected the president to resign after she humiliated him with the 1903 pamphlet. Instead, he stepped up his obsequiousness toward the founder, even kneeling to kiss her hand. It became apparent to Jane that he was battened down, awaiting her death. This led her to contemplate "the final remedy," according to Goebel: "the removal of the president."

Did Jordan know about the widow's plans? Goebel warned her that he had spies on campus—that he operated a moblike clique at the school, whitewashing trouble for friends such as Professor Gilbert and causing the same for his enemies. What's more, even the newspapers speculated that Jordan would be the next to go after the Ross affair, and others didn't see how he could show his face in academia at all after the way his own boss exposed him. Who else would hire him? The way Jane Stanford confided in Goebel made her lack of faith obvious, and by 1905 she was ready to act. William James was coming to campus, and if the president didn't like it, then maybe it was time for the school to find its second leader. But Jane Stanford never got to administer her final remedy. On February 28, 1905, she was poisoned to death.

Other People's Dreams

It's difficult to prove the specifics of a murder conspiracy over a century later, but historians have come to agree on that much: Jane Lathrop Stanford was murdered, and there was a conspiracy. There is a good circumstantial case against David Starr Jordan, consisting of his strong motive, his extremely suspicious behavior around the crime, and his low personal character. If he was willing to menace the librarian into exile to protect his friend, what wouldn't a self-interested sneak like him do to protect his professional position, his career, his pride, and his investments? For many decades the conventional wisdom was that Jane Lathrop Stanford died of being a crazy old lady, despite all the evidence to the contrary. These days, with the shine wearing off Jordan's reputation, he has come under suspicion. Though no one has produced a definitive smoking gun, it's no longer particularly controversial to suggest that Jordan was part of the conspiracy, most likely with Lady Stanford's longtime secretary, Bertha Berner.[12] What no one currently disputes is that Jane was poisoned. Twice.

On the evening of January 14, 1905, Jane Stanford drank her habitual bedtime glass of spring water, tasted something strange, and made herself throw up. The quick action saved her life: a pharmacist found that the water was laced with a lethal dose of strychnine. A month later she set sail (or steam, rather) for Hawaii.* Rumors swirled in the Palo Alto community that the widowed

---

* The Hawaiian territory was closely tied to the Bay Area, and Stanford served as a finishing school for the children of elite Anglo colonists. For example, following the 1893 overthrow of the Hawaiian monarchy led by Sanford B. Dole, the larger Dole family sent 8 of 13 college-age children to LSJU between 1895 and 1911, including some big men on campus. Wilfred Dole had just helped Stanford win the 1904 Big Game 14–0 with a touchdown, while his brother Norman set a pole vaulting record the same year. See David Starr Jordan, *The Days of a Man: 1851–1899* (Chicago: World Book Company, 1922), 710 (describing the Doles as "in a class by themselves" among the graduates from 1892 to 99); Gary Migdol,

founder fled the country after an attempt on her life. The *San Francisco Call*'s cascading headlines told one story:

TALE OF POISON CAUSES ALARM

Indisposition of Mrs. Jane Stanford Starts a Rumor That Is Quickly Denied

EXAGGERATED INCIDENT

Mineral Water Results in Nauseation and a Sensational Story Follows

The story ran on February 19, leaving boat-bound Jane unable to dispute the characterization. Nine days later, she was dead. Once again, it was strychnine in the bedtime glass of water, this time at the Moana Hotel in Honolulu. Jane was a guest of honor at the three-year-old luxury hotel, where she supped with the owner's wife on the evening of February 28. Having eaten too much candy, she asked for some seltzer. Her faithful secretary measured out the bicarbonate and added it to Jane's water. A few hours later she roused the hotel with cries of agony. "Bertha, run for the doctor. I have no control of my body," she cried. "I think I have been poisoned again."[13] Her jaw locked, and she gasped her last words: "This is a horrible death to die." An autopsy concluded that her death was caused by strychnine poisoning. (Suspiciously, Bertha Berner immediately accused the devoted Stanford cook of over 20 years, a Mr. Wing, who was quickly exonerated.)[14] As soon as he heard the news, Jordan decamped for Hawaii, where he immediately set about trying to dispute the cause of death. There was once again no poisoning, he insisted, though the undeniable presence of the founder's dead body made it a tougher case the second time around. Jordan offered his credentials as a scientist of international repute, though the relevance of his work in fish identification was never clear. He found his own doctor, who concluded, without examining the body, that the cause was a "heart attack."

"I don't care how many doctors or chemists in Honolulu make statements, or how many statements they issue," Jordan told the press, going on

---

Stanford: Home of Champions (Sports Publishing LLC, 1997), 32 (noting graduate Norman Dole was a pole vault world record holder).

to inexplicably imply that the Hawaiian doctors conspired to add strychnine to the bicarbonate postmortem to make themselves appear more important or increase their fees.[15] But Jordan knew how to work the media, and before long he convinced reporters (and through them the curious public) that there was no poison conspiracy, at least not premortem.

Unlike her husband's, Jane Stanford's will went off without a hitch, even though some of the Stanford branch of the family were not impressed with the $100,000 (approximately $3 million in 2022 dollars) that she left to each of the couple's relatives.[16] Jordan inherited control of the university (on behalf of the children of California, of course), and everyone seemed to forget how precarious his position at the school had recently been. He flexed his new administrative muscle and purged Julius Goebel, over the objection of the now-Janeless board of trustees. Jordan's move enraged the local German community, of which Goebel was a prominent member, and shocked the academic world. Harvard hired Goebel immediately in what was seen as a strong rebuke of Jordan. Charles Eliot, Jordan's counterpart at Harvard, was more explicit in a letter between the two: "I think I differ from you fundamentally on the nature of the responsibility of a University President. In my judgment he should be absolutely a constitutional and not a despotic ruler."[17] Jordan held his ground, and no opponent in the Stanford administration was able to dislodge him from the presidency until 1913. Unlike Jane Lathrop, he died on Stanford's campus.

Though he could clean house after the founder's assassination, Jordan couldn't undo the $5,000 offer Jane Stanford had instructed him to make to William James earlier that year. And in January of 1906 the philosopher arrived, unaware of just what had been going on behind the scenes at this "extraordinary little University," as he called it. In its utopian pretensions, the school was "a characteristic American affair!" And only one month into his residency, James already had a handle on Palo Alto: "There couldn't be imagined a better environment for an intellectual man to teach and work in, for eight or nine months in the year, if he were then free to spend three or four months in the crowded centres of civilization—for the social insipidity is great here, and the historic vacuum and silence appalling, and one ought to be free to change."[18] He understood the bargain immediately: nice weather, lots of space, but you mustn't ask about anything that happened there. Bluebeard's castle in terra-cotta red. James found himself beset by nightmares so strange that he wondered to himself in earnest italic dread, *"Am I getting into other people's dreams?"*[19] The campus gave him the "creeps." He didn't last the eight or nine months he first thought ideal for a Stanford stay. On April 18, 1906, a great earthquake shook the Bay Area, burning San Francisco to the ground and leveling millions of dollars' worth of university architecture—including Jane Stanford's monumental museum—as well as the Stanford mansion on Nob Hill.

Though the local Stanford family was extinguished in its entirety, the previously accused and exonerated chef Mr. Wing remained devoted. When the earthquake hit, he was on Nob Hill, acting as caretaker for the Associates' mansions. In the coming hours he watched as the fire got closer and closer: "I went out, looked around, but could [get] no one to help me to move out the valuables. I locked the door and went out. At Jones Street, I looked back and found that the Stanford House was in flame[s]. At this moment I thought of all the valuables in the house that were so pitifully destroyed."[20] He took the train to Palo Alto, where he informed administrators regarding the unfortunate state of the San Francisco properties. Mr. Wing stayed in the remains of the Palo Alto house and cared for the destroyed museum, the Stanford family's last loyal member. "My former employers were gone," he wrote. "Their house at San Francisco was completely burned. There was only one-half of the old house left. All these were too great a blow to me. I could not stay here in this country any longer to entertain such awful truths. I left here for my country to see my mother. I left here a few words that others might know of my state." The school canceled the rest of the semester and students camped on the quad and occupied themselves with relief work. William James, having fulfilled his contract to the best of his abilities, took a train home and was comfortably returned to Cambridge by the beginning of May.[21]

The Age of Synergy

The quake of 1906 gave Jordan's triumph over Jane Stanford an aura of divine approval. Faculty or buildings? God decided. The president's coup was so successful that the earth swallowed up his rival's works. Jordan moved to rebuild the church dedicated to Leland Jr., but the campus had seen the last of its West Coast Met—and of William James. Instead, Jordan turned Stanford into a new home for high-tech research and development. In many ways, this marked the emergence of Stanford and Palo Alto as the world still knows them.

In 1909, recent graduate Cyril Elwell turned to Jordan and the civil engineering department head, C. D. Marx, to help him start a West Coast wireless telegraph and telephone company based on a license Elwell acquired to use French transmitter technology.* The men jumped at the opportunity, and Jordan invested $500 of his own money and wrangled more San Francisco capital. In 1911, the Federal Telegraph Company (FTC) completed the first transmission between California and Hawaii. Stanford integrated its first tech start-up with the school's facilities, giving FTC access to the campus's high voltage laboratory for testing in exchange for some donated equipment.[22] Elwell had the foresight to take his transmitter to Washington, where he wowed navy officials with his machine's long range and silent operation. The officials ordered ten of them on the spot, but more important, they developed immediate brand loyalty, signing up FTC for increasingly big projects whether they matched the firm's existing capabilities or not. When America entered World War I, contracts and jobs flooded into Palo Alto, where FTC built a new, larger factory. Over the course of a decade, the rural university town became a regional center for the new radio industry.

Jordan had the right idea at the right moment. These were the high years of what historian Vaclav Smil calls "the age of synergy," when the inventions that powered twentieth-century modernity were born. A disproportionate number of those inventions came out of the San Francisco Bay Area, Palo Alto in particular. The next jump forward came from Lee de Forest, the vacuum tube inventor who found himself unemployed in San Francisco after his East Coast partners were arrested for stock fraud in 1910. Elwell brought de Forest back to Palo Alto, where by 1912 he perfected the vacuum tube for three uses: signal generation (as an oscillator), reception (as an audion), and amplification (as

---

* Marx was a founding member of the school's faculty and the brother of the Stanford mechanical engineering professor Guido Marx. Acknowledged as the "father of the Stanford engineer," C.D. was known as "Daddy" Marx. JudyAnn Christensen Edwards, "Palo Alto Has Its Own Marx Brothers," *Palo Alto Weekly*, February 12, 2007, https://www.paloaltoonline.com/news/2007/02/12/palo-alto-has-its-own-marx-brothers.

an amplifier). The result was phenomenal. "Vacuum tubes played a role in the electronics industry of the pre-World War II period analogous to that of the transistor during the postwar period," writes researcher Timothy J. Sturgeon. "They opened vast and unforeseen new market potential by increasing the capability and reliability of electronic systems while radically reducing their costs, power requirements, and size."[23] De Forest contributed an incredible amount for an individual, making it a no-brainer for FTC to post a $10,000 bond (approximately $300,000 in 2022 dollars) when federal marshals raided the company and arrested him in connection with his previous partnership.

In the first half of the 1920s, the nation's retail radio hardware sales increased from $2 million to $325 million.[24] At the same time, in San Jose, Stanford dropout Doc Herrold and his wife, Sybil, created commercial broadcast radio with channel FN, getting the power to transmit by illicitly tapping the streetcar lines.[25] Then Edward S. Pridham (Stanford class of '09) and his FTC coworker Peter Jensen spun off their own start-up speaker company: Magnavox. The hits kept coming from Stanford students in the interwar period, the most important being the Varian brothers' microwave-generating klystron tube and Charles Litton's tube manufacturing process, which he developed at FTC. And in the early '30s, this high-tech entrepreneurial breeding ground introduced students William Hewlett and David Packard, slamming the freshmen together on the Stanford football field.

The two young men didn't find themselves on the field for the 1930 try-outs by accident. Packard was high school class president, a standout math and science student, and an athlete who, at six foot five, couldn't help attracting attention. He was the kind of man David Starr Jordan—who died the next year—was counting on. Hewlett impressed the admissions committee less, but his recently deceased father had been a respected professor at the Stanford medical school campus in San Francisco, so both H and P were considered worthy of admission. Letting them in was the easy part, but Stanford did a lot more than that. One young professor in particular recruited them into the university's advanced radio program, where they toured the burgeoning Bay Area electronics ecosystem. It was through their immersion in this environment that the two friends developed their joint career ambition: They became electronics entrepreneurs.

In a mere 25 years, Jordan's plan transformed the town from a frontier university hamlet to a postindustrial center where men invented the tools that shaped the aerospace, communications, and electronics sectors and the era of American global domination they enabled. The university as led by Jordan nurtured industry with facilities, equipment, money, and, most important, human beings. By the Second World War, America (and the rest of the "free world") came to depend on the inventors of Palo Alto, just as he imagined. This human-capital factory had little to do with Jane Lathrop Stanford's plan to nurture the soul germ in the West, but after her assassination it was Jordan's school, now and forever, and he produced science in the form of men. Jordan tweaked the arc of history, but to what end or for what purpose? He wasn't thinking about vacuum tubes, so what exactly was the plan that culminated in Silicon Valley? What did Jordan really want, and why was it worth killing for?

Bionomics

Making Men — Lewis Terman and His Intelligence Quotient — Finding Genius in California — The Raisin Ku Klux Klan — The International-Radical-Communist Anarchist Club

The Stanford widow was out of the way, and Jordan was free to reorient the school toward his interests — interests not necessarily aligned with those of its founders. While Leland Sr. wanted a trade school and Jane a liberal arts palace, Jordan built a global headquarters of science instead. One new science in particular struck him as the foundation for the rest. It was "one of the most comprehensive of all the sciences," he wrote, "including in its subject-matter, not only all natural history, not only processes like cell-division and nutrition, not only the laws of heredity, variation, segregation, natural selection, and mutual help, but all matters of human history, and the most complicated relations of civics, economics, and ethics. In this enormous science no fact can be without a meaning, and no fact or its underlying forces can be separated from the great forces whose interaction from moment to moment writes the great story of life."[1] From the British polymath Patrick Geddes, Jordan took the name for this new science of evolution: bionomics, derived from the Greek words *bios* (life) and *nomos* (law). With an early professor recruit, the entomologist Vernon Kellogg, Jordan positioned the small department at the emerging frontier of life science. Though it didn't last long under that name, bionomics, with its vision of "degenerate" races and outstandingly normal heroes, underpins Palo Alto's ethos into the present day.

Jordan and Kellogg were popular professors, and their jointly taught course on evolution was so mobbed with enthusiastic students that attendees formed their own study groups. Experimentally, bionomics sought to study living organisms under artificial conditions made to mimic their natural environments, splitting the difference between naturalists observing plants and animals in the wild and the contrived tests of the biology lab. It made sense, then, that Stanford's two bionomics professors studied insects and fish, their habitats being relatively simple to re-create. From their study of the lower animals, Jordan and Kellogg derived not just a science of life but also an ethico-political program. Nature had no morality, they found, and degeneracy was not fully self-extinguishing. Negative characteristics as well as positive ones reproduced via hereditary means, and humanity was prone to developing "withered branches" on its evolutionary tree.[2] In a lecture on "degeneration," Jordan took students on an intellectual tour of the world's downward slopes, from the tropics (where life is too easy and the people are lazy) to the American South (where slavery stomped out intelligence all around) to the slums (poor moral incentives) to declining Europe (too softened by luxury).[3] Without new leadership, the species would surely degenerate; the fate of humanity hung in the balance. The implicit Goldilocks solution was white America, particularly in the West, where genius wasn't neurotic or tragic but unalloyed in the achievements of strong, well-rounded Anglo-Saxon settler men. "Great men live great lives," wrote Jordan; the bionomic proof is in the pudding.[4]

If bionomics was the theory, eugenics was the practice. Progressive breeding was the basis for the Palo Alto System—Leland Stanford and Charles Marvin pumped out new and improved horses by the tablespoonful—and under Jordan, the small, young university became a national center for controlled evolution. He was the inaugural chair of the Committee on Eugenics at the American Breeders' Association in 1906 and served as a vice president of the First International Eugenics Congress, in London, six years later: Signaling perhaps a fidelity to heredity, Leonard Darwin was president.[5] But the biggest impact Jordan had on the burgeoning field was at Stanford, where he forged a eugenic university. Key to the effort was Jordan's 1898 recruitment of his former Indiana student (and eugenics devotee) Ellwood Patterson Cubberley, who worried that new immigrants from southern and eastern Europe as well as Japan were diluting America's stock and causing "racial indigestion."[6] Assimilation, he believed, is best performed by the schools, which must prepare the foreign-born to blend into the American race.* In addition, the end of the nineteenth century marked the era of international competition and the recognition (pioneered by the Prussians) of the citizenry as a national resource.† There was, Cubberley wrote, "a new feeling of need for the transformation of all possible dependents into independent members of society."[7] Cubberley aimed for his own transformation, to take educational administration from art to science. He succeeded, creating a foundational literature for school administrators, and in 1917, Jordan gave him room to grow, establishing the Stanford School of Education, where Cubberley was to serve as dean.

In 1910, Cubberley's education department added another Hoosier: Lewis Terman, a Southern California school administrator and professor who was as concerned with the evolutionary implications of education as anyone. His early published work at Stanford focused on school hygiene, suggesting that the state had an interest in the wellness of students that on occasion superseded the rights of parents.[8] Children lost to preventable illness were "waste."[9] But Terman and the educational eugenicists did not believe that, even with all the environmental help the state could muster, every kid could achieve at the same level. Some had more to work with than others, and that diversity of inherent and immutable ability was important and, they believed, understudied. Without a way to test for superior ability, identifying it in students was haphazard and unscientific, and so was public education in general. If intellectual capacity were a single genetic trait—and they believed it was—then it should be testable. Terman set about making it so, adapting a French intelligence test used to identify students who were falling behind. Against the explicit warning of the test's author, Alfred Binet, Terman and his Stanford team reformatted it into a measure of inborn general intelligence, expressed in a single number, the ratio of "mental age" to actual age multiplied by 100.[10] From there

---

* Cubberley agreed with Jordan on the undesirability of support for the poor, arguing that by spending state funds on education instead of welfare they could eliminate poverty rather than maintain it. Ellwood Patterson Cubberley, *Public Education in the United States* (Houghton Mifflin, 1919), 58.

† In an 1872 lecture series, one young professor at the University of Basel complained that education was becoming about "discovering where and how a person can best serve state interests." That professor's name? Friedrich Nietzsche. Friedrich Nietzsche, *Anti-Education: On the Future of Our Educational Institutions* (NYRB Classics, 2015), 52.

Terman and company were off to the races, marketing "Stanford-Binet" tests, estimating the IQs of famous dead people, and looking for geniuses.

Lewis Terman's interest in "the science of individual differences and the diagnosis of personality" (as he called it) started early. In his autobiography, he recalls that when he was nine or ten years old, he and his family were visited by a book peddler:

> This one was selling a book on phrenology, the author of which I have forgotten. That evening, while we sat about the fireplace, the stranger discoursed on the science of phrenology and "felt the bumps" of each one in the family. Perhaps I remember the incident so well for the reason that when it came my turn to be examined he predicted great things of me. I think the prediction probably added a little to my self-confidence and caused me to strive for a more ambitious goal than I might otherwise have set. At any rate, I was greatly impressed and for several years thereafter was much interested in phrenology. As my older brother bought a copy of the book, I finally became familiar with its contents and believed in phrenology until I was fourteen or fifteen years old.[11]

It's a staggering origin story for a man who shaped ideas of intelligence testing and intelligence itself in the twentieth century. Terman's "Stanford-Binet scale" was bionomics for humans, a test meant to summon general intelligence from within an individual, pulling it out where scientists could capture and quantify it. The test in fact did nothing of the sort, asking questions like "What is Christy Mathewson's job?" (Answer: pitcher for the New York Giants.) Sports trivia was a fine way to test what was a rickety trait in the first place. The idea of a unitary general intelligence is a convenient myth, one that collapses as a scientific concept the minute you put any critical pressure on it. Plenty of Terman's contemporaries said as much at the time. But the IQ tests sold very well, and he followed with a Stanford Achievement Test that sold even better. Together they made their lead author a star in psychology. Terman became department chair in 1922, and the president of the American Psychological Association the next year. In 1925, his royalties from books and tests were around $11,000—over $180,000 in 2022 money, enough for him to subsidize his own research and, later, his son's.[12] Great things, as the phrenologist peddler foretold.

Though he sacrificed Edward Ross to the founders, David Starr Jordan successfully brought together scholars to push the Palo Alto System out of the barn and into the classroom. Like Leland, with his foals sprinting for a place on the Palo Alto Stock Farm starting roster, Lewis Terman developed a model for assessing how fast children could run, and the bionomists helped convince him that the results mattered. Applied to children, the Palo Alto System suggested both positive and negative eugenic practices. Budding geniuses needed to be identified and elevated, while young degenerates needed to be corralled where they couldn't dilute the national race or turn their underachievement into social problems. In the first half of the twentieth century, Stanford made large contributions to both strategies, promoting inequality as the only policy compatible with nature.

Great Men Live Great Lives

There's something of Calvinist predestination in Jordan's equation: Great men live great lives because they're great, they are not great because they've lived great lives. According to bionomics, their greatness is immanent, which means it can be found and nurtured in childhood. It was the job of scientist-educators to identify these exceptional individuals early — to spot the blood that trots young — on the nation's behalf. "We may all be equal in our right to receive a common measure of service from the state," Kellogg wrote, "but we are not equal in our capacity to give service. The state, which is simply all of us, needs the benefit of the best use of our best brains, and to get it we must see that these best brains have the best of training."[13] The bionomists also believed that the intellectual elite — a group in which they included themselves, naturally — were not deficient in some corresponding way, whether physically or emotionally, as stereotypes held. Geniuses were not sickly weaklings or fragile homos; they were simply better than other people.* American public schooling to this point was focused on educating up to a common standard, and these experts

---

* Without getting too far afield into psychologism, it's worth noting that Lewis Terman's young adulthood was marred by a long and debilitating course of tuberculosis, requiring his move to the mild California climate in the first place. For more on the era's conflicted relationship with genius, see Peter Hegarty, *Gentlemen's Disagreement: Alfred Kinsey, Lewis Terman, and the Sexual Politics of Smart Men* (University of Chicago Press, 2013).

worried that potential was going undiscovered. Terman's metaphor is revealing: "The use we have made of exceptional ability reminds one of the primitive methods of surface mining. It is necessary to explore the nation's hidden resources of intelligence."[14] Stanford produced mining engineers, so it produced intelligence prospectors.

In addition to genetics, the bionomists believed in the importance of an organism's environment. Jordan feared European softness, brought on by a lack of vigorous competition. Coddling wouldn't do. At the same time, America's best and brightest didn't belong in twentieth-century military combat, which bionomists saw as "dysgenic"—the bravest men were *more* likely to get shot and leave their fertile widows childless. "There was once a time when the struggles of armies resulted in a survival of the fittest, when the race was indeed to the swift and the battle to the strong," wrote Jordan in *Popular Science Monthly*. "The invention of 'villainous gunpowder' has changed all this. Except the kind of warfare called guerrilla, the quality of the individual has ceased to be much of a factor. The clown can shoot down the hero and 'doesn't have to look the hero in the face as he does so.' The shell destroys the clown and hero alike, and the machine gun mows down whole ranks impartially."[15] In 1913 Kellogg wrote in the *Atlantic* that militarism encouraged race deterioration, but he changed his tune after doing aid work during 1915 and '16 in German-occupied Belgium, where he found the German high command's evolutionary thinking far more martial than his own, leading him to the unhappy conclusion that America had to beat them by force.[16] He was right, and despite Jordan's misgivings, bionomics and IQ testing in particular got its biggest break with the American entry into World War I. After the war declaration, in 1917, the American Psychological Association convened a committee to decide how it could be of help. The APA president, Robert Yerkes, agreed with Terman about administering intelligence tests to recruits, and Terman pointed to the work of his student Arthur S. Otis, who developed a version of the Stanford-Binet test that could be administered to groups instead of one-on-one.[17]

The Army Alpha and Army Beta tests were designed to separate recruits into A–E categories: A was for officer material who should be kept away from the trenches; C was for soldiers who should fill the trenches; E was for washouts who probably shouldn't be allowed near a gun.[18] The testing was supposed to aid military personnel assignment, but there's a not-so-subtle eugenicist angle there, too: By separating recruits based on IQ, the psychologists could counter the dysgenic effects of war, keeping smarter men away from the line of fire and moving unexceptional men closer to it. There's not much evidence that the military took the testing effort very seriously, but as a result of the experience, the bionomists gave up on pacifism. If war was to be the way of the world, then Americans needed to improve their lethality, killing more of the enemy while losing fewer of their own. War became an efficiency equation. Combat in the twentieth century was won with science and by scientists; gifted citizens could contribute to the war effort using their skills, as Kellogg had observed in Germany, restoring the combat importance of the exceptional individual without risk to the gene pool. It seems like a jump from the bionomists' peace advocacy to their employment as military contractors in a march that culminated in nuclear war, but not from the perspective of the American blood-nation, as Jordan conceived of it. In both cases they were trying to protect the country's genetic future as best they saw fit, whether by peace or by bomb. But Terman and his team didn't know anything about bombs. To win the wars of the future, they needed to find the American geniuses of tomorrow, today.

Terman collected anecdotes about gifted children (identified by teachers and confirmed by IQ tests) starting in 1911, and in 1920 the university agreed to match $500 (half each from Terman and Cubberley) for a study of children with an IQ of over 140—the arbitrary cutoff researchers used for "genius."[19] The results from this first experiment were promising: The subjects weren't socially retarded, as some had expected, and they tended to be stuck, bored, in classes below their tested ability level. For Terman the actionable conclusion was obvious, and he offered it when he headed up a reform committee for the National Education Association in 1922. In their report, Intelligence Tests and School Reorganization, Terman called for breaking classes into five tracks (gifted, bright, average, slow, and special—echoing the A–E soldier ranking) based on ability, so that America might get the most out of its children.[20] The same year, Terman received larger grants for a longitudinal study unlike any done before. Relying mostly on the recommendations of teachers, he and his team expanded their sample to just over 1,500 California students of genius IQ. The study tracked these "Termites" over the course of their entire lives, testing hypotheses about the link between children's performance and adult life outcomes. Under the bionomic model, it also identified (what they believed to be) exceptional kids as state assets. In 2022, as I write, the study somehow has yet to be publicly concluded.

For the bionomists, there was no reason not to lane children as soon as they could be found. Their IQs weren't going to change. Just as the Palo Alto System did, Terman assumed that the adult's potential was always already observable in the child. The environment could, however, determine whether they lived up to that potential. And for the researchers, that was a question of national security. Though it ruined the scientific validity of what was already a dubious experiment, Terman couldn't help intervening in the lives of his subjects, helping them along and writing recommendation letters scientifically certifying their immutable genius, in which he fervently believed. Among the subjects was one young genius from whom he could hardly distance himself even if he wanted to: his son Frederick. There was never much doubt in Lewis's mind that Frederick Terman was gifted in the technical sense — genius being uncomplicatedly genetic, how could he not be? — and the test verified his assumption. The geniuses in the Stanford study did tend to outperform the average student in terms of their eventual accomplishments and prestige, and there were a few exceptional future adults among the kids, not least of whom was Fred. However, the researchers also missed a couple of future Nobel Prize winners, including the only child of a Stanford engineering professor named William Shockley. Bill Jr. was promising, but at 129 his IQ ranked slightly subgenius. If it's a confirmation of the experiment's hypothesis that Frederick and Bill Jr. became not only important human assets in the World War II Allied victory but also the two grandfathers of Silicon Valley, then it's the only kind of confirmation such a scientifically unrigorous study could offer: narrative. The genius study was a story, and many powerful people worked hard to make it come true.

At Stanford proper, eugenicist concerns and bionomic faith helped shape the student body. Recall that part of the plan for establishing the school's prominence was to train students in topics and fields that were increasing in importance so that the graduates might quickly become influential beyond their numbers. And if the university was going to place its bets on exceptional individuals, then it needed the best material to work with. Stanford itself was a self-consciously eugenic project: Administrators believed they were selecting for and promoting not simply the best young men and women but also the best *genes*. This led to some unforeseen problems, including a chronic issue with bed lengths. In a 1930 letter to the editor of the *Stanford Daily* a student named Hartwell Preston complained about the "at least fifty" Stanford men over six foot two who needed longer mattresses. The editors agreed, and in an editorial titled "Give Them Room," they made a special plea to the university president, six-foot-four former student Ray Lyman Wilbur.[21] But two decades later it was still a problem: TOWERING FRESHMEN OVERLAP ENCINA BEDS reads the 1950 *Stanford Today* headline. "When autumn quarter opened, University officials took one look at the height records of 716 freshmen men and put in an emergency order for more seven-foot beds." At a time when the average American man was around five foot eight, this was no coincidence; height was one of the easiest ways to evaluate genes. After all, the only way for Stanford to have height records for its incoming freshmen was to ask on the application, which the school did into the 1980s.[22] In this period of Palo Alto's history, the town's golden boys were noted for their athletic prowess, their physical attractiveness, and, not infrequently, the simple virtue of their size as much as their intelligence. All were evidence of the same underlying characteristic: evolutionary fitness. Once Jordan took control, it was bionomics all the way down.

The competition didn't end once students were accepted. Starting in the 1920s, they had to contend with Terman's new grading system, which ranked them on a curve of comparative rather than absolute achievement.[23] But the bionomists also needed an athletic substitute for combat, and Jordan believed that he found one in football. "[H]e felt football's combination of physicality and cooperation fit in with the spirit he wanted to see thrive at Stanford," writes California historian Kevin Starr of Jordan. "Football players offered an immediate and conspicuous paradigm of the Stanford Man as California gentleman: competent, self-reliant, possessed of a style and code having overtones of the Ivy League."[24] Stanford and Berkeley started a fierce rivalry, imitating Harvard and Yale in the East. Today the Bay Area teams have left the Ivies far behind, but it wasn't a smooth ride. Turn-of-the-century college football was violent—on and off the field, if you include the postgame beer riots. In 1904, Stanford players targeted the Cal captain, who was "battered into semi-consciousness and had to be carried off the field weeping hysterically."[25] In

1906, a study of the injuries to the Harvard football team concluded that the sport was unusually harmful, that the injury rate was largely unavoidable, and, worst of all, that "[t]he game does not develop the best type of man physically, because prominence is given to weight without corresponding nervous [meaning "nerve-related"] energy."[26] Jordan banned American football at the school between 1906 and 1918, but Stanford returned strong in the 1920s after the war behind legendary coach and youth football league namesake Pop Warner.

Stanford women didn't play football, but they did play sports, and the administration encouraged it. The school was designed to be coed, and Terman was interested in girl geniuses as well as boy geniuses, finding plenty of subjects worth his time. Relative to other colleges, Stanford seems enlightened with regard to gender equality, but within the bionomic framework women were meant for something different from men. "[S]ince women exist in the main solely for the propagation of the species and are not destined for anything else," Jordan declared in one of his evolution lectures, quoting the philosopher Arthur Schopenhauer, "they live, as a rule, more for the species than for the individual, and in their hearts take the affairs of the species more seriously than those of the individual."[27] In this division of labor, men pursue their interests as individuals while women consolidate men's achievements for the species — or, more precisely, the race. The Stanford woman, then, could not rest on the laurels of tradition if she was to be a worthy partner of the Stanford man, itself a controversial proposition when the Ivy League wouldn't finish integrating men and women for another 50-plus years.

A *Stanford Daily* editorial from 1930 outlines the particular Palo Alto feminism taking root at the time: "Co-education is representative of the western world, and while it may have its opponents, there is no reason why women should not be given the benefits of modern knowledge in order that they may use it in the home."[28] If men in general were inventing, then it was up to women to make efficient use of the latest plug-in technologies to assist their men in particular, whether husbands in the household or bosses in the office. The electric laundry machine is the typical example, sold for home use starting in the early twentieth century, but the electric typewriter is even better for this story. Only male engineers were allowed to design the complex machines, while only "girls" in the secretarial pool *used* them — in the American office,

men dictated and women typed, into the 1990s.* Stanford faculty wives were
at the vanguard of applied science, taking courses at the school and experimenting with new household diets based on (dubious) advances in chemistry. One even tried to study her maid's efficiency by strapping a pedometer
to her leg.[29] Equal in education but separate in function, the women of the
bionomic elite diffused men's scientific work throughout the western WASP
class.

Jane Stanford's rule of 500 held until the 1930s, when the gender ratio
began exceeding 5–1. The board of trustees decided to allow a 60–40 ratio,
maintaining coed scarcity at a sustainable level. And then there were the
babies. Women hold up half the double helix, and the quality the university
could attract to Palo Alto directly determined the quality of the next generation. Lewis Terman hired a number of women graduate students in psychology
to assist him with genius tests, and he mentored them within the profession. In
1928, when Frederick Terman was successful but still a bachelor nearing thirty,
Lewis set him up with Sibyl Walcott, one of his grad students. A year later, the
two were married with a son. Historians record a few variations on the story
about Fred checking Sibyl's IQ in the psych files, or Lewis checking for him,
but they're hard to believe. Lewis Terman would have known Walcott's IQ as
well as he knew her name—as he would have known all his graduate students'
scores, especially those of the women. Lewis Terman conducted a number of
sexual affairs over the years with his mentees, to the point where it was a joke
on campus. (Everyone seemed to know except Fred, who didn't find out until
the 1970s and was apparently crushed.) To the bionomists, smart women were
valuable, but primarily as men's companions and boys' mothers. When Lewis
saw those applications come across his desk—complete with test scores, headshot, height, weight—what did he think? Was he looking for mentees? Girl-
friends? A mother for his grandchildren? He found all three. Whatever else
it was at the time, Stanford was a positive eugenic project, breeding high-IQ
people to produce the next generation of Palo Alto residents.

The Shockleys are a good example of Stanford's reproduction strategy. Bill
Jr.'s mother, May, grew up in the West at the close of the century. Exceptionally

---

* As we'll see in a later section, this generation of white-collar men developed an unfamiliar-
   ity with the typewriter so severe that it may well have delayed the personal computer for a
   decade.

clever, she enrolled at Stanford, which she could do because it was coed and free. There she studied geology and, after graduating in the class of 1902 and operating a surveying firm with her stepfather, became the first woman to serve as a U.S. deputy mineral surveyor, which is how she met the pure-bred underachieving mine speculator William Shockley. He'd already spent a decade bopping around the world dipping his finger into colonially conceded resources—copper in Siberia, gold in Peru—and carrying out unsuccessful searches in Australia and Korea.[30] Shockley fled the Chinese mining concession he managed on behalf of a British firm with a price on his head. May ran into him in Nevada mining territory, where they both stuck out as sophisticates. He was fifty-one and she was twenty-seven; they soon married and headed for London, where they scraped by on Shockley's stock proceeds. After enjoying themselves among other American expat engineers—including another more successful couple of Stanford geology alums—the Shockleys moved to Palo Alto, where William Sr. got a job teaching at the university (on the recommendation of their influential friends) and May sold paintings.

Together the Shockleys homeschooled Bill Jr. for as long as they could, feeling particularly able. They cataloged his advancement scientifically, conducting experiments to track him. At one year old, he could count to four and could tell if one of six objects was missing. Bill Jr. attended the Palo Alto Military Academy for a few years in late adolescence and developed his early interest in physics with help from his next-door neighbor, a Stanford professor of the subject. After the elder Bill died in 1925, Bill Jr. enrolled at UCLA, then Caltech, the finest science university on the West Coast at the time thanks to an infusion of funds from the new aeronautics industry. But he went back to Palo Alto in the summer to take extra classes—from his former neighbor when he could. Palo Alto was Shockley's home, a fact that was to be of global importance, and it became his home in large part because that's where his mom went to college. Once he returned to town, in 1956, Bill Jr. stayed devoted to his mother in Palo Alto, where she lived until her death, in 1977, at ninety-seven years old.

May Bradford Shockley was ahead of her time in so many ways, from her STEM college education to her first-woman career, to her very intentional and then-unusual decision to have only one child and raise him in a style sociologists now call concerted cultivation or intensive parenting. She was disappointed when Bill Jr. missed the cutoff on Terman's genius study, enough so that she had him tested a second time—125, still close but no cigar. A few years later, Lewis Terman tested May's own IQ at an off-the-charts 161, indicating an exceptional facility with IQ tests. She apparently failed to pass on her full score to her son, but her child-rearing project worked. Shockley became a brilliant engineer, an athlete, a war hero without seeing battle, a celebrated inventor, an employee who rose to become a boss, a Stanford professor, a Nobel Prize winner, and the man who put the silicon in Silicon Valley, which made him substantially responsible for the success of the American economy in the 1970s, '80s, and '90s. Here was a great man; here was his great life.

William Shockley Jr. was also one of the most infamous American bigots of the twentieth century.

Cali Cartels

Shockley was obsessed with race and IQ his whole life, eventually devoting himself (and his office at Stanford) to the full-time pursuit of white supremacy. "The origin of Shockley's concept of race is unknown and unknowable," writes his biographer, Joel N. Shurkin, but given what we know about the Palo Alto milieu, that's an overstatement.[31] Eugenic thought was one of Shockley's hometown's biggest exports during the period, and everything the bionomists said about great men and their great lives had a corresponding flip side, a bottom to every top of the hierarchy, losers for every winner. As the self-styled scientists of the natural order, the bionomists developed their understanding of who belonged where. Scientific racists hailed the army intelligence tests, which showed racial minorities performing measurably lower than whites.* In 1919, one of Stanford's intelligence studies measured twelve-year-olds living in San Jose. The graduate student analyzing the results, Kimball Young, found that the incidence of "retardation" positively correlated with the number of Italian kids in the classroom, whom he believed to be racially "of peasant type"

---

* The validity problems with the experiment are too numerous and basic to list (see Stephen Jay Gould, *The Mismeasure of Man, Reissued* [Norton, 1993]; 192–233), but it's worth noting that Lewis Terman saw the army results as damaging to the hypothesis of white superiority because white recruits scored so *badly*, absolutely if not relative to other races.

and "Negroid."* The school superintendent agreed, and they worked together to lane southern Europeans away from other students.[32] At the border with Asia to the west and Mexico to the south, California was the frontier of Anglo white dominion, and it became a laboratory of racial classification. Shurkin thinks that because Shockley didn't encounter many black people in interwar Palo Alto—itself not necessarily a good assumption—his virulent prejudice must have been unusual or autochthonous. On the contrary: Racism was the foundation for California's prosperity.

When it came to translating bionomic insights into eugenic policy, California was ahead of the curve. Chinese exclusion made the country's racial health a question of border security, and the West was the edge of whiteness. At the same time, agricultural employers in the West needed a regular (though not constant) supply of labor, preferably with high skills and low wages. The Southern Pacific Railroad's strategy of importing vulnerable workers from abroad became integral to California's particular mode of production. Growers paid their workers by race, segregating them according to pseudo-scientific ideas about capacity and the intricate matrix of legal rights allotted to Americans by race, ethnicity, gender, immigration status, and national origin. When new profit opportunities arose, growers gathered foreign laborers; when the profit rates attenuated, the state expelled them. For example, in 1897, soon after Californians embarrassed the nation by forcing Chinese exclusion and abatement, a new American sugar duty (secured by a new American sugar trust) boosted West Coast sugar beet production, and the trust began importing Japanese agricultural workers by the tens of thousands.† These skilled gardeners transformed the industry, making the regional beet business the nation's most

---

* Terman advised Young's PhD, but Young later repudiated his own hereditarianism and became an outspoken critic of Terman's. A grandson of Mormon leader Brigham Young, Kimball assumed the presidency of the American Sociological Association as a social constructionist. See Fred B. Lindstrom, Ronald A. Hardert, and Kimball Young, "Kimball Young on Stanford and Oregon, 1919–1926," *Sociological Perspectives* 32, no. 2 (1989): 215–66.

† The emergence of beet sugar led to a collapse in the price of sugar, from over 30 cents per pound during the U.S. Civil War to under 4 cents per pound around the end of the nineteenth century. This hastened the end of sugar-based Atlantic colonialism and the twilight of the Spanish Empire. Max Beer, "The United States in 1898," in *Discovering Imperialism: Social Democracy to World War I*, eds. Richard B. Day and Daniel Gaido (Brill, 2011), 109–23.

profitable, and since beet labor was seasonal, the surplus of cheap skilled harvest labor made the further spread of off-season intensive (and expensive) crops such as strawberries possible. The value of California cropland exploded.

By 1907, the Japanese workers, who had just recently commanded the lowest field wages of any ethnic cohort, became the highest paid and began accumulating their own plots, which they made considerably more productive. However, as soon as they started getting their own land, "the Japanese ceased to be desirable aliens," writes Carey McWilliams in his masterly study of California agriculture, *Factories in the Field.*[33] As the most productive proprietors, small Japanese farmers could pay more than white farmers to buy and lease land, and the industrial growers began to resent the challenge to their position. The old fears that Chinese and Japanese workers would "under-live" Americans morphed into a new anxiety about being outbid.* San Francisco exclusionists attempted to segregate Japanese children out of the city's schools, causing an international crisis necessitating the intervention of President Theodore Roosevelt, who got the school board to back down and negotiated a deal with the Meiji emperor to confine the immigration of Japanese laborers to Hawaii. "The infernal fools in California, and especially in San Francisco, insult the Japanese recklessly, and in the event of war it will be the Nation as a whole which will pay the consequences," Roosevelt told his son, presciently, but California's Anglos kept pushing.[34]

Just as politicians stripped Chinese workers of the formal rights they used to secure a position in America at the end of the nineteenth century, California stripped Japanese farmers of their right to own land. The state's alien land laws passed between 1913 and 1920 made it increasingly difficult for any of California's Asians—the majority of whom at that point were Japanese—to operate their own farm concerns. Japan and the Philippines were spared the 1917 Immigration Act's Asiatic Barred Zone, which blocked immigration from the continent as a whole, but Congress added Japan to the list of banned nations in 1924. Their opportunities limited, second-generation Japanese-Americans left agriculture for the cities, and with immigration blocked, the big growers were finished with Japanese labor. California's farms absorbed a generation's worth of Japanese immigrants' work, skill, hopes, and dreams, and when the workers

---

* For a thorough investigation of this ideological tension during the period, see Colleen Lye, *America's Asia: Racial Form and American Literature, 1893–1945* (Princeton University Press, 2005).

threatened to assimilate or to carve out their own pieces, the state used race laws to group them, rob them, and drain them from the fields.

Whiteness as a legal fact made it possible for groups of European immigrants to follow a path similar to that of the California Japanese, and the California Chinese before them, but assimilate successfully. During this period, Armenian, Italian, and Portuguese immigrants all paid too much for substandard land and increased its value by growing expensive crops, such as grapes and artichokes. But unlike Japanese immigrants they were allowed to ascend to the ranks of the grower-capitalists, albeit under the terms of the already existing cooperatives and trusts, as one intransigently independent Armenian raisin grower in Fresno found out when night riders from the Sun-Maid Raisin Growers of California co-op burned his house down. East Indians, on the other hand, were in the barred zone, and the Supreme Court decided in 1923's *United States v. Bhagat Singh Thind* that Aryan heritage notwithstanding, Punjabis are not white.* Excluded by the land acts and with little prospect for legal advancement or family building, many of those who came to California, who helped to develop the state's rice production capacity in the same way that other immigrant groups improved the land, left.† Though as I'll explain, some of these men were running toward home rather than away from the United States.

Whiteness was a restrictive cartel, and the cartel model proved itself increasingly necessary in California as producers struggled with that old inherent tension: They wanted to sell as much as possible at as high a price as possible.

---

* The ruling in *Thind* followed the ruling in *Ozawa v. United States* the year before, in which the high court held that Japanese people are not white. The rulings in *Ozawa* and *Thind* resolved over 40 years of inconsistent racial jurisprudence in the lower courts, which (especially on the West Coast and Hawaii) struggled to categorize immigrants from India, Syria, and Armenia in particular. See tables 1–3 of "racial prerequisite cases" in Appendix A, Ian Haney-López, *White by Law: The Legal Construction of Race* (New York University Press, 2006), 203–8.

† A number began interracial families, the vast majority with Mexican women. Though anti-miscegenation laws still technically applied, racial formation remained undercooked in this period and in practice enforcement was left up to clerks, who filled out a blank field on the marriage license marked "race." Rather than the more detailed categories we'll see established, clerks used skin phenotype descriptions like "white," "black," and "brown," all three of which could apply and were applied to Punjabis. As long as they matched their proposed spouse, the marriage fulfilled racial requirements. See Karen Leonard, *Making Ethnic Choices: California's Punjabi Mexican Americans* (Temple University Press, 2010), 68.

But if all the producers in a marketplace try to grow and harvest as much as possible, they will oversupply the market, tank the price, and kill their profits. If a group of producers agree to restrain output in order to maintain a profitable level of scarcity, on the other hand, each has a powerful incentive to try to break the deal, and new participants have an equally powerful incentive to enter the market to the same effect. This tension helped produce the wheat boom-bust cycle as planters chased high prices until they caused them to drop. Falling cattle prices cut the throat on California Mexican land claims in the first place. Railroads hit the same problem, consolidating behind the Combine when speculators started to fear they had built too many lines. The redwood lumber industry tried to solve the problem by forming the Redwood Lumber Association in the 1870s, which then joined with the Pine Manufacturers Company to form the inclusive California Lumber Exchange in the 1880s, which successfully reduced timber production by over 20 percent between 1886 and 1888.[35] But the exchange was torn apart by the centrifugal force of high prices once it achieved them. Gold, as the money commodity, was immune, but the rest of California's products suffered from an excess of enthusiasm. For the capitalist class, there are benefits to seeing everything generically, without individual differentiators, but there are also drawbacks.

Planters premised produce production on premium prices, so they were vulnerable to market fluctuations. Crop diversity helped relieve the pressure, but the best truck farm practices ran counter to incentives to scale up and rationalize. As they scaled, growers also fell prey to middlemen packers and commission agents who could play them against one another. Already fed up with the situation in 1893, a German-born merchant turned orange grower in Southern California named P.J. Dreher organized some of his neighbors into a small cooperative so they could take over their own packing. They gained enough benefits from this vertical integration that others quickly joined. The California Fruit Growers Exchange (CFGE) scaled up, and by 1905 it had counted among its membership nearly half the state's citrus growers, a number that continued to plump. By centralizing packing beyond any individual grower's purview, the exchange could ensure that no one undermined the collective agreement regarding output. The group established fruit standards as well, and they shared marketing costs. By uniformly branding their own oranges, they made sure not to create free publicity for non-exchange fruit (from Florida, say), and the brand made it harder for would-be bad actors to betray the collective by dumping product. The name they picked, Sunkist, remains *the* brand for California citrus, which is why a soda company licensed the name many years later.

The CFGE didn't do all its own distribution in the early days, and on the faraway San Francisco market it relied on the assistance of a young hotshot commission agent named Amadeo Giannini. The Bank of Italy grew alongside the produce cartels in the first half of the twentieth century, and Giannini learned from Dreher's success. Dreher took part in Giannini's as well, helping the Italian outsider break into the Southern California market. Dreher joined Bank of America as an executive after retiring from fruit in the 1940s. In addition to consolidating California banking, Giannini financed the cartelization of California produce. His role in supporting the California Prune and Apricot growers is indicative: In 1916, when the Santa Clara–centered industry sought to sign up 75 percent of the state's acreage for the collective, they turned to Giannini, and he issued a public statement reprinted in the trade journal *Western Canner and Packer*. He used the royal we to issue his approval for the plan — speaking, I presume, for his banks.[36] The association came together and raised prices following the Sunkist model, and we still buy fruit under its Sunsweet brand. But Giannini was offering more than his opinion: In 1919, the Bank of Italy issued the association a $3 million line of credit to pay growers in advance, after a similar $500,000 move paid off the year before. Then he put over $2 million into the state's bean growers, allowing them to hold out for better prices.[37] Over the following years, he dropped over $10 million into the state's raisin cartel, which adopted the Sun-Maid name. The Bank of Italy made sure over 85 percent of growers joined, and marketing techniques — including packaging the fruit in little red boxes, putting raisins in cereal, and inventing raisin bread — nearly doubled the country's per-capita raisin consumption. Giannini helped the industry hold on until the federal government began supporting the produce cartels directly in the 1930s.

The grower cartels exemplified white ethnic assimilation in California as much as the Bank of Italy did — that is if we're determined to consider the bank and the growers as separate entities, which they weren't really. At a time when Asians (formally) and other nonwhites (informally) were prevented from owning agricultural land, the planters and financiers got together in exclusive clubs. The subscription drives shifted the basis of belonging from ethnic identity to the associations. "Class feeling between American, Armenian, Italian and Russian faded away into insignificance on the last few days as the need for unity became apparent," reported the *Fresno Morning Republican* about the Giannini-led Sun-Maid drive.[38] Finding yourself on the wrong side of the produce cartels was dangerous, and a number of Armenian growers in particular—among whom, it bears acknowledging, were recent immigrants who escaped a genocide—reported aggressive intimidation, including violence and property destruction. But the authorities played for only one team, and both the sheriff and the district attorney in the Fresno heart of raisin country openly supported the association. A Department of Justice investigator found ample evidence of what one independent grower described as a "reign of terror" by the "Raisin Ku Klux Klan," but Sun-Maid was too big to fail.[39] Expanded and more resilient with the inclusion of dark-featured immigrants, whiteness endured as California's core organizing principle.

Not everyone was thrilled with the idea of expanding the definition of whiteness, including those scientists who staked their reputations on the immigrant groups' insolubility. To maintain genetic health in the face of these assimilating ethnics, bionomists pushed eugenic sterilization programs across the country, nowhere more successfully than in California. In 1927's *Buck v. Bell*, the Supreme Court ruled that, based on hereditarian science, the state had a compelling interest in sterilizing a Virginia eighteen-year-old named Carrie Buck: She and her mother both scored too low on the Stanford-Binet scale.[40] In the first half of the twentieth century, American states sterilized 60,000 women, a third of them in California, and incarcerated more in asylums.[41] Writer Joan Didion, who grew up in Sacramento during the period, recalls trips to the local asylum to sing with her Girl Scout troop, along with the institutionalization of her grandmother's sister, who had come to live with young Joan's family after the death of her husband. In California, she writes, "the possibility that such a fate could strike at random was the air we breathed."[42]

Scaremonger Lewis Terman approved of the state's harsh mental hygiene regime, suggesting that 1,000 Harvard graduates would produce only 56 descendants in 200 years, while the same number of "degenerate" southern Italians would become 100,000.[43] But the high crop values, abundant food for consumption, seasonal labor, strong wages, and privileged positions reserved for white workers meant that European immigrants in Northern California could send their children to school at higher rates and for more years than they could in other parts of the country. In 1930, native-born whites in San Jose sent 94 percent of their children between the ages of fourteen to seventeen to school, while for foreign and mixed-white couples, the rate was 92 percent. In New Haven, Connecticut, by contrast, U.S.-born and immigrant whites sent their teenagers to school at 78.9 and 62.2 percent respectively.[44] The state's banks and aquifers financed white ethnic assimilation; only 100 years after Terman's dire prediction, California couldn't count its Italians if it tried.

The 1924 Immigration Act struck a delicate balance between racial and national distinctions—between admitting the workers American capitalists needed and avoiding the "racial indigestion" Cubberley observed. The law instituted a quota system, ranking Europeans by national-racial preference and admitting them accordingly, concocting a finely tuned racial diet for smooth white assimilation. Countries with racially unassimilable populations were assigned the minimum quota of 100 souls, but there remained a problem. What stopped a person of Chinese descent from immigrating through Mexico or Canada, which, along with the rest of the Western Hemisphere, were exempt from quotas? What stopped 100,000 of them? The 1924 act solved the problem by banning the immigration of anyone who was racially ineligible for citizenship—that is, Asians. "Congress thus created the oddity of immigration quotas for non-Chinese persons of China, non-Japanese persons of Japan, non-Indian persons of India, and so on," writes Mae Ngai in *Impossible Subjects: Illegal Aliens and the Making of Modern America*.[45] West of the Ural Mountains, people could become Americans, and it was up to the nation's scientists and policymakers to cook up the right ratios. The law separated whites into national groups, but only in order to incorporate them in proper proportion as white Americans. Black Americans secured their citizenship by force in the Civil War, and so the bill's logic required the annual admission of 200 black Africans: 100 each from the free nations of Ethiopia and Liberia. As for the rest of the racially undesirable world, European colonialism ensured that the most desirable whites—*defined as desirable in large part thanks to their success in colonization*—controlled those quota slots.

California's growers were still dependent on low-wage nonwhite workers, especially with the labor demand crunch of World War I, which meant they had to get by on loopholes. Fearing the quota consequences, growers began importing Filipino workers in large numbers starting in 1923, and they attracted over 30,000 workers to the state by the end of the decade.[46] As American nationals (the Philippines was a U.S. territory at the time), Filipinos were entitled to travel freely within the American empire; as phenotypically distinguishable from whites and Mexicans, they could be relegated by growers to a lower wage tier. It didn't seem to hurt that most Filipinos spoke English and were familiar with American customs and culture. With racial wage scales came a segregated production process: lower-wage Mexican and Filipino workers were overused in the fields, while higher-wage whites worked in the packing sheds and canneries. In the beginning, the Filipino immigrants worked for the lowest wages and under the worst conditions—their pay documented at under $10 a month—but the young Filipino men proved more assimilable in practice than growers and policy makers imagined. With their fluent English and American nationality, Filipino immigrants felt entitled to interact with white women, whether on the beaches or at the taxi dance halls, where (still relatively scarce in the state) women danced one-on-one in exchange for ticket vouchers. Under the law, the Filipino men weren't wrong; though California had banned marriages between whites and "Negroes and mulattoes" since 1850, adding "Mongolians" in 1905, Filipinos were "Malay" under the original eighteenth-century racial typology.[47] California, having relied on the broad stretch of the Asiatic Barred Zone to exclude South Asians up to that point, did not include them in the anti-miscegenation statute. But in 1933, as Filipino farmers posed an increasing sexual threat to white men (and as they organized for higher wages), the state added "Malay" to the rule.

White vigilantes didn't wait for the law to change before beginning abatement proceedings against Filipinos.[48] Once the Depression hit in 1929, white workers (with no assets to defend save their whiteness and masculinity) attacked Filipino workers and the farms that hired them. There was a fear campaign throughout Santa Clara County: A San Jose man was arrested in 1930 for dynamiting Filipino homes and meeting places.[49] But as Ngai points out, white workers weren't looking to leave the packing sheds and trade places with Filipino workers in the lettuce fields. They didn't *want* the jobs. Rather, "the central element of this hostility was the ideology of white entitlement to the resources of the West."[50] As scholar Geoff Mann writes, "Workers fought for a share of the surplus in addition to subsistence allowance at least partly because there was neither precedent nor functional logic to the region's profits, especially in the resource sectors that effectively industrialized the West."[51] As it did in the gold rush, the land held limited potential for advancement and assimilation; the bay was beginning to leach salt water into the already overused Peninsula aquifers.[52] Growers became frustrated with Filipino workers around the same time—as was their wont with imported laborers, who never seemed to stay in their place. And unlike foreign workers in the past, Filipinos couldn't be legally deported without their consent. That changed: The Philippine Independence Act of 1934 reclassified Filipino immigrants as aliens, even those already in the country. California began offering them free trips back, one-way.

The biggest and most permanent change to California's labor force in the early decades of the twentieth century was immigration of the Mexican proletariat. Following the American conquest, the collapse of the Spanish racial hierarchy into an Anglo-Chicano binary, and the expropriation of Mexican landowners, California was not an appealing place to immigrate to. But after the 1907 "gentlemen's agreement" with Japan to limit labor immigration, contractors looked to the south. World War I brought tens of thousands of workers a year northward for field work and the railroads.[53] Restrictionists introduced new hoops for Mexican workers to jump through, and employers helped them hop. Growers appreciated that Mexican laborers tended to go home when they weren't needed, something Chinese and Japanese workers couldn't manage, as well as their low wages and lack of labor organization. In the 1920s, the Mexican proletariat became the California agricultural proletariat, returned to Alta California to farm for Anglos. When the Depression hit, wages fell by over half, and Mexicans had to compete with white dust bowl migrants for agricultural work.[54] Suddenly the lax border enforcement tightened, and America began deporting Mexicans at a substantial rate, scaring (and angering) more of them into leaving on their own accord. Vulnerability to raids and deportation marked Mexicans in California as foreign in a new way, no matter whether their families had lived at that longitude and latitude for centuries or not. Immigration policy formalized national belonging according to the border, mapping the Anglo-Chicano racial binary to the north-south line. Maintaining a vulnerable racialized workforce that was relatively easy to import *and* deport proved very profitable for the state's capitalists. Unlike other racial groups recruited and then expelled from California's workforce, the Chicano agricultural proletariat still structures the state's demographics in a way that suggests a false continuity with white settlement, as if this is the way it had always been, as if the segregation were natural and Mexicans "belonged" in the fields.

California's agricultural capitalists pedaled the state's nonwhite labor like a bicycle: When they pushed one group down, another rose to replace it, and the whole contraption moved a little farther down the road. Via this continuous pumping motion they transformed the state's cropland, from low-value wheat to high-value fruits, vegetables, and nuts. The commodities were expensive and the profits were high, but it's the land itself where the real value accumulated. With mechanization and crop improvements, combined with suppressed labor costs, California's speculative promise swelled. The university suburb of Palo Alto grew increasingly prosperous as profits and rich kids began concentrating there. Stanford promoted an ideal Golden State lifestyle for its faculty, and the board of trustees wanted to make sure professors could afford servants, unusual for Americans of the period. Alongside campus developed one of the Peninsula's largest black communities, which provided much of the town's reproductive labor — in private homes, in restaurants, and at Stanford's fraternities and sororities. While in nearby San Jose most black residents were homeowners, in Palo Alto the figure was only 27 percent, the same proportion that worked as live-in servants.[55] After accreting value for 100 years, the Crescent Park neighborhood where Palo Alto's early twentieth-century black community lived is now home to multimillion-dollar mansions including the Zuckerblock, where the Facebook billionaire razed four homes and combined the plots.

The Bombs Are All Around You

As California's particular form of waged racial exploitation evolved in its workplaces during the first decades of the twentieth century, the strategy led to a set of unanticipated consequences. Planters gathered workers from around the world, counting on racial and linguistic differences to keep them apart. But bringing people together to work always risks bringing them together to do other stuff, like think, and sometimes what workers think about together is that maybe they shouldn't have to work so hard. California was a place where people from much of the rest of the world could come and find new lives, and that was a very appealing prospect for political dissidents who needed to disappear. As a result, the West Coast became a hotbed of revolutionary organization, a hub where anticolonialists and antimonarchists and just plain anarchists found one another. Despite Palo Alto's original purpose as a ruling-class safe house, not even Leland Stanford's suburb escaped the fray.

The first revolutionary party to form in California during the twentieth century was called the Social Revolutionary Party, and the society it sought to overthrow was Japan's. Its founder was Kōtoku Shūsui, a Japanese left-wing writer and organizer who came to the States in 1905 after being released from jail amid a nationalist crackdown in his home country. His 1901 pamphlet *Imperialism: Monster of the Twentieth Century*, written in conversation with both Western and Eastern thinkers and history, is one of the world's earliest and most coherent analyses of the phenomenon; Kōtoku had it pegged.* A translator of *The Communist Manifesto* and cofounder of the Social Democratic Party in Japan—based on the German party of the same name and banned immediately—Kōtoku was relieved to find that Japanese leftists had more breathing room in the Bay Area than they did at home. It was a crucial time in the development of the world's revolutionary political tendencies, and Kōtoku quickly came to reject ineffective parliamentarianism and embrace bomb-throwing anarchist insurrectionism as the only solution to the problem of empire. The Social Revolutionary Party wasn't based on the Germans, it was based on the Socialist Revolutionary Party of Russia, whose members, called SRs, sought the overthrow of the czar and the redistribution of royal land.

Kōtoku didn't become an anarchist in California—he thanked the emperor's jail for that—but his politics were further shaped there, and as the acknowledged leader of the Japanese ultra-left in the United States, he had his own serious impact on the development of the racially integrated West Coast labor movement. The California trade unions continued to exclude nonwhite

---

* "I believe that if the United States faces a crisis that threatens their national survival in the future, this crisis will not be caused by the smallness of their territory, but rather by their unlimited territorial expansion. It will result not from their failure to exercise their political power in the world, but rather from the corruption and decadence that has infected their own society, not from the small size of their market, but rather from the unfair distribution of wealth, from the destruction of freedom and equality, and from the rampant spread of imperialist and expansionist ideologies." Robert Thomas Tierney and Shūsui Kōtoku, *Monster of the Twentieth Century: Kōtoku Shūsui and Japan's First Anti-Imperialist Movement* (Oakland: University of California Press, 2015), 192.

workers, limiting their potential impact in the state. As a result, Kōtoku found his friends in the Industrial Workers of the World (IWW), or Wobblies, a revolutionary coalition of unions open to all laborers, which was founded the same year he arrived, 1905. Like the ultra-left factions in Germany and Russia, their idealized tactics were the general strike and the bomb, but the IWW was more like a militant labor union with big dreams than a revolutionary conspiracy. They scrapped with hired thugs at mines and sawmills throughout the West in particular. Compared to the craft workers of the American Federation of Labor (AFL), IWWers were rough-and-tumble, noted for getting in fights, moving around, and changing their names to escape bad reputations. The West, where they were strongest, was considered the country's backwater at the time, but the West was also closest to the Eastern Hemisphere, and the internationalist dissidents who made their way to the coast even temporarily, like Kōtoku — who was only in the country for eight months total — pulled still-emerging California into the global class struggle.

In 1907, the California Japanese SRs issued their biggest provocation to that point. On the emperor's birthday, they nailed an open letter to the door of the Japanese consulate in San Francisco. Full of revolutionary bravado, the threat was signed "Anarchists-Terrorists" and taunted the government with the doctrine of evolution, telling "miserable [Emperor] Mutsuhito" that he and his royal family were descended from apes, just like the rest of us. "Bombs are all around you, about to explode. Farewell to you," they signed off. The Japanese government took the letter seriously, producing a report on radicalism in California, including notes on the IWW. Kōtoku returned to Japan in the summer of 1906, and he led the revolutionary left under the banner of "anarcho-communism." Soon after completing their study of the SR milieu, Japanese authorities launched a new crackdown, using a bomb-plot pretext to round up leftists and execute a dozen people, including Kōtoku Shūsui. But though the California SR group only had a membership in the low dozens, and though its charismatic leader was murdered by the Japanese state within five years of the group's founding, the influence of this unusual organizational-ideological formation continued around the Pacific Rim.*

---

* For example, member Iwasa Sakutarō became the leading light of the Japanese anarchist movement during the twentieth century after his return to the country. Staying in California, SR member Tetsugoro Takeuchi founded the Japanese Fresno Federation of Labor

The California Japanese SRs were not the only West Coast diasporic revolutionary party to coalesce during the twentieth century's chaotic first couple of decades. While migrant laborers from the East Indian subcontinent were more likely to work in other Crown territories, thousands ended up in the fields of California, Oregon, and Washington, and fewer—but still some—in the local universities, including Stanford.* David Starr Jordan had a close relationship with the Japanese ruling class—as you will discover later in this section—and he even helped turn the school into an imperial listening post, but at the turn of the twentieth century he considered himself a fervent anti-imperialist. Unlike Kōtoku's, Jordan's issue with this neocolonialism was not that it was an affront to the equality of all people; rather, his problem was something closer to the opposite. As the United States gathered its winnings from the Spanish-American War—the Philippines, Puerto Rico, Cuba, and Guam—Jordan warned that

> the territorial expansion now contemplated would not extend our institutions, because the proposed colonies are incapable of civilized self-government. It would not extend our nation, because these regions are already full of alien races, and are not habitable by Anglo-Saxon people. The strength of Anglo-Saxon civilization lies in the mental and physical activity of men and in the growth of the home. Where activity is fatal to life, the Anglo-Saxon decays, mentally, morally, physically. The home cannot endure in the climate of the tropics.[56]

The Philippines, he suggested, should be developed independently with U.S. assistance before being turned over to a small European power for nonbelligerent safekeeping. Cuba, being so close, could be absorbed slowly in order to minimize domestic indigestion. In the European scramble for territory that

---

and led thousands of Japanese beet workers out on strike with the IWW in 1908. Masayo Duus, *The Japanese Conspiracy: The Oahu Sugar Strike of 1920* (Berkeley, CA: University of California Press, 1999), 25.

* According to an official count, writes Maia Ramnath, "only 6,656 South Asians entered the United States (legally) between 1899 and 1913," a majority of the estimated 10,000 South Asians in North America in 1914. Maia Ramnath, *Haj to Utopia: How the Ghadar Movement Charted Global Radicalism and Attempted to Overthrow the British Empire* (University of California Press, 2011), 17.

threatened to engulf the world, Jordan saw race suicide. "British people have been debauched by their course in India...the heart's blood has gone out of Great Britain as it has gone out of all countries which have engaged in constant wars."[57] And though he was convinced of colonized peoples' inferiority, Jordan sympathized to a certain degree with revolutionary nationalist movements that sought to pack up the Anglo-Saxons and send them back to their proper climate, especially when the movements were led by educated elites. British hegemony concerned the Stanford president more than Germany and Japan rising to compete, and he did his bit to try to keep the United States out of the polarizing alliances that eventually pulled the country into World War I. The circumstances yielded some strange bedfellows in Palo Alto.

When Jordan met Lala Har Dayal in 1911, I suspect what most impressed the president was the line in the twenty-seven-year-old's résumé about studying Sanskrit at Oxford, along with his salary requirements as an instructor of Indian philosophy: $0. FACULTY ELECTS A HINDU, announced the *New York Times*, elevating the story to a national one because Har Dayal was "perhaps the first Hindu professor to hold a position in an American college."[58] (The vast majority of so-called Hindus in California were Sikhs from the Punjab region, where British commodity wheat made the agricultural system fragile and nearly two million people died of starvation in the mid-1870s.)[59] Har Dayal's background was exceptional for a California East Indian: he was a highly educated young man from a Hindu family, another aspect of his credentials that must have attracted the elitist Jordan. What his new employer probably didn't know is that he bailed halfway through his Oxford scholarship to be a radical writer-editor and spread hard-line Indian nationalism. Politically, he swam in the same ultra-left streams as Kōtoku Shūsui did, reading Karl Marx and the Russian anarchists, including Peter Kropotkin (whom he met when he was at Oxford) and especially Mikhail Bakunin.* Har Dayal weaved together atheism, Buddhism, and Marxism into a single practice, one that involved personal asceticism and social extravagance. After spells in France, Algeria, Martinique, and Hawaii, and after an attempt to return to India, he came to the

---

* A contemporary and rival of Karl Marx on the international revolutionary scene, Bakunin helped lead the anarchist faction, influencing, among others, Kropotkin, whose concept of "mutual aid" pushed anarchism further away from formal politics toward a form of being in the world.

Bay Area, which was a center of East Indian labor on the West Coast as well as a global nexus for radical thought. The Stanford gig was little more than a cover, and Har Dayal used the position to gather the Palo Alto community's revolutionaries into what he called the Radical Club, or, in its full glory, the International-Radical-Communist Anarchist Club. Not exactly the "Indian philosophy" Jordan had in mind. As connected and experienced an intellectual as the ultra-left had on the West Coast, Har Dayal became secretary of the Oakland IWW.

It was soon apparent to the Jordan administration that, despite the headline news of his hiring, Har Dayal was not a good fit for Stanford after all. The tipping point seems to have been Jordan's receipt of notes from a Radical Club meeting on the topic of "heroes . . . who have killed rulers and dynamited buildings," but apparently the decision to part was mutual. At that point Stanford classes were the least important part of Har Dayal's work. A month after he left his position at the school, he launched the Fraternity of the Red Flag, an IWW-inspired revolutionary association committed to communism as well as the abolition of racism, patriotism, private property, marriage, government, religion, and metaphysics. A donation from a follower allowed him to set up the Bakunin Institute in the Bay, the first "anarchist monastery." But Har Dayal's internationalism took a back seat to anticolonial nationalism after a December 1912 bomb attack nearly killed the British viceroy for India, Lord Charles Hardinge. Har Dayal was overjoyed, and he captured his sentiments in a four-page propaganda pamphlet full of exclamation points and historical declarations. If Jordan feared that in the age of gunpowder the clown could shoot down the hero, Har Dayal rejoiced in the same potential: "When Caesar calls himself the 'Son of God,' the bomb answers that he is but the 'Son of Man.' "[60] He ended the call with: "Comrades of the Revolution in India, be up and doing. Organise your propaganda anew at home and abroad. Take new vows of service and sacrifice. Lo! the bomb has spoken. Let the young men and women of Hindusthan answer." They did.

The explosion energized the diaspora, and West Coast labor organizers began planning revolution in earnest. Among the East Indian labor leaders in the North American West was Tarak Nath Das, a farm worker turned UC Berkeley student who organized the Pacific Northwest from Vancouver to San Francisco. He knew Har Dayal from the Bay Area radical scene, and when this transnational milieu accelerated its independence organizing, it tapped Har Dayal to lead the propaganda and education effort. His organization became the Ghadar ("Revolt") Movement, which became the Ghadar Party and ultimately the Ghadar Mutiny. As he wrote his Stanford friend, the literary critic and English professor Van Wyck Brooks, a year after the bomb attack, the Ghadar press "prints about 1100 sheets an hour & we are printing tons of literature to smuggle into India."[61] As the imperialist powers drifted toward world war, the Ghadar Movement saw its opening. Part of the German strategy before and during the First World War was to encourage its adversaries' revolutionary movements. The most notable was the Reich's support of and transportation for Vladimir Lenin and his Bolshevik crew back home to Russia, but the Germans also backed what became the 1916 Easter Rising in Ireland. San Francisco was the portal for German support for Indian independence, which came in the twin forms of money and guns.

As an island of anti-English sentiment, Jordan's Palo Alto became part of that complex. The Germans helped Indian revolutionary Narendra Nath Bhattacharya escape to Stanford via San Francisco, where he took on the pseudonym M. N. Roy and met Evelyn Trent, a student protégée of David Starr Jordan from Utah who became, following a whirlwind courtship, Roy's wife. Roy and Trent studied Marx while they dodged British spies and Trent's rich family, escaping to Mexico in 1917 with Jordan's assistance.* There, in the wake of the Bolshevik Revolution, they were among the cofounders of the Mexican Communist Party. (Among other cofounders was the Japanese labor leader Sen Katayama, who organized between San Francisco and Tokyo and was delegated by the Communist International [Comintern] to help the

---

* If Jordan's small role in the founding of the Mexican Communist Party seems confounding, that speaks to the later split in anti-imperial politics on class lines. During this period, however, bourgeois anticolonial nationalists could make common cause with working-class radicals. For example, Sun Fo, the only son of Chinese nationalist leader Sun Yat Sen, was part of the Har Dayal circle while attending UC Berkeley, where he joined celebrations of the bomb attack on Lord Hardinge. The Ghadar Party itself included a future leader of the "Ad Dharm" anti-caste movement, Mangu Ram, as well as a future leader of the Hindu nationalist pro-caste movement, Bhai Parmanand. See Tim Harper, *Underground Asia* (Penguin Books, 2022); Maia Ramnath, *Haj to Utopia: How the Ghadar Movement Charted Global Radicalism and Attempted to Overthrow the British Empire* (University of California Press, 2011); Arundhati Roy, *The Doctor and the Saint: Caste, Race, and Annihilation of Caste, the Debate between B.R. Ambedkar and M.K. Gandhi* (Haymarket Press, 2017).

Mexican group.) Soon after, they accepted Lenin's invitation to the Second Congress of the Communist International, in Moscow. The two of them (and Katayama) spent the next years as globetrotting organizers for the Comintern until their separation in 1925. Trent returned to her family in the United States, but without her citizenship: As the wife of a man from the Asiatic Barred Zone, she was stripped of her nationality, and authorities warned her that if she resumed her political activities, she, a child of Salt Lake City, would be deported from the country of her birth as an undesirable alien.[62] The internationalist current could pull a Stanford student to the high council of world revolution in just a few years, a place from which it was hard to return.

Roy and Trent were just two West Coast targets of the British Foreign Office, which employed spies throughout the Pacific region. English officials continually complained to U.S. authorities that Har Dayal was obviously an undesirable alien, because he was publicly plotting to overthrow the colonial government by force. But the official position of the United States at the time was that, as long as you don't plot to overthrow *our* government, plotting to overthrow *other* governments is technically a freedom-of-speech question.* A few months before the assassination of Archduke Franz Ferdinand triggered World War I, immigration authorities finally hauled Har Dayal in to answer questions about his political views. He bailed out to continue his speaking schedule, and when the war started, he did the United States a favor and took off for Berlin. From there he helped coordinate the return of thousands of Ghadar members—a significant portion of West Coast East Indians—to India for the uprising. Leading the first crew was Jawala Singh, one of the main Ghadar funders and a truck farmer known as the "Potato King of California." In February of 1915, the revolt failed as government infiltrators thwarted plans for bomb attacks and Indian troop mutinies. Dozens were executed.

"What is puzzling about the Ghadar movement," writes historian Harjot Oberoi, "is the manner in which it virtually came out of nowhere and rapidly took over the consciousness of an entire diasporic community. What was so compelling in its message that it could uproot an entire project of migration and

---

* In practice, this safety depended on the state's whims, which changed as the United States shifted into long-term alignment (and international security cooperation) with the United Kingdom. See Moon-Ho Jung, *Menace to Empire: Anticolonial Solidarities and the Transpacific Origins of the US Security State* (University of California Press, 2022).

settlement and turn it upside down? Why would thousands of migrants, from different regions of India, but predominantly the Sikhs from the Punjab, suddenly become interested in waging an armed struggle against British colonialism?"[63] Oberoi's answer is to reconsider the Ghadar sequence in relation to the era's Russian anarchist revolts—no doubt an influence—but the similarities to the Japanese SRs are more dramatic. In fact, there were similar movements throughout the region.

Among the many political labels Har Dayal assumed was that of Magonista, a follower of the Mexican revolutionary anarchist brothers Enrique and Ricardo Flores Magón, ultra-left leaders of the Partido Liberal Méxicano (PLM). In 1907, after a failed revolt the year before, Ricardo fled to the Bay, where he helped weave revolutionary tendencies together. The IWW and PLM became nearly synonymous in the American West during the period, especially among Mexicano and indigenous members, and the milieu turned northern Mexico into an international revolutionary training ground. Unlike women in the trans-Pacific California communities discussed above, Mexican and indigenous women resided in California in large numbers, and ultra-left feminism found its real-world expression in militant leadership by women such as Basiliza Franco, Margarita Ortega, and Isabel Fierro as well as autonomous women's organizations under the radical banners.[64] The PLM-IWW alliance culminated in the 1911 invasion of Baja California from the north by 500 Magonista militants, including a polyglot crew of around 100 Wobblies.* Among those who crossed the border was Ghadar cofounder and UC Berkeley agriculture PhD Pandurang Khankhoje.[65] He found the revolution unexpectedly violent, which was not a great omen for the ill-fated Ghadar Mutiny.

The world's bomb throwers found cover in Northern California partly thanks to the brief periods of farmer diversity in the region. With the Korean peninsula under Japanese colonial domination starting in 1905, and emigration constrained, the Korean diaspora was small, but it, too, hatched a California bomb plot. Kim Chong-lim was a rice farmer north of Sacramento, and he accumulated leases on thousands of acres, entitling him to one of the region's commodity-product kingdoms and the title of Korean Rice King. Like Jawala Singh, he channeled proceeds into the nationalist movement. In

---

* Moderate elements betrayed the Magonistas, clearing the way for a right-wing coup soon after.

1920, Kim funded a handful of flight schools that trained a Korean air force in exile.[66] They planned to launch an aerial bomb attack on the Imperial Palace in Tokyo, and they deployed to Manchuria for the purpose. But the squadron's leader, Park Yong-man, was assassinated, and the group dissolved into the broader anticolonial movement, which itself took on a particular ideological character, as I'll explain below.

These Pacific revolutionary conspiracies stand apart from the U.S. political struggles of the era for the good reason that they were designed to. Despite the discrimination they encountered, Pacific dissidents—especially when they were looking at censorship, jail, or execution at home—found California a relatively safe place until the World War I Red Scare. And though this set of plots ended in misfortune, they formed the experimental foundation for what followed. The Bay Area was already a laboratory for radical thought and practice. In 1908, San Francisco Koreans demanded a meeting with Durham Stevens, the Oberlin graduate foisted on the Korean government as a foreign affairs adviser by the Japanese, who was on his way to Washington, DC, to explain the emperor's position. Stevens refused to retract a statement he made about the necessity of paternal control over the peninsula, and when he told the four Korean representatives that they had been gone too long to know what was really happening, they beat him with their chairs.[67] The next day, two local student independence activists, Jang In-hwan and Jeon Myeong-un, shot Stevens as he got out of his limo, mortally wounding the imperial hireling. Capital's strategy of pulling cohorts of desperate people from wherever it could reach and putting them to work transformed California for the profitable, but that combination was combustible, too. If Palo Alto wanted to stay rich—and it did—the town would have to get used to facing the consequences.

Chapter 2.3

Hooverville

Herbert Hoover and the Pioneer Class — Gold Mine
Market — The Neutral American — Commerce
Secretariat — California Bolsheviks

Born in 1874, Herbert Hoover was the middle child of WASP settlers (specifically, Iowa Quakers), his mother a schoolteacher and his father a blacksmith. Jesse Hoover was an ambitious young man in the age of the shopkeeper, and in 1878 he upgraded to an agricultural implements store. If that suggests an old-fashioned picture, it shouldn't; agricultural machinery was an advanced sector of the era's technology. The elder Hoover sold water pumps and sewing machines and was the town's first barbed-wire producer, using an apparatus that was invented only a few years prior. Professionally, the former blacksmith was more like an engineer who opened an electronics shop than a farmer. In his early thirties, Jesse was in touch with his time and riding an enviable trajectory. But despite being a modern man, he was living in liminal times, and contagious disease was a serious threat to everyone everywhere in the world. He died of pneumonia complications in 1880, and his widow, Hulda, followed him into the afterlife four years later (also pneumonia). Their three children, who just recently faced uncircumscribed opportunity as upwardly mobile white kids with education and a family business in the American West, were now orphans.

For orphans, however, they were relatively lucky. Herbert shuffled between relatives in Iowa until he reached adolescence, when the extended family, who shared his parents' belief in the value of education, sent him to an uncle in Oregon who was the doctor for and principal of a Quaker community school. When the uncle started a land-settlement business, teenage Herbert became an office boy. That's where he first met some engineers and became enchanted with the profession, which in the closing decades of the nineteenth century had many evangelists. After seeing an engineer coldly assess a mountain, Hoover decided he wanted to study mining. That ruled out the Quaker college in Indiana the family planned for him to attend, because it didn't offer engineering classes. But the teenager had an alternative proposal: He read in the newspaper that a new university was opening in California. It was free, and they were holding tryout exams in Portland. The fact that the interviewer was another Quaker doctor assuaged the family's concerns and probably helped young Herbert squeeze his underqualified way into the inaugural class of Leland Stanford Junior University—they're not called Friends for nothing. In 1891, when the Governor invited the pioneer class to Palo Alto and bestowed his son's fortune upon them, spreading the family curse for good or ill, he was speaking to Herbert Hoover.

Hoover had actually been on campus the summer before, taking some remedial instruction to prepare for his freshman year in accordance with his conditional admittance. At a school based on bionomics and a scientific understanding of immutable intelligence, Herbert made a surprising leader of the first class. He wasn't from an overly distinguished family, nor did he demonstrate exceptional gifts. In the first volume of his memoir, he recounts failing only one class (German), but getting zero As. He had, as he put it, too many "other yens and occupations in noncurricular activities."[1] These included a paper route and a laundry service that he established and then subcontracted to other students for streams of passive income. After an unspectacular stretch as a shortstop on the baseball team, he found a niche where he fit better, as the team's manager.

What Hoover was really good at was organizing. He had a talent for handling situations in a dignified manner, and at a time when Anglo California was still establishing its social structure, that talent was in high demand. The story of how he met President Benjamin Harrison is typical: When the president visited campus for a game at the unenclosed baseball field, no usher had the nerve to request his 25-cent entrance fee. When this information made its way to the team manager, Hoover, he went to Harrison and graciously requested the quarter. Harrison bought an advance ticket for the next game, too, and told the young man to keep the change from the dollar. Hoover demurred and offered another two tickets instead, which the president accepted. With so many of California's important fields metaphorically (and often literally) yet to be enclosed, the charm and instinct to navigate the open grass successfully was more important than a strong throw from the left side of the diamond or even straight As. Stanford added a football team and Hoover's fellows promoted him to athletic manager. A game between Stanford and Cal generated close to $1 million (2022 value) in ticket sales, putting Stanford student sports solidly in the black. Herbert was the kind of eighteen-year-old other students could trust with a genuine bag of gold.

In his senior year, Hoover and the so-called Barbarian slate (against the Greeks—get it?) beat the fraternity boys who had led the student government poorly for the university's first three years. The way observers recount the election and its consequences sounds more like great power politics than student council: "The movement was in reality a revolution," writes the inaugural head of the psychology department, Frank Angell, "which resulted in the practical suppression of the old athletic association and the establishment of the present constitution and of the Student Body Treasurership, with Mr. H. C. Hoover, '95, as treasurer—a reformer to whom the Student Body is exceedingly indebted for starting it on the straight and narrow road of business-like methods in its business affairs."[2] Herbert Hoover was the subject of boxy adjectives such as *straight and narrow* his whole life, and not just because his head and shoulders featured an abundance of right angles. He was a reformer like A. P. Giannini at Bank of Italy, but on a campus scale, forcing all the sports teams to keep standard books and pay their bills, to behave like twentieth-century bureaucrats and reap the resulting efficiencies. It's what the region and the world needed, and despite his lack of familial, academic, or athletic distinction, Stanford's leading men recognized their star pioneer when they saw him.

Hoover majored in geology, campus politics having yet to displace his engineering dreams. John Casper Branner was the department head, and he took a quick shine to the Quaker boy and put him under his wing, hooking him up with summer work for the U.S. Geological Survey mapping Arkansas coal deposits and tracing the gold rush placer mines back to their Sierra Nevada veins. When Branner overheard some other students complaining about Hoover's "luck," the professor snapped, "If I tell any one of you to go and do a thing for me I have to come around in half an hour to see if you have done it. But I can tell Hoover to do a thing, and never think of it again. I know it will be done. And he doesn't ask me how to do it, either. If I told him to start to Kamchatka tomorrow to bring me back a walrus tooth, I'd never hear of it again until he came back with the tooth."[3] Going to Kamchatka to bring back a walrus tooth is not so different from what mining engineers had to do in those days; they were expected to visit totally unknown locations and dig up fortunes. Herbert Hoover couldn't wait. The only obstacle was an English-composition graduation requirement that he couldn't seem to pass. Geology refused to see its golden boy fail, however, and a friendly paleontology professor appealed directly to the head of the English department. Hoover graduated with the rest of the pioneers.

Stanford gave the orphan boy so much—when he took ill with typhoid as a junior, Banner even paid his favorite pupil's medical bills—that it must have seemed like fate when in Hoover's senior year the geology department admitted its first female to the major. Lou Henry was his same age and also from Iowa, the eldest child of a small-time banker. She grew up as an outdoorswoman, camping and riding with her father and developing an affinity for rocks that rivaled Bert's own. Unlike him, though, she was academically outstanding, especially when it came to learning languages. He couldn't have asked for a better partner. Hoover was immediately smitten, and between meeting her, at age twenty, and his death at age ninety, he doesn't seem to have thought about another woman. At graduation, he promised to write and to build a career quickly so he could call on her in a more official manner.

First he got some low-level work in Nevada, pushing mine carts in the depressed 1890s market. He stepped up thanks to a recommendation from a professor, winning over skeptical miners across the West who weren't used to dealing with college boys. Hoover started with mine inspections, sending quick evaluative letters to the home office in San Francisco from Nevada, Wyoming, Idaho, and Arizona. He lived up to his reputation as a problem solver, and his Stanford education helped him perform inordinately well, considering his level of practical experience. Within two years of his graduation he was profitably managing a mine in New Mexico. That was when his boss sat him down: Hoover was being called up to the big leagues. The London mining consultancy Bewick, Moreing and Company wanted an American-trained engineer to evaluate gold deposits in western Australia ("Westralia"). They wired San Francisco, offering $600 a month for the best guy around—the low six figures in today's money—which was three times what Hoover was making in New Mexico. It was enough for him to support his older brother through Stanford in his wake. The only hitch was that Bewick, Moreing was expecting a middle-aged man, and Hoover was twenty-three years old. No matter; he could always count on his mentors to bend the rules for him, just as they could count on him to make them look good and repay favors without being asked. Off he went.

The Australia-London axis was a new central artery for gold, starting with some Australian forty-niners who couldn't help but notice that gold-filled California looked a lot like their hometowns. California engineers had a global reputation for high-tech methods and efficient organization, and Bewick, Moreing wanted one. While expertise was concentrated in NorCal, the best deposits were now elsewhere, as indicated by Hoover's travel schedule as a mine evaluator. Worldwide, those "elsewheres" were, geopolitically speaking, mostly English by possession or concession, which put London capital first in line for the world's up-and-coming mines. Hoover traveled around Australia inspecting rocks as an agent not just of the capitalists Bewick, Moreing but of capital itself. He rationalized the mines the way Giannini rationalized California's farms, standardizing the books and techniques, eschewing folk wisdom in favor of science, introducing labor-saving technology, and submitting every decision to the cold knife of profit calculation. Instead of promoting local miners to managers, he imported Stanford geology graduates and other Yankee college boys who shared his methods. Hoover also took some inspiration from the railroads, recategorizing expenses to show high operating margins, expanding the use of contract work, and bringing in Italian miners to reduce labor costs via racial rivalry with the English.[4]

One location in particular spoke to Hoover, and he advised his bosses to buy it, put him in charge, and invest a quarter of a million 1898 dollars in it. They went for it, and the Sons of Gwalia mine proved extremely successful under the Stanford athletic association treasurer, ultimately yielding an average of more than $1 million a year in gold for half a century of continuous operation.[5] Hoover took another jump in salary, to $10,000 a year plus expenses, including a cook and a valet. Some resented taking orders from the twenty-four-year-old—especially when he was lengthening the work week, cutting wages, eliminating overtime, and reducing staff numbers— and the Hoover reign in Westralia led to a wave of labor unrest. But Italian strikebreakers brought in via contractors kept everything under control, and the gold flowed.[6] Hoover did his job — for his Stanford professors, for his San Francisco boss, for his London employers, for himself, and for history. Thanks to him, tens of millions of dollars' worth of gold — gathered gram by subterranean gram — presented itself to Western capital in lumps and drove twentieth-century economic expansion. With the modern systems in place, Hoover could move on, and Bewick, Moreing was eager to see if he could work his magic on still another continent.

Chastened by defeat in the 1894–95 Sino-Japanese War, in the summer of 1898 the Guangxu Emperor instituted a series of modernization reforms designed to make China internationally competitive: a new education system, capitalist industrialization, and the abolition of aristocratic sinecures. Part of the plan was to exploit the kingdom's natural resources by establishing the Bureau of Mines. European colonial powers were in the middle of their "scramble" phase, and having divided the continent of Africa at the Berlin Conference in 1885, Western capital now eyed China's new mining concessions. The Bureau of Mines director, Zhang Yi, consulted with Charles Moreing, who was happy to buy up bonds from the Chinese Engineering and Mining Company (CEMC) and went as far as to propose his company's hotshot young mine evaluator to head up the technical staff.* Bewick, Moreing offered to double Hoover's salary to $20,000 a year (plus expenses, of course) if he would once again head into the unknown and bring back a walrus tooth. He wired Lou Henry back in California and asked her to marry him and join the adventure.

Despite his academic adviser's denial, Hoover was extremely lucky by any sort of standard. The $20,000 a year (plus expenses!) he was making by age twenty-five is over $675,000 in 2022 dollars, and he was already used to the burden of command. Like Leland Stanford, Hoover stuck with a favorite title throughout his life, but it wasn't President or Director; it was Chief, which is what miners traditionally called their bosses. That's what people were calling Hoover by the time he and his new bride arrived in Peking in March of 1899. It helped that he was a loyal boss *as far as technical employees were concerned,*

---

* That Hoover was an American didn't hurt, since any European, Russian, or Japanese manager might have appeared to prejudice the Bureau toward one of the contending nations, a list that did not include the United States.

and he sourced his new staff from his previous projects, a practice he continued throughout his life. The stars were crossed on his first trip to China, however, and by the time the newlyweds arrived, a conservative coup instigated by Empress Dowager Cixi had overthrown what became known as the Hundred Days' Reform. Instead of entering a modernizing country by invitation, they were now imposing themselves in the midst of an anti-foreign turn. Zhang Yi—who had substantial pecuniary motivation—said they would roll with it. The Hoovers set up a household in Tianjin, the northeastern port city where the Second Opium War concluded. After the treaty was signed, European powers established their own concession neighborhoods there as trade and administrative outposts. Lou set about learning Mandarin Chinese and collecting antiques while Bert directed expeditions into the interior looking for gold and then, on his own advice, coal.

In the winter of 1900, China's nativist sentiment was increasing. Hoover, as an American, seems not to have felt too implicated by the critiques of European imperialism, even though he was a manager at a British mining firm working with corrupt government officials to exploit Chinese resources. A new secret society began assassinating foreigners, and though Hoover's surveyors had just found the biggest coal deposit yet, in the spring he recalled his field expeditions. In June the Hoovers woke up to exploding shells as the Boxer Rebellion—the white name for it, but a cool one—attacked the Tianjin foreign quarters. Among those seeking security in the multicultural colonial settlement was Zhang Yi, who as a collaborator was as much a target as the Americans were. The Hoovers billeted down in their house with their engineering staff as the ad hoc international forces stationed in the district organized a collective defense. Under the supervision of a Russian colonel who took command, the Hoover engineering team built barricades with the help of Chinese Christians. The siege lasted around a month before an invasion by an eight-empire imperialist coalition (Britain, the United States, Russia, Germany, France, Austria-Hungary, Italy, and Japan) took control of the coastal zone.

Fighting continued for over a year, but the invaders didn't lose any time seizing compensation in forced Chinese concessions, a substantial number of which belonged to the CEMC. Hoover recalls: "The Russian Army seized the coal mines and the extensive shops at Tongshan. The British Navy seized the harbor works and coal stocks at Chinwangtao. The German Army seized the coal yards at Taku and Tientsin. The Japanese Army seized the company's offices at Tientsin. The American Army seized the twelve coal steamers."[7] Zhang feared they would lose it all, and he went to Moreing with a proposal: To avoid seizure they could convert the CEMC into a British-owned company, whose property rights the invaders were more likely to respect. Hoover claims that Zhang drew up the paperwork—but that's hard to believe, and historians mostly do not. Using the magic of finance capital and share issuance, Moreing and Hoover turned the Chinese company into a European one, stitching together London bankers and Belgian royal capital. Using free "promotional shares," the directors interested the financial elite, drawing in French, German, Russian, Hong Konger, and Japanese investors. The best way to avoid confiscation was to make sure everyone got a taste, and the only way to do that was to nudge out the Chinese. "Not to put too fine a point on it," writes historian Ian Phimister, "the previous Chinese owners were defrauded of their property."[8] With the country's mineral wealth, the team organized international ruling-class interests strong enough to supersede nationalist rivalries. Hoover got the new CEMC up and running, but he chafed under Belgian majority control and wanted to move on. In 1901 Bewick, Moreing welcomed him back to London as a junior partner—not bad at all for a twenty-seven-year-old.

Having taken the retiring Bewick's place, Hoover spent the next seven years bopping around the world for Moreing, serving as the California engineer par excellence and working on his growing global reputation. The company had assets everywhere: "coal mines in China, Wales and the Transvaal, a tin mine in Cornwall, a group of gold mines in Western Australia, New Zealand, South Africa, and West Africa, copper mines in Queensland and Canada, a lead-silver mine in Nevada, and a turquoise mine in the Sinai Peninsula of Egypt."[9] Plus they were always on the lookout for new opportunities, consulting for other owners and speculating when tempted by a good find. There were synergies to be found in a worldwide mining empire, too: After Hoover arrived in South Africa in 1904, Bewick, Moreing began shipping in tens of thousands of Chinese "coolie" laborers under the auspices of the CEMC, where Hoover remained a member of the board. This kind of racial arbitrage was standard operating procedure for Hoover; the Chinese gold miners cost Bewick, Moreing 45 cents a day compared to 60 cents a day for black South Africans.[10] Later when his labor record as a mine manager became an election issue he denied knowledge of and responsibility for the program, as he did with the CEMC contract.

In time, financiers began to doubt Hoover's golden touch. He seemed to be making more money with paper, on selling stocks, than in metals. Modernization was a good sales pitch but as was the case with the railroad, the financial mechanisms undergirding the process made capitalist "rationality" a peculiar type indeed. Prospective investors in Bewick, Moreing, like the Associates' prospective investors before them, became concerned that their money was padding the directors' pockets, which made it harder to raise money, which was a problem because that's how the firm *made* money. Eventually Hoover faced pressure from frustrated Bewick, Moreing shareholders, and he took a (substantial) buyout for his board seat in 1907 and left the firm entirely in 1908. He was going out on his own.

The Food Dictator

By the time he left the mining consultancy, Bert Hoover was wealthy and relatively famous, especially around Stanford where he exemplified what the school had to offer. An orphan made rich through education and hard work, an American out reshaping the world for progress. It was an image he'd been promoting for some time, telling the press he was the highest-paid man of his age (and variants of the description) beginning in 1901, when he returned from China. Back in Palo Alto, David Starr Jordan told the incoming freshmen of 1902 that Hoover was the university's ideal. As an independent financier the future president continued to tour the colonized world looking for resources to profitably extract, and he brought Stanford wherever he went, recruiting staffers, hosting expat alums, and entertaining visiting graduates. Hoover also channeled proceeds from his mines back to the school, starting when he secured his place in Australia. He paid the way for his brother, Theodore, to attend Stanford (in geology, of course—Tad joined Bert's consultancy and later came to head the university engineering department itself) and sent money to support his undergraduate chums, including Ray Lyman Wilbur, in postgraduate study. As his salary improved, so did his donations; he sent hundreds of books he acquired on his travels to the school library, along with money for an extra librarian. Never one to forget a favor, he also sent thousands of dollars to support his guardian angel, Branner.

Jordan, who won full control of the university after the convenient murder of Jane Lathrop Stanford, understood that the school's fortunes were intertwined with those of its lead pioneer. After Hoover left Bewick, Moreing in 1908, Jordan and Branner suggested that he move his family—Lou bore their sons, Herbert Jr. and Allan, in 1903 and 1907 respectively—to California full-time and take a place on the board of trustees. The Hoovers already had a cottage in town; Lou's family was close, and Herbert was not shy about his affection for the place. But he still had mining money to make, so instead he gave some lectures on campus and funded an exorbitantly expensive new student union building. Hoover was like a vacuum, sucking up precious metals from around the world and depositing a hefty share back into Palo Alto's giant tax shelter.

London remained the center of mining finance, and that's where the Hoovers set up shop, entertaining continually. Among those in their circle was another mining-engineer couple, he from MIT and she also from Stanford. Unlike Lou Henry, her friend May Bradford became a professional surveyor under her own name, breaking the gender barrier in Nevada before meeting her husband in the field. William Shockley Sr. traced his lineage back to the Mayflower, was two decades older, and liked to have a good time. The young May fell for the "engineer" (speculator) and they lived between luxury and penury; servants and landlords alike went unpaid while the couple partied with the Hoovers. Bill Jr. was born in 1909—after some pregnancy talk between the geologists Lou and May—and the broke Shockleys moved back to the States and in with May's parents in Palo Alto. There they finally found some good old bourgeois stability when their influential friends intervened to get William Sr. a job at Stanford in Branner's geology department.

A few years later in 1912, Hoover did step up to the Stanford board of trustees, and in 1913 Bert ushered in the university's first regime change, working out a face-saving compromise that moved the aging David Starr Jordan to the new consulting role of "chancellor" and promoted his own mentor John Casper Branner to the position of president. But as it turned out, Branner was too conservative and friendly with the faculty. Hoover wanted a proxy president who held a progressive perspective similar to his. When Branner tried to close the medical school, Hoover persuaded the board to give his job to the medical school's dean instead.* That was Ray Lyman Wilbur, Hoover's friend from student government days, whose medical studies he sponsored with his Westralia money. Wilbur was as loyal a deputy as the Chief had, whether he was literally in Hoover's employ or working collaboratively at a distance. He held the office for twenty-seven years, including four he spent in absentia as secretary of the interior, which count because the president of the United States forbade the school from appointing a replacement. Wilbur held Palo Alto down as Hoover country through the Second World War.

By the time he went solo, Hoover was less an engineer than what we might recognize today as the head of a private equity firm.[11] He had a few stakes in genuinely productive mines, and new techniques for processing mine tailings for their base metals led to novel Westralia revenue, but finance ruled the world now. He found that rationalization and efficiency were good ways to attract capital, but the ultimate results didn't always correlate with his gains. Hoover didn't have to invest a ton of money or reorganize production in order to prosper on a new project. He just had to convince other financiers that something previously uninvestable was now a good bet; then he could sell them his stake at a profit and do it again. Instead of South Africa and Westralia, his five offices were in San Francisco, New York, London, Paris, and Petrograd. In the years following settlement of the Russo-Japanese War he advised both the Russian czar and Japanese capital on carving up the Siberia-Korea-Manchuria nexus, but he spent most of his time in the world's Paper Belt, traveling between his five offices and Belgium, where a spike in rubber prices combined with the Crown's superexploitation of African slave labor on the Congo plantations enriched King Leopold II and his affiliated financiers.

By 1914, almost 20 years into his career, it looked like Hoover's luck was starting to run out. The shine was wearing off his singular status, and others began to see him as not just a common stock hustler but rather as one of the biggest culprits. The Chief long claimed that he resigned all his mining seats and directorships in 1914 to pursue a life of public service, but that's unlikely.

* Instead of running the school, Branner finally published three decades of his research on the Virginia Branner family, which continues to be recognized as an important work of early twentieth-century American genealogy. See John Casper Branner, *Casper Branner of Virginia and His Descendants* (Stanford University, 1913).

More recently, historians have suggested he fled an anticipated lawsuit from his ex-partner Moreing, which better explains why he left the chairmanship of the firm's Burma mine within a year of his appointment after serving on the board since its inception. In the spring of 1914, Herbert and Lou went to London on behalf of the coming Panama-Pacific International Exposition—despite Jordan's suggestion to President Wilson, Hoover didn't get the gig managing the construction of the canal itself—where he stumbled into public service doing what he did best: figuring stuff out by being a rich guy.

When the Great War kicked off, the Hoovers were half a continent away from the conflict in initially neutral England for summer vacation. Bert's first concerns were about liquidity and his various enterprises. With banks closed and credit tight he had to make sure he had cash on hand to pay his staff. It wasn't like the Boxer Uprising; no one was handing him a rifle. The Hoovers were content to wait for their regularly scheduled boat in August, which was set to bring them home in time for the boys to get to school in Palo Alto, where they were now enrolled. Not all the Americans in Europe were in such an enviable position, however, and soon a mob of a thousand of Hoover's countrymen assembled outside the consulate. These tourists and other travelers couldn't access cash or find boats home and no one had the capacity to handle them, never mind the many tens of thousands of Americans who were emptying the Continent through London's bottleneck. Local authorities appealed to Hoover and he took up the challenge, enlisting his whole network of connections to finance and process the torrential human flow.

Hoover wasn't a real boss or an official representative of the United States. He was simply the Chief, and the assembled staff—made up largely of his fellow stranded globe-trotters and American college students studying abroad—pledged their fealty by consensus. He pulled together a quick $1 million in credit among his rich friends, and their ad hoc bank doled out the borrowed money to get the stranded home. Standard accounts have Hoover taking everyone's word and coming out whole thanks to the constancy of American honor, but that's not what happened. Instead, the team set up a credit ratings board and arbitrarily assessed applicants into three categories. Those deemed reliable got white cards and the Hoover team took their checks from local American banks (or whatever other paper credit instruments they had to offer) and gave them cash. The perceived unreliables, however, had to call friends or relatives in the United States and wire funds into the Hoover team's London account to get the money — in effect they were denied credit. Those who couldn't manage even that were deemed "destitute," and they depended on private charity until a boat of American government gold showed up. Hoover describes this last group as "some thousands of colored porters and people of similar humble and useful occupations" — useful, but not creditworthy like white school teachers.[12] Hoover's team processed thousands of people a day, segregating them into groups so they could be dealt with efficiently, rationally, based on how much money they seemed to have. In the face of overwhelming need, the wealthy Hoover made his reputation as a brilliant action philanthropist *based on not actually spending any money*. With a couple of calls from the right guy to the right guys, the miracles of finance could turn stinginess into heroism. And Bert knew how to make his numbers good.

The rest of the family went to Palo Alto in August as scheduled and Herbert took up a new task. Imperial Germany overran Belgium, and the people were short on food. The kaiser's pointy-headed forces drained the country's resources, and London blockaded further imports from the West. Hoover had many associates among the Belgian elite, and they asked if he could solve their problem the way he solved the issue of the stranded Americans. During the year of U.S. neutrality, the Chief led his Commission for Relief in Belgium (CRB) as an independent transnational organization, flying its own flag and crossing the western front back and forth under unique permissions. Here's the way it worked: The CRB used monetary donations from the Allied governments to buy foodstuffs on the global market, ship them to Belgium, and distribute them to Belgian communal authorities, who then sold most of them to local shops, which in turn sold them to the customers who were still liquid enough to buy stuff under German occupation. The remainder went to canteens for the destitute. As before, Hoover's team worked hard to maintain functioning markets above all — and with them a class structure — in the face of leveling catastrophe.

By turning the CRB into a win-win for the belligerents, Hoover kept markets functional across the front. The Germans had a trusted partner who ran the blockade for them and kept the Belgians fed at no expense to the kaiser, while the British exposed influential Americans to the effects of German aggression firsthand. (For example, recall that Stanford bionomist Vernon

Kellogg's experience with the German command as a member of Hoover's staff convinced him that the Reich was on a collision course with America and that lethality had to replace peace as a eugenicist value.) The Belgian people didn't have to rely on their occupiers for food, and the Belgian elite no longer had to wait in bread lines with the poor. As for the Chief, he simultaneously negotiated a line of credit with the British government to cover his business debts that were financing ore shipments to blockaded Continental smelters. There may have been no cash value to report, but pounds were scarce and Hoover stayed highly leveraged, so the deal likely saved him a significant amount of trouble and might have rescued his whole concern. Critics complained that Hoover confederates in the food industries were getting preferential deals, but the CRB's press wing turned the Chief into an international celebrity: the strait-laced engineer above the war, feeding people with a neutral army of Yankee volunteers. Critics also complained that the reason Hoover's executive team could work for a dollar a year is that they were paid by agricultural-processing cartels and trusts—millers, refiners, canners, packers, and so on—to set high profit margins on sales to the CRB. But the critics didn't own as many newspapers as Hoover's friends did.

Like many global business elites, Hoover had believed the world's economies were too interconnected for all-out war on this scale. Skirmishes in and over colonial territories, sure, but the moneyed interests all swam in the same stock pools—recall that's how Bewick, Moreing settled the CEMC conflict in the post-Boxer China scramble, by making sure everyone important had a piece worth protecting. Hoover was a representative of the worldwide ruling class, super-imperialism personified; how could they fight if they were all his friends? The logic broke down as Chancellor Bismarck, in Giovanni Arrighi's elegant formulation, "realized that the verdict of the market on the viability of the German state and of German society was too harsh to take" and built the nation into a unitary imperial machine.[13] Still, the ruling class, with its business and personal relationships, endured above and among the states, and when they needed a front man, they turned to Herbert Hoover of Palo Alto, California.

Soon after America entered the war in 1917, Hoover prevailed upon Woodrow Wilson to build him an official version of his commission so that he could administer the nation's wartime food system. He wanted the unilateral power to set prices, establish acceptable profit margins, and control exports so as to make sure American civilians and Allied troops were well fed, and all without meddling from the beholden eggheads at the Department of Agriculture. He wanted to be Food Dictator, and over cries of "Who is this guy again?" from the Senate, that's what Wilson made him. Hoover openly staffed the new temporary department with volunteers from the industrial food processors. This experience transformed his position in U.S. politics, from unique rogue to federal operator, and set the course for the country's next decade. The voluntary association of leading men, he saw, could be more than just a lifestyle or a business strategy. It could become a whole ideology.

The Chief's primary stated goal was to lower the price of wheat in the face of intense global demand, which he did by setting the price lower, enraging farmers. The processors, however, had nothing to complain about. For them Hoover used a "cost-plus" formula, paying contractors an agreed-upon percentage above their costs rather than setting a price.* He earned the ire of staple-farmer populists, the loyalty of the processing industries, and the admiration of anyone who believed what was printed in the corporate press. America won the war, and the boys came home with an appreciation for canned food and candy. Rather than scale down mass production when soldiers went back to their local food systems, the processors plowed their wartime profits into advertising designed to convince the country that processed foods from national companies were better and safer.

After spending the postwar year directing American food aid to war-ravaged Europe, Hoover returned home to a hero's welcome. The war had been a morally discombobulated cautionary tale about war itself, a brutal clusterfuck of imperial ambition and meaningless death that covered no one but the cynics in glory. The Chief was the exception. Bert the Food Dictator fought with mustard, not mustard gas. He parlayed with savage Germans, fed

---

* Hoover kept the Food Administration–directed margin on value-added products very high—between 20 and 30 percent—which signaled the industry to expand production and domestic retailers not to worry too much about being assailed for wartime price gouging, a power the benevolent dictator elected not to exercise. As Paul Findlay ("Successful Grocer") wrote in his advice column for the *Retail Grocers' Advocate*, Hoover's unambiguous message was that they should "go as far as they liked" on processed goods and "get a margin when you have the chance." Paul Findlay, "California Grocers Advocate," *Retail Grocers' Advocate*, December 12, 1919, 21.

the desperate Belgians, and sent M&Ms to the boys Over There, all without becoming a personal burden on the Treasury. His mining-finance shenanigans faded to the background as his press agents went to work and his professional adversaries began to appreciate him as a valuable asset to their shared class.

As he arrived home in 1919, Hoover told his carefully cultivated friends in the press two lies. The first was that he was not a candidate for president of the United States. The second was that he was not worried about the Bolsheviks.

The Chief

When basketball players are on an exceptionally hot streak, they sometimes throw up a shot from too far away just to test their luck. It's called a "heat check," and it's a good description of what Herbert Hoover did when he got back to America. Ahead of the 1920 presidential primaries, the Chief had his confederates in the press put his name forward as a possible nominee for *both* the Republican and Democratic tickets. Hoover himself pretended to be extremely reluctant to disclose his ambitions, but his associates let it be known he'd be willing to accept the Democratic nomination if the Republicans didn't give him theirs. The strategy of the "make Hoover president" effort was to manufacture a swell of "grassroots" support for the Food Dictator that transcended partisanship, making him the obvious choice for whichever party wanted to win. But despite Hoover's having used government resources to popularize his character via Food Administration advertising, the parties picked their candidates from the top down and they didn't take kindly to Hoover's attempt to go over their heads to the voters. The campaign fizzled.

His failure to select a party wasn't merely an instance of miscalculated opportunism, a heat-check air ball. The First World War was ideologically disorienting for capitalist internationalists like Hoover. He grew up in a one-party state in Iowa in the post–Civil War years—in his memoirs Hoover describes the town's single Democrat as a disgraceful drunken shopkeeper, kept around solely as a lesson to the children. Palo Alto was a Republican place, too, the town's founder having been the state's first elected governor. But Hoover worked for the Democrat Woodrow Wilson and urged voters to back the president and his party during the war for the sake of unity. When he arrived home to questions about his political affiliation, Hoover (who hadn't spent a full year in America since he took off for Australia at twenty-three) answered that he was "a liberal," which wasn't easy to interpret but became a favorite response of the capitalist right. Some thought he forgot he was no longer in England, where there was a "liberal" party.[14] But Hoover represented a political synthesis that didn't fit neatly in either American organization: He was an internationalist like the Democrats but still conservative to his core. He believed in collective action but not by the government, unless the government was facilitating the public-private activity of men like him. He was a twentieth-century Capitalist with a capital C, and people (including the man himself) weren't sure what that meant yet, especially when it came to public service.

There was an inherent tension in Hoover's politics between the individualism he prized and the fellowship that he knew underlay any successful system. What was a man without his chums? And more important, what was a businessman without credit networks? Good clean competition was the basis for society, but unlimited competition led to price wars, which undermined profits and halted progress in research and development, which inhibited economic expansion. Forcing firms together under the aegis of the federal government, however, undermined their profit *potential*, which slowed investment and led to the same stagnation. The only solution was the free, voluntary association of businessmen in their common interest. As the agricultural cartels discovered, it was more efficient in the long term to centralize certain functions, such as marketing. Rather than let 10 raisin brands fight it out on the jingle battlefield, they could come together and pay a guy to invent raisin bread. Amadeo Giannini aggregated their interests, taking money he made off of them and investing in an agricultural research foundation on the whole industry's behalf. But these associations always threatened to split apart under the centrifugal force of individual greed. Successful capitalist modernization was a delicate procedure, and the Chief couldn't help but think he was the man to lead it.

The primary voters at least disagreed, but Hoover won over a fair amount of elite opinion makers, and his Food Administration advertisements made him a celebrity figure among American housewives. The Nineteenth Amendment was ratified in August, making 1920 the first presidential election in which women voters played an important role, and the government had been telling America's women to listen to Herbert Hoover about their household food decisions. When Warren Harding took the nomination, he and his team quickly resigned themselves to offering the Chief a cabinet position, if only to neutralize him as a potential weapon for the Democrats. Commerce was one of the youngest secretariats in the cabinet, having split with the Department of Labor in 1913, and business itself was changing so much in the era that Hoover would have an opportunity to set the department's agenda and direction, Harding promised. The Chief accepted, and once Harding won he set about expanding his corner of the executive branch. He wanted the Bureau of Mines from Interior; foreign trade from State; the Census Bureau; the Bureau of Markets from Agriculture...oh, and the Panama Canal. And airplanes. And patents. And radios. As far as Hoover was concerned, the Department of Commerce should *be* the government—just about any legitimate state function could fit under his mandate. Even when Harding later offered him departments higher on the succession chain, Hoover stayed in his niche, building Commerce into a mini government within the government with him on top.

Drawing from his extraordinarily eventful life, Bert pulled together something like a political philosophy. "Hoover in 1921 saw himself as the protagonist of a new and superior synthesis between the old industrialism and the new, a way whereby America could benefit from scientific rationalization and social engineering without sacrificing the energy and creativity inherent in individual effort, 'grassroots' involvement, and private enterprise," writes historian Ellis Hawley in his classic 1974 study of the Commerce secretariat under the Stanford engineer.[15] Hoover turned the fledgling department into Harding's agency for modernity, casting the mold for the relationship between the industries that made America into a superpower and state bureaucracy. Hawley calls it the "associative state"—note the resonance with the four Sacramento Associates who talked Abe Lincoln into footing the bill for their public-private railroad partnership—and that's what Hoover built, between his elevation to secretary with Harding's inauguration, in 1921, and his defeat at the hands of FDR in the presidential election of 1932. And though historians have long portrayed Hoover's three terms (two at Commerce, under Harding, then Coolidge, and one in the presidency) as a bust after the corporatist Roaring Twenties were indicted by the Great Depression and swept away by the New Deal, the country's turn toward corporate-cabal associative logic in the fourth quarter of the twentieth century suggests that they've understated the Chief's influence. From our perspective a century later, the difference between the associative state and the New Deal is subtler than we've been led to believe. In this section I'll trace the ways in which Hoover's associative model built the West Coast's twentieth-century agricultural and aeronautical industries, but that was just the beginning; Hoover's impact on the real estate and radio sectors was just as decisive and important. If most historians think FDR set the stage for American hegemony, the endurance of Bert's California suggests otherwise. By examining some specifics of the long Hoover administration, we prepare to understand the following hundred years.

The largest uncontested achievement of Hoover's leadership is the one that still bears his name: the Hoover Dam. By the time he got back to America, the plan to dam the Colorado River and thereby irrigate and power California's Los Angeles "Southland" already existed, but it took an organizer of Hoover's skill to bring several state and municipal governments, federal agencies, and private firms into agreement on how to divide such a massive bounty. He needed the entire length of his Commerce terms, but the Chief finally got the damn dam built in his image. First he got representatives from the affected states into a room and hammered out the Colorado River Compact over the course of two weeks. The interstate accord set the future direction of the river, but it was a stacked deck, because the congressional (Senate and House) as well as White House representatives all came from California. That's where the lion's share of the water and power went, too, as well as the biggest construction contracts. After a few years of procedural delay—a cynical reader might think some of the players involved needed time to secure a bunch of land titles—the appropriation passed, just as President Hoover installed his Stanford buddy Ray Lyman Wilbur at the Department of the Interior. This was engineering at the nation-building level; it's what the engineer in chief had prepared to do all his life.

Though it was finished in 1935, long after Bert had left Washington with his tail between his legs, the dam was his project, and it bore all the marks of the associative state. First off, it was a massive thing, the largest dam in human history and the biggest known construction project by volume since the Great Pyramids of Egypt. By 1940 the turbine generators produced one-eighth of the country's electricity and, along with the aqueducts, made it possible for Los Angeles to rise as California's second city. Behind the massive wall of concrete was an ad hoc coalition of relatively petty West Coast construction capital. They called themselves "the Six Companies" after the Chinese associations in San Francisco during the railroad days, but they were closer to the original Associates. Most prominent among their number were Warren A. Bechtel and Henry J. Kaiser, and Hoover's dam turned them into famous industrialists. The new Six Companies earned their place, building the project during the Depression with modern techniques and an all-American white male labor force—no union required, but Asian workers were banned by contract. The companies kept costs comparatively low in part by efficiently managing their workers' whole lives at the site, though it wasn't until a few years later that Kaiser figured out a way to incorporate health-care costs into his rationalized production equations by moving employees to a company medical plan. Until Roosevelt took over, the Six Companies paid partly in scrip, and in 1931 when the Industrial Workers of the World came by to agitate, site managers rounded them up and shipped them to Vegas. It was, in the words of historian Kevin Starr, a "demanding, if vaguely benevolent, dictatorship," paralleling the insurgent right-wing industrial cultures of Germany and Japan.*

At the tail end of this win-win dam were California's landowners and speculators, whose job in the whole scheme was to get rich. Behind the Six Companies (Kaiser in particular) with a big sack of money was A. P. Giannini, whose bank stood to gain the most from an increase in California land values. Hoover's private associates were up and down the project, especially the Southern California Edison chairman Henry Robinson, to whose firm Secretary Wilbur originally appropriated 25 percent (!) of the Hoover Dam power output, before criticism forced him to reduce it to 9 percent.[16] Harry Chandler—conservative publisher of the *Los Angeles Times*, Stanford dad, and Hoover's confederate on the university board—became the city's most important capitalist by riding the Hoover real estate and manufacturing boom into the 1930s. These men poured the concrete foundation for what was shaping up to be California's century.

---

* Starr's description of the work-site documentary photos blends Leni Riefenstahl and Tom of Finland, with the workmen as Nordic "Hoover hunks," "their chests bared despite the blazing sun, the low-slung Levis, the studied poses..." The author can't help but speculate: "Was there a gay sub-culture at Hoover?....There must have been." Kevin Starr, *Endangered Dreams: The Great Depression in California* (Oxford University Press, 1996).

In his last full-time job before committing to public service and passive income, Hoover went around reviving "sick" mines with a rationalized approach—or at least convincing investors that's what he was doing. As a national leader, he endeavored to perform the same function but for whole industries. America was supposed to be the land of dynamism, but a number of the country's advanced economic sectors were languishing, especially compared to how quickly Germany and Japan were developing under neo-imperial systems. Hoover understood that government had to establish a base level of coordination and standardization around novel technologies. Capital was stuck in Yogi Berra's "Nobody goes there, it's too crowded" contradiction: Investors were scared off by reasonable fears of free-riding on research and development, price competition, and a lack of standardization. No one wanted to be stuck holding the bag when the new rules came down. This is where the associative model came in: Hoover could provide not just physical infrastructure with water and power, but also the informational infrastructure new industries needed to become investable. He had a third gift for California, too, a gift that would soon provide Palo Alto technologists with their next frontier.

When Hoover formally entered the cabinet, the American airplane industry was severely underdeveloped. The first U.S. passenger had yet to fly, and there was no commercial air sector to speak of. When World War I ended, production cratered by over 98 percent as the market flooded with surplus war planes.[17] Independent pilots "barnstormed" the country and wowed crowds with stunts; flight was more or less an entertainment medium during peacetime. The Europeans, however, turned World War I into an air war by the end, and Hoover was convinced that the country had an existential need for a healthy domestic air industry. At the same time, he believed the government couldn't just build the planes itself efficiently without a profit motive. This sick sector was Hoover's first priority at Commerce, and a solid success for his strategy.

Bert's model was to get the federal government to set flight paths, research weather patterns, license pilots, and otherwise facilitate development in a general way. After some hemming and hawing about the "Air Dictator," Congress gave him the go-ahead in 1926 with the Air Commerce Act. He worked with the Guggenheim family—Hoover had almost turned down the cabinet seat offered by Harding to join them in a mining partnership—after patriarch

Daniel Guggenheim offered a $2.5 million fund to train aeronautical engineers, improve the technology, and push the industry as a whole forward in full cooperation with the Commerce Department in light of the agency's new powers.[18] They were the airplane Gianninis, bankrolling the industry's shared expenses out of a combination of public and private interest, no government coercion necessary. Stanford and MIT (among a few others) got new engineering programs, but Caltech in burgeoning Los Angeles ended up benefiting most, becoming home to a Guggenheim aeronautics lab that helped make the region into the world's plane and rocket headquarters.

The associative state didn't work without capitalists, and thankfully Los Angeles had its own Associates, among them Henry Robinson of Southern California Edison — he was also the head of the Security First National banking combine in LA, the only part of the state where Giannini found himself on the outside looking in — and Harry Chandler of the *Times*, who also owned half the city's best real estate and a large swath of the agricultural Southland. In 1920, Chandler led the financing for an ambitious pilot and aspiring airplane builder who found his way to his office and, like Theodore Judah with his railroad plan, couldn't get any other capitalists interested in his designs. Donald Douglas proved as able as Judah, and Douglas Aircraft won a number of military contracts. The experience must have favorably disposed Chandler toward the industry, and he underwrote pilot Pop Hanshue and his Western Air Express a few years later. Another pillar in Hoover's air plan was to spur the industry by awarding lucrative and exclusive mail delivery contracts; Western won the western contract, and when the Daniel and Florence Guggenheim Foundation sought a firm to run the first experiment in passenger travel, they picked Western, too.

After Charles Lindbergh survived his 1927 solo flight across the Atlantic, the Guggenheims paid him to barnstorm the United States to promote aviation. This, along with Hoover's election, was enough for Wall Street, and big finance piled into planes in the spring of 1929. The Lehman and Harriman banking fortunes teamed up with aircraft pioneer Sherman Fairchild (son of an IBM cofounder, as well as a future microchip financier) to buy a controlling interest in over 20 small airlines via a holding company. With a minimum of government money and intervention, Hoover successfully triggered a private air boom. In this context, it's easier to understand why, on the eve of destruction and for a long while after, he thought everything was working as planned. By the time he left the White House, the country was well on its way to being the dominant air power, military and commercial, regardless of the Depression, just in time for his successor to take credit.

Even when the associative state triumphs, there are always malcontents complaining about the relationship between capital and government. Once Hoover was gone, Congress took a closer look at the airmail contracts and the flurry of corporate activity surrounding them. Pop Hanshue told the legislators exactly how Western became so successful. Why had the company been confident it was going to get the mail contract? He testified that the company's friends Robinson ("the banks") and Chandler ("the newspapers") had friends in the Hoover administration.[19] He laid it out plainly, in a way that has convinced many historians that the whole mess was a corrupt blunder corrected by Roosevelt. But Hoover never hid his intentions. *That was the way it was supposed to work.* The government facilitated leading men, who in turn facilitated the government's facilitation. It wasn't corruption that enabled Herbert Hoover Jr., after being the first person to take a class in radio engineering at Stanford, to study aeronautical economics at Harvard on a Guggenheim grant and then get hired to run radio development at the Chandler-and-Robinson-financed federal-Guggenheim contractor Western Air Express. It was *coordination*, the way royal families arrange marriages. There weren't any planes and then there were a lot of planes—that was the important part, not who got rich. After all, somebody had to. The tangle of names and firms, partnerships and stock offerings and board positions, starts to sound less like the tense strings of a conspiracy network and more like the dull thrum of business as usual.

In the 1920s, the Chief was a good friend to have, and among his best pals were members of the California planter class. Upon his return to America, he became one of them. He joined with former state food commissioner Ralph Merritt (who also ran the Chief's ill-fated 1920 primary campaign) and some other men to start a large cotton farm in Kern County, north of Los Angeles. When cotton prices tanked, they switched some acreage to stone fruit. As far as the Chief was concerned, no industry needed his help more than commodity agriculture. In peacetime, the Food Dictator was absolutely opposed to price setting, but he also knew that agricultural overproduction was a global problem that couldn't be solved by allowing the government to dump surpluses overseas and that tariffs couldn't rescue an export industry. His solution was much like Giannini's: collectivize marketing and research while securing *voluntary* agreements to restrain production.

The Co-operative Marketing Associations Act—also called Capper-Volstead, for its sponsors—passed in 1922 exempting grower associations from antitrust law, but in the Harding administration Hoover often found himself thwarted by secretary of agriculture Harry Wallace, the leader of the Midwest farm populists, a group distinct from (and sometimes opposed to) the processor cartels. When Wallace died, in 1924, Hoover had a freer hand, and the Agricultural Marketing Act of 1929 was meant to halt the perilous price plunges plaguing producers by buying and storing surplus crops and lending money to the associations. If individual farmers wanted access to that money, they had to join up and conform to output agreements. Hoover's farming partner, Ralph Merritt, was by then encouraging growers to join cartels from the other side, managing the Raisin KKK as the director of Sun-Maid and distributing federal subsidies for the Chief.* After he finished his Stanford-Harvard MBA education and a stint at Robinson's Security First National Bank, Bert's second son, Allan, went to manage the Hoover Farm (now called the Poso Land and Products Company). The farm, of course, was mortgaged to Security First National.

The associative state failed to control agricultural output and prices not because the Chief misunderstood the problem but because it was an intrinsically hard one to solve. FDR struggled with the same issues, and his Agricultural Adjustment Act led to the famous scenes of farmers dumping milk and intentionally spoiling produce, cheered on by the feds so as to maintain high prices. It was New Deal government intervention at its most vulgar, which didn't stop even the Hoover Farm from taking its share of subsidies when the time came. Still, by Depression standards, California did well; there's a reason John Steinbeck's Joad family was headed west.† The invention and proliferation of electric water pumps in the century's first decades invigorated marginal lands, and the larger planters knew that more water and power was on its way

---

* This made him, at the end of the day, a functionary of the Giannini banks, which financed the raisin cartel.

† The California-born Steinbeck spent the early 1920s studying English at Stanford.

from Bert and Ray. As it did for the railroads in the 1890s, failure led to concentration. Someone had to own the land.

Besides federal connections, California agriculture's big advantage was how developed and central the packers and processors were. The state led the world in produce processing, canning, and transport by the end of the nineteenth century, as capital built the apparatuses necessary to get the Sun-Maid, Sunkist, Sunsweet, and Sun-everything fruits and vegetables to the national and world markets without refrigeration. As the country turned toward processed foods in the wake of the First World War—thanks in no small part to the Food Dictator—the West Coast led the way. Giannini cartelized the state industry, which existed on a comparatively advanced capitalist basis even before he came along, with its land highly concentrated and full of farm employees rather than yeomen. The Gianninis invested in agricultural research at the University of California, endowing Berkeley's Department of Food Science and Technology and financing research up and down the state in the midst of the Depression. Scientists looked into how food could be made more healthful with additives, and their findings served as advertisements for new products. (Not all research is productive, however—one unfortunate side effect was the emergence of California as a global center of fad diets, a deserved reputation the state maintains.) Agricultural profits lay in added value, not in growing stuff to eat per se, which made California's planter-processor-bank-university associations the model for making money off of food.

But there was something missing from their groups. Their problem was labor.

The Age of Expropriation

At least as much as Leland Stanford was, Herbert Hoover was a creation of the joint-stock company. These associations put capital to work without robbing investors of liquidity, which allowed owners to leverage enough money to accomplish epic feats on the state's behalf, like the transcontinental railroad and the Hoover Dam. Despite his misspent years of stock jobbery, the Chief worked hard to structure real long-term outlets for investment capital during his Roaring Twenties, succeeding epically in Southern California, where his relationships were strong and the region remained comparatively undeveloped.

The speculators recognized Hoover as one of their own, and the national markets boomed, beginning with his landslide election in 1928. Capital piling into stocks was an important part of the associative model; that's how companies got the money they needed to build airplanes, plan subdivisions, and invent new radios, all while staying nimble, without the fear that comes with being all-in on a single bet with your own money. Hoover strove to stay at a proper associative distance, intervening only to improve the sunny climate for capital, never threatening the future of any investment for fear of undermining its present value. Such intervention might as well have been Bolshevik confiscation. The government had to be careful only to help.

In return for his restraint, Hoover needed the bankers to stick together like raisins in a little red Sun-Maid box. Demand for stocks was shooting up, which compelled financiers to increase the supply. They designed new investment trusts, issued more securities, and enabled buyers to trade on margin. But if too many bankers tried to cash in too much at once, they would oversupply the market and cause a crisis of confidence that would tank the whole scheme. The Chief needed capitalists to match his restraint, or at the very least stop encouraging the public to invest with opportunistic scoundrels. He summoned newspaper editors, whose resulting editorials cautioning against stock-market gambling were ineffective, as were Treasury Department statements reminding people that bonds were safer than stocks. Maintaining his distance, in the spring of 1929 Hoover sent his favorite banker, Henry Robinson (of both Southern California Edison and Security First National), to New York to talk with his peers and report back. They said everything was great, and the president reassured himself that regulating Wall Street was not his job. That responsibility belonged to the governor of New York, the wealthy and connected Franklin Delano Roosevelt, and he seemed to agree with the local guys. Since Hoover was just the president, all he could do was warn them.

This narrative from Hoover's memoirs is no doubt at least a little self-serving, but in his dominant left-liberal history *The Great Crash, 1929*, John Kenneth Galbraith repeats it.[20] Historians today mostly don't fault Hoover's leadership for the crash in the fall of 1929, nor do they credit Roosevelt's New Deal so much as World War II for the rescue. At the time, however, the Chief endured one of the worst reversals in American political history. The self-made orphan got shellacked by a Gotham aristocrat on behalf of the common man, and his famous name became forever entwined with penniless squatters in their "Hoovervilles." It was not only the unemployed workingmen who abandoned Bert; so did a number of important capitalists, including A. P. Giannini (always too Italian for the bionomics crew anyway), Pierre du Pont, and media mogul William Randolph Hearst (who tired of alcohol prohibition, which the president favored). Even the Wall Street speculators who most proximately caused the crisis backed Roosevelt.

Conservative businessmen such as Hearst and du Pont came to regret their choice, but there was a big temptation to scapegoat Hoover at the time. A year after the crash, *Vanity Fair*'s Jay Franklin reported that "Poor Mr. Hoover" was the song of the day in Washington, but not in a good way: "For people have stopped blaming the President; they have begun to pity him; and though pity may be akin to love it is not a sign of political power."[21] The Republican Party considered pulling him from the ballot. The Chief was under attack from all sides: Conservatives were ready to throw him on the one-term heap, and a group he came to label "totalitarian liberals" promised direct government intervention in the economy.[22] The biggest threat, however, was from the workers and soldiers who kept showing up en masse outside Hoover's properties with an implicit threat to kill him and take all his stuff: the Communists.

The conventional wisdom is that communists became America's new bogeyman immediately following World War II, as Harry S. Truman squared up with former ally Joseph "Uncle Joe" Stalin for control of the postwar world. For the Chief, however, Bolshevism was a personal threat from the beginning, when they took his mines. Despite what he led people to believe, Hoover maintained a number of interests in the Russian czar's mines—recall that the two had been business partners and that Hoover oversaw the modernization of a copper mine and smelting complex as director, which he describes thusly: "At the top was a Russian noble family and at the bottom 100,000 peasants and workers, with nobody much in between but the priesthood and the overseers."[23] (He meant that in a good way.) Bert claims to have resigned the position and sold off all his Russian holdings when he took over Belgian relief in 1915, but it's an impossible claim to verify as well as exactly the kind of thing he tended to lie about, and I therefore find it implausible. Regardless, those workers who had seemed so content to him ("Everyone took great pride in our progressive and happy community") assumed control of the operation in 1917, and the new council passed three rules: expropriation of the ownership, expulsion of the management (including 60 or so Americans), and a 100 percent increase in wages.[24] Regarding his work in czarist Russia, Hoover later lamented, "Had it not been for the First World War, I should have had the largest engineering fees ever known to man."[25] The Romanov baron he so admired ended up a racetrack security guard in Shanghai, and that guy got off easy compared to other czarist collaborators. Hoover also knew on some level that had it not been for the First World War he could've found himself facing thousands of angry Leninists who wanted their money back.

As the director of postwar food relief, the Chief was one of the first ones into the Red Scare. Reports from Germany had the Spartacists—who opposed German imperialism from the inside—gaining public support as food stocks dwindled. In eastern Europe, the Soviets pushed to expand their revolution worldwide, and in China communists infiltrated the nationalist government, threatening to force a split. The Allied powers sent a harassing force into the Soviet west, and Hoover sent food in behind. Critic Albert E. Kahn later noted that, until it became clear the Reds in Moscow would not fall, American food aid seemed to concentrate in anticommunist areas, providing White militias the resources to bribe local populations and keep trying their luck against the Bolsheviks.[26] Hoover conceived of the food aid as an explicitly anticommunist program, hoping to give capitalist-aligned elements an incentive to overthrow leftist leaders. The plan was most effective in Hungary, which the Romanian army invaded and occupied, tossing out communist leader Béla Kun. But despite the Food Dictator's best efforts, the commies didn't budge, and he wasn't interested in another world war. Eventually Hoover capitulated, sending Soviet authorities a letter declaring that, no matter the rumors they'd heard about him, he made no personal claim on Russian resources.*

World War I ended with the collapse of Europe's global empires, and with them went the colonial model of the California engineer. As new countries formed, some repudiated the debts and concessions imposed on them by previous unelected governments. But if populations held some sort of fundamental right to cancel these contracts unilaterally under a principle we might call

---

* The Soviets, having unsuccessfully concluded negotiations for compensation with one of Hoover's mining associates (and with an understanding of capitalist government as indistinguishable from capitalist industry), must have found this a bit rich.

"economic democracy," then how could anyone make investments in the first place? And it wasn't just Europe and Russia; in Mexico, where a lot of California capital lived, the 1917 constitution declared that "the Nation shall at all times have the right to impose on private property such limitations as the public interest may demand, as well as the right to regulate the utilization of natural resources which are susceptible of appropriation, in order to conserve them and to insure a more equitable distribution of public wealth."[27] This began a two-decade process of expropriation as the Mexican state dispossessed American owners such as Hearst and Chandler. What was next—America's new Panama Canal?

Bolshevism directly threatened the Hoover model of global governance in a way that nothing else did. With no ability to reliably project protectable profits, capitalists couldn't invest, halting the engine of progress in its tracks just as things were getting good. Humanity would be stuck in the Dark Ages, ruled by rabble. For Hoover personally, the layer of international associates that made his entire adult life possible, from the Westralian gold boom to Belgian relief, would dissolve, its members subject to people's justice at the hands of their least satisfied employees. Given what his previous few years looked like, that would have been on trend for Bert. "Bolshevism," he beseeched the Paris Peace Conference, "is worse than war!"[28]

The Depression instilled in the Chief a new fear of his government's violent overthrow by communists. Self-described American Bolshevism didn't pose much of a direct threat to the forces of domestic order, but Hoover and what was left of his loyal following took the revolutionists at their word. As far as they were concerned, workers organizing to leverage their collective role in production were a menace to the capitalist system itself. Once they started thinking that way, what was to stop them from taking it all? Friendly unions could be useful partners in coordinating the associative economy—Hoover helped persuade the steel industry to voluntarily cut the workday from 12 to eight hours, for example—but only if they were ultimately dependent on the generosity of a boss patriarch.[29] The associationists couldn't help but see coordination behind mass action, and in the global context in which they lived, that could only mean one thing: The Reds were acting on their promise of world revolution.

There's nothing un-American about a crowd of veterans demanding that the government pay them early, but in 1932, in the midst of the Great Depression, when the Bonus Army—tens of thousands strong—showed up at the Capitol looking to redeem their service-bonus certificates for cash, Hoover saw a Bolshevik military plot. The certificates were earning interest until their 1945 redemption date, but the Depression left some people unable to wait, and the troops formed a motley crew, staging an event that was half protest and half bank run. The Chief didn't see anyone worth negotiating with on the other side, and the administration convinced themselves that they were under attack by armed communist forces looking to repeat the storming of the Winter Palace in the Washington summer. In reality, Moscow was frustrated with the American communists for *failing* to take control of the campaign, but Hooverites prepared for the worst.[30] Army chief of staff Douglas MacArthur was just as Red-scared as his boss, and together they saw this pitiful group of their countrymen camping in tents with their families as a godless revolutionary vanguard. (The revolutionaries had been poor soldiers in Russia, too!) MacArthur marched the cavalry into the camp, followed by infantry and five tanks with their caterpillar treads. They lobbed tear-gas grenades ahead of them, making use of the state's best war technologies, and when troops reached the Bonus camp, they methodically burned it down—on camera. Dozens were injured and troops arrested over 100 demonstrators. Hoover was unrepentant and the Roosevelt campaign looked on with glee. The Chief was toast.

Traumatized by the Bolsheviks, Bert took out his fears on the Bonus Army, hammering the final nail in his own presidential coffin. In the light of this Red dawn even Franklin Delano Roosevelt took on a pink hue, and in his mind Hoover's enemies blended together. The lame duck president hardened in his politics and sentiments. He planned to retrench in Palo Alto. But California wasn't safe, either.

The Reds

Bert and Lou cast their votes in the 1932 election at the Stanford student center they financed before retiring to their modern-style Palo Alto mansion, which the campaign had transformed into an Election Day headquarters. But by the time they got settled, the Hoovers didn't need a bundle of telegraph cables to know they were getting walloped. His fall from grace was steep,

among the quickest heel turns in the history of American politics. Hoover was
no revolutionary victim, and no one was going to string him up from an apricot tree for crimes against the people; he lost to the silver-spoon fancy man
Roosevelt, and despite the personal antagonisms between the two they were
members of the same class. The feds were not about to expropriate the Hoover
Farm and turn it over to the workers. (Adding insult to electoral injury, however, the Roosevelt administration did temporarily take Hoover's name off the
dam.) The Chief was not reassured, and the labor situation in California did
not comfort him.

The organized agricultural capitalists used the Depression to attack the
high wages that had plagued their regional industry since before the Anglos
showed up to steal the land. A surplus of desperate laborers made it impossible
to gain any leverage on the bosses even in the white-only canneries, where pay
fell from $16 a week in the summer of '29 to $8 four years later.[31] The cuts for
field workers were even more brutal.[32] At a certain point workers had too little
to lose, and they began organizing, complete with work stoppages protected
by hard pickets.* Harvest work is extremely time-sensitive, and the picket gave
laborers more leverage than they had on the glutted labor market. Workers
could control supply, too. Hoover escaped the feared Bonus Army onslaught
only to find himself at the Red heart of American Bolshevism. And this time,
he wasn't seeing things. Communists had inordinate success organizing California agricultural workers in the 1930s, more success than other labor groups
and more success than the Party had elsewhere. For a moment, the Soviet-
affiliated American subversives found themselves the right people in the right
place and at the right time, a rare confluence in United States history. That
place was the Hoover Farm.

There was no such thing as the Hoover Farm, Hoover angrily informed the
press. During his first July in the White House, *Time* magazine reported on
"three carloads of particularly luscious apricots" entering the eastern food market, each crate labeled GROWN AND PACKED ON PRESIDENT HOOVER'S RANCH,
WASCO, CAL. *Time* continued: "Careful explanations emanated officially from
the White House: President Hoover does not own a Wasco Fruit Ranch. He

---

* While soft pickets allow customers and replacement workers to enter through the protest
line, hard pickets do not.

does own some stock in Pozo [sic] Products Co. which in turn controls the ranch."[33] The Poso Land and Products Company was the name of the corporate entity, but that's not what they called the ranch when the consortium of agriculture-industry heavy hitters acquired it. "I bought thirteen hundred acres, selected it for Hoover, down in Kern County, and it was called the Hoover Farm," recalls government agronomist Wofford "Bill" Camp.[34] Though he initially planned to manage the farm, the southern cotton specialist Camp decided to stay at the Department of Agriculture after the cotton price tanked and the farm converted some of its acreage to those apricots.

Their plan was to run the ranch according to Hooverian principles: high tech, low wages, scientific information, rational planning. They were convinced that efficient production changed the agricultural model, promoting the idea of a farm managed by engineers rather than farmers. This was around the time of Hoover's return from Europe, at the height of his popularity, and his friends in the press ate the narrative up like a crate of particularly luscious apricots. But in truth the farm was a speculative play on cotton. Hoover and his managers planned to plant an especially good variety bred by the University of California and take advantage of high prices, but their timing was bad. The farm loaded itself down with high machinery costs and "apparently they never made much money on it," Camp remembers.[35] He was in a good place to know: Hired as the head of agricultural appraisal for the Bank of Italy, he was asked to review a new mortgage loan application for...the Hoover Farm. He knew the $400,000 or so the farm was asking for was the same amount the consortium—and he on their behalf—paid in the first place, and Giannini's bank turned the future president down.* The Hoover team went to Henry Robinson's Security First National instead, where they had fewer problems.

The California industrial agricultural community and Hoover-loving apricot consumers weren't the only ones paying attention to the Poso Land and Products Company. The *Western Worker*, print organ of the Communist Party USA (CPUSA) on the West Coast, announced HOOVER RANCH SYMBOL OF BANKRUPTCY OF CAPITALIST FARMING.[36] The paper published pictures of children cutting cotton and formally segregated worker housing under the

---

* Perhaps Camp was unfamiliar with Hoover's standard practice of staying highly leveraged—no reason to tie your capital up in a farm if you can use the bank's.

headline CHILD LABOR, JIM CROWISM ON POSO. What's more, the *Worker* came to the same conclusion Camp did, taunting the farm's businessman manager, who is quoted saying that he can't figure out how to make any money off the land. Poso became an election liability for Hoover when rumors spread that a sign posted at the farm stated NO WHITE NEED APPLY. Farm management quickly replaced black, Filipino, and Mexican workers with downwardly mobile white Okies, and Hoover denied the whole thing, as was his wont.

American trade union organizers weren't particularly interested in working with California's harvest laborers for a number of reasons. The workers were precariously employed migrants, spoke a lot of different languages, and didn't make enough money to contribute substantial dues. The bosses were vicious and intolerant of organizers, and out in the country they made their own law. In fact, they made their own law in the state at large: California passed a broad syndicalism ban in 1919 to target the IWW, a ban that provided cover for the Klan and other right-wing vigilantes acting on the planters' behalf. Organizers had to live like farmworkers, and the organizers didn't want to — though that only dramatized the need for help. As a result, since the turn of the century the state's agricultural workers have organized with rank-and-file leadership, starting with the 1903 strike of Japanese and Mexican beet workers in Oxnard, which planters put down with gunfire.[37] IWWism as an ideological formation is a theoretically informed, internationalist rank-and-file politics, and its mascot is the black cat of the unauthorized wildcat strike. Though the union is associated with dynamite and sabotage, violence was more prevalent in its rhetoric than its actions. For the Wobblies, militancy mostly meant a willingness to keep fighting even after they got beaten up, which made them the leaders of the California agricultural-workers movement in the first decades of the twentieth century.

By the spring of 1914, the IWW had 40 locals in California averaging over 100 members each, plus many dozens of full-time organizers sourced from among the working ranks. Their presence extended beyond the fields to the ports. World War I fanned anti-IWW sentiment, the internationalists out of step with the patriotic mood. The California Criminal Syndicalism Act of 1919 prohibited speech that suggested the use of violence for political aims, and with Wobblies prone to passionate speeches about world revolution, prosecutors used the act to turn membership into a crime. The law was also an

invitation to vigilantes; soldiers, sailors, and the Klan organized to raid Wobbly offices, beat members in the street, and then hand them off to the police for
jailing. In 1923, the superior court of Sacramento County issued an injunction
demanding that IWW members stop committing syndicalism by existing,
and thousands fled the jurisdiction to avoid what they knew were biased juries.
Wobblies filled San Quentin, the Bay Area's only prison, on bullshit charges
that could hold them for up to 14 years. In Southern California, the police
teamed with a resurgent KKK to bust the waterfront union, and the IWW was
lucky if the cops decided to merely stand by and watch. In one instance, Klan
members were accused of using the hot pot of coffee at an IWW gathering to
burn organizers' children.[38] By the end of the decade, the state organization
was jailed and beaten into submission. But they were no longer alone.

With Moscow's blessing, in 1929 the CPUSA began organizing independent revolutionary unions rather than trying to radicalize existing trade
groups. The Trade Union Unity League sent Party members to organize wherever there were gaps in existing representation, and California agriculture
more than qualified. Sam Darcy was a twenty-five-year-old New Yorker born
in Ukraine. The son of a Jewish garment worker unionist, he began his political work as a child laborer. When he was in his early twenties, the Party sent
him to Moscow, where he joined the executive ranks of the Young Communist International and taught at the Lenin School. Returned to New York after
some organizing in China and the Philippines, Darcy fell on the wrong side of
the CPUSA chairman, Earl Browder, and Browder exiled him to the West to
head up the Party in California, Nevada, and Arizona. With the Unity League
starting, Darcy had his work cut out for him, and under his leadership the
Party took up the mantle of the IWW—not what Browder had in mind, but
California was a long way away from the CPUSA's power base, and distance
allowed the young man some leeway.

Darcy's deputies were misfits as well. Caroline Decker was the anglonym
used by Caroline Dwofsky, a Party organizer even younger than Darcy, who
stood just over five feet tall in her trademark high heels. A Ukrainian Jew as
well, Decker grew up mostly in Syracuse, learning about radicalism through
her older brother and the communist friends he made at Columbia University.
She joined the Young Communist League as a teenager, and her youth, blond
hair, and femininity proved an asset: Comrades had her hold the Party funds

because the police wouldn't think to search her. Decker adopted that name (with her sister) when, forgoing college, the two deployed to Harlan County, Kentucky, where company thugs drove the United Mine Workers out of the coalfields. There she met hard-core communists and improved her organizing skills. From Harlan she jumped from demonstration to demonstration until she met Jack Warnick—a graduate student at UC Berkeley, a comrade, and "strikingly attractive," according to historian Kathryn Olmsted.[39] Smitten, she went with him to the American hinterland, where they fell under the direction of Sam Darcy. He sent the lovebirds to San Jose, where they helped lead the Cannery and Agricultural Workers Industrial Union (CAWIU), which they had to build themselves with virtually no money. They split the work: Handsome college boy Jack raised cash from liberals and Caroline went to the front lines to agitate. With her was Pat Chambers—also a pseudonym, in his case for John Williams—a mysterious Wobbly who'd been persuaded to join the Party rather than the AFL after the IWW fell down.* He was short, Irish, and could take a beating. Unlike Caroline, she wasn't much of a talker, but he knew what they were up against, and he never wavered.

The CAWIU's anglophone leadership was made up of marginal whites— the bad ones who picked radical internationalist politics over American assimilation—because those were the cadres the CPUSA, based in New York City, had. They were not, however, the bulk of the labor revolutionaries in California. To address labor shortages around World War I, contractors imported Mexican workers by the thousands. A number of them brought revolutionary military experience with them, and the global Marxist current was at least as strong in Mexico as it was in California. American military intelligence tracked Mexican communists through the CAWIU, singling out men such as Frank Samora (union secretary), Francisco Medina (chapter founder), and Fred Martínez (YCL organizer).[40] Behind them were the Chicana-led networks that ensured the strikers lived to see another day, financing the effort with sweat and discipline. Prominent radical Filipino labor organizers such as Carlos Bulosan and Larry Itliong cut their teeth in the same California 1930s farmwork milieu. The planters' depiction of the CAWIU as Mexican

---

* Politically active Bay Area longshoremen had to contend with employer-controlled hiring halls and a management-friendly union; they often adopted aliases to dodge the blacklist.

and Filipino workers misled by communists is belied by the obvious fact that a handful of underfunded outside agitators couldn't possibly have organized California's Spanish- and Tagalog-speaking agricultural workers the way the CAWIU did. Rather, Party organizers like Darcy and Decker eschewed the top-down turn in Moscow and fit themselves to the diverse rank-and-file tradition of California communism.

In the first years of the 1930s, the CAWIU operated as a kind of flying squad—a "little red fire brigade" in the words of historian Mike Davis, deploying with volunteer lawyers and mimeograph machines to support strikes wherever they threatened to erupt organically across the state.[41] The growers were operating from a place of strength after the IWW's defeat, and they treated labor stoppages as challenges to their authority. They busted pickets by force, kidnapped leaders, and armed scabs. The tide turned when a CAWIU-reinforced strike of fruit workers in Vacaville held out for two months against the bosses and their lackeys. In the spring of 1933, pea pickers went out in a general strike—like the packers and processors, they understood there was strength in unifying farms—and faced the same police and vigilante violence they were used to. But for the first time, the strike held, and the growers folded, doubling the price they paid per hamper picked. The CAWIU workers dominated the harvest of '33, winning spring strikes in cherries, peaches, pears, and grapes. Santa Clara County apricot growers offered a preemptive raise. No longer was the CAWIU dropping in: It was picking targets, and after Chambers led a successful action at the Tagus fruit ranch in the conservative San Joaquin Valley, another strike wave carried the union into the fall. Its next target was big—bigger than any agricultural labor action in American history to that point: the San Joaquin Valley cotton crop.* Which brings us back to the Hoover Farm.

The struggle between labor and capital now reached a fever pitch in California. Both the CAWIU and the growers were getting more organized, and both were looking to force as the only way to settle their conflict. To stop the planters from bringing in scabs, the union operated a flying picket, intercepting strikebreakers on their way to work at one of the valley's hundreds of cotton

---

*   Excepting the revolt of the enslaved during the U.S. Civil War, which W. E. B. Du Bois
     famously describes as a general strike.

ranches. Overwhelmed, the police deputized growers and their hired thugs, while their financiers stocked up on tear gas. Pickets threatened to leave crops rotting in the field, which capitalists viewed (not incorrectly) as a kind of sabotage by default. At Poso Land and Products, the farm superintendent got himself deputized, returned to the ranch, and promptly arrested 11 strikers for vagrancy.[42] A general strike at harvest time against one of the state's top cash crops meant whole enterprises could fail, whole banks. With so much at stake in October, a mortal feeling descended on the San Joaquin Valley: People were going to die.

On October 10, the day after a large rally whipped the growers into a frenzy, the shooting started. While Pat Chambers spoke to a group of workers in the town of Pixley, dozens of armed vigilantes fell upon the meeting. Chambers led the crowd into the nearby union hall, but Mexican consular official Delfino D'Ávila was there to mediate (on the planters' behalf, it's worth noting), and he didn't appreciate the interruption. D'Ávila approached the growers; they hit him over the head and shot him dead on the ground. Then they opened up on the crowd, killing striker Dolores Hernández and wounding many more.[43] On the same day in the town of Arvin to the south, capitalist forces opened fire on a picket, murdering worker Pedro Subia. Though the California farm owners had used Klan-style violence and intimidation to combat strikes before, these big attacks with live ammo were a significant escalation. This was open class war.

After the shootings, Sam Darcy told the strike committee to be prepared for a "businesslike demonstration" at the Hoover Farm.[44] The following day he was surprised to find both Okie and Chicano strikers bunkered down in a line of cars surrounding the farm, gun barrels sticking out the windows. Horrified, he asked field lieutenant "Big Bill" Hammett—a large militant Okie preacherman who, with his five large militant sons, gave off a John Brown vibe—what the hell was going on. Hammett, equally confused, answered that everyone had heard him loud and clear the day before: They were ready for business. If not for Darcy's intervention it could've been another Mussel Slough, Hoover following Leland Stanford into California absentee-landlord infamy.

Sam Darcy was not looking to use the rank and file for cannon fodder in order to raise his profile, contrary to popular stereotypes about communist Jews from New York City by way of Moscow coming to the rural West under assumed names to agitate workers and foment industrial disharmony—a description that despite its racist, paranoid character fits Darcy about as well as it's ever fit anyone. As the Party chair, he had to act locally while being accountable to a global movement. The world situation had changed since the Unity League strategy began: The German Reichstag burned in February and Hitler assumed dictatorial power; Japan consolidated control over Manchuria and menaced the Soviet and Chinese borders; FDR beat Hoover. The future Axis countries moved to exterminate their domestic communist parties, while the Soviets entered into negotiations with the Roosevelt administration to recognize the Red government, something the president's expropriated predecessor categorically refused to do. Darcy was supposed to be expanding the Party's membership in the West, not triggering an uprising that could push the American leadership toward the fascists.* Through a chain of fellow travelers that reached the top of the Department of Labor (just as the growers suspected!), strikers appealed to Roosevelt to step in and prevent further bloodshed and alleviate conditions in the worker camps, where babies were starving to death.

If it were almost any other sector, the Department of Labor could have intervened under its new industrial policy, but the New Deal excluded agricultural workers for fear of upsetting Jim Crow in the South and splitting the Democratic Party's racist base. This, however, was an emergency—and it was in California. A week after the shootings, the New Deal administrator for the state, George Creel, arrived in the San Joaquin Valley. Federal fact-finding found something close to the reality, and Creel made two unusual decisions: First, he decided as a matter of law that the strike fell under his authority, because California's agriculture production was so advanced that the labor dispute was "industrial." Second, he decided that the strike was reasonable, which meant the strikers qualified for federal food aid. While they were out, the government would supply the makeshift camp in Corcoran with enough to eat. Creel saw himself as a Solomon figure whose successful resolution of the strike put him first in line for the governor's mansion in Sacramento the following November. Farmers depended on federal aid to the cartels—including

---

*   Given Roosevelt's antipathy toward Hoover, perhaps it wouldn't have been as disastrous as
     Darcy believed. Regardless, CAWIU leaders displayed none of the heartless Soviet instru-
     mentalism that planters warned workers about.

$1 million invested in the San Joaquin cotton crop, according to Creel—which gave the administrator real leverage, especially when combined with his ability and willingness to feed the strikers. Having grown dependent on the state, planters found themselves subject to some attenuated version of economic democracy.

Creel held special investigative hearings in which he allowed Caroline Decker to serve as the advocate for the strikers opposite the growers' lawyer, whom she easily outperformed by all accounts. When the strikers refused to participate without the jailed Pat Chambers, Creel had him released. If the workers were determined to be represented by the CAWIU, the administration had to recognize them as a legitimate counterparty in the proceedings, communist or not. This was Hoover's nightmare—the American government ensuring something like a fair negotiation between investment capital and communist insurrectionists. This is why you don't take money from the government! The Democrats wanted the whole thing done with, and despite trying, they couldn't cut the Reds out. But Creel was no commie, and he had no intention of securing the CAWIU a permanent place in the state he planned to govern. The feds suggested a compromise: 75 cents per 100 pounds picked, up from 60 cents but short of the dollar strikers wanted, and no recognition for the union.[45] For both sides, with the federal carrot came the threat of its withdrawal. When the strikers held out for 80 cents, Creel canceled food relief and mobilized the United States Farm Labor Service to deploy 1,000 strike-breakers.[46] To sweeten the deal for planters, the feds assured them that the government bank would still declare cotton worth financing at 75 cents, while threatening to pull the loans if they refused.[47] The union leaders asked the strikers to accept the offer, and after some protestations they did, officially winning the strike and securing harvesters something like a $1 million raise.[48] Nonrecognition wasn't the end of the world anyway; they'd won without it before and could do it again. But they didn't.

After the mixed defeat of the cotton strike, California's capitalists were nervous. The communists weren't looking to settle for the fields, and IWWism returned to the ports as well. As soon as the Roosevelt administration affirmed the legal right of workers (outside of agriculture and domestic work) to join whatever union they wanted, left-wing seamen in San Francisco began organizing to separate first from the boss-controlled "blue book" union—named for the membership document workers in good standing were required to maintain—and then from the more conservative AFL affiliates. They formed the racially integrated Marine Workers Industrial Union (MWIU) under Darcy's leadership, which evolved into the International Longshoremen's and Warehousemen's Union once they began their "march inland" to organize all workers connected to the ports. A few days before George Creel arrived in the San Joaquin Valley, his appointed panel reinstated four longshoremen who were fired for not belonging to the company union. Led by Australian ex-Wobbly seaman Harry Bridges, the rank and file began seizing control of the docks. A convention at the end of 1933 pointed San Francisco toward strike.

Seen from Hoover's point of view—and his influence was rising again with capitalists, who had begun regretting their support for FDR—this was all part of one great big Red sequence of events. The people who confiscated his mines in Russia at gunpoint were the same ones who tried to take over starving Europe in the wake of World War I—the same ones who marched on the Capitol in 1932; the same ones who shut the Santa Clara orchards and surrounded the Hoover Farm in October; the same ones taking the ports. The waterfront was at least as logistically fragile as the cotton harvest, and with the industrial labor rights promised by the New Deal and a solid base of support in the city, the longshoremen were in a stronger position than the farmworkers, and the farmworkers were gearing up to build on their own mixed successes of 1933. Capital, the capitalists came to realize, couldn't afford another year like the one before, and they couldn't rely on Roosevelt to do what needed to be done if things got out of control—say, in a situation like the Bonus March. The corporate press (a repentant Hearst in particular) became increasingly hysterical, trying its best to marginalize the Reds as enemies of America and its people. But the press was a relatively weak tool, as Hoover found out during the run-up to the stock-market crash. What the ruling class needed to do was the same thing its enemies in the working class were doing: organize.

"The radicals almost, *almost* took over," recalled Bill Camp. "That caused the Associated Farmers to [come to] be."[49] With a name that evokes both Stanford's Associates and Hoover's associative state, the Associated Farmers of California (AFC) was a standing committee of California capitalists that existed to coordinate extralegal anticommunist activities in the agriculture industry and beyond.[50] The Confederate cotton man Camp, who served as both president and treasurer of the AFC, favorably compared it to the Reconstruction-era Klan, an organization to which his father proudly belonged. In his view, both existed for the same singular purpose: "All we were organized for and all we tried to do and did do was fight communists."[51] Unlike the cartels, the Associated Farmers wasn't set up to organize production, distribution, or marketing; the organization existed only to combat the CAWIU and its fellow travelers. For that reason it didn't suffer from the same dismembering spin that plagued the other producer associations as success reduced their incentives to cooperate. "We had too much of a fight against the labor organizers and the racketeers and things to be able to afford any fights. We couldn't afford the luxury of a fight amongst ourselves," planter politician Philip Bancroft told an interviewer in 1961.[52] If there's one thing the bosses could always agree on, it was grower control of the fields.

The AFC understood the agricultural and waterfront strikes as a single phenomenon. Starting in the spring of 1934, longshoremen started turning away trucks full of farm products. What was the point of paying to get the crops picked if they were going to rot on the road instead of the field? "The farmer's interest in his products does not cease until it is in the hands of the ultimate consumer," the group resolved, and they cooperated with the state's industrial capitalist associations to coordinate "anti-C activities," led by the chamber of commerce.[53] Made up of county chapters, the AFC aggregated sympathetic community organizations much the way the Communist Party did, but for the ruling class rather than the workers. For the first time since the state's founding, California's varied patchwork of right-wing vigilantes had a common body. The AFC raised money from growers and packers as well as railroads and oil refiners and banks, which were as much like "farmers" as anyone was, as far as the capitalists were concerned. The organization was connected first and foremost to local police in all jurisdictions, but it was also connected to the highway patrol, National Guard, and the governor's office. Even labor wasn't left out; the farmers worked with the conservative AFL against their common enemies in the canneries and on the docks. They chatted with Harry Chandler at the *Times* and put out their own literature.

Among the AFC's successful early interventions was creating and distributing a statewide database of radicals. By the end of 1934, it had assembled an index of over 3,000 four-by-six cards holding information about left-wing individuals, organizations, and groups — the Bank of Italy's credit scoring system retooled for counterinsurgency.[54] Consistently identifying communists was hard because the Reds used pseudonyms to confuse authorities and employers. When the AFC consulted with local police, even the feared anticommunist Red Squad in LA and its counterparts in San Francisco only had photos of around a hundred people each. The farmers assembled a file of 600 "known communists," with pictures, fingerprints, known aliases, and other identifying information.[55] Assisting the government, the AFC standardized anticommunist practices up and down the state, lobbying for and passing antipicket rules in dozens of localities.

The AFC's inaugural win was a Contra Costa County apricot strike in June of 1934. Authorities arrested the picketers en masse, held the CAWIU leaders on vagrancy charges, and expelled the rest from the county. The grower-friendly press portrayed it as a defeat for communist agitators. But only a few weeks later, San Francisco exploded. Longshoremen across the West Coast overthrew their company unions and, reorganized under rank-and-file leadership, struck for union control over hiring. Industry was unwilling to set that precedent and figured this was its one chance to bust the independent waterfront union and restore the status quo. In early May, the longshoremen closed the port of San Francisco; by the end of June, the city's leaders and employers had had enough. On July 5, 1934, the bosses tried to break the picket under the guns of the city police and the National Guard, which Governor Frank Merriam called in. Open warfare erupted on the waterfront. Ignoring the informal rules of a picket fight, police attacked union headquarters, drenching the Embarcadero in tear gas. One policeman fired into the crowd, killing strikers Howard Sperry and Nick Bordoise.[56] With these murders, the police convinced both sides that they had leverage — the strikers because they had a new moral authority with the city's workers; the Industrial Association of San Francisco because it had the military on its side. More unions joined the strike, and on behalf of the longshoremen and their martyrs, Harry Bridges petitioned the city labor council for a general walkout of all workers, a true general strike. AFL leaders weren't interested, but the rank and file was furious. On July 14, after the shippers refused to negotiate, 63 out of 115 union representatives voted to join. The next day, San Francisco's workers seized the city.

For four days (including Sunday), nothing moved without the union's say-so, and it didn't give in for anything but essentials. An employer plan for FDR to cruise into port on his way to vacation in Hawaii fell through when the pink-tinged secretary of labor, Frances Perkins, convinced the president that her sources in San Francisco were more reliable than the wails from industry men. Roosevelt steamed on by. Forsaken, the bosses shifted tactics and decided to use their new intelligence capabilities to split off the communists from the rest of the workers. The AFC relayed on-the-ground intel, such as where and when Reds were meeting, where they stored written materials, and whom in particular to look out for. Major General David Barrows led the National Guard; he was an anticommunist from the beginning, a veteran of the international anti-Bolshevik force that backed the Whites in the Russian Civil War. On July 17, the Guard surrounded Marine Workers Industrial Union headquarters, trained two truck-mounted machine guns on it, and grabbed nearly 100 people.[57] A series of targeted raids rounded up between 270 and 450 alleged communists, getting them off the street and holding them as vagrants.[58] At the same time, the AFC buttered up the AFL, publishing a long public letter to the strike committee asking it to distance itself from the anti-American communists and bring the strike to a close for the sake of the nation and the hungry women and children who needed their California produce. Behind the scenes, the AFC kept a constant flow of propaganda going to AFL leadership. It seems to have worked: Referring to the anticommunist military raids, the AFC's executive secretary, Guernsey Frazer, wrote in an internal letter, "The labor element in San Francisco was heartily in accord with the program and is believed to have materially assisted with the work."[59] The next day, with all the communists the city could grab in jail, the strategy committee voted 191 to 174 to end the strike and submit to arbitration.[60]

The owners pressed their advantage. Two days after the end of the San Francisco general walkout, Sacramento authorities raided the offices of the CAWIU and arrested the leadership in a decapitation strike, including Pat Chambers and Caroline Decker.[61] The district attorney, Neil McAllister, charged 18 with felony syndicalism under the 1919 act—punishable, recall, by up to 14 years in prison.[62] Though it was happy to simply keep the CAWIU leadership out of the cotton fields and avoid a repeat of the previous fall, the AFC recognized that this was also its big chance to vanquish the Reds for good. Associated Farmers officials assembled all the information they had in the state on the defendants and forwarded it to McAllister. They even sent up the Imperial County DA, who unlike McAllister had experience prosecuting syndicalism, to walk him through it.[63] The AFC took such an active role that McCallister shouted the organization out by name in his closing statement. At the trial's height, AFC leaders complained they were spending $1,000 a day supporting the prosecution—over $20,000 in 2022 value.[64] The Sacramento Conspiracy Trial, as it's become known, became a show trial, and after 118 reported ballots, the jury convicted eight defendants of conspiracy to commit syndicalism for their membership in the Communist Party. Decker was sentenced to one year; Chambers got five. Anyone still incarcerated was released on appeal in the fall of 1937, but the damage was done, and the CAWIU, along with the MWIU, was finished. Money well spent for the farmers.

It was common both at the time and in subsequent histories to think about the Associated Farmers and their vigilante gangs in the context of the fascist movements emerging concurrently in Europe and Japan. There are obvious parallels: The Salinas ax-handle brigades who tried to break a 1936 lettuce strike were the California equivalent of the brownshirts who shattered Jewish windows on Kristallnacht.[65] Feelings about the Hitler regime varied among the farmers and their social milieu, and Hoover would have done his damnedest to keep America out of the Second World War. Both fascists and their American cousins hated their local communists, who shared an attorney: California lawyer Leo Gallagher went from defending IWW icon Tom Mooney to George Dimitroff (ultimately convicted of burning down the Reichstag) to the accused syndicalists at the Sacramento Conspiracy Trial. And yet, the U.S. Hooverian tradition that stretches from the rationalized gold rush through the broken strikes and forced harvests of the 1930s is distinct, and it's worth understanding how.

It's often said that under capitalism, relations between people appear as relations between things. The butcher, baker, and candlestick maker vanish into the Bed Bath & Beyond. But there's a countertendency at work within the ruling class, among whom relations between things often appear as relations between people. Mr. Smith seems to have dinner with Mr. Brown, but behind the veil are the bank and newspaper sitting to sup. This is a virtue of the joint-stock model: Huge piles of capital, years of work extracted from labor and subsequently aggregated, meet as men. Capital's fundamental drive for better-than-average returns means that no operator can be satisfied with a tie, but in order to function the system needs superficial competition on a stone platform of cooperation. In the fascist system competition is external, between nations, its various components conceived as parts of a single body. Individual interest is subordinated to that of the group. That was anathema to Hoover and his fellows, who saw individual interest as the prime mover, society's engine. Capitalist collectivity emerges in two ways: First, there's exploitation, wherein capitalists extract bits of value from their employees' work and gather it up into lumps to reinvest. Second, there's association, in which investors pledge their gathered lumps to a common cause. Unlike an enveloping fascist state, an associative state comes together like an interoffice softball league, via the ostensibly free and voluntary association of participants.

The stone foundation of capitalist cooperation cracked during the Depression, as near-term self-preservation undermined long-term self-interest. The "Popular Front" alliance between leftists and liberals offered a different model, a democratic state that mediated between capital and labor much the way the associative state mediated among capitalists. The idea had a lot to offer, especially in the face of fascists on the right and communists on the left. The Stanford athletic association treasurer was abandoned, nearly alone in his fidelity. But he grasped something the others didn't: Financialization and economic democracy can't blend. If property rights are subject to popular control, then investors will encounter the public as an obstacle, a variable to be managed. For example, banks loaned credit to farms based on existing prices, which were based on the current cost of labor. Improving labor conditions by picket was an attack on property valuation, which thanks to financialization made it an attack on property, full stop. The Roosevelt coalition brought together capital and labor under one roof, but one partner always sought to dominate the other.

Bill Camp was an odd choice for a New Deal bureaucrat, but the banker, cotton planter, and proud son of a Klansman was the right wing of the FDR team, one of the Confederate Democrats who hadn't left the party yet, except for a single dalliance with the Chief in 1928. He was a link of continuity between Hoover's agricultural administration and the New Deal version.

When the Agricultural Adjustment Act came under legal challenge, Camp was introduced to the left side of the coalition, and he was shocked to discover that his very own lawyer was a communist. Camp knew one when he saw one, and when he realized that Department of Agriculture officials were planning to help the left-wing Southern Tenant Farmers Union get better conditions for cotton workers in the South—Camp's ancestral stomping ground—he denounced them. Camp called a handful of his conservative politician friends from the cotton belt and they went over the head of the agriculture secretary, Wallace (the new one), straight to President Roosevelt. The next day the president fired the left-wing lawyers, and Agriculture reversed a pro-tenant rule interpretation. But Camp couldn't forget about his commie lawyer, and when one of Camp's local congressmen wanted to make a name for himself exposing liberal Reds, Camp fed everything he had on Alger Hiss to Richard Nixon, helping ignite the congressional Red Scare.

Herbert Hoover understood that the social forces Bill Camp and Alger Hiss represented—the plantation owner and the plantation worker—no government could bring into harmony. Capital *by its nature* dominates labor, and if it fails to accomplish that, it ceases to exist. The rule interpretation Camp objected to bound planters to their existing tenants, which was an untenable attack on their profitability, even though at the time they weren't profitable at all without the government's help. The conflict was inherent, and it didn't take until the end of World War II for the Cold War to start or for liberals to reveal which side they planned to take. After George Creel lost the California gubernatorial nomination to the wacky socialist writer Upton Sinclair, he and FDR knifed the populist author. First they rewrote Sinclair's platform to moderate it, then they cut a deal with the Republican incumbent, Frank Merriam, anyway—the same Merriam who called the machine guns to the San Francisco waterfront. Merriam trounced Sinclair, who waited patiently for the Roosevelt endorsement that never came. "He didn't realize at first that communism was the threat," Camp recalled of Creel, regarding the official's work; "he became one of the greatest fighters [against communism]."[66] So much for the New Deal.

At the end of the day, Creel belonged to the same club as Hoover. The club was figurative, but in the world of the associative state, it was also literal: San Francisco's Bohemian Club. Every year the club brought California's elite along with their invitees to summer camp in the woods, the Bohemian

Grove, where the real business of the world could be done at a no-girls-allowed sleepover party. They performed skits and sang songs and told secrets. The Gianninis came, and the Chandlers—A.P. and Harry, and then their sons. Ray Lyman Wilbur was there, but so was Harold Ickes, his successor at Interior under Roosevelt (and future Stanford dad).* The club was the literal version of what Vladimir Lenin imagined as the figurative finance-led "personal union" established in this period "between the banks and the biggest industrial and commercial enterprises, the merging of one with another through the acquisition of shares, through the appointment of bank directors to the Supervisory Boards (or Boards of Directors) of industrial and commercial enterprises, and vice versa."[67] In California, they also merged by frolicking in the grove. Herbert Hoover, of course, was identified with the whole operation, and he anchored his own camp within the camp, where he continued to operate as a global kingmaker until his death, long after FDR's. It's comical to imagine them all lined up outside the dining hall in the summer of 1934 to ask attendee David Barrows, commander of the California National Guard, what it was like to kick all that commie ass on the waterfront in July, but this genuine scene was Hooverism at its purest: capital, in the form of men, slapping one another on the back while they coordinated their attack on labor.† Nothing could break that core unity, just as the people couldn't remove Hoover from power by voting him out. There could be no New Deal between the cotton picker and the plantation owner, no fair bargain between the exploiter and exploited.

Communism, Hoover and his allies saw, was not merely a political party running Russia or an economic philosophy. It was a real movement that threatened to abolish capitalist control over society and thereby destroy capitalism in its entirety. Communists were communists whether they realized it or not, even when they thought they only wanted better wages. It's easy now to look back and see the Hooverites as victims of a paranoiac fantasy about the world—to see them either as the only ones who really believed the Marxist

---

* Creel loved the Bohemian Club so much he made the San Francisco club his full-time home after his wife's death.

† An anthropologist by trade, Barrows was instrumental in American colonization of the Philippines and later served as the president of the University of California, Berkeley. See Montgomery McFate, *Military Anthropology: Soldiers, Scholars and Subjects at the Margins of Empire* (Oxford University Press, 2018).

revolutionary rhetoric or as cynical operators stoking an arbitrary moral panic. But Bert knew the global revolution was real. He saw it in China, narrowly escaped it in Russia, confronted it outside the window in DC, and heard it tear apart his farm in California. They took his mines, and they would kill him and take the rest if he wasn't vigilant, just like they did to his formerly privileged friends around the world. Still nursing his wounds from defeat but far from vanquished, Herbert Hoover devoted the rest of his life to winning the class war. Palo Alto became his watch tower.

First, however, America had another war to win.

Men with Potential

Blowing Tubes — De Forest's Triode — Avionics — The
Varian Brothers and the Rhumbatron — Fred Terman,
Genius Son — Internment of the California Japanese —
Ernesto Galarza and the Betrayal of the Popular Front

The path of the Bay Area electronics industry from Federal Telegraph to today's internet platforms does not appear linear. How do you go from radio transmitters to inert hunks of silicon? In roughly half a century, that's what happened in Palo Alto. Lee de Forest's multipurpose vacuum tube morphed into the silicon wafers that give the Santa Clara Valley its more popular name. The Stanford community rode radio waves to semiconductors, contributing well above its size and prestige to the birth and development of the American midcentury. World War II shifted California's national location as the country spread into the Pacific, linking the greater United States to the Asian continent. With a combination of invention, hype, government contracting, and stockjobbery, these men of the radio age cast the mold for more than a century's worth of local tech entrepreneurs. And as the world entered two wars, they became something more.

After Muybridge, Lee de Forest was Palo Alto's second star inventor. The self-declared Father of Radio came west after his partners in New York oversubscribed their stock issue and spun off the assets into a new company, leaving de Forest in a bankrupt corporate shell. Convinced he couldn't steer the firm back toward viability, de Forest writes that he "accepted the doom and reconciled myself to the fact that I must at once seek employment."[1] Luckily, through his work on the Pacific Coast, he had become friends with Cy Elwell, the Federal Telegraph founder and Stanford graduate, who jumped at the chance to hire him. De Forest only spent 1910 to 1913 at Federal, but his most important years were at this original Stanford start-up.

De Forest had been trying to make an improved radio receiver, which he did, but he didn't immediately realize what else he had accomplished. The tube diode sent a flow of electrons from the positively charged cathode to the negative anode relatively unimpeded, thanks to the vacuum. These tube devices could rectify the hectic household alternating current into a steady direct-current flow as well as receive radio signals. But by adding a third electrode—the grid or control grid—between the cathode and the anode, he inadvertently created a switch. And by floating a low-power signal across the grid, you could amplify it on the high current between the original diode connections. More or less by accident, de Forest had invented the triode.

Think of it like this: There's a giant airplane hangar, and on one end there's a door, and behind the door is an endless stream of hungry cheetahs. This is the cathode—remember "cat" for hungry cheetahs. On the other end is a pile of recently deceased antelopes—"antelope" for anode. When you energize the cathode, the cheetahs flow toward the antelope in that single direction (assume no vegetarian cheetahs). If we then add a set of supermarket-style sliding glass doors between our cat-ode and antel-ode, we can control the massive energetic flow from the pack of hungry cheetahs with only the tiny amount of energy required to tell the doors to open. Now we have an amplifier.

An amplifier was a big deal at a time when communications technology was limited by signal power; absent an amplifier, AT&T could only connect local calls, since signals attenuated over long distances. With refinement from engineers who understood the device better than de Forest did, the three-electrode Audion became the magic ingredient in radio broadcasting and reception as well as telephony. By using Audions to repeat signals when they grew faint, the telephone company could bridge indefinite stretches. In 1915, the year after it snagged the license from de Forest, AT&T announced the first coast-to-coast voice circuit at the Panama-Pacific International Exposition.

The head of Federal's vacuum-tube production was a young Stanford graduate from San Francisco named Charles Litton. Born in 1904, Litton was an amateur-radio enthusiast as a kid, like Fred Terman (who was four years older and grew up 30 miles south). Litton was a vacuum-tube prodigy, blowing and selling glass parts for radios before becoming the go-to tube guy at the Stanford communications lab. He graduated with degrees in mechanical and electrical engineering, in 1925, and Federal hired him to manage its tube operation three years later.* But Federal was now owned by the International Telephone and Telegraph (ITT) conglomerate, which soon consolidated its U.S. operations in Newark, New Jersey. Not yet thirty or a decade out of Stanford, Litton was confident enough to quit Federal and open his own shop, producing tube-manufacturing equipment. Maybe the California boy just couldn't stand to leave the Bay. Instead, he designed a glass-blowing lathe that mass-produced tubes of consistently high quality, a major upgrade from the hand-made industry standard at the time. Now the Litton process was standard.

Litton was an exceptional young man in a community of exceptional young men. If you were born within a decade of the turn of the twentieth century and were interested in radio technology, the San Francisco Bay Area was as good a place as existed in the world. Lee de Forest and Federal Telegraph made the region a paradise for amateur-radio ("ham") enthusiasts such as Ralph Heintz, Stanford class of 1920 and a World War I veteran of the U.S. Army Signal Corps, who cofounded the radio-parts firm Heintz and Kaufman with a Berkeley graduate. For most enterprising inventors in the West, the Bay Area was the nearest source of capital and skilled labor, as it was for the Utah-born Philo Farnsworth, who located his television lab at the foot of San Francisco's Telegraph Hill in the mid-1920s. (He invented television.) If San Francisco, with its investors and view of the Pacific, was like a receiver for regional talent, pulling the signal in from America's ex-Mexican territories, then Palo Alto was like an amplifier, blasting human potential back over the rest of the country.

Despite the concentration of technological development, there were limits to what a NorCal wireless company could accomplish on its own. After de Forest left Federal for a fancier offer in New York City, he found himself embroiled in a variety of intellectual property disputes. (The Audion's case wasn't helped by the fact that de Forest didn't quite understand how his own invention worked.) He and the American division of the ruthless Marconi Company fought each other to a standstill: Marconi owned the anode-cathode Fleming valve, while de Forest owned the third electrode. Each needed the other, and neither was inclined to yield. The war offered some relief by turning

* Federal was one of the only places Litton could make the de Forest–style device without crossing AT&T or the Wall Street–financed White House–approved monopolists at the Radio Corporation of America (RCA), which now held the treasured triode license for radio (rather than telephone) functions.

radio communications into military infrastructure. The feds forced a sale of the foreign-owned Marconi subsidiary to the all-American General Electric and obviated the patents for the duration of fighting, forcing the firms into a temporary cartel to their common advantage.

After the war, commerce secretary Herbert Hoover brought the major players together to find a profitable solution for the consumer radio boom. At the chief's urging, in the early 1920s, GE licensed its radio IP (including the Fleming valve) to a new subsidiary company called the Radio Corporation of America (RCA) before making a deal with the telephone monopolists at AT&T (who had a license to de Forest's third 'ode) and the electronics manufacturers at Westinghouse. De Forest's biographer James A. Hijiya describes how the Audion's inventor became the industry's odd man out: "AT&T gave RCA the right to manufacture triodes; RCA gave the right to GE and Westinghouse; GE and Westinghouse made the triodes, put them in radios, and sold the radios to RCA; RCA sold the radios to the public; and nobody had to buy anything from the Radio Telephone & Telegraph Company of Lee de Forest."[2] With capital concentrated in the East, Hoover's model of organized capitalism wasn't always encouraging for West Coast inventor-entrepreneur types in the short term.

De Forest wasn't the only radio-age engineer who ended up surrendering his creation; the same story recurred around the country as the industry consolidated. In 1930, Heintz and Kaufman sold a controlling interest in their firm to Dollar Steamship, which used their technology to communicate among its shipping lines.[3] Founded by West Coast lumber baron Robert Dollar, the company capitalized on the trans-Pacific trade, and it probably didn't hurt that Dollar was friends with Bert Hoover, with whom he was appointed to the International Chamber of Commerce in 1921.[4] Those connections were worth less after Dollar's death, in 1932, and once FDR took over, the new regulatory apparatus shut down the independent Dollar radio transmitters, effectively ending H&K as an innovative concern through no fault of its founders. With RCA and AT&T splitting the domestic telecom market (and ITT taking international), there just wasn't always room for the West Coast upstarts. RCA tried to buy out Philo Farnsworth and his television in 1931, driving him into the arms of Philadelphia's Philco and ultimately ITT. In the early days of the radio age, the Bay Area's inventions tended to end up in the hands of litigious East Coast capital, one way or another. This early trauma still lurks in Silicon Valley's unconscious.

Figuring out how to maintain control of their inventions and the profits they yielded was an iterative process for the Bay Area's entrepreneurs and engineers, and that process selected for adventurous types. Consider Alexander M. Poniatoff, a Russian-born tinkerer who flew in the czar's air corps in World War I and then fought with the Whites against the Bolsheviks. Defeated, he retreated through Siberia to Shanghai. He made his way to Schenectady, New York, and a job with GE designing new electric equipment. But life as a cog in the East Coast corporate monopoly machine didn't appeal to the Russian flyboy, and he went out to California, where he got a job with the power monopoly, Pacific Gas & Electric. Start-up life appealed to Poniatoff even more, and in 1934 he offered to work on spec for a young local engineer named Tim Moseley, who had set up his own machine shop, called Dalmo. Electrification opened the door to electric gadgets, and America had a new appetite for harebrained schemes. Together Poniatoff and Moseley did commissioned electric work and tinkered with plans for beauty devices: Poniatoff successfully patented one that put waves in women's hair. But they ran into trouble with another device, their so-called motorshaver, and in 1939 a lawsuit brought by the comparatively well-capitalized Schick bankrupted the small firm.[5]

That could have been the end of the road for the Dalmo shop; such bouts of bad luck and accidental confrontations with East Coast corporations had ended similar start-ups. Like the gold rush merchants who could be swept away by a flood or burned up in a fire, early gadget entrepreneurs encountered big capital as an elemental force that threatened to wipe them off the face of the earth via acquisition or competition, whether in the market or in the courts. The war granted a temporary reprieve as intercapitalist squabbles took a back seat to building national power, but the end of the Great War was supposed to spell the end of war in general, and East Coast telecom monopolists took off with the postwar peace. Luckily for NorCal's new tech entrepreneurs, not everyone got the memo about World War I having been the very last war. Electronics inventors would soon become the world's most dangerous weapons, and California was extraordinarily well armed.

Radar Love

During the interwar period, a plane all by itself wasn't much more than a toy;
to do anything purposeful with it, you needed ways to navigate and communicate. From the beginning, planes relied on ground and onboard electronics
systems to guide them. These systems were collectively called avionics after
World War II, but the Bay was a national center for avionics before anyone
called it that. In 1927, Hawaiian pineapple colonist and proud Stanford dad
James D. Dole sponsored a flying contest between Oakland and Honolulu.
Heintz and Kaufman outfitted one competitor with an advanced short-wave
radio system originally designed for ships, allowing the pilots to remain in
constant contact. In this case the radios worked better than the aircraft, and
ground crews listened in horror to the final SOS of the *Dallas Spirit* as it went
into a fatal tailspin 600 miles from the shore.[6] Tragedy is part of innovation,
and the loss of the *Dallas Spirit* preceded the use of H&K shortwave systems
in adventures around the world, including trips to the North and South Poles,
which helped persuade Robert Dollar to use the firm when he wanted to set
up a permanent communications network across the Pacific. The burgeoning
Stanford radio milieu was the key to connecting land, sea, and sky.

In peacetime, the newest technology can be a threat to established players;
with large investments in existing products and processes, big capitalists often
find it cheaper and easier to squelch upstarts and their improvements rather
than incorporate their advances. In times of war, however, the state does well
to put a damper on such domestic rivalries in the collective national interest,
which is what happened with the Fleming valve and Audion patents during
World War I. The next world war, however, gave Motorshaver Moseley another
chance to make good. Five years after Dalmo's forced breakup, he went back
to Poniatoff. According to Poniatoff, Moseley asked the ex-pilot if he knew
anything about radar antennas because the navy was looking to buy a new
one to stick in warplanes. Poniatoff didn't. "Neither do I," replied Moseley,
"but the contract says the unit must be completed in 100 days, so you can't
waste time."[7] The legend is that they worked the 100 days straight, and at the
end they presented their prototype to the procurement committee, which had
already tentatively awarded the contract to a group of big firms led by GE
and Westinghouse. But somehow the Dalmo antenna worked better—much

better. On the monopolistic free market, there's a good chance that Tim and Alex would have been squished again.* But with American boys' lives at stake, the state chose to play it straight and went with Dalmo's design. Having failed to beat them, the oligopolists at Westinghouse offered to expand the dinky Dalmo into a joint venture and handle production. Tim Moseley saw the writing on the wall and took the deal, turning Dalmo into Dalmo Victor and turning himself into a serious military contractor virtually overnight. By the mid-1960s, the company produced nearly all the country's submarine antennas; it was the largest contributor of airborne and spaceborne antenna equipment as well, picking up where H&K left off.[8]

Moseley's finesse, along with the war's exigencies, allowed Dalmo to persist and grow where other Bay Area telecom entrepreneurs got chewed up in the monopoly gears of the interwar era. The gadget makers (Moseley was into his forties, Poniatoff in his fifties) hit the big time, which is why Poniatoff was surprised when Moseley asked him to quit right away. His plan was this: They knew their antenna design was about to go into production, and they knew it required the precision motors they created, which no one else had for sale. If the two of them spun off a precision-motor company, they could supply the joint venture, avoid turning into Westinghouse employees, and start building a new pool of equity. Moseley put in $25,000; Poniatoff put in $5,000 and agreed to run it. They split the company 50-50 but put Alexander's name on it: Ampex, for Alexander M. Poniatoff Excellence. Poniatoff moved into a different floor of the Dalmo Victor building, Dalmo Victor bought Ampex motors for its antennas, Ampex recruited from Stanford's engineering graduates, and the Motorshavers had a second company. (Poniatoff's first hire was a recent Stanford master's graduate named Myron Stolaroff, who will play a larger role in the story once an LSD trip changes his career trajectory and perhaps world history.)[9] By cleverly pursuing his self-interest, Tim Moseley made something with what the military-industrial complex made with him, and the Bay Area's tech ecosystem benefited. In the Hoover tradition, self-interest became community interest.

The Second World War allowed Moseley to make himself one of the

---

* That's what happened to H&K: Boeing dropped H&K's superior radios from their planes after dominant components supplier Western Electric asked them to.

region's first successful electronics hustlers, but not everyone in the milieu pursued the antifascist cause with the same business zeal. The area also had an altruistic bohemian streak, epitomized in another pilot-engineer pair, the brothers Russell and Sigurd Varian. Born just on either side of the dawning twentieth century, the Varian boys grew up between Palo Alto and the theosophist utopian community of Halcyon, to the south, where their parents were movement leaders. Russell and Sigurd both inherited a left-wing public-mindedness as well as an out-of-the-box way of thinking, though it initially led them in different directions. Russell worked hard to overcome a learning disability and complete bachelor's and master's degrees in physics at Stanford, only to be rejected from the PhD program. Disappointed but still holding good credentials, he got a job at Philo Farnsworth's San Francisco television lab. His brother Sigurd was less concerned with academic achievement, and he dropped out of California Polytechnic (located in San Luis Obispo, near Halcyon) to pursue a more glamorous life. He took flying lessons and got his hands on a decommissioned World War I plane, taking up work as one of the barnstorming pilot entertainers touring the country and performing stunts. Described as dashing and adventurous, the six-foot-four Sigurd got a job with Pan American Airways captaining flights to Mexico and Central America. He married Winifred Hogg, the daughter of the British consul in Veracruz, and was able to save a decent amount of money. That's when he called his brother Russell and quit his job.

Growing up, Russell and Sigurd always planned to open an "ideas factory," combining Russ's patient diligence and Sig's enthusiasm and mechanical talents. The plan was for Russ to develop technical knowledge at school while Sig rustled up some money and brainstormed ideas. Though they were in their thirties, the younger brother, Sig, hadn't given up on the concept, and now he had some money and some ideas. Even better, he had a purpose. The later years of the interwar era brought the real militarization of the airplane as fascist governments synthesized flight and explosives to create the bomber. Unlike infantrymen, pilots could and did fly over front lines, indiscriminately targeting urban infrastructure and civilians. In Spain, Franco's forces (reinforced by Hitler's planes) bombarded Republican territory, most memorably captured in Pablo Picasso's lamentation for the city of Guernica. In Ethiopia, Mussolini's air corps sprayed wave after wave of poison gas. For a politically progressive pilot such as Sigurd, the harbingers of another war were horrific. Like most socialist-minded Americans, he expected a second confrontation with Germany, and looking down from his Pan Am clipper, Captain Varian saw disaster. He knew he was invisible to ground defenses when flying through clouds at night, and if he could bomb the Panama Canal, he knew the Nazi air forces would be able to do so as well. Even worse, if Hitler set up a base in the Western Hemisphere, long-range bombers could turn the whole country into Guernica. He was coming home, Sig told Russ, and they had to figure out a way to see planes at night. Everything was at stake. Russ quit his job, too, and the two of them moved back to Halcyon, where they set up shop.

Halcyon was a lot of things, but an experimental physics lab it was not. The Varian brothers had some ideas about how to proceed, but they needed facilities and tools that weren't available in the utopian community and they couldn't afford to buy them with the few thousand dollars of Sig's that had to serve as their bankroll. Russell reached out to his former Stanford roommate William Webster "Big Bill" Hansen, who was by then a professor in the physics department.* He was working on a resonating cavity—an empty box that pinged high-frequency waves back and forth, creating an electric field. Because the electrons appeared to dance as they moved, the young experimenters called the device a rhumbatron after the rumba dance craze. (When the stodgy physics department head sent them to the classics department for a solid Greek name, the professor replied that on the contrary, rhumbatron was a perfect name, from the Greek ρόμβος or *rhombus*, meaning "motion" or "spinning." Blessed by the Greeks, the name stuck.) The Varians thought they could use the rhumbatron to generate a controlled high-frequency "microwave" beam, which they could then send through clouds and bounce off enemy aircraft at night. Based on the ping's reflected characteristics, an operator could "see" where the plane was and respond accordingly, with ground or air defenses. Like little kids formally requesting a sleepover so as to continue playing into the night, Hansen and the Varians asked the Stanford administration if maybe they could find a place for them to continue their work on campus. The department—still run by David Webster, the man who rejected Russ's

---

* Not to be confused with California strike leader "Big Bill" Hammett, or, for that matter, IWW cofounder "Big Bill" Haywood.

PhD application—made a rather ungenerous offer: The Varians could use the facilities as unpaid researchers for one year in exchange for half the royalties from any patent. As for funds, the university could offer $100 toward materials.[10] Undeterred, the brothers accepted. They lived off Sig's savings and Palo Alto's fruit trees.

It wasn't long before they made progress. The young master Charles Litton tutored the underschooled but manually capable Sig on tube making, and he took to it quickly. (Litton also helped them make sure they didn't tread on de Forest's Audion patent, by then securely in the exclusive hands of the telecom oligopoly.) A plan to adapt a Farnsworth tube fell by the wayside as Russell Varian got hit with a stroke of genius: Pumping a stream of electrons through one charged rhumbatron generated bunches, as the constant stream met an undulating wave of encouragement and discouragement. Those pulses then got the next rhumbatron dancing as they transferred bursts of energy into the second cavity, like a wheel of fists against a dangling speed bag. The result was an amplifying oscillator that generated stable waves on the high-frequency microwave spectrum. Within a couple of months they had the major issues figured out, and Sig built their first prototype. After all sorts of tinkering, they flipped the switch and pulled out an old "cat's whisker" radio detector, and detect it did. Their math worked, and the device oscillated as the dual rhumbatrons danced. The room was full to the brim with 13-centimeter waves, leaving the Varian team bathed in their invisible success. Even Webster, the department chair, was thrilled, appropriating another $1,000 for materials and readying the team to talk patent. But first he sent them back to Hermann Fränkel in the classics department for another Greek name. Fränkel offered κλύζω or *klyzo*, a word that describes the action of the ocean's waves against the beach, an answer so concise and beautiful that it has come to exemplify collaboration between science and the humanities in the decades since. They called their gadget the *klystron*.

Today, when a team of Stanford physicists invents a new device that suggests improved combat performance, there's no need to contact the military because the military is almost always already there, having funded the research in the first place. But though the West is now deeply associated with weapons technology, in the pre–World War II era the feds still considered the area a bit of a backwater, and Palo Alto was a deluxe Hooverville in a Roosevelt country.

Besides, real science got done in the corporate labs and storied universities back East. The obvious peacetime use of the technology was a blind-landing system for pilots, but Sig was determined to get the tech into the army's hands before America had a need to use it. Unable to interest any military contacts, he approached the Oakland office of the Department of Commerce's relatively new aeronautics bureau, hoping someone there might at least understand the klystron's potential and move it up the ladder. No one there got it, either, but between that move and the buzz Sig was creating in the Bay's pilot community, the Bureau of Air Commerce gave him a call back. They happened to have two men arrived from the East Coast who would understand the device, and they were traveling with a representative from the Sperry Gyroscope Company, the avionics division of Sperry Aeronautics based in Long Island, where the Daniel Guggenheim Fund for the Promotion of Aeronautics financed a laboratory. Could they get a presentation? The cash-starved team agreed, and they duly impressed the visitors with Sig's prototype. The Commerce men offered to buy some klystrons to power an experimental blind-landing system, but the Varian team didn't have any to sell. The man from Sperry, however, had a different proposal.

Sperry already produced, among many other things, an air-defense machine that bounced waves off enemy planes to locate them at night. It was called a searchlight, and it used waves in the visible spectrum, pinging a beam at the sky and back to the waiting light receptors. What they had was a giant flashlight—the light receptors were, of course, eyes. The klystron suggested a step up, from the biomechanical to the electronic, and Sperry was interested. The company offered Stanford a deal: it would sponsor klystron research at the university in exchange for an exclusive license to the technology. Stanford, the Varians, and Big Bill Hansen split a 5 percent net royalty on the sales. From the beginning, the relationship with Sperry was uneasy. A Sperry gambit to passive-aggressively buy out the Varians collapsed when the convert Webster promised the corporate goons that the entire klystron team would resign in protest. But Sperry's scientists still didn't take the inventor brothers—who didn't have a single PhD between them—very seriously. At the beginning of 1939, Stanford announced the klystron to the public, focusing on the blind-landing applications, though the proto-radar function was clear to anyone who could read between the lines. (One newspaper headlined the Associated

Press wire story with ELECTRONS DO RHUMBA, GIVE SAVANTS NEW TYPE OF RADIO.)[11] It was equally clear to the klystron team that Sperry wasn't going to let them run the show much longer. Once again East Coast capital was a menace to California inventors.

The outbreak of war gave Sperry executives a good excuse to close up shop and move everyone back East, which is what they did. Not only were they shuttering the facilities and bringing the Varian team with them, they also outsourced elements to other conglomerates, including ITT and GE. The Varians came to New York with the whole crew except Webster. California commune boys Russ and Sig bristled at the East Coast corporate atmosphere and looked forward to their Best Coast return. Regarding the weirdos with the extra-thick eyebrows and no terminal degrees, Sperry corporate was also counting the days. But their original plan was a good one, and in 1940 the klystron became part of the Allied arsenal. Unbeknownst to the Varian team, the military in collaboration with the Brits already had the magnetron — ground-based electronic radar — but the klystron was high-powered for its weight, and unlike what they already had, it was designed to fit inside a plane. Only a few years after the friends Sig, Russ, and Bill set off in earnest, their device helped the antifascist alliance win the electronic arms race with the Axis powers and beat the fearsome Nazi air force. The Panama Canal remained intact, as did the continental United States (with the exception of some Japanese transoceanic autonomous balloon attacks). To turn the klystron into a battlefield weapon, however, it took another team from Palo Alto.

When last I mentioned Frederick Terman, it was as a subject of his father Lewis Terman's experiment into childhood genius. Unsurprisingly, given Lewis's ideas about the heritability of intelligence and his own lofty opinion of himself, Fred's test results showed the highest level of promise. It was in observing baby Fred's first encounters with the world that Lewis became really interested in children's thinking in the first place — Fred was the original child genius, the *ur-wunderkind*. Lewis was obsessed with his scientific practice, and he kept Fred home from school until he was nine years old, preferring the controlled application of his work to the early childhood education Palo Alto had to offer at the time. But Fred was growing up in the Lee de Forest era of Federal Telegraph, and the air hummed with invention — waves floating for anyone to grab, like fruit on the campus trees. Lewis was increasingly busy with his tests and grad students, and Fred was free to run around with other faculty kids and experiment with the latest radio electronics.* At the age of thirteen he entered the first graduating class at Palo Alto High School, but he got his most important education from the book *Wireless Telegraph Construction for Amateurs* (checked out from the Stanford library) and his own fooling around.[12] He was an early ham, and he built a Morse code transponder in his bedroom. Fred found willing companions in the neighborhood boys, including fellow radio enthusiast Herbert Hoover Jr. Like most of his classmates, the boy Terman enrolled at (tuition-free) Stanford, just across the street from Palo Alto High School. In accordance with his father's theories about accelerating gifted students he graduated early, starting at the university halfway through his sixteenth year, attending from his conveniently located family home on campus.

Raised to adulthood in town, Fred Terman was a direct product of Palo Alto. After he finished his first Stanford degree—in chemistry, at the age of twenty—he upgraded from ham to pro, working for a summer at Federal Telegraph before taking another Stanford degree, a master's in electrical engineering. His enrollment coincided with World War I mobilization, and the draft age fell to eighteen in the summer of 1918, two months after Fred's birthday—this gives a personal spin to Lewis Terman's fears that the army was going to waste particularly promising young men in the trenches. David Starr Jordan and Stanford's new president, Ray Lyman Wilbur, both had the same fear. The university applied for a Students' Army Training Corps unit, and Fred enrolled. Once again he remained on campus, pretty much the only home he'd ever known, as its functions stretched to accommodate and protect Fred and other promising boys like him. When the war ended, in November, he mustered out after one quarter of training, unsacrificed. His second Stanford degree completed, Fred readied himself for doctoral study. With his strong record and genetic pedigree, he was a shoo-in anywhere in the country, and Lewis nudged him toward the best: the Massachusetts Institute of Technology, MIT. He figured a terminal degree from the top technical school in the East would ultimately make Fred more attractive to Stanford than a third certificate from his home institution, a prediction he was qualified to make as

---

* George Branner, son of geologist John Casper Branner, had been toying around with radio gear in Palo Alto since 1907. C. Stewart Gillmor, *Fred Terman at Stanford: Building a Discipline, a University, and Silicon Valley* (Stanford University Press, 2004), 23.

a department head. Every year that Fred stuck on the genius path, the further he confirmed his father's theories. By the mid-1920s, they looked very good.

In that era, the new science of electrical engineering was about electrification: how to create, maintain, and improve a national network of electricity production and distribution. After all, the California gadget tinkerers needed to plug in to something. Terman distinguished himself at MIT working on the properties of transmission lines under the young and respected engineer-entrepreneur Vannevar Bush, whom he watched spin research on rectifying household current into an electrical appliance company called Raytheon. Three days after his twenty-fourth birthday, Fred Terman received his doctorate in electrical engineering from MIT, only the eighth person to do so. Still a genius, and still not much more than a child, considering how sheltered his life had been to that point, Fred was in demand. Both his alma maters offered him teaching jobs, but a bout of tuberculosis tipped the scale toward the West, as it did for his father. He returned home where he was put on bedrest, and he used the time to continue reading and thinking.

Lying in bed, Fred synthesized his teenage vacuum-tube radio experience and his MIT education in circuit design to establish the principles of radio engineering, a subject whose seminal textbook he soon wrote. When he was well enough to assume his first Stanford teaching duties he was thrilled to find that the single student in his advanced tutorial was none other than his childhood friend Herbert Hoover Jr., a senior at the school, and together they returned to their ham origins, turning Hoover's dorm into a makeshift radio station. Soon Fred was back in fighting shape and helping coordinate the still-growing radio scene from his office at Stanford, consulting for all the appropriate companies and helping guide the careers of talented students such as Charles Litton, Dave Packard, and Bill Hewlett. Led by Terman — the only member of the faculty with a PhD in the subject and thus "senior" despite his youth — the Stanford electrical engineering department became the solder connecting the regional industry's sundry parts. He took over and finagled increased support for the school's communications lab, assisted along the way by his father, who from 1925 on donated some of his testing royalties to support his son's scholarship. In 1939, it was Fred who explained to the Associated Press how the klystron worked, even though it was a project of Webster's physics department rather than the electrical engineering faculty.

Lewis Terman's work on child geniuses and bionomics writ large was about national resources: intelligence is one, and it takes the form of people. Fred Terman was a sharp tool, and he belonged to the United States of America. He did his job, advancing science and industry, starting with his hometown. (Lewis, recall, ensured his son's future genetic contribution by setting him up with a high-IQ—and, according to Fred's biographer, "vivacious"—psychology grad student.)[13] But after Vernon Kellogg's visit to Germany, bionomics took a martial turn. German imperial neo-Darwinism was unappeasable, and the country's leaders were determined to prove their national-racial superiority on the field of battle. Against the totalizing German state, the United States deployed its heroic individuals, not on horseback—where, Jordan complained, "the clown could shoot down the hero"—but from within secure facilities at home, wielding intelligence to increase lethality and assure triumph. Fred was a product of bionomist thought, and he was a weapon, not because of anything he learned in the training corps but because wars were to be decided by scientists and engineers. He barely avoided World War I, and three weeks after the Japanese attack on Pearl Harbor, Fred Terman's country finally called him up. But he wasn't heading for Manila or Paris; they called him back to Cambridge, Massachusetts, to one of those secure facilities from which countries fight modern wars.

The Radio Research Lab (RRL) at Harvard was a spin-off of MIT's Radiation Laboratory—confusingly, the latter was nicknamed the Rad Lab, a name that could easily apply to either facility. Leading the charge to militarize American civilian science was Terman adviser and Raytheon cofounder Vannevar Bush, who successfully proposed a National Defense Research Committee (NDRC) to FDR the summer before Japan's not-so-surprise attack. A collaboration between large defense contractors, New England's top universities, and the federal government, Bush's NDRC was the draft outline for the era of Big Science, but first it had to beat the Axis powers. Terman's job at the RRL was in the vanguard of the electronic arms race, devising countermeasures and counter-countermeasures to outwit German and Japanese engineers. Fred brought a grip of Stanford's top young guns with him, and at Harvard they devised ways to jam and distract enemy radar. These projects had goofy names like Tuba (a giant ground-based jammer set up on the English coast and pointed toward the Continent) and Carpet (an air-based jammer), but they were critically important to the war effort. Working with British scientists, the RRL enjoyed its biggest success with the development of "chaff" ("window" in the UK)—bunches of metal strips calculated to misdirect air defenses when dropped from a plane. Terman traveled to England to coordinate a U.S.-British team that deployed their devices as part of high-stakes operations. Their ultimate test came with the American invasion of Normandy on D-Day.

To prevent a bloodbath, the Allies needed to keep the Nazis confused about where in France they planned to land. That battle was fought in the electronics arena, on the radio and microwave spectra. With precise calculation they deployed their planes, which dropped so much chaff that the German radar showed incoming air and sea "ghost" fleets. Carefully, they used just enough jamming to make it look real without using so much as to fully camouflage their own spoof. Wave equations structured the battlespace on both sides, and once the Nazis bought the feints, they searched high and low for enemies who weren't there. Cut off from further instructions via jamming and unable to locate a target, the Luftwaffe drifted aimlessly in the wrong place. Once the Germans committed to chasing the ploy, the Allies hit the landing zone with a giant "Elephant Cigar" jammer. The series of moves was so effective that allegedly the first signal the Germans got that the invasion force was coming to Normandy was auditory, because the only receivers left working were human ears. But by the time they heard the ships coming, it was way too late. The Allies didn't know just how successful the electronic countermeasures had been until after the war, when the team went in to examine the German records and interview German scientists. What they found was staggering: After an early Nazi decision to rely on electronics for antiaircraft targeting, the countermeasures left their tech no better than the human eye, forcing them to resort to visual aiming. And because the radar fight was crucial, the Germans unsuccessfully redirected so many of their scientific resources that American investigators concluded, "The countermeasures program had nullified the German antiaircraft fire and the entire scientific program in general"—pretty good for a team from California.[14] By winning the electronics arms race, they reduced the enemy to its human senses.

Lewis Terman was right: A scientific approach to cultivating exceptional children's intelligence helped the Allies win the war for the future of the planet. Though he didn't encounter them all as subjects, Lewis had been looking in the right place: a milieu of brilliant electronics engineers raised in Northern California in the first decades of the twentieth century. His son Fred took up the mantle, communicating among his students, colleagues, friends: Bill Hansen at Sperry, Charles Litton at ITT (then making magnetron tubes, a contract Fred made sure Litton got), Bill Hewlett at the U.S. Army Signal Corps.[15] However, Fred Terman does not seem to have kept in touch with the one fellow genius test subject who was perhaps the closest thing to a peer he had in the military-industrial complex, another golden boy from Palo Alto who was forged into a powerful scientific instrument for the Allied war effort: William Shockley Jr.

When war research took over the American scientific community in 1939, Shockley was working at Bell Labs, trying to figure out why his model of a semiconducting transistor wasn't working in real life—more on that in the next section. With his MIT PhD, Shockley was considered a bright light in Bell's solid-state physics group, but in 1940 he shifted to militaryish work. Uranium was solid-state, too, and he researched that at Bell until 1942, when he got a call from his MIT mentor, Phil Morse at the Rad Lab.[16] Morse was recruiting for the Anti-Submarine Warfare Operations Research Group, and he wanted Shockley to be research director with a roving commission. He could do whatever he wanted, wherever he wanted, as long as it was blowing up Nazi submarines. The gig's strictures appealed to Shockley, and Bell Labs loaned him to the military, not for the last time. He immediately proved himself uniquely suited for the job when he solved his first problem in just a few days: Anti-sub depth charges worked when dropped from ships, but the same charges failed when dropped from planes. They exploded, but always harmlessly. The problem, he determined, was that the charges were rigged to explode at 75 feet under, which was great for destroyers targeting diving U-boats but too deep for bombers targeting submarines on the surface. The plane charges were reset to 35 feet, and within two months they increased the number of successful anti-submarine attacks by a factor of five.[17] Shockley fixed it.

Once he got in the groove, Shockley was using data analysis to crack the war's secrets. Unlike Terman he didn't have electronic help; the Allies' few vacuum-tube computers were otherwise occupied, as you'll read in the next section. But Shockley was a whiz with paper and pencil, and he stocked his team with actuaries. Together they created the field known as operations research, a term Shockley invented over the course of their work. By breaking problems down to mathematical questions, they reduced the war to a series of brain-teasers. Higher-ups had to shush the group when, looking to improve submarine targeting, they found the coordinate guesses were already too consistently accurate to be guesses—no one else knew that the Allies had broken the German codes. Other answers surrendered themselves: Fast bombers were less accurate than slower planes; cross-referencing meteorological data revealed that Axis bombers weren't using radar to target Allied boats; big convoys were less likely than small convoys to lose ships. Shockley was in demand, traveling the conflict's backstage from England to the Pacific front on a special pass from the secretary of war, which allowed him to board any commercial plane he wanted. The army shifted him to strategic bombing, and he reformed pilot training to teach airmen how to use their electronic tools. Everything worked better under Bill's genius pencil.

By the closing months of the war, Shockley was promoted to expert consultant to the secretary of war, working directly with the commanding general of the newly organized air force, Hap Arnold. His job as he understood it was to conclude the conflict as efficiently as possible, and in that capacity he employed terms like pay, cheapness, and profit, which made sense when he was comparing monetary costs, but his preferred measure was man-month. A bionomist to the core, Shockley knew that a society's central resource was its citizenry; everything could be reduced to months of generic labor. When he did the math, he found that the bombing of Germany hadn't really been so effective: in terms of man-months, building the bombs cost the Brits around a third of the damage they did to the Nazis. The numbers in the Pacific were even worse. But Shockley retrained the radar bombing crews, and in the spring of 1945 they began night raids with napalm and white phosphorus munitions, burning Japan's cities. These attacks included the March Tokyo sortie that torched half the city to the ground in the war's single deadliest night. Shockley's analysis that summer included a five-page memo titled "Proposal for Increasing the Scope of Casualties Studies." In it he projected that, in order to be successful, a mainland invasion needed to kill 5 to 10 million Japanese and that such an invasion would lose Americans at a ratio close to one to ten—one American for every ten Japanese killed, an unacceptably high number.[18] Shockley wasn't officially read in on what was going on at Los Alamos, but there's no doubt he was sufficiently informed to suggest that command should consider other, more efficient options, knowing full well what that meant. Two weeks after he sent his memo, America dropped an atomic bomb on Hiroshima. Shockley was awarded the country's highest civilian honor, the Medal for Merit, in 1946, a couple of years before they got around to giving one to his hometown rival Fred Terman.

The Joint Chiefs were thrilled with Shockley's work and the whole operations research concept, and they told Bell Labs as much, warning that they would probably want to borrow him again in the future. Before he went back to the transistor, Shockley wrote one more memo, the ominous "On the Economics of Atomic Bombing," for a Vannevar Bush working group on nuclear weapons that became the Atomic Energy Commission.[19] He opens by talking about the restriction of proportional war, in which any side must spend man-months roughly equivalent to the months destroyed on the other side. "This type of limitation," he writes, "has been largely overcome by strategic bombing," which, properly applied, does five months' worth of damage for every month spent. He figured that atomic bombs were 10 to 100 times as efficient. "This cheapness is a new factor and indicates that an unparalleled loss of human resources will accompany future wars." Following the idea to its logical conclusion, he writes, "leads to the picture of one man being able to unleash forces which would destroy the world." Still, he concludes with that big number: Given 100x efficiency, 500, maybe 600 man-months are destroyed for every one spent. At that ratio, you could rule the world with a button. His boss, Hap Arnold—now promoted to fourth in the military's hierarchy, fifth if you count Roosevelt—was impressed enough that he had Shockley expand on the memo and publish it under Arnold's name in a new volume of leading perspectives on the atomic age titled One World or None.[20] In between pro forma pleas for world peace, Shockley-as-Arnold laid out the postwar plan: strategic air bases around the world, dispersed weapons, mutually assured destruction before it was called that. What we needed was a bunch of R & D spending, especially on "pilotless" weapons similar to Germany's V-series rockets. Oh, and we shouldn't "trammel" scientists with security regulations, Shockley couldn't keep himself from adding. Whether he realized it then or not, he would play an important role in developing those pilotless weapons. From then on, Bill did his best to work under his own name, the one he shared with his father.

I would say the Stanford eugenics project was immeasurably useful for America and the Allies in World War II, but I'm sure Shockley could pull out some numbers. The Palo Alto System completed its second round of human production: Hoover and other miners tore open the earth, now the radio boys had lit it on fire. To be fair, the Nazis did start the fight, and the California contingent in particular was not excited to be fighting Japan, the Pacific's other colonial power. Stanford's bionomic theorists developed respect for the country's racial character, and the university cultivated good relations with imperial Japan's ruling class. David Starr Jordan cofounded the Japan Society in 1905 amid California's rising anti-Japanese sentiment. He lobbied for peace between the two nations and had a particular interest in Japan's fish, which he helped catalog on a trip to the country. He shared perspectives with the Japanese ruling class: Neither thought much of the Koreans or Chinese or, for that matter, Japanese peasants.[21] He didn't live to see his bionomic dreams come true—the best of his students realizing their potential on Tokyo. But his protégé, Yamato Ichihashi, did. The Stanford graduate made headlines when Jordan appointed him in 1908: JAPANESE BECOMES STANFORD TEACHER.[22] A first. Decades later, from inside an American prison camp, Ichihashi waited for reports as his students firebombed his hometown.

The Internment and Expulsion of the California Japanese

Thanks to the combination of its location, historical timing, and first president's affinities, Stanford has always had students of Japanese origin—even though Palo Alto had only a handful of Japanese residents, most of whom were domestic servants. The son of a downwardly mobile ex-samurai, Yamato Ichihashi followed his eldest brother to town in the mid-1890s, with a detour through San Francisco's public education system. He graduated from Lowell High School in 1902—avoiding the controversy over segregating Japanese students in "Oriental" schools by a few years—and was admitted to Stanford in 1903. In a climate of rising Japanophobia, Jordan took a shine to Ichihashi, who with his aristocratic bearing conformed to the university president's idea of the Japanese as the whites of Asia. Though Stanford was a young institution, Jordan was a powerful man for a scholar to have in his corner, especially after he seized control of the university. Jordan encouraged the immigrant Ichihashi to pursue an academic career in the United States. After graduation, a rejection from Columbia kept him at Stanford, where he received his master's in economics, studying with (among others) Thorstein Veblen. The economics faculty gave him work after graduation, conducting interviews with Japanese immigrants in California for a congressional study. His interaction with fishermen, sugar beet farmers, and asparagus pickers doesn't seem to have inculcated much sympathy for the working class in the self-important young man, whose identity was based in large part on his separation from such people. In 1910, he moved to Cambridge to complete his PhD at Harvard.

Like many Stanford graduates over the following decades sent East to mature, Ichihashi longed to return to California. After completing his coursework and beginning his dissertation on Japanese immigration to the United States (based in part on his postgraduate work at Stanford), he sent a letter to his mentor, Jordan, asking if his alma mater would consider employing him to teach a couple of classes while he finished his dissertation. The president encouraged Ichihashi to head back, and he stayed in San Francisco while he waited for the job to come through. Jordan's plan was to have prominent Japanese businessmen he met on a recent tour of the country endow a spot for Ichihashi at Stanford as a bridge between the nations, spreading mutual understanding close to the center of American anti-Japanese sentiment. The day after California's governor signed the Alien Land Law of 1913, prohibiting Asians from owning farms, the Japanese consul in San Francisco alerted Jordan that the money was ready. Ostensibly the money was from a bank and a steamship company, but it was likely from the Japanese government. Jordan and the rest of the Stanford administration don't seem to have cared, and even if he knew it's hard to imagine the president—who was politically, ideologically, and even socially aligned with the Japanese ruling clique—being truly upset. Ichihashi published pro-Japanese essays and tracts, distinguishing his countrymen from the Chinese, whom the author readily agreed Americans should view as inferior. The Japanese "businessmen" continued to re-up his contract through Stanford, which happily accepted the money. In 1921, they negotiated a larger sum from his patrons—over half a million dollars in 2022 money—and Stanford's trustees appointed Ichihashi to the university's very first endowed chair.[23]

While Jordan was thrilled about how everything worked out, the FBI wasn't so sure. In the wake of World War I, Ichihashi assisted Japanese delegations in Europe, doing translation, and perhaps—American intelligence feared—something more. In his introduction to Ichihashi's internment diaries, scholar Gordon Chang strongly implies that, while in Paris for an arms-reduction conference, Ichihashi was directly involved in a Japanese plot to acquire plans for a new weapon from the American inventor Peter Cooper Hewitt. After Hewitt threw Ichihashi out of his apartment at the Ritz Paris, the inventor (who was vice president of the civilian Naval Consulting Board) got sick and promptly died.* Hewitt's widow also refused to sell the plans to Ichihashi, and when she discovered that he had booked a ticket on the same boat back to America as she did, she notified the U.S. embassy and the navy that she feared for her life. The navy was convinced he was trying to steal the plans and kept the documents in Paris. On board, intelligence agencies jockeyed for position, British agents surrounding Hewitt's widow and Americans stalking Ichihashi in a scenario right out of a screwball comedy. The affair concluded without further incident, and the professor resumed his work, albeit under increased state suspicion.

In the following years, Ichihashi played an important role in Japanese-American diplomacy, helping negotiate agreements that forestalled conflict between the nations by foregrounding common interests among their elites. But though some in Japan clearly saw Ichihashi as an asset ("an effective agent who is supported by the Imperial Government to engage in indirect propaganda," as one former minister described him—internally, of course), others may have viewed him as overly westernized and compromised by his life abroad.[24] As parochial forces gathered power, his usefulness decreased, and he seems to have ceased any direct work for the empire, continuing as a Japanese-American academic under his own ideological steam, though the FBI continued to track his movements.[25] In the 1930s, his support for his home country was enough to get him in trouble with the campus community, where Chinese students outnumbered Japanese and turned the school's attention to imperial atrocities. "I felt as though I was being exposed as a criminal, trapped among accusers, and at the mercy of them all," recalls Noboru Shirai,

---

* Perhaps Ichihashi really was Jordan's protégé!

one of Stanford's 22 Japanese students at the time and one of only four issei (first-generation immigrants, born in Japan) on campus (as opposed to nisei — second-generation, their American-born children). "I tried to make myself as inconspicuous as possible so they would not notice me."[26] But the Japanese government wasn't making it easy to stay neutral. As the militarists set about conquering the Pacific, the local Japan Society converted itself into a fundraising front for the army. Unwilling to root against his home country in a war and at the same time not eager to defend the country's merciless attack on Nanking, Shirai was stuck. That one of his issei classmates definitely *was* a spy — a haughty aeronautical engineer named "Omori," who didn't go to class or hide his rank in the Imperial Japanese Army — didn't help Shirai or other Stanford community members of Japanese ancestry stay low-key.

Unsure if he could rely on Americans to hire him in the future, even with his Stanford degree, Shirai considered heading back to Japan in the late 1930s, as most of his classmates planned to do, whether they liked it or not. Another classmate, Kay Yamakawa, graduated with highest honors from Stanford's elite electrical engineering program in 1939 but couldn't find a single job in the U.S. radio industry.[27] He ended up relying on connections for a disappointing academic assistant position in Tokyo. But when Shirai pitched the idea of repatriation to some progressive-minded Japanese friends on a visit to the East Coast, they warned him against it. Better to be discriminated against in the United States than to die in a stupid war for the imperial ultra-right faction. Professor Ichihashi (about whom Shirai had mixed feelings) agreed with the conclusion if not the logic, and got him an assistant position in the history department. The two were the last issei men left on campus who weren't service workers for whites, and Ichihashi believed that if anyone would be spared whatever was coming it would be him, a full professor and personal friend of the university's president — who, recall, happened to be the former secretary of the interior. Unlike Shirai, Ichihashi was willing to defend Japan's occupation of Manchuria and the archipelago's other expansionist designs. It was simply, he argued (to boos) during a campus debate with his Chinese colleague Shau Wing Chan, a Monroe Doctrine for the Pacific to protect the region from communists. Surely in Hoover's town we could all agree on that?

A vision of Japan as the Pacific's anticommunist anchor appealed to the White House after the war, but December 7, 1941, answered any outstanding questions about immediate relations between the two countries. Ichihashi offered Wilbur his resignation, which the president rejected, offering a paid sabbatical instead. Ichihashi still had his powerful friends' support, but this time—as Lewis Terman discovered—there weren't to be any exceptions. In February, President Roosevelt authorized the War Department to designate security areas from which to exclude anyone of Japanese ancestry. On Saturday, May 23, Yamato Ichihashi and his wife, Kei, were notified to bring only what they could carry to the local Japanese-language school the following Tuesday. Like so many people around the world caught up in the war, 144 deportees from Palo Alto clutched their belongings and faced the fearful unknown at the mercy of a dehumanizing state.[28]

The Ichihashis were headed for a waystation in San Jose, and then to Tule Lake, where they were held until the American government said otherwise. Ichihashi's internment diaries and Shirai's memoir are surprisingly conflicted. Sometimes the food is better than expected, sometimes worse. Sometimes the whites are kinder than expected, sometimes more inconsiderate. Ichihashi works himself into an informal leadership position, but he's careful to draw his own lines about his cooperation: He won't do anything that could be interpreted as aiding the U.S. military, and he won't teach below his station as a full professor at Stanford University. In his diaries and letters, he is equally frustrated with his guards and his fellow internees, resenting the illogic of any system that views him and them similarly. Among the camp's most deplored aspects is the effect "communistic" living was having, dismantling family discipline and class distinction. Kei (who had already left him once for a substantial amount of time) drifted from his command. His son, Woodrow, joined a jazz band against his father's strong objection. Still, Ichihashi's influence didn't count for nothing, and he and Kei were allowed to leave early for an open-door camp in Colorado. Shirai, no security threat in the slightest, was kept at Tule Lake for the duration, thanks to his immigration status.

If Yamato Ichihashi had been strategic, he could have arranged for a teaching position outside the restricted area and spent the war in exile at an East Coast university. But he relished his life in Palo Alto, and he resisted all attempts to permanently settle him somewhere else. When the Japanese government included him on a list for a proposed prisoner swap, he spurned the offer, not out of American patriotism—surely this was a nadir in his experience of that particular feeling—but because he didn't want to give up on Stanford yet. He wrote to his best friend and fellow faculty member, Payson Treat, that Treat was right to deny a rumor that Ichihashi planned to repatriate after the war. Still, he wasn't sure he could still live in dignity in California. "Naturally we need not stay in a place we are not wanted; unlike Jews, we have our native-land, of which we are still citizens whose rights will be protected and respected. Old as I am, I am not yet a helpless creature, and I will not be a beggar or even an object of charity, for I am certain of my ability to earn enough to support my family," he wrote to Treat nearly a year after he was forced from his house. "I cannot and will not be content to exist in a place I am not wanted."[29] He wanted to go *home* to Palo Alto, not just back.

Japan's protection extended beyond the territory; the imperial government held American prisoners as well, and U.S. officials were worried that gross mistreatment in the internment camps would be felt by their own boys abroad. Tule Lake internees voted to invite camp inspection from a representative of neutral (fascist) Spain. (When two communists objected on political grounds, pro-Axis internees beat them into the hospital; Ichihashi implies they deserved it for snitching on pro-imperial Japanese to the Americans before internment.) Pro-imperial internees thought of themselves as prisoners of war, sometimes requesting that status. Left-wing and progressive internees—such as Shuji Matsui, a victim of the Tule Lake beating—took up the struggle on the inside, despite having been betrayed by the Americans and left at the mercy of their right-wing countrymen. It's hard to imagine supporting a government that is currently holding you in a concentration camp based on your race, and yet some did, not out of fear or complacency but out of deeply seated political commitment.

The truth was, left-wing California Japanese were not joining the American war effort against imperial Japan: The Americans were joining the left-wing California Japanese in *their* war effort against imperial Japan. As I mentioned above, a number of important Japanese dissidents fled political repression at home and moved to California in the 50 years prior, including Kōtoku Shūsui and his respectful rival Sen Katayama, founder of the Japanese Communist Party. While David Starr Jordan was off shaking hands with the emperor and categorizing fish, American police were rounding up Japanese leftists and shipping them back as undesirable aliens to face imperial justice. Domestic antifascists were, of course, enemies of the state, and thousands were held in Japanese jails, according to the fiery rhetoric of San Mateo comrade Hoko Hideo Ikeda. WE MUST EVACUATE, he telegraphed to the funeral of San Francisco labor legend Tom Mooney in 1942 after racist restrictions prohibited his attendance, BUT WHEREVER WE GO WE WILL CONTINUE TO FIGHT THE FASCISTS.[30] The LAPD Red Squads targeted Japanese antiwar protesters as they staged a sympathy demonstration outside the Chinese consulate. When a Japanese training ship docked in Los Angeles in 1929, communists distributed anti-militarist flyers to cadets; the Red Squads seized them back. American elites had more in common with their friends in the Japanese elite than with Japanese labor organizers, and they never forgot that.

Consider the case of Karl Yoneda, who helped lead the San Francisco longshoremen's strike in 1934 by persuading Japanese workers not to scab. He left Japan in 1926 to avoid being drafted into the army, and at the docks he organized pickets of war materials headed to Japan. On December 16, 1938, leftist workers including Yoneda joined a California Chinese picket at the San Francisco piers and talked the stevedores into leaving the ships.* Under the banner STOP JAPANESE AGGRESSION!, the interracial labor group held the empty boats for four days, making national headlines and drawing praise from Japanese-American peace groups. The San Francisco authorities (who, recall, fought a pitched battle with the longshoremen only a handful of years earlier) informed their Japanese counterparts about Yoneda, and imperial cops harassed his mother out of her home in Hiroshima. When the FBI picked up Yoneda in 1942, he was loading 16-inch cannonballs onto a ship bound for Manila, and in his pocket he carried a telegram to FDR on behalf of the 150 readers of his small political magazine, *Doho*, pledging their support to DEFEAT THE VICIOUS MILITARY FASCISTS OF JAPAN. The agents tossed him in a cell with other leaders of the Japanese community, one of whom pointed out the cell window and yelled, "Wait and see, the Japanese Imperial Navy will soon sail into the bay and free all of us here, except some of those Nisei, especially Yoneda."[31] The

---

* The action was, in a historical rhyme, 165 years to the day after the Boston Tea Party. Karl G. Yoneda, *Ganbatte: Sixty-Year Struggle of a Kibei Worker* (Resource Development and Publications, Asian American Studies Center, University of California, Los Angeles, 1983), 101–2.

FBI let him go after 36 hours; he stopped to send the telegram pledging his life to their boss on the way home.

The Americans eventually allowed Yoneda to join the war he had already spent his life fighting, and he served as a decorated intelligence officer in the Pacific theater, one of many left-wing California Japanese who did so. But not before he was interned at Manzanar.* As a prominent anti-militarist organizer, Yoneda was targeted by a transnational right-wing Japanese gang called the Black Dragon, and when he went to Minnesota to train, he left his wife and toddler son Tom (named for the boy's godfather, Mooney) in the camp.† Their lives continued under threat until white authorities released them back to California, having finally determined that the toddler child of a U.S. serviceman no longer endangered national security.‡ And while Yoneda's white coworkers and local comrades stuck up for him whenever they could, the CPUSA decided to suspend members of Japanese ancestry during the war for fear of appearing insufficiently pro-American, a cruel joke considering what those members had already risked to oppose Japanese militarism. Instead of contesting the decision at the time, California Japanese members simply ignored the order with the approval of local leadership and continued their Party work, which at the time consisted of trying to win World War II for the Allies. "Our rationale was we would lose all rights if the Germany-Italy-Japan fascist Axis powers were victorious. The menace of worldwide fascism was knocking at our nation's doorstep. We had to do everything to ensure Allied victory," recalled Yoneda in his memoir. "We had no choice but to accept the racist U.S. dictum at that time over Hitler's ovens and Japan's military rapists of Nanking. We

---

* His wife, Elaine Black Yoneda, a Russian Jew and California Communist leader, was one of the few whites to voluntarily intern with their husbands. Japanese wives of white husbands were not required to leave.

† The Black Dragon was named for the river separating Manchuria and Russia. The gang's primary task was warding off Bolshevik encroachment plus securing and expanding Japan's Chinese colonial territory.

‡ At the camps, nationality couldn't be used to distinguish staff and guards from nisei prisoners (who were by definition born in the United States), and so the segregated facilities were labeled by race, as a proxy for internment status. This still led to some jumbled circumstances, such as black staff assigned to "caucasian" facilities and the few interned white wives, like Yoneda, excluded from them. See Gordon Chang, *Morning Glory, Evening Shadow: Yamato Ichihashi and His Internment Writings, 1942–1945* (Stanford University Press, 1997), 169n.

would thrash out the question of our rights after victory."[32] Victory achieved, they never got the reckoning.

In a postwar American order that maintained fidelity to the Popular Front the way California Japanese leftists had during the war, we can imagine men like Karl Yoneda becoming official leaders. Charismatic in Japanese and English and uncommonly handsome, he had a workman's tan and seemed to inspire intense loyalty. As the editor of *Doho*, he was the model of an organic intellectual, a product of and credit to the Bay Area's transnational working class. He also remained connected to the anti-imperial movement in Japan; if the Soviets had been the ones to occupy the islands, as was planned before the atomic strikes in Hiroshima and Nagasaki, we have to figure he would have played some kind of direct high-level role in the postwar reconstruction. On his way home from India, where he spent his leave time meeting with labor leadership, Yoneda tried to assess what kind of country he was returning to:

Had my government and its capitalist system saved only a limited democracy in a war in which three hundred thousand Americans, including seven hundred Japanese Americans, had died? Would employers, who had raked in millions of dollars in profits from the war, open their gates to returning GIs, including those of us who were of Japanese descent? Would people of Japanese ancestry, who had been confined in U.S.-style concentration camps, be restored their full rights? Would civil and human rights be protected?[33]

Yoneda found out quickly. He looked for months for an apartment to rent, knocking on FOR RENT doors (wearing his army uniform) with no success. The family continued their activism, and the FBI began following their movements again, as if the whole war hadn't happened. That's how American authorities preferred it. With help from his old boss Herbert Hoover, General Douglas MacArthur redeemed Emperor Hirohito and most of the country's imperial clique. (He later repeated the feat in the Philippines, rescuing influential collaborators from their comeuppance, a decision that paid dividends in Palo Alto, as you'll see.) A few scapegoats paid with their lives, but there was no revolution in Japan. The only place for Karl Yoneda in the American-led postwar order was struggling to make a living and running from the cops, the same place he was before. During the war, America benefited from the commitment of California Japanese such as Yoneda, but the country didn't earn or deserve it. Whatever the historical narrative is, U.S. leadership didn't learn any better by beating the Axis powers. Karl Yoneda was a very smart man, and he knew what country he was headed back to.

Politically, most internees were like Ichihashi and Shirai—either stuck with a complicated set of allegiances and frustrations (Ichihashi) or trying to make a good life as an individual without having to worry about sides (Shirai). Japanese ancestry didn't necessarily prevent Americans from finding good gigs in the postwar environment; Shirai became president of the Asahi Homecast Corporation, bringing Japanese radio and TV programming to Los Angeles. Ichihashi ended up being a strong investment for both sides: for the Japanese government as an unofficial representative (let's say) and for the Americans as a professor. He came face-to-face with his work at Tule Lake: At the end of 1942, Caucasian authorities installed a new head of the camp, and when Ichihashi went to see him he was pleasantly surprised to see Harvey Coverley, Stanford class of 1924 and a student from two of his seminars. It was not a coincidence. In a real way, Ichihashi trained Coverley for the job. The university announced soon after that it was opening a training program for the future military administrators of occupied Japan (including its colonies and formerly conquered territories), a joint project with the Hoover War Library.[34] Karl Yoneda and his comrades were not invited to attend.

This was the era of young men with "potential," especially in California, but potential to do what? For whom? As Yoneda's example shows, potential meant more than courage, intelligence, and a winning smile—he had all three, and they earned him grief from authorities on two shores. It's worth retracing our steps to the Palo Alto System, in which potential counts for everything—but only a specific kind of potential. A colt that won't pull a cart is no good to the system, no matter how fast. And a colt that organizes all the horses to strike? That's no potential at all.

Home Front

The war's geography reoriented America's resources toward the Pacific, multiplying national investment in the West Coast weapons industries. Even though, as I've said, East Coast capital finagled much of the new high-tech industry out of the state, heavy industry was less mobile, and shipbuilding in the north and planes in the south led the regional economy to new heights. As a result, World War II permanently changed Northern California's racial character, baking the various European immigrants into one loaf of white bread, pulling black people from the South to the Bay Area in large numbers for the first time, reestablishing the Mexican proletariat in Alta California after the interwar deportations, and interning/expelling residents of Japanese ancestry. Wartime labor shortages nudged white women and migrant black workers into war work previously reserved for white men. In the wartime labor shake-up, planters and railroad capitalists found themselves left out. Their answer was the federal government's "Bracero" program, which brought Mexican agricultural and construction workers north under a reduced set of labor rights. Excluded from defense jobs because of citizenship requirements, temporary Mexican workers became a permanent solution for West Coast bosses. And when the war concluded with the occupation of Japan and western Germany, California was relocated from the hinterland of the nation to the middle of a U.S. empire that stretched most of the way around the world.

By the end of the war, the ingredients for the Golden State's postwar prosperity were all in place. Federal spending, along with the state's willingness to accommodate labor-starved employers, ignited the fuel in California's economic engine, starting the pistons pumping more air and gas into the combustion chamber. The Bay Area remained an entry point to the North American market for Pacific capital as that trade grew in size and importance, and Palo Alto grew with it. No longer would the West play the part of a minor league to the East's pros. America needed new men for its west-facing territory, and that's exactly what Stanford University intended to provide. Both Mexican farmworkers and interned Japanese counted members of the Palo Alto community among their leaders; so did the occupation forces and the prison camps. The "children of California" were on both sides of the era's conflicts, and only some could win the peace.

Born in 1905—around the same time as the boys of the radio pioneer milieu, and around the same time as Shirai and Yoneda—Ernesto Galarza fled Jalcocotán, Mexico, and the violence of the revolution as a boy with his mother and two uncles. They eventually settled in Sacramento, and Galarza's uncles worked in the fields and laid tracks to support the family. Unlike much of the rest of the country, California did not formally segregate its schools by race (after the San Francisco Unified School District's attempt to exclude Japanese children caused an international uproar that required President Teddy Roosevelt's direct intervention). Galarza's account of his elementary school sounds like what today's multicultural education advocates dream of: "My pals in the second grade were Kazushi, whose parents spoke only Japanese; Matti, a skinny Italian boy; and Manuel, a fat Portuguese who would never get into a fight but wrestled you to the ground and just sat on you," Galarza recalls in his 1971 memoir, *Barrio Boy*. "Our assortment of nationalities included Koreans, Yugoslavs, Poles, Irish, and home-grown Americans." The school was assimilative, but toward a diverse California rather than a white United States:

At Lincoln [elementary school], making us into Americans did not mean scrubbing away what made us originally foreign. The teachers called us as our parents did, or as close as they could pronounce our names in Spanish or Japanese. No one was ever scolded or punished for speaking in his native tongue on the playground. Matti told the class about his mother's down quilt, which she had made in Italy with the fine feathers of a thousand geese. Encarnacion acted out how boys learned to fish in the Philippines. I astounded the third grade with the story of my travels on a stagecoach, which nobody else in the class had seen except in the museum at Sutter's Fort. After a visit to the Crocker Art Gallery and its collection of heroic paintings of the golden age of California, someone showed a silk scroll with a Chinese painting. Miss Hopley herself had a way of expressing wonder over these matters before a class, her eyes wide open until they popped slightly. It was easy for me to feel that becoming a proud American, as she said we should, did not mean feeling ashamed of being a Mexican.[35]

Galarza saw the stakes of assimilation firsthand as he got older: During the school year, he worked at a pharmacy and delivered Western Union telegrams, and during the summer he worked in the fields and orchards at the mercy of labor contractors. During the school year, white adults encouraged him to pursue his education, taking personal interests in his success; during the summer, white adults exploited his labor every hour of the day without having to get close enough to see him. Understandably, Ernesto stayed in school, joining the first substantial cohort of Mexican-American college students. He attended Occidental College on a scholarship and found academic research a natural fit. In 1927, he became the first Chicano student admitted for graduate study at Stanford University, a feat he repeated at Columbia, where he earned his PhD with a dissertation on the development of the electricity industry in Mexico. Even in his Ivy League doctoral program, Galarza kept thinking about the plight of manual laborers in the Americas, from the Sacramento Valley fields he used to work in to the tin mines of Bolivia. He spent the rest of his career shoulder-to-shoulder in their struggle for dignity, trying to reconcile the conditions of their lives and America's social democratic potential. Galarza knew both intimately, yet it was a circle he could never square.

Instead of pursuing a tenured academic job (or, presumably, making lots of money as an expert on the Mexican electricity industry), Galarza used his education to advocate for workers in the Americas. He joined the Pan American Union (PAU, an international organization promoting hemispheric *hermandad*, later absorbed into the Organization of American States), which created a Division of Labor and Social Information for him to run. In 1943, he published a pamphlet titled "Labor in Latin America" under the auspices of the short-lived American Council on Public Affairs. In it, he argues for the inclusion of Latin American workers in an international popular front, because they've been in the "trenches of democracy" opposing Hitler and Hitlerism "even before the days when the appeasers permitted the destruction of Austria, Spain, and Czechoslovakia."[36] He saw the rising superpower and the influence it wielded over economic development in the Western Hemisphere. Hundreds of millions of dollars in U.S. capital traveled south of the border, he writes, looking for raw materials to feed to the war machine. If the policy of the FDR regime was to strengthen organized labor at home (in large part for political reasons), why not apply the same policy in contracts abroad? "American dollars should do a democratic job wherever they are spent," Galarza writes. "Will the enormous amounts of new capital correct or merely serve to enlarge the inverted pyramid structure of Latin American economy created by private interest in the last half century?"[37] It was a good question, and he hoped that American progressives had an earnest answer. He imagined a pan-American highway and international economic planning designed to raise wages across the continents. Galarza took the popular front internationalist FDR Democrats at their word. That, he came to realize, was a mistake.

. In the postwar period, Galarza found support from the web of civil-society organizations set up to promote liberal ideas as separate and distinct from the Soviet-led global class struggle. Galarza—a diligent scholar, passionate writer, and Mexican-American success story who believed deeply in the potential of internationalist social democracy—was like a poster child for U.S. liberalism, and the CIA-associated Ford Foundation funded his work. But he was also serious in his commitment to the working class, which the CIA was not. He quit the Pan American Union twice over the U.S. State Department's actions in Bolivia, where he was studying the conditions for tin miners. The first time was in December of 1942, when he complained in a letter to the State Department that the U.S. ambassador was lobbying against worker protection laws for fear of cost increases in raw materials needed for the war. The same day he sent the letter, Bolivian troops murdered hundreds of striking miners and their families in what became known as the Catavi massacre. Galarza's letter and the massacre combined to cause a scandal in Washington, and the Board of Economic Warfare committed to putting labor provisions in foreign supply contracts. The PAU begged Galarza back, but a few years later, when he caught word of American involvement in a successful assassination coup against Bolivia's pro-miner president, he left for good.*

Changing tactics, Galarza moved to organizing with workers directly, and after the American Federation of Labor and the Congress of Industrial Organizations merged into the AFL-CIO, the coalition recruited him to be the director of research and education for the new National Farm Labor Union. But he was never one for sitting in an office, and he took to the fields to lead agricultural worker strikes across the West and South in the 1950s: Florida, Louisiana, Texas, Arizona, California.[38] But leaders in the AFL-CIO were in a collaborative frame of mind when it came to negotiating with the bosses— something Galarza couldn't be accused of—and part of that bargain involved selling out farmworkers. He grew increasingly frustrated with the postwar

---

* Galarza seems to have written an account of the coup and American involvement for *Harper's*, which killed it after submission. Ilan Stavans, introduction to *Barrio Boy: 40th Anniversary Edition* (Notre Dame Press, 2011), xviii.

"consensus" climate of business unionism, which had no room for the men and women he represented and struggled alongside. The Bracero program in particular seemed to him an insurmountable obstacle: If workers were split into two tiers with one tier classified as conditional "guests" of the capitalist state, organizing couldn't happen. He turned back to writing, this time in the tradition of social reform essayists, and with his 1955 report, "Strangers in the Field," he galvanized public opinion against the program. Though he prevailed with regard to the Bracero program over the following decade, Galarza ran into new obstacles, including anti-union "right to work" rules and, most important in his account, the white union leadership's own indifference to Chicano farmworkers.

Galarza stayed flexible when it came to making himself useful, but even after the defeat of the Bracero program he found his ideas outside the mainstream. His dream was always an international organization of workers that operated on both sides of the border, one that could take practical steps to reduce the importance of that fence in their lives. But the new cohort of farm labor leaders took a hard line on so-called wetback labor, joining the state to marginalize undocumented workers in the interest of citizens. Galarza found himself alienated from his former organizations and his former ideology, and he took refuge in authorship and academia. As early as 1960 he was writing despairingly to his "liberal friends," and by '77, he was writing contemptuously about the "liberal conscience" and its "weakness."[39] It was a significant reversal for a man who once represented the best hopes of the Ford Foundation. Galarza began locating himself in a different lineage, writing about "class victims" and extolling the work of communist organizers like Pat Chambers and Caroline Decker. (He recounts meeting a depressed Chambers in Fresno and telling him, "If you hadn't been in the Imperial Valley ten years before I was, I wouldn't have been in the Imperial Valley at all.")[40] He ended up near the communists not because they convinced him of their ideas but because the liberal internationalists weren't as liberal or international as they claimed to be. Beneath the midcentury consensus were hundreds of martyred Bolivian miners, and Galarza didn't let the United States forget about them.*

---

* The Catavi massacre, as we'll see, is representative of the postwar order. In his intercontinental study of Third World anticommunist campaigns, reporter Vincent Bevins concludes that "the major losers of the twentieth century were those who believed too sincerely in the

Race hierarchy structured the California postwar period in decisive ways. Contrary to Popular Front rhetoric, America wasn't fighting to build a social order based on humanity's universal equality. Comparing Galarza to the radio boys from this chapter's first section helps us see how the proceeds from the era's progress accumulated in particular hands. Throwing in with American liberalism meant hewing to the national border and forsaking workers on the other side, even when they happened to work in America's fields. California built its hoard on "foreign" natural and human resources, and the ruling clique certainly wasn't going to surrender the rights thereto after *winning* the war.

Whiteness as a legal regime reiterated international inequalities at home, even for those exceptional individuals who focused their considerable potential in the right place. Art Fong was born in Sacramento in 1920, the son of Chinese immigrant grocery store owners. He interested himself in engineering and radios, and though he expected to keep working in his family's store, his teachers made sure he was enrolled in college at the new University of California branch in Los Angeles, where his family moved when he was fifteen. After two years he graduated to a job at the Los Angeles Bureau of Power and Light—there's always work at the power company—to save up for a transfer to Berkeley. Annual tuition, books, and fees together were around $100 at the time (a bit less than $2,000 in 2022 money), which is what Fong made at the power company in a month, so it wasn't an uphill battle.[41] Fong distinguished himself at Berkeley, and after the bombing of Pearl Harbor a recruiter from the Rad Lab came calling. (When Fred Terman got around to staffing the RRL, he was disappointed to find Fong already taken.) He jumped at the chance to do work in the microwave spectrum and was assigned to the test group.

Fong was as much a product of the California radio scene as any of the Palo Alto boys. Like the rest of them, he and his wife, Mary, couldn't wait to get back to California. After the war, he turned down a job offer in New Jersey and got an interview with a young signal corps officer who happened to co-own an electronics company. Bill Hewlett hired Fong to join the firm he

---

existence of a liberal international order, those who trusted too much in democracy, or too much in what the United States said it supported, rather than what it really supported—what the rich countries said, rather than what they did. That group was annihilated." Vincent Bevins, *The Jakarta Method: Washington's Anticommunist Crusade and the Mass Murder Program That Shaped Our World* (Public Affairs, 2021), 243.

started with his classmate Packard (which you'll read more about in the next section), and Art proved invaluable to the company's microwave division. But when the Fongs moved back to their home state, eager for their small part of the postwar American dream in the fast-growing suburb of Palo Alto, they couldn't find a house. "It was illegal for me—a Chinese American—to buy or rent a house in the desirable parts of Palo Alto," he recalls.[42] Restrictive covenants formally excluded nonwhite buyers, no matter where they were born or what they promised to add to the local economy—and regardless of their service to the country in the war. The Fongs found a plot at the city limits, and after going door-to-door, asking the neighbors how they'd feel about having Chinese-Americans living nearby, they built their own house. The price of postwar life in Palo Alto for Asians (and, Fong adds in his memoirs, "Jews, African-Americans, and Hispanics")—even for a promising California-born veteran who was recruited to the town for his exceptional skills—was immediately resigning oneself to second-class citizenship.[43]

The occasional nonwhite worker could find a place in the sun in postwar California, as long as he was willing to accept one at the edge of town. Things were expanding so fast that the edge of town turned into the center before long; today the Fong plot is near Palo Alto's incredibly expensive downtown. But for those people like Ernesto Galarza who hoped that with the defeat of fascism all the world's men could expect to be treated as equals in an American-led world order, the midcentury United States was an unending harvest of bitter frustrations and disappointments. The novelist Chester Himes lent voice to that despair in *If He Hollers Let Him Go*, the story of a black World War II California shipyard worker named Bob Jones. Uncommonly educated, Jones leads a crew at the interracial work site, but he struggles to endure the contradiction between the country's official line and his experiences. He confronts a white communist who feels entitled to Bob's support for the Popular Front: "Get these crackers to unite with me. I'm willing. I'll work with 'em, fight with 'em, die with 'em, goddamnit. But I ain't gonna even try to do any uniting without anybody to unite with. Do you understand that?... What the hell do I care about unity, or the war either, for that matter, as long as I'm kicked around by every white person who comes along? Let the white people get some goddamned unity."[44] Invited to get some goddamned unity, the whites united among themselves, with policies that effaced ethnic, regional, and (to a certain degree) class distinctions. Alexander M. Poniatoff—an uninvited white immigrant from Shanghai, and a czarist to boot—was awarded half a defense subcontractor; Art Fong was lucky his fellow children of California let him build a house at the town line.

America's postwar suburban culture wasn't white, patriarchal, and conservative by coincidence; it was a careful design. As Galarza discovered, the wealth distribution was an inverted pyramid balanced on the backs of the world's workers, just the way Hoover and his associates planned it. Despite the best efforts of "liberal friends," global inequality itself was the growth industry, and it took the form William Shockley predicted: a world ruled by bombs. All the better for Palo Alto.

Section III

1945–1975

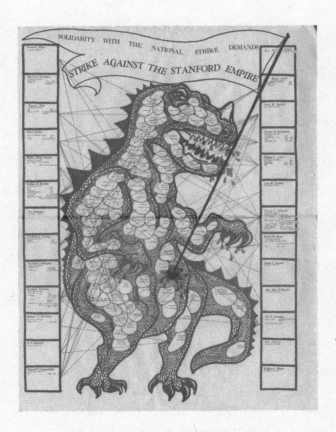

"Strike Against the Stanford Empire" (1970)
April Third Movement archive

Space Settlers

Missile Economics — Real Estate — Ghettoization of East
Palo Alto — Paul Baran and the Red Scare — The Cold
War University

Thanks to the militant anti-Roosevelt sentiment in the reigning Hoover cabal, Stanford — and by extension, Palo Alto — remained rural into the 1940s. Eschewing the race for big government war contracts, the school bided its time. It's not that Stanford's leadership opposed collaboration between state and academy in principle — Hoover himself led the effort for the National Research Fund as commerce secretary — but they dreaded what they saw as FDR's Bolshevism. If the state could use New Deal farm supports as an excuse to intervene on behalf of agricultural workers, there was nothing to stop them from pulling the same trick on private university administrators who accepted public subsidies or contracts. Stanford would sooner stick with the orchards. But with the end of World War II, Palo Alto caught a few breaks.

On November 17, 1944, FDR sent his head of the wartime Office of Scientific Research and Development (OSRD) a memo asking for guidance regarding the future of the OSRD's work after the war — specifically, how to make wartime technical advances available for commercial use, how to cure disease, what is the proper role of the government in research, and how to identify and develop American scientific talent. "New frontiers of the mind are before us, and if they are pioneered with the same vision, boldness, and drive with which we have waged this war we can create a fuller and more fruitful employment and a fuller and more fruitful life," Roosevelt wrote. The response from the OSRD head Vannevar Bush — a proposal for a National Research Foundation titled "Science, the Endless Frontier" — is a legendary document among scholars of postwar America, but by its July 25, 1945, postmark, the intended recipient had been dead for three months.[1] The memo made its way to Truman, and Congress began debating the future of federal scientific research.

Vannevar Bush wasn't a Stanford man, but he was one of the models for the archetype.* Operating at the highest levels of academia (MIT VP and dean of engineering), the tech industry (inventor and Raytheon founder), and the military state, Bush was just the sort of person who came to lead Palo Alto. Hoover even offered him the Stanford presidency on December 5, 1941, but the bombing of Pearl Harbor two days later made the choice for him, keeping Bush where he was needed, at the OSRD.[2] Regardless of his White House appointment, Bush was an anti–New Dealer, and when remnants of the Roosevelt coalition sought to organize postwar research under democratic rather than technocratic control, with commercial royalties going to the state rather than de facto ceded to corporations, he refused to budge.† Instead, he went with some trepidation to the military, and by the time the National Science Foundation was established by law, in 1950, the Office of Naval Research (ONR) was already dividing up Bush's endless frontier: It had 1,000 in-house scientists as well as 1,200 external sponsored projects spread over hundreds of institutions and supporting over 5,000 researchers.[3]

Despite the administration's grumbling, Stanford contributed over 40 professors to the war effort, including star radio engineer Fred Terman.[4] Recall that the second son of Stanford followed his father's advice to leave Palo Alto (so he could come back) and pursued his graduate work at MIT under none other than Vannevar Bush. In the 15 years since his first triumphant return— to a professorship at the age of twenty-five—he took after his adviser, helping seed companies and directing the growth of his field. In 1941, it was time for Terman to add the third leg on his tripod; the war state was calling. He packed up for Cambridge again, where Bush readied a dream assignment: Terman would run the Radio Research Laboratory out of Harvard. Frederick Terman's service at the RRL looked to be a final confirmation of everything David Starr

---

* No apparent blood relation to the Bush political dynasty.

† Bush was such a Hoover loyalist that, in wartime correspondence with National Academy of Sciences president Frank Jewett, he called Hoover by the insider nickname "Chief." Scholar Nathan Reingold writes of Bush's conduct under Roosevelt's successor, "by and large he was viewed as conniving against the Truman administration." Nathan Reingold, "Vannevar Bush's New Deal for Research: Or the Triumph of the Old Order," *Historical Studies in the Physical and Biological Sciences* 17, no. 2 (1987): 332.

Jordan and Terman's father, Lewis, thought Stanford could offer to America. This genius son had lived up to their expectations, not just in the magnitude of his intelligence and accomplishments but also in his purpose. When the nation called on the resources invested in him, he was ready to serve, pledging his superior smarts, scientific training, and leadership capacity to the war effort. And they won. More than Hoover's election, Terman's victorious return in 1945 was the culmination of Stanford's founding, and the school was ready to give him the keys to the sandstone kingdom. He was quickly appointed dean of the engineering school, just missing an overlap at the rank with his dad (Lewis retired in the summer of '45). In another decade Fred was provost, but it didn't take him that long to start making big changes.

The core of the postwar economy was not to be a civilian version of wartime industrial manufacturing. It was headed up, up, and away, into the aerospace, communications, and electronics (ACE) sectors, and Terman was ahead of the trajectory. His plan was to build skyward, creating "steeples of excellence"—specific exceptional competencies in growing ACE subfields that made Stanford an irresistible lure for federal and private research funds. Terman began with the technology that had produced Stanford's biggest prewar invention, the Varian klystron (which remained a source of passive income for the university), and in January of 1945 he talked the new president, Donald Tresidder, out of $25,000 to found the (not "a" or "Stanford," "the") Microwave Lab. It was a drop in the bucket, but Fred knew where to find the spigot: He nabbed an Office of Naval Research–led government grant for $225,000—annually.[5] Terman's relationship with the ONR was downright cozy, and his timing was great. Wartime Department of Defense administrators were used to writing blank checks for research and development, and now they were writing a lot of those checks to peacetime contractors like Stanford. That meant the government paid for new and expensive building-size research machines, including particle accelerators, nuclear reactors, and computers.[6] This led to some jurisdictional squabbling with the feds, especially around the Stanford Linear Accelerator Center, but no one can argue that the university's embrace of government contracts left it worse off.[7] By 1948, military contracts paid more of the Stanford physics department's bills than the university did.[8]

Terman conceived of research as falling into two categories—basic and applied—and while basic researchers could double as professors for undergraduates, the specialty work of applied researchers made them less useful in the classroom. So when administrators revived a Hoover plan for a research institute modeled on private industrial labs, that seemed a logical place to stick applied researchers. With Terman's help, the Stanford Research Institute (SRI) quickly began gobbling up DOD cash. President Tresidder, however, was another dogmatic Hoover selectee, and he saw research contracts in terms of government and private, with an anticommunist fear of the former. These conflicting interpretations came to a head when Terman sent a big ONR contract over to SRI, one that would have made the institute effectively a public charge. Even though Tresidder had been unable to attract private dollars to SRI, he refused to see Stanford turned over to the state. Fate complied: Tresidder fired intransigent SRI director William Talbot, and, a couple of months later, before picking a replacement, he had a heart attack and died.

While Tresidder believed that companies should simply donate to Stanford — since they would benefit from general scientific progress in the long run — Terman, as something of an entrepreneur himself, knew that wasn't a very attractive proposition for the companies. His experience with Varian Associates suggested a model: The government sponsored microwave research at Stanford; Stanford professors consulted for Varian; Varian hired Stanford students who were trained to make microwave tubes; Varian sold tubes to the government. Strengthening the win-win-win associative relationship between Stanford, industry, and the DOD could propel the university past its East Coast and West Coast rivals. The school had two big assets: classrooms and land. Terman made use of both.

Terman's vision for private research at Stanford was much more expansive than simply the establishment of SRI: With its 8,800 acres of beautiful Santa Clara County land (all of which the university was forbidden to sell in perpetuity), the administration should become a corporate landlord, he thought.[9] The first lease at the Stanford Industrial Park was granted to Varian's R & D department in 1953 — no surprise, because Terman was an investor and board member.[10] Soon followed fellow Terman advisee Hewlett-Packard with its corporate headquarters, along with major companies such as GE and Kodak. One bonus to being on campus was that under the Honors Cooperative Program companies could jump the admissions line and send their employees to Stanford for advanced classes in cutting-edge science — as long as they were willing to pay double tuition, which they were. The industrial park made Stanford appealing to entrepreneurial professors such as birth control pill co-inventor Carl Djerassi, who came to teach in the chemistry department and brought his company Syntex along afterward. Teachers and students circulated between the park and the school, profit and nonprofit blending in a smoothie. The park's biggest catch was Lockheed Aircraft Corporation, which in 1955 made plans to move its expanding missiles division to Sunnyvale from Los Angeles to be near NASA's Ames Research Center at Moffett Airfield, built with one of the region's relatively few large prewar defense contracts (in 1931, thanks to then-president Hoover).[11] With some prodding from Terman, Lockheed put a research complex in the industrial park the next year and followed that with a nearby manufacturing complex that made it the county's defining employer.

Vannevar Bush taught Terman what he had learned from Hoover: government money, private industry pursuing new technologies, and the academy in between added up to a booming economy and a powerful America. The younger man went home to prove it. The model worked, and Palo Alto changed. The orchard era was over, and the number of fruit-growing acres in Santa Clara County dropped from 101,666 in 1940 to 25,511 in 1973.[12] In the 1950s, Palo Alto went straight from rural to something like postindustrial, and the ratio of production to nonproduction workers decreased, even as the portion of the population employed in industry exploded and the median family income went up by 50 percent.[13] The space-age settlers who came west to explore the vertical frontier were making Palo Alto richer, younger, and better educated. *But what did they* do, *exactly?*

Postwar

The writer Michael S. Malone grew up in and with Silicon Valley, but he was born in Munich, Germany, in a country his father helped blow to smithereens from the nose of a B-17 bomber. The senior Malone was part of a new cohort of airmen who, operating with massive national support infrastructures (including those designed by Terman and Shockley), performed with unheard-of efficiency—which is to say they killed a lot of people very fast. After the war, he became a military liaison to the intelligence agencies, and in 1962 he sat helplessly at his teletype as the nation's computer systems escalated toward apocalypse. After the Cuban Missile Crisis and a heart attack, he grabbed his family and drove to California for a job at NASA. Here's how the junior Malone describes the wave of immigration that brought his family to Santa Clara County, "the fastest growing place in America":

> Young men, new families in tow, arrived by the scores each day, armed with a GI Bill degree in aeronautical, electrical, or mechanical engineering, and looking for a piece of the aerospace future. They bought their ranch-style house—or, if they were adventurous, a Bauhaus-for-everyman Eichler with an atrium—and drove off every morning to build ICBMs for Lockheed.[14]

Those were the same intercontinental ballistic missiles Malone's father read about on the teletype in 1962. Moving to Silicon Valley to escape thoughts of nuclear war is like moving to Alaska because the evening breeze in New York is too chilly. Why was the model product in the American postwar suburban economy an enormous, hugely sophisticated exploding rocket full of computers? Especially considering that, except during tests and as attachments to spaceships, America never launched one? Like the empty towns along the transcontinental railroad line, the signature products of postwar industry sat idle. It didn't matter that the country didn't use everything it built, at least not to the people doing the planning.

It's an understatement to say that much of the world was devastated by its second war, but the United States got off relatively easy. As one of the two superpowers left standing, America was responsible for rebuilding its half (or third, depending on whom you asked) of the world, and that meant getting money to flow through the global financial system again. The Marshall Plan to rebuild Europe and develop occupied Japan moved some cash, but the execution wasn't big or fast enough. In a memo titled "NSC 68," the secretary of state, Dean Acheson, and the chief of Truman's Policy Planning Staff, Paul Nitze, suggested a way to spend novel amounts of government money without appearing to crowd out private industry: rearmament. By paying for peacetime arsenals in America and western Europe (and "on behalf of" Japan), they could prepare for war with the communists as Shockley theorized it and boost global demand without driving down prices, kick-starting what we now think of as capitalism's twentieth-century golden age. This plan also rescued military contractors in the ACE sectors who were looking at peacetime layoffs. Acheson and Nitze wanted Truman to triple the Pentagon's budget ask for 1950.[15] Of all the smart-stupid state-capitalist plans, military Keynesianism, which called for the state to finance the expansion of the global economy by building machines designed to blow up the world, was one of the smartest-stupidest. And, of course, it worked.

If we look at Palo Alto and Santa Clara County, it's easy to see how rearmament funded suburbanization. California maintained its wartime gains in national steel-production share, and the timber industry in the Pacific Northwest grew from 41 percent of national output in 1929 to 60 percent in 1958, despite its comparatively high wages.[16] But electronics and ordnance firms came to provide a majority of the county's industrial employment, and between 1952 and 1968 they made most of their sales to the federal government.[17] Stanford was the conduit from the federal government to the regional economy for a disproportionate amount of this value, and that meant building more than weapons. As the space settlers poured into the Valley of Heart's Delight, they turned military spending into consumer spending, buying those newly constructed Eichler homes with mortgages backed by their stable, lucrative jobs making missiles. Demand for the accoutrements of suburban life surged: refrigerators, air-conditioners, cars, lawn mowers.[18] The university added housing subdivisions and a luxury shopping center, but took pains to control the nature of development.

Administrators did not want to spoil the bucolic vibe that they counted crucial to Stanford's success, so they issued a number of restrictions on industrial tenants: buildings no taller than two stories, no smokestacks, no offensive sounds or odors, and large suburban-style front-lawn setbacks.[19] These were the factories of the future, and residents shouldn't even know they were there.* If industrialization could be kept under control aesthetically while stimulated to run wild financially, then housing prices in the county would only increase as the space settlers kept coming. Companies began to offer stock options to employees, investing these workers directly in growth and keeping liquidity

---

* This effort has endured successfully for decades; if many office buildings in the Palo Alto area appear to be hiding behind bushes, it's because they are.

flowing back toward production. And what midcentury scientist didn't want to get paid in shares of the future? It being California, the especially ambitious could strike out on their own. The 1950 Defense Production Act (DPA) gave preference to small businesses in awarding contracts and loans to "incentivize the domestic industrial base to extend production."[20] Truman was not the FDR heir the Hoover clique feared, and the DPA was not a step toward nationalization: It was a giveaway for the space settlers.*

The foundation for space-settler prosperity, the cellular unit of postwar suburbia, was the house. As he did with agriculture and electricity, the Chief set the pattern for the Roosevelt program. Beginning in his first term at Commerce, Hoover applied his associative model to the real estate industry. His first task was establishing standards for city planning. He assembled a small committee of industry representatives (as was his wont) and they drafted a model zoning law for states—it was technically the minimal amount of power the federal government could exercise, but their pamphlet was very influential. What they established under the Chief's vague authority is that municipalities *under their delegated police powers* could, "for the purpose of promoting health, safety, morals, or the general welfare of the community...regulate and restrict the height, number of stories, and size of buildings and other structures, the percentage of lot that may be occupied, the size of yards, courts, and other open spaces, the density of population, and the location and use of buildings, structures, and land for trade, industry, residence, or other purposes."[21] States took up the language, and it helped permanently lodge a tremendous amount of authority in the hands of local governments and the landowners who ran them. They in turn shaped the lifeworld of postwar America. In particular, zoning became a powerful weapon in the retrenchment of residential segregation.

In the depths of the Depression, President Hoover became convinced he could unlock pent-up demand for houses by using federal resources to back private home loans. Every American family wanted to buy a home, he figured; the only things stopping them were that they didn't have enough money and there weren't enough houses. Home loans were high-interest and short-term,

---

* When Truman attempted (unsuccessfully) to nationalize the steel industry, it was at least as much an attack on labor as on capital.

and they only covered around half the purchase price. That suppressed building, and when the Depression hit and prices fell, home construction nearly ceased, exacerbating the housing crisis. In 1931, with radicals breathing down his neck, Hoover assembled hundreds of real estate and construction professionals at the President's National Conference on Home Building and Home Ownership, one of his classic associative state meetups. There they brainstormed how to fight their common enemy: the menace of public housing. Though the group failed to house the depressed masses, by designing a public model to finance private housing, they did achieve their central goals.

The conference came up with four tactics: creating long-term amortized mortgages, lowering interest rates, offering government aid for private housing for the poor, and reducing construction costs. All this was, as Kenneth Jackson writes, "a boon to [the] speculative builders, appliance manufacturers, and automobile companies" who created the postwar suburbs.[22] Hoover set up a national mortgage bank to supply credit to builders, but like Belgian relief, it was no charity project. The government planned to get every dollar back, and that made the program inaccessible to Americans in dire straits, the ones who really needed it. Exactly three families out of over 40,000 applicants received direct loans.[23] FDR expanded the program with the Home Owners' Loan Corporation (HOLC) and the Federal Housing Administration (FHA), and, buoyed by World War II, they accomplished precisely what Hoover and his hundreds of housing henchmen had outlined. America is still living with, still trying to come to grips with and understand, the consequences of this prosperity.

In his acclaimed 2017 book, *The Color of Law: A Forgotten History of How Our Government Segregated America*, Richard Rothstein uses Palo Alto as a paradigmatic case. The federal government acted as a superbank, backing private loans under a relatively broad set of requirements. Just as California's farms changed to fit the Bank of Italy's conditions, the housing industries shaped themselves according to the government's vision, which they helped set. Hoover's lost child, the FHA still had plenty of his DNA, and the lending program was designed to cost the government nothing. As long as it only backed solid enough borrowers, the tide of economic prosperity ensured that people could repay the loans and that the Treasury would never have to step in. That meant establishing data about where the good loans were, so the HOLC produced color-coded maps dividing urban regions into districts based on their investability. Red was for black, birthing the term redlining for the practice of isolating black and integrated neighborhoods from FHA loan-eligible areas. That's what happened when capitalists made the rules.

The state took for granted that black people and other minorities destroyed property values, which was the same as saying that white people would pay more to live away from them. Real estate agents made it a self-fulfilling prophecy by "blackballing" any of their colleagues who violated the map's lines—after all, the real estate industry drew those lines for the feds in the first place. As historian Thomas Sugrue writes, "Boundaries between the public and private sectors in housing were blurry in the postwar period. Leading developers, bankers, and real estate executives frequently traveled the road between private practice and government service."[24] Hoover's real-estate minions filled the public-private air like dandelion seeds, and his model lasted.

Restrictive covenants in land titles made sale to new buyers conditional on *their* only selling to whites in the future. But what about the Bay Area's famous good white liberals? It's not entirely a myth. In the late 1940s, a group of middle- and working-class residents called the Peninsula Housing Association of Palo Alto bought an undeveloped ranch near Stanford and planned to build a co-op subdivision with hundreds of houses as well as common spaces. But 2 percent of the first 150 families were black, which meant the feds wouldn't insure building loans, which meant banks didn't issue them.[25] On policy, Bank of America and others didn't make construction loans the FHA refused to back, even if it was a very good investment, like a 260-acre subdivision next to Stanford in 1948. The association gave up and sold the land to a developer that agreed to the FHA's conditions: whites only. The Ladera subdivision is still there; as I write, there have been 26 sales over the last 12 months, averaging between $3 million and $4 million.

Ghettoization, or blockbusting, was a parallel process, another one designed by real estate interests in association with the government, and again Palo Alto was exemplary. Into the 1950s, the new rules made it hard for nonwhites to find housing, even just to meet labor demand. (Recall Chinese-American HP recruit Art Fong's fruitless search for a Palo Alto rental when he returned from the war.) The solution emerged when a white resident in the eastern part of Palo Alto, on the other side of Highway 101, sold his home to a black family.

Under different circumstances perhaps the community would've forced the buyers out—that certainly happened elsewhere when individuals violated the color line—but this time the real estate agents and speculators saw a different opportunity. They went door-to-door in the white neighborhood warning that the block was changing, and whether it was the prospect of black people or the redline that scared them more, it meant the same: Prices are going down; sell now. Speculators bought up houses at fire-sale prices, then turned around and flipped them at a premium to black workers who were starved for Bay Area residential properties that they were allowed to buy. Within six years, Rothstein writes, East Palo Alto went from exclusively white to 82 percent black.[26] No one was keeping whites out, of course, but they couldn't get an FHA loan or guarantee an increasing home value the way they could in white-only neighborhoods; whites had to pay a premium to integrate, and as a group they declined to do so.

The FHA didn't lend to black buyers under any circumstances—they brought the red line with them wherever they went—so East Palo Alto's new owners were compelled to rent rooms to pay the loans they could get, leading to a density the suburban area wasn't built for. Palo Alto, however, zoned less than 10 percent of housing land for multifamily dwellings and established a minimum lot size for single-family homes.[27] The town didn't fully outlaw density the way neighboring municipalities such as Los Altos Hills, Atherton, and Woodside did, with their huge lot minimums and zero-percent multifamily zoning. Instead, Palo Alto played a calculated game that not only resembled but also exemplified the dynamics of postwar white ethnic assimilation. That meant yes to developer Joseph Eichler and his stylish, affordable tract homes—Palo Alto approved a dozen Eichler subdivisions in the expanding southern part of town, where they remain, though now they are less afford-able. But it meant no to high-rise apartment buildings, and in the early 1970s, the city board banned new buildings over 50 feet tall.[28] Shielded by official if not *de jure* housing segregation, housing development expanded in the 1950s and early 1960s, only to draw down sharply as suburban whites planned long-term solutions to the threat of "open housing."

Schools, like houses, were at the center of the desegregation struggle, and there, too, reactionaries had a zoning solution. As the East Palo Alto population increased, Palo Alto had to build a new high school. Liberals suggested a north-south dividing line to produce two integrated schools; that's not what happened. In 1958, the new school went right in the middle of East Palo Alto, segregating the teenagers for the first time in a manner that endures to the present day, with few exceptions. "Federal and state housing policy had created a slum in East Palo Alto," summarizes Rothstein.[29] Hoover's real estate plan produced white suburbs and corresponding black ghettos for the same reason: There was easy money in it. Whites who went along with the plan got rich, and the ones who didn't had to get out. Standardized mortgage instruments established through the Hooverian public-private associations Fannie Mae and Ginnie Mae helped banks relocate capital where it could grow fastest, out West. By the 1970s, Kenneth Jackson notes, savings banks in the Bronx invested only 10 percent of their funds back into the borough, effectively divesting the community from itself.[30] The new land boom enriched California real estate speculators, developers, and the agents they used, and the industry's power increased within the state's conservative movement, along with the influence of the banks, industrialists, and agricultural cartels. They helped finance and promote reactionary western politicians, who took charge of the national movement in the name of the suburban residents of stolen Mexico. The country's center of gravity shifted west, and the landowners cashed in.

Across the highway from the ghetto, the postwar ownership society took shape: a house with a white picket fence, a couple of white kids, a white wife at home (not working in an orchard or shipyard), a nice green lawn, and two cars—in your colors of choice! Round it out with a job making weapons of mass destruction, a new stereo, and a catalog of forthcoming products sitting circled on the kitchen table. Bank of America helped finance the dream, building up one $60 million portfolio mostly out of $200 refrigerator loans.[31] Eager to facilitate consumer spending, B of A started printing general-purpose credit cards; starting with California's agricultural centers where the bank had made its start, they bombarded customers with credit, mailing cards by the tens of thousands with no warning.[32] But as Michael Malone cautions us to remember, these people were hardly conservative "squares." In the two decades after the war, the space settlers were optimists who believed in far-out ideas like cybernetics and moon colonies. They were the audience for *Playboy*, and

they lapped up stories about the gadget-wielding secret agent James Bond.*
If you came over for dinner, they wanted to *show you something.*† These
were the shock troops of the American dream: younger, WASPier, and better educated than existing Santa Clara County residents. They were the vil-
lains on the 1970s California police procedural *Columbo*, in which they lied,
connived, and even killed to get ahead at work. The space settlers had their
cake with new consumer toys, and they ate it, too, with long-term assets
such as houses and stocks. The one thing the settlers didn't need? A labor
movement.

The postwar compact between labor and capital was that a privileged
segment of workers shared in the profits from rocketing productivity. In
exchange, the labor elite agreed to spend a lot and stay away from communists.
And build the best bombs in the world. But freed from the wartime no-strike
pledges, other workers—for whom suburban military Keynesianism looked
to be a Worse Deal—tried to pick up where they left off in the 1930s. The
postwar American economy was a site of high-stakes conflict: In 1946, the
country set new records for corporate profits *and* number of labor strikes.[33]
Both sides sought to consolidate wartime gains and claim larger shares of
expanding output, while workers struggled to keep up with rapidly increasing
consumer prices newly liberated from wartime controls. In Oakland, a conflict
that began with 1,000 striking department store workers escalated to a city-
wide general strike of 100,000.[34] But the evenhandedness that characterized
the Roosevelt administration's mediation (at its best) was gone.

One of Santa Clara County's virtues for firms looking to relocate or expand
there was the lack of a strong industrial union presence—not an uncommon
rationale for selecting a rural factory site. Like railroad engineers, salaried

---

* Bond's author, Ian Fleming, was a World War II British naval intelligence liaison and a
technology enthusiast himself. A literary voice for the space settler, Fleming also wrote
Chitty Chitty Bang Bang, a children's story about a robotic flying car that protects its inventor's family. Andre Millard, *Equipping James Bond: Guns, Gadgets, and Technological Enthusiasm* (Johns Hopkins University Press, 2018), 63, 175.

† One of these gadgets was the home movie camera. The Prelinger Archive has preserved
many dozens of tapes from the region and era and together they convey a postwar atmosphere of leisure and consumption among suburban families: weddings, vacation road
trips, amusement parks, children in big dresses, new cars and houses, men fooling around
on motorcycles, etc. That said, they couldn't film the PTSD nightmares.

engineers at firms such as HP and IBM remained tough to organize, but some hourly production workers armed themselves with the National Labor Relations Act and bargained collectively. At military contractor Westinghouse's Sunnyvale plant, the left-wing United Electrical Workers won an election to represent hundreds of workers, beating out more conservative unions. The UE entered the postwar period as the third-largest member union in the CIO with 700,000 workers, including around 300,000 women.[35] But the UE had a strong communist current, and in 1947 when the Republican congress passed the Taft-Hartley Act, which required union leaders working with the National Labor Relations Board to affirm that they were not communists, the UE refused to comply. Soon they split entirely with the CIO, preparing it to merge with the tamer and less radical AFL. Marginalized by the increasingly anticommunist mainstream labor movement and shackled by Taft-Hartley, with its ban on sympathy strikes, the UE withered. In 1956 it lost its Westinghouse reelection, and by the end of the '50s it was redbaited out of burgeoning Silicon Valley. This hit women on the production lines particularly hard. Historian Glenna Matthews writes that "[w]hen the UE lost its vital presence in the Valley, women workers lost their best chance of having labor commit resources to organize them."[36] Uncoincidentally, Silicon Valley firms used immigrant women to fill nonunion low-wage assembly jobs in the coming decades. Warned by example and freed from internal competition by Taft-Hartley, Santa Clara County union leaders stayed friendly with management.[37]

Manufacturers increased prices to offset the high wages that constituted their side of the compact, which made life hard for Americans whose pay wasn't tied to industrial revenues. As economist John Kenneth Galbraith wrote of the dynamic, "A passenger in even a very fast automobile is reasonably certain of keeping up with it. A man running alongside is not so well situated."[38] Suburban military Keynesianism was a speedy car, and not everyone was along for the ride. The program left workers behind in new ways. For example, the unionized fruit industry, with its relatively high pay, had been open to undocumented immigrants, but only U.S. citizens were generally eligible for defense work. Still, Northern California's Mexican population boomed as workers came from every direction toward the new center of prosperity, many solicited by regional labor contractors looking to fill jobs in the fields.* In 1948, the Supreme Court struck down restrictive real estate covenants, allowing documented Mexican workers to live anywhere they wanted, but the Supreme Court couldn't make high-technology firms hire them, even for nondefense work. Meanwhile, mechanization changed food production in California: The state's agricultural workforce declined (in absolute terms) by over 20 percent between 1949 and 1969, though workers harvested virtually the same amount of acreage.† Braceros, Mexican-Americans, and undocumented Mexican immigrants, cordoned away and together on the segregated labor market, all vied for the same shrinking set of jobs.

During World War II, hundreds of thousands of black Americans moved out of rural areas in the southern states to seek industrial jobs, and a solid portion came west. San Francisco's black population quadrupled between 1940 and 1945, from 4,800 to 20,000, filling neighborhoods without racial covenants, such as the Western Addition and its Fillmore district in San Francisco.[39, 40] In the East Bay, defense wages spun up vibrant black communities like the one depicted in Marlon Riggs's 1981 documentary, *Long Train Running: A History of the Oakland Blues*. The Oklahoma-born blues guitarist Lowell Fulson tells Riggs of playing packed Bay Area clubs during the war days, how he could hardly pull off his hat to the crowd before it was full of money. Downtown Oakland "became packed with a bustling twenty-four-hour street scene," writes scholar Chris Rhomberg. "Theaters and cafes stayed open all night to accommodate the swing shift, and dance halls, taverns, and other amusements sprang up to appeal to war workers with disposable income."[41]

---

* Dismayed by the sudden internment of the Japanese labor force, California's agricultural capitalists overcompensated, luring an oversupply of workers via contractors and advertisement.

† The small reduction in harvested California cropland between 1949 and 1969 is entirely due to a decrease in acreage devoted to barley, which peaked in 1955 and precipitously declined until its virtual elimination in the twenty-first century. Alan L. Olmstead and Paul W. Rhode, "A History of California Agriculture" (University of California Agriculture and Natural Resources, 2017), 3–4. Employment in the state's celebrated wine industry was also in a recovery period, between prohibition-wartime vine appropriation for raisins and the quintupling of wine output between the 1950 nadir and 1975. The level of employment in the industry didn't start increasing above its immediate postwar level until the early 1970s. Ann R. Markusen, *Profit Cycles, Oligopoly, and Regional Development* (MIT Press, 1985), 203–5.

But as shipbuilding declined with the end of the war, black workers were among the first fired: Manufacturing employment in Oakland fell by 70 percent between August of 1945 and February of 1946.*[42]

Like the white space settlers, these black Okies were younger and better educated than most people in the communities they'd left, and when the shipbuilding industry in San Francisco and the East Bay could no longer absorb them, thousands tried their luck in the South Bay. The black population in Santa Clara Valley more than doubled every decade between 1940 and 1980, jumping from 730 in 1940 to 4,187 in 1960, mostly in the growing black communities in San Jose and in and around Palo Alto.† But despite their manufacturing qualifications, black workers struggled to get hired in industrial jobs and often had to settle for janitorial positions. The historian Herbert G. Ruffin concludes that, contrary to the prevailing Great Migration narrative, wartime experience, trade unions, and federal anti-discrimination rules weren't enough to secure a significant role for black workers in South Bay manufacturing.[43]

Rearmament as a global economic stimulus program made perfect sense to a few policy makers, but what the country really needed was an expensive new shooting war, and American presidents have never had much trouble finding one of those. In a conversation about the eventual success of the NSC 68 rearmament plan at Princeton's Institute for Advanced Study, someone in J. Robert Oppenheimer's 1953 seminar reflecting on the Truman era posed the idea: "Korea came along and (saved?) us — did the job for us." Guest and NSC 68 architect Dean Acheson conceded, "I think you can say that."‡

---

* White women in war production jobs were laid off, too; for better and worse (and unlike most black workers) much of their labor could be absorbed in the white suburban household.

† One community open to migrants: the former Japantown in San Jose, redlined for black homeseekers during and after Japanese internment. Herbert G. Ruffin, *Uninvited Neighbors: African Americans in Silicon Valley, 1769–1990* (University of Oklahoma Press, 2014), 73, 80.

‡ A version of the full quote is often misattributed to Acheson, including in David M. Kennedy et al.'s textbook, *The American Pageant*. Sadly the transcript archived by the Truman Library doesn't label speakers other than Acheson, but among the seminar participants were Truman administration heavyweights like ambassador to the Soviet Union George F. Kennan, NSC 68 co-author Paul Nitze, secretary of commerce W. Averell Harriman, United Nations representative Philip Jessup, and assistant secretary of state for Far Eastern affairs Dean Rusk, all of whom were in a position to speculate. David S. McLellan, *Dean Acheson: The State Department Years* (Dodd, Mead & Company, 1976), 433n20. In any

Too Much Progress in the Burial Industry

Talking about the American early 1950s as a postwar period is misleading because there was a war. The plan that became suburban military Keynesianism sounded wacky to Truman, but the Chinese Communist Revolution and Soviet nuclear testing (along with an intensification of dogmatic American anticommunism) did suggest an inexorable drift toward round III. In 1945, the Soviets and Americans bisected Korea at the 38th parallel, creating North Korea and South Korea, and when North Korean troops blew by the line in June of 1950, American policy makers saw East Asia crumbling before their eyes: Red dominoes falling from Maoist China all the way down to Australia and Indonesia, where the popular Indonesian Communist Party threatened to take power by election or insurgency.* A U.S.-U.N. invasion force of 13,000, led by General Douglas MacArthur (the same one who burned down the Bonus Army camp for Hoover), pushed up the Korean peninsula toward the Chinese border. Mao responded with 400,000 volunteers, who promptly captured 7,000 American prisoners and drove the invaders back south. After Stalin's death, in 1953, an armistice reset the border.[44]

A draw between the great powers in military terms, the war was a disaster for the Korean and Chinese peoples. American strategic bombing had proved itself in Japan under Shockley's team of actuaries, and MacArthur began the war with a massive attack on North Korean cities and infrastructure. A RAND Corporation report describes the bombing campaign as "leisurely" because of the lack of enemy air defenses, and in less than two months American forces destroyed almost all their strategic targets. One crew was apparently so well armed that they chased a single enemy soldier on his motorcycle, dropping bombs until they hit him.[45] U.S. air forces dropped 635,000 tons of explosives during the three years of the war, more than the total used in

---

event, Acheson seems less wistful about Korea's role regarding NSC 68 than the misattribution suggests, though not necessarily more skeptical. "Transcript of Princeton Seminar Discussion, Wire VI, Dean Acheson Papers" (Harry S. Truman Library & Museum, July 9, 1953), 6, https://www.trumanlibrary.gov/library/personal-papers/princeton-seminars-file -1953-1970/july-8-9-1953-0?documentid=9&pagenumber=6.

* A 1949 CIA report warned Australian Communists were capable of "crippling Australian industry" from their trade union positions. "Communist Influence in Australia" (Central Intelligence Agency, Declassified and Approved for Release 2013/08/15, April 11, 1949), ii.

the World War II Pacific theater, including over 30,000 tons of napalm.[46] An estimated 400,000 to one million Chinese soldiers died, and according to the head of the U.S. Strategic Air Command, so did one-fifth of the North Korean population.[47] The United States lost fewer than 35,000 men, inaugurating the new epoch of American lethal efficiency.

The Korean War was the global underside of military Keynesianism. As bombers leveled North Korea's cities between 1950 and '52, military support for electronics research at Stanford tripled.[48] Stanford's leadership was wary of World War II—Hoover's preference had been to let Hitler and Stalin wipe each other out—but fighting communists was a different matter, and MacArthur himself remained a proud Hooverite, scheming with the ex-president against Truman while still in uniform.* The DOD's 1951 budget nearly quintupled, from $13 billion to $58 billion, and some universities became, in the words of C. Wright Mills, "financial branches of the military establishment."[49] Whereas only a few years before, William Talbot got kicked out of SRI for his profligate government contracting, Stanford's post-Tresidder president J. E. Wallace Sterling ("sufficiently anticommunist and anti-Roosevelt to please Hoover," writes historian Rebecca Lowen) promoted Fred Terman to provost in 1954, urging him to remake the rest of the university the way he remade engineering.[50] Terman had won another war, and with a Republican (Eisenhower) finally back in the White House, Stanford was no longer afraid of the state.

"[T]he solution to the economic crisis of the end of the war turned out to be simply not letting the war end," writes historian Walter Johnson.[51] The Cold War was a real, long war, and millions of people died. To speak of the American "postwar" economy or state into the 1950s is not to talk about a country at peace, but a country finished with peace altogether, a nation that has embraced a permanent conflict. "The world is squarely faced with Asiatic versus Western civilization," Hoover wrote MacArthur in his 1946 "John the Baptist" letter, in which he compared the general to the biblical preacher and urged

---

*   As president, Hoover appointed MacArthur army chief of staff and later supported his short political career. After MacArthur lost the 1952 Republican presidential nomination to Eisenhower, he moved into the Waldorf-Astoria in New York City, Hoover's East Coast home. A *New Orleans Times-Picayune* cartoon showed the two men shouting to each other: "Quiet and isolated, isn't it?" from the building's towers as revelers far below celebrated "Ike." Keith Temple, "Quiet and isolated, isn't it?," Library of Congress Prints and Photographs Division, https://lccn.loc.gov/2016684220.

him to start giving political speeches. "Western civilization cannot stand the shock of either Communism dominating the world or of another world war. Strength by the United States in preparedness and sense and courage in diplomatic action can prevent both."* Yet there were some diplomatic problems in a Shockley-Arnold preparedness strategy based on flooding the world with weapons. An Eisenhower plan to sell discount nuclear-tipped intermediate-range ballistic missiles to NATO allies in Europe (standard military Keynesianism) helped precipitate the Cuban Missile Crisis five years later, when the first-strike nukes showed up in Turkey, on the Soviet doorstep.† But missiles kept the suburbs growing and the Reds everywhere in check. And when they didn't, that's what 30,000 tons of napalm were for.

The conventional American narrative about the Korean War, to the degree that we bother to tell one, is about a country and a global order brought together. The United Nations, led by America, would now intervene to protect existing borders from communist aggression. Truman racially integrated the military, and the reimposition of price controls slowed down the runaway car of American prosperity so more people could jump in. America came together, even if we had to kill a couple of million East Asian people to do it. But the war had a domestic front, too. At the federal and state levels, the Red Scare kicked back into gear. The Immigration and Nationality Act of 1952 passed in the name of anticommunism over Truman's veto, reaffirming the 1924 country quota system and making anarchists and communists automatically deportable.[52] Radicals (particularly black radicals) found themselves surveilled, arrested, and, when possible under the new law, deported.[53] Even the military integration wasn't going as planned: Mass murder was not a strong basis for interracial harmony, and white American troops in Korea greeted their new black bunkmates with Confederate flags.[54] At Stanford, President Sterling announced that communists were not welcome to teach, and he

---

* The letter precedes NSC 68 in 1950 but suggests its shape, another testament to Hoover's influence long after leaving office. "Herbert Hoover to Douglas Macarthur, October 17, 1946," Herbert Hoover Papers, Post-Presidential Individual Correspondence, 1933–1964, Herbert Hoover Presidential Library, Box 129.

† In a confusing bit of loophole-based proliferation, the nuclear warheads technically still belonged to the United States, while the missiles were sold to host countries. Barton J. Bernstein, "The Cuban Missile Crisis: Trading the Jupiters in Turkey?," *Political Science Quarterly* 95, no. 1 (1980): 99.

began collaborating with the California Un-American Activities Committee. Sterling also worked with the campus Hoover clique to monitor and remove left-wing faculty.[55]

In the 1950s and early 1960s, no Stanford professor received more anti-communist pressure than economist Paul A. Baran.* When he was hired, in 1948, Baran was a great choice for a university that wanted a patriotic lefty econ professor. He was a Russian Jew by birth; his father was a Menshivik rather than a Bolshevik, and Paul finished his studies in Berlin. There he was taken under the wing of Rudolf Hilferding, leading light of the interwar German leftist economists and author of the magisterial *Finance Capital*—recall his early analysis of the railroads. When the left lost the struggle with Hitler, Baran fled, eventually to Harvard. Exceptionally brilliant, he found no shortage of American demand for his capabilities when World War II came. He worked in the Office of Price Administration, in R & D for the OSS, and for the Strategic Bombing Survey in Germany and then Japan. After the war he worked for the Department of Commerce and then the Federal Reserve Bank of New York. He was also an engaging lecturer, and he knew something about the emerging Soviet bloc. Though he didn't keep his socialistic tendencies secret, that wasn't a total deal breaker at the time—no member of the Communist Party, he wasn't even welcome in the USSR after helping the United States gather intelligence in reconstructing Germany. Stanford quickly promoted him to full professor and gave him tenure. That was a mistake.

Baran was a professional peer and (at least) an intellectual equal of the leading liberal economists. During the war, he worked alongside Galbraith, who called him "one of the most brilliant, and by a wide margin, the most interesting economist I have ever known."[56] But whereas others were eager to ride bombs *Strangelove*-style into the prosperous American half of the century, Baran loathed military Keynesianism. In fact, he thought its development discredited Keynesianism in a broader sense. Along with his Harvard friend Paul Sweezy, Baran became the strategy's most incisive critic within mainstream economics. In his 1957 book, *The Political Economy of Growth*, he argued that it *did* matter where demand was coming from, that stockpiling weapons of

---

* Not to be confused with Polish-American engineer and fellow Palo Altan Paul Baran, who's credited with designing data packets while working at RAND on nuke-resilient networking infrastructure.

mass destruction for the spending stimulus was "very much akin to the counsel to burn the house in order to roast the pig."[57] The oligopolies running the American economy followed the government down absurd R & D paths, failing to produce anything useful for the people. And on their own, corporate leaders only pursued investment that reduced their costs, avoiding plans to expand output, which (as we've seen) ignited price competition and lessened profits. For workers, living didn't get increasingly easy, as the Keynesians predicted. Under capitalism, people couldn't direct the nation's societal surplus to useful ends. Rather, the people's inability to control those resources in the face of oligopolistic control *defined* capitalism.

Baran's conclusions—representing the left wing of the left critique of left-Keynesianism—were controversial, but what really got him in trouble was Cuba. Part of his argument in *The Political Economy of Growth* is that America was unwilling and economically unable to tolerate any sort of popular sovereignty in what he called the "source countries."[58] It was the same conclusion Ernesto Galarza came to in Bolivia. No matter what type of government they pursued, Third World countries that sought meaningful independence had to expropriate foreign capitalists. Country by country, America put its fat finger on the scale in the 1950s, actively interfering in internal politics; Baran lists Venezuela, British Guiana, Guatemala, Kenya, the Philippines, Indochina, Iran, Egypt, and Argentina. Third World revolution suggested a new path to Baran, beyond American-Russian militarism. He visited Cuba at Fidel Castro's invitation in the fall of 1960, and he returned to Stanford after three weeks to report. Attendance at his public lecture overflowed. Baran praised Castro and warned that America would soon seek to halt Cuba's progress with a coup attempt similar to the one that overthrew the elected president of Guatemala, Jacobo Árbenz, in the interests of expropriated fruit companies, but he added that such a coup wasn't likely to succeed in Cuba.* A wire service picked up the story and it went national: Stanford had a commie economics professor, with tenure.

As long as he wasn't pro-Soviet, it was easy enough for most of the 1950s to write off Baran's professed Marxism as an intellectual orientation with no

---

* The Bay of Pigs was only about six months away; maybe the White House should have consulted Baran.

urgent political relevance. His Harvard degree, professional esteem, and long
résumé of American public service insulated him.* But paying a teacher to
shill for Castro in front of a giant crowd was too much for Stanford's conservative elements. Letters from alumni donors poured in. A Texaco executive
reminded Sterling about the company's $10,000 donation from the previous
year as well as the Castro regime's confiscation of $50 million in Texaco prop-
erty. If the school wanted more donations, it should do something about "a
professor who glories [sic] a sworn enemy of the United States and a robber of
one of the University's benefactors."[59] For capitalists, the global class war was
always personal. Sterling held a lunch meeting with large donors, including a
top executive from Transamerica Corporation, which is what Bank of America was then calling itself. University trustee and West Coast corporate leader
David Packard prepared a letter for the pro-Baran *Stanford Daily* suggesting
that the professor's salary be reduced by a dollar for every dollar he received
from the communists. Too inflammatory, it went unsent, but it reflected the
attitude of the Stanford board. The alumni outpouring was public anyway,
and the *Daily* ran a five-part series exposing conservative donor influence and
defending Baran. Provost Frederick Terman warned that they couldn't fire
the tenured professor for mere disagreeable scholarship without ruining the
school's reputation, something everyone involved valued very much. Instead,
they bullied him until he died.

A heart attack took Baran's life in 1964 at the young age of fifty-four. He
never got to see his masterwork, *Monopoly Capital*, written with Sweezy, published. Earlier that year, he complained to his writing partner, "For next year
I got a teaching load that is about twice as large as that of my 'peers,' with
pay of about 60 percent of theirs, and all this with a broad grin: 'Look at us,
how democratic and free and tolerant we are!' "[60] This while they knew Baran
was still recovering from his first heart attack. If it weren't for his son, Nicky,
he told Sweezy, he would leave academia and scrape together a modest living
as an honest Marxist intellectual, which is what Sweezy did at the *Monthly
Review* journal. Maybe if he'd had another year he would have done exactly
that; it's hard to imagine how much posterity lost to Baran's early death. The

---

* Willingness to live in the intellectual backwater of Palo Alto, California, probably didn't
  hurt; Harvard denied Sweezy tenure at the same time Stanford hired Baran.

reason we have so much information regarding the internal dynamics of the administration's decision making—including a Stanford official linking the "harassment" after the Cuba speech with Baran's health and a description of the kind of corporate-administrative strategy meeting we're normally forced to imagine—is that in 1971, in the middle of an even bigger campus intellectual-freedom controversy, someone broke into a locked room, stole the old file, and distributed copies. It's an important piece of local context for the eruptions that tore the school apart in the years following Paul Baran's death.

The historic irony is that Stanford's very inability to absorb Marxist intellectuals like Paul Baran during the 1960s confirmed Baran's theories. As *Stanford Daily* reporter Ron Rapoport noted at the time, Stanford was in the middle of a big fundraising campaign, attempting to raise $75 million to match a promised $25 million from the Ford Foundation.[61] Baran's work failed to flatter potential donors, and by lending legitimacy to the Castro regime he was an accessory to the expropriation of corporate property. As the Texaco letter made clear, Stanford University was in a zero-sum struggle against the Cuban people—as well as the Guatemalan people, the Iranian people, and the people anywhere Stanford donors owned stuff, which was a lot of places. In that fight, Baran was proudly on the wrong side. The middle-aged Harvard-trained economists dedicated *Monopoly Capital* in six letters: "For Che."

As a productive part of the American capitalist economy, Stanford faced some of the same limitations that capitalism did as a system. It was, as an institution, invested in profit and existing property relations. As I'll note in the rest of this section, in the electronics industry and way beyond, profit incentives determined Stanford's real shape. Not the school's own profit—nonexistent, of course—but profit in general. This was the role of universities in the Giannini cartel model: to take on research and development on behalf of the capitalist class rather than any individual firm. As Jordan designed it, Stanford's capabilities met America's pressing modern needs—"an adequate supply of suitably qualified technical personnel and a satisfactory number of first-rate scientists."[62] The fruits of this work, therefore, don't just "happen" to be bombs, ads, canned food, and Hollywood's "moronizing entertainment," Baran writes; for the capitalist system, all that is "the very basis of its existence and viability."[63] We've seen this dynamic play out with regard to the modern food system: The state demands canned food for war; firms invest in food processing; then, already halfway down the processed-food path, firms keep going, investing in advertising, shipping, mechanization, and additives research. What we're left with is a very profitable food system that's objectively harmful to people and to the rest of the earth. This same dynamic undergirded Provost Terman's Stanford and the wider "postwar" Palo Alto community.

Historians tend to excuse the defense-funded academic work of this period, since the researchers mostly believed they were using the government's largesse to pursue their own interests—though things might look a little different today if one of those Stanford-developed Lockheed ICBMs had leveled Leningrad, as they threatened to do every minute of every day for decades. But state incentives shifted priorities toward applied work, not only in engineering, but also in the new subfield directions shaped by Terman's entrepreneurial instincts: communications (replacing journalism), cultural anthropology, political behavior, and child development.* Stanford was quickly becoming a full-spectrum Cold War lab, and that led the school in disturbing directions, as I'll tell you about later in the section. In one early example, Stanford chemists produced an indeterminately toxic solution of zinc cadmium oxide that was then sprayed in a fog over slum neighborhoods in Minneapolis, St. Louis, and Winnipeg without warning in order to test...something.[64] In another example, Stanford psychologists, looking for new ways to spot the highest quality human capital, experimented with small children and marshmallows, seeing how long the former could delay consumption, searching for the promise of self-control in their toddling subjects. Inspired by the return of American POWs from Korea, policy makers and researchers titillated themselves with fantasies about brainwashing and body doubles as they pursued all sorts of bad science. These paths were largely dead ends, for the military and for humanity, but the checks cashed, which put the school in a place to guide the country and the world.

Wishful thinking and outright fraud were endemic to Cold War defense contracts. Asked to describe American 1950s military tech infrastructure, most people would probably walk away. But if they didn't, they might describe

---

* On the other side of campus, when a senior member of the classics department complained about cuts to their non-entrepreneurial subject, Terman wrote her views off as those of a "single woman—lonely—frustrated." Rebecca S. Lowen, *Creating the Cold War University: The Transformation of Stanford* (University of California Press, 1997), 159.

a dim room full of white-shirted horn-rimmed scientists, each monitoring a circular screen containing a continually updating radar map of North America. Those rooms were real; they were part of the Semi-Automatic Ground Environment (SAGE) system, a collaboration between the air force, MIT, and every major computer company, principally IBM. SAGE was the biggest computer system of the time: Operators fed punch cards coded with the planned air routes of the day's flights into the giant computers, and if radar hit on something that didn't match up, operators could deploy missiles or aircraft to intercept what they had to assume was a Soviet nuclear bomber. SAGE stations had computers that connected across the country by modem and telephone line, a first. The system was a PR coup for IBM, which produced a 12-minute advertising video called "On Guard! The Story of SAGE," a truly exceptional piece of Cold War propaganda, complete with Mom and Dad standing watch over their sleeping daughter: the parental dyad, a SAGE system of the home.* According to SAGE engineer Lester Earnest, it also didn't work—at all.† No one claims America ever used SAGE in action, but Earnest maintains that we never could have. He compares the system to Forrest Gump: "It was very fast, financially successful, and incredibly stupid."[65] For one thing, SAGE couldn't handle radar countermeasures, which the Soviets were already using. For another, ICBMs replaced bombers as the go-to nuclear delivery device, and those went above radar into space. At best SAGE was a glorified air-traffic control system; at worst it connected nuclear missiles to buggy code and unsecured phone lines.‡ But the Cold War power elite, congealing between the academy, the defense industry, and the military, had every reason to keep flashy scams like SAGE going.

With so much at stake, loyalty oaths and investigative checks kept potential security threats, whistleblowers, and malcontents outside the system, even when they had useful interests and talents. The promising UC Berkeley engineering student Lee Felsenstein had the offer for his work-study dream job at NASA's Flight Research Center rescinded when the university discovered that

---

* The IBM video also lends narrator samples to the lead track "The Buzz Kill" on the rapper Sage Francis's 2005 album *A Healthy Distrust*. See "On Guard! The Story of SAGE," IBM Corporation (1957).

† Earnest ended up at Stanford, where he worked on artificial intelligence and his eccentricity.

‡ There was no need to secure the network because the concept of a malevolent computer hacker didn't exist yet.

his parents had been members of the CPUSA. Discouraged about his future in the industry, Felsenstein dropped out of school before graduating.[66] Americans in general were getting better educated, but the military-academic-industrial complex threw up all sorts of barriers to education and employment depending on who—or, more precisely, what—you were. The result was an engineering elite of WASP men with an uncomplicated collective interest in the smooth continued expansion of American capitalism, nationally and around the world.

Fred Terman was squarely in the Cold War sun, but his father, Lewis, was drifting toward the shade. He envisioned his genius study as ultimately geared toward national service, but the nation didn't always feel the same way about all his geniuses. Terman's pleas couldn't stop authorities from putting at least two Japanese-American Termites (as his study subjects were known) in internment camps. "I tried hard to get an exception made in your case when the American-Japanese were being relocated," he wrote to Alfred Tadashi when Tadashi asked him if his connections could keep the man's biracial children safe, "but the military authorities were adamant."[67] He wrote to Ronald Talbot, another member of the genius-prone Tadashi family, "As an American citizen I feel greatly humiliated that any of my fellow citizens should show the racial intolerance that you and many others have suffered."* As HUAC blacklisted the Termite film director Edward Dmytryk as one of the Hollywood Ten, Lewis fumed over the new loyalty oath required from UC Berkeley faculty.† In 1952 he was retired and slightly outside Hoover's orbit, and while his prized son made a habit of denying tenure to liberals, Lewis took the biggest leftward stride of his life and voted for Adlai Stevenson.[68] To his dismay, individual IQ could not take precedence over America's structural inequalities; they're too closely related. Six weeks after the egghead Stevenson lost a rematch with the general Eisenhower, Lewis Terman died. His mistakes lived on.

---

* The Tadashis, having already moved to rural California farms, remained free through the war. Simply, they didn't come forward and no one found them. See Joel N. Shurkin, *Terman's Kids: The Groundbreaking Study of How the Gifted Grow Up* (Little, Brown, 1992), 130.

† To get out of prison, Dmytryk later named names to HUAC. See Henry L. Minton, *Lewis M. Terman: Pioneer in Psychological Testing* (New York University Press, 1988), 240.

The Solid State

Hewlett-Packard — Invention of the Semiconductor —
Shockley and Fairchild — Advent of Venture Capital —
Hoover in Germany and Japan — Chips on Ships

Despite the administration's reticence, Stanford and Palo Alto enjoyed more than their share of World War II contracts and subcontracts, though not as many as they nabbed in the years to follow and not as many as shipbuilding cities got. The Varian klystron, Poniatoff's antenna, and Litton's tube construction all played important roles in the Allied communications apparatus, not to mention Terman's leadership of the RRL. Vannevar Bush could be proud of his young protégé, and Bush was the man when it came to military research contracts. MIT and Raytheon benefited as much as anyone, but Bush and his newly established Office of Naval Research looked to Palo Alto, too. (It didn't hurt that politically Bush was still a Hoover man.) When Terman returned to his hometown, after Stanford made him dean of the engineering school, he threw himself into preparing the university and the local industrial community for the aerospace, communications, and electronics boom he knew was coming. With Bush and ONR's help, Terman made sure Palo Alto caught early Cold War funding by the ear, mounted it, and rode it to the promised land of space-age suburban settlement and prosperity that is the subject of the previous chapter. This chapter is concerned with the technological, commercial, and ultimately geopolitical developments that bridged the gap between de Forest's Federal Telegraph triode and the microchips of Silicon Valley. It's a much shorter distance than you might imagine.

First: How do you make a computer out of lightbulbs? It sounds ridiculous, but at the same time, we can picture the midcentury room full of lab-coated geeks racing to replace a burned-out tube in their giant calculating machine. They did exist; how did they work? The answer to that question helps explain

Palo Alto's quick transition from the capital of high-quality vacuum tube production to Silicon Valley.

Lee de Forest's Audion triode wasn't a whole lot more complex than a basic Edison bulb, and yet it was the basis for the whole vacuum-tube radio boom, as well as the microwave technology that kept David Starr Jordan's Palo Alto on the national map even after the telecom trusts left town. Still, the triode had a lot more to give, more than anyone first imagined. And while Fred Terman, Alex Poniatoff, Charles Litton, the Varian brothers, and the rest of the Stanford–Team USA radar squad used the power of tubes and waves to beat Hitler, other Allied groups pushed the triode into new territory.*

But just because you can do something doesn't mean there's a reason to: What can you do with an early computer? Practically, there's not a lot that jumps out, and it took roughly 35 years between the invention of the Audion and the first vacuum-tube computer. If necessity is the relevant mother, then Mom had a small centered mustache and beady eyes. Nazi Germany's coded messages presented a new challenge for the Allies' human computers, and age-old questions about how to calculate shell trajectories under various conditions offered a new opportunity. The Second World War was the igniting event for electronic computation, an occasion when the vast resources needed to realize the triode's promise finally encountered a situation with high enough stakes to justify spending them.

---

* How, technically, does the triode turn into a computer? Recall the metaphor about the Audion made of cheetahs and antelopes: With a diode, the two-part circuit either has electricity or not, there are cheetahs or there aren't. But a triode can turn on and off while powered up, the hungry cats are caught either scratching at the doors or munching on antelope. Now imagine there's a scale weighing the pile of antelopes, and when the number dips below a certain amount (due to being eaten by cheetahs), a light goes on. We have a binary switch: The light is on or off, the cheetahs are eating the antelopes or they're not. A switch like that is the fundamental element for a binary computing system, and when we start getting imaginative about how we put them together, they can form what are called "logic gates." Say we pair an antelope pile with two different glass gates (A and B) next to each other: The signal light no longer signifies "Yes, cheetahs!" as in a diode, it means "Yes, gate A and/or yes, gate B." If we put the gates one in front of each other, then the light signifies "Yes, gate A and gate B." Before you know it, you've built an "If...then" logic circuit out of hungry cheetahs. Then you wire the light from the antelope-ode scale to another, which triggers its own gate, and so on, through a theoretically infinite number of and/or/not conditions. That's how you build a computer out of hungry cheetahs and piles of dead antelopes.

Colossus was the name of the most successful British triode-based code-breaking machine, and its programmers and operators exploited a weakness in the Nazi system that happened to overlap with the era's limited processing capacity. Germans encoded their messages with rotor-based cipher machines, which automatically transformed letters. These devices were electromechanical, not electronic, which means they relied on the physical movement of parts for every encoding. The Nazis' Enigma machine, with its three rotors, was breakable with the same level of technology, but when they upgraded to a 12-rotor Lorenz cipher, the Allies were in trouble. The famed British mathematician Alan Turing found the vulnerability: Only one of the rotors advanced automatically with every keystroke; the other 11 depended on a change in input. With the first rotor cracked, they could test combinations for the rest by looking for an unusual proportion of matching bigrams—recurring keystrokes, which are more common in real messages than in intentionally randomized ciphertext. It was possible to do this by conventional electromechanical methods, but with so many rotors to crack, they couldn't get the information in a useful timeframe. Wars move quickly. By using triodes, though, it was possible to wire an electronic system that tested solutions at the speed of, well, electrons. Operators translated texts into binary, in which every letter is described with a series of five zeros and ones.* Once converted, the code could be translated into something physical, mechanical: Each letter was a row on a long roll of paper tape, a series of five punches or nonpunches, the computer ticking them through, pumping electrical impulses through a series of carefully arranged triode logic gates, outputting counts. The system worked, amplifying earlier techniques enough to make them useful, and the Brits built 10 of the machines and put them to work. It was the first triumph of electronics, with more to come.

In America, the first electronic computer was ENIAC, at the University of Pennsylvania, which was an upgrade on Colossus in that operators could program it (via switches) for several purposes—it was basically a superpowered calculator. (Or, by contemporary standards, a calculator.) Military-affiliated

---

* This alphabet requires five binary digits—known in computer science by the portmanteau "bits"—per letter in order to code all 26 letters. A is 00001, B is 00010, C is 00011, and so on.

scientists used it to pursue intense time-sensitive calculations, mostly those involved in nuclear weapons research and multivariable artillery projections. The engineers (and corporate contractors like IBM and Burroughs) succeeded, and despite its novelty the electronic triode apparatus easily outperformed existing electromechanical calculators. But compared to physical switch-and-plug systems, vacuum-tube computers were expensive and fragile, requiring thousands, then tens of thousands, of glass bulbs, one of which always seemed to be blowing. They weren't so fragile that they were inoperable—before engineers pulled it off, it was widely believed that the vacuum-tube failure rate multiplied by the massive number of tubes necessarily left such machines theoretically unable to function even under ideal circumstances—but the immediate commercial possibilities seemed limited. Reliable electromechanical punch-card counters and sorters of the type IBM made were much more evidently useful information-technology investments, and even the theoretical subject of electronics was shrouded in mystery. But Fred Terman had been behind the curtain, and he was coming home to Palo Alto. The seeds he planted before the war were sprouting.

While many of the Stanford area's young stars deployed for war tech work in one way or another—Litton to ITT in Newark, Hewlett to the U.S. Army Signal Corps, Fred Terman to the RRL in Cambridge (along with a crew of his favorites), Shockley to the Anti-Submarine Warfare Operations Research Group, the Varians to Sperry Gyroscope in New York, Hansen to MIT, and so on—Dave Packard was needed at home to keep Hewlett-Packard running. Even though they didn't have military contracts going into the war boom, the armed forces bought HP tools off the shelf, and the firm subcontracted for federal contractors. And when the American military moved to a war footing, it looked to HP for specialty radio and microwave assignments. The biggest one was the Leopard project, a radar countermeasure that issued phony locational pings to enemy scanners. Terman's radio work aided the war effort even beyond the RRL, in Leopard's case via the commercialization path he laid out for his students. Hewlett-Packard was Terman's first conscious attempt to matchmake an electronics start-up from the beginning, and though it seems to have been Packard who insisted on Hewlett at first, and though the two faced some bumps along the road with the Depression, things worked out much the way Terman had planned. When the military contracts and subcontracts started flowing, he knew where to place his students so they got wet. And in that way Fred's knowledge (and, his father would want us to add, his IQ) came to serve the American homeland, his hometown, and his home institution at the same time.

HP began with one-off custom electrical engineering projects for local businesses: a bowling-alley foot-foul indicator, some air-conditioner components, a failed harmonica tuner, what have you. Their first product success came with Bill Hewlett's design for a triode-based oscillator—a metal box that generates precise audio waves—which was based in part on Fred Terman's radio work. Hewlett's circuit used a small internal lightbulb as a kind of electrical exhaust pipe, which successfully reduced distortion. They endowed their inaugural box with the dignified name 200A, and priced it at $54.40, an arbitrary number alluding to the American expansionist slogan "Fifty-four forty or fight"— 54'40 being the latitude of the settlers' desired northwest border with Canada.[1] (The price was too low, and they were quickly forced to raise it.) They built a better mousetrap, and Terman gave them a list of around 25 potential clients.[2] But it was Bud Hawkins, chief sound engineer for Walt Disney, who placed the first big order. He picked up eight of the devices to use on the forthcoming film *Fantasia*, happy to pay considerably more than the original $54.40 since he was used to shelling out hundreds of dollars a pop.* In addition to making use of the newest advances, HP wasn't much more than H and P with little overhead, thanks to the good graces of the Palo Alto engineering community. Compared to its biggest competitor, General Radio, HP was light on its feet; in its artisan days, the firm not only avoided extraneous costs, it also offloaded a significant amount of them to the supportive local environment. Terman's golden boys had the run of the town, borrowing Stanford and Litton facilities as needed. It was a good investment all around, and the result for HP was that its oscillator, in addition to being as good as anything on the market, was

---

* The money came from Bank of America, of which Disney was effectively a subsidiary. A. P. Giannini financed other classics like *Alice in Wonderland, Bambi, Peter Pan, Pinocchio,* and *Snow White,* as well as the Disney studios and Disneyland theme park. Janet Wasko, *Movies and Money: Financing the American Film Industry* (Ablex Publishing Corporation, 1982), 172–74.

much cheaper, a small fraction of the competition's price. One counterintuitive lesson H and P learned from this first product experience is that if you were the obvious choice, you had a lot of price flexibility. If a buyer is expecting to pay $300, he doesn't much care whether you charge $50 or $100. It can't be gouging if it's a good deal.

When Hewlett returned from the signal corps to the firm that bore his name, he found that his place in the world had changed. What had been a sub-$40,000 concern in 1940 had grown to a genuine company, with over 200 employees and $1.5 million in annual revenue at the war's peak.[3] And though the founders were dealing with the Roosevelt government, Packard made sure the company had the profits to expand at 100 percent a year without turning to outside investors. Displaying the capitalist ideological fire that made him a trusted adviser to both Herbert Hoover and Ronald Reagan, he refused to comply with FDR's wartime Renegotiation Board. When two bureaucrats came to Palo Alto to tell Packard that the firm fell on the wrong side of regulations against excessive profits, he chewed them out about the free market, appealed above their heads, and got an agreement with "virtually everything we asked for."[4] Once again, Roosevelt's agents and the social democratic agenda found themselves nullified in California's Hooverville. When the war ended and the biggest contracts dried up, HP shrunk by around two-thirds. But thanks to wartime profits, it had the resources for a strong push into the postwar economy. H and P just had to decide what they were going to make.

Over the next decade, they learned what they didn't want to do from Palo Alto's Jimmy Stewart—the one-time magnetron king of California, Charles Litton. He is the cautionary tale that, even if they don't know it, haunts Silicon Valley entrepreneurs to this day. Like HP, Litton's business boomed through World War II and into the invasion of Korea. His magnetrons were in a class of their own, and his tube yield was so much better than that of his competitors' that he found himself dramatically underselling them, too. And yet even while offering the best deal on the best product, Litton saw his numbers run out of his control. He ran into the same problem Packard did with the Renegotiation Board: without excessive profits to plow back into financing its rapid growth, the company had to take on outside investment or intentionally scale back. Since the products were vital to national security, scaling back was not an option. Not possessed with Packard's willingness to tell the federal government to go fuck itself, Litton decided to spin off his magnetron business and sell it to a larger concern. Unfortunately for Litton, the feds also didn't want to see an increase in magnetron concentration and nixed any sale to the usual suspects. He ended up moving it to a group of engineers from SoCal's Hughes Aircraft who were spinning off their own start-up, Electro Dynamics. With the help of just under $1.5 million raised by the financiers at Lehman Brothers and Clark Dodge, they bought Litton's magnetron patents and the factory.[5] Looking for a way his top deputies could profit from the sale, too, Litton negotiated stock options in the new business at its early value for three employees, an unusual deal for the time.

Cutting every corner they could find, including negotiating Packard-style for huge exceptions to the excessive-profit restrictions (and then evading even those limits), the new owners turned a $2 million purchase at the end of 1953 into a business with an annual revenue of $180 million by 1961.[6] Litton's personal brand was so deeply associated with exceptional quality and price, especially among military procurement professionals, that Electro Dynamics swapped the name back to Litton within a year of its purchase. Charles Litton himself, having declined the stock options he negotiated for his deputies, was "the laughing stock of the business press in the late 1950s and the 1960s," writes historian Christophe Lécuyer.[7] While lesser men got filthy rich off his work and off his name, Litton took his glass lathes to Grass Valley to start over, out of the Bay and east of the Sierras. Bill Hewlett and Dave Packard wouldn't go down like that.

The Varians provided another example. The klystron team hadn't formed a legal entity before the war the way HP did in 1939 — they were guided by an antifascist mission rather than entrepreneurial ambitions. But in 1948, the Varian brothers, Sig and Russ, along with a handful of other former Sperry klystron engineers, formed Varian Associates back in the Bay Area. They were thoughtful and even ideologically rigid about how to set up the company. Russ in particular wanted an engineers' cooperative wholly owned by the workers and members of their community. New York capitalists inquired about investing, and the Varians sent them packing. Instead, they appealed to friends and family, including advisers and board members Bill Hansen, Fred Terman, and Dave Packard, who worked on the klystron project at Litton in the 1930s. In a move that seems cannier in retrospect than it might have felt at the time,

Hansen mortgaged his house to help found the firm. The Varian plan was to be a research and development lab, pursuing projects to the model or small-batch manufacturing stage before selling them to larger, better-capitalized producers in the event the product needed to scale. They were to be a boutique firm of inventors, without traditional office hierarchies or the distorting pressures of growth, more inspired by Halcyon than Stanford or Sperry. It sounded like a throwback to early gadget firms like Dalmo, but the klystron industry belonged to the military, because only it had the resources to contract the kind of adventurous research and development Varian Associates wanted to do. The exigencies of Cold War capitalism made quick work of the brothers' progressive plans.

Unlike HP, Varian and the team didn't capitalize on their war work, nor did they own their inventions afterward. Having made their discoveries on the government dime, the Varian team shared their war designs with the other local tube masters at Eitel-McCullough (spun off of defunct Heintz and Kaufman), which began mass-producing them for the military, quickly boosting the firm. Varian Associates' first big contract was with the Ordnance Development Division of the National Bureau of Standards, an office in the government responsible for explosive fuses soon to be transferred to the army but temporarily in the care of the Department of Commerce, where Hoover put it. The deal was for the development of a very precise klystron that served as a proximity fuse for nuclear bombs, tracking distance from the ground and triggering detonation at the right height for maximum destructive impact. It was a quick turnaround for the technology, which, recall, was originally intended to combat the horrific interwar fascist invention of strategic bombing. In the early 1950s, the feds stressed to Varian that the firm needed to expand quickly, pressuring managers to supply the Cold War military with progressively more specialty tubes as the armed forces became increasingly reliant on air power. Varian got a $1.5 million "victory" loan from the feds and increased production, most of which was dedicated to a new Stanford facility, the first in Fred Terman's industrial park.[8]

Only a few years in, and Varian Associates was miles from where the founders planned to be, though they hadn't left Stanford. The company wasn't a boutique engineering co-op; it was a large military contractor, and the requirements of that position overwhelmed the founders' bohemian intentions.

When anticommunist senator Joseph McCarthy's House Committee on Un-American Activities suggested there were Soviet sympathizers at Stanford compromising the security work being done on campus, three board members (including Terman — too associated with the school) had to temporarily step down as a gesture of fealty. It worked, and Varian grew rapidly with the Cold War bomb state, taking in millions of dollars in annual R & D contracts from the military and employing dozens and then hundreds of engineers. Its capital needs were no longer compatible with a cooperative structure, and what's more, the Varian worker-shareholders wanted to cash in, if not out. Technically, they owned significant shares in a very profitable major military contractor, but since Varian had to plow all its revenues back into growth, it couldn't pay dividends to the shareholders. Here was the problem with the workers' co-op model: It didn't create capitalists; it kept workers working. In the late 1950s, Varian tossed what was left of the founding ethos and floated on the New York Stock Exchange. Kept waiting for years, private capital jumped at the chance, pushing employees into minority ownership within a few years and supercharging the share price from $2 at issue to $68 by the end of the decade.[9] The firm used the capital infusion to dominate the ballooning klystron market, and the original Varian crew got rich. For Russ and Sig, the leisure proved fatal. Russell died in 1959 on a trip to Alaska where he was scouting future national park locations, and Sigurd died two years later when his plane crashed into the ocean between Guadalajara and Puerto Vallarta (he was flying the plane).

The whole regional industry thrived, the firms shaped in common ways by common pressures. While older, larger, better-capitalized companies in the East divided up the commercial telecommunications sectors and the lower-margin mass production of parts, the Stanford area specialized in experimental technologies. In an age of rapid progress the experimental was only a few years away from the standard, and these Bay Area concerns found themselves with sole-source contracts and monopoly profits, racing to scale. None of these companies made the jump from the first American air war to the second better than HP. Unlike the Varians, Hewlett and Packard had unimpeachable politics by HUAC standards, and unlike Charles Litton, they weren't afraid to stand up for their right to profit. Packard in particular was more comfortable than his peers with being a war profiteer, and that left HP better prepared.

For example, when Varian was trying to raise capital in its early days, it sold off rights to its microwave work for the bargain-basement price of $20,000.[10] The Varian owner-operators couldn't afford to keep it. Its coffers already full, thanks to the war, HP snapped it up and turned the technology into more than one multimillion-dollar product line.

Like the merchants in the early days of 1849, HP sold into price-insensitive markets. But the Cold War lasted much longer than the gold rush, and HP snowballed profits and even managed to reinvest its labor costs (via employee stock purchases) to keep expanding. Its research orientation kept it on the leading edge of product development and away from price competition. In 1957, following Varian's success on the public markets, HP had its first public stock offering, followed by a float on the NYSE in 1961. All this capital allowed the company to expand rapidly in a bunch of different profitable directions in the late 1950s and early 1960s. In the closing years of the decade, HP opened a manufacturing plant in the American-occupied sector of West Germany, followed by the Japanese joint venture Yokogawa Hewlett-Packard a few years later.[11] The firm also acquired smaller companies with related technologies, including Moseley, in 1958 (graphic plotters, which became general-purpose printers), and Sanborn, in 1961 (medical monitoring devices).[12] Expanding the HP product universe reduced the company's dependence on the military without taking the firm too far afield. If it could output a wave on an oscilloscope screen, which it had been doing since 1957, then there's no reason it couldn't output it on paper. A heartbeat was a signal, too, and HP could turn that into data.

Measurement and testing instruments were HP's bread and butter, and that made the firm a crucial element in the experimental electronics industry: What are experiments without measures and tests? To the twenty-first-century eye, these meters, analyzers, and generators all look the same: knobbed metal boxes with no obvious outputs of any kind. But to develop, produce, test, maintain, and repair—to make and use—any electronic device, everyone needed those metal boxes. Inside were vacuum-tube circuits hard-wire programmed to read and spit out wave signals across the radio and microwave spectra, depending on the device. The oscillator remained the spiritual core of the company as well as a lead product, and its brain was a set of vacuum tubes. HP was an information technology company, and its devices generated actionable data by dragging inputs through carefully designed circuits. HP devices pumped test signals through user machines just as a hydrolicker pumped water through a mountain. The gold was information, the same type of information Leland Stanford hired Edward Muybridge to generate from his horses. And like the zoopraxiscope, new technologies allowed for new modes of data capture. More, better, faster information was money saved, money saved was money earned, and everyone wanted a money machine.

Among its generation of local vacuum-tube peers—like Ampex, Litton, and Varian—HP was uniquely positioned to grow on its own terms. It was an important moment to have that kind of flexibility: Not many people knew it, but the tube's time as the crucial ingredient in electronics was already limited. The replacement was coming, and like the triode, it called Palo Alto home.

Junction

The first transistor was, at the most basic level, a triode. Like Lee de Forest's Audion, a transistor connects three (tri) electr(ode)s: an emitter, a collector, and a base. In the vacuum tube these are the cathode, anode, and grid respectively. The core operational principle was much the same: A change to the charge on the base connects or separates the electron flow between the emitter and the collector. The difference is that in a transistor the emitter and collector connect through a semiconductor instead of a vacuum. Most materials either conduct electricity (as many metals do) or don't (wood and rubber, for example, are called insulators), but some materials conduct or not depending on the situation. A vacuum doesn't do anything, because it *is* nothing—electrons can get through it, but they have to jump. While a vacuum is neither a conductor nor an insulator (again, because it isn't anything), a semiconducting substance is both, depending. A semiconductor (such as germanium) is a solid material with the functional properties of an electrical gate. Sometimes electrons can get through; sometimes they can't. As it does in the vacuum tube, the flow flips on and off, providing the basis for logic circuits. But semiconductors are theoretically much more stable than vacuum tubes. In vacuum-tube triodes, the electrons float as gas, pulled across the void by magnetism. They lose energy as heat. They are big and heavy and vulnerable to jostling and altitude shifts, and they break frequently. The warmth and light attracted moths, the original computer bugs. In transistors, electrons stay in a solid state, contentedly swimming from conductor to semiconductor to a second conductor. Transistors promised an end to overheating fragile tubes, as well as the thrilling possibility of fully mobile, miniaturizable electronics. In the first transistor, the conductors were made of—what else?—gold.

As to who invented the semiconducting transistor, it's a touchy subject. The matter of where is easier: Bell Labs, at the telephone monopoly's research center. The men who first realized the device were John Bardeen and Walter Brattain, but their manager ended up boxing them out for most of the credit. Bardeen and Brattain were hardworking, successful research scientists, and even after they won their Nobel Prize in Physics—one of two for Bardeen, a unique accomplishment—their lives remained much the same, and both taught (at the University of Illinois and Whitman College respectively) into their seventies. They were two of the many unassuming foot soldiers of the Big Science era, public-minded workers straddling industry and academia, secure and content in their upper-middle-class lifestyle and with no particular use for commercial extra credit. Their boss, however, was a different kind of man. He made sure his name was on the Nobel Prize and the patents, just as he made sure his name was on everything, even when he had to write it in.

After the war ended, Bell Labs installed researcher William Shockley as the head of a new solid-state physics group. It's clear why the phone company was interested in transistors: AT&T used a hybrid system of vacuum tubes and electromechanical switches to route calls between subscribers, and changing to a semiconductor base would make the whole system much more efficient and far easier to maintain. Shockley had a theory about magnetic fields, but none of the Bell Labs team could make it work. A lousy manager, Shockley worked on his own, and on his own design. But when Bardeen and Brattain finagled the point-contact model—working remotely without him in Murray Hill, New Jersey—Shockley rushed in to grab his share, to which, to be fair, he had a legitimate claim. For their part, Bardeen and Brattain were fine with sharing. Regardless of the other men's mild manners, Shockley's ego made the lab a tough fit, and after the point-contact breakthrough, he barged back in with an improvement: the grown-junction transistor. His model used a semiconductor crystal "doped" into layers by incorporating pellets of chemical impurity at the molten stage. After the substance cools, what results is a solid ingot, but at the subatomic level, it's a sandwich: negative-positive-negative (NPN) or positive-negative-positive (PNP) layers. The two junctions where the layers meet are as solid as the material itself because it was all grown together at once — thus "grown junction." For industrial purposes, the grown-junction transistor was a rock with three wires welded on. In the world of the vacuum-tube triode, it was a revelation, and Bell announced it in the summer of 1951.

Shockley had ambitions beyond the lab, and he had plenty of role models. At Stanford, Caltech, and MIT, he saw scientists use their inventions to become rich businessmen. David Packard was two years younger and already a nationally important leader of men. Shockley knew every business in the country was eventually going to need semiconductor devices one way or another. The AT&T–Western Electric conglomerate already faced antitrust pressure, and it would be forced to license Shockley's design; who better to manufacture it than he? He could be the Charles Litton of transistors. And with the tube triode's limitations surpassed, there's no reason computing couldn't keep scaling infinitely, tending toward full automation of production. Shockley was also probably more familiar with the military's advancing need for avionics equipment than anyone. Bell loaned him back to the government for a year, starting in the summer of 1954, which he spent as the research director of the Pentagon's Weapons Systems Evaluation Group (WSEG), the think tank that grew in part out of the proto-RAND work Shockley did during the war. The WSEG produced analyses that justified the weapons programs that consumed nearly the entire first generation of silicon chips.[13] Shockley had already worked up the equations on the government's behalf, and he knew that the lethality engendered by strategic bombing saved so many valuable American lives that the Pentagon's appetite for this kind of tech was effectively bottomless. His transistor was an all-purpose solution to the manifold problems they had with de Forest's vacuums. The second half of the twentieth century ran on semiconductors, and no one knew more about them than William Shockley — at least no one who wanted to be a capitalist.

Before he went to Washington for the WSEG contract, Shockley spent a semester as a visiting professor back at Caltech. He soaked in the California sun and didn't harangue any other Bell researchers, an arrangement that seems to have suited both parties just fine. And on the West Coast, Shockley was a hometown boy made good, whether in Los Angeles or the Bay. Though he still technically worked there, Shockley's time at Bell Labs was already over. The man was in his mid-forties and he was ready for a change, ready for a station in life that reflected his extremely high opinion of himself, one that might finally lift the chip from his shoulder. In February of 1955, he interrupted his government service to attend a gala in his honor thrown by the Los Angeles Chamber of Commerce. The gala was actually held in honor of two inventors: Shockley and the eighty-one-year-old Lee de Forest — the vacuum triode and the transistor that came to replace it, the two men behind the two doohickeys that created electronics.

Outstanding among the group honoring them was Arnold Beckman, founder of Beckman Instruments and the chamber's vice president. Beckman was a kind of SoCal analogue to Hewlett and Packard. Not quite as tall as Packard but still over six feet and remarkably handsome, Beckman was a Caltech chemistry PhD who, like HP, began with small-contract entrepreneurialism in the 1930s.[14] His first hit was a new non-clogging ink that enabled the U.S. Postal Service to stamp precise postage on letters and packages, but his equivalent of Hewlett's lightbulb oscillator was a vacuum tube–based pH meter for the Sunkist cartel, which needed to measure the acidity of lemon by-products. Using the advances of vacuum-triode technology, Beckman enabled the SoCal citrus industry to generate useful data about its own production process, the same function HP performed for the Bay Area's electronics industry. By the time of the gala, Beckman was the type of successful scientist-inventor-capitalist that the younger man aspired to be.

Later in 1955, Shockley called his former professor, Beckman, to ask him to join the board of the speculative Shockley Semiconductor Laboratories.[15] When Beckman heard about the plan, he became worried: He, too, saw a bright future for semiconductors, but Shockley didn't have a sense of the competitive environment. Shockley had spent his career to that point in the Big Science circuit of academia-military-AT&T, and assembling a corporate board was new to him. He tried to launch Shockley Semiconductor with East Coast capital directly, and a deal with Vannevar Bush's Raytheon almost went through, but he was not able to make it happen. (Perhaps potential financiers did some due diligence and talked to Shockley's colleagues about what the monomaniac was like to work with.) It must have been déjà vu for Beckman, who had a business relationship with Lee de Forest in the 1930s during one of the triode creator's many commercial misadventures.[16] Beckman made Shockley a paternal offer: Start the semiconductor firm as a division of Beckman Instruments. They nabbed a license to the transistor, and one year to the month after the gala honoring Shockley, they announced the new venture. Later that year, Shockley won the Nobel Prize with Bardeen and Brattain for the transistor, an auspicious sign for the enterprise and, unfortunately for him, the peak of success for Bill Shockley Jr.

Shockley Semiconductor Laboratory—true to his character, the founder refused to consider any other names for the Beckman subsidiary—was a disaster.[17] Beckman sold it off in 1960, and in those four years it never even produced a single silicon transistor. But Shockley is the founder of Silicon Valley the way a pile of excrement is the founder of a garden. There's nothing William Shockley liked better than evaluating other people, and hiring a research staff to do advanced work under his name was a dream task, especially after the Nobel cleansed his reputation. He wasn't looking for *éminences grises*; a true child of the Palo Alto System, he wanted the young guns. (Besides, there was no way Bardeen or Brattain was going to work for him again.) Long planning to start his own enterprise, Shockley kept his eye out, touring the country and even Europe looking for the best and brightest young physicists and engineers. Enough ambitious early-career scientists jumped at the chance to work with the demanding transistor inventor, even if it meant moving to the orchard suburb of Palo Alto, California.

Some (in particular Gordon Moore, one of Shockley's best hires) have claimed that Shockley picked Palo Alto because that's where his mom lived.[18] That's no doubt part of the equation, but Fred Terman's new industrial park was also the place to be for high-technology companies. Lockheed Missiles and Space moved there in 1956, which meant there was a lot of contract money sloshing around the neighborhood. Terman was connected not just to his fellow Palo Altan Shockley but also to various others in the Shockley orbit. One of Beckman's first suggestions as Shockley's partner was to bring in Terman, and the provost lobbied hard to bring the new subsidiary home. Beckman had also recently acquired the medical centrifuge manufacturer Spinco and was building its new facility at the industrial park, too.[19] Shockley immediately joined the Stanford engineering faculty as a lecturer, following the same path Herbert Hoover laid for William Sr. It was a natural fit, and the choice of Palo Alto was so right that even the firm's failure turned out to be a huge success.

The team Shockley recruited quickly realized that the man wasn't a normal boss. He put them through rounds of psychological examination, sifting through this best-of-the-best collection with a woven basket of IQ tests. The gold separated from the rest, he believed. What he ended up with was a strong and diverse collection of young white male scientists. Shockley's team reflected the leveling effects of the FDR–WWII years, the result of which was that a Jewish refugee and a midwestern preacher's son could look across the table at each other as colleagues in a California semiconductor company. Compulsory universal military service and the New Deal shuffled America's deck of white men, losing distinctions based on ethnicity and home geography. They all trained on the government's dime, and Shockley planned to use the military's investment in these men to produce semiconductors for a new generation of missile weapons, in effect selling the government's investment back to itself. It was one military-industrial-academic transistor block: the Solid State.

Among Shockley's recruits, the most famous group was a team Shockley later tarred as "the traitorous eight." It comprised the preacher's son (Robert Noyce) and the Jewish refugee (Eugene Kleiner), as well as Julius Blank, Victor Grinich, Jean Hoerni, Gordon Moore, C. Sheldon Roberts, and Jay Last. They were all in their late twenties and early thirties, accomplished in their own specialties, and strong believers in the technology. Moore was the only NorCal local, which meant the rest of the men were ambitious and adventurous enough to take a risk in California rather than settling into the comfy confines of academic-industrial Big Science, which was still an East Coast affair. Shockley offered the opportunity to play rebellious little brother, within the traditional hierarchy of prestige but without the stultifying pressure of life in a massive organization. But at Shockley Labs they ran smack into the downside risks of moving to California to work for a start-up. William Shockley was an awful boss, unbearable. Not content to let his all-star team work as one, Shockley berated his employees, constantly comparing them to one another and to himself. With the Nobel Prize secured, his ego was at its zenith, and he saw the group of hot young scientists and engineers as his lackeys. The tyrant Shockley became obsessed with his plans for a four-layer PNPN diode that would be able to perform more logic functions than a transistor, and forbade the staff from growing the silicon devices they'd been hired to make. It was untenable; the group just wanted the California dream they were promised.

Except for its disastrous manager, Shockley's was a very good business plan, an even better one than he had first thought. *Sputnik 1* launched in October of 1957, inaugurating the space race and a new immediate need for strong, dependable transistors. But it was too late: Shockley's senior group of eight failed to negotiate a deal for Shockley's departure with Beckman, and they resigned the month before, in September. This group of Greatest Generation clean-cut PhD military veterans wasn't anything like the smelly bearded geeks who became synonymous with tech start-ups in the following period, but they had a similar problem. They were a group of science inventor dudes who wanted to work together and make cool stuff, and to do that they needed approximately $1 million. None of them had that much to invest or knew anyone who did. The closest thing they had was Kleiner, whose father was wealthy enough to have an account with the New York investment bank Hayden Stone & Co. Alerted to the opportunity, Hayden Stone sent a couple of operatives to check out what the group of defectors had to offer as a prepackaged semiconductor subsidiary. What those operatives found instead were the ingredients for a viable start-up.

After striking out with a list of potential funders, Arthur Rock of Hayden Stone landed on Sherman Fairchild. The only heir in a rich family, Fairchild inherited his wealth at the young age of twenty-eight. He was an amateur pilot and inventor who moved from aerial photography to a very successful plane company and then, recall, to the Wall Street airline conglomerate. More important for the Shockley castaways, he was the largest individual shareholder in IBM, which his father had cofounded and led. Owning a contract supplier for a company you owned a large share of was a great way to make money—it's one Leland Stanford and the Associates used to suck funds out of the railroad—and Sherman Fairchild was familiar with the ploy as both an aircraft supplier to and shareholder of Pan American and various other airlines. In one particularly sophisticated move, he bought a 20 percent share in Mexicana de Aviación, which began flying Fairchild planes, only for Pan Am to buy the whole thing five years later, in 1930, earning him money three different ways in the middle of the Depression.[20] He was a canny operator, and so was his offer to the eight rebels: He would give them $1.38 million and let them run the company for two years.[21] If it worked, he would buy them out for $300,000 each (around $3 million in 2022), and they would become employees. If it didn't work, he would dump the whole enterprise. As a potential future subsidiary of Fairchild Camera and Instrument Corporation it was to be called Fairchild Semiconductor—none of this "Shockley" nonsense. They would stay in Palo Alto, where they had already begun work. The group agreed, appointing Noyce a sort of first-among-equals, with Moore as his deputy. It definitely worked.

Within a year of opening shop, Fairchild shipped circuits to IBM. Even though it was a small firm to be supplying such a big one, Sherman ensured the deal by meeting with the IBM CEO, Thomas Watson Jr.—a hard sit-down to get for others, but not so for the chair of the IBM executive committee. IBM bought 100 inaugural chips for $150 each, giving Fairchild something Shockley Labs never had: a silicon sale.[22] The team was off to the space race, leaving cheap commodity circuits to others and focusing instead on hyper-reliable specialty chips for government contractors working with NASA and the Pentagon. These buyers needed transistors that could go into space or operate through small-arms fire, and the Fairchild team came up with product designs and manufacturing processes to fit their needs as communicated to them through contractors such as IBM. Fairchild mostly declined to bid for military contracts directly, preferring the Goldilocks solution of subcontracting. Sent back to the drawing board in 1959 when he found he had misread the specifications in the request for a computer on the Minuteman 1 ICBM, Fairchild engineer Jean Hoerni worked out a new process based on the nonconductivity of silicon oxide to produce much more stable chips. The "planar" process used solvents to repeatedly etch holes in this insulating cover of silicon rust, exposing designated regions of the silicon to doping gases in order to create the NPN/PNP layers, then etching it again for neatly placed electrodes. With the insulating layer of rust protecting the circuit, these planar transistors were as reliable as required, a big technical jump for the industry. They were also extremely profitable objects; historian Leslie Berlin writes that they cost Fairchild 13 cents each to make and sold for $1.50.[23] As Jay Last recollects: "We didn't have competition and we could charge a lot for them so we had a lot of money floating around."[24] This was the signature commercial-technological advance of the missile age, and Fairchild discovered the wonders of monopoly profits.

The theoretical advances as well as the money from Hoerni's planar process put Fairchild just two steps away from the firm's next important invention.

To make its artisanal process cost-effective, Fairchild put several transistors on each doped silicon wafer before carefully slicing them into individual parts. Buyers then wired some of these transistors back together, along with resistors and capacitors, to create whatever complex circuit they needed. But if Hoerni could etch the pattern for several transistors onto a wafer, then why couldn't he etch a pattern that integrated these circuits on one wafer and save the splicing and reconnecting steps? All the engineers had to do was find a way to isolate the transistors and other sub-elements from one another on the wafer, then connect them in the right pattern across their electrodes.[25] The team got to work, and it wasn't long before they had their solutions. Sinking each of the components in a P-N junction moat made sure current couldn't flow between them, and a pattern of metal lines laid on top made sure it could. Noyce made the concept work, and he gets primary credit for the invention of the integrated circuit, but Jack Kilby at Texas Instruments figured it out first. The difference is that Fairchild's process was "monolithic": it established the metal reconnections by dissolving a film of aluminum over an etched pattern, while the TI model required manual wiring. From a production point of view, Noyce's was workable in a way that Kilby's wasn't. It's an advantage that's representative of Fairchild Semiconductor's edge in the industry, which it acquired by shaping its process for military and space needs while still prioritizing production efficiencies. Fairchild's immediate success spoke to Shockley's vision; it also dramatized just how bad his management truly must have been to single-handedly inhibit one of the era's strongest corporate ventures.

For the Fairchild rebels, however, there was also a drawback to working with a boss who *did* know what he was doing. When the two years were up, Sherman Fairchild exercised his option to buy out the semiconductor division, netting each of the technical cofounders around $300,000 in Fairchild Camera and Instruments stock. This didn't feel like a great deal for the men, considering that their semiconductor subsidiary was responsible for over $3 million in sales the year before, and, more important, they experienced the buyout as a demotion—from entrepreneurs to employees. Though the $300,000 didn't make them permanently wealthy, it was enough to take away their motivation at work. The semiconductor founders began leaking out of Fairchild to start their own new ventures, and a financing system that their success helped build was already waiting for them. Waiting with it was Arthur Rock.

After the lightning climb of Fairchild Semiconductor, investors saw there was a lot of quick money to be made in silicon in the Valley. Sherman Fairchild turned $1.5 million in cash into the country's second-largest semiconductor manufacturer in a matter of years, and he hardly had to do anything but accept the offer of young Arthur Rock and his colleagues at Hayden Stone. If Fairchild could partner with a Shockley Labs team, invest between $1 million and $2 million in their work, and have a profitable semiconductor operation in a couple of years, why couldn't someone else pull the same trick on Fairchild itself? The first of the spin-offs, or Fairchildren, was Rheem Semiconductor, formed in 1959. It was led by the Fairchild general manager, Ed Baldwin, and financed by the HVAC company Rheem Manufacturing.* It was an inauspicious beginning: Fairchild sued the enterprise for intellectual property theft and forced a sale two years later to Raytheon. It went better in the 1960s: In 1961, a group of Fairchild engineers started Signetics to do the integrated circuit work Fairchild developed but wasn't eager to exploit, since it already had the market cornered on high-margin planar transistors. Signetics got its $1 million via Lehman Brothers — which, you'll remember, made *very* good on its investment in Electro Dynamics, which allowed Electro to purchase Litton in 1953 — and the rapid shift to integrated circuits made Signetics a quick success. East Coast capital was starting to figure out how to make money in Silicon Valley.

Would-be founders sought out Arthur Rock — famous in the industry for his win with Fairchild — even though he had no actual knowledge of or experience in electronics.[26] In 1960, the two leads of Litton's (now fully corporate) electronics division approached him to finance their plan for a spin-off, which he did. They wanted to make the company into a conglomerate right off the bat; the idea was to buy up some small electronics companies and get to the stock market fast while investors were looking for an exciting tech opportunity. Hayden Stone secured the financing, a cinch for Rock.[27] One of the first things it bought was rights to the name Teledyne, which is what the founders re-christened the larger organization. Another purchase was Amelco, a tax write-off of a SoCal manufacturing plant. In January of 1961, Rock convinced

---

* Rheem was owned by the Rheem Brothers, whose father led Standard Oil of California (now Chevron). We will re-encounter them when radicals attempt to organize workers at an East Bay plant in Richmond, where Rheem emerged from a Standard Oil refinery.

four of Shockley's eight defectors (Hoerni, Roberts, Kleiner, and Last) to reinvent Amelco under Teledyne as a specialty circuit provider for the military. Within a year of founding, Teledyne had its initial public offering, making everyone rich, and they diligently reinvested in the local electronics industry.

Money flowed back the other way later that year when Rock spun himself off of Hayden Stone, moving to California to start his own venture capital fund with Tommy Davis, a vice president of the Kern County Land Company whose search for more exciting investments had led him to Fred Terman and the Stanford electronics community. Why should Rock work for Hayden Stone when he already made enough people rich to round up money himself? Among the initial investors in the firm, called Davis and Rock, were a Teledyne cofounder and all four ex-Fairchild Amelco founders. The company's VC fund knitted leading techno-capitalists together into a financing layer that could lie between Silicon Valley and East Coast capital, making sure inventors and their friends got rich first and reinvested in the community. It was the financial complement to what Fred Terman worked to establish with the industrial park.

For Davis and Rock's second investment, they poured a quarter of a million dollars into Scientific Data Systems, which planned to make relatively small, strong computers for research and enterprise using silicon (rather than the less tough but standard germanium) and Noyce's hardy monolithic integrated circuits when they became available. If you needed to put a computer on a boat or next to an oil well, they had you covered. Silicon was a success, and so was the company. Its Sigma series (started in 1966) was the closest thing IBM's legendary 360 computer had to a rival, and for a short while in the mid-1960s Scientific Data Systems became the thinking man's manufacturer. It was perfect timing, and in 1969 Xerox bought the firm for over $900 million in company stock (more than $7 billion in 2022 money), yielding Davis and Rock an approximately $80 million payout on its $257,000 investment.*28

---

* Scientific Data Systems founder Max Palevsky took his fortune and became a financier for Southern California's liberal politicians. He single-handedly saved *Rolling Stone* with $200,000 and joined the magazine's board with Arthur Rock. Hunter S. Thompson sent Palevsky some seeds of the "finest Chicano mescaline" as thanks, only for the two to fall out later over a $10,000 loan and the film rights to *Fear and Loathing in Las Vegas*. "As for Rock," Thompson wrote in a letter, "I definitely think he should be arrested. The fucker is floating around like some kind of un-programmed energy-bomb, adrift in the sea-lanes of

The limited partnership ended in '68, and both Davis and Rock started their own funds the next year. Among Rock's future investments was another computer start-up called Apple, and in between, on his own initiative, he set up the financing for Noyce and Moore who were finally ready to decamp from Fairchild and work on computer memory chips. Their NM Electronics became Integrated Electronics, which was later shortened to the catchy Intel. Eugene Kleiner followed Rock's lead a few years later, starting the largest VC partnership yet with the former general manager of HP's computer division, Thomas Perkins. The first round of Silicon Valley winners secured their spots and conspired to keep good opportunities in the family, making each other increasingly, outstandingly rich.

If Shockley Labs was the Valley's fertile pile of shit, then Fairchild Semiconductor was the silicon taproot, growing progressively more enterprises along with the deep financial roots to support them. Like Shockley himself, the Valley grew at the intersection of evolving triode technology and American strategic bombing, a combination that proved irresistibly profitable. After the failure of Shockley Transistor, he found a safe landing pad at Stanford, where Ampex endowed him a professorship. The path from the vacuum-tube triode to the silicon integrated circuit was historically short—a matter of a few decades—and geographically even shorter. Hewlett-Packard managed to bridge the two technologies cleanly, and that stability amid the churning start-up seas helped make it the region's signature firm, even as its followers overtook it in size. Unlike Litton or Varian, HP made it from the tube to the computer age on its own terms. More than Shockley or even Fred Terman, H and P were suited to the era.

Offshore

To understand the emergence of Silicon Valley, we need to grasp more than the procession of inventors and investors who came to define the region. We also need to understand the role Silicon Valley played in the transition from a

---

a reality he can't seem to mesh with . . . Hell, maybe we should run him for president in '72, on a national Freak Power ticket." Hunter S. Thompson, *Fear and Loathing in America: The Brutal Odyssey of an Outlaw Journalist* (Simon & Schuster, 2000), 360–61. The son of Yiddish-speaking immigrants, Palevsky bankrolled the McGovern presidential campaign instead, and Gore Vidal's 1982 Senate run, as well as a half dozen pictures at Paramount.

chaotic global order based on national rivalries and alliances to the Cold War's bipolar reorganization. To put the question simply: What did the United States want from the rest of the world, and how did pumping a huge amount of money through Palo Alto and the Stanford environment help the country get it?

The nation itself is a land of contrasts, but U.S. capital is univocal in its drive for ever-higher profits, and it's capital we're concerned with in this chapter. Securing as much of the world as possible for Team Freedom was essential for capitalists, not to secure trade access — socialist countries were happy to exchange goods across ideological lines — and certainly not to monitor "human rights," but because Freedom meant a state devoted to high profits. In capitalist countries, capital could rely on the state to both respect and enforce its property rights, even in the face of workers who organize for land reform and confiscatory taxation. Capital could rely on the capitalist state to take its side during labor conflicts and otherwise assist in controlling wages. Without those guarantees, U.S. investments abroad were subject to the political whims of local populations, and being subject to the political whims of local populations degrades an investment's expected return. As California's capitalists (such as Hoover) experienced so personally in the first half of the twentieth century, workers everywhere in the world were willing and able to seize control of their natural resources and means of production. By the end of the Second World War, socialism was as global as capitalism: two directly opposed systems vying for control wherever people worked. U.S. capital, hopped up on a decade of expansionary government infrastructure and war spending, was determined to win.

In 1959, in the middle of its own related expansionary run, Hewlett-Packard opened its first international manufacturing facility, located in Böblingen, Germany. The company's reputation was international, and recovering Europe needed high-quality testing and measuring equipment, but why expand from Palo Alto to Böblingen? When HP added a European sales office, it picked Geneva, Switzerland, a big commercial center that saw the war through unscathed. Böblingen was the opposite: On the night of October 7, 1943, RAF bombers successfully targeted the German industrial city of Stuttgart, but the evening was cloudy and the marking planes also hit Böblingen, 10 miles to the southwest. Bombs struck hundreds of buildings and killed dozens of people,

destroying most of the town.[29] But by the end of the 1950s, West Germany was
a hot spot of foreign investment, driven by world-beating profits and growth.
HP's factory was one part of an anticommunist project to ensure that former
Axis territories stayed within the Free community. The Western occupiers had
to put capitalist Germany and Japan on solid footing as soon as possible; Germany was the European border with the Soviets, Japan the East Asian. On the
postwar map the borders between the systems were always high-stakes. But
U.S. conservatives who hadn't wanted to fight in the first place weren't eager
to keep spending money abroad. Only one man could persuade them to unify
behind a generous reconstruction plan for the beaten enemies.

The federal food program still contained Hoover loyalists, and one convinced President Truman to meet with the ex-president. After their meeting,
Hoover toured the occupied territories with U.S. administrators, the Truman
government's expectation being that he would sell congressional Republicans
on an aid package. General William H. Draper Jr. was chief of the economics division of the Control Council for Germany in the wake of the war, and
he went over the situation with Hoover, whom he credits with securing the
needed budget. Their intervention wasn't really humanitarian per se: Their first
priority was getting the coal mines going, which powered the factories and the
larger German economy. Draper and Hoover increased the coal workers' daily
ration of calories to 4,000 and ordered them strip-searched at the mine gates
to make sure they weren't saving food for their hungry families.* Their wives
and children were not converting food into coal. Hoover understood that the
American occupation in the near term and Germany's position in the Cold
War in the long term were at stake. He and Draper came to the conclusion
that "if we wanted to bring the Germans back into the community of nations,
first they had to be fed, not too much, but they had to have enough to live."[30]
Draper—a New York investment banker in his civilian life—got promoted
to undersecretary of war in charge of the German as well as Japanese, Korean,
and Austrian occupations, joining a Hooverite military clique at the top of the
American postwar overseas administration with General Douglas MacArthur,

---

*   "Well, from the humanitarian point of view that's fine, but it couldn't work, and so we had
     to strip them of food and they had to eat it themselves." General William H. Draper Jr.,
     Oral History Interview, Harry S. Truman Library, interview by Jerry N. Hess, January 11,
     1972, https://www.trumanlibrary.gov/library/oral histories/draperw, 32.

who ruled Japan on behalf of the Allies. These men directed concern away from fascist-imperialist accountability and toward rapid economic redevelopment to ward off the socialist threat, which they understood to be the more pressing concern.

Draper was one in a two-man team of financiers sent to assess the Japanese economy in 1948, which ended up being the "death-blow to reform" in the words of researchers Sterling and Peggy Seagrave.[31] MacArthur, Draper, and the liaison to the Japanese imperial family, Bonner Fellers, all literally reported to Hoover—whether they were supposed to or not. Not only were they conservatives and loyalists who distrusted the Truman State Department, but, between Roosevelt's death in 1945 and Truman's inauguration in 1949, the Chief was also the most recently elected president. They conspired to divert blame from the Japanese ruling class and their representatives in the palace, and redirect attention and resources toward rapid industrialization. They brushed aside Soviet demands for the execution of the imperial leadership and even moderate suggestions that the occupation forces reorganize Japanese banks and corporations. The Hooverites opposed expropriation as a tactic, and if they were going to purge anyone, it was going to be leftists, which they did. Occupation forces prepared the ground for a quick, safe transition to capitalism in the Pacific. Bank of America was ready: When the fighting ended, B of A opened branches in the Philippines (Manila), in China (Shanghai), and two in Japan (Tokyo and Yokohama).[32]

HP—or, rather, Bill Hewlett—was in Japan as soon as America took control. Karl Compton, physicist president of MIT and Vannevar Bush associate, picked Hewlett, an MIT masters graduate and conscripted member of the U.S. Army Signal Corps, for the team that went in to analyze the Japanese science-and-technology industry. There he met with Japan's top scientists and engineers, whom he found to be agreeable and essentially blameless for the war.[33] These connections and Hewlett's familiarity with the nation's tech industry no doubt came in handy when HP announced its Tokyo-based joint venture, Yokogawa Hewlett-Packard, in 1963.[34] Unlike West Germany, Japan took a protectionist approach, excluding foreign capital, erecting tariffs against foreign goods, and cultivating monopoly networks called *keiretsu* in sectors where the country's powerful Ministry of International Trade and Industry saw potential. Without its overseas colonies, Japan didn't have the raw materials for most manufacturing, and the country redirected resources into the domestic tech industry. High profits took a back seat to growth, and though Hooverites might argue that the two were one and the same (as they were in West Germany), administrators were content to help Japan build on its own terms in exchange for an indefinite American military presence there and a hostile orientation toward newly Maoist China. Japan was more important as a forward base for the capitalist system in East Asia than as a source of near-term profits for individual foreign firms. And yet getting into Japan early turned out to be an important move for HP, maybe even a lifesaving one.

After the war, there were three ways for an American company to get capital into Japan: Either it could license its products to a local manufacturer or it could open a joint venture with a Japanese company as majority owner. Or it could do both. Our old friends at Ampex provided a cautionary tale about how not to navigate the system: After the war, the firm combined confiscated German audio-recording tech with 3M's new magnetic tape to produce the tape recorder, and it became a money-printing machine for Poniatoff's company after Bing Crosby started using it to tape-delay his radio show, in 1948. With the monopoly profits, Ampex dug into research and produced the VRX-1000 video tape recorder only eight years later. Effectively locked out of Japan and facing copycat threats, Ampex licensed its IP to companies such as Sony and Toshiba, which came to dominate not just Japan but also the world market for the products and derived technologies in the following period.* Like audio and video recorders, those chip exports turned into an existential threat for American electronics manufacturers.

HP didn't have those problems. With YHP, the Palo Alto firm got on the right side of Japanese productivity advances. Facing a domestic shortage of memory chips in the late 1970s, HP's computer division turned to Japanese suppliers and found that their chips were not just cheaper than the American

---

* Texas Instruments had similar problems, with Japan refusing to welcome TI into the country or recognize Kilby's integrated circuit patent until the end of the '60s, when Japanese pirate producers felt domestically secure and were ready to export chips. *Global Economy, Global Technology, Global Corporations: Reports of a Joint Task Force of the National Research Council and the Japan Society for the Promotion of Science on the Rights and Responsibilities of Multinational Corporations in an Age of Technological Interdependence* (National Academies Press, 1998), 26.

ones but also significantly more reliable. The company embarked on a concerted analysis and presented its findings to the industry in early 1980: American chips failed incoming inspection at a rate of between 10 and 20 per 10,000. Japanese chips didn't: their rate was 0.00, across the board.[35] In the quality composite index, which took into consideration factors such as costs and delivery, no tier of U.S. memory chips beat any tier of Japanese chips. Silicon Valley took the infamous Anderson Report hard, but Hewlett-Packard could take pride. Quality manufacturing required strong testing and measuring instruments, and HP benefited worldwide from the Japanese national investment in improved electronics manufacturing. It cashed in, while Robert Noyce at Intel burned miniature Japanese flags.[36] In 1983, 20 years after its founding and with the Japanese electronics industry no longer afraid of foreign capital, HP increased its ownership of YHP from a minority 49 percent to a majority 75 percent.[37] HP played the long game, using the founder's military and political connections to get an early bet down on Japan and its crucial place in Cold War geography.

As Hewlett-Packard proved in the immediate postwar period, there were profits to be made by rebuilding occupied First World territories. With some important exceptions, Americans responsible for rebuilding the Axis countries got along fine with the humbled German and Japanese ruling classes, largely for the simple reason that the fascists were closer to capitalists than they were to communists. In a 50-50 world, they were on Team Freedom, and America, including Hoover and the Hooverites, could see the logic in re-creating them as prosperous high-wage ramparts.* Strategic bombing created growth opportunities—the Allies leveled Böblingen, incinerated Tokyo—and Palo Alto helped make that happen, clearing ground for HP's foreign investments.

---

* This is the geopolitical situation that led Irish writer Leonard Wibberley to facetiously suggest Ireland invade the United States, with plans to lose and reap the rewards. He turned the idea into a book, which became the 1959 Peter Sellers vehicle *The Mouse That Roared*, about a small fictional European country that, with their sole national industry (wine) threatened by California exports—the California wine industry, recall, matured to export quality in the postwar period as it recovered from the fallow prohibition years—invades Washington, DC, with a crew of archers. The FBI later tormented Sellers's co-star Jean Seberg into a mental breakdown to punish her for supporting the Black Panther Party and other left-wing organizations.

The Stuttgart raid that mistakenly hit Böblingen was the first operational test of the "airborne cigar," an in-plane radar countermeasure designed at the RRL's British division; it worked.[38] The raid took out industrial capacity, and building it back under American auspices meant profits for HP. The raid also drowned 36 people in an underground shelter when a bomb damaged a water pipe.[39]

The strangest story of Pacific capital entering Silicon Valley after the war centers on a man named Joe McMicking. The son of the sheriff of Manila, McMicking came to California to study as a teenager and, along with his brother Henry, attended Stanford, where they rubbed elbows with the sons (and some daughters) of the western elite. Joe returned to the Philippines and worked in a camera store, and like a number of adventurous young men of his generation, he learned to fly planes. He joined the Army Air Corps reserves, and when the war broke out, he was recruited into General MacArthur's personal staff—the only one from the islands. Serving at one of the war's pivot points, he advanced quickly. MacArthur left to head Japan and McMicking stayed, liaising from Manila. Then, suddenly, Joe McMicking became very rich.

To the extent that it's discussed in most American histories of the Valley, the implied origin of the McMicking fortune is the Zóbel de Ayala clan. The McMickings grew up down the street from the house of Spanish-born capitalist Enrique Zóbel de Ayala during the period preceding World War II. Zóbel de Ayala was also a senior member of the Philippine Falange—the territorial chapter of the fascist Falangist international, which contained Franco's lead supporters on the islands. Like many leading colonists, the Zóbel de Ayalas were wealthy real estate financiers, and they socialized with the McMickings, which made for a cute story when Joe married the family's heiress and only daughter, Mercedes Zóbel de Ayala.* But her family, like many occupied capitalists who tried to walk the balance beam between collaborating with the occupiers and being expropriated by them, ended the war in a rough situation, the Japanese having held the country with an eye toward permanent control. It was a low point in the clan's fortunes, and some journalists and historians in the Philippines insist that McMicking saved the family's finances, not the

---

* Genetic diversity was a concern for the dwindling Hispanic overclass in Manila; Mercedes's parents were also cousins.

other way around.[40] Sterling and Patty Seagrave have an answer: McMicking got a share of the Japanese war loot that was buried in the Philippines after he helped oversee the torturous interrogation of a Japanese army major in 1945.[41] These funds—the significant discovered portion of Asia's entire gold wealth, systematically extracted by Japanese gangsters commissioned by the army— served the Hoover clique as an anticommunist slush fund.* The Seagraves write that Hoover held $100 million in Japanese war gold in an account under his own name.[42] His enduring cabal used the money to finance right-wing pol- iticians (particularly in Japan), pay bribes, and ensure capitalist governance throughout Asia without burdening the Treasury or incurring oversight.

It wouldn't be a Hooverite plot, however, if all the money went to politicians and governments. Joe McMicking, with his wife's family name as cover, built luxury real estate near a military base—an insightful bet on the American intentions for the Pacific islands that were in its now broad sphere of influence. The Ayala name, which dates back to a nineteenth-century Spanish colonial distillery, regained a prominence it maintains into the present, and the fam- ily advanced from luxury development to banking and food processing. The McMicking brothers also helped jump-start Silicon Valley in classic Hooverian fashion. In 1947 they formed an investment group in San Francisco, and their first buy was half of Ampex for $365,000—specifically, Tim Moseley's half.†[43] With Joe's military intelligence connections and an assist from board member Fred Terman, they turned the company into a defense contractor, supplying the NSA with the Nazi-derived tape-recording equipment that came to define the agency.

In 1952, the McMickings put together Ampex's first public stock offering, and its success was all the blood in the water Wall Street needed to start piling into West Coast technology stocks, starting the proto–venture capital model and giving the Stanford community its initial taste of instant tech wealth.[44] Stanford EE and MBA Reid Dennis had the good luck to run into Henry McMicking on campus, and McMicking persuaded Dennis (his friend's

---

* A part of this gold would have originated from the work of Chinese "Gold Mountain" families who returned with the proceeds of their years in California.

† It was not a bad deal for Moseley, who turned his $25,000 investment into $365,000 in four years. He split before East Coast capital and government profit controls started eating electronics start-ups for breakfast.

brother) to persuade his mom to let him move his $13,000 trust fund from Southern California Edison stock into Ampex. A few years later, that investment was worth close to $1 million.[45] Varian and HP took their defense contracts and followed Poniatoff's spin-off motor company onto the stock market later in the 1950s. Dennis worked at an insurance company, and he had done well to invest his boss's money in Ampex, too. With the huge returns, Dennis earned his firm's faith, and the management gave him relatively small amounts of capital to invest in West Coast electronics start-ups. At the time of this writing, Dennis is considered one of the Valley's most venerable venture capitalists.

The United States found a use for all the technologies Silicon Valley was coming up with—all the meters and the tubes and the semiconductors. Only a few decades old, the Palo Alto line of radio tools that started with inventor-stockjobber Lee de Forest and the antifascist Varian brothers became the silicon brain of the world's most fearsome killing machine. Military Keynesianism wasn't purposeless, the way a hoax like SAGE might suggest. These high-tech tools projected American lethality across the so-called Third World—not Team Freedom or the Evil Empire but the nonaligned nations of Asia, Africa, and Latin America: developing, low-wage countries, vulnerable to socialists and capitalists alike. This was the Cold War's real terrain of struggle as well as the real prize for Silicon Valley's electronics firms. In other words, Palo Alto was a conduit for the production of an outsourced capitalist planet.

Integration and Separation

With the planar transistor of the early 1960s, Fairchild had built a better triode. The main ingredient (silicon) is dirt cheap, and the batch-processing production method got the company's marginal cost down to 13 cents. Since the transistors went for $1.50—1/1,000th of the price Fairchild charged IBM for the company's first batch of circuits—the transistor had a profit margin above 90 percent.[46] But the company, with less than 10 percent of transistor sales, was still an upstart compared to the major non-silicon players such as TI and Motorola. The rapidly changing, capital-intensive industry made investments in new tech and production automation high-stakes and risky. Build the wrong kind of factory for the wrong process in the wrong place at the wrong time, and you could sink yourself. The profitable planar transistor gave the company capital to work with, but even though it made major R & D advances, Fairchild was hesitant to operationalize its own work, and this balk opened room for competing capitalists to do it for them, peeling off research engineers and anyone else in the company with a plausible idea. For the Silicon Valley electronics ecosystem, the Fairchild spin-offs were the start of a verdant flourishing to come, but for Fairchild Semiconductor's California leadership, they were worrisome. The company was stuck: It needed a way to invest in increasing profit rates without gambling the firm's future on any particular technology.

As far as the cost of materials went, the planar transistor was already a work of art, the singular product triumph of the Fairchild ethos. Only three of the 13 cents went to materials, which left a whole 10 cents for labor. There was a lot of work in a finished circuit, and it broke down into the fabrication of the silicon wafers (with the various doping and etching steps) and the circuit-board assembly. Once the big silicon wafer is done, workers need to slice it into individual components, mount and wire them on boards, test them, and package them. All of it is delicate work. In its early years, Fairchild vertically integrated these steps in its Bay Area facilities. The firm hired women to do the assembly work and men to supervise them, echoing the gender-segregated division of labor in the orchards and canneries.[47] Fairchild had three main ways to reduce labor costs: reduce the amount of labor per chip via automation, find a way to reduce the cost of the labor per chip, or, preferably, both. Automation was expensive and risky: Fairchild production supervisor Tom Maher tells the story of company engineers who designed a $1 million machine to automate an assembly step only to have a young engineer immediately come up with a way to do it three times faster with workers for a set-up cost of $60.[48] The Fairchild production chief "would not allow any spending for new automatic equipment for several months" as a result.[49]

That production chief was named Charlie Sporck, and at Fairchild, and subsequently at the spin-off National Semiconductor, he played an important role in directing the future of Silicon Valley and the American economy at large. In the early 1960s, only around five years after the company started, Fairchild opened its first overseas assembly plant, in Hong Kong. The move—suggested by Bob Noyce—surprised the rest of the industry, but with the low start-up costs for assembly lines, it was a textbook case of labor arbitrage.

According to Wilf Corrigan, who was promoted to oversee Fairchild's overseas manufacturing in the mid-1960s, the going rate for "semiskilled" assembly work was $2.50 an hour in the Bay Area (more than $20 in 2022 money) but only 10 cents in Hong Kong, a 96 percent reduction.[50] Fairchild was the innovator in what Corrigan called "jet-age automation" and what we have come to call offshoring.[51] At around $1 a day, Fairchild found a way to match the nominal cost of Chinese railroad workers a full century after they built the Central Pacific. Paying so little sounds dangerous, especially so close to Red China, but America's military bases provided sufficient security. The country's global anticommunist mandate (self-awarded) ensured capitalist governance, and that made offshoring a more promising investment than automation. Sporck replayed the same layoffs-first strategy at National Semi, and the rest of the industry followed suit.

Offshoring is an inexact term, considering that firms were perfectly willing to seek deals on work in North America, too, by building plants in Mexico. In 1965, Fairchild opened a factory on the Navajo reservation in Shiprock, New Mexico, taking advantage of high unemployment with a low-wage "trainee" program and $700,000 in loans from the Navajo Nation.[52] Scholar Cedric Robinson calls sites like Shiprock "production enclaves," places where corporations "could be guaranteed special privileges and higher rates of exploitation."[53] Whatever you call it, Silicon Valley reoriented around this labor arbitrage strategy, bifurcating high-cost engineering and design from low-cost assembly work—the Shiprock site quickly became New Mexico's largest industrial employer.[54] As we'll see, the strategy culminated in "fabless" (as in, without fabrication lines) manufacturing in the following period, divorcing design and production at the firm level. The First World's Cold War arsenal created the production enclaves where capital could count on low wages, freeing semiconductor firms and ultimately U.S. industry in general from domestic wage-price inflation. Besides, putting production in East and Southeast Asia kept electronics firms near their biggest customer: the U.S. military.

I don't know what possessed Hewlett-Packard vice president Bill Doolittle to submit to an interview with members of the Resolution film collective for their 1974 movie, *Redevelopment: A Marxist Analysis*. By today's corporate communication standards, what results is a disaster. Doolittle delivers a smirking monologue on the virtues of offshoring, which the filmmakers intercut with scenes of workers in Singapore. The monologue is fantastically concise and candid, and it's worth quoting at length:

> You could hire a girl there for $20 U.S. a month, 48 hours a week. We did not get any special concessions from the Singapore government at the time that we located there. We were attracted there because it had a good supply of labor. Their unemployment rate four years ago was 10 percent. It had a political and economic stability that we thought made sense for us to become involved in. They don't have all the social distractions that we have here. And as a result, when someone in these countries goes to work they don't object to sitting down and doing very tedious jobs on a continuing basis. Here in the United States, people don't like tedious jobs. You see this coming up in terms of the automotive industry. People now find that they don't like to sit on a line and put one bolt on a car every minute as it passes by. They want to have a job with more variety in it. Before we established our core-stringing operations in Singapore we had a pilot operations here in the Bay Area, and we found that people couldn't concentrate eight hours a day doing these tedious jobs and as a result the productivity was relatively low.[55]

When the prevailing wage is 1/25th as high, making the comparison about tolerance for tedious tasks is poor cover; of course the productivity per dollar was relatively low. And Singapore's political and economic stability was based on U.S. regional domination, which was in turn based on the American ability to sabotage, undermine, and eventually bomb the hell out of any country that starts to blush pink. Lewis Terman once dreamed that the United States could mobilize national intelligence to win wars; Fred Terman made it a reality, and the Stanford war machine he built equipped the country to rule the world in silicon and fire.

Like the components in an integrated circuit, America acted to isolate nations from the international current of socialist revolt *and* connect them in a precise pattern of capital investment, labor exploitation, and profit flow. The United States blocked refugees from the capitalist Third World, while soliciting them from Soviet allies under a new blank-check exception to American immigration law for anticommunists. It was a kind of semiconducting globalism, and HP was involved in that project from the beginning. Silicon Valley continued to cross-pollinate with the military command structure in the Cold War period. In 1959, former undersecretary of war General William Draper Jr. (recall his German calorie counting with Herbert Hoover) cofounded the first Silicon Valley VC partnership, Draper, Gaither & Anderson, beating out Rock and Davis.[56] (The Drapers have stayed in Palo Alto finance ever since: The general's son, William Draper III, founded Sutter Hill Ventures, and his grandson, Tim Draper, is a top VC today, with great-grandchildren Adam, Billy, and Jesse following in the family business.)* The Bay was called to make an equivalent offering, and in 1969 newly inaugurated Richard Nixon summoned Hoover trustee David Packard to the Pentagon as deputy secretary of defense.

The Bay Area electronics milieu earned its offshore factories by being instrumental to the state, building up an airborne fighting force of unparalleled lethality. Thanks in part to Fairchild's offshoring strategy, silicon chips advanced rapidly and cheaply enough to make the jump to the consumer market. The Big Science era was coming to a close, and in the shade of Silicon Valley's semiconductor orchards, a new industry began to sprout.

---

* While at Stanford, Tim interned — where else? — at HP.

Chapter 3.3

Personal Revolution

Computers as Human Augmentation — LSD as Human
Augmentation — Bob Kaufman: Black, Communist,
Beat — Ken Kesey and Other CIA Experiments

As so often happens on frontiers, land filled up fast in Silicon Valley, and settlers became workers. The Santa Clara County of the 1960s was heavily dependent on the federal government, and electronics industry fortunes rose and fell with defense spending like a small boat riding big waves. Scientists and engineers who felt so secure in the early days of the space settlers were tossed into the ocean of unemployment: 30,000 California engineers were laid off in 1963–64. As the Vietnam War wound toward its close, the engineer unemployment rate quadrupled.[1] These workers, many of whom hadn't wanted to encumber themselves with a labor union, faced uncertain prospects.

Colleagues they left behind started to feel dwarfed by massive machines, anonymous parts in the public-private defense bureaucracy. "By the end of the 1960s," writes economist Harry Braverman in his study of postwar shifts in the composition of the labor force, "rising rates of unemployment among 'professionals' of various kinds once more brought home to them that they were not the free agents they thought they were, who deigned to 'associate themselves' with one or another corporation, but truly part of a labor market, hired and fired like those beneath them."[2] The newest inventions and advances were for unused missiles. Making missiles and database systems was, if not morally repugnant, at least boring and pointless. Journalist Steven Levy writes that computers were "loathed by millions of common, patriotic citizens" who saw them as a "dehumanizing factor in society."*[3] The dull technophile

---

* As you'll read, the hatred was even stronger among non-patriotic citizens.

engineer with a new stereo became a stereo*type*, and the Japanese commodity-electronics industry threatened from across the Pacific.

Information technology was meant for more, and a line of theorist-administrators saw it coming together, starting with Vannevar Bush. In a 1945 article for the *Atlantic* with the clever futurist title "As We May Think," Bush described a possible synthesis of technologies that would allow individual professionals to store all their printed matter on a microfilm hard drive built into a desk, where it could be recalled and projected onto slanted translucent screens. "Trails" between documents would be easy to encode, leading to new ways to organize information:

> The lawyer has at his touch the associated opinions and decisions of his whole experience, and of the experience of friends and authorities. The patent attorney has on call the millions of issued patents, with familiar trails to every point of his client's interest. The physician, puzzled by its patient's reactions, strikes the trail established in studying an earlier similar case, and runs rapidly through analogous case histories, with side references to the classics for the pertinent anatomy and histology.[4]

He called this invention the memex, and despite Bush's influence it stayed speculative and his Raytheon didn't pursue it. But the vision of a desktop knowledge machine marched on. In 1960, betweeded and horn-rimmed, the former SAGE staffer and MIT professor J. C. R. Licklider published "Man-Computer Symbiosis," a paper predicting that soon the labor elite would outsource their rote tasks to "computers" (at the time a sketchy enough term to warrant putting it in quotation marks) — machines that would complete the tasks just as SAGE calculated trajectories and suggested responses to operators.[5]

The computer scene centered at MIT, but Fred Terman prepared the West Coast to compete. Radar was the first system that gathered complicated information from the world and automatically displayed it for a human operator to use, and that experience prompted the young technicians to imagine further uses for the human-information interface apparatus. One of those technicians was a young man named Doug Engelbart, who, with perfect timing, enlisted in the navy and qualified for elite radio training only to see the war end as soon as he deployed, shipping out to the Philippines on V-J Day. No matter;

he was a good investment for the military regardless. He spent his short tour in Manila Bay, and on the way there he happened to read Vannevar Bush's *Atlantic* article reprinted in *Life* magazine.

In 1950, Engelbart was twenty-five and working for NACA (soon to be NASA) at the Ames Research Center at Moffett Airfield in unincorporated Santa Clara County as an electrical engineer when he decided to decide what to do with the rest of his life. He had a sense of himself as an important, complex, expensive tool, which is exactly what the military built him to be, the human half of a hybrid man-machine radar apparatus. He was like an especially quick colt at the Palo Alto Stock Farm who halts his trot to think: What do I want to be when I grow up? A tractor? A fire truck? A cannon? He was good: *but for what*? He had three flashes of insight. First, the world's problems were increasing in difficulty faster than the human ability to solve them; second, improving mankind's ability to solve problems is a worthwhile activity; and third, a vision of himself, sitting at a screen, operating what we now know as a general-purpose computer. He saw men sharing information in new ways—in theaters, watching a big-screen presentation together, or in offices, sending data to and from their own screens. Information could move as fast as they needed it to. Text and graphics would combine to represent anything and everything, infinitely adaptable to the needs of a protean world. Pretty much everyone he told about it thought he was nuts. He quit his job and enrolled in a Berkeley PhD program.

Even his fellow Berkeley grad students thought Engelbart's idea, which he was calling "human augmentation," was wacky, so he kept his head down and got his degree without making too many waves. After he graduated, he got himself recruited to SRI, where he eventually got a small grant from the air force to draft a report on "augmenting human intellect." The report he returned in 1962 included the future possibility of "the digital computer as a tool for the personal use of an individual."[6] This caught the attention of Licklider (whom he cited a couple of times) and Bob Taylor, a Licklider protégé at NACA. Licklider gave Engelbart some funds from the new Advanced Research Projects Agency (ARPA), where he was helping direct computer research money. With his focus on MIT, Licklider didn't have a lot of faith in this guy out in Palo Alto, but "he's using the right words, so we're sort of honor-bound to fund him," Licklider allegedly told a friend.[7] Taylor directed funding to Engelbart so he could create a computer pointing tool—a contest won by a device that became known as the mouse—and when Taylor joined the Information Processing Techniques Office at ARPA, he buried Engelbart in more acronyms and money, setting him up with the Augmentation Research Center (ARC) at SRI.[8] America hadn't yet reached the moon, but already this group of powerful men at the academic-military nexus was looking to the next frontier.

In retrospect, the ARC has a magical aura, but at the beginning it was the black sheep of SRI. During the early days of NACA's support for the center, Engelbart's manager made clear to Taylor that he could back the crackpot if he wanted, but otherwise the institute couldn't afford to feed him. A straitlaced adopted son of a Methodist minister, the Texan Taylor came to engineering through psychology, and from there he jumped into the growing aerospace industry. Though he later objected to and even tried to obstruct the hippie turn in computing, the pipe-smoking former basketball coach shared the augmentation dream, and in 1968, when Engelbart wanted to show off his first attempt to the public, Taylor awarded the ARC another blank check. The center spent $175,000 in 1968 dollars on the single day's demo—$1.5 million in 2022 money.[9] But Taylor got his money's worth. The oNLine System (NLS) was a leap forward in computing technology, and if you watch a video of the charismatic Engelbart wielding it at the "Mother of All Demos," you'll see that it's still a somewhat recognizable interface today.[10] The mouse moved freely in two dimensions; there were windows and linked hypertext. Engelbart gave the demo on a keyboard-mouse-screen terminal in San Francisco, wirelessly connected to the computer itself at the ARC, in Menlo Park, via microwave transmission. He video-chatted live with the team at SRI, and the audience was riveted.

The next step was to transform the performance into a prototype, but that wasn't on the philosopher Engelbart's agenda. Meanwhile, Bob Taylor left ARPA after funding cuts and a disillusioning trip to Vietnam to try to coordinate the war's chaotic information streams.[11] He went to the University of Utah in 1969, where his ARPA munificence funded one of the nation's top computer science programs, but the next year, when corporate copy giant Xerox invited him to help build out the Computer Science Lab (CSL) at the company's new Palo Alto Research Center (PARC), he headed for the coast. Xerox wanted Taylor for his contacts—as the Santa Claus of computer research at ARPA, he knew the best recruits and how to get them on the phone. And not only did everyone in the field know him, they all owed him, too. Taylor raided Engelbart's lab for lead engineer Bill English, and the small, struggling Berkeley Computer Company for another half dozen top talents.[12] He didn't have his own PhD, but the ex-general Taylor did have an army of top scientists and engineers, and he led them to the promised land of the first personal computer.

Xerox PARC gets conflated with the CSL and the CSL with Taylor, a set of impressions Taylor worked hard to deliver and that drove his coworkers nuts. That said, the CSL's accomplishments are impressive: Within five years of the Engelbart demo, PARC had its Alto, a stand-alone personal computer system with a screen, a mouse, and a body that fit under a desk. It had Ethernet networking and a laser printer and a friendly graphical user interface. PARC did it, and then Xerox fumbled the ball. That's the traditional business-history story. Xerox had the future in its hands at PARC, but the large firm was too bloated to act fast, and the various Alto innovations slipped through its fat corporate fingers. There's some truth to that, and Xerox didn't cash in on PCs or networking, but the laser printer did so well for the company that it more than covered the whole pricey R & D effort. Merely making money is only a problem by Silicon Valley standards, and Xerox is from Rochester. Still, Licklider and Engelbart couldn't help feeling like there was something about the work that their eastern bosses didn't get.

In his conceptual framework for augmenting human intellect, Doug Engelbart posed the question of whom to augment first. His unsurprising conclusion was that computer programmers should be at the head of the line—specifically, those working on human augmentation, because the more they self-augmented, the faster they could produce further augmentations. They are "developing better tools for a class to which they themselves belong," he wrote.[13] (Engelbart saw this cycle as obviously virtuous, but today's reader can detect other possibilities.) Xerox as a company was doing the same thing, and when executives finally commercialized the Alto in 1981 with the Star system, they had themselves in mind. It was an office workstation—high-powered, very big, and so expensive that a large employer had to pick up the tab. It flopped. The personal computer wasn't just for work; it was also for a whole *person*, and if computer executives weren't turned on to the personal revolution, they would never understand their industry. If only they had listened to Myron.

At forty years old, Myron Stolaroff was the senior employee at the familiar Silicon Valley electronics company Ampex. Drafted out of Stanford, he was Poniatoff's first full-time hire. But now it was 1960, and Stolaroff had a plan to launch his firm into the future by augmenting the creativity of his fellow engineers. Like Engelbart, he saw how important individuals were becoming to innovation. In the electronics industry, getting the right person to see from the right perspective at the right time could mean year-size jumps in technology and millions or billions of dollars in monopoly profits. Stolaroff's solution wasn't to give them computers; he wanted to give them LSD. The rest of the management committee at Ampex did not think dosing their top men with a powerful and ill-understood psychedelic was a good plan, but Myron was a true believer, and he had plenty of success in casual settings turning on friends from the informal but powerful Stanford engineering fraternity, including employees from HP and SRI as well as Stanford professor Willis Harman. Wealthy enough by then to go at it alone, Stolaroff left Ampex to found the International Foundation for Advanced Studies in Palo Alto, where he "augmented" the engineering elite with LSD.[14]

During the first half of the 1960s, the foundation guided hundreds of subjects through personal LSD trips at $500 a pop (around $5,000 in 2022 money), and the reviews were raves.[15] Palo Alto was the glowing center of the bourgeois acid scene, a vindication of drug pioneers such as Timothy Leary, who imagined a trickle-down liberation of the American mind. A team including Stolaroff's deputies Harman and James Fadiman (of Engelbart's augmentation center at SRI) published their preliminary findings a few years later, summarizing the experiences of professional men who took acid and tried to solve work problems. In addition to the LSD effects we now take for granted (a broadening of context, access to the subconscious, increased empathy), they reported slightly improved work performance across a number of categories.[16] One engineer described the experience thusly: "I began to see an image of the circuit. The gates themselves were little silver cones linked together by lines. I watched this circuit flipping through its paces." An architect found himself with a perfect design: "I drew the property lines.... Suddenly I saw the finished project. I did some quick calculations.... it would fit on the property and not only that....it would meet the cost and income requirements....it would park enough cars....it met all the requirements." The foundation was at the edge of a breakthrough—a planned visit from some high-placed federal officials—when the politics of LSD shifted, and in 1966 Stolaroff found his clinical research abruptly shut down.

Luckily, Palo Alto contained plenty of other well-funded nooks and crannies. Harman got a placement at SRI, too, and he quietly resumed the acid experiments under the auspices of the Alternative Futures Project.[17] Fadiman has continued the work into the present, and his 2011 book, *The Psychedelic Explorer's Guide: Safe, Therapeutic, and Sacred Journeys*, inspired a surge of interest in "microdosing," now a popular performance-enhancing method in Silicon Valley tech circles that involves taking tiny amounts of LSD before work, a practice first proposed by Fadiman that's sometimes imagined as a twenty-first-century off-label use of the drug.[18] But acid was marketed to Bay Area knowledge workers as a productivity aid from the beginning.

The personal revolutions in computers and consciousness weren't just concurrent; they were also overlapping.* Aided by LSD (directly and environmentally), technologists were going out on limbs too slight for even California's big corporations to follow, and the government's support peaked, then declined. Silicon Valley's defense dependence posed a real risk: The electronics industry always relied on America's military and its big corporate contractors. Who the hell else would buy a computer? Who else *could*? Some California drug freaks were convinced that the answer was soon to be "everyone," including individual households. Whereas selling to the military was a relatively simple case of "know-who" among sophisticated technocrats, making the case for the home computer to the public required a salesmanship that was not yet a big part of the Palo Alto package. But the hype around computers and LSD was similar: People were either haves or have-nots—those who were "turned on" and those who were still off; the augmented and the rest. Marketer turned poet impresario Allen Ginsberg turned on to acid under the observation of Palo Alto's Mental Research Institute a few years after he piqued America's interest with his claim to know the best minds of his generation and where to find

---

* Celebrated books like *What the Dormouse Said* and *From Counterculture to Cyberculture* have drawn different versions of this Venn diagram, but Stanford and the Palo Alto community are always smack in the middle.

them.[19] A Stanford creative-writing hotshot named Ken Kesey was turning on around the same time, right down the road.[20] It was all so characteristically binary, and it appealed to the cultural elites in a rising generation, one with an ambivalent relationship to conventional success.

Beat

On March 31, 1973, at the Palo Alto Culture Center, the poet Bob Kaufman recited a speech from T. S. Eliot's verse drama *Murder in the Cathedral*.[21] Insofar as Kaufman was known at all, it was for his extemporaneous public readings, so the recitation wouldn't have been surprising except that he had barely spoken in a decade. There's some controversy regarding the circumstances of his silence—whether it was in response to the JFK assassination, Buddhism, or the Vietnam War—and whether the vow really kept him from asking people for speed and money. Regardless, there's consensus that Kaufman was in bad shape. He had chronic injuries from a lifetime of abuse: being hung from his thumbs overnight as a child by a lynch mob in Louisiana; a later beating that knocked out some teeth and permanently ruined his hearing.[22] He was also an addict. Kaufman received electroshock treatment at Bellevue Hospital in New York, lived on the streets of San Francisco, and in Paris they called him "the black American Rimbaud."[23]

Americans are coming to recognize Kaufman as a central figure in the development of Beat poetry and the larger aesthetic. San Francisco mainstay publisher City Lights put out his collected poems posthumously, in 2019; he's the subject of the 2015 documentary *And When I Die, I Won't Stay Dead*, directed by the great California talent Billy Woodberry; and it's not like Kaufman never got any attention while he lived.* But it was other people who

---

* The poet Steve Abbott recalls a night in North Beach in 1975: "The club seemed full of basket cases and I wasn't surprised when a thin ragged Black man wandered in, took a swig from a bottle, and jumped up on stage spouting some haunting words that were barely audible to most of the audience. The MC, an attractive blond wearing a medieval pageboy costume, then took the microphone. 'That was Bob Kaufman, founder and greatest poet of the Beats.'" Steve Abbott, *Beautiful Aliens: A Steve Abbott Reader* (Nightboat Books, 2019), 200. Asked about poets of the Beat community, artist Joe Overstreet recalled, "The poets were Bob Kaufman. I didn't believe anybody else could ever be a poet but Bob Kaufman." Oral history interview with Joe Overstreet, March 17–18, 2010, Archives of American Art, Smithsonian Institution.

made sure the work got out, who made it possible for him to win a National Endowment for the Arts award in the last years of his life, who kept him alive to the age of sixty. As pretty much any poem of his will tell you, Kaufman was moribund; his central creative notes were defeat and self-destruction. "My face is covered with maps of dead nations," he writes.[24] When you look at pictures of him, it's hard to disagree. He writes under the mushroom clouds of Hiroshima and Nagasaki, standing on unmarked Indian graves. History knocked Kaufman around, and he knows it when he sees it:

> Alien winds sweeping the highway
> fling the dust of medicine men,
> long dead,
> in the california afternoon
>
> Into the floating eyes
> of spitting gadget salesmen,
> eating murdered hot dogs,
> in the california afternoon.[25]

There's nothing of the personal revolution in Kaufman's poetry, no sense that something better is on its way. He is from a different tradition, one that doesn't overlap much with gadget salesmen. Kaufman joined the merchant marine at around seventeen, a classic outlet for restless young men, and he spent World War II shipping American goods (including arms) around the world. Within a couple of years, barely out of his teens, Kaufman was organizing with the National Maritime Union (NMU), a radical seamen's association affiliated with the CIO. In 1945 he represented the NMU as part of a delegation to Congress in support of anti-discrimination rules and led a sound-truck campaign to tell the public about the union's wage drive.[26] Stories about Kaufman organizing in the Deep South line up with the CIO's Operation Dixie, during which union organizers (including those from the NMU) went to sign up shops in the low-wage nonunion South at great personal risk.[27] But white reactionaries took control of the NMU in the late 1940s. Its vice president, Ferdinand Smith, the highest-ranking black labor leader in New York City, was expelled from the union and deported to Jamaica.[28]

Was Bob Kaufman a communist? The FBI sure thought so. As they did a lot of black labor leaders in the early years of the Cold War, the feds kept a close watch on Kaufman. They tracked his movements and activities and harassed his family and associates.[29] They were convinced he was recruited into the CPUSA in 1946 and advanced quickly. Informants told the FBI that the next year Kaufman became a member of the executive committee of the CP's Waterfront Section in New York. After Smith was kicked out of the NMU but before his deportation, he founded the Harlem Trade Union Council (allegedly at the urging of the CP), and the FBI has Kaufman as an employee in 1949, working with youth.* In 1950, the feds believed he attended Communist Party "leadership training school." But Kaufman, in his mid-twenties, got involved in the Harlem drug scene and was expelled from the Party in January of 1951 after admitting he "took the needle" himself. The FBI followed him to Los Angeles, but in 1956 they were convinced he was done with politics and closed the file. That's when Kaufman moved to San Francisco to check out the poetry.

It's tempting to see Kaufman as a one-of-a-kind poetic consciousness, the "best of the Beats" as some have it. So Beat he could barely get through the day, but throwing off gems as he staggered. A street poet for the canon, a black Beat. But Kaufman was also part of a working-class lifeworld torn asunder by postwar anticommunism.[30] "[W]e were outnumbered because the anti-[c]ommunist thing became a banner—a tent under which...racist elements could assemble and cover their flanks," recounts fellow NMU organizer Jack O'Dell of the South during Operation Dixie. "[Union officials] teamed up with the police and the Klan...to run blacks out of the Union hall. It was almost like a Reconstruction thing you read about—how they overthrew the government, the blacks are forced to flee, and so forth. It was that kind of atmosphere they were able to create."[31] After the Korean War began, the Cold War division went national, especially in industrial unions dependent on military spending.[32] Communists in the NMU (suspected and actual) had trouble shipping out, and O'Dell moved on to advise Martin Luther King Jr. before he was publicly red-baited out of the civil rights movement, too. Kaufman was

---

* The FBI believed the CP instigated the founding of the HTUC to counter the influence of A. Philip Randolph's anticommunist Negro American Labor Council. Federal Bureau of Investigation, "A. Philip Randolph, File No. 100-56616," n.d., 78.

among the youngest members of the Old Left—he was born the same year as Malcolm X—but he represented a whole population.

"Why do winos lie so much?" Richard Pryor jokes in his 1986 semi-autobiographical comedy, *Jo Jo Dancer, Your Life Is Calling.* "You give him a bottle of wine and talk to him a little bit, and he start lyin': 'I was with the FBI'; 'Me and another black man started the merchant marines'; 'Shit, I've been around the world, swam the equator twice.'" These were those guys, and they had good reasons, both to drink and to lie, just in case someone was listening too closely.* And behind the booze and tall tales were big, sad stories from real history. Many of them *had* been around the world—and some of them no doubt did inform on their coworkers to the FBI. There was Henry Thomas, fellow seaman and Spanish Civil War veteran, who got drunk all day at a bar near the San Francisco docks and sang "The Internationale."[33] There was Joe Overstreet, a Bay Area kid who joined the NMU, learned politics from Kaufman, and became a bohemian painter in Harlem.† And there was Kaufman's friend Jimmy Carter (of no apparent relation to the ex-president), another black communist sailor who was red-baited out of UCLA and became a renowned San Francisco jazz drummer. Carter was a poet, too, and a model for Kaufman, but he purposely never wrote anything down.[34] It's from this beaten black political milieu that the Beats got their sense of what it meant to lose.‡

---

* Pryor spent most of 1971 in Berkeley and around the East Bay's black political-artistic-intellectual scene. See Scott Saul, *Becoming Richard Pryor* (HarperCollins, 2014).

† "I came out of a society in San Francisco and in California of where I was with the Merchant Marines and they had taken our union—you know, and they had—we were mess boys and cooks anyway. So they had taken that and taken it from us and put us in jail and called us communists." Oral history interview with Joe Overstreet, March 17–18, 2010, Archives of American Art, Smithsonian Institution.

‡ Allen Ginsberg was a red diaper baby and describes the American overthrow of the Mossaddegh (Iran) and Arbenz (Guatemala) governments in the early '50s as important for his consciousness, but he characterized himself as "neutral" in the Cold War, against Eastern Bloc authoritarianism and homophobia. In Ginsberg's diary he recounts a dream I read as particularly meaningful: "Emerging up from 3rd class to First on great oceanliner—up the staircase to the deck—First thing I meet, huge faded negro Paul Robeson—in officer's uniform—I salute him introducing myself which doesn't mean much to him—he bows— I begin scheming immediately—Being a big officer Communist negro all these years perhaps he could get me a book in the NMU so I can ship out? I see he's working on an open deck hole with a lift truck & wire lift placing faded 2nd hand turkish rugs in the hold— Old communist, I notice I am amazed at his calm—he is folding the dead in to carry that way (Won't they not smell up the exported carpets?)—I see one corpse in the hold lying face up on rug, he's getting a layer of carpet to cover that. The corpse is a middle-aged man

The radical labor movement was defiantly interracial—in certain ports, NMU sailors were known for integrating bars by force—and with its national defeat, segregation shaped the Bay Area's culture.* We can't know how America would have been different if Popular Front culture had held its ground, but there are some indications. Instead of coworkers and comrades, the period's dominant white artists approached black people as material or inspiration, as symbols rather than humans. The internment and expulsion of the California Japanese also influenced the scene in ways it's hard to see now. The most famous artist-entertainer to grow up in Palo Alto during the interwar period was Paul Wing, an American-born Chinese tap dancer who graduated from Palo Alto High in 1932. The Wings were one of Palo Alto's founding families: Paul's parents ran a laundry and a women's clothing store on Emerson Street in the downtown area that seem to have been financed by his father's uncle Ah Wing ("Mr. Wing"), Jane Stanford's longtime cook, who after being cleared of her murder received the $1,000 earmarked for him in her will—over $30,000 in 2022 dollars.[35]† Paul's well-educated mother, Rose Tong Jew, who was born in San Francisco's Chinatown and raised bilingually fluent and literate, was the nexus between Palo Alto's white community and its early Chinese population. The Wings were almost certainly the first Chinese-American family to buy property in town.

Touched by the dawn of Hollywood's golden age, Paul loved showbiz from his early years, training himself in tap despite skepticism from his parents about their eldest son's vocation. But Paul had an uncle who found some success in vaudeville (as well as a bunch of younger siblings for his parents to worry about), and he vigorously pursued a dance career despite the paucity of Chinese-Americans in the industry. He teamed up with a young

---

dead-faced & slightly rotten lying on a rug drest in a blue business suit. I wonder if I have the guts to face corpses like that negro communist." Allen Ginsberg, *Journals: Early Fifties, Early Sixties* (Grove/Atlantic, Inc., 2007), 177–78.

* The Maryland NMU chief recounts going into waterfront bars with an interracial group of sailors, and if the owner objected that the business was segregated, he would throw a beer glass through the bar's mirror: "There, you've just been integrated." Gerald Horne, *Red Seas: Ferdinand Smith and Radical Black Sailors in the United States and Jamaica* (NYU Press, 2009), 141.

† Jane's maid Bertha Berner allegedly accused Wing, who after her death worked to preserve the Stanford family's memory at the Leland Stanford Jr. Museum until it was destroyed in the 1906 earthquake. This failed scapegoating attempt by Berner strikes me as one of the strongest pieces of circumstantial evidence against her.

Los Angeles–raised performer named Dorothy Toy, whose Russian ballet instructor traded meals at the Toy family Chinese restaurant in exchange for lessons. (Paul Wing dined there with his uncle as well, when he was in town.) The duo branded themselves as Toy & Wing and hit the road, winning plaudits for his quick feet, her Russian-inspired kick moves, and their natural chemistry. Fans called them the Chinese Fred Astaire and Ginger Rogers, and they signed with the top-shelf William Morris Agency in New York, making it all the way to Broadway. Hollywood was feeling them out, too, and they performed in the 1937 punny film short *Deviled Ham*, about an infernal revue.* Toy & Wing were supporting Chico Marx on tour and planning to shoot their first feature film when they got the news: Someone had snitched out Dorothy Toy, whose birth name was Takahashi. The Chinese Ginger Rogers was really the Japanese Ginger Rogers; they couldn't go back to California. Dorothy and Paul stayed in New York while her parents were interned in Utah. They never made it to the movies, and American culture suffered for it.[36]

Embracing white supremacy and segregation meant sacrificing a certain amount of nonwhite talent. This is what horrified the racialist Lewis Terman, who spent so much time trying to locate exceptional youngsters, about Japanese internment and expulsion. Considering its human capital goals, it's hard to account for what the state wasted, the degree to which California retarded itself in the process. Once again, there are some indications. For example, the sculptor Ruth Asawa was born to small farmers in Southern California in 1926, and she became a major influence on public art in San Francisco, but not before a long detour. First her family was interned with other Japanese-Americans, and as a young adult she remained formally excluded from California and was instead resettled in Wisconsin. Unable to pursue teaching because she was an American of Japanese ancestry, she found a home in the avant-garde at Black Mountain College in North Carolina via the communist art scene in Mexico City, where she learned weaving practices that inspired her signature wire forms.[37] At a time when the Bay Area's artists began toying with Japanese ideas and forms, artists of Japanese heritage were banned from the state. Asawa didn't regret her path, but she ended up on the artistically

---

* The Internet Movie Database and the Library of Congress both have the short's title recorded as the plural *Deviled Hams*, which though it is perhaps more clever and descriptive is nonetheless incorrect, as evidenced by the title card.

fertile margins because of her race, and she had to do it while segregated out of her home state. Meanwhile, urban redevelopment in Oakland and San Francisco refashioned the cities into destinations for suburban consumer spending and investment capital, wrecking communities in the process and leaving the city's experienced working-class organizers fighting for survival just as moderates pushed them out of the unions. The personal revolution became a spatial movement as well, as white homeowners bailed on cities and took their tax dollars with them, undermining urban public life. The hippies wanted out, too, going "back to the land," or at least taking some really long road trips. In the process they rebranded what it meant to be down and out.

Surrounded by so much historical unfairness and noble defeat, how did white suburban winners in Palo Alto come to convince themselves and a surprising segment of the world that they were the real loser rebels? The case of Ken Kesey is illustrative. A college wrestling champion at Oregon, Kesey polarized the creative-writing community as a Stanford graduate student in the late 1950s. Program director Wallace Stegner thought the charismatic and rebellious Kesey a clown, but other faculty spied promise, including novelist Malcolm Cowley. When a friend told Kesey that the veterans' hospital was paying local volunteers to take exciting new drugs, he signed up, had his mind blown, and got a job at the Menlo Park VA, where he had unfettered access to experimental narcotics. Kesey started bringing drugs home, where he gathered a scene about him.[38] His 1962 debut novel, *One Flew Over the Cuckoo's Nest*, was an instant hit, romanticizing the patients Kesey saw at work as exemplars of independent consciousness. The men in *Cuckoo's Nest* are not insane — they're mentally subjugated, and the Kesey character, Randle McMurphy, is there to liberate his fellow patients with swaggering masculine megalomania. Kesey's success allowed him to assume the McMurphy character (without having to continually wheedle people out of money, as McMurphy does in the novel), and Kesey started throwing large drug-fueled parties that, ever the jock, he made competitive and styled as acid "tests."

Outside the various electronics and tech industries, excluding the political ideologies of Jordan, Hoover, Terman, and the rest, Kesey is probably Palo Alto's most important twentieth-century cultural product. *One Flew Over the Cuckoo's Nest* is a distillation of hippie thought and it became a sensation. Kesey drew a distinct opposition between individual consciousness and a system of social control, which he called (in a throwback to Leland Stanford) the Combine. The word *computer* doesn't occur in the book, but a whirring mainframe was part of the evil Nurse Ratched's apparatus of domination.* It's man against machine, but the novel is politically clueless. Whereas the rebels are alienated white men (and one mute Indian), the proverbial Man is an overbearing nurse, backed up by her black "boy" orderlies. McMurphy's uprising is about the men reclaiming their masculinity in the face of a castrating state authority. Like Steinbeck before him, Kesey sublimates the era's struggles into existential melodrama, one in which his stand-in is the tragic protagonist. If rebellion was a matter of a man's individual mind frame, then it was perfectly compatible with augmentation, though not IBM mainframes. Like Chief Bromden at the end of the story, the new rebels smashed the punch-card machine and escaped through the window of individualism, a dynamic image Silicon Valley would use to represent itself to the world in the years to come.

But unlike Bob Kaufman, Kesey wasn't a patient.† He worked there. What, exactly, does a champion wrestler do at a psychiatric hospital? And why did those disabled veterans need all that LSD, anyway?

Evil in the Basement

There were a lot of LSD experiments in Palo Alto in the 1950s and '60s, and in a lot of institutions. The town was a, if not the, national epicenter of psychoactive research, with the possible exceptions of Cambridge, Los Angeles, and a mansion in Millbrook, New York, where Timothy Leary hung out. While the psychedelic explorers at SRI and the International Foundation for Advanced

---

* "Everything the guys think and say and do is all worked out months in advance, based on the little notes the nurse makes during the day. This is typed and fed into the machine I hear humming behind the steel door in the rear of the Nurses' Station. A number of Order Daily Cards are returned, punched with a pattern of little square holes." Ken Kesey, *One Flew over the Cuckoo's Nest* (Penguin Books, 2016), 28.

† For all his big talk, when confronted with an actual mental patient who was also an artistic genius, Kesey missed it. In 1976, Kesey told the poet Tony Seymour that he had a run-in with Kaufman's drive-by poetry on the street in the '60s, but that he "didn't really appreciate him as a poet until much more recently, within the last four or five years. In rereading his stuff I could trace back and see how— 'Yeah, yeah! That's where Ginsberg got that riff, here's where Kerouac picked up that thing, and that's where Cassady picked up…'" quoted in Steve Abbott, "Bob Kaufman: Hidden Master of the Beats," *Beautiful Aliens: A Steve Abbott Reader* (Nightboat Books, 2019), 201.

Studies dosed their engineer buddies to get them thinking outside the box, stodgier scientists used the same drugs to break down prisoners and replicate schizophrenia. Kesey wandered into one of those latter kinds of experiments as a student volunteer and liked it so much that he stuck around backstage. But the drugs he got his hands on at the VA mostly weren't for him; they were for testing on the patients. In the real *Cuckoo's Nest*, McMurphy doesn't hand out the LSD—Nurse Ratched does. But if acid is liberating, why would the government administer it to the people it locked up in jails and hospitals? The short answer is that the CIA wanted to see what happened. MK-Ultra was a suite of 183 subprojects financed by the CIA and conducted across North America by contractors at civilian institutions between 1953 and 1973.*[39] It's often referred to as a mind control program because some of the projects focused on using drugs to break down the mental defenses of enemy prisoners during interrogation, but they had a wide range of objectives, from research on blood types to building a miniature lie detector, and those are just a couple of the experiments conducted at Stanford that we know about.†

When Stanford turned itself over to Frederick Terman for a transformation, he remade it into the archetypal Cold War university. That meant a reversal of the school's fortunes, driven in large part by a flood of defense and defense-affiliated spending. He shaped Stanford to attract outside funds, and in the decades that followed state priorities drove the evolution of Palo Alto as a whole. That meant weapons research at the industrial park and missile building at Lockheed, as I've said. But Terman pushed other parts of the school to replicate the successes in engineering. In 1955, Stanford ceded 87.5 acres to the federal government so it could build a veterans' hospital on campus.[40] We could interpret this as a charitable gesture of a university in a country that spent most of the preceding decade at war, but it's also in line with the Terman

---

* The program was preceded by "Project Artichoke," which was a similar but more vicious program conducted at American bases in West Germany, France, Japan, and Korea. Stephen Kinzer, *Poisoner in Chief: Sidney Gottlieb and the CIA Search for Mind Control* (Henry Holt and Company, 2019), 56.

† The public only found out about MK-Ultra because a couple boxes of files were misplaced and then discovered, saving them from a document purge. In 1977, when the CIA notified Stanford president Richard Lyman of the secret research, he released the records. Central Intelligence Agency, "Project MKULTRA Collection" (Stanford Digital Repository, 1977), https://purl.stanford.edu/xf259xw8228.

strategy to maximize opportunities for outside support. The VA was spending twice as much per patient as state hospitals were, and patients were an experimental resource, as were students.[41] The Cold War required novel techniques, and the development of novel techniques required test subjects. Without the administration's approval, and sometimes apparently without the knowledge of the researchers themselves, the CIA spent hundreds of thousands of dollars supporting Stanford faculty working on MK-Ultra subprojects in the 1950s and early 1960s.*

The doctor who oversaw Kesey's first dose was named Leo Hollister, and he played an important role in Palo Alto history. Trained at the VA in San Francisco under the auspices of the navy and then recalled during the Korean War, Hollister decided that, if the United States was going to have so many wars, he'd be better off making a career in the VA than in private practice. He became an internist at the Menlo Park VA hospital and had a breakthrough in the early 1950s using a hypertension drug to treat schizophrenia. By 1959, when he attended a CIA-funded conference on LSD, Hollister was medical director at Menlo Park and a leader in psychopharmacology. When presenters suggested that LSD ingestion mimicked the schizophrenic state, Hollister was skeptical. The CIA was happy to pay him to check it out.[42] That's how Kesey ended up trying every drug in the government's medicine cabinet, from LSD to psilocybin to mescaline to morning glory seeds. Kesey was free to consent and consent and consent—as a Stanford student with an outside shot at the 1960 Olympics, he was a solid specimen by any bodily standard. Not all Hollister's patients were in the same boat. After Stanford opened its campus VA site, Hollister moved there, where he managed research. This is how he later described the (then brand-new) hospital: "Barbaric, by today's standards; we had patients in the Palo Alto VA who had been [in the VA system] for fifty years, since World War I, never left the hospital, stayed there until they died. We had about a thousand patients and most of them were very, very quiet."[43]

---

* Appalled to find out they'd been working for the intelligence agency, two Stanford neurology researchers told the press that they were sure their colleague Wallace Chan was the CIA liaison, and reporting seemed to bear it out. Chan later became a vice provost at UC Davis. Bob Beyers, "Stanford Reveals CIA Links," *New Scientist*, October 13, 1977, 81; "New Vice Chancellor at Davis U.C. Named," *Daily Independent Journal*—San Rafael, September 14, 1962, 21.

Like criminals with long sentences and prisoners of war, catatonic patients were good subjects for sketchy experiments. Whom could they tell?

MK-Ultra gets a lot of buzz in large part because of how outlandish and methodologically suspect the work was, but it wasn't so different from a lot of the other federally financed research going on at Stanford at the same time. The destroyed evidence makes it difficult to see where the rogue CIA program ended and regular university business began; Leo Hollister's experiments, for example, do not seem to have been grouped under the program, though they were funded by the agency and are often discussed as part of MK-Ultra. It's hard to say what exactly *was* the CIA, anyway. During this period the agency worked through dozens of front and pass-through organizations with innocuous names such as the Knickerbocker Foundation, the Michigan Fund, and the Munich Institute.[44] Stanford kept its fingers in everyone's pies as a landlord; the CIA was a customer. The agency sent a team to check out Xerox PARC—the CIA being a valued Xerox client—and after Engelbart and English visited CIA headquarters at Langley, a man with no name came (with a contract) to SRI to be briefed on the augmentation center's work.[45]

And then there was Al Hubbard, the LSD pioneer behind the LSD pioneers. A conservative Catholic, Hubbard was an alcohol runner turned prohibition agent, a weapons smuggler for the CIA's predecessor OSS during the early days of World War II. Hubbard was a drug "researcher" with lax distribution standards and a bankroll that made him Sandoz Pharmaceuticals' best acid customer, flying around on his own plane with a black bag full of premium quality LSD. He was, as one history of the era puts it, "not a CIA operative per se."* Instead he operated in a gray area between industry, organized crime, and the security state—no wonder he ended up in Palo Alto. Hubbard lurked behind Stolaroff's International Foundation for Advanced Studies, and when that shut down, Willis Harman hired him for "security" at SRI's Alternative Futures Project. He ran LSD trips and gathered opposition data about the student New Left, a job description about as bizarre as Hubbard's uniform: khakis, gold badge, pistol, and a belt strung with bullets.[46]

And yet Stanford's most disastrous government experiment didn't even

---

* Apparently he was pissed off that they never paid him money he was owed from the OSS. Martin A. Lee and Bruce Shlain, *Acid Dreams: The CIA, LSD, and the Sixties Rebellion* (Grove Press, 1985), 52.

involve the CIA. The money for social psychologist Philip Zimbardo's infamous six-day research project in the summer of 1971 came from Stanford's dear old friends at the Office of Naval Research.[47] After the Holocaust, the field of social psychology rose to consider and explore questions of discipline, conformity, and obedience—the most famous being Stanley Milgram's electroshock trials in which participants were supposed to have believed themselves to be shocking another volunteer on the orders of the experimenter. These experiments tended toward the theatrical, with experimenters assuming the role of the (implicitly Nazi) state. Zimbardo's study was about the dynamics between prisoners and guards, so he recruited some young men from the Palo Alto community and built a small jail in the basement of Jordan Hall. He flipped coins to assign participants as prisoners or guards, while Zimbardo was the superintendent. To maintain realism, he had the Palo Alto police pick up the "prisoners" at their homes, handcuff them, and bring them to the basement jail, where guards looked after them. Much of the experiment was captured on video, and you can watch the interviews with the young men, who all seem like chill dudes in that California '70s way, though less so after they were arrested without warning on a Sunday morning.[48]

At the jail, the abuse began immediately. It did not occur to the guards that their job involved anything but tormenting the prisoners, and they quickly invented psychological punishments: numbers for names, forced push-ups, food control, sleep disruption, withheld bedding, interminable repeat-after-me drills, mock rape. The prisoners started breaking down on Monday. When one of them demanded to be let out, Zimbardo refused to leave his superintendent role, suggesting that the young man could become his informant instead. On "visitor's day," when a prisoner's parents complained that their son looked to be in bad shape already, on day two, Zimbardo consciously appealed to the father's masculine pride: "Don't you think that *your son* can take it?"[49] Guards forced prisoners to write happy form letters to their visitors, and it was only Wednesday.[50] When Zimbardo brought his girlfriend, Stanford psychology grad student Christina Maslach, to the jail, she saw what was going on and prevailed on him to shut it down on Friday morning, eight days before the planned end.

In his recollections of the experiment, Zimbardo leans toward infernal metaphors. His bestselling book about the experience didn't come out until 2007, in the wake of the Abu Ghraib prison torture scandal and the subsequent trial, in which Zimbardo testified as an expert for the defense. He called the book *The Lucifer Effect: Understanding How Good People Turn Evil;* for some the walk into Jordan Hall was a "descent into Hell";[51] he considers what happened in that Stanford jail to have been an experiment in the "psychology of evil." But for a guy who "accidentally" summoned Satan into his office basement and did the Dark Lord's bidding for a week, Zimbardo is not particularly apologetic. He takes clear pride in how influential his little play has become, and he was certainly rewarded, including with Lewis Terman's old chairmanship of the American Psychological Association. If you think of this situational evil as a kind of demonic possession, it makes sense not to feel too bad about being a host, but Zimbardo created the situation, or at least part of it. The Stanford Prison Experiment is supposed to be a lesson about a species (humans) rather than a place, but generalizing from the behavior of young men in Palo Alto is unscientific. Part of the play's drama comes from the contrast: Look at these nice college boys and how quickly they turn to monsters! But the experiment was in *Jordan Hall*. From the perspective of the state, college boys were an essential national resource; they were already doing war work. *So was Zimbardo*.* The situation was broader than Zimbardo understood it to be, even in retrospect, with decades of distance. Turned into jailers, led by a Stanford scientist, those young men behaved exactly as California's white settlers usually have: with a useful excess of sadism.

A professor in a hastily constructed basement jail taking notes while he pays out of the defense budget for one group of college students to torture another was a natural result of the Terman postwar plan for Stanford. So was a campus hospital full of 1,000 very, very quiet veterans swallowing whatever they were given. So was the personal computer. And all of it was war work in the global struggle against communism.

---

* The ONR funding gets a single half-sentence in *The Lucifer Effect*, on page 236.

How to Destroy an Empire

ChiCom Cuts the Paper Tiger in Korea — Domestic
Decolonization — Rise of the Black Panthers — Third
World California — The War in Palo Alto

At the close of the Second World War, America stood head and shoulders above the international community. Not only did the United States captain the democracies to victory, it also did so without significant damage to its home territories. While the Soviets and Europeans rebuilt, America amassed weapons of mass destruction, strapping the country to a ballistic missile and launching it into the economic future. Using Shockley's man-month efficiency equations and the nuclear bomb, the country readied for a qualitative jump in national power. Now America could project its authority everywhere with the push of a button, the cost in its own blood and treasure reduced to new lows. Strategic bombing made victory so comparatively cheap that political changes anywhere in the world became subject to internal American deliberation. Washington was the capital of the free world, and soon that would be the whole world, an ever-vigilant bald eagle tucking the grateful planet into bed.

Just one problem: It wasn't really working. The Allied victory elevated and strengthened left-wing forces around the world, led by the Soviets — a people who spent nearly the entire first half of the century at war. Russia exited 1945 as battered as any nation ever was but triumphant, with a claim on the future at least as strong as capitalist America's. And if the West had a monetary advantage, the Communist International was better positioned when it came to the main political issues in the postwar Third World: decolonization and land reform. Fascism interrupted the conflict between deputized colonial leaders installed near the close of the nineteenth century and the national liberation movements that opposed them. The sides paused and realigned according to the war alliances. But the core issues of popular sovereignty and economic democracy were yet unresolved across the colonized world. As soon as the World War II guns stopped firing, the anticolonial struggle resumed.

The Soviets and Americans divided the globe in half, one for each super-power. Capitalist and communist forces bordered each other amid the sun-dered empires of Germany and Japan—the latter of which, recall, included much of East Asia—like a giant dog and fox chasing each other's tails around a line of latitude. In some places, the war shook colonial relations so deeply that they couldn't be restored. India won independence from Britain and, following the partition from Pakistan in 1947, moved to consolidate French and Portuguese colonies on the subcontinent. The Netherlands was overrun at home by the Nazis and in the East Indies by the Japanese; freed by Japa-nese occupiers and empowered by the emperor's defeat, an anticolonial leader named Sukarno declared a free Indonesia in 1945. He governed for more than two decades. Chiang Kai-shek's Chinese nationalist government was forced into a popular front against the Japanese with the communists, who were his main internal opponents, but his forces were wrong-footed when the civil war resumed. The communist People's Liberation Army drove his weak regime to full exile in Taiwan by the spring of 1950.

Capitalist forces had not reoriented around the Hooverite understanding of insurgent world communism fast enough to support Chiang and the Chi-nese nationalists to victory. Mao Zedong's campaign against the corrupt and flimsy Chiang was ambiguous at first as far as American policy was concerned, but Mao's clear decision to side with the Soviets made "losing China" the ini-tial serious trauma for U.S. Cold Warriors.* Suddenly, their understanding of the world map changed: Communist internationalists were on the march in Asia, and if the capitalists didn't unite to halt them, the whole continent would fall. National communist parties sprouted all over, including in the West— the Parti Communiste Français was France's largest postwar governing coali-tion partner, undermining the recolonial fight from inside the metropole. The

---

* Pankaj Mishra notes that the Bolshevik revolutionary government's unilateral renunciation of Russia's special concessions in China was important for building the moral authority of communism in colonized nations. Pankaj Mishra, *From the Ruins of Empire: The Intellectu-als Who Remade Asia* (Farrar, Straus and Giroux, 2012), 194.

communists threatened to lead the worldwide anticolonization movement, which put Americans cleanly on the other side.

The next flash point was in French Indochina, which Paris planned to reoccupy after Japanese withdrawal. Nationalist forces disagreed, particularly the Viet Minh, led by communist Ho Chi Minh. When Japan surrendered, Ho declared Vietnamese independence. Chiang's Chinese nationalists agreed to withdraw from the north and stay out of the dispute in exchange for French withdrawal from and renunciation of its prewar Chinese concessions. France invaded carrying the tricolor, but by the decisive defeat of Dien Bien Phu in 1954, America was paying near 80 percent of the war bill, more than $1 billion that year.[1] Mao's victory helped turn the tide as he reneged on Chiang's deal with the French and joined the Soviets in lending material and training support to the Viet Minh. Their success forced a temporary compromise, arbitrarily dividing Vietnam into a communist north and capitalist-proxy south. The Vietnam War, as Americans call it, started long before the 1960s; its roots went deep into the nineteenth century and the worldwide struggle over European colonization.

Understanding the Viet Minh's struggle for Vietnamese independence in those terms, going back at least to the organization's founding, in 1941, clears up the Cold War timeline, which in the U.S. imagination centers on the official deployment of troops to Asia: Japan, then Korea, then Vietnam. But we can only get a sensible grasp on the postwar period by decentering U.S. military history. Seeing it this way doesn't remove America from the story or even from its important role, but it does change the narrative arc. Just as Karl Yoneda and Ernesto Galarza discovered, U.S. betrayal shaped the Cold War world order.

Consider the Philippines: The archipelago's leading men collaborated with the Japanese occupation beginning in 1942, which left the United States supplying the left-wing peasant Huk (or people's) resistance. But after victory, as in much of the world, the Americans backed the collaborator-landowning class rather than take a chance on their recent small-d democratic allies, who belonged to coalitions that included communists. The Huks continued the fight against their exploiters, who now flew an independent national flag rather than a Japanese one. Willing to grant independence but unwilling to cede the territory, which remained an important base for U.S. resources in the crucial region, America's new Central Intelligence Agency helped turn the islands into the prototype for the period's anticommunist "dirty" wars, terrorizing peasants and disappearing their leaders. Financed by the Americans, the Filipino government fought a decades-long war against its own working classes, culminating in the Ferdinand Marcos regime and martial law.

The Korean War—again, as it's known to Americans—was the outcome of a structurally similar U.S. betrayal. Korean insurgents had fought against Japanese influence on the peninsula since Japan began exercising it, toward the end of the nineteenth century. Resistance formalized in the early 1930s with the Japanese invasion of Manchuria and the creation of the Manchukuo puppet state. Japanese colonization divided the Korean people into a large class of peasants and workers and a small class of local overseers, much like European colonization did in the rest of the world. Under the Cold War's binary organization, the two groups could only align one way, and Korean communists continued their resistance against the domestic collaborator class into the postwar period.

Because Korea lies near the nexus of Japan, Russia, and China, the country's militants had plenty of opportunities to practice and train, and the leftists among them made up an important part of the Chinese Communist Party in its insurgent phase. This group included the young man who came to lead the Korean communists. He was born Kim Sŏng-ju in 1912 and moved to Manchuria as a child. Kim was from a nationalist family, and he joined the communist underground as a teenager, in advance of Japanese occupation. As a guerrilla leader in the 1930s, and like many of his comrades around the world, he took a pseudonym: Kim Il-sung, which didn't prevent the imperial Japanese from finding, kidnapping, and murdering his first wife. During World War II he maneuvered his division to Soviet territory, where he joined the Red Army and trained further. With strong links to the Russians and Chinese, along with some reputation for military leadership and an uninterrupted commitment to the cause among his countrymen, Kim made a fine appointment to lead the north portion of the Korean peninsula, which the superpowers arbitrarily partitioned into communist and capitalist halves, the same solution they used a decade later in Vietnam after Dien Bien Phu. For the south, the Americans selected Syngman Rhee, an older independence activist with degrees from Harvard and Princeton who spent most of his life in self-exile in American territories, unsuccessfully lobbying for Korean independence. As it did in France, the postwar situation pitted left-wing partisans against moderate exiles in a contest for control.

The contrived lines that bisected former Japanese territories in Southeast Asia were not expected to hold. At the very moment these national peoples won their independence and self-determination within the country system — a designation they'd been denied for as long as that system had existed — here came a new foreign power to deal with. The Americans collected and empowered anticommunists, brokering compromises between Anglo-friendly exiled resistance leadership (often religious Christians, it's worth noting) and local remnants of the landowning collaborator class. Rhee, for example, came to accord with Japan's quislings and they filled in the Republic of Korea's power structure. In Korea and Vietnam, in the north and the south, all four parties planned to unify their countries under their own administration. But democracy was a risky game for the southern bloc, and the leaders (and their handlers) weren't going to risk the future of the free world on a show of hands. In Vietnam, a promised election came and went. In the Republic of Korea, Rhee's parliamentary installation was preordained by American occupiers.

From the perspective of East Asia's indigenous anticolonial movements, the Cold War reoriented but did not recast decades-long conflicts. For the region's peasants, economic democracy was about avoiding or managing proletarianization, about land reform and the national ownership of national resources in the true national interest. Like most of the agricultural strikers in California, the "communists" in East Asia were more often working people struggling to reduce their level of exploitation via collective action in the face of modern capitalists who were always finding ways to get more for less, new ways to grind their laborers down. The Huk Rebellion in the Philippines was left-wing, but it wasn't led from Moscow.* The same was true in Jeju Island, off the Korean peninsula, where autonomous local popular committees governed until the Americans landed in 1945. Capitalist proxy governments had no choice but

---

* In fact, the U.S. connected the Filipino farmworker struggles: "American authorities believed that a worldwide communist conspiracy was at the root of political unrest in the former U.S. colony and that Filipino labor activists in the United States communicated with insurgents in the Philippines through an elaborate spy ring that linked left-wing cadres across the globe." Rick Baldoz, "'Comrade Carlos Bulosan': U.S. State Surveillance and the Cold War Suppression of Filipino Radicals," *Asia-Pacific Journal* 11, no. 33 (August 19, 2014): 1.

to treat these forces as capital-C Communists, both because that's how the American handlers saw them and because if these economic democrats were to take power they would encounter strong incentives to align with the Soviets (as Mao did) or at the very least stake out neutral ground. In the late 1940s, Rhee's RoK authorities responded to protests in Jeju with a counterinsurgency operation. They killed tens of thousands of suspected leftists while American military occupiers watched.[2]

The Truman administration's containment doctrine marked a new Cold War unity between the Democrats and Republicans behind the Hooverite Red Scare perspective. The short, uneven era of Frances Perkins and White House neutrality in the war between labor and capital was over. Government purged leftists, and Soviet sympathizers were no longer considered Americans in good standing. Over outraged pleas from around the world, federal authorities executed Julius and Ethel Rosenberg on flimsy spying charges, alleging a nuclear conspiracy that didn't exist. Prosecutors convicted Bill Camp's New Deal commie lawyer, Alger Hiss, of perjury in the first days of 1950 for lying about aid he lent to the Russians. The likes of him were no longer welcome at the State Department, at least not in the open. America tended toward corporate-military leadership, and it saw the world as one big chess board, countries full of people just pieces to handle. The ascendant American anticommunist strategy collided with East Asian anticolonial movements that, in the wake of imperial Japan's defeat, were finally breaking through. The Chinese Communist Revolution changed the balance of power: Americans and their European allies weren't ready for a third world war in Asia against the combined forces of the Soviet Union and ChiCom (as America called Mao's government, since China was officially exiled in Taiwan). In the summer of 1950, Kim Il-sung moved to unify Korea.

Since the fall of the Soviet Union, anticommunism has collapsed as an all-purpose rationale for postwar U.S. foreign policy. Insofar as Americans think about the country's Cold War interventions in Asia, it's as mistakes or miscalculations, examples of psychological principles such as groupthink, or of over-zealous "humanitarian interventions," retroactively applying a more recent Western frame of military justification. These are weak explanations; contrari-wise, putting the anticolonial struggle at the center of the postwar world lends clarity to America's own domestic history. Thinking about global events in relation to Third World fights for land and freedom makes it easy to uncover links, symmetries, and analogies that otherwise remain obscure. It's worth reconsidering American history in this revised light if only because that's how most people in the world understood it at the time. And not just foreigners.

"The white man can never win another war on the ground," declared Malcolm X in the spring of 1964. "His days of war, victory, his days of battle-ground victory are over. Can I prove it? Yes. Take all the action that's going on on this Earth right now that he's involved in. Tell me where he's winning—nowhere. Why, some rice farmers, some rice farmers! Some rice eaters ran him out of Korea—yes, they ran him out of Korea. Rice eaters, with nothing but gym shoes and a rifle and a bowl of rice, took him and his tanks and his napalm and all that other action he's supposed to have and ran him across the Yalu. Why? Because the day that he can win on the ground has passed."[3] Years before the 1968 Tet Offensive demonstrated that Red Vietnamese forces couldn't be bombarded into submission, Malcolm X saw the writing on the worldwide wall. If America was unable to restore the colonial status quo with air power in aerially undefended Korea, then there had to be a problem with the rule-by-bomb equations.

One faction, led by hard-core anticommunists including Douglas MacArthur and Curtis LeMay, thought the country lost its nerve in Korea by refusing to use nukes and fighting for a draw with Kim and his ChiCom backers. The nuclear-button strategy, they figured, only works if you're willing to push it. But the problem in Korea wasn't lack of U.S. firepower or destructive will; America had all that in spades, and the campaign devastated the peninsula, methodically destroying the north's ability to feed its people. The bombing was worse, on average, than it was in Germany and Japan. The United States destroyed most of 18 of the north's 22 biggest cities.[4] Still, Koreans built tunnels and kept fighting the most recent invaders. Shockley's equations were supposed to inaugurate an era of U.S. domination, an era in which combat was so cheap for America that the country could afford a casual attitude toward war. In Korea, anticolonial forces proved that wasn't a winning strategy. You couldn't suppress popular liberation campaigns with tools built to defeat fascist imperialists, and there is no such thing as a cheap war. The West has been slow to absorb these lessons, and postwar leaders followed their fear and excitement down bizarre tactical dead ends, as I argued in the previous chapter.

Centering the insurgent anticolonial movement, rather than the rise of the capitalist superpower and the era of U.S. consensus, in our understanding of the 1950s and '60s helps explain the current of dread running beneath all the alleged prosperity. As the missile suburbs boomed, a new, broader cohort of white Americans had access to privileged positions in the world. Their benefits were based on continued military spending, and yet all that military spending implied the possibility of defeat and thus the disappearance of those same privileges. It was an intrinsically anxious position. They were able to cash in on whiteness just as the worldwide racial division of labor that Hoover and his fellows engineered at the end of the nineteenth century came under attack. Dust bowl Okies, too, found their share of the American dream, and they weren't interested in sharing. "I'm sure those very people, after World War II came along, and they got jobs in defense industries, and they bought tract houses and TV sets and cars," lefty New Deal bureaucrat turned full-time reformer Helen Hosmer said of the once hungry people she told Dorothea Lange to capture in her famous Depression photographs, "they became the backbone of the support, I'm positive, which elected Ronald Reagan governor."[5] They landed in Hoover's Southern California, which in seeming contradiction bloomed into prosperity and became a world capital of insecure right-wing reaction at the same time.

As decolonial leaders evinced a willingness to reassess the existing division of property — as decolonial leaders must, by definition — communism became an American euphemism for decolonization and economic democracy, for land and freedom. United States leaders demonstrated a clear preference for authoritarian leaders over noncommunist social democrats in the Third World (if not among European allies as well), making the capitalist superpower an enemy of most people. Development, once capitalism's watchword, became a threat. Its occasionally progressive tendency to transform feudal power relations — the way capitalists destroyed clerical rule in Alta California, or the way they pitted free trade against slave monopoly in the West Indies — reversed, and the U.S.-led bloc found itself a consistent defender of the Third World's archaic authorities: priests, landowners, kings, sheikhs, chiefs, husbands, fathers. Suddenly many white Americans felt they had a stake in the world struggle. They mourned not just the draw in Korea but the victory of the Mau Mau rebellion against British colonial control of Kenya, a fight the United Kingdom lost in the mid-1950s despite its use of asymmetrical airpower. And though this concern manifested itself in ways most Americans now recognize as hysterical (exemplified in Stanley Kubrick's *Strangelove* cabinet), the Red Scared whites weren't exactly *wrong*.

Americans like Ernesto Galarza who tried to stay faithful to their internationalist Popular Front ideals found themselves isolated and abandoned by the country, just as their counterparts in Korea and the Philippines did. Industrial labor's corporate revenue share had never been so high, and those workers weren't incorrect to sense that their interests were involved. Mainstream unions led by the AFL backed an aggressive Cold War foreign policy and purged leftists from their ranks, as I've said.

What happens to history if we reimagine America's postwar domestic conflicts not merely in the specific light of the anticolonial narrative but as part of it? What if, instead of stories about Oedipal family disputes and youthful self-expression, or even instead of legislative compromises arcing toward justice, we saw the interrelated U.S. campus, antiwar, and civil rights movements of the postwar period as part of the global struggle against domination by Western capital? A lot of things start to make sense, such as why the Black Panthers sold Mao's little red book, trained in Algeria, and escaped to Cuba. And why campus radicals flew the North Vietnamese flag. And why Malcolm X wanted to take black people's case to the United Nations instead of to the White House. For U.S. rebels in the third quarter of the twentieth century, decolonization started at home.

Fire Comes Home

The Malcolm X quotation about the white man's vulnerability on the ground comes from a 1964 speech titled "The Ballot or the Bullet." It's a landmark work of political rhetoric, and in it he makes the explicit case for understanding the United States in colonial terms: "America is just as much a colonial power as England ever was. America is just as much a colonial power as France ever was. In fact, America is more so a colonial power than they, because she is a hypocritical colonial power behind it. What is twentieth—what, what do you call second-class citizenship? Why, that's colonization."[6] Black people were a *domestic colony*, he said, an analysis black American communists put forward in the 1930s. And like the rest of the world's colonies in the 1950s, '60s, and '70s, black America was in crisis.

At the 1964 Democratic National Convention, held some months after Malcolm's speech, the more liberal of the two parties had a golden opportunity to bring the civil rights movement inside the tent. In Mississippi, black organizers (with some white supporters, as you'll see) risked their lives registering black voters in the face of white terror. The Student Nonviolent Coordinating Committee (SNCC) led a coalition of groups (the Council of Federated Organizations, or COFO) in an effort to build an integrated Democratic Party that would parallel and, they hoped, replace the Dixie-holdover whites-only state party, which was out of step with the new Democrats of the Civil Rights Act. The effort that culminated in 1964's Freedom Summer brought together some of the South's most legendary organizers, including Ella Baker, Fannie Lou Hamer, Bob Moses, Amzie Moore, and a young man named Stokely Carmichael. When the integrated Mississippi Freedom Democratic Party delegation showed up in Atlantic City for the convention, they had an obvious moral case for why they were the state's true representatives. LBJ, running to win the presidency that fell into his lap, had a chance to seat the integrated delegation, a chance to anoint Freedom Summer's peace militants as his party's future. It would have been a perfect origin story for the modern Democrats, a clean break with the segregationist past in favor of young black-led organizers who risked and sometimes lost their lives to gather votes for a party they couldn't be sure even wanted them.

That's not what happened. Instead, the Democrats stuck with the Dixiecrats, turning their nose up at the sacrifices in Mississippi. When Mississippi organizer Fannie Lou Hamer appeared on the television broadcast to testify about her struggles to register to vote, the president intervened to get the camera off of her. It was a clean stab in the back from the national Democrats, and the bitter meeting determined the shape of America's own decolonization struggle. The 1964 convention answered Malcolm X's question: No to the ballot. The next year's Voting Rights Act was too little and far too late. By the next convention, it was war in the street.

For a white majority West Coast institution, Stanford's students had an unusually close view of the Mississippi campaign and this whole sequence. This was thanks to one Allard Lowenstein. Like Ernesto Galarza, Lowenstein was a hard-core liberal striver, a son of immigrants who was really good at school. After graduating from Yale Law and spending two years in the army, he moved between working in universities (including a stint at Stanford) and foundation-approved international travel, writing quixotic reports meant to secure U.S. support for noncommunist liberals. Lowenstein aspired to be a heroic white liberal politician—a common career goal in his post-JFK cohort—and it led him into a career-long relationship with the CIA, an organization that men of Lowenstein's ilk hoped could be a force for good in the world. After a tour of greater South Africa resulting in an anti-apartheid tract that included an introduction from Eleanor Roosevelt, Lowenstein joined his home country's decolonization movement at North Carolina State, where he taught. In the summer of 1963, when he heard that the southern movement was fresh out of white legal observers, he jumped at the chance. "I expected it would be like North Carolina but somewhat worse," Lowenstein later recalled. "Instead it was like South Africa but a little bit better."[7]

The movement had a lot of needs, and that an unknown white guy like Lowenstein became as influential as he did as fast as he did is a testament to that. He was no silver-spooner, but he knew a lot of them, and he suggested that bringing in white volunteers from elite colleges could help solve a number of problems at once: First, they were eager to do organizational office tasks, freeing black organizers to spend their time in the community. Second, as fundraisers, they could pay for themselves and then some. And perhaps most important, they would attract media attention, which might lend local leaders a bit of safety, which was a principal concern for organizers, who spent every day not only risking their lives but asking black Mississippians to risk theirs, too. Lowenstein recruited 50–100 volunteers from his contacts at Stanford and Yale to come down and support a voting dress rehearsal in the fall of '63 that was meant to demonstrate black appetite for the ballot, a reality that some in the white power structure refused to acknowledge.[8] The project was a landmark event in the history of interracial organizing tension, but it did achieve its narrow goals, including the novel presence of FBI bodyguards. It didn't hurt that one of the volunteers from Stanford was Harold Ickes Jr., the son of the FDR interior secretary and Bohemian Club member of the same name.[9] SNCC leadership agreed to support an expanded program for the following year, organized by Moses with Lowenstein.

The Freedom Summer, in 1964, and the betrayal in Atlantic City reshaped the landscape of left-wing struggle in the United States in general and in Palo Alto and the wider Bay Area in particular. The white SNCC veterans brought their experience home and made it part of their own narratives. One of Lowenstein's protégés was David Harris, who got elected president of the Stanford student body on an antiwar platform.* After graduation he started a group called the Resistance, which urged young men to refuse to cooperate with the draft system as a form of peaceful protest and go to prison if need be. He spent nearly two years in prison himself, and the draft resistance escalated nationally. The organization raised funds in part thanks to a poster featuring three groovy twenty-something Palo Alto sisters. The picture showed the daughters of Stanford physicist Albert Baez sitting on a couch under the slogan GIRLS SAY YES TO BOYS WHO SAY NO.[10] One of the three, folk singer Joan Baez, definitely meant it: She briefly married David Harris. Many of the Friends of SNCC—as Lowenstein's volunteers were called—soon found their way into the establishment's upper ranks: After suffering the blow of Bobby Kennedy's assassination, Lowenstein worked to build Eugene McCarthy's liberal-radical coalition. He eventually got elected to Congress, as did his recruit Barney Frank. Joe Lieberman became a notoriously moderate senator from Connecticut and 2000 vice president manqué. Former SNCC chair John Lewis joined them in Washington in 1986. Harris wasn't so lucky, and he lost his race for a congressional seat in 1976.

But back in 1966, the SNCC moderates and the white Friends were on the defensive. Democratic voting rights activist Stokely Carmichael led a turn toward Black Power politics, and though American popular history often presents this as a deviation from the civil rights movement, in the context of decolonization, it's one straight line. The connections between the southern movement and the nationalist movements in Africa weren't subtle or subterranean. SNCC's slogan in Mississippi was "One man, one vote," a simple and precise attack on apartheid states everywhere—which is why the All-African People's Conference adopted it as a continent-wide plank in 1958.[11] The SNCC organizers themselves paid close attention to the full range of African struggles, from the relatively peaceful and bureaucratic to full-scale guerrilla war, debating where exactly America fell on the spectrum. The nonviolent N in the

* No relation.

leading organization's name included a solid exception for self-defense, and where that line belonged was a frequent topic of debate.

Lowenstein was solidly in the reform-not-revolution camp, and he soon grated on the movement's left-wing strategists, including Moses and James Forman, who both quickly understood what Lowenstein was about.* He used his access to credentials (as a lawyer) and elites to exercise undue influence over the civil rights movement on the ground on behalf of white liberals who sought to control it; that black leaders understood the situation and yet remained powerless to change it demonstrated a limit to the egalitarian potential of interracial organizing. Lowenstein's presence rendered their true self-determination impossible, and he made sure to be present. It's too simple to say that Lowenstein was a CIA asset who turned a group of up-and-coming black activists off of the idea of working with white people by being an overbearing liberal elitist who sought to manage and moderate the movement, but that is undeniably part of what happened.

The mixed success of the campaign—successfully forcing black voting rights in the South onto the national stage but failing to replace and integrate the Dixiecrat power base in a second attempted Reconstruction—pushed the American decolonization movement to intensify. If in 1964 the ballot and the bullet could fit as two possibilities within one mind or personality, then in the following years the paths began to diverge. The Klan in its hooded and besuited versions escalated its reactionary violence. In January of 1965, the Congress of Racial Equality (CORE) joined with the Deacons for Defense and Justice to formalize the armed defense of their Louisiana registration project.[12] The next month, Malcolm X was gunned down, and young activists took up his call of Black Power. The southern campaign famously, on the counsel of Ella Baker, opted for a diversity of tactics, registering voters and running candidates while maintaining direct-action agitation for integration.[13] And much

---

* Lowenstein's role in the southern movement is a heatedly contested historical question. I'm inclined to give credence to James Forman's account. Forman knew Lowenstein through SNCC and before, in the National Student Association. Based on an abundance of evidence, he came to suspect Lowenstein was "close to CIA circles if not actually on its payroll." Regardless of the exact nature of the relationship, Forman understood Lowenstein's role in the southern movement as infiltration on behalf of "liberal-labor" social democrats to control the opposition and marginalize radicals. It's an understanding others came to share after working with Lowenstein. James Forman, *The Making of Black Revolutionaries: A Personal Account* (Macmillan, 1972), 358.

like people's liberation armies throughout the decolonizing world, COFO organizers found themselves doing development work to counter the forced underdevelopment endemic to colonial exploitation, which meant setting up "freedom schools" to teach literacy in particular.[14] Among the outside organizers, the willing ones learned a lot from the rural workers they were there to organize as well, not least about the vital importance of guns to the movement's self-defense.

Into the mid-1960s, white violence and the experience of black community endurance shifted the consciousness of organizers. The SNCC field secretary, Charles E. Cobb Jr., recalls that in a meeting in the summer of '64, the Mississippi staff reaffirmed the organization's policy of not carrying weapons. That was an official line they would not cross, Cobb writes, "but when Stokely Carmichael asked who was carrying a gun at that moment, about a dozen were produced."[15] In the southern movement, the ideological line of armed struggle trailed the practical necessity. But the gap was closing: In 1966, committed Gandhian John Lewis was defeated by the more ecumenical Carmichael in a tight election for SNCC chairman. Organizers paid close attention as independence movements in Portugal's African colonies, facing the continent's most intransigent European occupying regime, reached the end of the reform line and turned to military strategies in Angola, Guinea-Bissau, Cape Verde, and Mozambique. Algeria and Cuba proved that young idealist intellectuals could revolt and win, while Korea and Vietnam showed America to be a "paper tiger" at the end of the day, with lots of sound and fury but no way to win wars against the world's exploited majorities. One cartoon published in the fall 1964 issue of Black America showed an American cop with his dog labeled VIOLENCE attacking a small black figure labeled U.S. NEGRO, but the black figure points behind the cop where four giants dressed in different regional Third World garb (labeled NON-ANGLO-SAXON WORLD) point their own gunlike fingers at the cop's back. The speech bubble: "You a majority Charlie? Just look behind you!"[16]

There are other, more popular interpretive frames for American politics in the 1960s: There is the Oedipal one about generational struggle; the cultural one about the disillusioned shift to individualism; the patriotic reformist one about protests moving a nation's heart and securing formal equality.

It has been made difficult to see the country in a global-historical frame, as one nation among many that came together in their current forms at the end of the nineteenth century and have teetered on unstable foundations of colonial exploitation ever since. These countries faced a set of analogous pressures in the years following the Second World War, and despite its unique position America wasn't exempt, especially if we're conscious of the country's timeline of development and expansion. California had more in common historically with South Africa than with England. France incorporated Algeria in 1848, only two years before California statehood; Algiers to Paris is much shorter than DC to Sacramento. The American South threatened to *include* Cuba for much of its history, as the regional oligarchy considered the island a natural extension of the territory, language and the Straits of Florida notwithstanding. It's a mistake to read the comparisons between what was going on in America and what was going on in the Third World—comparisons that were continual at the time and came from both the insurgent and government sides in roughly equal measure, in public and in private—as mere bombast or paranoia. Only in the context of global decolonization can we understand how California became a worldwide revolutionary touchstone in the 1960s.

The story we usually get about the West Coast in the '60s centers on the Free Speech Movement fighting for the right to speak out of turn about the war or whatever—the Summer of Love, hippies, LSD, the Merry Pranksters, the Grateful Dead. This is the scene Wallace Stegner contrasts with the real western individualists in *Angle of Repose*—the nineteenth-century mining engineers who conquered the continent. But as I suggested in the previous section, the personal revolution didn't have much to do with protest or collective action except in the existential sense. Politically, the Ken Kesey types were worse than useless to leftists. Many of them were war workers, engaged in the global decolonization struggle but on the colonists' side. Think of the Alternative Futures Project at SRI, people getting high out of their minds and hunting campus communists at the same time their office mates dreamed up strategies for obliterating Vietnamese villages. Their anti-authoritarian style didn't translate to the real world, leading to some misunderstandings, such as the one that occurred when Kesey was given the mic at a Berkeley antiwar demonstration, only for the Stanford author to harangue the crowd about how they were

overly attached to their egos—quite a claim for a man lecturing a movement.*
That the feds and hippies both liked dropping acid doesn't mean as much as
we've been led to believe by '60s nostalgics and cynics alike. (Acid is fun.) Posi-
tioning the personal revolution against the state is based on a deeply confused
set of coordinates, a special kind of convenient distortion native to the United
States that involves forgetting that the rest of the world exists. At the time, on
the ground, the division between the personal revolutionaries and the California decolonists was much clearer: One side tossed rocks at the other.

There is no single line that connects California to the world anticolonial struggle; they are embedded in the same history, as I contended in the first section. It
was *colonial exploitation* that linked these conflicts in the first place, not the spread
of doctrines or encounters between individuals. We know this is the case because
when large-scale street violence and conflict kicked off in California in the 1960s,
it wasn't thanks to an armed insurrectionary party. Riots that went beyond organizational politics—the organic black-led uprising of the urban exploited, what
King called "the language of the unheard"—erupted across Johnson's America.
Police abuse incited rebellions in California's black ghettos: in Watts (Los Angeles) in 1965 and in Hunter's Point (San Francisco) the following year, and on a
smaller scale in East Palo Alto in 1967, which fit the category by then. The only
outside agitators required to start military-scale conflict in America's streets were
the police commuting from their white neighborhoods. That said, there's value
in identifying some particular individual connections between the Bay and the
rest of the colonized world. In this period, Californians took conscious political
action to join the Third World struggle, even when that meant declaring war on
their own government. After all: Isn't that what colonized people did?

In 1964, UC Berkeley student Ernie Allen went on a trip to revolutionary
Cuba sponsored by Progressive Labor, a section of the communist student network Students for a Democratic Society (SDS) that later split from the larger
body. Allen made it to Berkeley the hard way, as a black working-class kid

---

* It was still a step up from his fellow LSJU novelist John Steinbeck. Also presumed progressive based on his earlier work, Steinbeck was rabidly pro-war, and he turned himself into
a militarist pundit. He even sent the White House a letter suggesting the Defense Department develop napalm grenades—American boys were already being trained to throw
baseballs. He proposed to name the weapon the "Steinbeck super ball." His letter was forwarded to the Department of Defense. Robert M. Nee, *Napalm: An American Biography*
(Belknap Press, 2013), 110–11.

from Oakland who transferred from Merritt Community College.* SDS was a racially integrated group to start, but around the Mississippi campaign, revolutionary black organizers began talking about Black Power, and they intended to organize without the paternal, moderating influence of whites like Al Lowenstein. Before going to Cuba, Allen was part of the Afro-American Association at Berkeley and his brother Doug was still an organizer at Merritt, which put Ernie at the very center of a left-wing network of young black organic intellectuals in the East Bay that included Huey Newton and Bobby Seale, future founders of the Black Panther Party, who, like the Allens, both grew up in the Bay's new working-class black milieu. Both of them had parents who fled racial terror in the South after the defeat of Reconstruction. One way to think about these future militants is as chickens who have come home to roost in California—the embodied consequences of the original bargain between Golden State capitalists and the Confederate Redeemers, who consigned black people in the South to apartheid conditions indefinitely.

Allen (who for a period named himself Mkalimoto) picked a great time to go to Cuba, which temporarily became an organizing center for black American leftists in addition to an inspiration.† The iconoclastic leader of the Louisiana NAACP, Robert F. Williams, whose call for black people to arm themselves for war with the Klan went contrary to the organization's strategy, took exile with Team Castro and set up a propaganda radio station (Radio Free Dixie) appealing to his people back home from the island's relative safety. Williams attracted black organizers looking for an ideological path through the southern movement and on to something more militant and less American, a path Williams walked down early, thanks to his heterodox embrace of firearms.[17] This group included a young man from Philadelphia named Max Stanford, who was forming a new Black Power organization: the Revolutionary Action Movement (RAM). Allen met Stanford, as well as a black delegation from Detroit, on the PL trip. When the group returned to the States, RAM had three chapters: Philly, Cleveland, and Oakland. They took close notice

---

* The school's namesake is the childless, brotherless Samuel Merritt—original Oakland developer and no near relation to Hoover associate Ralph or the Tagus Ranch owners.

† William Anderson notes that the sanctuary Cuba offered to black radicals was limited, especially if the guests' ideas veered too far to the left. See William Anderson, *The Nation on No Map: Black Anarchism and Abolition* (AK Press, 2021).

when, after the Atlantic City betrayal and the 1965 marches from Selma to
Montgomery, some SNCC organizers (including Carmichael) stayed down in
Alabama to join locals and help form the Lowndes County Freedom Organization, a black third political party that ran its own candidates against the
white Democrats. Of particular interest was the party's icon: a black panther,
ready to strike.

There's a temptation to see the left-wing organizational splits in this
period—which was full of them—as products of clashing egos and the nar-
cissism of minor differences. No doubt some were, but as I write 50-plus years
on, I think we benefit by extending some intellectual generosity. The era's militants were dealing with all sorts of fast-moving variables, trying to fashion a
viable revolutionary movement during an undeclared world war, negotiating
through new compositional developments in race, class, gender, education,
and ideology. RAM acted through front organizations and by infiltrating
more mainstream groups, which meant it was party to a number of these
splits. But what RAM itself had to offer was a revolutionary vision, one its
members put the work in to develop and one that transcended its organization: armed anticolonial revolution across the United States, led by an alliance (and categorical overlap) of black college students (who linked with the
global movement) and ghetto youths (who burned the cities). Malcolm X was
their model—a consciously political former street kid, smart and dangerous
in equal measure—but they tapped into some Old Left currents, too, looking
to the Detroit Marxists James and Grace Lee Boggs and consulting the Black
Bolshevik himself, Harry Haywood. RAM is best remembered today for one
of its front groups, one that split almost immediately.

In Max Stanford's account, the Black Panther Party started in 1966, when
RAM asked Carmichael if it could use the name for a Harlem organization meant
to support and extend the Lowndes County party, a request that the SNCC
leader approved. Stanford is careful to list the Oakland chapter last.[18] He writes
that the rascals Huey Newton (excluded from RAM for being too bourgeois and
waving guns around) and Bobby Seale (expelled for alleged drunkenness and
theft) of RAM's Merritt front, the Soul Students Advisory Council, more or less
hijacked the name for their own "adventurist" group. Newton's account has them
quitting the RAM front at Merritt because the organizers were boring college
students who only wanted to talk about armed revolution and weren't shooting or

helping anyone. In his telling, the Black Panther Party for Self-Defense emerges from bull sessions with Bobby about Mao, Che, Frantz Fanon, Robert F. Williams, and Malcolm X. He writes that they happened on the Black Panther name in a pamphlet about SNCC's work in Mississippi. Says Huey in *Revolutionary Suicide*, "Bobby and I finally had no choice but to form an organization that would involve the lower-class brothers."[19] Seale's account is like Newton's, adding an anecdote about kicking the door in at a RAM leadership spot, deciding that if they weren't willing to fight him they weren't willing to fight the government. "Later for these dudes," he writes, "I'm going to find myself a righteous partner to righteously run with."[20] Of the two stories, Stanford's is more credible on its face, but Huey and Bobby won the split and RAM abandoned the name.*

The version of the BPP's formation we get in *Revolutionary Suicide*, which remains the most influential account, describes the organization as emerging fully grown from the heads of a couple of college bros hanging out with some wine and talking about books, like Athena curling out of a half-smoked joint. We can imagine how in its simplicity that was an appealing account for readers; it's not unlike the standard personality-centered origin stories used by inventors, politicians, and even capitalists. The fuller picture isn't as clear, but it sets us up to ask important questions about the version of the Black Panther Party that developed in the Bay Area and became the most important American communist party since the Popular Front. Such as: Why California?

The Belly of the Beast

California is at first blush a strange location for an important node in the global black revolution. On founding, the state didn't go so far as Oregon and ban black people entirely, but it was discussed. In 1940, Santa Clara County

---

* RAM's enduring cadres pursued different lines: The Detroit chapter switched its revolutionary subject to the black industrial working class and members General Baker and Glanton Dowdell helped form the Dodge Revolutionary Union Movement and the League of Revolutionary Black Workers. Ron Karenga in Los Angeles wooed the black middle class with the US Organization. Others moved to create an underground military fighting force, a Black Liberation Army to parallel the liberation armies at work from China to Yemen to Namibia to Colombia. RAM leadership asked poet Amiri Baraka to try and bring together a national front including RAM, BPP, US, and SNCC, but the parts were insoluble and the 1967 Newark Black Power Conference went on without the Panthers. *The Autobiography of LeRoi Jones/Amiri Baraka* (Freundlich Books, 1984), 279.

still had fewer than 1,000 black residents, predominantly in domestic service.[21] As historian Herbert G. Ruffin details in his essential study of African Americans in the Valley, *Uninvited Neighbors*, the black people of suburban California balanced uncomfortably on history's edge. High-wage defense jobs brought black workers and their families to the coast during World War II to fill in for the white men off fighting in the segregated army. For the migrants, these jobs represented a big step away from Jim Crow labor relations toward a solid middle-class lifestyle. The jobs in ship and plane construction and the like were "in-the-car" jobs, to employ Galbraith's useful metaphor about postwar wage-price inflation. It was an overdue step, and it only happened thanks to labor shortages.

However, the whole point of Shockley's man-month analysis and the American postwar military strategy was to fight efficiently, without the overhead cost structure involved in the World War II effort. Per destructive unit, nuclear bombs were way cheaper to make than ships. Better to pay one aeronautical engineer than 12 welders—plus, the engineers weren't unionized. When the white GIs returned from Europe and the Pacific, they edged out their black temporary replacements (as well as white women who performed the same function and a small number of black women who were recruited near the war's close), a move immortalized in the phrase "Last hired, first fired." It was among the earliest in the series of American postwar betrayals. Though the jobs that lured them to California were gone, black migrants of this period were not looking to return "home" but rather were determined to make new homes. The result is that black Californians were among the first groups of American workers to face the blunt thump upside the head of deindustrialization, knocked out of the high-wage manufacturing car onto the low-wage service asphalt, left dazed while national prosperity sped away. The California suburbs mostly absorbed black labor the way they had for years, in domestic and janitorial work, both of which they had an increased demand for given the arrival of the space settlers.

The influx of a new cohort of black workers to the California cities and suburbs set up a clear division within the regional black community. Ruffin writes that the recent migrants were "more unapologetically southern, younger, relatively more educated, and were not content with racial injustice and menial jobs."[22] These "suitcase Negroes" worked with existing organizations such as the

NAACP and black churches in coalition with a substantial population of white liberals. California facilities, schools, and stores weren't formally segregated, as they were in the South, but as I've pointed out, housing discrimination was a strong skeleton, subcutaneously shaping the suburban society. This was the era of silent marches and protesters in suits, modeling integrated dignity as an argument. In Palo Alto, a small number of black space settlers led organizations that punched above their weight. Stan Puryear (later Muata Weusi-Puryear), a computer programmer who moved to the area in the early 1960s to pursue a doctorate in symbolic logic at UC Berkeley, became president of the Palo Alto–Stanford branch of the NAACP, which swelled with professors and students and was able to funnel substantial funds to the southern movement, in addition to organizing protests against new attacks from the real estate industry.[23] Palo Alto SNCC and Mid-Peninsula CORE worked to desegregate employment, education, and housing individual by individual. That meant negotiating for affirmative action in hiring at shops, getting signatures for open-housing promises from homeowners, and "sneaking out" black kids into white liberal houses so they could access the residentially segregated Palo Alto schools. If the suitcase cohort could not for the most part access the integrated middle-class lifestyle held out as a lure during the war, they worked hard to prepare their children for such opportunities and to prepare the world for their children.

It was, however, an uphill battle. As I've said, there was a lot of money at stake in California segregation. White suburban prosperity depended on colonization at home and abroad, and the terrain shifted quickly in the 1960s. The annulment of the 1963 Rumford Fair Housing Act by the following year's Proposition 14 was a harsh blow, led by the white population of Southern California, which also happened to be where most of the state's black people lived. It passed in Santa Clara County, too. Given the progressive narrative about American apartheid—and we have been given it—it's hard to understand that black communities in California experienced a drastic downturn in their quality of treatment, but that's what happened. The army integrated just in time to send young black men to die in the Southeast Asian imperialist campaigns. The red-lines hardened, and as young activists turned toward militancy and an anticolonial understanding of their lives, the older cohort tried to stall them, saying the area "was not always like this."[24] But that was part of the point.

This was the situation when Al Lowenstein came calling for volunteers from among the Stanford students. A campus-area Friends of SNCC organization had already coordinated support for the southern movement among white students, and a Stanford group toured the South during the 1960–61 winter break.* Lowenstein found 14 people who would take leaves in the fall of '63 to back up COFO's work in Jackson, Mississippi. Their experience was influential in the Palo Alto community, as was the larger group's when they went south the next year. And they returned to a local black population facing a set of circumstances that was looking more "southern" every day. Submerged strains of California fascism perked up, especially in the bottom half of the state, where the dust bowl Okies jealously guarded their newfound rocket-based prosperity, as Helen Hosmer described it. In the Bay, the Oakland Police Department was rumored to intentionally recruit new white officers from out of state, in the Deep South. Perhaps the OPD leadership imagined this was a natural solution to the FDR-era labor recruiters who brought black workers from the South to man the Oakland shipyards. Then again, as Gene Marine, an editor at the radical investigative magazine *Ramparts*, notes, a lot of the area's white migrants came from the South anyway, and they didn't leave their race hate at home.[25] Maybe the rumor was just an explanation for the level of white brutality, a way to distance that behavior from the Bay where it existed regardless.

After the Freedom Summer, Palo Alto's civil rights organizations followed the national groups into a Black Power orientation, and they relocated from Stanford–Palo Alto to East Palo Alto. This shift was concurrent with a change in the leadership composition, from elite college students and respected community members to junior college students and ghettoized teenagers. The era of silent marches and church leadership was over; from a purely descriptive perspective, the movement was looking closer to what RAM theorized than the left wing of the Roosevelt coalition that led the South Bay organizations. The Marxist anticolonialists may have seemed all talk to Bobby and Huey, but they played an important role preparing the ground. "We wanted a different kind of analysis, a politics that emerged from an analysis of race in America and

---

* The group included a single black person, a Stanford grad named James Maina from independent Kenya, who recognized Alabama as a "police state." Herbert G. Ruffin, *Uninvited Neighbors: African Americans in Silicon Valley, 1769–1990* (University of Oklahoma Press, 2014), 154.

race in the globe," Cedric Robinson of the UC Berkeley NAACP recalled.* The group cosponsored a Robert F. Williams visit to campus in 1961, in which he talked about armed resistance and Cuba, followed two months later by an off-campus lecture from Malcolm X, who proved to the assembled college students that education and intelligence are two very different qualities. "Shortly after the minister's visit," writes historian Donna Jean Murch, "the campus NAACP dissolved."[26] In its place rose the Afro-American Association, whose members provided the core for the East Bay chapter of RAM after Ernie Allen's trip to Cuba a few years later.

From their perspective, the situation was accelerating fast. Williams was chased out of the country months after his Berkeley talk, framed for kidnapping a white couple in North Carolina. After Williams escaped, Malcolm X became the formation's chief domestic theorist. He's the one who told an eager Max Stanford (known as Muhammad Ahmad after 1970) that he should start something different instead of joining the Nation of Islam, with which Malcolm was becoming disillusioned. According to some accounts, Malcolm was one of RAM's officers, all of whose names were kept secret from the public for understandable reasons. His assassination confirmed his prophecy: the ballot or the bullet. And while the standard narrative is that Malcolm's turn to internationalism was cut off incomplete, those with ears to hear already knew his anticolonial critique well, and they saw America in those terms. Working with white liberals and the few existing black missile engineers wasn't just untenably frustrating, it was also contrary to RAM's analysis. By the time Carmichael won his SNCC election, in 1966, Bay Area revolutionaries had joined the world movement, advancing to the next stage of struggle.

At this point, with a structural analysis of the region's past 100 years, we're prepared to examine what put Californians in place to lead the national movement. "We say that black people are the vanguard of the revolution in this country, and, since no one will be free until the people of America are free, that black people are the vanguard of world revolution," wrote Huey Newton.

---

* Robinson took the lead in organizing a campus protest against the Bay of Pigs invasion of Cuba that Paul Baran predicted after his trip. Regarding the rule that demonstrations required a week's notice, Robinson told Berkeley administrators that the U.S. had given Cuba no such notice. He was suspended for a semester. If this kind of restriction on student speech sounds outrageous, many Berkeley students soon came to agree. Joshua Myers, *Cedric Robinson: The Time of the Black Radical Tradition* (John Wiley & Sons, 2021), 57.

"We inherit this legacy primarily because we are the last, and as the saying goes, 'The last will be the first.'"[27] In addition to describing the vanguard political role of black people in America, "The last will be the first" is also a good insight into technological development and California. As the edge of the world and all of Western civilization, investment accumulated in California and settled in this final location. As I've said—and please forgive me for repeating the point because it is an important one—with a scarcity of available wage workers, labor-saving machinery forged ahead of the national pace and turned Alta California into a high-technology zone from the beginning of Anglo colonization. The region's quick but uneven industrialization produced a high-low juxtaposition that was still somewhat incongruous in the 1960s—think microchip foundries abutting fruit orchards. But technology is more than what meets the eye; in addition to the metal machinery coming out of the ironworks and the electronic instruments coming out of Stanford, the region led the world in biological engineering, with its designer seeds and superhorses. And the key to all these systems was *human* capital. The state was exceptionally good at educating its newcomers, even compared to the East Coast academic centers. Here, too, the last became first.

So far, I've focused on the state's elite higher-education institutions—Stanford, for obvious reasons, and the region's first large university, UC Berkeley—but a number of historians give the California community college system at least as much credit for the region's exceptional success in developing its various tech industries. California capital has had a more or less consistently desperate need for "skilled labor" throughout its Anglo history. In the early twentieth century, cartelization and advanced monopolies made it easy for California capitalists to support public funding for higher education, since they could be relatively sure the value was coming back to them one way or another. One of the country's first two-year degree-granting colleges was an extension of the high school in Fresno, which emphasized classes in soil studies and agricultural crops. After the end of the First World War, the University of California system began accrediting junior colleges. By the end of the 1920s, the state had 15,000 students across 34 junior colleges, more than one-third of the country's junior college students among less than 5 percent of the U.S. population.[28]

At the end of the 1950s, California recommitted to public higher education, beating the federal Higher Education Act to the punch by five years. The 1960 California Master Plan for Higher Education hugely expanded post-secondary schooling in the state, offering the elite UCs tuition-free and opening admission to the junior colleges, along with a guaranteed transfer for graduates to one of the state's public four-year programs. It was a concession to history, a subtle acknowledgment that in the face of deindustrialization most workers required some level of higher education if they wanted a middle-class lifestyle. The two-year schools switched their focus to vocational preparation, which critics alleged was designed to keep working-class youths away from professional paths, while defenders said it upheld the state tradition of the upwardly mobile technician. Graduation and transfers were relatively uncommon, but one of the early students to make use of the protocol was Ernie Allen, who graduated from his local Merritt Community College, in Oakland, and moved on to Berkeley, where he and his classmates jumped into history. It wasn't impossible for a working-class black kid from Oakland to get into Berkeley straight away, but it was uncommon enough that, as historian Robin D. G. Kelley recounts, when Cedric Robinson went to sign up for classes in 1959, his dark skin and confidence on campus made the registrar ask the eighteen-year-old (who was born a straight four-mile shot south) if his home government would be paying his fees.[29] They assumed he was one of the new self-liberated Africans, come to gather knowledge for his people. In a way, they weren't mistaken.

The community colleges and the Cal State and UC systems on top of them provided an interface within the black Bay Area between young radical academics, self-identified "lumpenproletarian" street intellectuals, and disillusioned military veterans. This was just the potent combination that the RAM milieu theorized would lead America into world revolution. It was a conjunction the American state brought together by necessity—the space and arms races were accelerating, and the Soviets caught the United States with its developmental pants down. The Russians planned their human-capital production very carefully. America needed mechanisms to find capable young men and draw them into the new industries, and making efficient emergency use of the country's raw material meant including a certain number of black, Latino, and Asian people.

One well-known image exemplifies the way Cold War competition pushed

California colleges and their black students onto the world stage. Relying on black people while exploiting and mistreating them has been one of the keys to America's success since the beginning, and that is a risky proposition. The Cold War contest extended beyond science and technology; the Soviets dominated international athletics, and some American colleges systematically recruited black athletes to try to improve their positions. San Jose State University was one of those schools, and the year after the master plan was announced, the school nabbed a runner named Harry Edwards, who used the opportunity to study sociology. After some graduate work at Cornell (where he, too, got to see Malcolm X in the minister's last year), Edwards returned to SJSU to teach in 1966. He was only a few years older than his youngest students, and as one of only two black professors for 72 black students (out of 24,000), 60 of whom were athletes, as he'd been, he attracted a following.[30]

Edwards helped organize his students so they could improve their treatment at the school, and they forced the cancellation of a football game—the ultimate act of university sabotage. Governor Reagan wanted to send in the National Guard to police the field; the RAM milieu offered Edwards its own guerrillas if need be. But the school had to face a hard truth: It couldn't operate without the participation of black students. The game was not played. The "revolt of the black athlete," to quote the title of one of Edwards's books, that began in San Jose and spread across the country attracted international attention and embarrassed the American government, which from the state's perspective defeated the whole point of international sport. But despite the drama, SJSU had a very strong program, especially in track and field. One of Edwards's protégés was a national champion sprinter, and the school recruited a second from Texas. Only after Olympic organizers agreed to exclude South Africa from the 1968 games in Mexico City did the SJSU sprinters agree to represent the United States. When the teammates took gold and bronze in the men's 200-meter, there must have been a moment when Team USA's white leaders patted themselves on the back. Then Tommie Smith and John Carlos mounted the podium in stocking feet, bowed their heads, and raised their fists, one black glove each. The gesture humiliated America on the global stage, turning a national triumph into a searing Black Power tableau, an indelible salute of international solidarity. The last will be first, and then: Look out!

At the College of San Mateo (CSM), liberal efforts to recruit black, Chinese, and Chicano students were so successful that they undermined themselves. A minority-student retention program, for example, succeeded in scaring the board of trustees, which defunded it to death, leading to protests and the birth of a CSM Third World Liberation Front (TWLF) coalition. The state recognized its interest in providing more nonwhite students with at least vocational higher education, but the people hired to run these programs tended to be sympathetic to the radical critiques—when they weren't directly involved in the radical projects themselves. Bob Hoover, the Stanford grad student whom CSM hired to help run the retention program, was a good example. Hoover and his wife, Mary, were both SNCC veterans and Stanford grad students studying education, and like other black people with impressive qualifications, they could not live in Palo Alto. Instead they bought a house across the highway, and after a visiting Stokely Carmichael advised local education organizers not to try too hard to integrate into the proverbial burning house, the Hoovers helped start the Nairobi Day School in East Palo Alto to teach black students an anticolonial curriculum.[31]

One member of the TWLF at San Mateo was a young Chicano from South Texas named Aaron Manganiello. He moved to the Bay as a teenager and joined the antiwar movement in the early 1960s. As a CSM student, he volunteered in Hoover's minority-student retention program. Like most leftists, he radicalized in the '60s, particularly around the Black Panther Party model. In 1966 when two Los Angeles Chicanos, Carlos Montes and David Sanchez, founded the Brown Berets, he persuaded them to let him set up some Northern California chapters. After the CSM board killed the retention program, Manganiello teamed up with other TWLF students to help them set up their own experimental college programs. They enlisted the help of Bob and Mary Hoover, and together they built two independent Third World community colleges: Nairobi College, in East Palo Alto, and Venceremos College, in Redwood City's Chicano section. The contradictions in the country's Cold War human-capital strategy rose to the surface: White America needed black and Chicano people but didn't want them. The Hoovers and other East Palo Alto SNCC veterans turned Nairobi College into the kind of community college they thought black youths deserved, teaching an Afrocentric curriculum and channeling students into professional occupations rather than the vocational roles the state had planned for them. As far as the state was concerned, though, that wasn't the worst possible outcome. At Manganiello's Venceremos, they channeled students into armed communist revolution.[32]

America remained dependent on the next generation of workers, even though the human-capital production system was hostile to everyone except certain white men, as eugenicists designed it. Yet some individuals made their way toward places in the skilled labor car. Bobby Seale, for example, was an air force vet studying engineering and design at Merritt while he worked at Kaiser Aerospace.[33] Huey Newton was in and out of prison as a kid, and he disdained the substandard Oakland schools until he made his way to Merritt, where he studied law and thrived. There they got pulled into the RAM milieu, from which Newton and Seale spun off their own, distinct local analysis. Democrats were not totally insensitive to the situation's perilous dynamics. Johnson's War on Poverty attempted to alleviate the urgent pressure in the ghetto as unemployment mounted, partly by hiring black college students and recent graduates to do community work. Critics on the right called the programs bribes to the black communities, while critics on the left said they were the state's one step forward to go along with capitalism's two steps back. The Office of Economic Opportunity (OEO) put federal funds in the street, especially in the summer months when white fear of unemployed black teenagers was at its peak. In the summer of 1966, Newton and Seale both got OEO jobs. At the North Oakland Neighborhood Anti-Poverty Center, Seale oversaw 200 teenagers, teaching literacy and small-job skills, and keeping them busy.[34] In January of 1967, with the money from their OEO gigs, Seale and Newton opened the first office of the Black Panther Party for Self Defense, a few blocks away from Merritt College.

Instead of the mythic, individualist founding story, in which young Bobby and Huey suckled from a mother panther's teats, we have a multifarious account. There was SNCC and the southern movement, with its successes, failures, and concluding splits between liberals and radicals, black organizers and white supporters; there were the community colleges and the OEO; there were the anticolonial struggles around the world, from China to South Africa; there were the street riots and police violence and unemployment and criminal gangs and discrimination and assassinations; there were the revolutionary black student associations, with their heterodox Marxisms and passionate guest speakers; there were the cultural nationalists, with their Swahili classes and new names. And there was the black American tradition of armed self-defense, the one they had used to free themselves once before. The BPP came to a synthesis of these influences the same way SNCC found itself with its pockets full of pistols: Once they were determined to intervene in history, it was a practical necessity. That determination was the one thing that wasn't predetermined, the imaginative wriggling of butterflies that threatens to bring history's glass display case to the ground in pieces. Pound for pound, no American political group had nearly as big an impact during the period, and it's worth going through a brief but detailed history of the Oakland BPP to frame the next section, when we will return to Palo Alto proper.

Studying constitutional law at Merritt and at an OEO library, Newton became convinced that people had a right to police the police with their own guns, as long as they were very careful about how they did it. These community patrols enraged the cops. When they confronted the patrols, BPP members recited the specific law and affirmed their compliance. The patrols oversaw arrests to prevent brutality and followed arrestees to lockup and bailed them out when they could. Kids, teenagers, and young adults in the community were enraptured, and the BPP recruited quickly. It didn't hurt that Seale had spent the summer as a mentor to dozens of unemployed young black residents. The Panthers also had style, which developed into the beret-and-leather-jacket uniform. Coming out of the highly intellectual RAM milieu, they had a detailed explanation for the importance of looking cool, drawing on Freud and Fanon. Disdainful of cultural nationalism—or what they called pork-chop nationalism—the Panther leadership nonetheless recognized that black pride was an essential part of Black Power.

Unlike the RAM groups, the Panthers were gender-integrated in a serious way. Within months of the Oakland office's opening, a sixteen-year-old student at Oakland Technical High School named Tarika Lewis walked through the door and asked Bobby Seale two questions: "Can I join?" and "Can I have a gun?"[35] Seale said yes. Lewis was a born activist, organizing the high school's black student union, hanging out with older activist cousins, and ditching school to sit in on lectures at Merritt. (Other Oakland Tech students were early members, including Bobby Hutton—one of Seale's OEO mentees—and Reginald Forte, the younger brother of a Merritt student organizer.) In her book *The Revolution Has Come: Black Power, Gender, and the Black Panther*

Party in Oakland, Robyn Spencer explains that the insurgent Panthers made for a more appealing movement home for young women in Oakland than other militant organizations did. The party combined Maoism's strict gender egalitarian orthodoxy with the reality of women's community leadership, the latter of which structured the southern movement's gender dynamics. By staying underground, RAM could remain male-dominated despite its declared feminist convictions. The Panther tactic of bearing guns near the police was too recklessly open for RAM, but it also guaranteed women's participation. Panther women are often associated with the party's community survival programs, particularly their work clothing, feeding, and educating children, but the armed patrols, too, were gender-integrated from the beginning, and patrolling with arms is what Tarika Lewis joined to do.

The armed cop-watch strategy relied on California's liberal gun law, and soon after the Panthers started patrolling, the state legislature moved to tighten it. In their most visible action to that point, the BPP went with their guns to the state capitol building, in Sacramento, to protest the gun-control bill — another legally protected activity. Guards couldn't find any statutory reason to keep them out of the gallery, and the images of armed Panthers in the capitol astounded the country. (The pictures are still somewhat astounding today.) By the time the Panthers were ready to drive home, local police had figured out an excuse, and Seale kept the armed standoff from turning into a shoot-out. The organization had an international profile now, and new chapters started popping up around the Bay. In the early days, when people in other states called and asked how they could start a chapter, the Oakland Panthers told them to just go for it. The party in the late 1960s had a pragmatic, ad hoc flexibility that contrasts with the organization's later rigid centralism. Though they had understandable reasons for that, too.

RAM's main critique of the Panther strategy was that the police would immediately find ways to destroy the organization. Asymmetrical guerrilla war was one thing, but you couldn't expect to win public standoffs with the police. If they didn't shoot you dead in the street, they could kill you in jail or assassinate you any way they pleased. (The poorly explained death of left-wing Congolese independence leader Patrice Lumumba, in 1961, was never too far away in the Pan-Africanist mind.) The first months of 1967 suggested that was an exaggeration, that the Constitution *did* provide some level of protection, even for armed black militants calling the police pigs.* But after the Mulford Act passed in record time, the loaded guns had to stay in pockets and trunks. In October, a car stop gone awry left one pig dead and Huey under arrest for murder. In April of the following year, the assassination of Martin Luther King Jr. set off riots across the country, but not in Oakland, where Panther strategy opposed spontaneous uprisings. Instead, they planned a community picnic. The night before the planned gathering, a shoot-out erupted between Panthers and cops; the Oakland PD murdered the teenage Bobby Hutton while he surrendered, stripped down to his underwear to prove he was unarmed. If you patrolled with guns and talked about war— within your rights as Americans or not—the pigs were going to take you up on it.

"Free Huey!" became an international rallying cry after his conviction for voluntary manslaughter, in 1968. The Panthers fought "in the belly of the beast"—taking it to Uncle Sam within the country's own borders, exposing the contradictions at the empire's core. That meant political repression—or, rather, an intensified version of the political repression black people already faced in the United States. After surviving the shoot-out that killed Hutton, Panther minister of information Eldridge Cleaver skipped bail and fled to Cuba, then to Algeria, where he set up an international section of the party. In Los Angeles, the FBI pitted Ron Karenga's cultural nationalist US Organization against the Panthers with infiltrators and poison-pen letters, and after a UCLA black student union meeting, a US member shot and killed Panthers John Huggins and Bunchy Carter. It had been less than a year since Carter founded the chapter. Newton was freed in 1970 after an appeals court ordered a new trial, and the prosecution found itself unable to convict him in several attempts. The feds understood the Panthers as the country's biggest domestic threat, and the Nixon administration's FBI pursued them under a wide-ranging counterintelligence program (COINTELPRO), treating the organization as the revolutionary vanguard it claimed to be.

While at San Quentin, Newton allied with a black Marxist revolutionary prison group led by a young intellectual named George Jackson, who became a Panther field marshal on the inside.† After Jackson was moved to Soledad

---

*   Obscenity was a statutory offense, but you can't ban the word *pig*. So: Pigs.

†   The same historical demographic phenomena that formed California's new black population also shaped California's growing black prison population: "With its explicit reference to and rigid policing of racial hierarchies, the South's political geography seemed to mirror that of

State Prison, he narrowly avoided a race riot in the yard during which guards killed three black inmates.[36] Four days later, Jackson, Fleeta Drumgo, and John Clutchette allegedly killed a white guard in retaliation, for which they would surely be sentenced to death.[37] This led to one of the era's most dramatic moments, when George Jackson's teenage brother, Jonathan, led an armed takeover of the Marin County courthouse and demanded the release of George and the other two Soledad Brothers, as they were popularly known. Jonathan, three of his comrades, and Judge Harold Haley were killed in a shoot-out. The guns were registered to Communist Party USA leader, UCLA philosophy professor, and friend of the Panthers Angela Davis. She went on the lam, a global resistance icon for the age. The FBI finally caught up to her, but an all-white Santa Clara County jury found Davis not guilty of all charges in 1972.[38] Soledad guards killed George Jackson—during an escape attempt, they said. The state's violent machinations—perhaps epitomized in the blatant assassination of Chicago Black Panther leader Fred Hampton in December of 1969—seemed to confirm the Panther analysis.

Despite the state attacks, the Panthers inspired Americans the way no domestic left-wing group had, at least for the previous few decades. They disciplined and radicalized other organizations on the left by example. They provided a revolutionary model, and not just for black revolutionaries. In the summer of '69, the Panthers led the United Front Against Fascism conference in Oakland, bringing together the broad interracial Bay Area left under one (sometimes contentious) roof. (Frustration with white participants from SDS led the BPP to redouble service efforts in Oakland's black community, leading to a vast proliferation of programs, including sickle-cell testing, clothing and food drives, transportation to visit incarcerated loved ones, education, child care—the list goes on.)* A number of new organizations drew explicit

---

the prison. And in California, many of those who led uprisings, wrote exposés, or otherwise populated what was called the 'prison movement' were southern migrants or their children, shaped by southern racial hierarchies and modes of resistance. Their understandings of the violent and racially polarized world of confinement joined the southern collective memory of chattel slavery with the Western experience of police brutality and hyperincarceration to arrive at their critique of prisons as a form of slavery." Dan Beger, *Captive Nation: Black Prison Organizing in the Civil Rights Era* (University of North Carolina Press, 2014), 16.

* Between sponsoring Ernie Allen's Cuba trip and the UFAF conference, the SDS Progressive Labor faction took a hard doctrinal turn against all nationalisms including black nationalism, straining relations between PL militants and everyone else.

inspiration from the Panthers: the Red Guard Party, out of San Francisco's Chinatown; the Brown Berets, organizing Chicanos; the Young Lords, for Puertorriqueños; and even the midwestern Young Patriots, for poor white proletarianized Appalachians. Panther leaders, comparatively experienced with regard to the anticolonial question in America, nudged other Third World groups toward revolutionary internationalism rather than cultural or mere representational politics.

Although the Panthers were clearly and unapologetically black as an organization, they did not see their role as limited to the black community. If the last were now first, that put them in a leadership position. We can observe how BPP members handled that responsibility at another California school, San Francisco State College. SF State existed at the nexus of several nonwhite communities, and the school featured an advanced internationalist milieu. That was in large part thanks to George Murray, a SF State graduate student in English, popular freshman instructor, black student union leader, and minister of education for the Black Panther Party.[39]

Murray was an avid internationalist, and he led the BSU into a coalition with the campus's other Third World student groups, which became the Third World Liberation Front. Murray exemplified black student-instructor radicalism, and he and others like him drove Governor Ronald Reagan nuts. At an international conference in Cuba in the fall of 1968, Murray affirmed Panther support for the North Vietnamese, telling the crowd that every American soldier killed in Vietnam was one fewer they had to deal with at home. The governor put pressure on the state board of trustees to deal with Murray, and Murray pushed right back. In front of thousands of students at Fresno State College, where trustees were meeting, Murray told the crowd that the country needed "an old-fashioned black-brown-red-yellow-poor-white revolution."[40] Quoting Mao (as was the Panther wont), he said, "We maintain that political power comes from the barrel of a gun. If you want campus autonomy, if the students want to run the college, and the cracker administrators don't go for it, then you control it with the gun."[41] The BSU began pushing for a student strike to test its support on campus, and the Monday after his Fresno State appearance, Murray got up on a cafeteria table and encouraged students to arm themselves. The college president reluctantly suspended Murray; the BSU went on strike, joined readily by the whole TWLF and a group of white supporters. They were out from November to the following March, when the school agreed to establish the country's first ethnic studies department, though not to rehire Murray.* Some things were beyond the pale.

The BPP's heyday was extraordinarily short. In less than 10 years, the party fell apart under repressive pressure from the government and ethical inconsistency from its leadership, which centralized authority and became increasingly punitive and masculinist. Considering what the state put this group of people through, it's no surprise that some Panthers turned on one another: They *were* infiltrated by government agents planning to imprison and kill them. The RAM milieu was right about that (and it had a much higher survival rate), but it's objectively mistaken to see the Black Panther Party as a failure. It synthesized political currents from the Civil War and the Cold War, and the model it produced took the world by fire. In the Panthers' analysis, they combined the psychological heat of anticolonial struggle with an ice-cold understanding of capitalism as a worldwide *impersonal* system. That's what allowed them to uphold the seemingly contradictory truths of Black Power and Marxist universalism at the same time. Strategically, it allowed them to understand that changing hearts and minds could never abolish global capitalism. The Panthers showed that the war was always already here at home. The question was how to fight and win.

Shoot the Computers

As our focus jumps from the postwar period to the twentieth century's final quarter, we are ready to assemble the last few chapters together into a context, but a context for what? The threads spliced apart and examined above get pulled together into a tight knot in Palo Alto in the late 1960s and early 1970s. With so much going on politically, socially, economically, and technologically in such a small space and period of time, it's tempting to silo, say, the missile suburbs, microchip invention, the personal computer, and the political '60s. But these developments weren't just connected, they were the same thing. Although the events are separate on the surface, Palo Alto radicals made

---

* It's worth noting that without the intellectual movement catalyzed at SF State during these protests, writing this book would have been impossible.

it their mission to pull together what was going on in their town with what else was going on in their town, singling out Stanford's industrial community and its role in the Vietnam War specifically and capitalist imperialism generally. And once they got their collective finger pointed in the right place, they attacked.

Like the rest of the left-wing scene in the Bay Area from 1966 to the mid-1970s, Palo Alto organizers existed in the Panthers' shadow. Using the BPP's advances in theory and practice, they transformed the political landscape. As the Maoist Progressive Labor faction turned against the Panthers and the North Vietnamese, the SDS network split at the national level. The other leading faction was the famous Weathermen, who went underground and began bomb attacks on the capitalist state apparatus. In the Bay Area, however, the main challenge to PL came from a group called the Revolutionary Union (RU), which brought together pro-BPP (predominantly white) leftists to support the party and work under a similar anti-imperial analysis. The RU began in the East Bay, organizing communists in support of a strike by Standard Oil workers and connecting their action with the concurrent Third World Liberation Front strikes at SF State and Berkeley. Students went to support the oil workers, and some oil workers repaid the favor, sending delegations to the student pickets at SF State. This moderate success suggested an opening, and the East Bay group called a meeting that included various unorganized defectors from PL and the traditional Communist Party as well as a new Maoist group from Palo Alto: the Peninsula Red Guard.

Not to be confused with the San Francisco pan-Asian radical organization, the Peninsula Red Guard was a hard-core Maoist group based in Palo Alto. The group distinguished itself during a campus sit-in at the end of the 1968 school year, using small crews to make sure everything moved smoothly in the larger body of students. It greatly impressed a reporter for the *Berkeley Barb*, who concluded, "If you want effectiveness, this form of organization is hard to beat."[42] Among the early Peninsula Red Guard members was Chris Milton, a white Berkeley student who spent some of his high school years in Beijing, where he joined the genuine Chinese student militant Red Guards—an impressive résumé line in the radical scene. But the lead organizer of the group was at Stanford, where he was a well-respected associate professor of English literature.

If history rhymes—and I think we have seen some strong evidence that it does—then H. Bruce Franklin was something like the second coming of California CPUSA leader Sam Darcy: He was a short Jew from New York who moved to the West Coast and tried to run a communist party. Born in working-class Brooklyn in 1934, Franklin made his way to California the same way most men of his generation did: war. He was the first in his family to go to college, working his way through Amherst, where he found the preppy New England WASP atmosphere stifling. To avoid being drafted to Korea, Franklin joined the ROTC and spent three years at the end of the 1950s in the air force, which he concluded as an intelligence officer with the Strategic Air Command, assigned to a refueling unit for long-range bombers. By the end of his tour, he couldn't get away from the military fast enough. He found a loophole in the rules that let him leave a month early if he became a graduate student. Franklin located a program with the right dates and was accepted at Stanford University, in Palo Alto, California, where he would pursue his doctorate in English literature.

As a graduate student, Franklin was a hotshot, even by Stanford standards. (It's funny to think of an atmosphere in which a knowable and even obvious hierarchy of participants attaches to the study and interpretation of literature, but such is the academy.) Though he was an upwardly mobile air force intelligence officer, Franklin was "not what Californians think of as a Stanford type," as the *New York Times Magazine* euphemistically put it later.[43] Still, he must have impressed the hell out of the conservative English department with his work on Hawthorne and Melville. His thesis was based on a close reading of *Moby-Dick* and Melville's polyphonic use of mythology, just the kind of thing advisers love. Franklin finished his doctorate in a shockingly quick two years and, confirming his golden boy status, the department asked him to stay on as an associate professor, an invitation they hadn't offered one of their own grad students in more than 30 years. Four years later, in 1965, at the age of thirty-one, he received tenure. He wrote introductions for new editions of Hawthorne and Melville and could look forward to a long career as a prominent Americanist, as they're called. But then there was the war.

By the time Franklin left the air force for Stanford, in 1959, the Cold War was well underway, and Lieutenant Franklin knew more about how it actually worked than almost anyone did. The Strategic Air Command was the centerpiece of American military strategy, and he saw its underside. Government records show that at the time of his hurried discharge the young man was fully disillusioned with the institution. He understood for a fact that the Soviet nuclear threat was not just overblown but also manufactured—science fiction. The Soviets didn't have the range, either on missiles or bombers, and it was part of Franklin's job to keep that quiet. That is, when he wasn't "engaged in midair refueling of B-47 and B-52 bombers on routine espionage and provocation overflights of the Soviet Union."[44] After his bitter but honorable exit, he watched jingoist politicians and military contractors scare the country with fantastic tales of Soviet bomber armadas. At this point Franklin considered himself a Democrat in the Adlai Stevenson tradition, and the all-male, all-white Stanford English department offered a refuge from politics and current affairs.

The Vietnam War brought Bruce and his wife, Jane Franklin, into activism, and at first they had enthusiasm but little direction. Like the rest of the community in the early 1960s, they had a tactical commitment to nonviolence, in the SNCC mode. But things were moving quickly, and the Franklins found themselves in a very active ferment. (He went to a demonstration at the College of San Mateo in '65 to support a Chicano jazz musician who kept getting tossed off campus for selling peace buttons and antiwar tracts: Aaron Manganiello.) The multi-tendency peace group at Stanford combined pacifists, Marxists, and people who just wanted it all to be over. In early '66, a worker at a Bay Area military contractor got word to the peace movement that the company had won a contract to produce the new highly efficient napalm B—a horrific incendiary munition made of jellied gasoline, a skin-melting refinement of the Tokyo aerial hellfire strategy. Production was set to escalate quickly. Led by a Chinese-Jamaican grad student in the English department named Keith Lowe, the Stanford group initiated a campaign centered on napalm, designed to halt production.

In a scene reminiscent of Frank Norris, Franklin and three other delegates from the group got a sit-down meeting with Barnet Adelman, president of United Technology Center (UTC), to try to talk him out of napalm. Because of his air force experience, Franklin was assigned to do the lion's share of the research, and he explained to Adelman that the firm's paymaster, Dow Chemical, produced the Zyklon-B tablets for the Nazi gas chambers. Was he—a Jew, like Franklin—prepared to join that history? Adelman, an alumnus of the Caltech Jet Propulsion Laboratory and a model space settler, was unmoved. "Napalm will help shorten the war," he explained, leaving out *how* exactly it would do that.[45] Besides, he added, echoing Norris's railroad baron Shelgrim, he had no choice but to take the contract; it was the only way to stay in business as a chemical explosives company. The Stanford group had only slightly more luck with the plant workers, persuading a few to quit rather than make the bombs. Stokely Carmichael was a frequent visitor to East Palo Alto, and a few months before his SNCC election he joined the Stanford campaign, attending an organizing meeting and speaking at a rally outside the UTC plant.[46] They tried a public petition, exhausted their municipal bureaucratic appeals, phoned in to radio shows, and printed leaflets. Aaron Manganiello, serving out a suspension from CSM for distributing the peace buttons, began a one-man hunger strike outside the gates. Workers hosed him down with cold water every night, and he developed pneumonia. No one can say the group didn't work through the nonviolent civil disobedience handbook. Four members, including Manganiello, were arrested for lying down in front of a UTC truck.

The Palo Alto group was successful at building a national campaign against Dow Chemical and napalm. It may be one of the few things people remember about the antiwar movement besides the fact that the participants dressed funny and smelled bad.* But they didn't stop the bombs, and with victories like that, the war kept expanding.

The Franklins might well have radicalized ideologically in the Bay Area— they were well on their way—but that's not how it turned out. In 1966, Bruce took a year's assignment with the Stanford overseas study program in Tours, France. Thanks to some Ford Foundation munificence, the university had established the first European study abroad program, and it was meant to be a cushy assignment. But France was in the midst of its own New Left radical turn, and the Franklins found themselves engaged intellectually in a different way from what they had experienced in California. They read Marx. Moving to the City of Light for the second half of their trip, the Franklins helped set up the Free Uni-

---

* Revisionist reactionary propaganda. In the early 1960s, antiwar campaigners were particularly clean-cut, in the southern-movement tradition. Third World radical leftists did their best to dress sharp.

versity of Paris, parallel to similar projects back home. The city was the capital of
Euro-Maoism, and when they arrived back home at the end of the 1967 semester,
they were no longer the starry-eyed peaceful protesters demonstrating outside the
napalm factory. The Franklins were Palo Alto revolutionaries. Bruce changed his
"Hawthorne and Melville" class to "Marx and Melville."[47]

The Bay Area and the wider American left endured a similar political transformation while the Franklins were gone. Carmichael steered SNCC toward
Black Power; the Panthers were up and running in Oakland; SDS led the campus antiwar movement. When Bruce reconnected with Aaron Manganiello,
they were delighted to find they had followed similar theoretical paths from
general antiwar politics into revolutionary Marxism. Manganiello was building up the Bay Area Brown Beret chapters, and the Franklins decided to start
another organization from which they could work in a multinational coalition
with the Third World groups. This was the Peninsula Red Guard, and working in and around the Stanford SDS, they helped revitalize the white left on
and around campus before merging into the Bay Area Revolutionary Union
with the Richmond group led by Bob Avakian, who worked from a similar
playbook.[48]

You wouldn't necessarily know it from the way they're depicted in twenty-
first-century popular culture, but the Panthers spent a solid amount of their
rhetorical energies warding off narrow cultural nationalism and defending collaborative work in integrated fronts. The case of *Los Siete de la Raza* shows
how the BPP's Black Power politics empowered the broader community. *Los
Siete* were seven young men charged after a familiar incident in 1969. Two
plainclothes San Francisco cops went to hassle a group of young Latino men
moving furniture into a house. A struggle ensued and one cop ended up shot
dead and the other injured.* The police laid siege to the house under the mistaken impression that the men were inside, and the suspects escaped — to a
friend's house in Palo Alto, it turned out. That's the crime-report version, but
it's lacking the political context. The young men were College of San Mateo
students, part of the world Aaron Manganiello tried to build. Manganiello
followed the Bobby and Huey example, working an OEO community job in

---

* The young men were Gary Lescallett, Gio Lopez, Tony and Mario Martinez, Danilo
Melendez, Jose Rios, Nelson Rodriguez. The officers were Joe Brodnik and Paul McGoran.

the summer and organizing out of the community college during the school year, channeling kids into revolutionary study and organization. *Los Siete* were part of that Brown Beret scene, and they organized other young Latinos in San Francisco's Mission neighborhood.[49] The police knew them. And they might well have known those officers in turn, despite the plainclothes and unmarked car—these were notorious anti-Red cops, remembered for beating San Francisco State strikers.[50] The shooting was a domestic skirmish in the Cold War.

The Bay Area left sprung into action to back *Los Siete*, rallying support and linking their case to those of the Soledad Brothers and Huey Newton. The SDS-affiliated filmmaking collective Newsreel made a 30-minute documentary about the conditions underlying the case.[51] One of the suspects, Gio Lopez, hijacked a plane and escaped to Cuba, which was a relatively normal thing for communist fugitives to do at the time. The other six stood trial, defended by BPP lawyer Charles Garry, and they were all acquitted.[52] During the 18 months they spent in jail between arrest and trial, their defense committee blossomed into a Panther-style pan-Latino "serve the people" organization. The experience pushed Manganiello away from the Brown Berets, which he saw as becoming Chicano cultural nationalist, closing itself off to Central American and black organizers. *Los Siete* were Guatemalan, Salvadoran, and Nicaraguan—not Chicano but de la Raza—and at the start they found some trouble attracting support from mainstream Chicano groups. It was the Panthers who stepped up, donating $25,000 (over $200,000 in 2022 dollars) and connecting them with Garry.[53]

This was the Panther model at its most successful. Working-class Third World youths were recruited into the revolutionary milieu, educated around if not exclusively by the community college system, and they expanded the scene, recruiting their friends and others on the block who were inspired by their example.* When the police came to hassle them, as they were bound to, the youngsters were mentally and physically prepared to defend themselves. The community got them to safety, organized their legal defense, *and channeled that organization back into the community* with service programs. In this way, organizers produced a virtuous circle as revolutionary activities and institutions built on themselves, drawing progressively more people into the

---

* We can always see the imprint of Malcolm X and his autobiography.

widening gyre of political struggle. The Panthers sent many other nonblack Bay Area communities spinning.

Thanks to economic pressure and Bureau of Indian Affairs urbanization policies, by the end of the 1960s the Bay Area had the third-largest urban Indian population in the country.*[54] In 1969, a Panthers-inspired group called Indians of All Tribes occupied Alcatraz Island, claiming an American Indian treaty right to unused federal property.† Militants held the former prison for over a year and a half under the slogan "Red Power." Leading organizers included a college student named LaNada Means (later LaNada War Jack), a member of the Shoshone-Bannock Tribes who grew up in Idaho Indian country and relocated in the 1960s to the Bay Area, where at UC Berkeley she helped lead the Third World Liberation Front movement. The occupiers intended to turn Alcatraz into an indigenous people's college. Newly self-identified Asian-American students in the Bay organized as the Asian American Political Alliance and helped stop the redevelopment of a low-rent residential hotel in downtown San Francisco for nearly a decade, while the Red Guard Party emerged out of conflicts between the police and Chinatown youths.[55] But where did the Panther model leave the Franklins and the rest of Palo Alto's white radicals?

Here I think it's important to pause and examine what some might find a touchy subject: Jews and the New Left. The truth is that if it hadn't been for assimilating Jews, there wouldn't have been much of a white radical left at the time. Paul Berman of the Columbia SDS wrote on the question that two-thirds of the white Freedom Riders who traveled to Mississippi were Jewish; a majority of the steering committee of the 1964 Berkeley free speech movement was Jewish; the SDS chapters at Columbia and the University of Michigan

---

* Midcentury Indian policy centered on the "termination" of tribes and the attempted assimilation of members into Anglo-American society. "By 1970," writes historian David Treuer of the result, "half of all Indians lived in urban areas, the single largest demographic and cultural shift in Indian country in a century and arguably more pervasive and transformative than the reservation system established in the mid-nineteenth century." David Treuer, *The Heartbeat of Wounded Knee: Native America from 1890 to the Present* (Riverhead Books, 2019), 278.

† Richard Oakes, a Mohawk SF State student on an OEO grant, was the first to step on the island, where he read the "Alcatraz Proclamation." Damon B. Akins and William J. Bauer, *We Are the Land: A History of Native California* (University of California Press, 2021), 281–82.

were more than half Jewish; Penn State's chapter was almost half; at Kent State in Ohio, where only 5 percent of the student body was Jewish, Jews constituted 19 percent of the chapter.[56] (Berman's Columbia comrade and fellow Jew Mark Rudd adds that, though Jews were an overrepresented one-fifth of the Kent State chapter, *three of four* students gunned down by the National Guard on the campus in 1970 were Jewish.)[57] Stanford was no exception. That's notable, even if it's uncomfortably close to anti-Semitic fantasies about cosmopolitan cabals of Jewish communists conspiring to undermine America.

And yet, at a time when anti-assimilationist nationalist politics were the wave, Jews in the New Left mostly kept quiet.* While black militants adopted new names, their Jewish comrades held on to their anglicized ones, even though they were in large measure only a couple of generations old. What explains it? Part of the issue was the right-wing character of pan-Jewish nationalism, or Zionism. Israel was a colonial project, stealing land from Palestinians and combating anticolonial Arab armies in alliance with the West. Domestically, the Jewish Defense League claimed to be the Jewish Panthers, but they were a right-wing group that attacked Soviet property in the United States to protest the treatment of Jews in the Eastern Bloc. Also, the assimilation of white Jews into white America was smoothing out in the postwar period; lobbying for resources and autonomy the way Third World groups did was unnecessary and would put them in unfair competition that might lead to resentment. At the same time, they faced pressure not to be the "wrong" kind of Jews, the racially undesirable sort. According to a university alum who served as a student admissions representative at the time, Stanford semi-openly maintained a suppressive Jewish admissions quota in 1968.[58] With no strong incentives on either side to draw attention to themselves, New Left Jews confined their ethnic expression to pointed Holocaust references, as in the confrontation between Bruce Franklin and napalm executive Barnet Adelman. As a result of these unique circumstances, Jews constituted a ready base for multinational or intercommunal formations such as the Revolutionary Union in a way that other assimilating white left-wing communities in California— notably the Irish—had not in the past.

---

* The exception to this trend was perhaps the Yippies, the group led by Abbie Hoffman and Jerry Rubin. They worked in a tradition of Jewish humor that wasn't afraid of alienating the goys. Which it did. A lot.

In a 1968 interview from jail with the journal *Movement*, Huey Newton tackled the question of the white radical directly:

> As far as I'm concerned the only reasonable conclusion would be to first realize the enemy, realize the plan, and then when something happens in the black colony—when we're attacked and ambushed in the black colony—then the white revolutionary students and intellectuals and all the other whites who support the colony should respond by defending us, by attacking the enemy in their community. Every time that we're attacked in our community there should be a reaction by the white revolutionaries; they should respond by defending us, by attacking part of the security force.[59]

This line represented a shift from the Friends of SNCC model, in which the role of white radicals was to support the organizing activities of their black comrades, both by performing ancillary office tasks and by putting their bodies at risk alongside those of the more vulnerable participants. As nonviolent strategies (if not tactics) fell away from the insurgent-left playbook, the white radical's job changed. The Revolutionary Union continued trying to fill in gaps between organizational bodies in the region, but it also assumed a more confrontational role. It was up to white radicals to attack imperial infrastructure in their own communities. Now, where could Stanford students find some of that?

It's important to remember that the 1960s left-wing milieu, on campus and off, was intellectual to a fault. Despite the critiques of the RAM and other "all talk" groups, research and even scholarship were key left-wing activities. The anti-napalm campaign was a model for the Palo Alto left going into the late '60s: direct action backed up by detailed study of the military-industrial complex. This idea fits with Aaron Manganiello's goal for Venceremos College—to produce "revolutionary technicians" who would turn their professional-caliber training into an anticapitalist weapon and put it at the community's disposal.[60] And these technicians were not just engineers; one example was the San Jose Chicano playwright Luis Valdez, who as a San Jose State University student in the early '60s developed a new form of street theater that he then brought into the grape fields to support farmworker organizing.[61] Teatro Campesino's syncretic agitprop started a true artistic tradition, and Valdez's successful play about the Zoot Suit Riots secured that story's place in the history books.* Could white Stanford students learn from Third World revolutionaries (at home and abroad) and put their education to work for the revolution? Everyone knew they were willing to talk, but were they willing to fight?

We can see the tensions on the Stanford left in a documentary about the 1968 SDS occupation of the university president's office. The viewer watches activists debate whether to frame their confrontation in deliberative or aggressive terms. Bruce Franklin clutches his head in his hands, cigarette dangling between his fingers as he argues that talking with the administration wasn't going to do any good, no matter how solid the research they brought to the table was, something he learned from the napalm campaign. "This whole idea: talking and talking and talking and all of a sudden people will see the light and they'll pick up *The Communist Manifesto* and race into the streets and join with—it's a bunch of shit! When does talking with people become relevant? Past a certain point."[62] An immanent critique of the university—calling on the school to live up to its ostensible principles regarding learning and debate—was misleading because it meant activists had to pretend not to have already come to a conclusion about Stanford's role in the world. They had to take down the capitalist university, not reform it; agree to a conversation, and that's all you could win. The viewer follows Franklin as he participates in the SF State strike, taking mental notes out loud about the Third World Liberation Front tactics and rhetoric. In an interview segment he laments that ruling-class Stanford students need more help than SF State students do to understand capitalism.[63]

In January of 1969, the Revolutionary Union announced itself with what it called a Red Paper, the communist equivalent of a corporate-academic white paper, the first in a series the organization published promoting its formula of

---

* The idea of the revolutionary technician leached into the mainstream in unpredictable ways. Stephanie Rothman's low-budget soft-core erotica *The Student Nurses* (1970) depicts a nursing student who falls for a Chicano militant and turns down a hospital job in order to bring medicine to the people. "Who've you been shacking up with, Chairman Mao?" her friends tease. "Where's your gun?" "In the glovebox!" she answers. "Wanna see?" The girls walk away together, still laughing, but not joking. The film includes an extended anti-imperial street theater performance by El Teatro Popular, a real Valdez-inspired group from Los Angeles.

a pre-party formation. (The debt to Paul Baran is right there on the surface: The "statement of principles" uses the phrase "monopoly capital" 28 times.)[64] The second pamphlet declares, "No individual or organization can be considered revolutionary who at this time does not defend the Black Panther Party and learn how better to defend them."[65] In 1969, the Revolutionary Union changed the Stanford left's primary target, from men to forces.

Stanford's Applied Electronics Laboratory (AEL) was an important stone in the military-industrial complex wall. Built by Fred Terman and the Office of Naval Research in the early 1950s to house the many offshoots of his wartime electronics work (it was originally called the Electronics Research Laboratory), the AEL was more or less the postwar version of the Radio Research Lab. But this time Stanford was calling the shots, and Terman successfully positioned the AEL between military contractors and the government. Along with the industrial park and the research institute, the AEL helped turn Stanford into a new academic home of the arms industry, surpassing every American university but MIT and Caltech in defense contracts by 1967.[66] Thanks in part to support and patronage from Dave Packard and Bill Hewlett, the lab grew to become one of the country's main sites for combat electronics research during the Korean War, producing important advances in military avionics, which were key to the strategic bombing model.

SRI technically spun off from the university after World War II, but it remained wholly controlled by the trustees—a who's who of military contractors, including Hewlett, who supplemented his HP income with a board seat at the Food Machinery Corporation, which had added antipersonnel munitions to its agricultural technology. At SRI, as you read in the previous chapter, researchers pursued bizarre tactics under the new strategic line of counterinsurgency. Mao said the guerrilla must "move amongst the people as a fish swims in the sea," and around the world militants heeded his words. At SRI they tried to figure out how to solve this fish-sea problem, attacking it using anthropological and sociological approaches, not just technology per se. Academics tried to figure out what made certain counterinsurgency campaigns effective (in Malaysia and Thailand, for example) and others ineffective (in Cambodia and Vietnam). There they helped develop the CIA's "strategic hamlet" plan, which involved relocating entire villages by force. By 1968, millions of dollars in annual military and intelligence contracts flowed through SRI. If

Stanford students wanted to attack America's imperialist war machine, they didn't have to go far. They didn't even need to leave campus.

In fact, student militants could hardly throw a rock on Stanford's 8,000-plus acres without hitting some piece of Cold War military infrastructure. Recall that accumulating public and private defense contracts was precisely the strategy Provost Fred Terman used during his ten-year tenure (1955–65) to build the university from a well-regarded private school in the California suburbs to an essential American institution, with corresponding effects on the town. The connection between the campus where they lived and the American military wasn't the grasping work of stoned conspiracy theorists; rather, as historian Rebecca Lowen said in the title of her book on the school, Stanford was the prototypical Cold War university. As the school reorganized with the influx of resources, the AEL became the home of classified research on campus. Its director was Bill Rambo, one of Terman's bright young men from the RRL, and when students and faculty began complaining about military contracts on campus, Rambo tried to play down the secrecy: "This building [AEL] has a sinister reputation not fully deserved; most of it is freely accessible to all. This is well known to many faculty, staff, and students outside of [Electrical Engineering], in large part because the Sergeant of the Guard, a slightly built man in his seventies who does not carry a gun, makes what is reputed to be the best coffee on campus," he told the faculty's academic council in 1966.[67] That's what's called foreshadowing.

In 1969, student activists noticed that the guards outside AEL suddenly *were* carrying guns, and it wasn't just one old man anymore.* A group went to ask the provost to research what was going on in there and what it had to do with Vietnam. He told them it was "defensive weapons," just "ECMs," nothing to worry about. According to one activist who was present, that took the wind out of their sails for a second. If they didn't know what ECMs were, how could they demand that the university stop making them? Then an English professor spoke up: "Those are electronic countermeasures," Bruce Franklin said. "They are used by our bombers to jam enemy radar so that the bombers can get through and bomb sites in Vietnam. If you think that's 'defensive'

---

* The upgrade in security was no doubt in part due to two arson attacks at the end of the 1967–68 school year: one on departing president Sterling's office, the other on the Naval ROTC building.

you're out of your mind."[68] Not only did the administrator lose the argument, he also revealed too much about what was going on in the AEL to someone who knew how to understand it. Oops.

After a meeting of campus radicals (including Franklin) in the spring of 1969, members of the resulting April Third Movement (A3M) decided to occupy the AEL and demand the elimination of classified research. Led by Revolutionary Union cadres, they held the building for more than a week. The rebels appropriated the AEL printers and used hundreds of thousands of the lab's sheets of blank paper to print and distribute their propaganda. At the beginning their messaging was chaotic—an early flyer misidentified the AEL as the Atomic Energy Lab, one of the few military science subfields in which Stanford did not excel—but the occupiers soon turned the space into their own research station. They put out daily issues of a journal called *Declassified*, which included agitprop, explanations, and leaked material from the AEL files. Issue 1 assailed the lab for anti–sex education pamphlets found stacked near the printers. Each edition included a profile of a different university trustee, detailing his ties to the military-industrial complex. Issue 5 featured the "Song of the SRI Researcher." ("I have never killed a man. / I have never seen him die. / These formulas: they could be / for jelly. I don't think I know.") Bobby Seale and SDS leader Tom Hayden, both under indictment for allegedly disrupting the 1968 Democratic National Convention, in Chicago, came to lend the occupation their support. Seale gave it the BPP stamp of approval, linking the occupiers' work with the world decolonial struggle in Angola, South Africa, and, of course, Vietnam.

The AEL occupation ended with the removal of classified research from campus, a real victory. But in addition to that met demand, the occupation was a step forward for the movement, a model for action. The A3M not only halted classified research at the AEL during the occupation and after, they converted the technology resources into community assets. In doing so, the members transformed themselves into Aaron Manganiello's revolutionary technicians. Lenny Siegel, for example, was a Stanford physics major looking forward to a career in the computer industry until he got thrown out of school for plotting the trajectory of a police tear-gas canister through a second-story window at SRI. A one-page essay in the seventh issue of *Declassified* makes the explicit argument for popular control over technology: "The university is deeply involved in production for private profit," the authors write. "It produces, often at public expense, skilled labor and scientific knowledge. This university isn't a temple of the intellect or a place where disinterested scholars examine the world. It is a center for the development of knowledge and resources for human use."*[69] Who controlled that use was a matter of dispute, specifically between classes. The occupation was a powerful real-world example, and when the BPP updated its 10 Point Plan a few years later, it added "people's community control over modern technology" to the list.[70]

This action was part of a staggering nationwide series of attacks by antiwar militants on America's fragile information, or DP (data processing), infrastructure. Students at Boston University and Loyola University in Los Angeles destroyed school computers in the spring of 1969, in Boston with acid and wire cutters, in LA with what quickly became the preferred method: bomb. Analog files weren't safe, either: The Catonsville Nine Catholic activists burned hundreds of paper draft files in a Catonsville, Maryland, draft board parking lot. After the Nixon administration announced the escalation of the Vietnam War into Cambodia at the end of April of 1970, the home front escalated in return. The National Guard killed protesters at Kent State and Jackson State University, pouring fuel on student-movement militancy, which turned toward the bomb.

Militants in the 1970s bombed a lot of stuff, especially on the West Coast—Bank of America averaged one bombing per month among its California branches for two years—and campus computer centers were particularly good targets.[71] At California's Fresno State College, students Molotov'ed a million dollars' worth of data equipment.[72] At NYU, students "kidnapped" a particularly expensive computer, hanging it with bombs and demanding $100,000 for the Black Panthers—or the robot gets it![73] The University of Kansas computer center was bombed, and in the most notable action of 1970, militants at the University of Wisconsin parked a van full of dynamite next to the school's Army Math Research Center and demolished the building, accidentally killing postdoc researcher Robert Fassnacht, the bombing wave's only casualty.[74]

---

* Baran's theoretical fingerprints are all over *Declassified*, from the critique of counterinsurgent land reform in Vietnam to the section on military-financed paths of technological development. Issue 7 printed Paul Sweezy's eulogy for his friend, along with some kind words from Che for his favorite economist.

Damage estimates from the Wisconsin attack included $1.5 million in computer equipment, $5–6 million in facilities, and, most important, 1.3 million man-hours of data.[75] To a military that thought in terms of man-months, this was the kind of blow that counted.

These computer center attacks became an endemic problem in the industry, as reported in *Computerworld*, the "newsweekly for the computer community." In between stories about the latest mainframe model and corporate mergers were articles such as "Violence by Rebels Threatens Centers."[76] In an August 1970 piece, *Computerworld*'s Phyllis Huggins quoted the coordinator for computer activities at the UC system, who explained that the schools couldn't keep potentially militant students out of the computer centers because the same students were also potential programmers. He suggested that the computer industry could win them over once inside. That didn't work for Fresno State's Virgil Lewis, who was charged with firebombing the same center where he trained on an OEO grant, Huggins notes dryly.[77] At the University of Pittsburgh, black students leveraged a computer-center takeover in negotiations with administrators.[78] The campus conflict also penetrated the industry: When math prodigy, professional programmer, and New York Black Panther Sundiata Acoli was charged along with 20 comrades in a bombing conspiracy, the judge rejected a bail payment from an ad-hoc group of Acoli's coworkers calling themselves Computer People for Peace.[79] IBM offices in New York and San Jose were bombed.[80] Things got so bad so fast that by the end of 1970, *Computerworld* featured a note (joking?) about a new "bomb suppression blanket" for computers from the Pinkerton company: "Worried about those long-haired, dope-smoking, glue-sniffing, bomb-throwing anarchists putting bombs under your printer?"[81] They were.

The AEL occupation shifted the strategic orientation of the Stanford campus militants, in line with the acceleration of campus conflict in 1969–70. The militants kept the A3M organizational branding and kept moving, next into a quick occupation of an administration building, Encina Hall. It ended after an arrest threat, a first for the A3M, but not before the occupiers raided private personnel files. We know one they got away with because they released it the following year: Paul Baran's, which showed once again how corporate interests controlled Stanford academics. Gone was the "hearts and minds" strategy; A3M militants weren't trying to convince anyone anymore. "We are engaged in a conflict with the kind of men—and some of the very men—whose interests got us into Vietnam, and whose disenchantment with the rising costs of that conflict will eventually get us out," they wrote in a pamphlet explaining the Encina raid. "As the War goes on, their university moves closer and closer toward becoming one of the costs: their control is threatened. The struggle at Stanford, then, is a microcosm: the trustees' intransigence will not give way to moral persuasion or majority votes any more than our outcries have ended the war. If this view is correct, then the trustees will respond only to rising costs."[82] On May 7, 1969, an anonymous Molotov attack burned down the Stanford Naval ROTC building, which was undergoing repairs from the previous year's Molotov attack.

On May 16, the A3M moved to its next target: SRI. At this point, Stanford administrators and local authorities could no longer afford to treat student militants as if they were engaged in respectable protest behavior. These kids were a threat to national security. Even Bobby Seale said so! The flyer calling students to action on the sixteenth was headlined in a scrawl: SMASH WAR RESEARCH. On the back was a map of relevant targets in Palo Alto: SRI, the Hoover Institution, the Stanford business school, Varian, HP, Lockheed, IBM. Under the map it read in the same scrawl: SINCE WORLD WAR II—HOW TO RUN AN EMPIRE FROM PALO ALTO and then MONDAY—HOW TO DESTROY AN EMPIRE.[83] The sixteenth was Friday, a dress rehearsal; Monday the nineteenth was Ho Chi Minh's *and* Malcolm X's birthday, so that's when things would really kick off.* On Friday morning, outside the SRI counterinsurgency office, hundreds of students blocked the street with a school bus and Ping-Pong tables. They linked arms to prevent SRI employees from entering, always offering to explain why, of course. These were no longer the well-behaved Friends of SNCC from the early 1960s, but the A3M still remained ready to explain itself, at length, in detail.

This time, however, the authorities didn't want to "rap"; they wanted these kids to get the fuck out. At around eleven that morning, the protesters were met by dozens of police officers firing tear-gas canisters ahead of their advance.[84] Led by the aggressive Harvey Hukari Jr., observers from the

---

*   In another one of history's strange rhymes, both Ho and Malcolm worked at the Parker House Hotel in Boston, MA, though a couple decades apart.

campus chapter of the ritzy conservative organization Young Americans for Freedom (YAF) applauded the police as they liberated SRI.* The YAFers took notes on their radical classmates, whom they knew better than the authorities did and hated at least as much. Also taking notes were members of a new anti-militant Coalition for an Academic Community and their leader, Eckhard Schulz—German graduate student, the head of the engineering fraternity, and a protégé of the electronics lab director, Rambo.

The problem with mounting an insurgency against an institute for the study of counterinsurgency is that it's like trying to rob a gun store: they're ready. On the eighteenth, SRI got an injunction against all the participants in the Friday action, including 27 known individuals, 12 organizations, and 500 "John and Jane Does"—everyone else.[85] The emergency restraining order enjoined them from entering, obstructing, defacing, or throwing things at SRI and summoned them to court later in the month. The Monday action was unusually peaceful. The SRI president, Charles Anderson, sent the staff a memo on Tuesday explaining the events of the previous days. As for the temporary restraining order, he wrote, "Several members of the staff, who appreciate how long this process can take, have expressed some surprise that we were able to get the restraining order so quickly that several of the named defendants had been served by midnight Sunday."[86] He explained that anti-militant Stanford students had furnished "hundreds of photos" from the demo, and worked through the weekend with SRI staff and lawyers making identifications. To back up the official complaint, SRI attached a number of sworn affidavits testifying to particular people's observed actions, including one each from the conservative student leaders Hukari and Schulz.† *That* is how you separate the fish from the sea.

Events at Stanford petered out for the summer. The school fully spun off

---

* Hukari led the doctrinaire libertarian Stanford chapter in a membership-card burning later in the year after a YAF split along traditionalist and libertarian lines. See Gregory L. Schneider, *Cadres for Conservatism: Young Americans for Freedom and the Rise of the Contemporary Right* (NYU Press, 1999), 138.

† One name on the TRO sticks out among the Semitic patter of activists narc'ed out by the YAF: Levin, Weissman, Cohen, Friedman, Siegel, Weinberg, Bernstein, Braunstein—Bechtel. Lauren Bechtel (class of '71) doesn't seem to have been an active radical, but she was identifiable in the Friday rabble. I suppose, even in Stanford's rarefied atmosphere, everyone knew who Stephen Bechtel's granddaughter was. The injunction didn't prevent her from joining the Stanford board of trustees as an adult philanthropist.

SRI, which the radicals had expected. It looked like a concession to the protests, but the radicals themselves were more circumspect. They understood that the newly independent SRI was taking on the AEL's classified contracts. But the summer of 1969 was for dealing with internal movement business, after the previous year's chaotic Democratic National Convention. At the SDS convention that summer in Chicago, the group began its organizational descent. SDS expelled the PL faction, which sought to explicitly subordinate the issues of black nationalism and women's liberation to a class line. As the Weathermen moved toward a guerrilla orientation (before his murder, Chicago BPP leader Fred Hampton famously condemned the fall 1969 Days of Rage strategy of frontal attack in Chicago as "Custeristic"—as in loser general George Armstrong Custer) and the Bay Area Revolutionary Union became the national Revolutionary Union, the RU ended up one of the largest aboveground factions and America's leading multiracial Maoist student-worker organization.

The organizational splits, however, weren't over. Buoyed by the RU's success, Bruce Franklin invited his friend Aaron Manganiello to a meeting. Manganiello was ready to be part of a multinational organization, but instead of Franklin talking Manganiello into the group, Manganiello talked Franklin and his faction out of it. The Richmond group, led by Bob Avakian, was becoming frustrated with the way the emphasis on Black Power was hurting its efforts to organize white industrial workers. At the local Rheem factory, for example, "they didn't like cops when it was a matter of their own lives or their union struggles, but they would support the cops in the black community," as the RU's Steve Hamilton reported back with disappointment.[87] These workers understood—not without reason or tradition, as you've seen—that they had something to lose as white people in addition to something to gain as workers.

Avakian became increasingly rigid and authoritarian both in his thinking and behavior, a problem with many if not most male leaders on the New Left. Franklin argued that the organization needed to embrace armed struggle in the immediate term and continue attacking the war machine, driving up the cost and building revolutionary capacity. The FBI did what it could via informants and poison-pen letters to open the split, but it's more or less the same ideological perforation along which SDS divided, with Franklin playing Weatherman and Avakian as the PL. The strategic and analytical differences were as deep as the tactical ones, and all three went further than the personal gripes and COINTELPRO plots the histories often focus on. The BPP underwent a similar internal conflict, between a faction focused on community service and municipal politics and one pushing for violent confrontation. Bruce and Jane Franklin were expelled from the RU, and they took around half the regional group with him, a couple of hundred people. They joined Manganiello's Venceremos organization, which developed from an experimental community college to a Chicano-led multinational militant group committed to armed struggle.

As far as the feds were concerned, the split was for the best nationally, damaging the RU while pushing it in a more moderate direction. It's the end they were looking for when the FBI targeted Franklin under the notorious COINTELPRO counterinsurgency, as it did his Panther comrades. But a perhaps unintended result was that militants concentrated in the Palo Alto area, and the split let them loose. In addition to the large campus demonstrations, underground groups committed acts of sabotage—it's hard to call them terrorism, since these destructive attacks successfully avoided harming people, always calling in warnings to give them time to evacuate. At the end of the 1970 school year, militants ignited the Center for Advanced Study in the Behavioral Sciences, a Ford Foundation–funded campus institution built in part to conduct anticommunist research. The attack led President Nixon to condemn student radicals as "bums blowing up the campus" and nearly destroyed the single copy of visiting philosopher John Rawls's manuscript for his book *A Theory of Justice*, which he was in the process of finishing at the center.*[88]

Within two months of the Venceremos split from the RU, the Stanford struggle accelerated. In February, alerted that the campus computation center was working on an SRI project modeling a Vietnam invasion, militants invaded the center. According to the head of security, they cut the power and went right for the computer's data storage drums. That's where the government kept the man-months. Violence, including some minor gunfire, broke

---

* According to Rawls's wife, Margaret, the philosopher's first reaction to the early morning phone call was to "turn pale and say 'I can't do it again.'" The (notoriously long) manuscript was wet from the sprinklers but legible. See William A. Edmundson, *John Rawls: Reticent Socialist* (Cambridge University Press, 2017), 186.

out between the radicals and conservative students. Activists also targeted the school's most successful alumni: They chased David Packard around the Bay trying to effect a citizen's arrest. "Packard before Calley!" they shouted, unfavorably comparing the town's paternal figure with the country's most notorious war criminal of the Vietnam era. When Packard's Western Electronic Manufacturers Association moved his speech to San Francisco, Venceremos announced it as a "people's injunction" keeping him out of Palo Alto. The radical press release declared that Packard was "afraid to return to the city that he owns."[89] They firebombed Bill Hewlett's house.

Despite the federal informants placed throughout the scene, Palo Alto's radicals were hard to catch red-handed (so to speak), and the situation was rapidly becoming untenable. The university, however, knew where to start: The West Coast's leading white proponent of armed struggle worked in the English department, where he was still writing critical studies of *Moby-Dick*. There was, however, a problem: In an era full of purged left-wing teachers, Mr. H. Bruce Franklin had something the others didn't—he had tenure. Franklin also had a perfectly respectable scholarly output. In fact, his departmental colleagues recommended him for a promotion to full professor the year before—they were turned down, ostensibly because rules prohibited such a quick advance. To fire him solely for expressing unpalatable political views would outrage the academic community and damage Stanford's reputation. That would be to concede that the school's contradictions couldn't hold, that politics and academics couldn't be separated while the world was on fire. But if you couldn't dismiss a professor for leading students to destroy school property, where was the line? Was the capitalist university doomed to suffocate in its own academic freedom? After the Fresno State computer center attack, Stanford explored moving its own to an off-campus location, but the insurer said no chance. Such an installation would be a sitting duck for waiting guerrillas. The only way to insure a computer center was to keep it on campus, under a general policy. In December of 1971, militants bombed the Stanford Linear Accelerator Center.

The Stanford administration began building its official case against Bruce Franklin back in August of 1971, when he allegedly heckled the U.S. ambassador to South Vietnam, Henry Cabot Lodge. *Speaking* controversially was one thing, but *interrupting* someone else's speech was anti-scholarly. When

Franklin pressed, the Stanford president, Richard Lyman, admitted it wasn't enough to revoke his tenure. Instead Lyman tried to "Baran" him with a suspension and a reduction in pay. Franklin said he'd fight it, and in January he looked likely to win. But after the attack on the computation center in February, Lyman felt empowered to move decisively. Two days later, he suspended Franklin, obtained a court injunction banning him from campus, and started the permanent removal process. For the English department, firing a tenured professor was even more unheard of than hiring one out of your own graduate program. Lyman's case put a new constituency in Franklin's corner, winning him the support of free-speech liberals who couldn't stand behind or anywhere near the content of the Venceremos line. His die-hard supporters were still with him in armed revolt, too. In April, following Franklin's suspension and the official invasion of Laos, Stanford suffered a series of bombings: the campus police station, the Pacific Gas and Electric station, President Lyman's office. The war continued.

The administrative attack on Franklin was far from exceptional in the era. UCLA fired Angela Davis in 1969 for being a capital-C Communist; there was the case of Black Panther George Murray at San Francisco State; at Fresno State in 1970, the president purged the new ethnic studies department, dismissing eight instructors. It was also common for campus struggles to degenerate into free-speech debates around faculty dismissals. At Palo Alto's Cubberley High School, protests in the summer of 1969 centered on the dismissal of the popular New Lefty social studies teacher Ron Jones, whose Third Wave experiment, in which he turned his students into a fascist party, confusedly straddled a line between insurgency and counterinsurgency and presaged Zimbardo's Stanford prison.[90] These were among some of the best-known cases, and they no doubt stand for a wider body of politicized employment practices. What made Franklin's case different was that he had tenure and it took place at Stanford, which made it a national story. "At Stanford University, football has come roaring back like a flying wedge," announced *Esquire* magazine in its 1971 back-to-school issue regarding the team's surprise Rose Bowl win. "But if the quarterback has a big following at the school, so does Bruce Franklin, a Maoist English teacher."[91] He became a national cause célèbre, refusing to moderate his tone. Jane showed up at a January press conference toting a rifle, to remind everyone where power came from.

Venceremos split in the fall of 1971. A faction behind Miriam Cherry renounced armed struggle and joined the Oakland BPP as the Intercommunal Survival Committee to Combat Fascism, resurrecting the Friends of SNCC model to support the increasingly moderate and electorally oriented Panther faction. "We have other priorities," Cherry told the press. "We don't see spending a lot of time fighting—by leafleting, in rallies, going to Bruce's class—to fight for a white male intellectual's job, when we know there are people sitting on death row."[92] The Venceremos self-identified "brown leadership" denounced the departing white group as "racist sissies." Franklin for his part never failed to connect his case to other cases of academic repression in which instructors didn't have tenure to offer them due-process protections. Still, by moving to a deliberative free-speech struggle controlled by the university, the Venceremos message got muddled, even if its actions remained more or less consistent. In January, the administration finally rid itself of Bruce Franklin.

Facing increased repression, Venceremos and other armed-struggle groups tended toward underground actions, and, for the first time, some sought bloodshed: While breaking a friend out of jail, members executed an unarmed guard.[93] Venceremos officially dissolved in September of 1973, less than a year later. From there the tendency trickled into adventurist rivulets. The Red Guerrilla Family continued the bombing strategy, hitting a number of high-value targets around the Bay in the mid-1970s, including FBI and ATF offices, the Iranian consulate, and a fancy new Hewlett-Packard lab in Palo Alto.[94] They stuck to the 10 (or so) point plan, but the mass pre-party orientation as well as most of the theoretical and investigative work fell away. The dramatic dead end of the Bay Area armed struggle was a May 1974 shootout in Los Angeles, in which the Symbionese Liberation Army cadre lost a gun battle with the LAPD. The police exaggerated the connection between Venceremos and the SLA, and leaders, including Franklin, rejected the group that kidnapped Patty Hearst and assassinated Oakland schools superintendent Marcus Foster, but the Bay Area armed-struggle scene was only so big and some overlaps were to be expected. And though the Palo Alto empire did not fall in the 1970s, the communists and Third World liberationists could point to important victories. The Monroe Doctrine has yet to recover from the Cuban Revolution. And America surrendered in Southeast Asia, falling back to South Korea, which remained only half a nation. In the defining conflict of the

American anti-imperial struggle during this era, the communists won. This was not the world Shockley's equations promised.

Even with a whole jungle full of sensors, bombs, and defoliants, the Solid State couldn't beat Vietnam. "Ho, Ho, Ho Chi Minh, NLF is gonna win!" Stanford SDS protesters yelled before the 1968 president's office occupation, and they were right.[95] When campus militants trashed computer labs and war research offices and raised the NLF flag, they weren't just trying to stop the war; they were trying to help win it, to win it the same way their enemy countrymen were: by the man-month. In 1972, members of the Weathermen faction exploded a bomb in a women's bathroom at the Pentagon, damaging targeting computers and disrupting air operations in Vietnam for a week.[96] The A3M line about the war becoming too costly, about capitalist imperialism only speaking one language, was precisely correct. Battered first in Vietnam by the Vietnamese people and second on the home front by the Third World solidarity movement, America's leadership came to grips with the unthinkable: losing the war. To survive this world-historical setback, the country and the global economic system it helmed were forced to change.

As you'll read in the next section, capitalist reaction to the liberation struggles of the 1960s and '70s structured the fourth quarter of the twentieth century. One of history's truths—as observed by Huey Newton—is its snaking tendency: The last comes first; the loser wins. Partial defeat in the Cold War's first half catalyzed a conservative revitalization as America's ruling class came to understand the stakes and shook off what was left of its New Deal–Popular Front fetters. Liberals turned on their countrymen, reversing the Johnson administration's half steps. They abandoned the "compensatory state" and its equalizing mission for a focus on individual rights. As the American public sphere shrunk, so did the number of democratizing claims that could be made of it. After jumping more than 20 percent between 1966 and '76, spending on "human resources" as a percentage of federal expenditures began to stagnate and fall.[97]

Part and parcel of this shift was the rapid change in California's orientation toward public higher education. Having expanded greatly in the previous decades, in the late 1970s the state stopped. Conservatives, led by Governor Ronald Reagan, turned an attack on the New Left campus movement to an attack on students in general.[98] Tuition and fees at the University of California system doubled in the '80s, then tripled in the '90s.[99] Right-wing lawyers attacked affirmative action, posing individual white claims against black group claims. In the landmark *Bakke* ruling of 1978, the Supreme Court struck down the UC system's racial admissions quotas—themselves a compromise with the open-admission demand from the Third World student movement—which steered liberation struggles toward an individual anti-discrimination orientation. Backed by campus reactionaries, school administrators relaxed their inclusion efforts.

One good example is that of Cedric Robinson, the Berkeley organizer and intellectual from Oakland. After graduating from UC Berkeley (despite his pro-Cuba suspension), Robinson began his postgraduate work in political theory at SF State, where liberation struggle was also an epistemological fight to bring new kinds of knowledge into the academy. In the wake of black student protests at Stanford, the university made a point to increase its recruitment, pulling in the obviously brilliant Robinson to finish his doctorate there. Recruiting working-class black intellectuals from the Bay Area who were writing on black political theory was just what the department should have been doing, according to activist pressure, and they did try it. But when Robinson critiqued his discipline's concept of leadership and offered counterexamples of African "stateless societies" or "tribes without rulers"—particularly the anarchistic Tonga—the political science department lost its integrationist nerve.[100] Faculty members declined to sit on his committee, passive-aggressively consigning Robinson to academic purgatory. He had to make a credible threat to sue the school before it handed over his PhD.[101]

As capitalists locked down public resources through privatization, tax evasion, and austerity, the high-growth technology industry hardened its defenses, erecting literal and metaphorical walls between the people and computer power. "Such elaborate precautions may have appeared unnecessary up to now to the managers of most computer installations," a security consultant told *Computerworld* in 1970. "But with the growing unrest in the country, the increasing sophistication of saboteurs, and the potential that computers offer for easily inflicted and costly damage, major precautions are necessary for data processing managers to fully protect their computers."[102] He recommended not only closing public access to the labs but also removing their locations from all maps. MIT's famous anti-authoritarian hackers constantly thwarted administrative attempts to lock down their AI lab, proving repeatedly that there was no lock for sale that they couldn't crack. But when Massachusetts militants planned to demonstrate at their beloved lab, the programmers didn't object to the steel plates and Plexiglas. "Though previously some of the hackers had declared, 'I will not work in a place that has locks,'" writes Steven Levy in his account of the lab in *Hackers: Heroes of the Computer Revolution*, "after the demonstrations were over, and after the restricted lists were long gone, the locks remained."[103] It was the end of an era.

Locking down was easier for corporations than it was for public and pseudo-public institutions such as universities. For example, in 1975, after a wave of layoffs at the Fairchild assembly plant in Shiprock, New Mexico, on the Navajo reservation, American Indian Movement (AIM) activists occupied the plant, demanding the workers' reinstatement. Instead, Fairchild permanently suspended the plant. Property rights, aggressively enforced by the state, were a layer of insulation: The Bay Area AIM chapter decided on a sympathy demonstration at the Fairchild headquarters in Silicon Valley, hoping to encourage workers to walk out in support. Led in part by former Fairchild assembly line worker Roxanne Dunbar, the activists arrived to find "police snipers lining the roof of the plant building and tactical squads swarming the place in riot gear."[104] They felt compelled to retreat, and the workers stayed inside. By going private, SRI distanced itself from the democratic aspects of the Stanford community while maintaining its beneficial connections to Palo Alto's ruling cliques and most skilled workers. Shrinking collective computers into personal property also reduced the democratic pressure on the hardware. As I'll spell out in the next section, the personal revolution was in part a functional fix to the demand for people's popular control over modern technology.

"This bombing occurred in Palo Alto, but it could very well have happened at any other of our facilities in the U.S.," Bill Hewlett wrote to his employees after the Red Guerrilla Family hit the HP lab, in 1976. "Although the problem may seem more apparent and critical in Palo Alto than elsewhere, one should not labor under the misconception that the problem is *limited* to Palo Alto or to the United States." The world, he wrote, is "ever more violent," and "as the company grows larger it is a more attractive target for sabotage, theft and violence."[105] Instead of examining the correlation between violence and the firm's growth, between HP and RGF, HP had a different solution: It surrounded the new Palo Alto lab's 52-door open campus with a guarded security fence.[106]

Section IV

1975–2000

Security fences being built to protect HP's Deer Creek laboratory in Palo
Alto after a bomb attack, in *Measure*, August–September 1976

Chapter 4.1

California über Alles

Silicon Canneries — The End of the '70s —
Civic Vigilantism in the Suburbs — New Walls
Everywhere — "What about Jensen?" — A Union of
Homeowners

"It was a great feeling to be part of the team that tied the lace on the shoe that took that giant step for mankind. You don't get that feeling from building a goddamn missile." Thus opens the 1977 movie *Fun with Dick and Jane,* as aerospace engineer Dick Harper and his boss lament the state of the post–moon walk industry. "Can I level with you?" the boss asks Dick. "Sure," says Dick. "You're fired," says the boss. Unable to find a comparable job, Dick tumbles down the American class pyramid, falling through the shredded social safety net and, with his titular wife, into street crime. Dick makes it back to his old firm after he cannily steals the company's sizable cash bribe fund. Unable to report the loss, the Lockheed-esque enterprise hires Dick back instead, now as management. In the last quarter of the twentieth century, the California economy followed one rule: Cut or be cut. Get ahead or get left behind. The only way to take advantage was to be a Dick.*

While big cities suffered from the collapse of military Keynesianism after the country's defeat by the Vietnamese national liberation forces, Silicon Valley came into its own. Industrial commodity production faced new competition, especially from Japan and Germany, which implemented state industrial policies from under the free (but pricey) U.S. security umbrella. Faced with the costs of the Cold War arms race and the domestic demand for more social spending,

---

* *Fun with Dick and Jane* is also one of the Paramount films funded by Max Palevsky of Scientific Data Systems fame. The movie features a scene in which the protagonists rob the local Pacific Telephone office while another customer exhorts them to "Shoot out the computors [*sic*] while you're at it."

government debts mounted. In October of 1975, the city of New York nearly defaulted, saved only by the teachers union, which reached into its pension fund.[1] This situation led to what geographer David Harvey calls the "solution of the '70s": the re-empowerment of owners relative to workers after the uprisings at home and abroad via "unemployment and deindustrialization, immigration, offshoring, and all manner of technological and organizational changes (e.g. subcontracting)."[2] Firms and municipalities alike made their numbers fit by reducing their commitments to workers. It was a solution devised by capitalists to the problem of labor, and it was particularly suited to Palo Alto. Once again, the town's fortunes rose counter to the well-being of the country's working class.

Two of the tactics on Harvey's list seem to contradict each other at first: immigration and offshoring. If the region's companies were offshoring production, then why would immigrants be coming to town looking for work? But these are two sides of the same coin. In both cases, firms were taking advantage of regional disparities in the standard of living. Electronics manufacturers chased low wages both abroad, where they built new assembly lines, and at home, where they could swap in even lower-wage migrants for the women who assembled the first generations of silicon chips.

(Recall that electronic component manufacturing is separated into two main operations: fabrication—which includes the various doping, etching, and baking processes, as well as the slicing of individual chips out of the big wafer—and assembly, which involves wiring the tiny components together into a functional circuit and packaging them for sale. The first is performed in "clean rooms" at laboratories, making it resistant to offshoring, while the second takes place on traditional assembly lines. Fabrication is a chemical engineering process involving several categories of hazardous compounds, and because the parts involved are so fragile and are affected by the smallest trace residue of material in the wrong spot, they require continual cleaning with harsh solvents.)

U.S. chip manufacturers kept pace with Japan by recruiting a global workforce of women. Firms offshored the vast majority of fabrication work to Mexico, South Korea, Singapore, Malaysia, and Thailand while filling local manufacturing roles with Vietnamese and Filipina women. Domestically, employers relied on the pseudoscience of racial difference: They believed Asian women were less likely to organize for higher wages than Chicanas, whom they feared were susceptible to the era's revolutionary rhetoric. "Small, foreign, and female" is how one manager described the qualifications for semiconductor production jobs.[3] Immigrant women in the Bay Area from Mexico and increasingly from Central America weren't the right kind of "foreign," and they found themselves relegated to domestic service work, an area in which they had fewer rights. Just as it served growers during the interwar period, formal and informal labor segregation by race, gender, ethnicity, nationality, and immigration status boosted Silicon Valley's profitability and kept the Bay Area growing while the nation's other regional economies fell into recession.[4]

After communist North Vietnam defeated the south and its U.S. allies, hundreds of thousands of Vietnamese refugees fled to California, and immigrants have been following them ever since. Santa Clara County, undergoing a simultaneous boom in electronics production, was a leading receiver of refugees, especially in San Jose. These workers tended to be skilled, politically conservative, and desperate—just the combination that appealed to employers. By 1984, Hewlett-Packard employed 4,000 Vietnamese immigrant workers in low-level jobs.[5] This was something of a consolation prize for electronics executive and Pentagon hand David Packard. No doubt if America had been able to overwhelm the NLF, HP would have offshored some production to the country. But if Packard couldn't win the war, then at least he could get a new low-wage group of employees. It's not a coincidence that the South Bay maintains the country's largest concentration of Vietnamese immigrants to this day: Silicon Valley firms were ready to absorb thousands of refugee workers at the same time and *for the same reason* they were refugees in the first place.* War spending jump-started the civilian electronics industry both by funding R & D and by bombing a new cohort of Asian workers onto the California production lines.

Although the Bay Area was adding manufacturing jobs while they disappeared elsewhere in the country, the electronics industry used significantly fewer production workers than American manufacturing in general did. By

---

* Though the Los Angeles–Long Beach–Anaheim metropolitan area has a larger absolute number of Vietnam-born residents (for similar historical and geographic reasons), at 1.9 percent they are a much smaller part of the population than in smaller San Jose–Sunnyvale–Santa Clara, where they make up over 5 percent of total residents. Laura Harjanto and Jeanne Batalova, "Vietnamese Immigrants in the United States," Migration Policy Institute, October 15, 2021, Table 1, https://www.migrationpolicy.org/article/vietnamese-immigrants-united-states.

the 1970s, mechanization reduced the proportion of production workers in semiconductor employment to less than half, while the relative share of managers, engineers, and marketers increased.[6] Firms adapted a bifurcated labor model, holding manufacturing wages 20 percent below the national average while electronics professionals did significantly better financially than professionals in slower industries did.[7] Again, this was no coincidence: Electronics firms rewarded their managers for controlling labor costs. It seems counterintuitive to pay some workers not to pay other workers, but by using stock options and grants to align professional employees' interest with ownership, firms could provide a paternalistic atmosphere for high-value engineers while keeping the aggregate wage low enough to generate double-digit profits even as prices fell.* Chip makers pursued a similarly bifurcated model for sales, vending monopolized custom setups at high markups and mass-producing other chips so cheaply that competitors couldn't compete. Foreign capital poured into America and into Santa Clara County in particular as investors looked for ways to hedge against inflation, which soared above 10 percent. If any regional sector in the world was likely to stay ahead of a steep inflation curve, it was California's electronics industry.[8]

A bet on Silicon Valley was a bet on the future, and the future after the solution of the '70s meant driving down labor costs. The number of union members as a percentage of American employed workers began falling dramatically in the early 1970s, and Palo Alto was leading the trend. While big industrial cities battled legacy unions, this labor-hostile suburb kept its production wages low by locking organized labor out of its factories. For reasons that recall the agricultural struggles of the 1930s, large unions were not particularly aggressive about organizing the chip industry's low-wage, polyglot workforce of immigrant women, while professional employees were mostly too well rewarded and pretentious about their work to be interested.[9] What organizing there was had to come from the rank and file—it wasn't worth anyone else's time. Or, rather, almost anyone else's. Stanford graduate Amy Newell

---

*   In the 1994 tech industry thriller *Disclosure*, adapted by author Michael Crichton from his novel of the same name, Michael Douglas plays a manufacturing executive at "DigiCom" who, upon learning that he might be out of a job ("You gonna be okay? You want a Prozac?"), bravely reassures the higher-up, "Yeah, no, you don't have to worry about me. I'm a stockholder. Whatever's best for the company."

came by her labor politics honestly, as they say, meaning she inherited them. In the 1940s, her father, Charles Newell, was the business manager for the United Electrical Workers (UE) at the Pittsburgh Westinghouse plant, where he helped lead the left wing of the left-wing union, and her mother, Ruth, organized for the UE at a Sylvania plant.[10] After, in 1953, Charles was named as a member of the Communist Party by notorious FBI spy Matthew Cvetic at the Senate Judiciary Committee hearings into "subversive influence" in the UE, the family moved to Watsonville, California.[11] Amy graduated from Stanford in 1969, having witnessed the militant turn in the campus antiwar movement, after which she enrolled in a doctoral program at SUNY Buffalo. On a visit to her parents in 1972, she saw the semiconductor workforce shaping up and thought she could help them organize. Newell persuaded her boyfriend to drop out of graduate school with her, and the two of them moved to the South Bay to start as "salts"—workers who get jobs with the ulterior motive of unionizing their coworkers. A couple of decades after the UE got run out of Sunnyvale, after Taft-Hartley purged avowed communists from the official labor movement, the Reds were back. Newell agitated from the line at her job with Siliconix, and with other rank-and-file semiconductor workers, she started organizing at the shop level at firms such as National Semiconductor, Siltec, Fairchild, and Semi-Metals.*

Soon after Newell arrived, she spearheaded the UE Electronic Organizing Committee, which built a registered membership of over 500 across a number of fabrication plants ("fabs"), and published a newsletter in English, Spanish, and Tagalog. The committee targeted large plants because, according to Newell, "the capital investment was so large there. They were the big players, and we wanted to go for the heart."[12] The UE national office consulted, but the

---

* Among the few other early salts in the industry was revolutionary organizer and historian in training Roxanne Dunbar (later Dunbar-Ortiz), who met Newell on the line at Siliconix. Dunbar attempted to put her experience in the feminist and Maoist movements— she had joined the Bay Area Revolutionary Union just before the Franklin/Avakian split, siding with the former—to work in the UE campaign, but found UE organizers too committed to a trade-union strategy built by and for white men, one that ignored the immediate needs of the largely immigrant workforce of women, needs like maternity leave, child care, and freedom from sexual harassment. "When I suggested to the union officials that a union program offer the women workers free martial arts training," she writes, "they laughed." Roxanne Dunbar-Ortiz, *Outlaw Woman: A Memoir of the War Years, 1960–1975* (City Lights, 2001), 388.

rank and file were once again mostly on their own. The lack of support from national unions was one of many challenges the South Bay semiconductor labor organizers faced, including a multilingual workforce; an industry that—because it had to rebuild its quickly antiquated systems every decade or so—had a lot of opportunities to relocate production; high employee turnover; and workers who expected to advance on employers' terms within a skyrocketing industry. It was also a bad time to be an American union organizer in general: Between 1970 and 1988 the percentage of California workers represented by unions fell from 36 to 22, a nearly 40 percent drop.[13]

Perhaps the greatest challenge was well-organized employers, who shared information about union efforts among themselves and, under the auspices of the Packard-founded American Electronics Association (AeA, or the Western Electronic Manufacturers Association, before 1977), split the costs of anti-union campaigns, just as the Associated Farmers before them did. The competitors were able to come together after getting spooked by a 1968 strike of 5,000 Bay Area electronics workers across three firms (including Ampex), which lasted a week—the kind of interruption the fast-moving semiconductor industry couldn't afford.[14] Offshoring and the threat of unemployment was a good issue to rally workers around, but it was also the boss's trump card. It's a card the video-game manufacturer Atari played in 1983 after the Glaziers' union neared its goal of an election involving several shops. Rather than face its workers across a collective bargaining table, the company laid off 1,700 people and closed two of its three Silicon Valley factories, moving production to Hong Kong and Taiwan.[15] Unsurprisingly, the Glaziers found it too difficult to organize Atari workers at the remaining domestic line. Despite the efforts of Newell and other rank-and-file workers, the UE's organizing attempts failed repeatedly, as did limited campaigns by other national unions—notably, the Teamsters at Intel. In 1994, scholar AnnaLee Saxenian described the results of the previous couple of decades in her comparative study of Silicon Valley and the Massachusetts tech industry: "There are approximately 200,000 union members in the four-county [Bay Area] region, but virtually none work in high technology industries. No high technology firm has been organized by a labor union in Silicon Valley during the past twenty years, and there have been fewer than a dozen serious attempts."[16] It was a brutal period for workers and a correspondingly excellent one for the men who employed them.

Without many traditional labor allies in the South Bay, organizers took a different tack. Despite the suburban look cultivated by early planners, Silicon Valley was an environmental hazard, with workplace injury rates twice as high as they were in general manufacturing, mostly because of the prevalence of toxic chemicals.[17] As members in an environmental justice coalition with local liberals (including a smattering of homeowners), labor organizers could pursue pro-worker ends without triggering the union alarms at the AeA. The Santa Clara Center for Occupational Safety and Health formed thanks to the efforts of three women: Robin Baker, Amanda Hawes, and Pat Lamborn, only one of whom was a production worker. The group leveraged new nationwide concerns about how pollution was affecting American families to lobby for safer labor practices. Describing the campaign to ban the toxic semiconductor cleaning solvent trichloroethylene, Hawes writes, "Its origin and focus was always on the workplace." The environmental-justice message the group tried to hammer home, in the face of popular stereotypes about hard hats facing off against tree huggers, was that "if hazards faced by workers are not made a priority, we will all suffer the consequences."[18] That was a safer and more compelling angle than "Workers of the world, unite!" in a place where so many workers identified as engineers, homeowners, or parents first. The group and its numerous spin-offs had successes holding semiconductor manufacturers accountable for their environmental impact, but by its nature the organization and its affiliates weren't building worker power as such in California.

U.S. capital was so afraid of unions that the United Auto Workers in Northern California found itself beholden to an unlikely savior: Toyota. Japanese companies had a bad reputation at the time for taking "American jobs" by outcompeting domestic manufacturers. Once again, whites in California resented and envied Japanese efficiency as it rose past American levels. Car manufacturing was a particularly sensitive area: Formerly a symbol of American power, ingenuity, and good middle-class jobs, the industry now came to represent national malaise. In 1982, General Motors closed its beleaguered plant in Fremont, California, which had been leaking workers from its 1978 peak of 6,800 down to 3,000 by the time it closed.[19] Morale was reportedly so bad at the GM plant that one worker recalled, "I couldn't have cared less if somebody had driven a forklift right through a wall just to break the monotony. And sometimes we did."[20] Two years later, in 1984, Toyota made a deal with GM to take on the factory as New United Motors Manufacturing, Inc., or NUMMI. The idea of a Japanese automaker hiring from the UAW flew in the face of conventional beliefs about jobs and international competition, but NUMMI agreed to hire the large majority of its hourly workers from the laid-off GM group, even if they had previously been prone to a little bit of sabotage once in a while.

At first, the NUMMI plant was a global success story. Japanese management techniques improved plant efficiency and output quality enough to restore it to competitive shape; the workers seemed to like it better, too. NUMMI amicably negotiated a contract with the UAW, but production workers also seemed to appreciate the tenets of the cohesive Toyota Production System. The factory grouped workers into teams, reduced the number of job descriptions, and rewarded suggestions from the line. A stated "no-layoffs" policy put everyone at ease, and a doctrine of "continual improvement" invited workers to contribute to increasing efficiency. Compared to the stultifying atmosphere at GM, NUMMI valued workers as thinking people, which turned out to work just fine. It was an ideological leap: NUMMI's production system transcended the dichotomy between standardization and autonomy. Workers at the factory had room to use their brains — as the rebels used to demand — but in the service of uniform production. Business analysts celebrated the solution, which was rare for a unionized project. "Taylorist time-and-motion discipline and formal bureaucratic structures are essential for efficiency and quality in routine operations. But these principles of organizational design need not lead to rigidity and alienation," wrote Paul Adler in his 1993 *Harvard Business Review* case study celebrating the plant. "NUMMI points the way beyond Taylor-as-villain to the design of a truly learning-oriented bureaucracy."* GM took the lesson, adopting its own "Global Manufacturing System" cribbed from the Toyota system.[21] At the hinge of East and West, the Bay Area could perhaps open the door on a new age of unionized American manufacturing after all.

Not so. GM pulled out of NUMMI as part of its bankruptcy restructuring after the 2008 financial crisis, and Toyota shut it down in 2010. "What we're dealing with here is the kind of corporate treachery toward workers and their

---

* Frederick Winslow Taylor is credited with bringing scientific management to the organization of industrial production, around the turn of the twentieth century. Adler, "Time-and-Motion Regained."

local communities that has ruined countless lives over the past several decades and completely undermined the long-term prospects of the economy," wrote *New York Times* columnist Bob Herbert of the company's decision.* But it wasn't the Bay Area's economy that was in trouble.

The End of the '70s

The official labor movement—the workers led by the AFL-CIO coalition as well as whatever was left of the more radical trade-union currents—was back-footed by the shift of manufacturing growth into the virulently anti-union high-tech sector. There were no doubt strategic mistakes involved, but the official movement was contending with difficult historical circumstances. It was riven by the same internal contradictions that made California's workers so difficult to organize over the course of the previous century. But what happened to the radical left-wingers?

In cultural accounts, the curdling of the radical 1960s is associated with two murderous events. First was the 1969 Altamont concert, headlined by the Rolling Stones (and set to feature a number of local California bands, including Palo Alto's Grateful Dead), at which the semi-deputized Hells Angels motorcycle gang ruined the show and stabbed a man named Meredith Hunter to death.† That was in December, months after a group led by singer-songwriter Charles Manson committed a dramatic spree of killings in Los Angeles. Though the Black Panthers played an important role in their confused cosmology, the Manson Family, unlike the Symbionese Liberation Army, didn't have even a distant connection to the left. The Altamont crew was a little closer, associated with the San Francisco anarchist Diggers, but they were a cultural and mutual-aid group rather than a self-identified revolutionary organization. By connecting these gruesome and unfortunate incidents to the Third World solidarity movement, popular historians are somewhat misleading. America's left-wing radicals were in the middle of their work at the

---

* Bob Herbert, "Workers Crushed by Toyota," *New York Times*, March 15, 2010. The next year, Herbert, his attention on U.S. inequality and the plight of the working class out of step with the prevailing mood of liberal elites during the Obama years, was also out at the *Times*. "Corporate treachery toward workers," indeed!

† The Dead declined to take the stage after seeing members of their road crew assaulted, a wise choice in retrospect.

time, as you've seen, and their relationship with the "counterculture" was complicated at best. The pat narrative that left-wing radicalism leads to a break with reality and the emergence of evil forces is weak for a number of reasons, including the fact that the counterculture was always violent and masculinist in practice. Its deterioration narrative is largely overstated, as is its connection to radical politics.* Lots of people liked the Stones.[22]

The end of the 1970s has more to teach us about the left's break than the violence of 1969 does. I've already covered how California's insurrectionary tendencies came to a close, but what of the groups who split and opted for base-building strategies? The Revolutionary Union persisted without the Franklin faction, doubling down on its appeal to relatively conservative white workers. The organization reconstituted itself as the Revolutionary Communist Party (RCP) in 1975 and infiltrated Vietnam Veterans Against the War. But tailoring its work to its conception of the white industrial working class led the RCP into reactionary positions against gays, women, and racial minorities, whose movements they derided as bourgeois distractions. The group's most shameful moment came during the Boston busing crisis in the mid-1970s. Instead of siding with the black liberation movement and the left to defend school integration, the RCP called for the working class to unite and *defeat* busing as a divisive attack. According to one account, during a 1977 fight to protect a working-class San Francisco residential hotel from redevelopment—a watershed moment in Asian-American coalition politics that I mentioned earlier— RCP members harangued supportive gay activists, telling them to "go back to Castro Street."[23] Since then, under "Chairman Bob" Avakian, the RCP has become a marginal personality cult that operates through opportunistic formations such as Refuse Fascism. If shooting at white supremacy didn't fix the problem, neither did telling everyone to ignore it.

One notable left-wing strand of 1970s Bay Area Maoism took a different and somewhat surprising cultural turn in the 1980s. Tim Yohannan was part of the Bay Area Revolutionary Union scene in the early '70s, though not a particularly active participant, and he soon focused his attention on a community radio show called *Maximum Rocknroll*, devoted to the emerging genre of DIY

---

* The involvement of black American entertainers in radical politics is correspondingly underrated. Mick Jagger didn't offer to pay Angela Davis's bail, Aretha Franklin did.

punk music. Promoting and being promoted by the extremely controversial Bay Area band the Dead Kennedys, *Maximum Rocknroll* expanded to become the original punk 'zine and, in 1986, a concert space in Berkeley. The Gilman Street venue catered to the "misfits among misfits," writes music historian Dan Ozzi—"kids who weren't old enough to get into shows at bars and weren't tough enough to survive shows at violent punk venues."[24] Course-correcting a culture that was increasingly violent and masculinist, Gilman Street was known for its list of rules, written on the wall.

NO RACISM

NO SEXISM

NO HOMOPHOBIA

NO ALCOHOL

NO DRUGS

NO FIGHTING

NO STAGEDIVING

Tim Yo, as he was called, brought the rigid discipline of "democratic centralism" to a scene in which that attitude seemed counter to the prevailing ethos. But *Maximum Rocknroll* did as much as any single band did to define that ethos, and Tim Yo took that responsibility seriously. For him, punk was a left-wing revolutionary political vehicle, and he refused to feature or promote bands that were bigoted or corporate in any way.[25] This led to many accusations of tyranny, and he was a very polarizing figure. But though some bands—including Green Day, a product of the East Bay punk milieu—spit on his grave in the years after he died, most interviewees now credit him with gluing the scene together and making space for kids who found themselves outcast in Reagan's California.*

If you were a radical punk band and you were in an emergency—a Venn

---

* Tim Yo lives on as the subject of a bunch of songs, from the still-mad "Platypus" by Green Day ("And now your time is up / It brings me pleasure just to know you're going to die"—recorded while he was dying of cancer), the cleverly needling "I'm Telling Tim" by NOFX ("You better watch out you better not cry / You better put out records DIY"), to the folk-heroic "Timmy Yo" by Millions of Dead Cops ("He labeled himself / A musical commie / When in fact he was acting like / Everyone's mommy / Gave all them kids / A place to go / And unheard of bands / Somewhere to show"), and more.

diagram that tends toward the circular — Tim Yo was the guy to call, because
he channeled his increasing 'zine revenue back into the scene, sending FedEx
envelopes stuffed full of cash wherever they were needed. *MRR* became the
model for the subculture, and as one looks through its early issues, its debt
to the Bay Area radical intellectual scene is obvious. Issue 2 features a one-
page intelligence report on the local and worldwide activities of the secretive Bechtel Corporation opposite a report-back on liberation movements in
Europe and a table of data on political violence in El Salvador. The next spread
is an interview with the band Hüsker Dü.[26] *MRR* linked punks across the
country and even across borders. In addition to old-fashioned internationalism, Tim Yo brought a belief in armed self-defense to the scene; participants
credit him with passing out the baseball bats the first time Bay Area punks
bashed back against skinhead Nazis determined to infiltrate their safe space.[27]
Besides Green Day — banned at first (under the name Sweet Children) by Tim
Yo for being insufficiently punk — the milieu produced bands like Operation
Ivy, Jawbreakers, Rancid, NOFX, AFI, and Pansy Division. Hardcore music
didn't bring on the revolution, as the Bay's punk tyrant hoped, but the scene
he structured was an important reservoir for disillusioned white kids, the same
demographic courted by neo-Nazis and Reaganites. Punk was a helluva lot
better than the conclusions the mainline of the RCP came to, and even if a
lot of the adults who were in Tim Yo's child army have some less-than-sweet
memories, the story troubles a just-so narrative about left-wing hierarchy's
inexorable slide into murderous violence.*

And besides, eschewing the heat of radicalism for an establishment suit was
no guarantee against getting burned. Allard Lowenstein spent his life trying
to cool down the hard-liners and bring them into the left wing of liberalism.
When last we left him, he found himself disinvited from the southern movement for a combination of white chauvinism, red-baiting, sketchy relationships
with powerful people, and generally being a dick. He betrayed the movement
at the Atlantic City DNC, where the SNCC-led organizers were left at the

---

* As the noted exception to the Gilman Street "no fighting" rule, Dead Kennedys frontman
Jello Biafra might disagree. He was beaten up in the pit in 1994 after demanding the ID
of an aggressive "slam-dancer" known as Creton, who had allegedly crashed into the Bay
Area punk icon, breaking his leg. Biafra told *Rolling Stone* that a gang yelled, "Sellout rock
star, kick him," while they kicked him. Michael Goldberg, "Jello Biafra Attacked," *Rolling
Stone*, July 14, 1994.

altar of democracy; he returned to his base milieu and counseled a compromise with the segregationists. But not all the people Lowenstein brought into the movement left with him. Among the most prominent remainders was Dennis Sweeney, a likable Stanford scholarship student from Oregon with a hard family life. Lowenstein was a mentor to Sweeney from his administrative role at the school, politicizing the directionless youth. Sweeney was one of the first people he recruited to go to the South. There Sweeney volunteered for the toughest assignment, in McComb, Mississippi, where he survived arrest and a dynamite attack.

One of the few white college volunteers who grew up poor, Sweeney earned the respect of and built a genuine rapport with black organizers in a way that Lowenstein did not. But Lowenstein had an agenda as well, one that involved his handpicked crew. Another volunteer, a dentist, fixed Sweeney's teeth, prettying him up for the cameras and the future. But Sweeney dropped out of Stanford to return to Mississippi, and even broke with his mentor to stay with the movement. Later he joined the Resistance campaign with his former classmate David Harris and lived in a Palo Alto–area commune and dropped acid and drove motorcycles. But Sweeney broke with Harris, too, finding Harris's decision to surrender himself for prison rather than go underground to avoid the draft self-indulgent and indicative of a martyrdom complex. Sweeney had already dodged martyrdom a couple of times in his young life, and he didn't see any strategy in it per se. Instead, he flirted with more radical elements on campus and seems to have participated in an arson attack on an ROTC boathouse. But he was uncomfortable with the tactic. After all the campus peace groups denounced the action, he joined a traveling rock group and left the West Coast in 1968.

A 1967 article in *Ramparts* revealed Central Intelligence Agency support for the National Student Association, seeming to confirm the rumors about Lowenstein's connections to the government.[28] In the summer of 1965, Lowenstein tried to recruit Sweeney into a delegation to the World Youth Festival in Algeria, about as obvious a CIA pass as you could get. Sweeney found the request revolting, just as he found Lowenstein's attitude toward SNCC after its black nationalist turn. Like a lot of liberals, Lowenstein called SNCC racist, infuriating Sweeney. Increasingly isolated, Sweeney left the scene, finding work as a carpenter. But he was haunted by voices, one voice in particular: Al

Lowenstein's. He became convinced that his former mentor and friend was tormenting him and trying to have him killed — that Lowenstein was transmitting his voice into his head via CIA implants in his bridgework, the work done at Al's behest by the volunteer dentist. In 1969, Lowenstein got elected to Congress from New York, serving one term before being redistricted out. He spent the next decade working on liberal strategy in and around the government, and losing close races for Congress in an effort to return to elected office. Dennis Sweeney filed down his teeth with a hacksaw.

Most of the people who served with Sweeney in SNCC and know what he and others went through were not surprised that his life took a sad turn. His ex-wife and fellow SNCC worker, Mary King, writes in her memoir that she knew at least four others from the campaign who developed similar psychoses and mentions the concussion Sweeney suffered as a result of the 1964 McComb freedom house bombing.[29] A Harvard volunteer named Greg Craig recalled that when he met Sweeney, in 1965, "he just seemed to be like the first person back from Dachau, not able to talk about it, his very demeanor bearing witness to the atrocities that he had seen."[30] When he didn't talk about Lowenstein or the CIA or his teeth, Sweeney was lucid, but the voice wouldn't go away. He was convinced he had to make a deal, that Lowenstein could make it stop if he could just persuade him to. Stanford friends raised money to send Sweeney to a clinic in Connecticut, but it didn't work. In 1973, he wrote a somewhat rambling but not totally incoherent letter to a couple of leading student radicals asking for advice. Trying to explain his situation and why he was being targeted, he seems to suggest and then rule out his brief foray into arson, before coming to what he believes is the real source of his suffering: "More likely, I think, is that my whole life since early childhood is tangled into a kind of self-aborted preparation for social democratic leadership, where the lines of responsibility for thought and action are very muddy. Unwilling to live my life on the terms that have been revealed recently, that is as a component in a vast communication system, I think I am simply being pressured to leave the country."[31] He wasn't wrong there, but he had nowhere to go. Sweeney was in anguish, alone, for years. In a confusing world where resignation offered one of few paths to clarity, there was a nobility in his struggle not to stab his friends in the back and turn over his life to the new liberals. Instead, in the spring of 1980, Dennis Sweeney went to Al Lowenstein's office in Manhattan and shot him to death.

For liberals, the assassination was a cruel marker of the end of an era: one more in a cohort of great potential leaders, taken in violence. Lowenstein was a close adviser to Bobby Kennedy, and like others he consciously modeled himself on the martyred brothers. If his mentees who spent their careers in the Democratic Party—such as longtime legislators Joe Lieberman and Barney Frank—are any indication, who knows how far Lowenstein could have gone?* It was a tragic waste, a final lesson about misguided radicals. But for the radicals themselves, it was something a little closer to "Chickens come home to roost," as Malcolm X famously said regarding JFK. Rejecting the *Washington Post*'s obituary frame, which suggested that some left-wing children of the 1960s and '70s became "ordinary people with special memories" while others "never truly reconciled ideas and reality," an article in the *Workers Vanguard* announced, "No Tears for Allard Lowenstein!" The unsigned editorial questioned what so many Americans have come to take for granted:

> Were the choices really adjustment to capitalism's decaying racist status quo or madness? Were those others who refused to become 'ordinary people,' dirt farmers or Hare Krishnas destined to become mad assassins?
>
> No, the political activism of the 1960s did not merely evolve into the '70s as youthful idealism into the "reality" of adulthood. There was a political fight. Sides were taken and there were victories and defeats.[32]

There was a political fight. Sides were taken and there were victories and defeats. That's as good a summary as I've found.

White Riot

The solution of the '70s wouldn't have been possible in California without a few carrots in the pile of sticks, at least for white settlers. Asset ownership in the form of appreciating houses and stocks was an alternative path to wealth, and

---

* Greg Craig, the volunteer who saw in Dennis Sweeney a kind of traumatized heroic ideal, went on to law school with Bill and Hillary Clinton. A lawyer by trade, he served in the Clinton White House, including as the director of the president's impeachment defense. Later, he served as White House counsel for President Obama, where he was seen as botching the effort to close the Guantanamo Bay torture prison by pushing too hard. No matter how much he compromised, it was never enough. So much for the inside strategy.

coming to own land is what settlers are good at. White working-class home-owners began to identify as white and homeowners more than as members of the working class, and not without reason. If their human capital was depre-ciating rapidly, their home values jumped. In Santa Clara County, the house price index doubled two and a half times between 1975 and 1990.[33] With home ownership also came guaranteed places in the California public school system, where the professional workers of the future (with their in-the-car wages) were trained. America's society kept bifurcating, and without a powerful labor move-ment to push back, people were left trying to navigate their own families to the correct side. In that environment, the continued assimilation of migrant groups presented a pressing threat to white homeowners. They feared that non-whites would undermine home values by moving nearby and that their children would take advantage of public programs funded by white tax dollars and end up competing with white children for future advantages. Equalizing opportu-nity sounds nice in theory, but in practice the attack on wages meant there was less of them to go around. For white settlers, equality was a step down.

In 1963, the California legislature passed the Rumford Fair Housing Act, propelled both by the moral suasion of the movement for black freedom and a fear that segregated black slums could erupt into violence. The law banned restrictive covenants, by which sellers excluded nonwhite potential buyers. This was unappealing to a large number of white homeowners, but it was intol-erable to real estate agents. The industry used segregation to maintain high property values, both in exclusive white neighborhoods, where skin privilege pooled and consolidated, and in *excluded* nonwhite neighborhoods, where would-be owners were stuck paying more for less and couldn't count on the same appreciation. An individual seller might have been able to get as much or more money for a house from a nonwhite buyer—undermining the claim that minority owners sunk prices—but by cooperating on these boundaries, agents cashed in on the whiteness cartel. Fair housing, they worried, meant cheaper houses. In March of 1964, the directors of the California Real Estate Associa-tion (CREA) met at Palo Alto's fanciest hotel—the Cabana—and announced their intention to fight fair housing on the grassroots level, through the initia-tive process. The NAACP and CORE organized an orderly protest of over 500 people outside the hotel, on El Camino.[34] Hotel security had a harder time the next summer, when the Beatles stayed there midmania.

Proposition 14, as the pro-segregation plan appeared on the ballot, framed the question in terms of homeowners' rights to sell their houses to whomever they choose. In reality, it freed up the CREA to continue setting segregation standards across the state. Though the language was technically race-neutral, it was a clear rallying cry for national hate organizations such as the White Citizens' Councils and the John Birch Society, which followed well-trodden racist paths to the West Coast. The initiative proposed to alter the California state constitution in a way that would not only negate the Rumford act but also prevent any state legislature or even *locality* from taking any similar action in the future. It banned fair housing everywhere in California, forever. The referendum was racism on the ballot, pro or con, plain and simple. It passed, and by a large margin. Even Santa Clara County, with its large nonwhite working-class population of San Jose, approved Proposition 14. The Rumford act went into effect in the summer of 1963, and by the election of 1964 the ultra-right California real estate community—historian Robert O. Self describes the CREA as "a more consistent reservoir of conservative politics in 1960s California than the Republican Party" and "the principal force in the state opposing liberal or social democratic claims on private property"—had run a successful campaign to permanently override the legislature.[35] It was a magnificent example of property holders organizing for rapid-response collective self-defense at the state level, and it became the model for reactionary politics into the present. Call it the white man's veto.

Courts negated Proposition 14 within a couple of years, but the proposition system turned into a standard tool of the radical right in California, with capitalists mustering white voters into the civic vigilantism that had been part of western settlement since Leland Stanford was paying militias to hunt Indians. Whiteness intertwined with home values in new ways in the last quarter of the twentieth century, but the California dream was always about land speculation premised on racial exclusion and domination. This relatively populist mode of wealth accumulation provided a safety valve for corporations as they competed to boost profits by reducing their commitments to society. Expanding suburbs bid down their business tax rates to lure industrial jobs, and the state's tax burden—both in the rapidly growing 'burbs and in the urban districts that capital abandoned with equal and opposite speed—shifted to individuals. For some homeowners this was a perfect storm: The state assessed their homes at skyrocketing prices while sales and income tax rates went up, too, all while high inflation undermined their spending power. Elderly homeowners who faced the prospect of being taxed out as their property assessments raced ahead of their fixed incomes were particularly sympathetic. On the left, organizers called for corporations to pay their fair share, but the right had an alternative solution: No one should. In 1978, California passed Proposition 13 by almost exactly the same margin as it passed the defunct Prop 14. Proposition 13 changed the property tax system, fixing assessments at 1976 levels (plus 2 percent a year for inflation, max) until a property is sold and capping the tax at 1 percent of that property's value. Like the discussion surrounding Prop 14, the rhetoric around Prop 13 framed the issue in terms of fairness for individual homeowners, but the benefits disproportionately accrued to organized capitalists. Over 60 percent of the relief mandated by Prop 13 went to landlords and corporations. In Fremont, which voted pro at a three-to-one margin, the rule cut GM's annual local tax bill for its factory from $3.8 to $1.1 million, saving millions that no longer flowed into public services.[36]

With civic vigilantism, California's white homeowners joined with organized capital to defeat the global working-class uprising that shaped the decade between 1965 and '75. There was a certain amount of trickery and salesmanship by the business community involved, but the homeowners got their votes' worth. As historian Mike Davis writes, "Proposition 13's explicit promise to roll back assessments and let homeowners pocket their capital gains was accompanied, as well, by an implicit promise to halt the threatening encroachment of inner-city populations on suburbia."[37] These California homeowners were on the vanguard of an international shift in value creation, from the wage-price inflation that characterized the previous period to asset appreciation. Wages were down; consumer prices were down; but houses? Houses were up.

With this new value shielded from taxation by Prop 13, whatever social democratic ambitions existed in the state withered fundless on the vine. The collective pot evaporated, and public services deteriorated as homeowners walled themselves off in the suburbs. Civic vigilantes worked to make sure white discontentment expressed itself along racial and property lines rather than as a working-class demand. Part of the U.S. reprisal against the global working class in the 1960s and '70s was the criminalization of Chicano labor.

As a portion of federal immigration apprehensions, Mexicans increased from half in 1965 to 94 percent in 1985, cementing an identification between the two in the Anglo popular imagination.[38] As asset holders increased their wealth, the demand for casual labor increased—in contracting, landscaping, cleaning, and other domestic tasks. These workers could be paid in cash off the books—another way to choke off taxes—and with immigration authorities on the hunt, they had little recourse in the event of mistreatment.* As Mexican workers came into increased contact with Anglos who didn't depend on their agro-industrial labor, white hate attacks increased and vigilantes pushed the state to militarize the border.[39]

While the regular Anglo vigilantes attacked Mexicans with fists and rifles, the civic vigilantes kept using the law. In 1986, voters passed Proposition 63, an official designation of English as the state language, a transparent attempt to marginalize Spanish speakers in particular by suggesting that they aren't entitled to public accommodation. Proposition 187, in 1994, made the implication explicit, requiring the state to maintain a citizenship database so that residents without valid documentation could be prevented from accessing public benefits at the point of service—specifically, in schools and emergency rooms. It was an assault on the most vulnerable—children, the sick, the wounded—denying them membership in society, never mind a road to assimilation. It passed, and again the courts had to rein in the state's Anglo population, whose racism was too extreme even by U.S. standards.

Throughout the twentieth century's fourth quarter, these reactionary referenda frightened Democrats, who were loath to oppose the state's richest supermajority. Suburbanites tinkered with tax rates and expenditures to isolate the poor and cut off their access to public dollars. As geographer Ruth Wilson Gilmore points out, California's voters were perfectly happy to raise taxes during the late 1970s and throughout the '80s, just as long as the money was staying inside their segregated communities.[40] With Prop 13 making houses easier to own and harder to buy, homeowners could easily perpetuate de facto

---

* The employment of off-the-books domestic labor became so prevalent among professional American families in this era that when new president Bill Clinton went to appoint the country's first woman attorney general, his first two choices withdrew from consideration after both were revealed to have relied on undocumented workers to care for their young children. The media called it Nannygate.

residential segregation, which in turn allowed them to use community as a proxy for race-caste, and vice versa. Education improved for the rich and got worse for the poor. The state's child poverty rate climbed. Bifurcation was an all-purpose solution to the crisis of the 1970s, and that meant a defeat of communism at home and abroad, a defeat of the New Deal social democratic program, a defeat of the civil rights movement, and a defeat of organized labor in general. To California's organized capitalists and their leadership faction in Herbert Hoover's Bohemian Grove, all those were always one and the same anyway.

Palo Alto in particular never believed in the New Deal vision; bifurcation built the town. The whole world invested in the Silicon Valley economy and the profit promise of inequality, and the value of both the land and the companies located on it sped skyward. The remnants of this process were explosive: a nonwhite working class sliding down the hill of generational progress, stuck in depopulating cities with fewer good jobs and declining public services. Wages stagnated for those without college degrees. Organized labor in the full range of its expressions, from communist to liberal, was defeated. But what happens to the defeated? The specter of crime haunted the suburbs, the only way homeowners could acknowledge that the booming economy was throwing off manufacturing jobs, even in electronics. Unemployment and underemployment meant more workers were forced out of the legal job market, through the new holes in the safety net, and into the streets. As the Immigration and Naturalization Service and the border vigilantes knew, criminalized labor was vulnerable labor. Black Americans took their rights by force in the Civil War, but slavery lived on in the Constitution, behind the bars in the country's prisons and jails. As part of what Mike Davis describes as "the deterioration in the labor-market position of young Black men" during this period, the state criminalized its urban population writ large, placing a rapidly increasing number of black people beyond the protections of the Thirteenth Amendment.[41] Crime was a growth industry, and California's politicians found a way to take advantage, replacing rural manufacturing work with new jobs building and guarding the cages. California embarked on "the biggest prison construction project in the history of the world."[42] The state paid one part of the working class to lock up the other, a classic move.

Walls went up: at the border, around the jails, and around new elite gated suburbs. California's apartheid strategy succeeded in steering the state (as a financial aggregate) through the recession rapids and into the tranquil postindustrial lagoon that Palo Alto's founding engineers dreamed of once upon a time. Even as Cold War defense spending came down to earth, Stanford and its environs nabbed a lion's share. But more important, Silicon Valley was the regional economy that made the strongest jump from defense dependency to commercial independence. Organized capital's Palo Alto faction bet big against communism and social democracy's Popular Front, and though Hoover didn't—realistically, couldn't—live to see his final triumph over the New Deal, it's his vision that won out—over the moderate wing of the GOP, the Democrats, the country as a whole, and history's twentieth century.

Hoover's Return

Though the actors were heavily constrained, it still took some thinking and planning to bifurcate California to the core the way capitalists and property owners did during the twentieth century's closing decades. Organized capital had to find a way, in theory and in practice, to reconcile the expansion of the world's enfranchised population as a result of the previous period's liberation struggles with a fixed system of arbitrary inequality. If the American masses voted themselves a greater share of the domestic product through social democracy, and if the Third World threw off its chains and reappropriated its natural resources, then investors would find themselves cornered, boxed out from paths to profitable growth. In a cutthroat contest with international communism, organized capital couldn't risk those kinds of stumbles lest the dominoes all fall down. The Hooverites likely overestimated the danger they faced, but at the same time the demographic threat was genuine: By definition, Anglo-American domination couldn't survive in a world where everyone was equal. The supposedly natural pigmentocracy threatened to crumble, which would reveal it to have been, in retrospect, unnatural, merely imposed. As a bastion of American anticommunism, it was Palo Alto's job to rediscover and refound inequality.

While Eisenhower Republicans imagined a Pax Americana anchored in rising living standards for a broad swath of citizens, the Hoover faction saw the existential threat on the horizon. Though he was out of step with some national trends, Hoover spent the years before his death (in 1964, at the age of ninety) securing a space at Stanford for a counterstrike. He transformed the collection-minded Hoover Library into the political force of the Hoover Institution, its purpose "by its research and publications, to demonstrate the evils of the doctrines of Karl Marx whether Communism, Socialism, economic materialism, or atheism—thus, to protect the American way of life from such ideologies, their conspiracies, and to reaffirm the validity of the American system."[43] The institution's tower loomed phallic over the town, attracting right-wing thinkers and donors to the university, spewing anti-collectivist theory across the nation for many years to come. But though Hoover's last erection was a beacon for right-wing thought on campus, there was plenty to go around. In the fourth quarter, Stanford helped forge the three talons of the ideological grappling hook that neo-Hooverites used to scale the state: genetics, demographics, and property rights.

After his failed run at the semiconductor industry, William Shockley was left with his intellectual reputation, if not his business reputation, intact. A Nobel Prize was a Nobel Prize, and he'd played the media well enough to retain credit for the semiconductor and Silicon Valley. The logical landing place for the physicist was Stanford, where his mother had studied and his father had taught and where the world's most brilliant minds were always welcome. The Ampex Foundation donated money for the Alexander M. Poniatoff Professorship of Engineering Science, where, beginning in 1963, Shockley could sit and figure out what he wanted to do with the rest of his life.[44] The inventor moved on campus to the beautiful and technically unownable "faculty ghetto" and even joined the Bohemian Club. It's easy to imagine him fitting in there out by the water among the conspiring masters of the universe; maybe it's the only place the homeschooled hyper-elitist could. As for his work, he began by designing a system to teach thinking—which is to say, thinking like him—and he set up a program to teach it at Wilbur Junior High in Palo Alto, for which he received a $100,000 federal grant.[45] (The school, which I attended, is now known as Jane Lathrop Stanford Middle School, or JLS.) But Shockley quickly focused his attention elsewhere: the genetics of intelligence.

In 1965, Shockley gave a wide-ranging interview to *U.S. News & World Report* in which he posed a whole lot of questions about the "quality of the population," banging the gong for a new round of eugenics discourse.

Shockley's words could have been coming straight from Lewis Terman ("If that woman can produce 17 children in our society, none of whom will be eliminated by survival of the fittest, she and others like her will be multiplying at an enormously faster rate than more intelligent people do") and David Starr Jordan ("We live in such an abundant welfare state that the forces which, in the past, led to the evolution and development of man are playing a little role").[46] He was not a geneticist, but as a reputed scientist, Shockley claimed to be—and was presented as being—in a good place to ask important, taboo-breaking questions. Asked to what extent heredity may be responsible for "the high incidence of Negroes on crime and relief rolls," Shockley lamented, "We lack proper scientific investigations, possibly because nobody wants to raise the question for fear of being called a racist."[47] His implication was that genes, when we found a way to correctly interpret their language, would explain the dominant conventional wisdom with regard to the supposed order of the races.

Biologist Joseph L. Graves describes Shockley as probably the period's "most outspoken scientist on the danger of dysgenesis," always a competitive event in the United States.[48] Shockley availed himself of every media opportunity his Nobel Prize could offer, wasting none of it when it came to casting aspersions on the scientific basis of racial equality. In 1970, he testified against school integration in the House of Representatives, telling the Subcommittee on Education that "[t]here exists between the white and black races a well known and often measured difference in learning skills," a difference that was "of a hereditary character which no change in school environment can overcome."[49] Shockley knew how to phrase racism in neutral scientific argot while offering ludicrous proposals—such as a controlled study of the cross-racial adoption of black babies into (white) Jewish homes and a bank of genius sperm for use in the event of nuclear catastrophe—and the mainstream media lapped it up, handing him progressively bigger megaphones from which to blare his white-power noise.

People who don't know the whole history of Terman and the IQ tests might think it a strange deviation for the physicist, but Shockley began his career weighing lives for the Pentagon, and then he did something similar for Fairchild. The man was obsessed with comparative intelligence his entire life, and surfing the early swells of the backlash he saw coming, he appointed himself a scientific spokesman for the white race. For the rest of his years he used whatever attention his formidable efforts could attract to allege the scientific inferiority of nonwhite people.

Whatever the university's role was in forming these ideas in young Shockley in the first place, Stanford hired him in 1963 to be a physicist (or whatever), not a professional racist. Student protests from Venceremos and the ad hoc Third World Coalition Against Shockley disrupted his classes and put a public microscope on his theories. Pushed by radicals, the administration decided he couldn't teach race science, even as a no-credit elective. Shockley found a smart solution, aimed at one of the school's soft spots. As long as he could attract outside money for his "genetics" work, the university had to let him continue or be charged as censors, violating the academic freedom of another one of its distinguished professors. He applied for money from eugenics organizations and rich enthusiasts across the country and met with success, raising tens of thousands of dollars from the jump, including recurring grants from the eugenicist Pioneer Fund, which was growing rapidly. Right after purging Bruce Franklin, Stanford's administration affirmed that if Shockley could bring home the bacon, he could cook it however he liked. Shockley's association with the university was invaluable, not only because it lent him stature and a mailing address. As Shockley's biographer Joel N. Shurkin notes, the Stanford University News Service worked diligently to promote the professor in the media, which is where he spent most of his time after 1970.[50] In terms of his white-power agenda, however, it was his proximity to other scholars that proved most important.

In 1966, the educational psychologist Arthur Jensen came down from his professorship at UC Berkeley to spend a year at Stanford's Center for Advanced Study in the Behavioral Sciences, the Ford Foundation project that kicked off in 1954 as part of the revenue-inspired militarization of the school's social science faculties under Frederick Terman (the same center that campus militants later burned down, in 1970).[51] The relatively early-career Jensen had received his PhD from Columbia ten years previously, and he was at Stanford working on the question of differences in children's educational achievement—a question close to the school's heart as well as Shockley's. When Jensen heard that the Nobel Prize winner wanted to meet he was excited, as most academics would be. After Shockley in his gruff way determined that Jensen was intelligent enough to be worth his time, he set about winning over the junior scholar. Jensen was inclined to attribute nonwhite students' lower scores to their social exclusion, but Shockley convinced him that IQ was something you either had or you didn't, and some races tended to have more of it than others. There's no zealot like a convert, they say, and Jensen turned out to be a more effective advocate for race science than the boiling-over crackpot Shockley ever was. Stanford's focus on financial efficiency left the school community open to co-option by outside parties with their own agendas, such as the Ford Foundation and the Pioneer Fund.

Jensen's 1969 piece for the *Harvard Educational Review* summarized the change in attitude the author underwent at Stanford. It was the longest article in the journal's history, filling pages 1–123, and it was a bombshell, propelling "Jensenism" into mainstream American politics. Tasked with addressing the failure of American schools, after formal desegregation, to educate black and white students up to the same test scores, Jensen lays down his cards in the first sentence: "Compensatory education has been tried," he writes, "and it apparently has failed."[52] The paper is a kind of common ancestor of contemporary varieties of American race science, relying on a mishmash of pseudoscience and appeals to racist "common sense." "When bridges do not stand, when aircraft do not fly, when machines do not work... one begins to question the basic assumptions, principles, theories, and hypotheses that guide one's efforts. Is it time to follow suit in education?" he asks.[53] For Jensen and Shockley, Occam's razor said black people were inferior to white people, and denying that was a denial of science. It was an idea whose time had come in the white backlash to the Watts rebellion and the wider urban crisis as well as in the segregated fight for scarce tax dollars. The two men were certainly aware of the political implications of their ideas, and so was everyone else. A 1970 *Life* magazine profile of the duo outlined the stakes in clear terms:

> Incredible as it may seem, in a country littered with the physical and moral debris of hundreds of ghetto riots, Jensen is in effect saying that, if his studies could only show blacks that their lower IQ scores are a product of genetics, they would stop complaining about imagined insults or alleged discrimination—or at least that they should. "I don't see why people should be disturbed by unequal representations of different groups in different occupations—or educationally, *if* it should be found that there are real differences," Jensen says.[54]

Jensen, of course, was claiming to have established just those differences. In some ways the new iteration was more flexible than previous race science gambits. Using population-level probabilistic correlations allowed for the existence of black individuals who were just as gifted as any white individual—a hard idea to contest in a world that bulged to contain Paul Robeson, to cite just one dramatic example—while offering *tendencies* that aligned the races according to dominant conventional beliefs, yielding the infamous overlapping bell curves of racial intelligence. DNA offered a place in the body where racists could find racial hierarchy, a code they could unwind to verify their prejudices and justify their advantages. If equality wasn't taking then it had to be unnatural, at least at the population level.

This argument delighted conservatives. Representative John Rarick, a white supremacist anticommunist Democrat from Louisiana, approvingly read articles about Jensen into the Congressional Record within months of the *Harvard* publication. By 1970, Jensenism was the talk of a Nixon cabinet meeting. According to Daniel Patrick Moynihan, someone asked "What about Jensen?" As the room's expert on the "Negro problem" and a social constructionist, Moynihan gave the strongest indictment of this new attack on black people that his white liberalism could muster: "The President asked me if I knew anything about it and I briefed the Cabinet: who Jensen is, what he said, the essentials: that it was merely a hypothesis, that in fact we have no direct knowledge of a genetic basis for intelligence, only inferential knowledge, that nobody knows what a 'smart gene' looks like, that Dr. Jensen is a thoroughly respectable man, that he is in no sense a racist—but that it is merely a *hypothesis*."[55] He doesn't mention what "What about Jensen?" was a response *to*, but in a larger sense we know: It was the question of black equality.* In the country's highest office, at the highest level of policy discussion, one *hypothesis* regarding black people's equality no one was prepared to rule out was that, as a question of science, they weren't.

---

* In an interview, Jensen agreed with a "Jensenism" defined by three tenets (which he claimed were empirically derived): "(1) the failure of compensatory education, (2) the evidence for a genetic basis to IQ, and (3) the likelihood of some genetic component to the Black-White IQ difference." Jensen was a racist—a professional one, at that—and Moynihan's statement to the contrary revealed that liberals of his ilk were mentally and rhetorically unprepared to contest the argument. Arthur Robert Jensen and Frank Miele, *Intelligence, Race, and Genetics: Conversations with Arthur R. Jensen* (Westview Press, 2002), 39.

Shockley and Jensen waged a successful "war of position" for racist ideas, which included a fight within the country's scientific establishment. Shockley in particular maneuvered for stage time at the many august venues to which he as a Nobel laureate had access. Eventually he wore down the National Academy of Sciences, and the organization created a committee to study Shockley's proposal for an endorsement of eugenics research. It was a chance for the academy to announce a refutation of racialism, but Shockley got lucky: The committee's head was Kingsley Davis, a Berkeley sociologist—one of the strongest believers in the use of inequality and a neo-Hooverite of the highest rank.

Like most other scientists, Davis was skeptical about a unitary IQ with a simple genetic explanation, but the committee's report was positive toward Shockley's racial science, which makes sense considering Davis's own work. Davis made his academic bones on the Davis-Moore hypothesis, explained in a short 1945 paper written with Wilbert E. Moore called, innocently, "Some Principles of Stratification." The core of the hypothesis is that social stratification is a "functional necessity" because the hardest, most essential jobs require high incentives to attract the "proper individuals."[56] The obvious implication is that society's elites deserve their rewards, and in fact threatening to confiscate them in a misguided attempt at equality undermines the fragile but optimized division of labor. Davis's other famous idea was his contribution to demographic theory—the concept of a steady-state population, in which births match deaths. He's credited with coining the term *zero population growth* or ZPG, which quickly became the watchword of the population-control movement.[57] Whether he was influenced by his encounter with Shockley's ideas or just the larger climate, in the years following his committee work for the NAS, Davis's ideas became increasingly racialist.

The narrative for Davis's demographic theory goes like this: A population starts with high birth and death rates, then technological progress represses the death rate, leading to a glut, but the population compensates by reducing birth rates, stabilizing at low-birth and low-death ZPG. In the 1970s, Davis was one of a number of demographers who pointed toward an imminent crisis in the Third World. In his formula, the ease with which medicines and other death-halting technologies spread across borders threw population transitions out of whack, growing "free rider" populations out of control at a time when developed countries headed toward ZPG. The result, he warned, was waves of immigration, permitted or not, that would overwhelm these developed countries, reducing the resources per capita, stunting technological development, and undermining wages. "As a result of the displacement and mixing of races there are more racial problems in the world today than at any time in the past," he wrote in a 1974 feature for *Scientific American*.[58] The article included a graph that showed Mexican immigration to the United States far outpacing the numbers from any other nation. It recalled Edward A. Ross on the Japanese as well as Lewis Terman's warnings about Italian immigrants reproductively outpacing the native-born. Davis's scaremongering was influential, and it helped make him a good match for the Hoover Institution, which he joined as a senior fellow in 1981 and where he stayed until his death in Palo Alto in 1997. But Davis wasn't the Jensen of demographic threat, not even in the Stanford community. That was biology professor Paul Ehrlich.

Ehrlich's 1968 book (written with his uncredited wife, Anne), *The Population Bomb*, didn't explode at first, but a couple of appearances on *The Tonight Show* triggered a blast of sales. The problem, he argued, was simple: There were too many people, and population growth outpaced food growth. That left population control and "the death solution" as the only options: Either we slow birth rates or a lot of people are going to die. Disgusted by the crowded streets of Delhi, Ehrlich suggested the sterilization of all men in India who had at least three children. America, he writes, should have volunteered logistical support for the operation, since its success is our concern as well. "Coercion? Perhaps, but coercion in a good cause."[59] The Indian government sterilized more than 10 million people in the 1970s using a range of coercive techniques, pushed by the withholding of American food aid, a stance Ehrlich publicly supported.[60] While the world community got population growth under control, migration controls were needed to "prevent swamping of aided areas by the less fortunate."[61]

Though Ehrlich leaned heavily on his credentials, *The Population Bomb* was not a scholarly book. It was, rather, "largely a work of science fiction," concludes historian Emily Klancher Merchant. "It devoted considerable space to spinning out horrific and highly speculative futures, including global nuclear conflagration and massive famines.... Such speculation clearly exceeded Ehrlich's expertise in butterfly biology. Few of his claims about the dangers of population growth were backed by empirical research."[62] Yet this unreconstructed Malthusian bionomics found purchase, thanks to just these predictions of imminent catastrophe, and in California in particular it gave a green sheen to the era's suburban conservatism. ZPG became a slogan for the elite environmentalist milieu—distinct, usually, from the environmental justice movement, which grew out of workplace organizing—and Ehrlich cofounded an advocacy organization of the same name. Immigration restriction quickly became the organization's domestic policy focus, especially with the ascendancy of the restrictionist John Tanton to the presidency of ZPG in 1975. A few years later, frightened in particular by Davis's predictions in his 1974 *Scientific American* article, Tanton spun off the Federation for American Immigration Reform (FAIR), ridding himself of the moderate environmentalists in ZPG and focusing his attention on Mexico.[63] Ehrlich would prefer to be remembered as one of those moderates, but he joined and led FAIR from the beginning, including with the coauthorship of *The Golden Door: International Migration, Mexico, and the United States*, a tract that strains to avoid the appearance of anti-immigrant alarmism but nonetheless concludes with a call for readers to join FAIR.[64] In 1977, the professor cosigned a mass-mailed letter referring to illegal immigrants as a "human tidal wave."[65] Ehrlich joined some of the country's most organized bigots, lending their propaganda a respectable Stanford face.

Tanton became perhaps *the* major player in what we might without much hyperbole call American Nazism.[66] Through another spin-off organization, American English, specifically dedicated to undermining interracial social democracy, Tanton created and pushed for Proposition 63, the successful attempt to write the English language into the California state constitution.[67] He was trying to get rid of, among other things, multilingual ballots, excluding non–English speakers from political representation entirely. FAIR remains the go-to organization when restrictionist lawmakers need an "expert" to testify, and Tanton kept spinning off more dedicated organizations, including Numbers-USA (a "grassroots" version of FAIR) and the Center for Immigration Studies (the policy arm). If there has been any anti-immigrant effort in the United States between 1980 and today, it's a virtual certainty that some part of the Tanton complex is involved.[68] He died in 2019, living long enough to see a new generation of mainstream bigots like Stephen Miller and Kris Kobach pick up the reins.

In the late 1970s, demographic threat grew into a central focus for

California's neo-Hooverites, and in the following decade they took the concept national, where it remained an important element in the right-wing mental landscape, especially when combined with Jensenism. Together—and they usually were—the two concepts crystallized into a racist phantasmagoria: decent white property owners losing control of their communities to inferior blacks and Mexicans who are taking over the government, using up all the tax dollars, allotting themselves unfair advantages via affirmative action and social programs, despoiling the environment with their fertility, undermining the quality of America's human stock, and destroying property values. And because of these shifting demographics, soon there would be nothing anyone could do about any of it. Bienvenidos a Soviet América. Underpinning the persecution fantasy in the 1970s and '80s was Stanford's supposedly hard new science in genetics and ecology, making it difficult for liberals to refute or reject.

Democracy in the shape of the Roosevelt coalition was a problem, perhaps *the* domestic problem for the Hooverites, neo- and paleo- alike. If wealth is controlled by a minority, but political power is controlled by the majority, then the majority is liable to vote the minority's wealth away via taxation and redistribution. Political democracy would lead to economic democracy, which, given the Hooverite understanding of *inequality* as the world's natural state, could only be a kind of tyranny by mob. Back in the day, Hoover's solution was to make sure enough of the population was sufficiently invested in the defense of property rights to render calls for confiscation scary rather than exciting. People had to become owners without leaving the workforce, where capitalists still needed them. The solution was homes. In 1931, at his Conference on Home Building and Home Ownership, where he outlined the plan for a government-backed private boom in home construction, President Hoover put the question in racial and political terms. "There can be no fear for a democracy or self-government or for liberty or freedom from homeowners no matter how humble they may be," he told the 3,000 delegates, contrasting owners with renters and tenement dwellers, who have less to lose. "That our people should live in their own homes is a sentiment deep in the heart of our race and of American life."[69] Hoover proposed not public housing—vulnerable as it is to democratic control—but government financial backing that allowed lenders to lower deposit requirements, so long as those provisions benefited the right buyers buying the right houses.

Hoover had to watch his plan work from the sidelines, justifiably chagrined as FDR got credit for the suburban home boom. During the 1940s and '50s, Californians increased their homeownership percentage from the low 40s to the high 50s.[70] Hoover lost the presidential battle, but his faithful servants in the real estate industry took off through history like an army of flying monkeys. As the shock troops of white reaction in California, they wrote and enforced segregation rules until the feds made them stop writing it all down, though that hardly ended enforcement. The "taxpayers' revolt" that began with Prop 13 in 1978 and never really ended was part of the Hooverite solution to the threat of economic democracy. Leading the movement was seventy-six-year-old Howard Jarvis, a retired businessman and press officer for the 1932 Herbert Hoover presidential campaign. It took almost 50 years, but Hooverism was back on the march. The New Deal coalition fed itself a poison pill, basing the boom on a private housing system that, as we've seen, made a mint out of segregation. By financing the expansion of property, the state expanded the constituency for *property rights* as a counterclaim to the linked social democratic demands for racial equality and tax revenue to redistribute. The more white people who owned homes, the more who could be mad about the government giving their property tax money away. Emboldened, a new cohort of California Republicans picked up where Bert left off.

Ever since Franklin D. Roosevelt smoked Herbert Hoover in 1932, the hard-core anticommunist contingent of American capitalists found themselves on the defensive, even when they were ostensibly in charge. Hoover himself died in 1964, having backed a series of right-wing losers, including his former general Douglas MacArthur and, right before his death, reactionary Arizona senator Barry Goldwater, whose obliteration he didn't quite live to see. But LBJ couldn't hold his progressive-cop coalition together, and it split like a demonstrator's head under a Chicago police baton in front of the infamous 1968 Democratic convention. After decades on the presidential outs, the conservatives had their opening. They resubmitted the SoCal Quaker anticommunist workhorse Richard Nixon, who had been valuable as a member of the House Un-American Activities Committee, as a senator, and as a foreign-policy vice president for Eisenhower. Bert never really liked Dick with the chip on his shoulder, but as an avatar of the Los Angeles white-power missile suburbs, he represented a big step back toward the Hoover plan.*

But Nixon found himself embattled, stuck in a foxhole not all that different from the one where his predecessor perished (politically). Dick surrendered in Vietnam and recognized Mao's China. His administration couldn't fend off democratic demands on the federal budget, and the White House kept printing checks to support groups the president personally detested. If there's any anecdotal proof that presidents are puppets of history, it's that Nixon and his deputy secretary of defense, David Packard—top-level adepts of missile Keynesianism—felt compelled to pare back Cold War military spending to free up government funds for social programs. American industry stumbled as the state pulled the war rug out from under the economy. Packard barely saved Lockheed Martin, the Valley's leading employer, when it mortally over-invested in a new fighter jet. Layoffs rocked the whole sector. But the crisis allowed employers to shake off their powerful employees, who had been leveraging their key role in the war state for double-digit wage increases. That bargain, which kept war workers so invested in anticommunism that they were willing to make napalm bombs even after they saw what their work did, was finally preempted. In 1972, Nixon's Pay Board stepped in to blunt aerospace wage demands in the name of inflation defense when management couldn't hold them under 10 percent.[71]

There was no "peace dividend" to go with the drawdown in Southeast Asia; instead, as any slowdown is wont to yield in a financialized economy, debt crises hit the country. Companies that wanted to survive did their best to limit their obligations both to their workers and their communities. Capital searched out low wages and low taxes, lengthening unemployment lines and

---

* Once he joined the West Coast political elite, Nixon was a regular visitor to the Bohemian Grove. He even gave the ritual Lakeside address in 1967 as a tribute to the deceased Hoover, who usually gave the speech. "Two thousand years ago when these great trees were saplings—the poet Sophocles wrote, 'One must wait until the evening to see how splendid the day has been,'" he told the forest cabal. "Herbert Hoover's life was eloquent proof of those words." Later, when the Nixon tapes were released, the country got to hear the president describe the Bohemian Club as "the most faggy goddamned thing you could ever imagine." Richard M. Nixon, "Address to the Bohemian Club" (1969), U.S. Department of State Historical Documents; James Warren, "Nixon on Tape Expounds on Welfare and Homosexuality," *Chicago Tribune*, November 7, 1999.

further exacerbating local budget shortfalls. A 1973 oil-price shock engineered by the international cartel pushed prices higher, though wages stagnated and unemployment mounted. The Watergate controversy pushed Dick Nixon of Yorba Linda, California, out of the presidency, where he didn't prove all that useful to his home milieu anyway. If the real estate agents and missile sales-men wanted to run the world in their own interests, they had to do better than Nixon.

The Hooverite brew had bubbled in the Palo Alto cauldron since the defeat of 1932, and though the Chief and his institution flirted with potential heirs such as MacArthur, Nixon, and Goldwater, it was half a century before the potion was strong enough to take down the Roosevelt coalition for good. "Hoover people assume the country is getting more conservative," a former institution fellow told the *Christian Science Monitor* in 1980, "and if Ronald Reagan wins the election they will ride to glory on his coattails. After the [1979] invasion of Afghanistan, they began to talk in Hoover Tower as if they were on the verge of public policy hegemony."[72] They weren't wrong.

War Capitalism

Hoover Institution — Ronald Reagan's Dirty Harry
Situation — The Office of Technology Licensing and the
Privatization of the Cold War University — Wiring the
Asian-American Circuit — Computers for Dictators —
Iran-Contra Net

How did the relatively unimpressive actor Ronald Reagan get picked as the avatar for the new right? *Who* picked him? Associations of capitalists and asset holders get short shrift in the historical literature compared to labor unions, and it was the former groups that took the offensive. Devoted Hooverites maintained networks of association during the midcentury wilderness years, carefully shaping America's priorities from revolving places within the government, corporate directorates, and the military. Thanks to partisan technocrats including Vannevar Bush and William Draper, Hooverism stayed relevant without a popular mandate. But in the 1960s and '70s, anti-Eisenhower Republicans drafted a plan to turn the "silent majority" of resentful whites into a new base. The Hooverites were coming out of the tower and into the streets. And to seize their own party and national power from the liberals, free-market capitalists had to persuade a sufficient slice of the public to side with them in the battle with labor over squeezed profits.

With its high profits and bifurcated labor force, California modeled capitalist discipline for the nation. Investment capital fled west, rewarding the state's owners. Between 1979 and 1986, total manufacturing as a share of gross national product stayed nearly flat, but the sector's composition changed a lot.[1] Computers and machinery, electronic and electric equipment, instruments, and aircraft increased their percentage share by double digits, while all other manufacturing categories declined. Primary industries such as metal, oil, coal, and lumber took the biggest hit, along with the offshored cars and textiles.[2] This wasn't deindustrialization; it was Californication.

The state's political class presented corporate divestment as inevitable, pitting stockholding homeowners against the beneficiaries of the compensatory state for whatever scraps were left on the table. This polarization reframed the domestic decolonization struggle: Innate white supremacy wasn't a viable answer after Vietnam, but "individual rights" spun the progressive demand for personal freedom into a defense of the conservative status quo. To the *demand* of open housing, conservatives could answer with the *right* of property. Democratic control of resources in the collective interest was out; the sovereign individual was in.

Thanks to his friendly associations with various incipient industries, Hoover left a large ideological footprint in the American historical mud. In the squelching vacuum of his death, a menagerie of capitalist creepy-crawlies came forth to continue his work with the same messianic fervor. In her book *Invisible Hands: The Businessmen's Crusade Against the New Deal*, the historian Kim Phillips-Fein reveals that Hoover affiliates played major roles in keeping the anticommunist torch lit during the long FDR-plus liberal era. Leonard Read (a Palo Alto real estate agent turned chamber of commerce leader) was flipped against the New Deal by W. C. Mullendore (Herbert Hoover's executive secretary, who became the president of Southern California Edison) back in the 1940s, and Read became an early evangelist for hard-core anticommunism through his propaganda outfit, the Foundation for Economic Education (FEE), which promoted fringe arch-capitalist thinkers such as Ludwig von Mises, Friedrich Hayek, Milton Friedman, and Ayn Rand.

Organizations like FEE assembled ideologically committed wealthy people to fund them, strengthening ruling-class bonds and bringing big-shot reactionaries out of the woodwork. Names like Du Pont, Coors, and Pew headed the donation lists, along with Hoover himself and later David Packard. They published newsletters, sponsored lectures, and offered fellowships.* "Over the course of the 1950s, dozens of new organizations devoted to the defense of free enterprise and the struggle against labor unions and the welfare state sprang

---

* Among the works published was FEE founder Read's 1958 essay, "I, Pencil," told from the perspective of the titular commodity. The pencil is composed of different materials from different places that, thanks to the market, spontaneously combine themselves. More than 20 years later, Hoover economist Milton Friedman repeated the story on his PBS show *Free to Choose*, where it became one of the era's most influential lectures. See Anne Elizabeth Moore, "Milton Friedman's Pencil," *New Inquiry*, December 17, 2012.

into existence, with the support of business-oriented conservatives," Phillips-Fein writes.[3] Along with FEE, other groups set the stage for this reactionary movement: The Mont Pelerin Society (1947) was like an international version of FEE, and the American Enterprise Institute (1938) provided a venerable conservative counter to the liberal Brookings Institution. But chief among the anticommunist think tanks was the Hoover Institution.

Founded to house Hoover's accumulated historical records in the wake of World War I, the Hoover Institution moved in the early '40s into the tan priapism of Hoover Tower, where its mission expanded from securing a Hooverian understanding of the past to promoting a Hooverian vision of the future. As the Chief's remove from the national mainstream deepened during FDR's World War II heyday, he pushed his institution further to the right, building a watchtower for the anticommunist international in his Palo Alto backyard. By grafting itself onto the university, Hoover's institution pushed the school and the community rightward as well. By the end of the 1960s, Stanford had a strong left-wing movement, but the left-wingers met their match in the right-wing student counterinsurgency, as you read in the previous section. Members of the Stanford chapter of Young Americans for Freedom, a campus feather in the philanthropy complex's right wing, tried to lure radicals into physical fights and twist the uprising into a contest. They came to one 1969 antiwar protest armed with rolls of pennies—brass knuckles for the Hoover set.[4] The right adopted what it saw as the New Left's minoritarian tactics, gaining power by disrupting its enemies while pressing on elite connections and intervening at the weak points of civil society.

Residential segregation provided the social base for reaction, unifying white people as homeowners and parents across strict class lines in homeowner associations, school districts, parent-teacher organizations, churches, and other locally financed community institutions. They shared an interest in protecting what they had, including and especially their expectations for future success, from the decolonization movement at home and abroad. Once again, California led the way for reaction. The state's white community was well organized, with its deep vigilante tradition and cartelized business culture. As the right's disdain for official government intensified, its leaders began to see politicians as employees—and not particularly skilled ones at that. Nixon was an eager hireling, not nearly likable enough to make it very far in corporate life. Barry Goldwater had to be shoved into the presidential race by a network of capitalist ideologues and their white community organizations. Compared to the discretionary power someone like David Packard wielded at his firm, any political job would have felt like a distraction, a hassle, and, at the end of the day, a demotion. The right's leaders didn't want a Herbert Hoover with strong new ideas about how the world should work; they wanted someone to sell the ideas developed in the think tanks, using marketing from the advertisers. They wanted a brand ambassador for free-market capitalism, individual rights, and anticommunism. A vessel for white ruling-class reaction who was rigid enough to face down the Russians without Nixonian compromise but who was supple enough to glove an iron counterattack on the working class. The situation called for a precise performance.

Business conservatives got used to hiring people to promote their ideas, dressing up financier concepts of freedom in reading glasses or a kitchen smock, depending on the audience. They countered ideologically committed left-wing entertainers by promoting their own, led by John Wayne. But they also hired performers straight-up; the singer Anita Bryant, for example, became a national figure by leading an anti-gay crusade from her job as a spokeswoman for the Florida citrus cartel. The best professional capitalist spokesman was an empty-headed actor who distinguished himself from his fellow liberals by testifying to HUAC against communist influence in the film industry. The fink found himself on the outs in Hollywood, and he took refuge in television. At the time, sponsors played a larger role in developing programs than they do now, and Ronald Reagan worked not for CBS where his program aired, but for the title sponsor General Electric. In addition to hosting *General Electric Theater*, as part of his contract Reagan toured GE plants, giving a generic motivational speech to workers at each location. Under the mentorship of his wife, Nancy Davis, and his GE companion, Lemuel Boulware, Reagan's "the Speech," as it came to be known, grew political and right-wing. His liberal anticommunism morphed into the pro-business Christian conservatism for which he's known.

Boulware was such a tough manager at GE that he got his own labor-relations eponym: "Boulwarism" still refers to the take-it-or-leave-it non-negotiation approach. He climbed the ladder to vice president at the major industrial concern, but like other conservative corporate ideologues, he had extracurricular intentions. "Boulware believed that it was not enough to win over company employees on narrow labor issues," writes Thomas Evans in his history of Reagan's GE years. "They must not only accept the offer but pass on GE's essentially conservative message to others, helping the company to win voters at the grassroots who would elect officials and pass legislation establishing a better business climate."[5] Ronnie practiced the Speech and learned about the free-market thinkers and the true evils of communism. In 1962, with Boulware retired, he went freelance, voicing campaigns against gun regulation and socialized medicine. By the mid-1960s, Reagan had put a decade of practice into the role of conservative spokesman, and he was among the movement's best.

When Reagan debuted a version of the Speech on the national stage in 1964 in support of the Goldwater campaign, it hit like lightning out of a clear blue sky. In the middle of the compromising '60s, he was uncompromising, and a group of SoCal capitalists led by auto dealer Holmes Tuttle bought him a slice of national airtime in which to make his, and their, pitch. Reagan assailed not just government spending in general but also the crown jewel of the New Deal state: Social Security. Foreign aid was a waste, except when it came to the poor refugees of Castro's Cuba. He quoted Karl Marx to draw an equivalence with LBJ: Pink was just a weak shade of red. "The spectre our well-meaning liberal friends refuse to face is that their policy of accommodation is appeasement, and appeasement does not give you a choice between peace and war, only between fight and surrender," he intoned in his practiced cant. "We are told that the problem is too complex for a simple answer. They are wrong. There is no easy answer, but there is a simple answer."[6] That simple answer was not the flyboy department-store scion Barry Goldwater, who was rough around the edges and out of step with the still workable civil rights coalition. When Republican voters went to the polls in November, some of them wished it was the silky spokesman on the ballot instead of the craggy cowboy.

Americans as a whole weren't ready for a full-blown reaction, but the Golden State was. In January of 1965, the same cabal of California capitalists who bought Reagan his national advertising time returned to ask him to run for governor.* Reagan wasn't a California Okie bootstrapper, but he did play one

---

* Carey McWilliams, California's Depression-era moral voice, saw it all coming. In 1966, a month before the election, he wrote that "The Ronald Reagan campaign is more, much more, than a mere Republican Party effort to elect a Governor. Essentially, it is a carefully contrived campaign to strengthen and perpetuate right-wing control of the GOP machinery." Carey McWilliams, *Fool's Paradise: A Carey McWilliams Reader* (Heyday Books, 2001), 251.

in the movies once. In *Juke Girl* (1942), he was a migrant fruit picker who had to face down the local packer capitalist. (Movie critic J. Hoberman called it a "bargain basement *Grapes of Wrath*.")[7] One supporter of the real radical fruit pickers won by Ronnie: James Cagney, the actor who was red-baited by California authorities after his name was discovered in letters between Caroline Decker and a leading fundraiser. Like a number of his contemporaries, he took a rightward turn, and Cagney campaigned for his once-upon-a-time costar Reagan in every election he had. When Cagney died, in 1986, Reagan eulogized him as "the classic American success story, lifting himself by determination and hard work out of poverty to national acclaim."[8] What else would anyone want to be?

Elected in 1966, Reagan was the stern face of the establishment against the black radicals and the Chicano radicals and the feminist radicals and the campus radicals, all of whom could be aggregated at will into *them*. Between fight and surrender, he chose fight, deploying the classic anticommunist militia the California Highway Patrol and then thousands of National Guardsmen to Berkeley to handle the students. Though Reagan didn't go further with his own anti-government radicalism than California's liberals let him, he made the left into his foil, scoring points with scared suburbanites by vilifying Angela Davis and the Panthers. In two terms in Sacramento he became the go-to Cold Warrior for the right, and in 1976 he came within a hair of snatching the GOP nomination out from under the incumbent President Ford. The 1980 contest was not so close, and neither was the general election. In an era obsessed with left-wing brainwashing, the people elected a man who repeated pro-market propaganda until there was little else in his head. The solution of the '70s had its guy, and he came from California in a big hat.

The Hoover Institution did more than back Reagan; it *was* Reagan, at least as much as anyone not named Nancy was. In the 1960s and '70s, fellows hung his portrait in their offices, and not just because he was the governor. The obscure ideological notes Boulware whispered in Spokesman Ronnie's ear were the same ones broadcast from Hoover Tower like a capitalist call to prayer. Among Reagan's key advisers was Martin Anderson, a hard-right economics wunderkind with bushy eyebrows who, as a finance professor at Columbia in the 1960s, hovered in the middle ranks of the Ayn Rand circle. He had also been a senior fellow at Hoover since 1971, at a relatively junior thirty-five years old. Some presidential advisers were surprised to find out just how empty a suit Reagan was, but Anderson and his clique had been with the campaign since the 1976 primary; they weren't confused about the president because his employers were also their employers. It was Anderson who set up an important meeting at the Palo Alto home of former secretary of labor (and Treasury) George Shultz, who was at that point, in 1978, a Bechtel executive. The group included Hoover economists, future Reagan cabinet member Ed Meese, the one and only Alan Greenspan, and the Bechtels themselves.[9] At dinner, Reagan began winning over this group of Nixonites, who didn't foam at the mouth the way his Goldwatery lead supporters in the Stanford milieu did. They weren't part of the loser silent majority; these men were more interested in what they had to gain than worried about what they had to lose. The Hoover Institution filled in the GOP's coalition cracks with the caulk of free-market orthodoxy, which appealed to forward-looking rich men like Shultz as well as scared suburban homeowners. It's hard to describe this group as a "core" of the Reagan administration, which was characterized by giant flocks of advisers who had to run the country around their ostensible boss, but that dinner is representative of the way a clear right-wing account of the world quickly came to dominate American politics.

When they won the White House, Anderson came prepared. In the late 1970s, between Reagan presidential campaigns, he initiated a project at Hoover to devise a program for the next decade. The brick-size text was called *The United States in the 1980s,* and it contained contributions on particular policy subjects written mostly by Hoover area experts, leading with essays on economics by Milton and Rose Friedman (economic freedom) and Alan Greenspan (risk of inflation). Citing anti-government feeling following defeat in Vietnam, the group saw an opportunity to put its spin on the prevailing mood. The whole Reagan agenda is in there: reducing taxes and government spending; cutting regulations, entitlements, and foreign aid; opposing affirmative action; fighting wage pressure from organized labor; increasing market competition in health care; getting tough with the Soviets; letting the CIA off the leash. Building lots of new high-tech weapons and bigger missiles and bombs was actually anti-government because it was anticommunist, and communists were the most pro-government of all. Anderson, who became a senior adviser to the president on domestic and then economic policy, contributed a piece about "welfare reform," which is to say ways to restrict access to it. This was the playbook. The Soviets, who shared the American elite's understanding of capitalist politicians as mere lackeys for the ruling class, knew what was going on. Meeting with George Shultz, by then the secretary of state, in advance of his first sit-down with President Reagan, an apparently fed-up Mikhail Gorbachev produced a copy of the giant Hoover tome and waved it in Shultz's face. "Don't tell me that! We know what you think!" said the new general secretary of the Communist Party of the Soviet Union. "We have read this book and watched all its programs become adopted by the Reagan Administration."[10] Anderson uses the anecdote to lead off his memoir—a good one for him, no doubt—but the confused reaction he writes for Shultz is silly: Of course Shultz knew about the book. From simultaneous positions at Bechtel and the Stanford business school, he led the volume's four-man advisory committee.

In *The United States in the 1980s*, we can see the nimble set of moves the Reagan brain trust made to stitch together a cross-class coalition to attack the New Deal legacy. "The United States did not have class consciousness of the English variety, but enough developed to fire the business-labor animus and to produce clear and consistent differences between middle-class and working-class Americans on a variety of discrete issues," the book's editors write about the long Roosevelt era, in an essay on policy and public opinion.[11] Pointing to the coalition behind California's property-tax-limiting, state-gutting Prop 13, they write that the old division was dissolving under inflation pressures, resulting in what they call "the new ideological admixture."[12] The authors link the break in American class coherence to the concurrent collapse of the brief black-white civil rights coalition: "the more recent focus of the movement on substantive equality and forced integration has pushed it up against the individualistic, achievement-oriented element in the American creed. As this has occurred the consensus has broken."[13] This contradiction made affirmative action a rotten beam in the liberal house, and they sought to exploit that weakness. Though their main mode of organization was the cabal, individualism was the Reaganite hammer, and the president's advisers saw a new national frame just waiting for them to nail its parts together.

They could not do it alone, however. How would they sell individualism to the unemployed? Promising to whip inflation helped, but elements of the working class had to be persuaded to accept a cure that, for them, was probably worse than the disease. California, where liberals experienced serious setbacks as wealth flowed into the state, suggested a plan. By reducing the size of the social surplus available to the working class and poor, they could deepen fissures within the broad category of wage earners. Cutting taxes, especially for the rich, thinned the budgetary air for everyone else. Spending lots of money on defense, particularly the Silicon Valley high-tech kind, redirected tax revenue back into ownership pockets and expanded its non-union bifurcated labor forces. Whereas Nixon cut defense in order to provide social services, Reagan increased defense spending to justify a cut in social services. Like conservatives in California, the Reagan administration expected a significant portion of white people to abandon the liberal consensus in favor of a new vibrant conservative individualism.

When it came to mobilizing a cross-class coalition of white people against the political left, California had a long history to offer the Reagan team. As I've said, white vigilantes were longtime crucial, if junior, partners of the state's capitalists. In this period, YAF brought the "disorder in defense of order" tradition to college campuses; a rejuvenated Klan claimed responsibility for patrolling the southern border; the ultra-right John Birch Society reveled in Reagan's victory; a hard reactionary subculture polarized itself against non-whites, leftists, women, and queers, claiming that compensatory demands and the rigged labor-state crowded out individuals—hard-working, skilled, yet humble white male individuals who only wanted a fair shot. The amount of power American whites were willing to surrender to their black compatriots was not sufficient to yield social peace, but the idea of their increased taxes going to fund social programs that paid and trained anti-American black communist revolutionaries—a genuine phenomenon in California, as you've read—was more than some patriots could handle. If the biggest assets most suburban white people had were houses in exclusive zones, school seats to go with them, and preference on the segregated labor market, then "forced integration" (as the Reaganites called it) threatened all three. And how do good Americans respond when someone threatens them? When someone threatens their family? When someone threatens their children's future?

Reagan's real home milieu, Hollywood, readied itself to surf the backlash, and they used the Bay as a set. Urban renewal and the Californicating economy made the region a sponge for investment capital in the 1960s, but the Bay Area also developed a global reputation as a magnet for freaks and weirdos. The San Francisco mayor's office enticed local film productions with financial incentives only to see the filmmakers turn around and portray the city as depraved and crime-ridden. "Wildly popular and profitable," writes historian Josh Sides, "the San Francisco vigilante films of the late 1960s and 1970s portrayed a city that spectacularly exceeded Americans' worst impressions of San Francisco."[14] Manhattan's famous Fear City public-revenge cinema movement of the 1970s and '80s—featuring movies such as *Taxi Driver, Ms .45,* and *Death Wish*—was playing catch-up; the archetype who gave a silver-screen face to white vigilantism was Californian through and through.*

Clint Eastwood was born and raised in the Bay Area; his youth included a stint at Oakland Tech, future high school home of the Black Panther Party. Starting in 1971, Eastwood helped fill in the self-portrait of the white vigilante as SFPD detective Harry Callahan. "Dirty" Harry wasn't going to let criminals get away with crimes just because the liberal Supreme Court said they had a bunch of new rights; he would simply shoot them. It's okay that he used racial slurs, the movie tells us, because he discriminates indiscriminately. Besides, his wife was dead and he fought in a war (Korea), so he was owed in a general sense. *Individuals*, such as his partner Chico Gonzalez—a "college boy" recently graduated from San Jose State in sociology—were okay if they could take a joke and help Harry do his job (shooting criminals). Harry's signature lines were invitations to compete, the kind you offer with a gun. In 1978, a right-wing member of the San Francisco Board of Supervisors and ex-SFPD officer named Dan White assassinated the city's liberal mayor, George Moscone, and his own liberal colleague Harvey Milk, who was a leader in the city's gay community. Smirking conservatives turned the murderer White into a mascot. In 1982 in Detroit, two white auto-workers made headlines when they beat a young Chinese immigrant named Vincent Chin to death. In January of 1989, a gunman opened fire at a Stockton, California, elementary school, murdering five Cambodian and Vietnamese children and wounding dozens more. These shocking public instances stood for a deeper climate of

---

* Scripted for New York City, *Dirty Harry* was forced to move to San Francisco in order to support my narrative as written. Balancing the scale, Abel Ferrara, don of New York crime cinema, spent the early 1970s studying film at the San Francisco Art Institute.

order-maintaining white violence that crowded the full range between a lawful increase in imprisonment and individual hate crimes.

Dirty Harry and his many incarnations gave a voice to white frustration that didn't relocate it within class conflict, even when the narratives touched on political subjects. They were part of the new ideological admixture: angry at groups and institutions of all sorts. John Rambo of *First Blood* (1982) can't stand the police *or* antiwar protesters. George Nada (*They Live*, 1988) gets a pair of glasses that reveal the evil aliens in control of society, and like Holden Caulfield with a shotgun he goes after the phony people, capitalists and labor leaders alike.* Both Rambo and Nada are unemployed, but their problem isn't the rich per se. They portray a fed-up conservatism that looks forward and back, a conservatism about preserving the status quo for the (read: our) next generation, and they echoed the rhetoric of California's Anglo settlers. They didn't really want a job — not the ones that were on offer, anyway; not the ones in the lettuce fields then or on the electronics assembly lines now. They wanted to hold on to their ownership stake in the American dream, even if they had to kill for it, which many of them already had anyway. After all, it was their property, and that was a right, too. "I have my veto pen drawn and ready for any tax increase that Congress might even think of sending up," Reagan told the American Business Conference in 1985, gearing up for reelection. "And I have only one thing to say to the tax increasers: 'Go ahead, make my day.' "[15]

Privatizing Life

Individualism, privacy, property, competition: This conceptual constellation gave the political right a way to talk to people beyond the material appeal of their policies. Rather than the government providing a basis for individuality

---

* An unimpressive addition to the list was 1975's *The Human Factor*, in which the protagonist NATO bureaucrat goes vigilante in order to take down California student radicals conspiring to murder Americans in Europe. An artificially intelligent computer mainframe tells him whom to kill. It was a sad end to the career of Terman subject and blacklist victim Edward Dmytryk, finally allowed back into Hollywood after renouncing his communism as well as his HUAC intransigence. "When *The Human Factor* is dismantled," writes film scholar Bernard Dick, "Dmytryk's contempt is laid bare: contempt for the material, the characters, even for himself." Bernard F. Dick, *Radical Innocence: A Critical Study of the Hollywood Ten* (University Press of Kentucky, 1989), 165.

by spreading the costs of independence and creating a fair field of play, the Reaganites promised to simply get the state out of the way. But the irony of Hooverian governance is that it requires a fleet of government bureaucrats in order to oppose government bureaucracy. As the Hoover Institution entered the White House, Anderson and company became strange technocrats, tweaking the rules in little ways that they predicted would make big differences — the definition of efficiency, after all. Their main tools were deregulation, privatization, and tax cuts, which all reinforced one another. They continued work already begun by congressional Republicans, who cut the capital gains tax back down to Jazz Age levels and sliced the top marginal rate so hard that they redefined the levy from something political and more or less confiscatory to just another tax. Deregulation made new gains easier to invest, and stocks reversed their 1960s and '70s slide and even longer period of relative indifference. The rusty gears of financial capitalism creaked and turned once more, beginning two decades of explosive American stock growth. Organized labor was able to soften the blow of industry deregulation to some degree by pushing workers' pension assets into the booming equities market. Here was an alternative road to socialism: Workers could *buy* the companies, just like anyone else.* But the unions didn't generally manage their voting shares — that job went to the banks they hired, and the banks voted with management when it came to undermining workers. Instead of purchasing the means of production, they ended up loaning their retirement accounts back to their bosses. Labor bifurcation drove stock and home prices higher as the economic surplus flowed to upper-income Americans, who were more likely to buy houses and stocks. The Bay Area led the trend; median home prices nearly tripled in San Francisco and Santa Clara Counties during the 1980s.[16] Consumer credit expanded via loans, home equity lines, and credit cards. Existing owners benefited, even if they were also on the wrong end of bifurcation as workers. This was the new ideological admixture made flesh.

It was hard to believe that California could continue its postwar hot streak, especially after the end of the space race and the defeat in Vietnam. The resulting wave of layoffs confirmed the widespread suspicion that it all couldn't last.

---

* This was an original revisionist interpretation regarding the rise of finance capital. German theorist Eduard Bernstein argued that the spread of shares tended to expand the middle class, rather than concentrate it away.

In the next chapter I'll cover the personal computer industry, which started the accumulation cycle over again, but the Mac and PC weren't the only things Palo Alto had to offer. Finance capital always did like the suburbs. Novelty is high-growth, and Palo Alto built an incubator for new technologies. The huge capital-gains tax cut—more than 50 percent—and pension-investment deregulation helped turn venture capital from something small groups of well-connected buddies did in Cambridge, Massachusetts, and the Bay Area into a national growth strategy. Money raced from all over the world to Palo Alto's Sand Hill Road, capital's new capital, and into the hundreds of venture funds springing up like apricot trees. Capital in the funds quadrupled in the early 1980s, from $1 billion at the close of the 1970s to $4 billion in 1983.[17]

With Hoover goons at the national levers, Silicon Valley capitalism came into its own. Like Hoover himself, paving the runways for the commercial plane industry, the Reagan administration set up the legal infrastructure for a new round of high-tech investment. The microelectronics boom was one of the first instances of a fully military technology—integrated circuits—finding a real commercial home, and knowledgeable venture capitalists bridged the gap between military contractors and the consuming public. Decades after government computers plotted pretend Soviet missile trajectories, America's latch-key children could do the same in for-profit arcades and then in their private bedrooms. That is, if their parents could afford a console. Reagan triggered the new stock boom without taking government ownership of the investments, just as Hoover did with the aviation industries. In fact, with the 1980 Bayh-Dole Act, the feds turned over their proprietary interest in technologies developed with government dollars. Contractors and, crucially, universities could hold on to their intellectual property and flip it into high-growth start-ups that absorbed large amounts of venture capital, then large amounts of investment capital on the stock market. Counterintuitively, the Reagan administration's Palo Alto brain trust argued, privatizing public knowledge ensured its best, fullest use for the public.

This line of thought was in accordance with a fable that capitalists adopted from the Stanford eco-racist anti-population milieu: the "tragedy of the commons." In six pages published in the journal *Science* in December of 1968, the Stanford-trained ecologist Garrett Hardin asserted that the public "commons" was by its nature subject to abuse by maximizing actors. A bigot and cofounder of the anti-immigrant group FAIR, Hardin was worried about population specifically. "In a welfare state," he begs the question, "how shall we deal with the family, the religion, the race, or the class (or indeed any distinguishable and cohesive group) that adopts overbreeding as a policy to secure its own aggrandizement?"[18] One step away from neo-Nazism, this rhetoric wore the cloak of environmentalism during the Nixon years, but by the time of the Reagan administration, the musing philosophy paper that had no business in a scientific publication in the first place had ballooned to an existential truth that applied to public goods in general. As the economy advanced, the state had to "enclose" an increasing number of commons to make sure they weren't misused, either by overexploitation or, just as concerning, *under*exploitation, since, as we know, capital is reluctant to enter new markets where it can't protect its initial position. This represented a change in the ideology, from recognizing the need to build up an intellectual-property commons for new industries to creating the best investment climate possible by *constraining* the spread of new tech. Whereas lively antitrust enforcement ensured the proliferation of the first transistor licenses, the new state religion encouraged techno-monopolism on the public dime.

The poster child for this government-funded stockjobbery was an organic product of the Bay Area's new synthetic environment. In the 1970s, scientists at the Bay Area UCs and Stanford worked on ways to design DNA sequences and insert them into living things, the basic building block for what became biotechnology. Concurrently, Stanford looked to commercial licensing as a way to secure long-term financial benefits from campus research. A Stanford bureaucrat named Niels Reimers created the Office of Technology Licensing (OTL) in 1970, a decade ahead of the government's official policy change.* The OTL was operating in a gray area, especially in 1974, when it filed a patent for the recombinant DNA process along with the UCs on behalf of the scientists Herb Boyer and Stanley Cohen. Could you even patent DNA? A lot of scientists in the community said no, and they knew from firsthand experience that it took a lot more people than Boyer and Cohen to develop recombinant

---

* His office was in Encina Hall, and he was present when the A3M radicals busted in and turned the place upside down. Reimers was "ready to smash a guy," but seems to have restrained himself. Leslie Berlin, *Troublemakers: Silicon Valley's Coming of Age* (Simon & Schuster, 2017), 58.

DNA. The U.S. Patent and Trademark Office demurred, but Boyer, along with a venture capitalist from Kleiner Perkins named Bob Swanson, saw a road to the market for biotech, and they formed a company in 1976 planning to license and use recombinant DNA. Following the day's simple scrunching naming conventions, they called it Genentech. Instead of hiring employees, they outsourced work to the Beckman Research Institute, as in Shockley investor and citrus pH measurer Arnold Beckman. If they were going to fail, they were going to do it fast and on the cheap, in accordance with the Palo Alto System.

They did not fail. Things came to a head in the fateful year of 1980, and the OTL got a series of green lights to leave the gray area. First, in June, the Supreme Court cleared up some of the ambiguity in *Diamond v. Chakrabarty*, which explicitly allowed people to patent synthetic organisms—privatizing life.[19] With that promising indicator, Genentech hit the public markets in October, turning Herb Boyer into a multimillionaire when the share price doubled on the first day, *even though the company didn't have a product.* In December, following the clarity established in *Chakrabarty*, the patent office approved the recombinant DNA application, and before the end of the year, Congress passed the Bayh-Dole Act. The Genentech model had a seal of approval from the government and Wall Street, if not necessarily from all the scientists involved. Like Walter Brattain and John Bardeen, the traditionalists could content themselves with prestige, while the scholar-entrepreneurs, such as Boyer, cashed in big.

Though it contrasted with accepted scientific practice, "[t]he focus on intellectual property was thus developed as a prominent business strategy for securing the infusion of venture capital at early stages of research and development," writes Doogab Yi in his book *The Recombinant University: Genetic Engineering and the Emergence of Stanford Biotechnology.*[20] Stanford pulled in over a quarter of a billion dollars in commercial royalties from the OTL's share of the recombinant patent.[21] Critics said the patent obviously led to underutilization, locking out small start-ups that didn't receive the grace of VCs. But in terms of dispersing the tech, it's hard to look askance at the licensing fees and Genentech's success. At the end of the 1980s, after making many people in Palo Alto very rich, the company was majority-acquired by the Swiss multinational pharmaceuticals conglomerate Roche. By getting the government out of the way, the Bay Area's capitalists and scientists turned a legally dubious piece of paper into a real company that made drugs that people used. It was their payout for rescuing recombinant DNA from the tragedy of the commons. Boosted by the OTL's DNA IP, Stanford quickly became the top university in the country in terms of patent income.[22] What the public gained or lost in the process is hard to calculate.

It was an era of trade-offs, even for an institution like Stanford, which grew around finance capital like beans on a trellis, and the administration had to navigate between the opportunities opening up in the private sector and the reduction in public resources. Despite the Chief's warning, LSJU adapted itself to the liberal consensus and its fat government contracts. But Palo Alto hummed along in the final quarter of the twentieth century, a nexus between the national defense industry, technology start-ups, and academic research. The Reagan administration turbocharged defense R & D spending, looking for a new Cold War knockout punch.* American military spending returned to Vietnam levels, in peacetime.[23] Computer augmentation was no longer an LSD fantasy; the new weapons were full of computers. By 1983, the university had secured 23 percent of all federal university research contracts, including more than $30 million in annual on-campus Department of Defense spending.[24] But less than ten years later, the campus was crawling with dozens of federal investigators, a government audit was in the newspapers, and the school's president resigned in shame. What happened?

Stanford's whole existence as the exemplary Cold War university depended on its relationship with the Department of Defense, and its relationship to the DOD was mediated through one of the department's branches. Universities negotiate aspects of their overall relationship with the department through a single agency, and Stanford worked with the Office of Naval Research—the same one that helped the school build out the campus's postwar facilities, the same one that financed the infamous Stanford Prison Experiment and who knows what else. For many decades that relationship was exceedingly cozy, leading to the aforementioned millions of dollars in annual grants, and Stanford got really good at getting the most out of those awards.

---

* On a return trip from NORAD, when Ronald lamented there wasn't a way to shoot Soviet missiles out of the sky, Martin Anderson suggested there might be, leading to the spectacular "Star Wars" boondoggle. Almost as ineffective, at least the SAGE system inspired movies rather than being inspired by them. Martin Anderson, *Revolution: The Reagan Legacy* (Hoover Institution Press, 1990), 83.

When universities get grants, the schools charge the granting institution a fee for indirect costs—cleaning the buildings, keeping the lights on, and other expenses—so for every dollar, the university gets an extra fraction for its overhead. Stanford led the country in indirect-cost accounting, going from a high 58 percent in 1980 to an absurd 78 percent of every dollar in 1991.[25] As the Cold War drew to a close, so did the need for a Cold War university, and Republicans and then Democrats started worrying about deficits and government bloat more than they worried about the Soviets. In 1988, the Office of Naval Research's representative at Stanford, Robin Simpson, who presided over the escalating indirect-cost rate, got a promotion. His replacement, in a turn of bad luck for the university, was an accountant named Paul Biddle.

As Biddle talked to faculty, he found that the high indirect-cost rate made some of them worry that the school was pricing them out of contention for grants. As an accountant, unlike his predecessor, Biddle wanted to see the books. Stanford was not forthcoming; under the terms of 100 or so agreements (memoranda of understanding, or MOUs, an aggressively efficient mode of [de]regulation) with Simpson during the 1980s, the school avoided performing audits. What the ONR rep Biddle found when he got into the books is what eventually propelled Stanford's spending into the national news media: $6,000 for cedar-lined closets at the president's house, $2,000 each month for flowers, $1,200 for a fancy toilet, $7,000 for sheets, and a 72-foot luxury yacht outfitted with wood stoves and a Jacuzzi.[26] This is the kind of overhead the public was funding.

Stanford tried to go around Biddle by appealing to Simpson directly, a ploy that further angered the accountant. But when Biddle tried to move his findings up the ladder, bosses at the navy weren't interested in pursuing fraud at Stanford—perhaps the feds were concerned that too many people in Palo Alto knew where the bodies from the government's postwar human experiments were buried, so to speak. But Biddle was determined, and the information he had was explosive. He took it to Michigan congressman John Dingell, a fellow army veteran and the chairman of the House Committee on Energy and Commerce. The resulting hearings were a brutal embarrassment for Stanford and a warning shot to other profligate research universities. Dingell dragged the school and its president on the record as well as Simpson and the ONR hierarchy. "The initial charges reveal... over $1,000 a month for laundry charges at a

French laundry," he said. "I'm Polish and I have my laundry done at a Chinese laundry."[27] Stanford made a perfect target for outrage: elite academic liberals wasting the people's money on effete frivolities. The jokes wrote themselves. The congressman lauded Biddle, threatening the ONR if anything were to happen to him.

Flayed in front of the nation, the university president, Donald Kennedy, had no choice but to resign, along with some red-handed underlings. The navy disciplined Simpson and honored Biddle, giving him the Meritorious Civilian Service Award. Biddle wasn't content: He figured that Stanford owed the federal government $200 million, and if he won a whistleblower suit, he could be entitled to 30 percent of that. But as with Rambo, the system didn't want to hear Biddle's truth. The court threw out the whistleblower suit.[28] Stanford paid back only a tiny fraction of the hundreds of millions of dollars allegedly owed. "Do we get to win this time?" Stallone's one-man army pleads in *First Blood*, knowing that the answer is no. A few heads rolled, but the model kept working. In fact, it was accelerating. Kennedy was too wishy-washy for the board anyway. Abolishing the liberal consensus didn't end government waste; it just transferred it to the private sector and, in Stanford's case, the expanding big-money public-private nonprofit sector.

American leadership placed its best hopes for growth in asset prices rather than wages, and in-demand workers traded guaranteed pay for stock options, cannily throwing their lot in with the owners. "National prosperity and high wages could no longer be ensured by a contract among the state, capital, and trade unions: it could be secured only through the ability of national economies to attract global investment funds," write scholars Lisa Adkins, Melinda Cooper, and Martijn Konings in their study of the asset economy, which is emerging at this point in our narrative.[29] The new industrial focus on intellectual property was one part of this shift, and local lawyers assumed a prominent place in Silicon Valley, presaging their important role in structuring a profitable software industry despite the challenge of a marginal production cost that dances close to zero. Thanks to the flexibility of financial capitalism, lawsuits within the community could usually be avoided, especially when both sides used the same law firms, as was not infrequently the case. It is easy to waive conflict of interest when both sides are interested in avoiding a conflict. Besides, there were enough shares to go around, and if there weren't, you could print more, especially if you had some cool intellectual property to show the market. Genentech proved that the right IP could be enough to make investors millionaires on the mere promise of a product.

If capital was in increasing supply, thanks in large part to the Hoover cabal policies, what about labor? Particularly the trained labor these high-tech firms needed? The Reagan strategy of choking off public resources undermined the programs they relied on for skilled workers. And the ones who did graduate could pass their costs along to employers via wage demands, since there was a constrained supply. One solution was the privatization of education—steering students away from democratically controlled community colleges and toward for-profit "technical" trade schools, led by DeVry, a private academy franchise cofounded by triode inventor Lee de Forest as a training school for radio repairmen. If students paid to attend a technical school, the thinking went, rather than going to community college for free, they would value their education and feel compelled to seek a return on their investment. Companies opened their own proprietary training institutes, in which they got to tailor the curriculum and charge tuition.* The next Bobby Seale could train for a tech or an aerospace job, as Seale first intended, without running into political distractions. Free of public control, these schools only taught skills for which there was a private demand, ensuring the best use of the country's human capital, according to the market's transindividual superintelligence. Apparently the market approved, launching DeVry stock from $10 to $24 a share on its first day of public trading in 1991.[30] Now capitalists could not only get their workers to train themselves, they could also make them pay for the privilege. To keep up, the community colleges invited tech companies to take over class periods and even set the curriculum for publicly financed courses.

There was a central irony to the official individualism of the Reagan years. As a result of the reduction in social services provided by the state, people's life chances came to depend more on the circumstances of their birth—the one thing in our lives to which we contribute nothing as individuals. In the high years of postwar American liberalism, federal programs leveled differences

---

* Vincent Chin graduated from one of these corporate institutes, owned by the Control Data Corporation, where he trained in computer programming and operations. Helen Zia, *Asian American Dreams: The Emergence of an American People* (Farrar, Straus and Giroux, 2001), 58.

between white men, as I've said. The military draft pulled promising American boys into higher education and professional science based on the state's needs. The Department of Defense operated a constant talent search, newly indifferent to white recruits' origins. Later anti-poverty programs and the expansion of public higher education brought a broader range of people into the federally funded opportunity industrial complex. That system spun out of control, contributing to the birth of the Black Panther Party and inspiring a generation of rebels. Reaganism was an emergency treatment for what the right wing saw as an overdose of opportunity. Conservatives—and not just conservatives—found justification in the Palo Alto idea of a new inequality located in the genes. The compensatory state only distorted the natural order, which comprised a set of unequal distributive tendencies. Of course rich people tended to do better under the new order, they figured: Genetic superiority is how their families got rich in the first place! (This is part of a common confusion: A trait's heritability does not indicate a genetic component. Home ownership, for example, is heritable but not genetic.) Privatized life didn't mean individualism in terms of effort but rather a resurrection of classed IQ logic and the recentralization of inheritance. Increasing the cost of being a college student not only kept the commie bums out, it also turned higher education back into a family investment.

Instead of treating human capital as a national resource the way David Starr Jordan and company first planned it, America's new leaders applied Garrett Hardin's tragic-commons logic: If they were giving it away, people would go to school and, say, invent radical new theatrical art practices instead of building bombs like they were supposed to. With education enclosed, on the other hand, the market could properly value it and ensure its best use. Students began to think of themselves in the same terms, as a walking, talking set of investments; in a bifurcated world, they couldn't afford not to. Silicon Valley employers, meanwhile, used their two-track labor force to keep unions out of the regional industry. For the highly waged, firms introduced all sorts of fun perks, from team getaways to gourmet meals and free beer. National Semiconductor invested millions of dollars in a 14-acre "Employee Recreation Park."[31] Referral bonuses encouraged workers to talk up their firms to their friends. Bosses eschewed formal hierarchy and opened up the floor plan. Fighting alienation at work by making the workplace more fun, more *personal*, was a flexible way to attract workers and keep labor organizers at bay—these free-bies were easier to withdraw in lean times, such as the early '80s downturn, which briefly reached the Valley in '82, than wages and promised benefits. "The Pentagon is an active collaborator in union-busting," wrote scholars Ann Markusen and Joel Yudken at the time, and the state encouraged investment in non-union areas.[32] Three of the top four counties for prime DOD contracts at the end of Reagan's first term were in California, including Santa Clara at number 3.[33] The county nabbed 3 percent of all DOD contracts in 1980, five times its fair share by population.[34] Silicon Valley became a labor-relations model, and the CEOs became national figures. "Organization in a high growth company is people oriented," the ASK Computer Systems founder and CEO, Sandra Kurtzig, explained to a joint congressional committee in 1984. "The company functions as a family. It takes care of employees who perform, but nonperformers are unwelcome and unwanted. And we're fortunate that we don't have labor unions in Silicon Valley because of the orientation toward people."[35] What a strange family.

New World Order

The Reagan era—which includes Carter's presidency as well as George Bush Sr. and, arguably, Clinton, George Bush Jr., Obama, Trump, and Biden, at the time of this writing—put America back on its narrative track. The coun-try's time in the sun wasn't over; it was just beginning. "Morning in America," as the slogan went. Economically, it made the leap from industrial to postin-dustrial, jettisoning midcentury labor models along with the mines, mills, and factories. If the country couldn't beat the world market in primary materials and heavy manufacturing, then it would play to its own advantage: making shit up. Innovation was the national watchword, high-tech the new Ameri-can brand. But what made this strategy more successful in this period than it was in the preceding years? Computerization didn't add enough efficiency to the country's classic manufacturing processes to keep them competitive. The U.S. tech strategy failed miserably in Vietnam, particularly as it was applied in strategic bombing and in the military's effort to use sensors to render the bat-tlespace calculable—never mind the LSD. The rapid Soviet ascent in science and technology, culminating in Sputnik, proved that there wasn't anything special or inherently faster about the capitalist developmental road. How, then, did the United States turn its series of lost battles into a victory in the Cold War? This is when, in the words of Hungarian philosopher István Mészáros, the progressive "cunning of history" flipped into reverse gear.[36]

A big part of the problem was solved at home, where capital broke organized labor and began the deunionization and wage-repression trends that have defined American society ever since. This was accompanied by a shift in investment toward the South and West and toward computers and other electronics that are made using bifurcated labor. Capital-friendly reforms accelerated the process. But for the capitalists, the decisive Cold War fight was in the Third World. America's life-and-death race with the Soviets was about which side could assimilate the global South into its circuits of production and consumption. The military Keynesian strategy succeeded in securing a border with the Reds—Japan, Taiwan, South Korea, and West Germany remained a solid buffer against falling dominoes—but imports from these countries rapidly sabotaged domestic profitability. The California magic of finance capital had to solve the unsolvable once again.

With Reagan in office, the hard-core ideological capitalists running the White House used American might to leverage a global policy revolution along Hooverite lines. By shifting the balance of class power everywhere toward local elites, they triggered a virtuous cycle of financial growth, analogous to the one that drove domestic asset prices up. Overseas capitalists had to invest their profits, and since they were subject to the same global-historical pressures as American capitalists, their money tended toward the same financial sinks, a disproportionate number of which were headquartered in the United States. Instead of supporting allies with Marshall Plan funds and secret war-gold stashes, the United States and U.S.-led institutions offered these countries large loans, which could be paid by privatizing public assets and even forgiven in exchange for Hooverite reforms. Undemocratic leaders had plenty to gain from the loans (which supported extravagant lifestyles and loyalist coteries), the privatization (which offered opportunities for bribes and self-dealing), and the reforms themselves (which shifted the economic surplus in their favor). They could also afford plenty of American weapons, which helped make it possible for the regimes to protect themselves by attacking their own working classes. As capital concentrated in fewer hands, it grew easier to get everyone on this same page, a page later named the Washington Consensus.

To wrest American trade policy from democratic control, capitalists pushed "free trade," which meant moving authority for agreements to the executive branch and using tariffs to undermine foreign support for their industries. But with the exception of extremely high-growth Japan, this created a familiar problem in capitalist South and East Asia. By bifurcating developing economies, the leaders reduced the functional demand for goods and services across the broad working class, which meant potentially destabilizing levels of unemployment, particularly among upwardly mobile professionals. You could snap the population in half, but you had to deal with the people in the middle. Nonaligned India, for example, was oversupplied with engineers after a couple of decades of urbanization and playing the United States and the USSR against each other in an effort to secure educational support. South Korea and the Philippines suffered similar human-capital gluts, especially in medicine: dentists, doctors, nurses, pharmacists. "The problem," writes scholar Ronald Takaki regarding the Philippines, "stemmed not from too many doctors but from too many poor people."[37] Under Reaganomics, demand without money doesn't count, even when it's the demand of a toothache for a dentist. Bifurcation meant reducing the working-class demand for medical care the hard way, by leaving needs unmet. The "problem," however, was also a solution, depending on your perspective. For the United States suffered from a chronic *under*supply of skilled labor, at least at the price capital was willing to pay, and disappointing skilled workers from East Asia was an American specialty.

Not only was American capital ready to make use of a new immigrant labor force, American law was ready, too. In 1965, supposedly as part of the Johnson administration's janitorial bipartisan anti-racism efforts, the country liberalized its immigration rules, removing the racial requirement for naturalization. In its place was a pseudo–merit system, offering additional points for professionals and relatives of legal permanent residents, which made it possible for one "skilled" (or very hardworking) immigrant to anchor a family. Aspiring Americans who were bringing capital with them could come through a side door in the law. The country was open to the East for the first time, and immigration to the United States served as a safety valve for the regimes of Indira Gandhi (India), Park Chung-hee (Republic of Korea), the Chiangs (Republic of China, or Taiwan), and Ferdinand Marcos (Philippines), as well as, in an opposite way, Ronald Reagan (United States).

The comparatively privileged people in Vietnam, Cambodia, and the People's Republic of China also sought to migrate, for understandable reasons, as did some in Cuba and the Eastern Bloc. America was willing to absorb defectors, because they represented a transfer of resources in terms of their labor, skills, and whatever capital they could bring. The "parole" provision of U.S. immigration law was built for individual cases, a sort of pardon function, but in the 1950s the authorities began using it to admit defectors en masse. By the end of the '70s, 99.7 percent of the more than one million people admitted under parole were from communist countries.[38] The first wave of Vietnamese refugees tended to be more educated, fluent in English, and from professional or managerial households. Chinese defectors came through Taiwan or Hong Kong and split down the middle into high-wage professional/technical/managerial and low-wage menial workers, accompanied by a new cohort of mainland immigrants as relations between the countries warmed.* Refugees from Cambodia and Laos came with much less, as did a second wave of Vietnamese refugees in the late '70s. With the exception of die-hard anticommunists who—encouraged by elements within the U.S. government—still expected to take back their countries, the post-1965 cohorts of Asian immigrants were not planning to return, as past cohorts had been. These were families coming to settle in the United States, and this wave of immigration profoundly shaped the country in ways that many take for granted. "Asian-American" as an identification comes out of this period, along with the pan-Asian solidarity movement, which I wrote about in the previous section. This "Asian" abstraction—a new imaginary place, very different from the one the ancient Greeks and colonizing Brits used that word for—came partly from the grassroots anticolonial pan-Asian movement and partly from American law, but it clearly contained a lot of diversity. Rather than mix everyone into a national melting pot, capital put that diversity to work.

Without the national restrictions, the Hoover team's market superintelligence had to decide how best to allocate all this incoming capital and labor. Work background and education level helped organize immigrants, but

---

* This led to conflicts in the United States between KMT loyalists and supporters of the PRC as Beijing's flag began to displace Taipei's in Chinese-American communities. This conflict is the political background for Wayne Wang's excellent Pynchonesque 1982 independent film *Chan Is Missing*, set in San Francisco's Chinatown.

language skills and access to capital were at least as important. Professionals with English facility—who tended to be from India and Hong Kong (colonized by the United Kingdom) as well as South Korea, South Vietnam, and the Philippines (colonized by the United States)—had a decent chance of finding jobs in their fields, though not at the level of seniority they could have reasonably expected. Working-class and poor immigrants without English facility—more likely to be Chinese, Khmer, Lao, and Hmong—found work in factories and assembly lines in non-union sectors such as electronics and textiles and in low-wage service work. Professional and managerial immigrants without strong English skills, of which there were a fair number, particularly among Koreans, found themselves caught in the middle of a bifurcating economy once again. But Reagan's America had an answer, as long as you could come up with, say, $10,000.

Talking about how the American labor market channeled various groups of post-1965 immigrants risks repeating tired ethnic stereotypes that still plague the country's psyche. But *not* talking about it risks naturalizing the same patterns, reinforcing false ideas about ethnic suitability for certain jobs and the role of Asian immigrants in general in America. Only by putting this sequence in its global economic-historical context can we understand, for example, the relationship between Korean immigrants and urban corner stores. A disproportionate number of post-1965 Asian immigrants gravitated toward small-business ownership for a whole slew of reasons: If they bought one, immigration rules permitted individuals to enter the country regardless of their point-system scores; small businesses allowed families to informally employ their own members at low wages, lending the enterprises a competitive advantage; as their own bosses, immigrants didn't exaggerate the necessity of English language skills, as an anglophone employer might; members of a generation of white ethnic small-business owners were nearing the ends of their lives after having successfully assimilated their children into professional jobs and felt compelled to sell their shops; educated professionals who couldn't traverse the American credentials system had access to modest loans and pooled capital from their community networks; suburban expansion in the South and West created demand for small concerns to fill out the new strip malls. Low-capital, labor-intensive businesses such as restaurants, doughnut bakeries, small groceries, auto-repair garages, newsstands, motels, nail salons, liquor shops, and convenience stores were viable enough, but small profit margins meant that self- and family exploitation was the only way to make any money. Ronald Takaki calls it an "opportune moment" to become a shopkeeper, and yet he also notes that a "study of Korean business owners showed that more than 90 percent of them worked harder and lived more frugally here than they had in Korea."[39] It's this decline in living standards that Reagan admired when he hailed Asians and Pacific Islanders as model minorities: All workers should work so hard and live so frugally! The president sounded a lot like his forerunner in Sacramento, Leland Stanford, at least when the robber baron was feeling charitable toward his laborers.

It's hard to read an account of post-1965 immigration from Asia without running into comparisons to the American assimilation journey of the Italians and, in particular, the Jews. "The easiest way for Americans to make sense of Chinese history is to compare everything to Jewish history," writes Eddie Huang in his memoir *Fresh Off the Boat*, about growing up as the child of Taiwanese immigrants in the suburban America of the 1980s and '90s.[40] But the easiest way is probably not the best, and the striver story we get about Jews is already too simple. In the network television adaptation of Huang's book, Eddie's parents are close to the Reagan ideal: His dad, Louis, is an affable, creative, and romantic restaurant owner; his mom, Jessica, is a demanding, no-nonsense "tiger mom" who picks up real estate sales. They're both here for opportunity and freedom and to do hard work, values they transmit to their boys, with a complementary twist from American culture. It's a just-so story of Asian-American success. But the book version is more complicated and more interesting. Huang writes that his mother's parents were millionaire migrants, taking capital from their Taiwan textile factory to open a furniture store in suburban Virginia, which expanded. His father, in the book version, is a semi-reformed gangster who came to the United States as a student looking for casual sex, knocked up Eddie's mom by accident, and probably still messes around behind her back. He also messes around with his arsenal of guns in the family living room. Louis figures that a restaurant in Orlando, Florida, is a good bet, works a couple of weeks as a line cook, then opens his own spot. "Landlords would give you a restaurant with no key money and three months free rent if you'd sign a lease," writes Huang of expanding Orlando. "It was a theme-park and sunshine-fueled boomtown."[41] The two versions aren't totally incommensurable, but the book emphasizes specific historical contexts, his parents' differing relations to them, and how that affected their immigration narrative, while the sitcom puts a version of their personal-cultural values first in a way that obscures what was going on. In the discrepancy we can see how the history of the successful post-1965 cohort, which unfolds during the Reagan-era shift from labor to inheritance, has been rewritten in favor of bootstrap clichés.

One thing that's confusing about the intercontinental Pacific flows of labor and capital in this period is that, at the same time as immigrant labor and capital crossed to the United States, U.S. companies were offshoring production to those very places: Taiwan, Hong Kong, South Korea, the Philippines. Why would U.S. capital want to go to Asia at the same time as Asian capital wanted to come to the United States?* One reason is that the very political stability achieved through immigration made the capitalist East safe for foreign investment. And for the ruling class in the various Yankee-aligned dictatorships, there were downsides to investing their extracted gains in the expansion of domestic production: It's too easy to tax and confiscate, and it's too hard to grab and run. Like their U.S. equivalents, capitalists in other countries distanced themselves from their popular obligations. America also strongly preferred that its allies bank in New York (or San Francisco or Los Angeles). As David Harvey describes it, an agreement to do just that is what saved the Saudis from a U.S. military invasion to break the oil cartel in 1973.[42] The United States held on to Saudi cash until the kingdom was ready to distribute it to U.S.-based multinational contractors, a process that contractor John Perkins describes from personal experience in his *Confessions of an Economic Hit Man*.[43] Returns on American investments abroad and on foreign investments in the United States both jumped, but the former jumped higher. The difference between the two was America's reward for keeping the world safe for capitalism, and this neocolonial tribute channeled value from workers everywhere into American financial institutions and assets, narrowing and strengthening the international ruling class.

When the Soviets suppressed consumption and increased labor in order

---

* Huang can only speculate why his mom's family left their factory in Taiwan; no one could ever explain it to him.

to mobilize against counter-revolution in 1918, they called it War Communism. In the 1970s, with military Keynesianism—both too much and not enough, too strong and yet too weak—on its last legs at home and abroad, the world capitalist forces needed their own version: War Capitalism. Only by reversing the Nixon capitulation and redirecting working-class demand into capital growth could America win the Cold War as the economic race it was turning out to be. The obscene increase in consumption by the wealthy was merely, in the broad scheme of things, their deserved payment for services rendered as henchmen for the capitalist superintelligence, to whom they offered the world's resources for improved use. Emergency may suggest a need for a decrease in executive salaries (to communists), but to capitalists it signals the opposite. That better use was often—as in the cases of market-darling high-tech companies such as Atari, HP, and Fairchild—moving production to enclaves where labor was cheaper. Returned to its point of extraction, this capital pushes the same cycle forward, further running up returns for investors and undermining workers. Rushing back and forth around the world at the speed of information, capital shook off its local accountability; the international system of property rights was now the supreme law. As creditor and financial nexus, America claimed a referee role, vowing to police any substantial tack to the left anywhere within the capitalist world as the crime and rights violation that a reduction in profits was. And as usual, when global exploitation increased, California and Palo Alto thrived.

The system did not work perfectly. Many American-backed leaders were extremely unpopular, which is often (though not always) a feature of authoritarian kleptocracy. Mohammad Reza Pahlavi, the shah of Iran, was one of the unpopular ones. Installed by a 1953 CIA coup to replace social democrat and oil nationalizer Mohammed Mossaddegh, Pahlavi restored the foreign corporate partnerships. Thanks to rising oil prices the country modernized at a rapid clip, and its economy intertwined with America's. The shah proved a valuable ally during the 1973 Arab oil embargo, pushing up Iranian production and urging the participants to fold. Through the *New York Times* he asked Arab leaders: "What's the use of all that money in the bank if the whole system crumbles?"[44] During the 1970s, Iran was rewarded with $700 million in American corporate investment across 500 firms, and a dozen international banks built up a $2.2 billion profile of Iranian assets.[45] Meanwhile, the Iranian investor class moved capital to . . . California. In the second half of the decade, Iranians invested in farmland, small businesses, and real estate. One broker estimated to a reporter that in the years following the embargo, when oil prices and production increased, Iranian nationals were buying $20 million worth of real estate annually in Beverly Hills alone.[46] The shah tightened the relationship with the West Coast by becoming America's largest weapons customer as well as the biggest exporter of students — by number, even, not per capita — to the United States.[47] Some were exiles and political dissidents, but others were the regime's allies, picking up technical training to bring home and performing the international public-private you-invest-in-me, I-invest-with-you finance tango.

Iran was the model for the new version of American international influence. The country was growing fast enough to satisfy its working, middle, and capitalist classes, as well as foreign investors and banks. A secret police organization trained with American help and notorious for brutal torture kept dissident Marxists and Muslims in line. The shah's Iran was a very strategic geopolitical ally, the informal headquarters for the CIA in the Middle East and a rare friend of Israel. The shah himself was also a pro-growth populist capitalist navigating a river of petrodollars, a poster child for team freedom in the post-colonial world. That's the picture the shah offered, and the West seems to have bought it, which is why it was such a surprise to them when Iran's own new ideological admixture of leftists and political Muslims seized the country and American hostages in 1979. Both sides confiscated and froze the other's assets, but tens of billions of Iranian dollars in American-controlled banks gave the United States a stranglehold on the post-revolutionary economy.[48] In the 1980s the two sides came to the table and Iran compensated American corporate victims of expropriation one by one.[49] Embedded in the same financial system, even anti-American revolution couldn't sever the neocolonial relationship between the countries: Iran still needed to buy computers and oil equipment. Meanwhile, the shah's luckiest men were already settled in California, having avoided the dueling asset freezes by reinvesting in the American dream. The great market superintelligence minimized losses automatically.

For cronies attached to America-supported regimes, California was irresistible. A cornucopia of start-up and suburban development and shopping-center and office-tower projects promised high returns on big investments under safe conditions, even if things went badly at home. "They come over here with shopping bags full of money—real money," one Palo Alto real estate agent told the *San Jose Mercury News* in 1985, regarding Filipino investors.[50] The article was part of an investigative series by the *Merc* into capital flight from the islands to the Bay Area, which revealed a network of elites affiliated with President Ferdinand Marcos siphoning billions of dollars out of the country's coffers into their own accounts and portfolios—billions the regime had borrowed from international lenders on their people's credit line. Corrupt authoritarians had to invest, too, and among the best ways to do it was to dump a pile of cash on a California lawyer's desk.

In one case, a government fund directed by the infamous embezzler (and first lady) Imelda Marcos invested millions to acquire three Silicon Valley tech firms through a holding company.[51] Prominent among the elite Filipino investors in California was Enrique Zóbel, whose namesake, recall, was the Falangist father-in-law of Ampex co-owner Joe McMicking. Now that the family fortune was restored, Zóbel's Ayala International controlled two hotel projects in San Francisco and Los Angeles worth a combined $73 million.[52] "They have money in Switzerland and money all over," one Silicon Valley electronics executive told the *Mercury* about the Filipino investors he worked with, "but the really wealthy put their money over here, always with the expectation something could go wrong. One man told me: 'As long as I can get out of the Philippines and get to a telephone, I'm in no trouble.'"[53] Investing in California meant, whether a communist revolution or democratic regime change, the country's rich could stay rich. The *Mercury*'s "Hidden Billions: The Draining of the Philippines" series created a stir on the islands. Local papers repeated the articles in excerpt and in full. At a time of financial hardship, this "dollar salting" took food out of hungry mouths, retarded economic development, and ran up a $28 billion tab.[54] The ensuing scandal helped pressure President Marcos to concede to the early elections that removed him from power.

If the Filipino elite were to blame for their country's condition, then Cold War financiers were accessories to the crime. Just as the Soviets supported development in aligned countries, international financial institutions took the petrodollars glutting their coffers and loaned them to the rest of the capitalist Third World. There was no reason for oil-consuming countries to suffer just because prices were up; they could borrow the cash they needed, invest it in growth, and pay it all back later. It was an irresistible deal to unaccountable leaders like the Marcoses, who could funnel the money into their own pockets instead. (As reported, those pockets often took the form of houses in Palo Alto.) Bank of America created a "world banking" division and dove headfirst down the petrodollar waterslide.* A 1975 ad for the new division showed a wooden globe carved into four pieces, a folding knife lying open beneath it.[55] In 1980, B of A president and Bohemian Club member Tom Clausen was appointed president of the World Bank.†

This cycle sucked borrowing countries dry. Once on the hook, countries had only one thing to offer their creditor nations and institutions: sovereignty. Taxes went to servicing debt instead of social spending; leaders sold off state assets; and national economies switched to low-wage export models of development in order to keep needed loans and investment coming in. Latin America in particular lived under the Damocles sword of international debt, the people's necks held fast on the chopping block by military dictators and their personal friends in the CIA. Operation Condor provided American support for a continent-wide campaign of terror in South America starting in 1975, in which the coordinated right-wing security forces of Argentina, Bolivia, Brazil, Chile, Paraguay, and Uruguay kidnapped, tortured, raped, murdered, and stole children from tens of thousands of people in the name of anticommunism. The

---

* Even before the world banking division, Bank of America cofounded the Bank of Credit and Commerce International with Sheik Zayed bin Sultan al-Nahyan and other Gulf oligarchs. It was a money-laundering operation of global scale that specialized in hiring the relatives of powerful people within authoritarian Third World governments. In addition to banking solutions for the growing South American cocaine cartels, BCCI was accused of providing financial conduits for "terrorist" campaigns in the Middle East. Steven Mufson and Jim McGee, "BCCI Scandal: Behind the 'Bank of Crooks and Criminals,'" *Washington Post*, July 28, 1991.

† "I remember sitting lakeside at the Bohemian Grove in the summer of 1980 ... Somebody from Washington sidled up next to me and said, 'You should know that your name is really all over town, that they want you for the next president of the World Bank.' So there it was again. Saul Linowitz, the former CEO of Xerox, told me, 'The whole Grove is talking about it.' In the evening, people would sit around the campfires, have a drink and talk before turning in and I guess I was the focus of discussion of a good many camps. I was told that one camp had an informal discussion of who ought to be the next president of the World Bank, and I was kind of elected by that camp as being the strongest candidate." A. W. "Tom" Clausen, "A Legacy of Leadership: CEO of Bank of America and President of the World Bank" (Oral History Center, Bancroft Library, University of California, Berkeley, 1996), 167.

intelligence services coordinated through an encrypted telecommunications system based in the U.S. Panama Canal Zone.[56] "U.S. Personnel played a central role in setting up Latin American intelligence bodies that used computers to upgrade their lethal capabilities, agencies such as DINA in Chile, La Técnica in Paraguay, the intelligence apparatus in Guatemala known as the Archivo, Department 5 in El Salvador, and, later, Battalion 3-16 in Honduras," writes scholar Joan Patrice McSherry. "These intelligence organs soon became known for their savage violence."[57] This debt-based neocolonialism was Cold War on the cheap. The United States invaded Grenada (1983) and Panama (1989) as quick police actions, sorting out moments of political instability—ostensibly to protect in-country Americans and their stuff—and then leaving. Elsewhere American agents and assets *generated* instability, making it hard for elected social democrats such as Jamaica's Michael Manley to maintain order and hold their people's confidence. Meanwhile, the Soviet Union bogged down in its own Vietnam in Afghanistan, thanks in no small part to CIA-backed mujahideen insurgents. America was building what economist Samir Amin came to call the Empire of Chaos.[58]

War Capitalism could put on a blindfold and run into a maze of horrific, absurd plans with confidence because it had class-power echolocation for a guide: As long as the rich strengthened and the working class weakened, then things had to be going in the right direction. It didn't matter that capitalists were investing in finance sugar highs, monopoly superprofits, and an international manufacturing race to the bottom rather than strong jobs and an expanded industrial base. The twenty-first century was going to be all about software anyway, baby. The robots will figure it out. Silicon Valley leaders sat on top of this world system like a cherry on a sundae, insulated from the melting foundation by a rich tower of cream. As far as they could see, it was their far-out new ideas that were driving history. If their government customers wanted to bring a computer to Chile, it wasn't a programmer's job to know that the end user needed it to index future murder victims. Computers can be used for lots of things. Serenity was Palo Alto's prize for excising its radicals; Stanford was an innocent boy once again.

In 1983, no one batted an eye when a rich Iranian immigrant and a recently retired air force intelligence officer joined to form a vague company called Stanford Technology Trading Group International, registered in Los Gatos, California. That was the most normal thing in the world.

Stanford Technology

If this all sounds complicated in the abstract, it is not less so in the concrete. But an anecdote might lend some clarity with regard to Silicon Valley's place in the new world order and the motivations of the people involved. Let's start with Hewlett-Packard, an easy orienting fixture located only a few degrees from Leland Stanford and just as few from the present.

Nothing was more genuinely "Stanford technology" than HP. And in the 1970s and '80s, as you'll recall, the company focused on broadening its global production and customer bases with the projects in Germany and Japan as well as the Swiss sales setup. In 1973, David Packard testified before Congress on behalf of his regional trade group, the Western Electronic Manufacturers Association, in favor of liberalizing trade.[59] In particular, he argued that export controls unfairly limited the sales of civilian technology just because the tech *could* be used to strengthen authoritarian militaries. Computers could be used for lots of things. HP found its way through the rules, and by 1991, overseas sales constituted 60 percent of the company's revenue.[60]

One of the factors that made military export deals like these so appealing was the corruption. Everyone in the chain marked up their costs and tucked something extra into their pockets, which was easy to do at electronics companies, whose products were high-margin and poorly understood by anyone who didn't already have their own stake in the sales.* That also made it possible to export electronic systems that weren't technically supposed to get exported, as long as you knew how to break them down into acceptable parts and then rebuild them on the other side. A layer of wheeling-dealing middlemen connected Silicon

---

* Such "profit pyramiding" was standard operating procedure for U.S. military contractors and subcontractors, selling at home and abroad. Economist James M. Cypher offers an example: "Imagine a contract of $1 billion, where the prime contractor charges the $1 billion to the Pentagon, with 8 percent labeled 'profit'—or $80 million. Putatively, the cost is $920 million. However, the first-tier subcontractor charged $500 million as a cost (with $40 million in profit) and the second-tier company charged $300 million as a cost (with $24 million profit). Total profit on the $1 billion means $80 + $40 + $24 million = $144 million, or 14.4 percent on the sale. But the record would normally show only the 'reasonable' markup of 8 percent, not the overall 14.4 percent armaments profiteering rate here noted (which included estimated 'pass-through charges' of the subsidiary and the first-tier contractor)." James M. Cypher, "The Political Economy of Systemic U.S. Militarism," *Monthly Review*, April 2022, 32.

Valley and Third World governments, nabbing no-bid contracts and scooting around the export laws. In the 1970s, one fast-growing market for HP was the shah's Iran, which had a number of uses for HP's signals and communications technologies. HP's sales agent for the country was a man named Albert Hakim. He was connected to the head of the Iranian air force—who happened to be the shah's brother-in-law—which made Hakim a central conduit to the biggest and most lucrative American arms market. He called his American company Stanford Technology Corporation (STC), which is apparently what you called a tech company if you wanted to impress dictators.

STC was helping the shah's secret police get its hands on phone-intercept technology so it could spy on the country's citizens when Hakim ran into the CIA and U.S. military intelligence, who had their own plans for Iranian signals systems. Project Ibex was an American operation designated to turn Iran into a forward base for signals intelligence into the Soviet Union and the Afghanistan battlespace. Whereas Hakim had been dealing in multimillion-dollar projects, Ibex was magnitudes bigger—$500 million, and that was the starting price (it soon doubled). Hakim and STC integrated themselves into the project and won the telephone monitoring system contract, too. Hakim's specialty seemed to be knowing whom to bribe. The lead contractor for Ibex was a firm called Rockwell, but HP got what *Computerworld* called a substantial subcontract.[61] The industry paper reported on the fishy deal after three American Ibex contractors were shot at point-blank range in Tehran. In 1979, with impeccable timing, Hakim immigrated to the San Francisco Bay Area and bought a $500,000 house.[62]

STC must have done a good job, because soon after, in 1976, the company was approached by a man named Frank Terpil. He said he was an active CIA agent, and he was there for a job. An STC executive claims that the agency, when asked, didn't say Terpil wasn't an agent, and so the partnership hired him, and he brought on his fellow not-so-ex-CIA pal Ed Wilson. As a CIA affiliate, Stanford Technology expanded its business. It snuck a legally restricted radar jamming system to Egypt's Anwar el-Sadat and set up computer intelligence systems for Idi Amin (Uganda) and Muammar Gaddafi (Libya). Terpil and Wilson expanded the services offered, from electronics systems to small arms and explosives, then assassinations. Their relationship with Gaddafi in particular seems to have been close, and they contracted the training of his internal security forces, as well as supplying him with 20 tons of C-4 plastic explosives.[63] Things came to a head at STC when Wilson got busted selling the code from a satellite imaging system meant for Iran—repackaged as agricultural technology—to the Soviets. The CIA and STC both cut Terpil and Wilson loose, backdating the end of the relationships, and the two were convicted in absentia of dealing arms to Libya. Later tracked down by a journalist and asked whether he sold torture equipment to Idi Amin, Terpil responded rhetorically, "Well, what *is* torture equipment? I could take a pair of pliers and make it very unpleasant for anybody."[64] He did concede that he could hear screams from his office. Terpil stayed on the run. Wilson was caught and jailed in 1982, but he went free in 2004, after a court concluded that the CIA, contrary to its attestations during the trial, remained in contact with Wilson during his activities. Instead of imprisoning or blacklisting Albert Hakim, the CIA gave him a new partner.[65]

In the mid-1970s, the deeply unpopular U.S.-aligned Somoza regime in Nicaragua came under assault from a left-wing coalition called the Sandinista National Liberation Front (FSLN). For the hard-core anticommunists, it was vitally important to prevent the establishment of a Red beachhead in Central America. From there it was only a few borders to California. At the same time, Somoza was no better a leader for his people than the new world order model asked him to be, and his people didn't have oil reserves to cushion the blow. An earthquake wrecked the capital, Managua, in 1972, and Somoza channeled hundreds of millions of dollars in aid into his own pocket while Nicaraguans suffered.[66] The American right wing, coming into its own at the time, tracked the developments in Nicaragua closely, and it was worried. When Carter took office, in 1977, Stanford Technology/the CIA—correctly fearing that the new president would cut off military aid to Somoza—made contact with the dictator through another shell company and Ed Wilson, offering a security package including Cuban expat bodyguards, in-country trainers, and the same search-and-destroy assassination program it built for the shah. Somoza quibbled about the no-doubt-inflated price until the beginning of 1979, when it was already too late.

In the Bahamas, where Somoza fled, he met with Stanford Technology point man and Bay of Pigs leader Chi Chi Quintero, and they agreed to continue the collaboration with STC, only now with the aim of overthrowing the government of Nicaragua rather than bolstering it. These counterrevolutionaries, or *contras*, became an obsession for the far right, which desperately feared the spread of Cuban influence onto the mainland.* But Nicaragua also became a line in the sand for liberals, who were sick of the CIA operating its own foreign policy, which for some reason always seemed to involve supporting authoritarian torture squads. The Sandinistas won fair and square, and by most accounts they were better leaders. Congress fought the incoming Reagan administration's efforts to restore Somoza. Capitalism couldn't survive on public money; it had to find a way to protect itself.

Stanford Technology Corporation and its many subsidiaries had been supplying the contras since they were the government of Nicaragua. Hakim and STC were recruited into the CIA plausible-deniability apparatus early in the firm's existence, but the self-destruction of Terpil and Wilson left the private firm mostly selling physical security systems rather than the exotic stuff, like assassination packages. In 1983, the CIA sent Hakim another "retired" operative named Richard Secord. The fifty-year-old Secord was a career military man, and he moved up the ranks rapidly, thanks to his facility with covert operations. As a flight instructor, he piloted into places he wasn't supposed to be and trained pro-American mercenary air corps. Later, as a U.S. liaison to the Iranian air force, he met Albert Hakim, whom he incorporated into Project Ibex. Secord left the military as a major general and an assistant secretary of defense, in which capacity he was responsible for covert actions in the Middle East, Africa, and South Asia, which included the Ed Wilson shenanigans. Unlike Wilson and Terpil he wasn't disavowed, but he did officially switch to the private sector. It was a convenient cover for what he was really up to: Operation Tipped Kettle, a deal with the Israelis to ship over $15 million in Soviet-made weapons confiscated in Lebanon to the contras in Nicaragua via a private channel.[67] In 1983, Hakim hired Secord at STC, and they cofounded the Stanford Technology Trading Group International subsidiary as, of course, a joint-stock company. They split the shares 50-50.[68]

STTGI—continually confused with STC, for many good reasons—broadened the firm's covert Third World small-arms distribution activities

---

* The Sandinistas quickly acquired top-level status in their larger neighbor's paranoid imagination. In the 1984 movie *Red Dawn*, U.S. high school students turn to guerrilla war after the country is invaded and overcome by a sneak attack from the Soviet Union, Cuba, and Nicaragua.

with Secord's help. Serving in Vietnam, Secord was part of a CIA apparatus that flew planeloads of gold into Laos and bribed tribal groups to join America's efforts. To incorporate these groups into the world market as fast as possible, U.S. operatives helped expand regional opium production and hooked up smuggling lines, including avenues to American troops, who then directed the contraband into the United States, where it had a deleterious effect on U.S. city life.[69] Secord denied not only his own participation, but the existence of any commercial opium operation in Laos during the period.[70] Heroin was valuable per kilo, and drug smuggling helped keep costs down, though clearly not down far enough to win the war. Major General Secord considered himself an expert in countertrade, large-scale barter-swaps involving cash substitutions, and now he got to fill his own pockets, legally. Every dollar Secord and Hakim made increased their ability to affect world politics. Meanwhile, Congress cornered the Reagan administration on Nicaragua, banning CIA money, and then, when the White House used National Security Council money instead, banning all money. How do you fight a war with no money? How do you get a war to build itself, the way a railroad does?

As the arms-trade circuit designers, Hakim and Secord acted as a sort of Robin Hood for the anticommunist international, upcharging right-wing rebels in Afghanistan and Angola and redirecting savings to the embattled insurgents in Nicaragua.[71] This was the kind of plausibly deniable operation the pro-contras in the American government needed, and the CIA director, Bill Casey, assigned a newly promoted lieutenant colonel on the NSC staff named Oliver North to coordinate the operation with Hakim and Secord. Since the White House couldn't spend American money, the feds leaned on allies to pitch in, particularly the extravagantly wealthy authoritarian leaders who depended on U.S. support. The biggest contribution came from King Fahd of Saudi Arabia, who donated $32 million to the contra cause, followed by $10 million from the sultan of Brunei and a couple of million bucks from Taiwan.[72] Smaller amounts came from South Africa and the Republic of Korea, and nonmonetary assistance for the project came from Israel, Chile, Singapore, Venezuela, England, Panama, Honduras, El Salvador, Guatemala, and Costa Rica.[73] Hakim was an expert at Swiss banking, having spent years in Geneva at Hewlett-Packard, and he handled finances for what became known as the Enterprise. With Secord, Stanford Technology was full-service; it even worked out logistics to get guns from contra warehouses near Costa Rica to the frontline troops.

This public-private operation definitely contravened the intention of Congress, but there wasn't much dissent about it in the Reagan White House. George Shultz (State) played dove in public while Cap Weinberger (Defense) played hawk, but they were both Bechtel-Reagan men, and they knew about arms dealing. It was Shultz's idea to approach Brunei, though he ended up sending his deputy, Elliott Abrams, to make the ask.* The contras got another $10 million from the Medellín drug cartel, which though not technically a country, was definitely capitalist and preferred the contras, who were full of drug traffickers, to the Sandinistas, who were commies. Besides, using the same Central American airfields as the CIA had its advantages.

The first American official to put down on paper that the contras were trafficking cocaine was a young man named Robert Owen, and though we haven't met him, we already know him in the abstract.[74] At six foot four, Owen probably fit in at Stanford as well as he could have fit in anywhere. He studied political science and was a fervent anticommunist, idolizing his older brother who was killed doing special operations in Vietnam. He tried to join the military and the CIA, but thanks to an old knee injury he couldn't make it. Still he found ways to be useful to the right, starting in the office of the conservative senator Dan Quayle, who was close with the CIA director Bill Casey. That's how Owen ended up the courier for Oliver North. His entrepreneurial cover

---

* The $10 million from Brunei is one of the most intriguing loose threads in the Iran-Contra narrative. It never made it into the contra bank accounts, and apparently no one went looking to see what happened. Instead, it ended up in the Swiss account of one Bruce Rappaport, an Israeli money-mover with close relations to the country's government. The simplest explanation, offered by Israeli arms dealer and intelligence operative Ari Ben-Menashe, is that it was an unsuccessful bribe meant for Israeli leaders in order to ease the flow of weapons. (Ben-Menashe claims to have helped sabotage the move.) A more exotic explanation, suggested in independent counsel Lawrence E. Walsh's report on Iran-Contra, is that Rappaport was concurrently tasked with seeking Israeli approval for an oil pipeline from Saudi Arabia to Jordan on behalf of the contractor leading the project (Bechtel), and was encouraged to believe the NSC's "piggy bank account" had millions available to him for that purpose. There's no reason Rappaport couldn't have been working on both with the same $10 million. When investigated, the Stanford Technology explanation for the missing money was that the expert financiers accidentally transposed a 6 and an 8 in the destination account. Ari Ben-Menashe, *Profits of War: Inside the Secret U.S.-Israeli Arms Network* (Sheridan Square Press, 1992) 172–73, 181; Lawrence E. Walsh, *Final Report of the Independent Counsel* vol. 1, 197n42.

was a 501(c)(3) nonprofit he created called IDEA—the Institute for Democracy, Education and Assistance—which received a government grant to administer humanitarian aid in Nicaragua. In reality, Owen became North's errand boy, flying to the rebel camps to take weapons orders and de facto representing the National Security Council to the anticommunist militia. It was a dream job for a right-wing partisan like Owen, and like most of the men involved, he came to admire and even revere Oliver North. When later compelled to testify, Owen read a free-verse ode to his boss into the record, including the following stanza.

Fear, anguish and despair are with us daily, yet in our darkest hours we
have three things that help sustain us: our faith in God Almighty, the
love and support of our families, the knowledge that on this troubled
earth there still walk men like Ollie North, men that have shown bravery
in their youth, wisdom in their adulthood, and patriotism throughout
their life.[75]

What more could a right-wing radical hope for than to serve a man like that? But when he was in Nicaragua, Owen couldn't help but notice that a fair number of affiliates and even contra leaders themselves were drug traffickers. It was the 1980s, and the cocaine industry was growing. The Nicaraguan cocaine-trafficking and country-exploiting milieus overlapped, and it wouldn't have taken a countertrade expert such as Secord to realize that flying empty planes back to the United States after dropping off supplies was a missed opportunity. The Medellín cartel was already using a route north through the area. Still, the idea that the contras were funding the war with drugs doesn't seem to be the case, at least not significantly so—though it certainly made a good story for Nicaraguan traffickers.

One reason the money didn't go to the contras is that the traffickers weren't really freedom fighters; they were drug traffickers. But another is that, thanks to international donations, profits from other weapons sales, and misappropriated American government funds, the contras were in good financial shape. While their supply requirements topped out at around $2 million a month, Stanford Technology and related schemes look to have channeled nearly $100 million to them in a couple of years, more than twice what was needed.[76] As adepts of the free market they couldn't let money rot in a bank account, so they invested the surplus in short-term certificates of deposit, pumping it back into the financial system.[77] A lot of it simply disappeared. Hakim and Secord got their biggest deal acting as a new back channel between the West and the new regime in Iran. The CIA director, Bill Casey, became convinced it was a good idea to sell the ayatollah $12 million worth of missiles to fight Soviet-supplied Iraq, prompted by the Israelis, who wanted to see the regional rivals continue their fight to mutual self-destruction.[78] It was standard for Hakim's group to mark up goods, but for official enemy Iran, they went out of their way, netting a whopping $16 million in profit, of which only $3.8 million was channeled to the contra effort.[79]

As it did during the investigations into MK-Ultra, the national security infrastructure, when caught, fell back on a cover story it could live with, even if the story was outlandish. Iran-Contra was a clever scheme to get funds to Nicaraguan freedom fighters at low or no cost to the taxpayers, contravening the spirit of the law but adhering to a deeper, more important spirit of American ingenuity and loyalty. Besides, how could North and his team be supporting Iran if they were price-gouging the government? Hardly a betrayal, this was self-sacrificial patriotism. Noble Oliver North took the fall, and his three felony convictions were overturned in the early 1990s. There's no proof he took bribes from Hakim and Secord, though there's lots of evidence they supplied them.[80] The expert Hakim, who understood how expensive college was getting, worked with North's wife to set up a fund for their children. The congressional hearings focused on who knew what when, in particular President Reagan. This was a distraction; the whole group of men at the top of the Reagan administration fervently believed in a free-market capitalist system in which people *didn't need to know* what was going on for it to all work out. This was the central insight of Friedrich Hayek, the economist who along with Reagan was one of the Hoover Institution's first three honorary fellows. The president himself famously couldn't keep Central America's countries straight.

And yet the system worked. The flow of guns and money, missiles and cocaine, didn't overthrow the Sandinistas, but it did make it difficult for them to develop and build a socialist society. The Stanford Technology enterprise sabotaged efforts throughout the Third World, transferring resources from durably unequal capitalist nations such as Saudi Arabia and Taiwan to the global struggle against peasant and working-class self-determination, which is to say economic democracy, wherever it was happening. The effort included multimillion-dollar wire transfers, but also a trip to New York by our lanky Stanford courier Robert Owen to pick up a $9,500 wad of $100 bills from a Chinese corner store on the West Side and deliver them back to Secord in Washington.*

This is the system that ultimately won the Cold War; it was guaranteed to turn any Third World country where the people were considering socialism into a massacre site, and at prices that weren't about to trigger a domestic inflation spiral. It ultimately worked well enough in Nicaragua, but the strategy was more effective to the north, where Honduras and El Salvador suffered what were later categorized as human rights violations at the hands of right-wing soldiers and paramilitaries, which kept the countries in the United States' sphere of influence. Yankee affiliates tore liberation movements apart for the sake of doing so, bribing the most craven commanders to seek aggrandizement through civil strife with former comrades. Authors Joe Bryan and Denis Wood note striking similarities between the ways highland tribes in Cambodia, Vietnam, and Laos were integrated into the international market through the dual paths of the American war effort and the opium trade and the experience of the Miskito Indians of Nicaragua with cocaine and the contra war.[81] The writers do not note that both groups enjoyed the managerial presence of Dick Secord, but if it hadn't been him it would have been someone else.

It's no challenge to locate conspiracies within this global network of arms dealers, dictators, and capitalists. The most famous was the one sketched by *San Jose Mercury News* reporter Gary Webb, who connected the Los Angeles–centered crack cocaine epidemic to the blind eye the feds were turning to contra-aligned smugglers.[82] Via the diluted rock cocaine, anticommunists enlisted the country's declining ghetto economies in the Cold War struggle,

---

* When Owen suggested that maybe the Taiwanese corner store owner had taken a 5 percent fee, Secord explained that the odd number was to stay under the $10,000 legal threshold for transporting undeclared currency on international flights. "North Aide Tells Probers of Cloak-Dagger Trip to N.Y.: Says Secord Sent Him to Get $9,500," *Los Angeles Times*, May 19, 1987.

roping poor black and brown Americans into the Third World drugs-and-guns circuit. In the words of Stanford anthropologist Philippe Bourgois, who compared his field experiences in El Salvador and East Harlem, authorities were able to transmogrify the direct political and structural violence of class struggle into the decentered, depoliticized everyday violence of capitalist terror, under which the strong and lucky are forced to outrun their own families just to survive.* This formulation is structurally similar to the domestic new ideological admixture the Hoover Institution strategized to exploit through Reagan: Confuse class relations by foregrounding the individual. Capital-gains tax cuts accomplish that, and so does shooting into a crowd of civilians with a helicopter gunship.

Does it matter who knew what and when? Those knowledge questions are what the investigations came to focus on, including the Iran-Contra hearings and the controversy over Webb's *Mercury News* series. Reagan was symbolically acquitted of foreknowledge, which left him convicted of being an old fool who wasn't really running the country. Better that than to end up like Nixon, in charge and in trouble. For Reagan, there was no single mastermind — not Martin Anderson, not North, not Terpil or Wilson or Hakim or Secord, not even George Shultz or Bill Casey or Caspar Weinberger, the latter of whom, in his capacity as general counsel for Bechtel, happened to have met productively with Albert Hakim in the early days of Stanford Technology.[83] The buck never stopped; it circulated. This decentralization of responsibility was one of the beauties of War Capitalism. Even when one plot failed, there was always another in the works. The cabal could plan and coordinate without assuming centralized responsibility, as long as members were willing to accept that around half the money was going to go missing, which they were as long as it would find its way back to the banks one way or another.

That a firm called Stanford Technology coordinated funds for the

---

* Bourgois was working in El Salvador (on what was almost certainly, to someone, counter-insurgency research) when he was caught in a large body of civilians as they were fired on by military helicopters and ran for their lives for 14 days. The event became known as the Santa Cruz Massacre, one of many such attacks in the region and throughout the world, but one of the few that happened to contain a Stanford anthropologist, which enhanced the story's credibility in the bigoted Western media. Philippe Bourgois, "The Power of Violence in War and Peace: Post-Cold War Lessons from El Salvador," *Ethnography* 2, no. 1 (2001): 5–34.

anticommunist flow of weapons around the Third World is a nice connection for my central theme, as is the 1978 Palo Alto meeting that yielded much of the Reagan administration leadership and the Hoover Institution plan for the 1980s. But the structural connection goes deeper than that. Palo Alto's new tools were suited to this new form of social war. It's not a coincidence that Albert Hakim worked as an HP sales agent; it's a confluence. "One of the most intriguing things that [Oliver] North did was to establish his own worldwide communications network—secret and totally secure," writes Martin Anderson, admiringly. "From virtually anywhere in the world—from Nicaragua or Honduras, from Europe or the Middle East, from any part of the United States—his colleagues and coconspirators could send messages to one another in unbreakable code."[84] Here was real human augmentation, a gadget that allowed 15 people to run a shadow world government: a portable, folding computer.

To connect his intercontinental cabal, Oliver North used a top-of-the-line device, a set of some of the first laptops, produced by the venture-funded Xerox PARC spin-off GRiD Systems Corporation, the first to fit a portable computer into a briefcase.[85] The slick black computer with a clamshell plasma screen was too expensive for all but the most elite businessmen, but the National Security Agency saw it as a good deal and paid extra to wire in proprietary encryption chips. North commandeered 15 of the devices and set up a remote access network connecting the capitalist insurgency.[86] Despite the high-margin computers involved, for the feds it was a bargain, *the* bargain that could pull capitalism out from between wage-price inflation and the Red menace. GRiD remade itself as a defense contractor and its private shareholders got rich when one of the big computer firms—Tandy—purchased the company in 1988 for over $50 million in stock.[87] Everybody involved paid a small capital-gains tax. The computers were made in Mountain View in the South Bay, probably at least in part by Vietnamese refugees. It was game over: America won the Cold War, and Silicon Valley invented the personal computer.

Chapter 4.3

Jobs and Gates

Pong — Mac and the PC — De Facto School Segregation and the Production of Mean Nerds

The new privatized order called forth various plans and various people to execute them. The first generation of digital pioneers had their eyes on the office, not the home. Tech companies such as Hewlett-Packard and Intel sold their products to other companies, not individuals, even though the occasional engineer wielded his own HP calculator as a point of pride. It wasn't that they couldn't imagine a future in which computers were made cheap and small enough; the problem was that these midcentury men didn't know what people would *do* with them.

The postwar boundary between home and the office was newly thick, and engineers had trouble thinking of domestic purposes for their inventions. Tech sprinted ahead of society in the 1960s and early 1970s, and executives across the industry nixed PC projects. Intel's Gordon Moore — no pessimist when it came to progress in tech production efficiency — turned down an engineer's plan for a home computer: "The only use he could come up with at the time was, a housewife could put her recipes on it," Moore recalled in 1993. "And I just couldn't imagine my wife sitting there with her computer cooking dinner."[1] The manufacturer Honeywell offered just that for the holiday season of 1969, repackaging a corporate minicomputer into an attractive case and marketing it as the Kitchen Computer in the year's Neiman Marcus catalog for $10,600 (over $86,000 in 2022 money).* Computing was work, and home

---

* Misremembered in many histories as a product failure with no sales, the Kitchen Computer was rather a surprisingly successful marketing gimmick, generating orders that the company had not been expecting to fill. Design historian Paul Atkinson describes it as a "non-product," a kind of "vaporware." Paul Atkinson, "The Curious Case of the Kitchen Computer: Products and Non-Products in Design History," *Journal of Design History* 23, no. 2 (2010): 163–79.

was supposed to be a place of rest and relaxation for men, and companies didn't see women as a market for very expensive machines that didn't as yet do much. The home computer project remained a recurring but mostly insubstantial glint in engineers' eyes.*

But by the mid-1970s, falling chip production prices made it impossible for smaller electronics shops to keep competing with the big semiconductor firms, which could count on a cheap and steady supply of components. One of those firms was the Albuquerque, New Mexico–based MITS, run by one of America's many postwar boy rocketry enthusiasts, this one named Ed Roberts. He followed the hobby-electronics yellow brick road, from toy rocket lights to kits for pocket calculators and digital clocks, building MITS into a respectable midsize company. But as prices continued to fall and the industry consolidated behind companies such as Texas Instruments and the Fairchildren, MITS and all the firms like it were in trouble. In 1974, the company was $365,000 in debt ($2 million in 2022 value), but Roberts had one advantage: He knew Intel's forthcoming 8080 chip, significantly cheaper and more powerful than the 8008, was going to deliver a knockout punch. Roberts used imminent doom as a stepstool to the future, negotiating a bulk deal with Intel for 8080s and pivoting MITS to produce a DIY computer kit. The time had finally come, and *Popular Electronics* editor Les Solomon was determined to get a picture of the company's product on the cover before another magazine announced an 8080 kit. When the prototype Roberts sent got lost in the mail, Solomon decided to trust the blueprints. Someone — accounts differ — named it the Altair, after the destination planet in an episode of *Star Trek*.† In January of 1975, the personal computer era kicked into gear with the glossy national announcement of the Altair 8800, and mail orders, complete with hundreds and even thousands of dollars, poured into Albuquerque.[2]

Artisanal hippie entrepreneurialism was in the NorCal air, and not just among the early computer hackers: A three-man team led by two Stanford students started selling a beginner's guide to "juggling for the complete klutz" in late-1970s Palo Alto, adding a second book on the official stoner sport Hacky

---

* The Alto, out of Xerox PARC, was the first production desktop computer, but the desk in question was the digital office.

† One early internal MITS memo suggested calling the kit Little Brother, an indication of Apple commercials to come.

Sack in 1982. The company became the publisher Klutz, which sold in 2000 for $74 million and is now a subsidiary of Scholastic.[3] Noel Lee left a laser fusion engineering job at Lawrence Livermore National Laboratory to tour with his all-Asian country rock band, Asian Wood, in the 1970s.[4] They got stuck in Hawaii, and when Lee got back to NorCal he started making his own audio cables. Launched in 1979, his high-margin Monster cables redefined the industry, and his company grew to $100 million in annual revenue.[5] It was a good time to get lucky with a product or business plan. The personal computer boys had that good historical timing and something more: They had a community and even the beginnings of a subculture. Somewhat to Ed Roberts's and MITS's surprise, the home computer revelation already had its zealots, including the two two-man teams that lugged the device into the twentieth century's fourth quarter.

Starting in 1975, at Silicon Valley's Homebrew Computer Club, the Bay Area's techno-freaks and anarchist hackers gathered regularly to share their parts and progress, their designs and dreams, in a communal atmosphere. The scene brought together antiwar technologists from Berkeley, young employees from the tech companies, and even a few local boys, the first offspring of the suburban Keynesian baby boom to be left in control of their own initial adult choices, the Vietnam War having ended without them. The personal revolution was coming into its own, finding its organic base in these young California men who combined a libertarian ethos with entrepreneurial ambitions. For a meeting place, the group settled on a Stanford auditorium. Two of the younger Homebrew acolytes were from local Homestead High in Cupertino and named Steve: Jobs and Wozniak. (Jobs, the younger of the two, graduated after joining the club.) Wozniak was a good-humored junior engineer at Hewlett-Packard who liked building stuff, and Jobs was Jobs, a hustler hippie reeking of arrogance and body odor. Though he was not a good fit for a staid workplace like HP, he was just what a young company like Atari was looking for, and after an aborted attempt at Reed College in Portland, Oregon, Jobs moved back to the Bay in 1974 and demanded his way into a job at the hot game company. He had just turned nineteen years old.

The first video game wasn't as big of a step as it seems in retrospect. Recall, the first computer system to incorporate (pseudo) real-time interaction with a visual output was the (nonfunctional) SAGE air defense system, headquartered at MIT's Lincoln Laboratory, which was established in the mid-1950s. From there it was only a few years and an on-campus skip and a jump to *Spacewar!*, Slug Russell's 1962 game, which took the war-trajectory premise and put it in outer space, where the feel was a little less apocalyptic. To show it off, Russell and other early MIT hackers had to feed 27 pages of paper-tape instructions into a DEC PDP-1 mini-computer, which they hooked up to a big oscilloscope display.[6] The same year, MIT AI pioneer John McCarthy left for Stanford's new Artificial Intelligence Project, which became the Stanford Artificial Intelligence Laboratory (SAIL), bringing his trusty coder, Russell, along with him. At SAIL the game became a kind of institution, and a group of three programmers led by Palo Alto–born Bill Pitts tried to commercialize it, installing coin-operated cabinets loaded with *Galaxy Game*—it was an antiwar scene, at least among the customers—at a Palo Alto coffee shop and a bowling alley in 1971.[7] Meanwhile, a young engineer over at Ampex named Nolan Bushnell had the same idea, and he designed a cabinet-based variant called *Computer Space* for an existing company called Nutting. Their initial test was at a Menlo Park bar-restaurant called the Dutch Goose frequented by nerdy Stanford students, who lined up to play. But taking war out of the title couldn't change the game's origins, and *Spacewar!* was built on the military-industrial complex's quarter.* The game makers made their own use of the downtime on federally financed machines, but when it came to spinning off a frivolous version with private capital, the minicomputers were way too expensive. The *Galaxy Game* cabinet, with its PDP-11, cost $20,000 (more than $145,000 in 2022 dollars), fronted by one of the cofounder's wealthy Palo Alto parents, which was too many quarters to recoup. Computer programmers loved *Spacewar!*, but without taxpayer-subsidized processing power, the numbers weren't there.

Bushnell read the writing on the wall, and he left *Computer Space* to Nutting and convinced some Ampex coworkers to give video games a new, different spin. This time they employed a hobbyist's rather than a military-industrial approach, cutting costs wherever they could. The result was *Pong*,

---

* The games couldn't avoid it, either: *Galaxy Game* used joystick controllers built for B-52 bombers, picked up at a military surplus store. Bushnell first encountered *Spacewar!* at the Bob Taylor–created graduate program at the University of Utah, where he was a student. Pitts sat around at Lockheed waiting for them to buy the PDP he was hired to program, moonlighting with *Galaxy Game*. You could do this all day; *Spacewar!* and its variants were a byproduct of military Keynesianism.

an aggressively simple Ping-Pong-type game hacked together by the lead Atari engineer, Al Alcorn, a former television repairman who knew how to get the most out of analog hardware. "The whole idea is to get the maximum functionality for the minimum circuitry," Alcorn recalls. "It worked. We had $500 in the bank. We had nothing and so we put it out there."[8] Bushnell had Alcorn try to design *Pong* to be small and cheap enough for the home, but the original 1972 version belonged in arcades.* There *Pong* was a hit, and Atari bolted ahead of its competitors. The enfantrepreneur Bushnell, who held meetings in a hot tub and named products after the hottest ladies on the assembly line, proved irresistible to investors. Fairchild veteran Don Valentine was founding what became Sequoia Capital at the same time, and his first investment provided Atari with the money it needed to get into the home market with *Home Pong*.[9] By the mid-1970s, Atari wasn't the biggest computer company in the Valley, but it was the most fun.

By all accounts, Steve Jobs's biggest contribution to Atari was bringing Wozniak around. Unlike Jobs, Wozniak was a brilliant coder, seeing eye-to-eye with Alcorn and building on the analog hacker's work. Still at HP, Wozniak subcontracted a single-player *Pong* variant called *Breakout* for Jobs at Atari, getting swindled by his best bud in the process (Jobs famously quoted Wozniak a much lower price on the contract than what Atari offered him, subcontracting his friend and pocketing the difference). But more than money, Wozniak wanted challenges, and his Homestead High partner in crime kept finding ways for them to make some cash while Woz solved puzzles. When he wasn't doing his own job or Jobs's job, Wozniak was moonlighting at his HP desk on his own computer circuit design, challenging the Altair as his own one-man hacker band. Like other men before him, Wozniak dreamed of a minicomputer wedged inside a terminal, the personal revolution taken to its domestic conclusion. The Intel 8080 was still too expensive for his purposes, but a renegade group of Motorola engineers left to design a low-cost, high-performance chip for competitor MOS Technology, releasing the game-changing 6502 in the fall of 1975. By the next spring, Wozniak had his

---

* Magnavox—one of the first generation of spin-offs from the original Stanford start-up, Federal Telegraph—released the first home video-game console, *Odyssey*, in the fall of 1972, but, selling only out of corporate dealerships as an add-on for the company's televisions, it floundered, despite having the first Ping-Pong game.

computer, and the other Steve convinced him that they could make a batch for $20 and sell them for $40 (a little over $200 in 2022 money). That circuit board was the Apple I.

Though Jobs eventually earned his reputation as a business shark, no one could accuse the Steves of refusing to dance with the ones that brung them. Wozniak, ever conscientious, offered his invention to HP first — reasonably, since he developed it as an HP employee with HP resources. His boss turned him down, seeing too much of the hacker ethos in Woz's board. Jobs, eyeing Bushnell's pockets, offered him a third of their start-up for the arbitrary figure of $50,000. He declined. Within the year, Bushnell sold Atari to Warner Communications, and within two years he was working on his real passion project: a chain of pizza restaurants featuring animatronic animal entertainers.* He sent Jobs to Valentine, who also declined to invest until later, and fobbed him off onto Fairchild-Intel vet and young millionaire Mike Markkula, who joined the team and provided the business sense (and personal credit) necessary to make Apple investable. The hobbyist-board Apple I became the sleek product Apple II in 1977, in time to compete with similar new microcomputers from Commodore and Tandy/Radio Shack. With its color output and spreadsheet program, the Apple II (and its peripherals) quickly turned into a $100 million product line, launching the company into the top rank of the 1977 microcomputer pack. Apple scored a coup in 1979 when an independent software company introduced a spreadsheet program called VisiCalc that worked exclusively on the Apple II. The first "killer app," it let users serry their data in rows and columns and then apply functions, taking the microcomputer from a toy to a tool. Small businesses became the company's biggest customer group.

But being a big fish in the home computer pond still left Apple closer to a video-game company than to an industrial giant like IBM or Xerox. Apple closed the 1970s in a precarious position, even as one of the hottest tickets in the country. Large office-technology firms that already locked down monopoly superprofits — like IBM, with its mainframes, and Xerox, with its copiers — were so well capitalized that virtually as soon as they decided they wanted their own retail microcomputers, they could have them. Everyone knew IBM

---

* The inane "Pizza Time Theater" became Chuck E. Cheese, an era-defining children's entertainment business.

would build its version eventually, and competing with IBM was corporate suicide. Intel decided to stick to being a supplier, and other chip makers made the same call. Xerox invested considerably to build the Alto at Bob Taylor's Palo Alto Research Center, and even still they were slow to commercialize it, lest they stumble into their rival's stampeding path.

This was the context for the 1979 show-and-tell between PARC and Apple that led to the Mac. The meetings were a condition Steve Jobs placed on a million-dollar investment from Xerox. A chance to buy 100,000 big shares of Apple at $10.50 was, in retrospect, quite the opportunity, but that wasn't what the copier company was really after.[10] The investment was a way for the bigger firm to secure a stake in what it hoped would be a contract manufacturer for the retail Alto. It wasn't a crazy idea; Warner-owned Atari was making an unsuccessful pitch to IBM for the privilege of building a Blue microcomputer at the same time. Apple, however, had other plans, and Jobs was up front (if bratty), telling the PARC team that he had no intention of building the Xerox machine. He wanted Apple's engineers to learn from the Alto's unique user interface—and its legacy all the way back to Engelbart, NASA, and the Stanford Research Institute's Augmentation Research Center—to build the next generation of Apples. The result was the Apple all-in-one personal computer we've come to know.

Getting some of the benefits from Xerox's massive PARC expenditure helped, but if Apple was going to compete in the 1980s appliance-computer market, it needed capital. A lot of capital. But 1980 was a good time to be asking if you were a fast-growing technology company. People who had invested in Apple to that point multiplied their money, and anyone who cashed out (as did the faithless Don Valentine) left much more on the table. At the end of 1980, Apple went public and the markets went mad, snatching up the 8 percent or so on offer for nearly $100 million, giving it the capital to develop and produce two new computers for the decade.[11] There was the Lisa, a high-end "workstation," and the Macintosh.* Market confidence buoyed Apple through

---

* There are differing accounts of the Lisa naming, ranging from the founder slyly acknowledging the parental obligations he otherwise dodged to the one I find more believable: Senior Apple employees named the computer as a "fuck you" to the child-abandoning egomaniac Jobs. It's also worth mentioning that team member Larry Tesler had a daughter named Lisa, too.

the misstep of the Apple III and the Lisa to the Macintosh, the spiritual successor to the Alto, the personal revolution in a beige box.

Jobs gifted Macs to the children of John Lennon and Yoko Ono and Mick and Bianca Jagger, paying tribute to the counterculture and squeezing Apple into the lineage. The company announced the product launch to the public with an iconic commercial that aired during the 1984 Super Bowl. Directed by Ridley Scott (then recently of *Alien* and *Blade Runner* fame), the one-minute ad showed a scene right out of George Orwell's *1984*, as rows of worker drones listen to Big Brother on a big screen. In runs a braless blond woman (Anya Major) chased by police, breasts bouncing in an Apple tank top. She wields a giant hammer, which she flings through the propaganda screen. "On January 24th, Apple computer will introduce Macintosh," the narrator intones as the words scroll on the screen. "And you'll see why 1984 won't be like '1984.'" Faced with a cease-and-desist order from the *1984* rights owner, Apple only aired the ad twice—once during the biggest advertising event of the year and once the month before in the tiny market of Twin Falls, Idaho, in the middle of the night to qualify it for advertising awards.[12] The ad was a hit, but the Mac didn't have the same immediate effect. Compared to other computers at a similar price point it was underpowered. Wozniak was checked out of the company, and Jobs guided development by instinct, absolutely nixing any cooling fan because he didn't like the whirring vibes, for example. The Mac was a cool toy for rich children, but it was not a muscular computer for the price—Apple's third technical disappointment in a row. And now the company had a bigger problem, a Big Brother problem. IBM was here.

Trey

After it turned Atari down, industry commentators assumed IBM would enter the U.S. minicomputer market via a Japanese partner, and in 1981 Matsushita (the Japanese conglomerate behind Panasonic) admitted that the two firms discussed a deal.[13] Why not just make the computer in-house? Xerox's example is instructive. The office-solutions company was stuck with giant legacy cost structures—collective-bargaining agreements with manufacturing unions, high-salary salesmen, and internal repair divisions with proprietary replacement parts—none of which fit with the hobbyist-led retail microcomputer market. One Xerox engineer famously joked that if the company sold a paper clip it would have to retail for three grand.[14] Burdened under the cost structure, the Star system blinked out, too expensive even for the large enterprise customers. Xerox wanted businesses to buy the whole suite: a bank of computers networked by Ethernet to one another and a laser printer. The costs could run into the hundreds of thousands of dollars, around $30,000 per user ($100,000 in 2022 money), a risky move for purchasing managers considering that it was a new platform and most men outside the computer industry *still didn't type*. It was a lot to spend to improve secretarial efficiency, and at Xerox's crucial moment the target market preferred not to.

Since a post-1977 pricing war drove microcomputers down to a few hundred bucks at the low end, Big Blue would have to upend its whole production system if it wanted to get into the same stores. When IBM finally accepted the reality of the personal computer, it created a secret project in Boca Raton, Florida, to build an IBM consumer appliance computer, codenamed Chess, eventually to be the PC, as in "the PC." The developers had it in a year. The incipient office-microcomputer industry spent its whole short life worrying that IBM was going to jump in and squash them all with a cheaper, better machine. And then it did. That everyone expected it made the Boca Raton blowout less interesting than start-up stories like Atari and Apple from a narrative history standpoint, but the way it happened determined the shape of the industry long after "PC" became a generic term.

The jump from making mainframe computers to microcomputers looks small in the rearview, but there was a big difference in the corporate structures behind the products. IBM had to find a way to get out from under its own prohibitive cost structure and into direct-to-consumer retailers and catalogs. Computer retailers were eager to put a new IBM in their windows, but they wanted customers to be able to bring their computers in for repairs and modifications without IBM's oversight. The solution was for Big Blue to start thinking like a hacker: Instead of building its PC from the ground up, it assembled off-the-shelf parts bought from contractors. Intel's new 8088 processor was the brain; Zenith made an iconic green monitor; Epson made a printer; Bob Metcalfe's PARC networking spin-off, 3Com, contributed the Ethernet board.[15] That was one configuration, but there were plenty more, depending on what you wanted the computer to do and how much money you wanted to spend.

By assembling contracted parts, IBM incorporated start-up geniuses who got pushed out the door at Xerox. As the programmer Larry Tesler replied to Bob Taylor when the boss told him PARC could just hire any of the hackers smart enough for the big leagues: "It's not going to work like that."[16] Taylor was used to running ARPA during the draft, when he could virtually conscript any bright young man in the country, moving his recruits around military and pseudo-military installations like pieces on a board. But the draft was over, and in 1980 Tesler followed PARC's clever guests back to Cupertino, accepting a job offer from Jobs. Xerox sold off its whole workstation division within the decade, including its investment in the never-was contractor Apple.

IBM, on the other hand, was known as the purchasing manager's best friend. "Nobody ever got fired for buying IBM," went the saying, because IBM products were the standard for corporate data technology not just across industries but across Industry. These were not Apple's customers—the nation's newsletter publishers and the other small-business elder children of the personal revolution—this was the professional managerial class, bureaucrats wielding organizational capital and trying to keep up without rocking the boat. They redefined the computer markets, lifting IBM over companies that never really dared imagine themselves to be its rivals. With its off-the-shelf cost structure, the IBM PC retailed below $5,000 (under $15,000 in 2022 money), less than a third of the price of a single Star workstation, which more than made up for a substantial discrepancy in reliability. The PC also stomped the Apple III, the company's attempt to step up to the corporate world. For companies looking to computerize, IBM built an obvious choice, just as everyone expected it was going to—but even more so. In fact, IBM's PC sales got off to such a strong start that it surprised the company itself: BIG I.B.M. HAS DONE IT AGAIN announced the *New York Times* in the spring of 1983, suggesting the product was so successful that it threatened to cannibalize the firm's business at both the high end (mainframes) and the low end (word processors) at the same time.[17] Besides selling too many of them, IBM had one big problem with the PC: If it was made from off-the-shelf parts, then anyone could go to the electronics store, buy the same parts, and make their own PC. What's more, anyone could go to the electronics store, buy the same parts, and *sell* their own PC. Like the chemist Victor Frankenstein losing ownership of his surname forever, IBM didn't just build a single monster from scraps. It birthed a whole category.

Cloning was said to be a perennial problem in computers, depending on whom you asked. Copying was also an important way the science and the industry advanced, no matter whom you asked. Firms frequently faced questions about how they were going to interact with one another, when and what they would share, and what they would protect.* There were good reasons to embrace openness: As Apple showed with VisiCalc, the software tail could wag the hardware dog, and some other team's work could make you rich.

The biggest customer for all its contract suppliers, IBM also dictated a lot of production terms without being on the hook for implementing them. The chosen suppliers, for their parts, became the dominant players in their particular markets without signing away exclusivity. IBM orders buoyed contractors with scale and gave them a competitive leg up on further development as well as support in lean times. Following the PC's release, with the American semiconductor industry losing its brutal price war with Japanese firms, IBM bought 12 percent of Intel for a quarter of a billion dollars, allowing the company to survive the downturn and refocus on high-end microprocessors.[18] Meanwhile, dozens of firms of various sizes started selling their own PC clones.[19] Compaq's Portable debuted in spring of 1983 for less than $3,000, and the company sold over $100 million worth the first year.[20] HP followed in 1985 with its compatible Vectra and more or less scrapped the company's own incompatible 8088 microcomputer after only two years. IBM, with no protectable PC intellectual property, triggered an attack of the clones that quickly swamped the 1977 generation of microcomputer companies, including Apple.[21]

The IBM PC was a departure point for the home computer's intellectual property regime, raising and answering questions in equal measure. By effectively waving away IP claims on the market's hottest commodity, Big Blue made room for some of its contractors to pursue their own. Two of these contractors in particular hitched their chariots to the winged horses Copyright and Trademark, escaping the gravitational pull of linear growth and launching

---

* Different firms tackled compatibility in different ways. Magnavox, recall, decided to only sell their *Odyssey* game system at company stores, sabotaging the product. Apples were decidedly closed, with the Mac and Lisa lacking even a networking port. The rising power IBM threw open the frontier with the PC: Anyone could make a PC, sell a PC, whatever. Enterprise would buy the IBM version for the support as long as they kept it competitive, and the more compatible the platform, the more people could contribute to improving the PC without planning or investment from IBM.

into the sky, surpassing even IBM itself. More than the commercial tower PC's successful originators at IBM, Microsoft and Intel came to define the product. As of this writing, Intel's market cap is almost twice IBM's, while Microsoft holds an unseemly advantage that nears 20–1. IBM's choice to create an IP-less PC was smart from the perspective of development speed, and it made the giant untouchable to antitrust authorities. But the real money from the PC boom went to firms that used the law's protections to secure monopoly super-profits.* That's how Bill Gates became, for a time, the world's richest man.

Gates grew up as Trey, the third in a line of William Gateses, but the real family money was on his mother's side: The Maxwells had worked at family banks since Trey's great-grandfather went west and founded Seattle's National City Bank at the turn of the century. Trey attended the exclusive Lakeside boys prep school, where he met his future cofounder Paul Allen. That's also where he first started using a computer. At $1,475 a year when Trey enrolled, Lakeside was pricey.[22] In 1968, one of the things students got for that money was access to a terminal connected to a DEC PDP-10 in downtown Seattle. The Lakeside Mothers Club raised thousands to pay for their boys' computer time, and Gates got hooked. His career started when, after crashing the whole time-sharing computer, the company C-Cubed offered Trey and his buddies free hours in exchange for their help recording bugs.[23] There the budding programmers happened to meet *Spacewar!* creator Slug Russell, who was recruited away from SAIL by the Seattle time-sharing company after the 1968 protests. He needn't have worried; when SAIL did get firebombed, in the early 1970s, no one was injured.[24]

Trey went away to Harvard, but only long enough to re-create his great-grandfather's westward flight. Gates was entrepreneurially minded, and the computer industry was on the other side of the country, or at least its future was. He and Allen saw the Altair on the cover of *Popular Electronics* in January of 1975 with everyone else and drew a similar conclusion: The micro-computers were coming. Gates and Allen offered to translate a version of the programming language BASIC for MITS, built using an Intel 8080 emulator Allen whipped up on the much more powerful PDP-10, simulating the new

---

* Antitrust was a real concern for IBM, which spent the entire decade of the 1970s embroiled in one of the country's biggest antitrust cases.

category of microcomputer hardware on the minicomputer. Albuquerque was skeptical, but the college kids delivered, and as the early birds they got the worm, establishing themselves as the contractor for Altair BASIC as sold in the MITS catalog for between $60 and $350 depending on the specifications (roughly $300 to $2,000 in 2022 dollars).[25] They were the first ones writing commercial microcomputer software, and they named the company accordingly: Micro-Soft.

Unlike hardware, which had to be fabricated out of toxic materials in real life by workers, new software had a very small marginal cost. It was just information, after all. Duplicating information was the same as sharing it, and sharing information was the basis for the entire burgeoning hacker-hobbyist microcomputer milieu. "Anyone who owned an Altair had probably written a program for it at one time or another," write Paul Freiberger and Michael Swaine (without exaggeration) in their history of the era.[26] To use the first microcomputers, you had to be more than a consumer; users were part of a collaborative community by default. That community's center was the Homebrew Computer Club. Some Homebrew members owned early Altairs, and they hyped each other up about the new tech. Homebrew's Steve Dompier was so excited and curious that, after MITS returned half his $4,000 check because the company didn't actually stock all the products in its catalog yet, he flew to Albuquerque in person, then reported back to the club on the ramshackle state of the New Mexico operation.[27]

In June of 1975, the MITS caravan literally rolled into Palo Alto, setting up shop at the Hyatt Rickey's on El Camino.* The road-show Altair was hooked up to a teletype, with which it could load the Micro-Soft BASIC (punched on a roll of paper tape) and then interact with users. If you loaded the BASIC and typed "2+2," it printed "4." Without the language, the Altair 8800 was merely a box of switches. The Homebrew Computer Club needed it, but they weren't about to pay hundreds of dollars each to be able to use the machine they already bought, and perhaps more important, they weren't going to wait until Altair was ready to start using it. Someone snagged one of the BASIC paper rolls from the MITS box and handed it off to club member Dan Sokol, who worked at the Fairchild spin-off Signetics, where he had access to a

---

* Rickey's was also where Stanford militants forced David Packard to cancel his WEMA speech.

PDP-11 with a high-speed tape-copying machine. Sokol showed up at the next Homebrew meeting with 50 copies, asking everyone who took one to come back with two to share. The pirated BASIC spread quickly through the small microcomputer community, pushing the platform's software development forward and enraging Gates, whose company was supposed to be pulling in a royalty for every copy in use. Then 20 years old, Trey Gates was going by the more relatable name Bill, and when he wrote his famous "Open Letter to Hobbyists," he signed it as "Bill Gates," without the "III" but with "General Partner, Micro-Soft." He complained that, though their BASIC was popular, only 10 percent of Altair owners had purchased a licensed copy. "As the majority of hobbyists must be aware," Gates wrote with indignant sarcasm, "most of you steal your software. Hardware must be paid for, but software is something to share. Who cares if the people who worked on it get paid?"[28] The fight over consumer software piracy is as old as consumer software itself— maybe older, since Homebrew was swapping BASIC before it shipped to buyers.

Hobbyists didn't buy Gates's arguments any more than they bought his BASIC interpreter. They didn't believe Micro-Soft had spent all that much developing it, certainly not enough to justify charging $100 for the pattern to a series of punches on a paper tape. Some of them took the assertion that hobbyists wouldn't write their own BASIC for free as a challenge, assembling their own Tiny BASIC for which they charged only $5 by mail or passed along free at in-person meet-ups. Others griped that BASIC was a taxpayer-funded language in the first place and that Gates snaked time on an ARPA PDP-10 at Harvard to do the work, which was true, and that Allen probably used another PDP at his job at Honeywell.[29] Why was that so different from the Homebrew Club meeting at the Stanford Linear Accelerator Center or Sokol borrowing time on the Signetics tape-copying machine? Hobbyists used their access to mainframes and minicomputers as employees and students to work on microcomputers, and the big computer industry was built on taxes. Trying to profit off that was uncool, and getting all high-and-mighty about it was worse. The responses were so numerous and strong that Gates felt compelled to issue a second note ("Unfortunately, some of the controversy raised by my letter focused upon me personally..."), more amicable than the first.[30] At the end of the day, Microsoft owed the antagonists: The controversy helped make it the logical choice when, just a handful of years later, IBM went looking for an operating system for the PC.

Microsoft didn't have an operating system for the PC's Intel 8088, but another Seattle computer company, Seattle Computer Products (SCP), did, and Gates finagled a middleman deal to provide the Quick and Dirty Operating System (QDOS) to an undisclosed client (which Gates knew to be IBM) for a bargain cost to him of only $25,000. Following the Boca Raton strategy, IBM's license for what was now PC-DOS was nonexclusive, which meant Microsoft could sell a compatible version to every PC clone manufacturer, which it did under its own brand name MS-DOS. By then Gates, having already nabbed the Big Blue deal, hired away the QDOS author, Tim Paterson, and bought out SCP's software permanently for a measly $50,000. As IBM PCs recomputerized the office and PC clones computerized the home, Microsoft built up a monopoly position, dominating the market for PC operating systems as the bargain option.* The original IBM license was unlimited and perpetual for a fixed price near $100,000—more than Microsoft paid for SCP's entire software operation—which allowed IBM to offer it to customers cheaply.[31] But as its position solidified, Microsoft settled on a new model, one in which manufacturers paid a license fee for every central processing unit (CPU) sold, regardless of whether it was loaded with Microsoft software.[32] No matter who built the PC, no matter if it used MS-DOS (or later, Windows), Gates got a cut. Since they were paying for it anyway, licensees might as well use it every time, which they did.

Nerds

Americans like to tell the story of the early microcomputer industry in Silicon Valley as a history of invention. At its most facile, this manifests itself in stories of individual iconic businessman geniuses: David Packard, Gordon Moore and Robert Noyce, Steves Jobs and Wozniak, Bill Gates and Paul Allen. Even if they may not have been the best engineers or programmers in the region — only a couple of them were even in that conversation—they were *visionaries* who saw the future in advance. The true path of invention is rarely clean or simple, but when scientific credit fails to align with net worth, the second

---

* Mainframe servers mostly used non-Microsoft operating systems, a fact that Microsoft lawyers cited to argue that the company did not have a monopoly on the operating system market.

trumps the first in public memory. After all, crediting inventors is notoriously difficult; every innovation building on the last, every inventor inextricably embedded in a series of communities. Two or more often alight on the same idea at the same time. Money provides a sort of scoreboard, an equivalent by which we can compare the otherwise incomparable. Steve Jobs goes on the THINK DIFFERENT poster, just as Leland Stanford stars in the Southern Pacific's celebratory painting. Judah and Wozniak go down in history as the brains behind their operations, and the workers who built the tracks and assembled the chips are background figures at best.

An alternative way to think about this period of postindustrial history is to look at the regional business environment. Accounts of this are principally concerned with *how* Silicon Valley was able to nurture such a concentration of economic success, not among individual leaders or firms but as a project that exceeds any single one of them. Here it's the connectors who are more responsible than the inventors or even the specific siloed visionaries — men such as Frederick Terman, who coordinated the birth of Silicon Valley from the Stanford provost's office, or the venture capitalists who adopted companies into corporate family structures inspired by the Japanese. More sophisticated than the Great Man version, this ecosystem analysis still takes its object for granted. The Great Region histories, like AnnaLee Saxenian's *Regional Advantage* and John Markoff's *What the Dormouse Said*, see Silicon Valley as a place of creation rather than transformation. By placing these stories in the context of statewide, national, and global changes in the relations between workers and owners, we can better understand the microcomputer industry. Steve Jobs and Bill Gates are very important characters in the story, but they're more meaningful as personifications of impersonal social forces. As Frank Norris said through his composite oligarch, "You are dealing with forces, young man, when you speak of Wheat and the Railroads, not with men." The same goes for computers: If Jobs and Gates hadn't been themselves, some other guys would have been them instead. But as personifications, they can help make sense of those forces, help characterize them.

Like a not inconsiderable number of other people, Bill Gates was in the right place at the right time to write an operating system for the first generation of personal computers. That he did *not* write one of them isn't surprising, since a lot of other people didn't, either. What distinguishes Gates is that, unlike everyone else, he came to own the legal rights to PC-DOS. Why him, and how? The "Open Letter to Hobbyists" helps explain. It's a landmark assertion of property rights within the community: It attempts to draw a thick line between the hobbyist era and the microcomputer industry, and it's characteristic of the way Gates made his billions with Microsoft. The Homebrew pirates saw computer science as essentially a public domain, and in the 1970s, in a descriptive sense, they were right. Public dollars paid for almost all the computing power in the country, even when the computers were technically privately owned. The hackers could point to Gates's use of the ARPA PDP at Harvard not only because they had experience pulling the same con, using official processors after hours for personal projects, but also because there were only so many computers he could have used to write the BASIC interpreter. They all learned to code on publicly financed Big Science machines, whether at universities, at commercial defense contractors, or in the military itself. With a draft on, where exactly individuals fit in this complex wasn't usually up to them anyway. The knowledge products of that work, like BASIC, belonged to the people. It was acceptable to use the knowledge to make products and sell them — hobbyists were always first in line to buy, too — but to fence off an important set of instructions and start charging monopoly rents for them was an audacious move. Where did Gates get the nerve? There was an important difference between him and the hobbyist community: Trey Gates didn't learn to code on a public system, not mostly. He was an elder child of a new age, a new age in the organization of wealth and privilege as much as in technology.

It's not complicated to see why the decision makers with access to time on powerful microcomputers didn't let literal children use them. The machines were very expensive, very fragile, and important systems depended on them. Of all the things in the history of the world that you wouldn't let a child play with, the military-industrial complex's early computer systems is a strong contender for the top slot. The SAGE operators themselves couldn't stop bugs from making their nuclear response apparatus spontaneously ready itself for war. Even if they didn't trigger Armageddon — the plot of *WarGames* (1983), a movie that apparently terrified the simpleminded President Reagan — kids would no doubt break the delicate systems that were at best always threatening to quit on skilled users. Not to mention the fact that computer time was pricey. At Lakeside in Seattle, the teenage Gates had access to a mainframe terminal as a sanctioned learning tool, something almost no one his age had ever had before. The PDP-10 was a new machine and a transformative one. Lakeside contracted with General Electric for a teletype terminal right away, but the mothers' club's whole budget for mainframe time was spent in weeks. In the fall of 1968, four computer experts from the University of Washington got capital from Seattle-area investors to start the Computer Center Corporation, or C-Cubed. With its leased hardware (including the PDP-10), C-Cubed offered "the largest concentration of timesharing computer power on the West Coast," which it planned to sell by the hour to companies such as Boeing.[33] One of the C-Cubed partners was Monique Rona, who just so happened to be a Lakeside mother, and the school moved its time-sharing contract to the start-up. The timing was perfect for Gates and a few other boys: As I mentioned, after Gates predictably crashed the C-Cubed PDP-10, the company agreed to give him and some friends free time on the system if they made a note of every bug they found. They learned what they needed to on the C-Cubed computers in order to sneak illicit-to-semi-licit time on various systems over the following years, becoming some of the most advanced teenage programmers in the country.

A few time-sharing companies succeeded, but C-Cubed wasn't one of them. They closed their doors quickly, in 1970. It probably didn't help that Boeing started its own time-sharing system in 1969, a year after C-Cubed opened. In fact, the generous deal with the Lakeside boys wasn't really as generous as it seemed: As part of its rental deal with DEC, C-Cubed could delay its payments if it found bugs in the PDP-10's code. DEC was basically contracting work to its customer, which subcontracted it to the unpaid teenagers. The boys eventually got the operating system code (out of the trash, Gates recalls) and found so many bugs that DEC pulled the deal.[34] But by the time C-Cubed failed, the boys were good enough programmers to be employable on their own, especially since the PDP-10 they knew from the ground up was a standard and unusually long-lasting piece of industrial computer equipment. Gates got his computer training via an exclusive private school contracting with a private company that was financed by private capital. He got his connection to IBM through his philanthropist mom (who sat on the United Way national board with the company's chairman, John Opel) and got his legal advice from his attorney dad. For Gates there was no such thing as society — just family and businesses. He didn't owe the people shit, and he acted like it.

Trey Gates was an avatar of suburban bifurcation. He grew up in Laurel-hurst, the tony lakefront district next to the University of Washington that the Home Owners' Loan Corporation labeled "best" in its 1936 map, the same map that redlined nonwhite borrowers away from the water and into the industrial districts.*[35] Bankers like the Maxwells got rich off the segre-gated housing boom — recall that the HOLC's "best" designation referred to the quality of investment — rich enough to avoid the threat of integration. In 1962, when Trey was in first grade or so, the NAACP sued the Seattle school district, seeking to integrate in the long wake of *Brown v. Board*.[36] The dis-trict agreed to a voluntary busing program, but in 1966, after years of delayed action, protests started in earnest. Organizers led the city's black students in two days of walkouts.[37] The following year, SNCC leader Stokely Carmichael gave an inflammatory speech at Seattle's de facto segregated Garfield High in front of a crowd of 4,000, calling for black people to resist the draft. "So you tell them they better be happy with Dr. King, 'cause when some of us get guns, we know who we going to kill," he told the crowd. "Our guts and blood have been spilt for this country and we go to the worst schools this country can pro-duce! We who have spilt our guts and blood for this country. Our guts and our bloods have been spilt for this country, it's time we spill them for our people."[38] When King was assassinated, the next year, black Seattle high school student leader Trolice Flavors was already in a jail cell, waiting on bond after leading a rally at Franklin High.[39] Seattle's schools were a battleground. In 1968, while Gates formed the Lakeside Programmers Group (with the recent public-school transfer Paul Allen), across town some other Seattle youths were helping form one of the first Black Panther Party chapters outside California.[40] The Panthers wanted people's control of modern technology; the Lakeside Group was pri-vate control.

The solution of the '70s shaped the kind of people and institutions that suc-ceeded in the period. The giants of Silicon Valley's pre-silicon days tended to be handsome, athletic, and likable. These were the all-around outstanding

---

* In 1976, on New Year's Eve, the George Jackson Brigade bombed the main transformer powering Lakehurst in solidarity with a strike by City Light power workers, reassured they could sabotage the whole "very rich" neighborhood without inconveniencing the working class. Workers refused to do the repairs, forcing supervisors to restore power to Lakehurst themselves. See "New Year 1976 Communique from the George Jackson Brigade," January 1, 1976, https://socialhistoryportal.org/sites/default/files/raf/0419771200.pdf.

young men of the bionomics age, "gifted" with superior genes and anointed by their professors. The individuals who won wars for America from the air and from the laboratory were selected early by institutions, often channeled into their future fields before they had any experience at all in the subjects, based on the sense that they were the kind of dependable, respectable men who belonged at the top of big companies. Bill Gates and Steve Jobs, by contrast, had poor personal hygiene, didn't play sports, and were both noted jerks. Neither served in the military, and both dropped out of college quickly. They ended up with two different corporate strategies, and occasionally became business opponents, but they personified the same historical forces. They weren't serving the public, and they didn't need approval from clean-shaven authoritative professor-administrators like Fred Terman or military bureaucrats like Bob Taylor, which left them and the cohort of tech workers they hired free to smell bad. (Historian Charles Petersen describes the transition as one from "bureaucratic" to "nerd" masculinity.)[41] These repellent young men were the tools that got capital from the crisis of the 1960s to the "greed is good" '80s, and an unwillingness to wash and feed oneself began to seem indicative of programming skill and economic value.

Unheard-of sums flowed through these men; what did Gates and Jobs represent to the money they attracted? The Xerox PARC visit infused Apple's Mac with years of prized research and development, and they didn't do it because they liked the boss—Jobs literally stunk up the place—or even for the opportunity to invest. Contracting with Apple was a way to solve the problem of the company's labor costs, secured by the firm's workers during the previous decades, when big business, big government, and big labor collaborated to split the proceeds of racing growth. Apple combined great branding with the worst of Silicon Valley's labor practices. Journalist Michael Malone, fellow son of the Bay Area space settlers, described the hypocrisy: "While the company propaganda stressed its community, its democracy, its adherence to the ideals of the Howdy Doody generation, each day an unmarked car picked up blank boards and boxes of chips from Apple's back door and delivered them to a roomful of Filipino women and housewives in a Saratoga home, who watched soap operas and stuffed boards at piece rates."[42] That network is what really made Apple a desirable partner.

At its simplest, Xerox wanted Apple because Apple could make computers without unions, which meant it could develop production efficiencies without worrying about the impact on employees: offshoring, subcontracting, technological speedup, hiring and firing according to the market's real-time demands.[43] Santa Clara County claimed the country's highest concentration of temp workers.[44] Any laborers a company couldn't easily replace were aligned with ownership via stock options: The professional employees swapped their guaranteed pay for a more direct stake in growth. Through bifurcation, they turned labor into a mere cost. Without a solution like that, Xerox couldn't compete with low-cost Japanese manufacturers. But instead of contracting to make a computer, Apple built computers for contractors.

The company's advertisements tell the story: Early Apple ads suggested a computer so multifunctional that the manufacturer didn't want to tell you what to do with it.[45] To close the 1970s, Apple offered $250 in credit to the 16 users who sent the best story about how they used theirs. "What in the name of Adam do people do with Apple Computers?" the ad asked. "You tell us." The picture showed a musclebound blond man, naked, holding an Apple II over his genitals. A large snake bends toward his ear as he smiles and shrugs, as if to say, "I don't know what it is, either!" But they figured it out, and the '80s ads featured inventors such as Thomas Edison and Henry Ford. "What kind of man owns his own computer?" asked one. "If your time means money, Apple can help you make more of it," says the body copy. "You concentrate on what you do best. And let Apple do the rest." Above, an excited Ben Franklin designs a kite on a color monitor. Another ad is more explicit, profiling an optical engineer named Reddy Chirra who used to work for "big companies" with "big mainframes." When Chirra started his own consulting business, he bought an Apple II, no time-sharing or per-hour mainframe charges necessary.* For small businesses, a personal computer reduced the marginal cost of work hours, allowing companies to pay a flat fee for unlimited processor time and compete with established firms via increased self-exploitation. Though Apple computers after the II were overpriced relative to their power, the company maintained a dedicated core of users who appreciated the friendly operating

---

* With a Desi STEM-professional small-business owner in the ads, and underpaid post-1965 immigrants building the chips, Apple incorporates and exemplifies the bifurcation of Asian-American labor in the period.

system, allowing Apple to adhere to a high-price, high-profit strategy while other microcomputer companies competed one another into the ground.*

But Apple didn't become one of the world's biggest companies because millions of people started their own businesses, at least not exactly. The shift from minicomputers to microcomputers made it possible to use them as educational tools for kids in secondary and primary schools, which in turn increased human capital production as children trained on their future business machines. And it was Apple—inspired by the past generation of scientists and engineers, who preferred to use the same brand of tools they used in college labs after they graduated—that made a distinct push to be the education computer. If kids got familiar with the unique Apple operating system and brand, they would likely buy their own when they got older.[46] After a successful 1978 pilot in Minnesota, Steve Jobs lobbied the California legislature and the governor, Jerry Brown, for a bespoke tax credit: 25 percent of the purchase price for every computer donated to schools. In 1983, he offered each of the 9,250 eligible schools in the state an Apple IIe system, and almost all accepted.[47] The company's huge profit margin combined with the offsetting tax credit meant that Apple was paying an estimated 5 percent or less of the ostensible bill—and that's just what the company said publicly.[48] Jobs found a way for Apple to pay California taxes in trade, in bougie electronics. It was part of a sneaky pattern, and by 1990, forsaking the paternal style of HP, Apple was selling two and a half times as much per employee as Wozniak's old employer.[49]

The socioeconomic forces of the '70s produced the classroom Apple II like a diamond, pressure accumulating until it took objective form. And despite the friendly interface, Apple computers were a signature commodity in a world that was getting rapidly worse for most people. That's what the lucky bid to invest in; that's what made them rich.

---

* This changed in 2020, when Apple began using its own high-power "Apple silicon" chips. Tom Warren, "Apple is switching Macs to its own processors starting later this year," *The Verge*, June 22, 2020, https://www.theverge.com/2020/6/22/21295475/apple-mac-processors -arm-silicon-chips-wwdc-2020.

Americas Online

San Jose Sharks — The Tiger Woods Economy —
Cocaine and Cappuccinos — Web Yahoos —
Broken Windows — Pets.com

Now that the gamers, hackers, and small-business owners had shrunk computer power down to personal size, they had to reconnect. Single-player games and sole proprietorships gave Apple a customer base, and Steve Jobs famously left the Ethernet connectivity port behind at Xerox PARC. Bob Metcalfe encouraged Xerox to license the board cheaply. The inventor got in line himself and started looking up venture capitalists. Ethernet boards were expensive, and bootstrapping wasn't feasible, but the venture capital industry was coming together after the Fairchildren and Atari wins as well as some helpful deregulation in the financial sector. They absorbed plenty of PARC spin-offs, and the VCs ended up competing to give Metcalfe money. Metcalfe called the company 3Com, for the three "coms": computer, communication, and compatibility. As the office model shifted from one mainframe computer with many terminals to a series of office PCs, Ethernet allowed firms to stitch their boxes into a local network even if they weren't all the same brand. It extended compatibility beyond what IBM accomplished, projecting a space where computers interacted like people — or, rather, where people could interact through computers. That place, clearly, is where we all live now.

Computers have been networked for as long as there have been what we recognize as computers; recall that nationwide computer networking was one thing the SAGE program did manage. To do it, scientists developed a device that turned the computer code into audio signals that could be transmitted over phone lines and then recoded on the other side. These modulator-demodulators became known as modems. As postwar computer research spread across the country, researchers connected to one another according to their programs. ARPANET connected Bob Taylor's defense-funded computer teams across the country in the 1970s, and at the end of the decade SATNET connected it with a heterogeneous system in Europe. In the Hawaiian archipelago, where long-distance wired networking between terminals and computers was less practical, scientists built ALOHAnet, the first wireless network, using radio.* The American network expanded in the '80s along with civilian funding for university computer research. CSNET connected computer science departments to five new supercomputers financed by the National Science Foundation. NSFNET hooked up the dozen or so regional academic networks that extended from university communities and, led by Stanford's Vint Cerf, developed the use of a standard set of transmission and networking protocols, which became the two-part Transmission Control Protocol/Internet Protocol, or TCP/IP, still in use today.† To implement this code, researchers assigned it to dedicated computers that became known as routers for the way they routed traffic according to a given protocol.

But meanwhile, at Xerox PARC, where Bob Taylor ended up after overseeing the failure of computerized war in Vietnam, the Metcalfe-led team was working with its own transmission protocol. These were the Rambo days, and part of the PARC plan was that the company could move faster and more nimbly than institutions in the public sector could, with all their bureaucrats and stakeholders. They drove ahead and completed their protocol suite before the feds did. The PARC Universal Packet (PUP) system wasn't universal at all; it was proprietary. When the corporate bosses wouldn't share with MIT's AI lab, the guys over there came up with their own Chaosnet protocol. Xerox developed PUP into the commercial version XNS with the help of Yogen Dalal, a PhD student of Cerf's at Stanford.‡ The result was that in the early '80s Palo Alto was computorily multilingual, at a geographic overlap between the Xerox PARC protocols and DARPA's—the added *D*, for "Defense," was an attempt

---

* One of Bob Metcalfe's most famous achievements was convincing Xerox to send him to Hawaii for three months to study ALOHAnet to begin his employment at PARC.

† For a summary of these networks and their development, see Katie Hafner and Matthew Lyon, *Where Wizards Stay Up Late: The Origins of the Internet* (Simon & Schuster, 1996), 219–46.

‡ Dalal was one of the engineering students who oversupplied India in the period, graduating from the Soviet-supported Indian Institute of Technology Bombay in 1972 before pursuing his electrical engineering doctorate (and resulting fortune) in Palo Alto.

to conform with a congressional restriction on civilian research by the DOD.[1] The researchers could talk to computers halfway around the world but not to the ones next door. Within Silicon Valley, whose job was it to make sure everyone was speaking the same language?

With Palo Alto suffering from an embarrassment of protocol riches and stuck trying to integrate the public and private information roads, even the most hardened Hooverite would say that figuring out the traffic signs was a job for the state. But it was the '80s, and the technology was ahead of the regulation. Before the government could get the industry to settle on TCP/IP, someone built a box to translate.

Stanford, as the pseudostate governing Palo Alto, is where the public and private roads met. Xerox programmers gave hints about their protocol to the school; employing Cerf, Stanford was already one of the couple of world centers for TCP/IP. A staff research engineer at the Stanford medical school named William Yeager was the first to rig up a translator, coding a multiprotocol routing program to hop the Xerox fence. A request from the university's director of computer facilities led the vast, distributed Stanford computer brain trust to put together a device that routed between devices across campus. The router included a few different networking circuits and ran on a new high-power computer board based on the Alto and designed by a Stanford graduate student named Andy Bechtolsheim. Combined with an upgraded version of the Yeager code, it worked, and they quickly built and distributed a couple dozen. In the public-private era of the proto-internet, Stanford *was* the multiprotocol router, translating between state investment, academic research, and the profit motive. Making all three compatible, however, meant compromises.

The multiprotocol router was a Stanford campus hack, the kind of device you need at a white-hot geographic center of computer R & D—internal demand was solid, and other universities wanted some, too—but probably not anywhere where there wasn't an extraordinary concentration of computing power. At least that's what most of the computer scientists thought. But three of the computer support staff saw an opportunity. Leonard Bosack and Kirk Lougheed inserted themselves into the multiprotocol router project, and Bosack's wife, Sandy Lerner, worked with it as the head of computer systems at the business school. At the end of 1984, with Bosack and Lougheed still working for the computer science department, Bosack and Lerner formed a company to commercialize the routing technology, against the express wishes of the university. (Lougheed later joined.) When the irascible comp sci boss, Les Earnest, found out his employees were sneakily redirecting Stanford resources into their private start-up, going so far as to sell boards that were made on campus, he forced their resignations.

For a while, the conventional wisdom about the creation of cisco Systems— all lowercase to start, as in the last part of *San Francisco*—was that Lerner and Bosack were inventor-entrepreneurs, icons of a new wave of Silicon Valley start-ups and founders of the fastest-growing company in American history. The couple in charge was portrayed as naive even, getting pushed out of their own company by conniving venture capitalists, a cautionary tale for the inventors who followed. But after Bosack's and Lougheed's former boss on the router project, Tom Rindfleisch, published his revisionist account in 1999, Yeager and the broader Stanford network got more credit.[2] The cisco team, on the other hand, gets credit for pursuing an ask-forgiveness-later strategy to wild success. At Stanford, responsibility for the situation fell to a new part of the bureaucracy: the Office of Technology Licensing, headed by Niels Reimers. In a March 1987 electronic letter (no doubt sent over a Yeager-and-company coded router), Reimers outlined the school's options: "1. Do nothing. 2. Go to court. 3. Try to make the best of a bad situation. None of the three are palatable; the first isn't even digestible. The second may make us feel good but would accomplish little else. So that left us with the third course of action."[3] The deal was for less than $200,000; Yeager gave 80 percent of his share back to the school. The cisco team violated the rules again, advertising their router on the anti-commercial ARPANET. But it worked, and as the VCs propelled cisco onto the stock market, everyone involved in the company got filthy rich, even if everyone involved in the technology didn't.

Internetworking raced ahead of government standardization, and cisco began by selling to places that had Stanford's luxurious problem of too much computing power. But that computing power cheapened very fast, and by the closing years of the '80s, cisco was targeting multioffice corporations, for whom connecting existing systems was more cost-effective than buying new standardized gear. To keep up with growth, cisco turned to Don Valentine at Sequoia Capital, who nabbed a controlling stake. Valentine brought in an aggressive new CEO (from the Stanford business school, via spy contractor

GRiD Systems), put the company on the NASDAQ at a quarter of a billion dollars and growing, and ousted the founding team. Live by the sword, die by the sword. They did die well, however; Bosack and Lerner donated millions of dollars to their own animal welfare foundation, including a spay/neuter clinic at Tufts University's school of veterinary medicine named for Lerner's cats.* The capitalized Cisco went on an acquisition spree through the '90s, leveraging a high stock price to expand by purchasing smaller firms, and the company built an oligopolistic position in the built internet infrastructure, supplanting (though not destroying) 3Com.

In this period of the early web, similar market and technological pressures shaped a generation of new complementary firms. A category of appliances was becoming something more: a networked ecosystem where circuits of all sizes and types could converse with one another. We have come to call this electronic web the internet, a unique—though no longer proper—noun. Internetworking began, like so many things in this story, in the space between the military and academia, before moving to start-ups and the big corporations. Palo Alto companies like Cisco and 3Com took advantage of public infrastructure such as telephone lines and, with the help of the still new but increasingly established and powerful venture capital scene, spread internetworking like a chorus of trickster gods. Everyone was finally starting to speak together.

That was the hardware, but what about software? After working on a failed database contract called Project Oracle for the CIA at Ampex, three employees, in the proud tradition of Ampex itself, took off to start their own database company. (Think of it as a spreadsheet company like VisiCalc, but one that was dealing with such large, complicated sets of data that in addition to writing software, it also needed to process and store information for customers.) On its third naming try, the founders landed on Oracle Systems. Its first customer was the CIA, which found the name (then being used for the firm's first product) an audacious repurposing of public resources. But the CIA also found the advertised idea of a relational database software that ran on several systems very appealing, since the agency tended to buy everything. The Reagan CIA sent big checks in plain white envelopes with no return address and

---

* The couple divorced, and Lerner went on to found the iconically mordant Gen X makeup brand Urban Decay.

didn't mind that the first few versions didn't work—or that it had to serve as Oracle's debugging team. "We bought this thing knowing damn well it wasn't going to work. We're buying an idea," an Oracle engineer recalls being told.[4] Thanks to the Reagan defense buildup, Oracle had the time and money to develop its product, and eventually it did work. In 1983, Don Valentine and Sequoia Capital helped boost the firm onto the commercial market, and after the Oracle version 5 software debuted, in 1985—the eccentric CEO Larry Ellison started at version 2—the company went public, in a spring cluster with Microsoft and a new Palo Alto computer company called Sun.

The personal computer was, from the first Alto with its Ethernet board, the interpersonal computer. When Andy Bechtolsheim built the computer board for the router Cisco appropriated, he was building a knockoff version of the fancy workstations donated by Xerox. Altos were the first of their kind, and by realizing Engelbart's dream of human augmentation, the copy-machinists financed the industry push to the personal computer. The conventional account foregrounds Apple's access to PARC, but the Altos set up at Stanford were at least as important. To see an Alto was to want one, but Xerox wasn't going to manufacture it anytime soon, which made the Alto nothing more than a luxury prototype, like a futuristic car built for a movie, a car that no one can repair. Bechtolsheim's goal was to build his own Alto-type workstation the IBM way, by wiring together generic modular parts. These workstations took advantage of rapidly improving processors, and, as with the Alto, users could use them to perform sophisticated design tasks. They plugged into the new Stanford University Network, whose routers also ran on Bechtolsheim's board. The university built some of these generic Altos, but Stanford wasn't a computer manufacturer. When no firms jumped at the opportunity to license the design for a general-purpose modular workstation, Bechtolsheim teamed up with two Stanford MBAs—Vinod Khosla and Scott McNealy—and a Berkeley engineer named Bill Joy to start the workstation company themselves. Unlike Cisco, they didn't steal the Stanford network, but they did port the name: Sun Microsystems.

Once it was ready to scale beyond its revenue, Sun took on venture capital and built a Sun-2. Like Cisco, Sun sent its first version to other universities. News spread of the new "micro" computer workstation that was almost as powerful as the minicomputers, but a full order of magnitude cheaper.

Unlike Apple, Sun wasn't committed to its own branding, and when the OEM market came calling, Sun was first in line to build workstations for whoever needed one. The first big sale was to Computervision, which sold computer-aided design (CAD) systems. For Computervision and other niche system producers, making the switch from mini to micro—and picking the right manufacturer—was essential for staying competitive in the '80s. After some hard negotiating, Sun scooped the $40 million contract.[5] It was in the race.

Sun hit the NASDAQ in '86, and though Oracle and Microsoft stole its thunder, it quickly captured a growing quarter of the workstation market. From there the company pursued the kind of deals that Apple turned down with Xerox and that Atari couldn't negotiate with IBM: It became a contract producer for large industrial concerns, making generic workstations that the big guys branded for their own use. Kodak bought 7 percent of the company, then AT&T bought 19 percent, elevating Sun into the top tier of computer manufacturers, and without the big revenue from mini and mainframe systems.[6] Even when fourth-place HP bought second-place workstation manufacturer Apollo, Sun kept gaining. Sun made a symbolic jump to HP status when, as its forerunner was first into Japan and Germany after the war, it was first into Moscow in 1992, scooping up the Soviet supercomputing team like a privatized telephone network. McNealy kidded that maybe he could help the new San Jose hockey franchise grab some Russians, too.[7] The Sharks unexpectedly made the second round of the playoffs in 1993, behind ex-Soviets Sergei Makarov, Igor Larionov, and Sandis Ozoliņš. Though I can't imagine the two were actually connected except via shared historical circumstance, McNealy did later join the board of the team's parent company.

In the heavenly ledger where the contributions and rewards of various Silicon Valley figures are weighed and recorded, Andy Bechtolsheim ranks high on both lists. From his start as a would-be Intel intern in the 1970s, the German immigrant contributed to the Palo Alto ecosystem, taking, giving, recycling, and, when that's what the world told him to do, commercializing.[8] His Alto-inspired board ported a whole series of functions to microcomputers. In addition to the multiprotocol router, it was the basis for another big Stanford start-up's product: the graphics terminal from Silicon Graphics, Inc. (SGI). Led by electrical engineering professor Jim Clark, Silicon Graphics turned the Sun board and a bunch of grad-student labor into a specialized display terminal for architects and engineers. That became a series of high-powered workstations that made the second generation of computer special effects possible, including the liquid-metal Terminator in *T2*.* SGI and Sun also built the technological infrastructure for Pixar's genre of computer-animated films, such as *Toy Story* and *A Bug's Life*, a pop-culture beachhead for Silicon Valley as well as a $1.5 billion IPO for Pixar in 1995.[9] This stuff wasn't "online," but it was part of the internetworking phase of computer development.

Though it's easy to think of them as sequential—first came the PC, then everyone plugged them together—the personal computer and the internet reflected somewhat different theories about how to distribute and arrange computing power. As I've said, Steve Jobs and Bill Gates embodied the Reagan-era tendency toward private household ownership, and so did their companies and flagship products. For Sun and Oracle, however, "a minicomputer in every pot" was an illogical idea. Academic and corporate networks that connected thin client terminals to heavy-duty processor and memory system nodes were much more efficient. "The network is the computer" became Sun's slogan, and though the company did make a desktop play, its next real success came in the new market for big computers that sat in closets. These powerful server computers hosted files and programs that skinnier client devices could access through a network. The backbone for the network of networks was still the NSFNET, and a commercial ban limited the internet's spread through the '80s. That's when Tim Berners-Lee at CERN, in Switzerland, published the code for a web browser program called WorldWideWeb that allowed users to post and retrieve multimedia—photos and audio in addition to just text— and a program for a web server computer that always stayed on and hosted sites with pages. The Stanford Linear Accelerator Center (SLAC) installed the hemisphere's first web server at the end of 1991, allowing Berners-Lee to demonstrate the system by browsing from a conference in France into the SLAC bibliographic database. The NSFNET commercialized at the same time, and as the world went online, Sun sold the gold pans in the form of powerful web

---

* In her recent book, scholar Julie A. Turnock questions the Silicon Graphics PR claims regarding use of the company's workstations on films such as *Jurassic Park* and *Death Becomes Her*, claims which have become accepted as fact. More likely, she argues, persuasively, those effects were accomplished on regular Macs. Julie A. Turnock, *The Empire of Effects: Industrial Light & Magic and the Rendering of Realism* (University of Texas Press, 2022), 139.

servers and the universal web programming language Java, which did for web coding what the multiprotocol router did for networking.

These were the first internet boom years, when vast arrays of internet-worked hardware promised to disrupt every industry in the world. Companies raced to snap up networking and hosting equipment from 3Com, Cisco, and Sun as well as the software-as-a-service offerings of Oracle. Buoyed by market enthusiasm, the firms scaled by acquisition, interweaving into friendly *keiretsus* through their shared shareholders. In 1995, Bechtolsheim left Sun to found a company devoted to speeding up Ethernet, which was quickly snapped up by Cisco for a cool $220 million, a nice payback to Bechtolsheim for designing the company's original computer board.[10] The firm 3Com got so big that it bought the naming rights to Candlestick Park, home of the San Francisco Giants and 49ers, a venue previously named for the chilly promontory where it had sat since the baseball team moved there, in 1960. Though I have it on good authority that some fans declined to use the privatized name, it marked a new era for the region, which had become something different over the previous decade and a half. Palo Alto and Silicon Valley and Stanford and tech and the internet stood for more than the newest electronics; that cluster of nouns meant a new way of doing business, a new plan for growth in a unipolar American capitalist world. They stood for getting fucking rich.

One of the reasons capitalists were so excited about these internetworking companies was a principle outlined by Metcalfe that—as Silicon Valley is wont to do with regard to useful insights about business and technology—has been elevated to a law. Metcalfe's law simply asserts an exponential relation between a network's nodes and its value. The more users there are, the more valuable the existing connections. In other words, these companies got big extremely fast, and these networks tended toward monopoly and oligopoly. Meaning that if these firms could use marketing and low prices to expand their user bases exponentially, they could jump from zero to billion-dollar monopolies in a process that looks more like the flipping of a binary switch than growing a company. Sophisticated and risk-tolerant venture capitalists could take an idea, just a prototype and a few sheets of paper sometimes, and build it into one of these firms in a year or two. (The expansion of consumer credit helped, too, and early start-ups were often financed on a house of founder credit cards.) Of course there were many millions of dollars in public money underlying those ideas, but Bayh-Dole and Stanford's OTL gave the spin-off model an academic Kosher stamp. The exploding stock market learned to love these start-ups and their whirring boxes, and once again value sprinted from around the world into the Bay Area. Assessing this period, the analysts Martin Kenney and Urs von Burg write that business-model innovation was "almost on a par with the importance of technology itself in the history of Silicon Valley's development."[11]

The internet's business implications were huge. Long before the Valley became associated with "disruption," Kenney and von Burg pointed out that, with internetworking, "industries that appeared to stabilize, in terms of organizational forms or business models, could be reopened for new rounds of firm formation."[12] That meant growth—albeit the destructive kind—and Silicon Valley became a bipartisan darling as it promised a new phase of postindustrial American expansion. The NASDAQ composite index grew from under 200 in the 1982 recession to over 5,000 in the spring of 2000. With support from the so-called Atari Democrats such as Paul Tsongas, Gary Hart, and Al Gore, the tech industry sealed the precepts of the Reagan Revolution into new and seemingly permanent layers of national infrastructure, from defense and finance to computing and telecommunications to who knows what else. These lean tech firms wiggled out from under the obligations of the New Deal and compensatory versions of the state, and it showed in their numbers. Capital utilization was high, as was revenue per employee, and their profit margins reflected their monopoly positions. Key employees were committed to companies through stock options and grants. One hundred years or so later, it was strikingly analogous to the railroad boom. And as in the joint-stock model back then, the financial regime was about as important as the underlying technology.

For some capitalists, the internet was like the arrival of the messiah, the prophesied jump forward for which they'd been waiting. The stock performance was the miracle that proved its divinity. There had been plenty of successful start-ups from the Bay Area in the past, but the speed and scale displayed in the 1980s and '90s was of a different order. For those nearby it was not hard to believe this was a new phase of society, that the tech industry had found a way to make everything more efficient by transcending old limits, and they convinced a lot of other people of that, too. Comparisons between the internet and fire or the wheel were common.

The techies found their sporting equivalent in Tiger Woods, a young California-born golf prodigy who was breaking record after record in the late 1980s and early '90s. Intensively trained from infancy in a manner that the reader can recognize as the Palo Alto System, Tiger was significantly better than other golfers, so much better that it suggested he'd figured something out, that he was permanently changing the game. Just as the internet was taking off, Woods enrolled at Stanford, where he won nearly everything there was to win in two years before turning pro. Nike signed him to a reported $40 million endorsement contract, the most ever for a professional golfer, before he played a single round of professional golf.[13] It was an exceptionally good investment, and Tiger continued to transform the sport. He was objective proof that you could instantly change an old game, a powerful metaphor for Silicon Valley. And though he only stayed two years, Woods kept some of his millions in Palo Alto, investing with the VC Ron Conway and serving as an early "angel" for a web search company at Stanford.[14]

In those frothy days, some people felt like they missed out, even if they made a lot of money by normal standards. But part of the playbook at the time for VCs was replacing founders with seasoned professional managers: Bosack and Lerner were the cautionary tale, particularly because they sold their stock after getting the boot instead of holding on and letting the suits make them 50 times as rich. Jim Clark of Silicon Graphics was a big personality, and he chafed at his VC managers. He became obsessed with the Valley's big fortunes, figuring he was as entitled as anyone and mad that the finance goons were getting too much credit. Weren't the engineers the ones creating the real value? At the beginning of 1994, Clark left SGI with a single purpose: getting very rich. He told people he was going to make $100 million. He was off by a factor of at least ten.

In looking for the next great internetworking tool, Clark landed on Mosaic, an improved browser out of the supercomputer center at the University of Illinois, one of the research institutes the NSF funded to create CSNET. The free program put a pretty skin on the World Wide Web—it presented images in-line, on pages, instead of as pop-out files, for example—making it easier to use, and brought the internet into the home and onto Microsoft-powered personal computers. Mosaic rapidly expanded the internet user base, and it was obvious to Clark that the browser was the next thing, even if it wasn't obvious how to make money off of it. He got in touch with the leader of the Illinois browser project, a young man named Marc Andreessen, who, luckily, had just moved to California. Drawing on their networks at SGI and Illinois, the two formed a company that used the Mosaic name until the university gave them a hard time. They changed it to Netscape and they called their version of the Illinois browser Navigator.

The projections for rapid adoption were right on, and though the web wasn't fast enough to enable most people to download the free software, it spread via floppy disk. The company's revenue model was as low-tech as their product model was high: the honor system. Individuals were welcome to use the program for free forever, while enterprise users were asked — sometimes by phone — to send a check for a license. Some did, but Netscape was losing investor money, and voluntary payments weren't going to make Jim Clark rich. He steered the company straight to the stock market. Less than a year and a half after he and Andreessen formed the company, they had the era's most successful initial public offering, more than doubling the $28 floated price, which itself was doubled at the last minute to match market enthusiasm. Thanks to sharklike deals with Netscape's VCs, Clark had his $100 million and then some, within two years of leaving SGI. "No longer did you need to show profits; you needed to show rapid growth," writes finance journalist Michael Lewis in his book about Clark. "Having a past actually counted against a company, for a past was a record and a record was a sign of a company's limitations."[15] Once again we see finance tending toward a version of the Palo Alto System, in which speculative potential is the metric that matters and winners are chosen early, before there is too much damaging competition. This binary culture could be as harsh as it was rewarding. Silicon Valley decided that Netscape was going to be the next hit from the first day, and missing out on such opportunities was increasingly unbearable. When Glenn Mueller — Clark's venture capitalist from the SGI deal — found out he didn't make the Netscape funding round on incorporation day in 1994, he shot himself in the head.[16]

Coffee, Computers, and Cocaine

As in the days of LSD, there was more than one way to augment a programmer in the 1980s and '90s. Computers and the network between them enhanced individual productivity in the tech industry itself, just as Engelbart once imagined. Silicon Valley was a great advertisement for Silicon Valley's products. The implicit message was that firms and individuals who adopted the region's orientation and tools would see the same breakthrough gains and efficiencies. Between the internet and the stock market, the Valley became an increasingly evangelical culture, both externally — pushing national and international adoption and investment — and internally, as firms jockeyed on imaginary fields of reputation and momentum as much as they did on the retail market.

With so much activity between firms and between individuals, the Bay needed a physical network of neutral public places. Silicon Valley became known for its coffee culture: not the relaxed boulevards of Paris, but laptops and lattes and "informational meetings" and overheard industry gossip. Its rise was concurrent with the "second wave" of American coffee, which began at Peet's Coffee in Berkeley and spread to Starbucks in Seattle, and from there around the world.[17] Cyber cafés offered internet access by the minute, and the web itself was built on java. The idea of the café as a creative node became so central to the Silicon Valley self-conception that firms later re-created full coffee shops inside their plush offices. But the transformation of the coffee-house into the office of the future masked a worrying shift in employment trends. Some of those people sitting at Starbucks were rich or getting there, but an increasing number of their tablemates didn't have a desk or a workplace to go back to. Much of Silicon Valley's value to the global capital markets came from the new business models, but business-model innovation was in part a euphemism for the new employment models, and the new employment models were unfortunate for most people involved.

One premise of technological development was always that computers would automate manufacturing activities. In 1975, Harry Braverman was already writing about how punch-cards were changing production work, about how they transformed manufacturing workers into technicians who worked with numbers as much as steel.[18] But when firms looked for places to locate their new facilities, they often as not picked somewhere offshore, combining efficiencies for super-duper efficiency. Rather than galloping ahead on electronic legs, American manufacturing growth declined, propped up by the pricey computer equipment itself. "By the year 2000, 76.6 percent of all computers used in business were being used in retail and service firms," writes scholar Fred Turner, yet "this sector of the economy had seen little in the way of productivity gain."[19] Rather than expanding the pie, the new Silicon Valley labor regime was good for shifting the rewards from labor toward the overlapping groups of bosses, managers, and stockholders.

Tech companies were "lean" or "virtual," which is to say they outsourced as much work as possible. The ideal for these firms was a pure idea company, one that produced intellectual property and hired out for the rest. For manufacturing, that meant outsourcing to domestic contract firms with names like Solectron and Flextronics, as well as the Taiwan-based Foxconn.[20] In this way, internetworking firms like 3Com and Cisco got closer to being software companies while still benefiting from the big margins that came with selling little whirring boxes. Sun assembled its own workstations at first, but the firm's origins lay in combining off-the-shelf parts that were, more likely than not, manufactured by companies like Solectron and Flextronics. When things got tough, Sun outsourced assembly as well. Empowered by a weak labor movement, large firms such as HP sold off much of their manufacturing infrastructure to contractors, then contracted with them. IBM took it a step further and spun off a whole contract manufacturing firm, Celestica, in 1997.[21] In the '90s, while Santa Clara County's overall numbers dazzled, its manufacturing wages declined, including in the electronic equipment sector.[22] Firms outsourced high-wage work, too; the famous Palo Alto industrial design consultancy IDEO opened in 1991, encouraging tech start-ups to further narrow their focus, and discount imitators followed. One analysis found that likely well over half—up to 80 percent—of the county's employment growth between 1984 and 1997 came in the form of externally contracted workers.[23] And those were the jobs kept onshore; statewide, electric and electronic manufacturing employment fell 38.7 percent between 1980 and 1995.[24] The issue wasn't just that capitalists were thriving while their workers suffered; with output growth stalled, it was all about the split. Capitalists were winning *because* their workers were losing, a reality well camouflaged by the whiz-bang excitement Silicon Valley produced.

But how could the world's highest-technology firms outsource their work to low-paid contract workers? More easily than you might imagine. As you read in the previous chapter, Apple got its boards stuffed at unregulated low piece rates by contracted immigrant employees, and Apple was far from alone. An estimated one-third of the region's Indochinese immigrant population was employed assembling printed wire boards in the 1990s, a whopping 40,000 people.[25] The increasing sophistication of Taiwanese contract manufacturers—led by the Taiwan Semiconductor Manufacturing Company (TSMC), which was founded by former Texas Instruments employee and Stanford electrical engineering PhD Morris Chang in 1987—also allowed firms to outsource progressively more work. In China, Deng Xiaoping's pro-market policies allowed the Taiwanese contractors to "onshore" production to the mainland in turn, where firms enjoyed the privileges that came with the People's Republic's first capitalist production enclaves. All this distancing of companies from production, shoving it into the home and over the border, also pushed the environmental and health hazards of an extremely toxic industry onto someone else's books. Being lean had legal efficiencies, too.

America imported a bifurcated cohort of immigrants to fit a bifurcating pattern of employment, and for every Silicon Valley investor or board member or founder from the Third World, there was a family of refugees in a local basement performing the low-wage manufacturing labor that animated the computer industry's numbers. Neocolonialism provided more than a market for Silicon Valley's defense-ish electronics; it provided a labor force as well. Immigration from Mexico increased rapidly starting in the 1970s, followed in the '80s by Central Americans fleeing societies intentionally destabilized by American meddling. In this time of growing inequality and immigration, many found their work absorbed by the bifurcated winners, in the forms of domestic service, maintenance, and construction work, which was often informal and left these laborers unprotected from above-average levels of exploitation and abuse. During the 1980s, the share of U.S. Latino workers in the relatively poorly paid service sector increased from 28 percent to 61 percent.[26] As contracted janitors, these workers led the regional tech industry's only successful union drives in the early 1990s, putting pressure on Apple and HP by connecting the big brands with their labor contractors. But when workers tried to expand the action to the assembly line at the IBM chip assembly contractor Versatronex, the company shut down the factory.[27]

In terms of solid, middle-class careers, the Bay Area had less to offer every year, thanks to the decline in defense dependence. If you couldn't count on the Cold War, what could you count on? There were fewer government jobs available, and you certainly couldn't depend on the new tech companies, which provided stock options in lieu of retirement benefits and job security. Even company founders were fired with no compensation, depending on the contracts they signed with their investors. If you didn't invent the newest new thing—or convince rich people that you might—then the best option seemed to be going ahead and developing skills that were tied to the high-tech industry. If you were a capable programmer or engineer, you at least had something to leverage in the marketplace. These computer skills might not get you a permanent job, but they were in demand, and they could earn a check. And all sorts of institutions needed their own "information technology" staffers to maintain what were still fragile computer systems. Workers could be certified in one or another of the internetworking systems in a single-year program and become eligible for a tech job. Insofar as Silicon Valley yielded something like a new middle class in the 1990s, this was it.

In her study of South Asian teenage life in Silicon Valley, scholar Shalini Shankar finds that these "gray-collar" jobs exerted a powerful pull on her subjects and their families:

> New types of technology jobs offered middle-class Desi teens an inroad into the white-collar world. Between highly skilled engineering positions and grueling assembly line work emerged an intermediate category of technology workers: systems operators, Microsoft Windows administrators, and other "low-tech" entrees into the high-tech world. More prestigious than assembly line work yet far less upwardly mobile than engineering jobs, such categories of work offer the distinctive title of computer professional as well as monetary benefits in an industry that signifies modernity and progress.[28]

In a tighter labor market, Microsoft, Cisco, and other firms would have had to train people to keep their unstable systems running for clients, but with few paths to career employment open, tech companies relied on striving members of the middle class to pay and work hard to learn. This model forced students and workers to assume all the risk, and when the systems and technologies changed, they could update their own skills or get out of the way. In a sequence that I find hard to interpret other than as an act of collective punishment for the uprisings of the 1960s and early '70s, California's informally segregated, formally choked-of-funds public schools no longer prepared black and Hispanic students for the tertiary education required for technology jobs of any collar. Assembly-line managers preferred foreign-born workers, who had fewer rights than their American-born colleagues. Members of the region's black working class found themselves, like an increasing share of the population in general, boxed into the low-wage service and informal sectors of employment. In a documentary, one man who grew up in the 1970s in LA recounts that after graduating he planned to go to a technical school, as some of his classmates did, but his inability to read put a hard block on his continued education.[29] Rick Ross became the West Coast's most infamous independent cocaine distributor instead.*

Coffee and cocaine had a lot in common for the Bay Area tech milieu: Both came from the Americas as part of the restructuring of Third World economies toward consumable exports; both were increasingly available at several price points; and both made people go fast for long periods of time. Following Miami, Los Angeles, and New York, Silicon Valley was the fourth corner of the American coke binge. Thanks in part to the industry's cozy relationship with elements in the U.S. federal government, the international cocaine trade increased in volume during the period. In the 1980s, street and wholesale prices fell rapidly while purity increased.[30] Blow became as central to the tech industry as it was to Hollywood or Wall Street, and Palo Alto gave the drug its own nerdy spin. "The valley's would-be titans of industry preferred their cocaine at the office, or at house parties where husbands gathered together to talk incessantly about computers, while ignoring their wives," writes scholar Charlton D. McIlwain. "Cocaine retained every bit of its glitz and glamour. But in the valley, it was all designed to push the work. Cocaine labored in service of the dream. For most, the dream was a fantasy, but they chased it nonetheless. Cocaine kept them in the race."[31] Michael Malone describes the era as a white-powder blizzard — the only kind the Bay ever saw — complete with coke mirrors made of clean silicon wafers purloined from work.[32] The drugs

---

* Oakland rapper Too $hort tells the same story in his novelistic 1992 song "No Love from Oakland": "So why commit the crime? Don't ask me / Went to school every day, and I still can't read."

certainly help explain both the wacky business models and the general surfeit of enthusiasm—as well as the country's highest divorce rate.[33]

Just as the internetworking companies rendered ugly, incomprehensible code into the nice smooth websites Americans were getting used to trusting, the tech industry presented very sketchy business practices as the spotless work of clean-room engineers. Even authorities were convinced, which left the San Jose Police Department surprised when a sting operation for thieves ended up catching electronics workers. The SJPD secretly opened its own bar in the early 1980s and put the word out that it was a safe place to fence stolen goods. They expected to get the regular jewelry and such; instead, they got disk drives and microchips. Workers were stealing equipment and selling it to scrap dealers and secondhand computer merchants—for cocaine money in particular, the police suspected.[34] Valuable materials such as gold wire tended to go missing from company labs. Even the occasional spy (international, industrial, and both) cut a deal for some important information. But that kind of thing was the price of doing business in the culture Silicon Valley encouraged. Managers at the brand-name firms distributed drugs to employees: cocaine for the coders, cheaper crystal meth for people on the assembly lines. Speed was more important than accuracy, and parts failed at high rates. No big deal: With margins so large, just send a free replacement. That was cheaper than implementing real quality control in the first place.

The same changes to employment echoed up and down the intercontinental supply lines. "The average Colombian is affected by the drug trade in roughly the same way in which workers in other third world countries are affected by international subcontracting," writes Philip Mattera in *Off the Books: The Rise of the Underground Economy*, in which he tracks the growth of informal labor in the 1980s. "Instead of working directly for foreign capital, they are employed by domestic suppliers who enjoy astronomical rates of profit."[35] Countries that didn't have oil or electronics manufacturing capacity had to find something else to trade for dollars; like those other international commodities, cocaine was valuable per unit and allowed for good profit margins. The leaders throughout the Americas who captured U.S. support tended to be involved with drug trafficking for the same reason the leaders of the United States tended to be involved with electronics trafficking: It was a good business for bosses. Of course, the drug cartels kept a lot of their money in Western banks, just as everyone else did.*

Without getting into chemistry questions that are beyond my field of expertise, I think it's relatively uncontroversial to describe heroin and cocaine as habit-forming. But these compounds had other magical properties as far as capitalism was concerned: Expensive, portable, and peasant-grown, they pulled people into the price system on both sides of the pipe. Poor producers, who could no longer make a living growing anything else, met poor users, who had an urgent new reason to make themselves useful to the market. This was a cruel distortion of Third World unity, a fun-house image of the decades before, when messages of solidarity traced the same lines. Some 1980s subcultures, including the straight-edge punks, made a point of rejecting all drugs as capitalist poison, and they had a point. In the black (and increasingly Chicano, Southeast Asian, and Central American) ghettos, drugs funneled money out of communities already suffering from divestment. If the wealth accumulated by dealers and distributors sometimes trickled down to the corner, that amount could never exceed a portion of what came out of the streets in the first place, as in a pyramid scheme. Drugs didn't produce anything, not without an assembly line. Reagan's "Just say no" anti-drug policy didn't fool anyone who was paying attention. A satirical ad featured in the early internet-era San Francisco print rag *Processed World* pitches one of the ubiquitous get-rich schemes: "How to stop working and earn $30,000 a year." The answer? "Become a Freelance Drug Merchant!" Just make sure you say yes to "American-imported Afghani hashish, Pakistani and Burmese Heroin, Paraguayan and Bolivian Cocaine" and no to "other syndicates."[36] The cutout postcard expressing interest in a drug career is pre-addressed to the White House. The actual *Processed World* article, about the Bay Area's very uncool 1980s drug scene, is full of goofy *MAD* magazine–style illustrations, but the article's contradictory headline is evocative: A CORROSIVE SOCIAL CEMENT. The flow of drugs into Silicon Valley completed a productive circuit: California exported microchips and

---

* In 1986, the Treasury Department imposed a record $4.75 million fine on Bank of America for failing to report cash transactions across its California branches as required by anti-laundering regulations. Nathaniel C. Nash, "Bank of America Is Told to Pay U.S. $4.75 Million Fine," *New York Times*, January 22, 1986.

imported drugs; the drugs powered the labor that went back into the micro-chips; and so on. With every circulation, capitalists strengthened themselves in relation to workers by peeling off a growing share. The drugs were part of the corrosive social cement, binding populations together in the acid embrace of dispossession.

This was the shape of the unipolar capitalist world, and though the authorities denied their role when it came to cocaine, the international coffee market was legal and on the record. In his study of that market, scholar Joseph Nevins finds that the big changes occurring between the mid-1970s and the mid-1990s are related to the "longer-term struggle over the distribution of income related to the crop."[37] In the early part of this period, growers pulled in an average of around 20 cents for every dollar of coffee revenue. They were aided by an agreement called the International Coffee Accord (ICA) of 1962, which acted as a sort of cartel plan, constraining and arranging supply. In the wake of the Cuban Revolution, the Kennedy administration supported the ICA and its concessions to Third World workers as a Cold War tool to head off communist onshoring in the Western Hemisphere. But as the U.S. strategy changed, the country and its free-market Latin American proxies abandoned the ICA in 1989. The results were quick: By the mid-1990s, the grower share was down from 20 to 13 percent. Roasters, traders, and retailers in the drinking countries improved their share from 54 to 78 percent. That big, fast shift was partly thanks to repressed grower wages, partly thanks to repressed domestic service wages in the West, partly thanks to consolidation in the industry, and partly thanks to new high-priced coffee drinks. Starbucks went public in 1992, and if it seemed to be growing like a tech company in the '90s, that's because both thrived on the same social changes.

Worsening conditions for workers in Mexico and in the rest of the Americas pushed people north, rapidly increasing the undocumented immigrant population in the United States. The Bracero program was over, but the jobs still needed doing. Caught in between employers who were hiring migrants and nationalist restrictionists, the Reagan administration legalized a few million undocumented workers while increasing border enforcement. Even though the vast majority of narcotics came into the country via legal ports of entry, conservatives and liberals alike framed border enforcement as a central front in the war on drugs. Increasing the costs of crossing couldn't stanch the increase of people — they were responding to larger factors: Out-migration from Mexico's coffee-producing areas increased after the dissolution of the ICA, for example. This tendency intensified after the North American Free Trade Agreement went into effect in 1994, pushing Mexico further toward cheap manufacturing exports and cheap imported American corn.

The glut of cheap labor and commodities in this period undermined labor protections in the center as well as on the periphery, and the United States lost union jobs at a rapid clip. Reagan undermined the bulwark of government jobs by bringing Boulwarism to the White House. His signature incident occurred in his first year, when he fired more than 11,000 striking air traffic controllers and decertified their union. To the press, the president quoted an air traffic controller who quit the union and reported to work as ordered: "How can I ask my kids to obey the law if I don't?"[38] Once again, questions of individual criminality put the Reaganites on firm ground. Organized labor took to rearguard action, holding on to its institutions by agreeing to two-tiered contracts that reduced benefits and protections for new or future members. Capital shook off the midcentury labor agreement like a bad habit, reducing its accountability to its own workers the way it previously reduced accountability to the broader communities. The second part didn't require as many votes.

Organized labor was on its back foot, a back foot that was stuck in the quicksand of "business unionism." The capitalist and political constituency for that form disappeared, and anyone who wanted to improve the situation for workers had to find another model within the moment's ideological limits. Collective strategies like the strike grated on a public primed by an unrelenting cascade of individualist propaganda. Political associations — often centered on the welfare of women, children, and particular minority groups — put pressure on companies in an attempt to relink them with their social responsibilities. Protests targeted public-facing brands, holding them accountable for conditions in their supply chains, since the ability to sully brands was one of the movement's few points of leverage over the private sector. The endgame for this strategy was a reform promise from the target, a sort of DIY regulation without the state. Going after individual violators was an anticapitalist strategy for the war-on-crime era, and brand-heavy offshored textile companies were especially vulnerable. Most famous was Nike: Activists successfully associated the trademarked Swoosh logo with children working in Third World sweatshops, yielding a wide-ranging series of promises from the cofounder and CEO, Phil Knight (Stanford MBA '62).*[39] These agreements were not an effective way of improving labor's situation, and few involved were under the false impression that they were. These were bad days for working people. You could tell because the stock market was going up.

Not many trends can match the stock-market surge that defined the twentieth century's fourth quarter for volume. Plenty of individual firms flopped, but the indexes climbed with univocal intent, and most people who invested in "the market" made real money. Despite the growth graphs, this was a zero-sum era, and workers around the world lost a lot; it had to go somewhere. Russia got its own set of capitalist oligarchs, and corporate multinationals helped them carve up the region's privatizing assets. Vietnam, so recently a symbol for communist victory, is where underage workers were stitching soccer balls for Nike. Capitalism's grimy slip covered the globe, as if a cosmic titan had grabbed the planet by Cuba and dunked the blue ball in used cooking oil. We've seen how the United States and its allies created new forms of social control through violent disorder, using cliques of gangster capitalists to discipline local populations and drive the global price of labor down with every massacre. But what about the domestic scene? How could authorities maintain social balance during the long Reagan era if they weren't willing to pay workers enough to go along with it? Even if the individualist propaganda was very effective, people had to find ways to live. If the formal jobs didn't pay— and they didn't—then workers had to find informal ones. Like tech, drug and crime networks were monopolistic and came with high profits. New and powerful guns flowed alongside the drugs, and American cities destabilized with the rest of the hemisphere, even as the skyscrapers hosted ownership-class profit orgies.

To speak about crime in this context, even critically, is to accept a classed definition. Wage theft, stock fraud, and tax evasion are serious crimes, and they escalated dramatically in this period, but those are not the traditional referents for the 1990s "crime wave" discourse, because we have come to see ruling-class violations as part of a system that encourages cheating and corner

---

* Coincidentally, Knight overlapped at Stanford with TSMC founder Morris Chang. Though their firms came to represent different moments in the globalization sequence, we can recognize them as two principals in the same ballet.

cutting rather than as individual acts of social antagonism.[40] The crime wave refers to crimes that interest the police and prosecutors, which is to say crimes committed by working-class and poor people, which also increased during the period. Any serious analysis of this kind of crime puts labor conditions at the forefront rather than some individualist idea of criminal intent; there was never much mystery to the phenomenon from a sociological point of view. But administrations from Reagan through George Bush Jr. (at least) understood that, to avoid risking another wage-price spiral, they had to deal with crime as a problem of too many criminals rather than too few good jobs.

In this period, state authorities expanded their domestic counterinsurgency campaign from left-wing groups to all forms of organization by poor people. The policing strategy called for total domination of the streets, and it was based on research from a familiar figure. Philip Zimbardo, working on a small government grant in the late 1960s, tried a casual experiment with some cars. A couple of years ahead of his famous prison experiment, he abandoned two vehicles, one outside New York University's South Bronx campus and one outside Stanford. A confederate reported that the New York car was stripped for parts quickly, after which locals turned it into a jungle gym. Zimbardo speculated that urban anonymity enabled antisocial behavior, which he contrasted with Palo Alto, where the car went untouched.[41] Ever the dramaturge, Zimbardo pushed his Stanford scenario further: He instructed two of his grad students to take a sledgehammer to the car, at which point a crowd got into it, encouraging them to "hit it again, harder!" In his presentation of the research, he captioned a photo of the scene "The awakening of dark impulses at Stanford University."*[42] From this shallow pool of evidence, Zimbardo further imagines that the disintegration of the social fabric begins with a "releaser cue," and the more anonymous the society, the weaker the cue required. All it took to put us on the path to hell, he figured, was someone to break the first window. A decade or two of social-science telephone later, and the police were implementing an intensive "broken windows" strategy, which reclassified all undesired behavior as crime. Based on the study, the implicit idea was to make

---

* Zimbardo does not seem to consider that passersby correctly assumed that the graduate students had permission from the owner to destroy the car for some inscrutable scientific purpose related to the university and that they were not engaged in any criminal or even (directly) antisocial conduct.

the country's cities more like Palo Alto. The real social disintegration, however, was less about graffiti and litter than the increasing involvement of police in American life.

In 1988, California passed the Street Terrorism Enforcement and Prevention Act (STEP), which targeted what the legislature claimed was "nearly 600 criminal street gangs" operating in the state. The law gave the state's increasing number of police a blank check to target gang members, as well as broad latitude to define "gang member." The reasoning is worth quoting: "The Legislature hereby finds and declares that it is the right of every person, regardless of race, color, creed, religion, national origin, gender, gender identity, gender expression, age, sexual orientation, or handicap, to be secure and protected from fear, intimidation, and physical harm caused by the activities of violent groups and individuals." The lawmakers used the language of civil rights to proclaim an individual freedom from the tyranny of groups; it could be Reagan talking about air traffic controllers. By the late 1980s, incarceration was already manifesting a stock market–esque trend, as governments at all levels put the last phase of the solution of the '70s into action. As detailed by Ruth Wilson Gilmore in her invaluable study *Golden Gulag: Prisons, Surplus, Crisis, and Opposition in Globalizing California*, the state led the country into jail.

Unlike some commentators, Gilmore doesn't see the police and prisons as military Keynesianism by other means but rather as a different form of social control, required for a different historical situation. Still, she writes, the point isn't to "wax nostalgic for Keynesianism" but that "with [the] disappearance of the congeries of policies that to some degree guaranteed effective demand and provided — however haphazardly and stingily — incomes and services for the most vulnerable workers in the racial state, some other form of social control will, indeed *must*, step into the breach..."[43] California's ruling class was in a strong place to design that form, which historian Vijay Prashad describes as relying "less on factory discipline than on the discipline of starvation."[44] The state's voters gave their leaders a huge mandate for "tough on crime" policies, passing 1994's Proposition 184 with a 72 percent majority.* This "three

---

* Like many of California's trailblazing laws, this one was contested to the Supreme Court, where a conservative majority upheld the statute on a 5–4 vote. See "Excerpts from Supreme Court Rulings on California's 'Three-Strikes' Law," *New York Times*, March 6, 2003.

strikes" initiative established a long list of "serious and/or violent" crimes that, on a third conviction, send the perpetrator away indefinitely regardless of mitigating circumstances. Other states followed, and the federal government's concurrent crime bill distributed billions of dollars in support of police and other punitive solutions, though the crime wave itself had already peaked. As a result, the country's incarcerated population rose alongside the NASDAQ, as if the two were connected.

Too Many Assholes

Netscape was a game changer for the capital markets. SILICON WEALTH EXPLOSION, *Forbes* announced on the cover of its 80th anniversary issue in July of 1997, WHO REAPS THE NEXT TRILLION DOLLARS?[45] Not only did Jim Clark accomplish what he set out to do, and on a fantastically short timeline, he also made it look easy. The Netscape IPO prospectus contains some hints about what made the company so paradigm-shifting for investors: The firm reported only 257 employees — 114 in R & D; 114 in sales, marketing, and customer support; and 29 in administration and finance. In the six months before the prospectus came out, Netscape pulled in over $16 million in revenue, which meant that each employee generated more than $100,000 a year, an outstanding number for a company that was still figuring out its business model (and losing more than $10,000 a day doing so).[46] Among the revenue models Netscape was exploring at IPO were: the IStore virtual storefront infrastructure, including transaction processing; support for ad- and subscription-supported online publications; and a social network of virtual communities based on interest. All these ideas eventually did turn into successful web plays — though not by Netscape — so there was plenty of potential there, and besides some servers and office space, the firm was untethered from physical restrictions, leaving it able to pivot on a dime and scale up without a clear limit. The stock performed similarly.

Netscape straddled the line between the internetworking companies discussed in this chapter's first section — the round of devices that evolved from Bechtolsheim's circuit board like different organs from the same stem cells — and the true web start-ups of the internet boom. Navigator was software, leaving the silicon to someone else — they just had to get disks to users. If the idea of being mailed a physical copy of a single program sounds woefully inefficient now, the idea of downloading a file so large over a phone line was preposterous at the time. The browser was a layer between the internet's hardware and its content, and Netscape staked out a large swath of that territory. Virtual space seemed intrinsically valuable the way real estate was, and the Netscape IPO was the starting gun for the internet land rush.

Microsoft, the consumer software monopolist, felt threatened. If Netscape could place itself between all computers and the internet, it could become the standard digital interface rather than Microsoft's Windows operating system. Following the IBM playbook, Microsoft blitzed its own (licensed) browser onto the market: Internet Explorer, which the company packaged as part of the Windows OS. By reducing the browser license cost to zero for enterprise users, too, Bill Gates showed early that price competition got ugly fast in the internet sector. The move was transparently anti-competitive, and Microsoft didn't make a secret of its intention to dominate as much space as it could. Gates had been on the government's radar since 1990, and he successfully weaseled out of charges throughout the decade with appeals and consent decrees, though regulators stalled a merger with the tax software firm Intuit to death. To press its case against Microsoft, Netscape hired a surprise ringer: Robert Bork, legendary conservative, one-time Supreme Court nominee, and author of the prevailing theory of antitrust. If even Bork said there was a monopoly, there probably was.

The Clinton administration filed suit and Microsoft hired its own ringer— a recent head of the DOJ antitrust division, natch. Still, the district judge didn't like Bill Gates, and he didn't like Microsoft. He ruled for the breakup, which made for dramatic headlines, but Microsoft won the appeal and later negotiated a lenient settlement with the extraordinarily pro-business George Bush Jr. administration. In 2001, a month before Microsoft argued the browser wars appeal, MGM released *Antitrust*. The movie starred Tim Robbins as a transparent Gates send-up and Ryan Phillippe as a Stanford computer science student planning to cofound a tech start-up when Robbins recruits him into not-Microsoft NURV. Phillippe discovers that NURV is literally murdering start-up founders to steal their code, and he has to use fake-Gates's network against him. Despite being the richest man in a world that worshipped wealth, pop culture treated Gates like a serial killer. The public didn't have to like Bill Gates, but they did have to pay him. Monopoly was the model; when asked what he would consider success, internet start-up winner Mark Cuban cited Gates and said he wouldn't be happy until he, too, was sitting in front of congressional antitrust investigators.[47]

Despite some victories on the cultural and legal fronts, Netscape had to match Microsoft and give up on charging users in the meantime. Software tended toward free, and the internet was made of software. Netscape pivoted to advertising, which became the standard move for companies with nothing to sell but user attention. Still, early investors were not too worried about how web start-ups were going to eventually make profits; it was a land rush, so they pushed in and kept their eyes fixed on the IPO horizon. Established banks were happy to play along, especially considering the inflated fees they could charge players in the frothy sector. Remember that people were doing a lot of cocaine.

After the browser, the next place for capital was individual websites. The early sites reflected the same artisanal orientation as the first software developers and the Apple II's user cohort of newsletter publishers. It was a world of enthusiasts: Literary Kicks archived Beat literature. San Francisco's fog got its own site, as did the band Megadeth. Legacy media institutions put up their sites only to find themselves sitting alongside Buzzweb.com and random guys named Justin and Glenn and Jerry posting links to sites they liked. But in these early days, it was unclear where the line between the web's overlords and users was going to go. Were these user sites the web's content or its infrastructure? Venture capitalists looked for equipment opportunities. The internet already traveled through a series of bottlenecks: from the operating system to the router and the modem to the servers and the browser. Each one of those steps was worth a lot of money, and they all had to be established. What was one more? Investors looked for new layers to sit on top of the web. One of those link sites from 1994 was called Jerry and David's Guide to the World Wide Web, after its curators, Jerry Yang and David Filo, Stanford electrical engineering grad students and web enthusiasts. Buoyed by the inordinately online Palo Alto community, their directory was getting a lot of traffic. Once people got online they had to figure out where to go next, and that was Jerry and David's layer. They renamed the site Yahoo! and locked down a few million dollars from Sequoia Capital in the spring of '95. A year later, the site's IPO made them one of the first true web-stock success stories.

This "portal" layer was the most valuable spot on the web for an obvious reason: Users went through it no matter where they were going. Yahoo! had to scrap it out with a handful of competitors, including the face of anti-competitive tech, Microsoft. Gates wasn't content to let competitors snap up doors between Windows users and content, so Microsoft used its operating-system revenue to support attacks on web competitors. Before the decade was out, Netscape succumbed to Internet Explorer pressure and sold itself to the ill-fated internet service provider America Online in a complicated three-way deal with Sun. But thanks to big cash infusions from the market, some start-ups, including Yahoo!, could compete with the big guys by acquiring other start-ups. That's what Jerry and David did, buying a games company, a DIY website company (GeoCities), a groups company, and a messenger company in quick succession. Microsoft kept pace, buying the free email site HoT-MaiL in 1997, along with its user base. For start-ups like HoTMaiL—bought within 18 months of launch, for an undisclosed amount, reportedly $400–500 million—an acquisition could be just as good as an IPO.[48] Investors were happy to finance the feeding frenzy by bidding stock prices up. Microsoft went from under $7 in '95 to $58 by the end of the decade, keeping Trey Gates the wealthiest man in the world. Yahoo! skyrocketed over $110, a classic example of what the Federal Reserve chair, Alan Greenspan, famously called "irrational exuberance."

Greenspan's speech came at the end of 1996, during an annual dinner put on by his friends at the American Enterprise Institute. David Packard died earlier that year, but before then he invested heavily in the AEI, leading fundraising for the institution and establishing it as an important part of the right-wing intellectual circuit.[49] It was a natural place for Greenspan to address some concerns to the financial elite. "Where do we draw the line on what prices matter?" he wondered. "Certainly prices of goods and services now being produced—our basic measure of inflation—matter. But what about futures prices or, more important, prices of claims on future goods and services, like equities, real estate, or other earning assets? Are stability [sic] of these prices essential to the stability of the economy?"[50] Those prices were not stable; they were headed straight up, and though that was great for everyone in the room who wasn't clearing the tables, some couldn't help wondering: Was it too great? Obviously something in the market wasn't working normally, but was that a problem? Where was the cause for pessimism? The investors thought they saw an ambush of Tigers Woods, not a brewing storm.

The question wasn't whether there was a connection between internet stocks and what Greenspan called the "real economy"—the economy of production, jobs, and commodity prices—but rather what the precise nature of the relationship was. Greenspan's worry was that a popping asset bubble could take it all down. Whether it actually would in 1996 was an open question. Maybe the hit would just go to fancy investors and their stock-optioned coders; part of the appeal to these companies was that they didn't have many workers to lay off anyway. As Microsoft hunkered down to fight the browser and portal wars, entrepreneurs looked for profitable ways to integrate the web with the real economy. The trick was not just selling internet tools to enterprise sectors but also spreading the web's disruptive tendencies to its new hosts. The big money lay in realigning whole industries under the network of networks, the way Giannini's banks once pulled California's farms into finance cartels. And the man to make it happen was Jim Clark.

Since the dramatic Netscape IPO, Clark had become a regional guru. He was an engineer who dictated terms to the Valley's biggest VCs, got away with it, and got incredibly rich, too. No longer would entrepreneurs have to cower before the money men: It was the dawning of the age of the founder and Clark looked the part. At six foot three, he was handsome in a white billionaire way, with suitable hobbies: driving motorcycles, flying planes, yachting, getting married to younger women, and thinking of new ways to make a lot of money very fast. A seat in the same room with Clark was like a golden ticket in those days, and with demand for his ideas so high, he was free to reduce supply. "He felt that pretty much the entire American economy was up for grabs, thanks to the internet," writes Michael Lewis.[51] The only restriction was to build something quick and foreign enough to Microsoft to avoid the beast's attention. Exemplifying the kind of thinking Silicon Valley made famous in the twenty-first century, Clark went to a doctor's appointment, after which he decided to change the whole health-care industry.

Clark figured that the huge sector was made up of nothing but doctors, patients, and a bunch of waste. The internet could handle all the information between the people who struck Clark as useful and cut out the ones who seemed extraneous. His business plan could fit on a cocktail napkin, and with

VCs and engineers desperate to sign up for whatever he scrawled down, he didn't need much more than that. It was a diagram, with "payers," "providers," "consumers," and "doctors" arrayed around a central node, which was the company. That was most of what Clark was willing to contribute, and he figured the idea was worth a quarter of a trillion dollars a year in revenue. At least that's what he told people. By the time it got to the Wall Street bankers, the Healtheon pitch was more detailed but structurally the same: all the stakeholders in a trillion-dollar industry arrayed around the new start-up. To get buy-in, they would persuade the biggest players to sign up as partners, promising them the internet tools to squish their competitors. "We want to empower the doctors and the patients and get all the other assholes out of the way," Clark told Lewis, "except for us. One asshole in the middle."[52] Healtheon used the land-grab metaphor explicitly; the bankers couldn't afford not to buy.

The model for using the internet to disrupt a brick-and-mortar industry was Amazon. An internet bookstore in Seattle founded by a young hedge-fund hotshot named Jeff Bezos, Amazon was among the most Gen X things in existence. Books were an arbitrary choice, a cheap, nonperishable commodity that seemed suited for the web. Thanks to early investment from his stepfather, an oil engineer for Exxon who left Cuba as a teenager after Castro nationalized his father's lumber mill, Bezos built and scaled the concept so fast that even a responsive, well-heeled competitor like Barnes & Noble couldn't keep up. Amazon was *the* internet bookstore. The stock debuted under $2 in 1997; around a year later, it was up tenfold. Between the summer of 1998 and the fall of '99, demand was so high that the stock split an unbelievable three times. Amazon closed 1998 with more than a half a billion dollars in revenue, and Bezos plowed money back into the business, making a firm choice for growth over profits. The company bought a couple of European competitors and expanded into music and movie sales. With help from outside investors, Amazon made large investments in other consumer-delivery start-ups, forming a Bezos-led *keiretsu* with the self-explanatory Drugstore.com, HomeGrocer.com, and Pets.com.[53] Bezos was the ultimate middleman merchant, inventing and dominating an online layer between commodity producers and consumers, starting with physical media and expanding rapidly from there. Throughout the late 1990s, Silicon Valley was awash in "Amazon for X" start-ups. Suddenly, the popular business plans looked much more like Jim Clark's asshole diagram than the exalted Fairchild tank of geniuses.

Though the aggregate measure of the '90s shows a strong upward line for tech stocks, and that impression is correct, on the ground it was a bit rockier. There were good times and bad times, periods when no pitch seemed like it could lose, and moments when it looked like the whole region was going to capsize. Party nights and hungover mornings. If a deal got caught standing when the music stopped, things could go bad fast. *Wired* magazine's parent company had a plan to expand into an Amazon of internet-age media content, with more magazines, a book publisher, and a web publication. The firm spent investor money and distributed stock options as an internet company would, and it needed a lot more cash to scale. It planned an IPO, with top-shelf Goldman Sachs agreeing to handle it at a huge $447 million valuation, a multiple appropriate for "the kind of high-flying internet companies *Wired* magazine wrote about rather than the sorts of print publishers Wired Ventures resembled," observed Jerry Useem in his postmortem.[54] It was a miscalculation, and a small dip in enthusiasm for Silicon Valley left the big institutional investors cold on Goldman's presentation. Soon after the release of Wired's first book, *Mind Grenades: Manifestos from the Future*, they called the whole thing off.* In a priceless bit of '90s color, Useem writes that the *Twin Peaks* theme was floating through the office when employees got the email with the bad news.

Recall the origins of the railroad crisis in the 1870s: too many roads to too few locations. Like the web, the tracks weren't built for price competition; they were monopolistic plans, and that made them brittle. "You're either a zero or a one. Alive or dead," repeats the Tim Robbins version of Bill Gates in *Antitrust*, describing both the Valley's business climate and its spree-killer competitive ethos. For investors, that meant they priced firms not based on expected returns per se but on the odds that they would become ones rather than zeros. Venture capitalists always played that way, with a few big winners picking up the slack (and then some) for a bunch of losers. The Clinton administration did what it could to encourage the boom in the late 1990s, including imposing a bipartisan Reaganesque cut to the capital-gains tax in 1997. Climbing stocks gave big internet fish the jaws to nibble start-ups the way VCs might,

---

* *Mind Grenades* is a fantastic early-internet object. It's a big picture-book, with out-of-context quotes from futurists like Alvin Toffler and Marshall McLuhan over post-psychedelic visuals. The form is indistinguishable from financial services advertising. One two-page spread reads MONEY IS JUST A TYPE OF INFORMATION, attributed to magazine editor Kevin Kelly.

or even consume them whole. A lot of founders got rich offloading what were more or less duds. Mark Cuban, the Bill Gates wannabe, is among the most famous, unloading his IPO'd but still money-losing Broadcast.com to Yahoo! in 1999 for more than $5.5 billion in stock. As the *New York Times* noted at the time, only speculative internet companies could afford to make bets like that. "Internet companies simply cannot be bought by established companies where stocks are valued on profits, not promise," wrote journalists Saul Hansell and Laura M. Holson. "Thus Broadcast.com is out of reach for such logical buyers as CBS or Walt Disney. But it is an easy bite for Yahoo, which can simply exchange its highly valued stock for that of Broadcast.com."[55] Yahoo! could also afford to downsize Broadcast.com a short couple of years later, taking a bath on the buy.

When the railroad bubble popped, at the close of the nineteenth century, it was the demonetization of silver that threw so many designs into question. For the web bubble at the close of the twentieth, it was a sock-puppet dog. The Pets.com mascot didn't actually *cause* the blowup of internet stocks in the year 2000, but the hyper little salesman, voiced by comedian Michael Ian Black, became the bubble's icon, and he's as good an entry point as any out there. The puppet's campaign, designed by the same Chiat/Day advertising firm that did Apple's 1984 ad—a top outsourcing option—was so successful at grabbing attention that it came to overshadow the company itself, which was a monopoly play in the pet-supply delivery space, bleeding millions and losing money on every transaction in order to build a user base. A lot of that money went into ads featuring the puppet, which people found about as goofy as the idea of shipping 30-pound bags of dog food in the mail. For Pets.com, and other start-ups like it, the only way forward in the medium term was by the grace of the capital markets. If investors supported their plan, they could keep buying customers, but a waver in confidence was a gust of wind through a house of cards. The $50 million that Pets.com raised from Jeff Bezos and friends in 1999 wasn't enough to finance a build-out of the physical shipping infrastructure, nor was it enough to cover the transactional losses, the advertising, and buyouts of competitors at the same time. And it's not like the firm could, as the old joke goes, make it up in volume.

It was one thing for a web company to pour tens of millions of dollars out of its financial arteries onto the sidewalk with little to show for it but a ledger of losses; it was another to do all that while everyone watched a giant balloon of your stupid advertising puppet marching around Central Park like a capitalist kaiju in the Macy's Thanksgiving Day Parade. The company spent $1.2 million placing a 30-second Super Bowl ad, a landmark of dot-com profligacy. But despite spending $10 million a month on marketing—far more than the site's revenue—and despite getting help from Amazon and institutional investors such as Disney, Pets.com wasn't establishing a big enough lead over its competitors, including Petopia.com, Petsmart.com, and Petplanet.com.[56] Each of them had a napkin like Jim Clark's, but the "one asshole in the middle" strategy didn't work with four assholes. (Clark ran into the same problem with Healtheon; he made the best of it by selling out to WebMD in 1999, soon after he found out the site had an investment from the only asshole bigger than he was: Bill Gates.) To kill a site like Pets.com, investors didn't have to lose faith entirely; a mere pause in the momentum was enough. A robust business can handle a negative readjustment in expectations, but these were not robust businesses—they were gambles. And gambles pay off or they don't, one or zero. By the end of 2000, Pets.com was the latter, and a whole cohort of start-ups followed it off a cliff.

The Y2K bubble was overdetermined; it had more causes than it needed. One was that technology hedge funds bid up stock prices with a plan to jump out at the high and leave less sophisticated capital holding the heavy bag. That strategy worked well enough, and the funds mostly came out of the experience surprisingly whole.[57] But if Pets.com brought global investors to their senses and tanked the NASDAQ as capital shifted out of technology stocks, then perhaps the coked-up sock puppy did some good, stopping people before they threw more money down the dog-food-delivery garbage chute and wising everyone up for the next time. In the period after the pop, many in Silicon Valley talked like dreamers awakened. There were jokes about "Cement .com," an imaginary web delivery platform for giant bags of Quikrete. Analysts wrote off whole e-commerce sectors as folly. In a 2001 interview about his case study of the grocery delivery site Webvan, Harvard Business School professor John Deighton said that direct-to-consumer internet advertising was here to stay, but "home-delivered groceries? Never."[58] There was no way to compete with supermarket efficiencies. Deighton's prediction was—not to belabor the point—wrong. But whereas the conventional narrative was that dot-coms drowned themselves in wasteful spending, Deighton did see that it was the relation between the internet and the real economy that needed to change. As it turned out, it wasn't the internet that had to do most of the changing.

The real problem with the delivery dot-coms was that the people running them didn't understand their historical context. In 2013, Peter Relan, the founding head of technology at Webvan, published a post on TechCrunch discussing why the company failed and how the next round of delivery start-ups could avoid the same fate. Webvan's strategy, he wrote, was to offer "the quality and selection of Whole Foods, the pricing of Safeway, and the convenience of home delivery."[59] But according to Relan, the company shouldn't have invested in so much infrastructure. Webvan built high-tech distribution systems from scratch: giant networks of new algorithms, miles of conveyor belts, fleets of custom trucks with PalmPilot-wielding delivery drivers. At its short peak, Webvan had a billion-dollar contract with Bechtel to build new distribution facilities around the country. This was the utopian vision of e-commerce, one in which the web's efficiencies generated gains for everyone involved: investors, workers, and customers alike. In a 2000 report to the Securities and Exchange Commission, Webvan bragged that all its couriers "are Webvan employees.... The courier training lasts two weeks and includes 36 hours of classroom training, 12 hours of driving training and 28 hours of on the job training.... Webvan's couriers receive a competitive compensation package, including cash and stock options..."[60] Commentators pegged Webvan's delivery-labor costs at $30 an hour, or over $50 in 2022 money.[61] Of the company's 4,476 reported employees on January 1, 2001, 3,705 worked out of the "real" operating facilities spread over nearly 1.5 million square feet of rented urban warehouse space across seven metropolitan regions.[62] The company filed for Chapter 11 bankruptcy in the summer of 2001 after losing hundreds of millions of dollars the year before.[63]

Webvan successfully lured workers out of grocery and meatpacking unions with stock options, and it used the same overvalued stock to devour the Amazon-funded competitor HomeGrocer. The firm's model was haphazard, though not in the way that seems obvious. Big investments in fixed capital and labor training were the key to decades of American prosperity, but that was a different era. Just as capitalists came to understand that they weren't going to win the Cold War with high wages, no dot-com was going to win its particular race by handing out stock to delivery drivers. Pets.com was making a similar push to expand its in-house warehousing and distribution system when the firm's bubble burst. Industry leaders had to put the win-win-win tech-economy fantasies aside; that's not what the internet was for. After their capitalist predecessors spilled blood around the world to get them out from under obligations to anyone except their shareholders, these fluffy web companies were being *too* responsible. It was all fine and good to issue press releases about how the web was going to improve life for everyone, but you weren't supposed to actually spend billions of dollars investing in that image. "Move fast and build things" wasn't going to cut it; what Silicon Valley needed was a reversion to Reagan.

Section V

2000–2020

An Anduril autonomous surveillance camera on the Southern California border
United States Customs and Border Protection photo

B2K

Palo Alto for Bush — The Internet After 9/11 — Scrapers
Eat the World — Amazon Thrives — The iPod

For many years, American cultural and political commentators have advanced theories about why Republicans so strongly disliked Bill Clinton, what made him appear as an existential threat to conservatives. On domestic and foreign policy, Clinton ran to the right with the times but wore a blue outfit, inheriting the Reagan-era mantle of law-and-order small government and a tough military. As another indication of how large tendencies structure presidential agendas, it's hard to plot the former Arkansas governor's policy orientation to the left of Richard Nixon's. And yet Republicans couldn't stand him. They couldn't stand his rural lumpen origins, his easy manner, his professional wife, his lucky historical timing. He got to bask in the unipolar American consensus that Cold Warriors fought to ensure, and if Republicans couldn't find a strong way to differentiate themselves during an ostensibly prosperous era, they would continue to lose on style alone, the same way Clinton beat them twice in a row, in 1992 and 1996. If the economic questions were settled, then the GOP couldn't win a cultural fight with progressives; it needed a new move. Rich, old, and having narrowly avoided jail, the Hoover-Reagan crew came back for one last score.

The capitalists' investment in the right-wing ideas complex continued paying dividends, even as they fretted about becoming a permanent minority party. Extreme free-market orthodoxy, once the purview of crackpots and discredited policy makers, swam its way firmly into the center of the political mainstream. Capitalists pushed their agenda efficiently, building a large infrastructure of professional operators and campaign hacks, a coterie of Reaganites lurking in the country's shadows. One of those operatives was named Karl Rove. A backlash child of the mountain West, Rove swore his life to the

Republican Party under Nixon and never looked back. He stuck with the Bush family after RNC chair H. W. selected him for chair of the party's college branch after a contested election. Rove's ticket to the top was H. W. Bush's son, and not the smart one. George W. Bush was a goofball rich kid who spent the end of the Vietnam War flying around Texas and collecting uniformed photos to use later. It was hard for such a person to fail in the 1970s and '80s, and despite being a doofus, W. made money by being a guy who owned companies. Nobody argued that he was an expert in oil drilling or baseball or stock trading, but that didn't preclude his moving up in the world. Bush and Rove started running for office in the late 1970s and they didn't stop until the Constitution said they weren't allowed to win anymore.

In 1998, with the junior Bush on his way to reelection in the Texas governor's race, the old gang called him in for a tryout. George Shultz reached out to Rove and asked if he and his candidate wanted to spend a day in Palo Alto after a planned fundraiser in San Francisco. Not many people can call an out-of-state gubernatorial candidate for a daylong chill session, but Shultz was near the top of the list, and Rove had the schedule rearranged. They met at the Shultz compound on campus (located just around the corner from the house Lou Henry Hoover built) with a crew from the Hoover Institution: economists Annelise Anderson, Michael Boskin, and John Cogan; Annelise's husband, the senior Reagan puppeteer Martin Anderson; and former NSC staffer and then Stanford University provost Condoleezza Rice. Though Junior was running for a lower office, everyone knew the meeting's purpose. He proved himself willing and able to hear and repeat Hoover policies, which pleased his hosts. As the visitors were leaving, Shultz took Rove aside and gave him the thumbs up: "Ronald Reagan had a meeting just like this in this room before he ran for president," he said.[1] From that moment in Palo Alto, Bush was the prohibitive favorite in the 2000 GOP primary.

Shultz wasn't the only one who noticed the repetition of the Palo Alto meeting; the *Christian Science Monitor* published a story about the importance of the Hoover Institution to the Bush campaign that was strikingly similar to the one they ran about the Reagan administration. Quoted in the piece, Martin Anderson exaggerates Bush's competence, and it's clear to the author why: "No one is sure when or if Bush's heavy reliance on the West's citadel of anticommunism will recede, but Anderson has a file of concrete tax-policy proposals he's just waiting to run by the presidential hopeful."[2] The *Monitor* describes the Hoover crew as "a collection of battle-toughened conservatives who have emerged as the early core of Mr. Bush's braintrust." Whereas Bush's dad considered himself a thinker, Bush and Rove conveyed that they had a Reagan model in mind—the chief executive as a cartoon hammer formed from a buzzing hive of advisory bees. Anderson, Rice, and Shultz flew to Austin for another meeting soon after, adding new members of the inner circle, in particular the former secretary of defense and Halliburton CEO, Richard "Dick" Cheney.[3]

With the Cold War decided and the compensatory state dismantled, the 2000 election seemed unusually low-stakes. When the close race came down to a street fight in Florida over the recount, Democrats—including one of Al Lowenstein's old recruits from Yale, vice presidential candidate Joe Lieberman—lost their nerve. Bush came to the Oval Office with a job requirement like Reagan's: He had to keep top-heavy finance-led growth going without coming off as unlikably harsh or insensitive to the people whose state benefits he was selling away. It was still about individual rights, but Bush and his copious staffers pitched a softer, friendlier version. As with Reagan, the effort wasn't very successful on its own terms, and Junior spent his second term with his approval rating under 50 percent and falling. But like his benefactors in Palo Alto, he used war to float his numbers.

On September 11, 2001, a team made up mostly of Saudi twenty-somethings executed a spectacular attack on the United States, hijacking four planes and crashing three of them into high-value targets, killing more than 3,000 people in New York City and a smaller number at the Pentagon. It was a shock, and the nation needed a cheerleader, which, coincidentally, the junior Bush had been at Andover and Yale. Standing atop New York City rubble with a megaphone and impeccable styling, he whipped the country into a war frenzy. The selected target was Afghanistan, a hideout for the plot's funder, Osama bin Laden, and a country where elements in the White House once channeled weapons to anti-Soviet militants. It was a vengeance mission. The American-led invasion force pushed the governing Taliban out of power temporarily and installed a standard clique of unpopular Western-educated technocrats supported with billions of dollars flowing in large part through contractors and subject to the same disappearing tendency exhibited during the Stanford Technology era. The United States and its oversupplied proxy forces lost the war slowly over the next two decades, and the Taliban officially retook power in 2021.

The Bush war cabinet overlapped with the Reagan team in rhetoric, strategy, goals, and personnel, including Shultz staffers Paul Wolfowitz and Elliott Abrams. Condoleezza Rice, Shultz's mentee and his personal selection for the Chevron board of directors, signed on as national security adviser, before a promotion to secretary of state in the second term. Shultz himself advised from his seats at Hoover and the Bay Area biopharmaceuticals company Gilead. Dreamed up by VCs at Menlo Ventures and led by an ex-Genentech scientist, Gilead was one of the most successful of the 1980s and '90s biotech start-ups, and the company did send Bush a cabinet member: the Gilead chairman, Donald Rumsfeld, resuming the secretary of defense role he held under Ford. As a pharmaceuticals executive at a different firm, Rumsfeld once served as Reagan's special envoy to the Middle East, famously meeting with Saddam Hussein in 1983, where he found time to push the Iraqi leader on Bechtel's oil pipeline proposal.* Shultz's deep and experienced advisory team continued to pull the junior Bush's strings. In 2003, the state launched another war of aggression, this one on Iraq, advanced by a "shock and awe" combination of missiles and video technology meant to demonstrate total command. The Saddam regime fell, and the "coalition of the willing" took over. For a moment it seemed to some like the Shockley model of domination by rocket bomb was finally operational, the world controlled by Californians sitting at computers. The occupation caused violence and destabilization, including the concerted rise of the Islamic State tendency. Examining the many studies on the question, John Tirman concludes that, by 2010, America's invasion caused perhaps as many as one million Iraqi deaths.[4]

The firms with direct links to the administration benefited handsomely. Bechtel and a Halliburton spin-off called KBR in particular received lucrative contracts to rebuild Afghanistan and Iraq, as well as to support the occupation

---

* Of the 61 declassified documents compiled by George Washington University's National Security Archive regarding this meeting, a cable from George Shultz about financing the Aqaba pipeline is the only one missing a page. Department of State Cable from George P. Shultz to the United States Embassy in Sudan, "Briefing Notes for Rumsfeld Visit to Baghdad [Page Missing]," March 24, 1984, https://nsarchive2.gwu.edu/NSAEBB/NSAEBB82/iraq48.pdf.

forces. High oil demand sent prices and energy-sector profits soaring. An expansion of Medicare's prescription drug benefit funneled tens of billions of dollars in annual bonus profits into the pharmaceuticals industry. It was a pro-business atmosphere, and asset owners thrived across the board, though production-output growth stalled. Martin Anderson got his tax cuts from George Bush Jr.—on capital gains, on high earners and dividends and corporate profits—just as he got them from Reagan. Investors got the signal, and with the invasion of Iraq, in the spring of 2003, the S&P 500 turned and began reversing its almost three-year slide, which began with the dot-com bubble. The junior Bush's administration was full of unresolved conflicts of interest, but the officials didn't need quid pro quo corruption to make sure their buddies prospered—that was an unavoidable consequence of their declared policy agenda. Hell, that was an unavoidable consequence of the Democrats' declared policy agenda, too. Both parties agreed that it was time for the capitalist class to take a real Cold War victory lap, and with the exception of the perennially frustrating Social Security privatization, the Hoover agenda was law once more.

What about the tech companies? Given Al Gore's personal support for the high-tech industry—as a congressman, he led the push for the civilian supercomputer infrastructure—one might imagine that Bush had to write off support from Silicon Valley, but not so. The *Weekly Standard* detailed the campaign's regional push in 2000.[5] The Bush campaign relied on ideologically committed executives to wrangle their fellows, and the team split its appeals by generation. For those under forty, there was Gregory Slayton, an energetic, wild-eyed evangelical Christian with a circle beard and a baseball cap who made millions selling a company to Silicon Graphics and was then CEO of an email marketing company called ClickAction that, naturally, contracted with GOP campaigns. Tim Draper, third in the Silicon Valley Draper VC line and grandson of Herbert Hoover associate General William Draper, took the fortysomethings.* The Netscape CEO Jim Barksdale took the next decade. Heading the whole operation and covering the old guys was E. Floyd Kvamme, an early Apple executive and Kleiner Perkins director. Only Draper forwent an appointment: Barksdale joined the President's Foreign Intelligence Advisory

---

* Tim Draper's father, William III, attended Yale with George H. W. Bush and joined the same Skull and Bones secret society. William III was also a funder of young fuckup George W. Bush's Texas energy firm—a worthy investment after all.

Board—not an organization covered with glory during the Bush administration; Kvamme led the President's Council of Advisors on Science and Technology; and Slayton, with his permanent grin, became consul general and chief of mission to Bermuda. The team wore buttons with the slogan B2K—not to be confused with the boy band of the same name—and they got public support from executives at leading companies like Intel, Microsoft, Oracle, HP, Cisco, and National Semiconductor.[6]

When it came to White House policy, Silicon Valley's central concerns at the time were federal regulation of the internet, which was completely up in the air, and finance-led growth. *Computerworld* and *ZDNet* reported that the industry was thrilled with the nomination of arch-conservative John Ashcroft to head the Department of Justice.[7] Traditional civil libertarians deplored Ashcroft—a paladin for the Christian right—but the new AG preferred a hands-off strategy for corporate regulation, leaving user privacy questions up to the companies themselves. He was also flexible on antitrust, which he proved by dropping the case against Microsoft, and he promised to relax export controls on multiuse tech. As you'll see, this policy orientation came about at a decisive time in the web's development, and Ashcroft effectively carved it in stone.

Part of the administration's pro-market thinking was that, if there were national security reasons to surveil users on the internet, then officials would be quiet about it, not undermining public faith in the web services. One issue was the Carnivore system, an FBI device used to tap internet service providers (with their knowledge) for targeted monitoring. The tool became a flash point when it was exposed in the last days of the Clinton administration, and industry lobbied for a partnership model over court orders and physical taps, as long as the government was willing to indefinitely indemnify corporate cooperants. The panicked Patriot Act allowed the state to dip into people's data flows on suspicion, without a specific order. Instead of imposing a new box on the ISPs, Ashcroft's DOJ opted for commercial software solutions. As surveillance increased and disappeared into the corporate code, the official number of annual FBI internet wiretaps dwindled into the single digits.[8] The public assumed its internet communications were legally private, whether that's what the user agreement said in the fine print or not.

At the same time, Silicon Valley companies jumped into the post-9/11 information arms race. The CIA started its own venture capital program called

In-Q-Tel, pumping tens of millions of dollars a year into early-stage national security tech from an office in Menlo Park.[9] But that was a drop in the bucket compared to the billions in "nat sec" spending, including the new Department of Homeland Security. Silicon Valley's self-styled anti-authoritarians got patriotic very fast. Leading the race was database contractor Oracle and its aggressive CEO, Larry Ellison. Within two months of the attacks Oracle had a new division dedicated to designing and selling homeland security and disaster recovery solutions, headed by a 32-year CIA veteran named David Carey, whose last agency title was executive director, number 3 on the organizational chart. "How do you say this without sounding callous?" Carey wondered in vain to *New York Times Magazine* reporter Jeffrey Rosen. "In some ways, Sept. 11 made business a bit easier. Previous to Sept. 11, you pretty much had to hype the threat and the problem."[10] There's no nice way to say that Osama bin Laden did you a solid.

In a November 2001 meeting with Vice President Cheney, Ellison was quick, perhaps a touch *too* quick, to offer technical support for a national identity program, the very project Americans rejected in the mainframe days. Ellison lobbied for a total government information system of digital ID cards linked to a central database, with thumbprint and iris scans. Optional for citizens, mandatory otherwise. He met with Ashcroft and apparently convinced him, because the attorney general nearly pushed it through, thanks to bipartisan support from Ellison's senator in California, Dianne Feinstein. Privacy safeguards were absurd, Ellison told Rosen when the interviewer expressed concerns about the plan: "We already have this large centralized database to keep track of where you work, how much you earn, where your kids go to school, were you late on your last mortgage payment, when's the last time you got a raise. Well, my God, there are hundreds of places we have to look to see if you're a security risk. I really don't understand. Central databases already exist. Privacy is already gone." Our lives are at risk, not our liberties, the Silicon Valley software leader argued. It wasn't an uncommon view in the Valley; Ellison was echoing what Sun's Scott McNealy had been saying for years. Oracle didn't win its proposed state-information monopoly, but it did get a lot of contracts, including one to unify all the DOD's civilian personnel databases and another to work with Lockheed Martin on an (optional) iris-scanning system. Oracle's revenue doubled during the Bush years.

There are risks to relying on military contractors, as Machiavelli once said, but they have been a cornerstone of America's economic growth strategy, as well as best friends forever with the country's formal leadership. Billions of dollars in public money flowed unchecked into giant weapons conglomerates and fly-by-night operations of all sorts, with disastrous consequences. The worst, as far as the public is aware, was a nine-figure (!) contract to two psychologists who claimed they had an innovative way to extract the truth from people "detained" for suspected links to terror networks.[11] Ex-navy pseudo-academic consultant hucksters Bruce Jessen and James Mitchell flitted between U.S. black sites, purposelessly torturing kidnapped Muslim men in the name of science, commerce, and the American way. At times there were more contractors than U.S. soldiers deployed in Iraq.[12] But with wages and most consumer prices well under control, there was little danger of a wage-price inflation spiral, and it was considered unpatriotic to pit the national security budget against social spending. Whether or not there would be butter was a separate question; there would be guns.

Privately owned Bechtel raked in many billions of dollars in war on terror contracts, comfortably placing KBR, the spin-off from Vice President Cheney's old firm. Indemnifying private contractors was also simpler than constructing elaborate government war-crime cover-ups. The Valley's big high-tech companies continued the proud wartime tradition of doing business with the government as subcontractors. They worked through the aerospace and telecom big shots like Boeing, Lockheed, Raytheon, Northrop Grumman, AT&T, and Verizon, thereby avoiding even lenient direct oversight. These companies had to get their semiconductors somewhere, had to host their files on servers and manage databases; subcontracting was a good way to expand fast and flexibly, and they did.

You were either with us or against us in the war on terror, the president said, and Larry Ellison more or less spoke for the sector when he joined the decade's long "U-S-A" chant. Still, despite its role as the Western citadel of anticommunism and the world's most exciting investment opportunity, Silicon Valley began as a minor partner in the George W. Bush coalition. The Cold War was over, and the region was still recovering after the dot-com crash. Winners were busy snapping up the losers, completing the scavenging phase of the West Coast electronics-industry life cycle. But now Silicon Valley was growing in the war on terror's blood-soaked dirt, and what grew there grew fast. By the time the Ashcroft internet policy of oversight by honor system and regulation by terms of agreement was no longer tenable, Palo Alto's new ruling firms were not minor anything.

Unpredictable or Incorrect Behavior

In the Bay Area, in the new century's first decade, there were two kinds of scrapers. First, out of Oakland and the wider East Bay, was a specific type of tricked-out car. An element of the hyphy regional subculture, scrapers are not-particularly-fashionable American cars souped-up with aftermarket rims and other custom modifications. Imagine grandma's Oldsmobile meets *The Fast and the Furious*. As a play on Reagan-era suburban material culture, scrapers lent even more postmodern flair to the Bay's roads, which were already lined with inscrutably named tech companies. The other kind of scraper is a genre of computer application.

When computer systems talk to one another, they tend to do it efficiently, in code. When computer systems talk to end-users, the programmers force the silicon to speak in human language. Scraper and crawler programs are exceptions to these rules: They can "read" human language output and reinterpret it as code. Because computers are faster readers with better memories than humans, even in our own languages, scrapers do not have the same relationship to information as we do. When a person reads a book, they have a memory of it; when a scraper reads a book, it has a copy of it. And scrapers can read a lot of books, very fast. (Crawlers do the same thing, but instead of html content they look for links between pages.) The internet promised to speed information flows, and scrapers threw settled questions of intellectual property into chaos. The typical example of this conflict is the music industry, but that's because we have already come to take so much about how the web functions for granted.

At the close of the twentieth century, the Ticketmaster company dominated online ticket sales. Venues were dependent on the contractor, and Ticketmaster charged inflated fees, making it one of the decade's most hated companies among concertgoers and sports fans. It was the one-asshole-in-the-middle strategy. The firm adapted quickly to the internet, leveraging its scale and snapping up regional competitors, just as A. P. Giannini bought small-town

California banks. By the late '90s it was selling 60 million tickets a year.[13] But the company had a problem: scrapers, and not the car kind.

Ticketmaster.com assembled the web's largest index of event listings, which was something other sites found useful. If I read the listings and tell my friends about a show next week, no one would accuse me of theft. I'm just a user, using the site properly. But if I scrape the site, I have a full copy of its listings. If I crawl the links to the Ticketmaster purchase pages, I can reproduce the function of its site up to the actual sale and stick it on my site instead. This appealed to web portal providers, for whom events were a big user interest, one they could satisfy on Ticketmaster's dime. When Microsoft copied the Ticketmaster links (and logo) for its own local services site, the company sued, arguing that the "deep links" to individual pages on its site (rather than to the homepage) were protected property. They settled—no huge surprise considering the companies' overlapping directorates—and Ticketmaster agreed to licensing deals with Yahoo! and the newspaper chain Knight Ridder that allowed them to use the listings. But Tickets.com was a different situation.

Tickets.com sold most of its tickets face-to-face and over the phone, but as the name indicates, it saw the sector moving online. One way it tried to compete with Ticketmaster was to index the market leader's tickets, too, using a crawler and deep links. By combining the Ticketmaster listings with its own, Tickets.com surpassed the monopolists, and at a tiny cost. For Ticketmaster, which paid employees to produce those listings and reaped advertising revenue when users navigated to them from the homepage, handing everything over to a competitor was suicidal. And yet, they *had* to make the information available to users so that people could buy tickets. It was the crawler catch-22. Ashcroft's laissez-faire DOJ left the civil courts in charge, letting the capitalists battle out the law themselves. Ticketmaster sued in 1999, and Tickets.com IPO'd, giving it enough money to fight.[14] The competitor did agree to stop deep linking eventually—once you're established it doesn't make a ton of sense to send sales to your rivals—but not before a judge ruled that crawling and deep linking weren't illegal.[15] Using a computer to do something legal but faster and more efficiently was not a crime; that was progress. District Judge Harry Hupp also ruled that the Ticketmaster site's terms of service weren't binding because they were too unobtrusively tucked at the bottom of the page. Haphazardly, the scrum of interested parties wrote the rules of the internet.

Linking to whatever you want has been legally unproblematic since *Ticket-master v. Tickets.com*, but errant crawlers could still get squashed if they wandered into the path of the wrong corporate megafauna. Ever since Ampex's introduction of audio and video recorders, home recording technology has presented the problem of bootlegging, and in 1984 the Supreme Court ruled that equipment manufacturers were not liable for copyright-infringing use of their products, siding with an amicus brief written by the tech-forward attorney general of Missouri, John Ashcroft.[16] The legislature affirmed it with the Audio Home Recording Act of 1992. Media industries worked with the FBI to stop organized infringement for profit, but enforcing the law against individual users duping tapes was impractical, and the music and movie cartels mostly satisfied themselves with physical media's huge margins. Less worried about piracy than they were excited about a new format, the recording industry pushed digitization. That plan went extremely well in the 1990s, as the proliferation of compact discs compelled listeners to rebuy their favorite tapes and records, but computers were coming for them sooner rather than later.

Just as computers can read better and faster than people, so can they listen. Scraping CDs for universal MP3 audio files was called ripping, and ripping CDs was easy. Free audio programs like Winamp and RealPlayer assembled the files for playback, and as long as your hard drive was large enough, any PC could put the biggest CD changer to shame.* Borrowing an album from a friend took on new meaning—you could have your own copy as fast as it took to listen to it once. Hewlett-Packard brought consumer-affordable CD writers (or "burners") to the market at the end of the '90s, and within a few years no desk was complete without a spindle of blank discs. Teenagers filled CD binders with generic silver or white recordable CD-R's, the album titles written in Sharpie. Though some bands thrived in the sharing-heavy culture, and independent artists found it newly simple to distribute their own work, CD burners upset the existing ecosystem from the financial top to the bottom.†

---

* For readers unfamiliar with the technology, a CD changer was a piece of stereo equipment that held many discs and could switch between them. Users had to remember which CD was in which numbered slot or maintain their own index.

† In 2004, when young NorCal screenwriter Alex Tse needed a way to bring three of San Francisco's segregated ethnic communities together, he wrote a conflict between a local black rapper and CD bootleggers in Chinatown. Showtime didn't pick up the series, but

But like young Bill Gates, the Recording Industry Association of America (RIAA) was not about to roll over for pirates.

In the late 1990s, when a company called Diamond Multimedia introduced a $200 Rio digital music player that could hold an album's worth of MP3s, the RIAA sued to block the whole technology.[17] The courts dismissed it, and MP3 players went ahead, consigning proprietary media players such as Sony's MiniDisc to the dustbin. Digital music melted into air, evaporating from physical media entirely, and that was a problem for people who sold records. More worrisome than the new bootlegs was direct file sharing. The dam broke with the launch of Napster, a web program that aggregated and indexed users' hard drives, allowing people to download directly from one another. File servers are older than the internet itself, but as storage got cheaper and people packed their drives with tunes, each became its own potential hub, a tiny personal vault of music that might be worth flipping through, like a CD binder. This peer-to-peer (P2P) sharing upset the web's monopolistic hub-spoke server-client model. By limiting its role to scraping users' file information, presenting it for search, and connecting peers for downloading, Napster kept its operational costs relatively small and, it had good reason to believe, legally protected itself from the record companies. The program was a national phenomenon, perhaps the web's first to transcend all subcultural barriers, and Napster received over $15 million in venture capital, even though it *really* had no business plan — not besides selling T-shirts with the site's snazzy cat logo.[18]

The reason Napster felt somewhat safe despite being a hub for pirated content is that it seemed to fall into a category that the law calls a safe harbor. The Digital Millennium Copyright Act is a '90s law that brought an international agreement to protect digital intellectual property to the home front. America's content cartels wanted a way to protect their discs and corral overseas copiers; Congress passed the domestic version with a full consensus, from both parties. George W. Bush's attorney general, John Ashcroft, chaired the committee that drafted the Senate bill language while he represented Missouri in that chamber, a continuation of his pro-tech work that began with the friend-of-the-court brief he wrote in favor of VCR manufacturers in the '80s. One of the

---

the movie-length pilot directed by Spike Lee, *Sucker Free City*, is an account of the era that's too often overlooked.

reasons the law faced no opposition is that it outlined an exception for internet companies. As long as they made an effort to take down offending content when notified by the owner, providers couldn't be held liable for infringing material posted by users. This insulated service providers such as America Online, web portals, and a host of arriving sites featuring user-submitted content, as long as they played ball with the content rights holders, which during this music-swapping era was principally the RIAA. Tech firms tended to err on the side of caution, deleting when alerted of a violation without investigating the underlying complaint. The law was Hooverian in that it worked like a series of intellectual-property traffic lanes, clarifying who was to drive where and how. That allowed investors to pile money into disruptive and sometimes dubious internet plays without worrying that they would deflate to zero with a prick from the recording industry. And yet that's exactly what happened to Napster.

The program's creator was a working-class coder kid from Massachusetts named Shawn Fanning. Along with his internet friend Sean Parker, Fanning applied scraper logic to the file sharing that online kids like them were already doing using chat programs. If you could copy one song from your friend, why couldn't you copy any song from any person in the world? If you could deep-link to a corporate web server, why couldn't you download from your buddy's file server? Napster let users search one another's shared files and download them as if it were one centralized database when it was technically more like an aggregated menu; Napster didn't actually have any food. But when the nation's teenagers logged in, they saw a search field where they could type in the name of whatever song they wanted and download it for free. The recording industry saw the same thing, and it wasn't hearing any of the arguments about P2P and safe harbors. Napster, a free music machine, was giving away its product, often leaking songs before they were released. It was an existential threat, and the record cartel sued as hard as it could.

As Fanning and Parker discovered the hard way, there was no viable path back from the wrong side of the RIAA, at least not for Napster. Fanning didn't release Napster as a way to get rich; he released it as a cool hack. Scrapers and crawlers move so fast that a teenager can turn an industry on its head with nothing more than a team of friends. Users came running and capital followed, but the RIAA already had its mind made up. The courts didn't rule that Napster was wrong; they didn't get the chance. A preliminary injunction from a U.S. District Court told Napster it had to immediately cease allowing the download of any copyrighted material. Napster argued that it was only the menu—that it could do its best to exclude protected content but there was no way to guarantee the quality of every dish. Not good enough, said the court. Napster tried hand-sorting files, but the automated crawling is what made the site workable in the first place. VCs weren't going to pay for this fight, and Napster had no choice but to settle with the labels and shut down. Fanning and Parker landed on their feet for a number of reasons—they were very young; Silicon Valley is forgiving when it comes to talent; Chapter 11 bankruptcy is made for such situations; their investors were used to taking total losses—and offshore Napster clones popped up immediately. P2P sharing was, in some ways, an irrepressible technology. And yet, as you'll see, the RIAA clawed its way back by teaming up with a Silicon Valley force that understood how monopolies and cartels are supposed to work.

The rule for the scrapers and crawlers after Napster was not to piss off powerful incumbents before you could survive an injunction. Smart founders figured out that though they could get a lot of users fast by sticking it to the man, their projects were better off in the medium term if they had symbiotic models and offered significant value to everyone involved. That's not what the Stanford computer science students Larry Page and Sergey Brin were thinking about when they were building Google, but that's what they found. Both were born in 1973, which made them young PhD students in the late '90s. It had been almost a generation since Jobs and Gates, and to get to the top of the class it was no longer enough to be a curious kid with access to a computer. Both Brin and Page were sons of college professors, in math and computer science respectively, and both had relatively univocal trajectories. That's how you get to Stanford comp sci, which following the internetworking era became a very well-funded millionaire factory.

Larry's dissertation involved mapping the connections among the internet's pages, producing a picture of the web as a web. Sketching out all the links by hand was impossible, but that kind of thing is a perfect task for a crawler. Page enlisted a sizable portion of the department's computing resources and sent the crawlers out into the web, like radioactive dye through a patient's circulatory system. Hopping from link to link to link to link to link the crawlers put together a graph of the 'net. What Page was left with (and later, what he and Brin were left with) was more than a cool infographic; it was an index of citations. If one assumed that, as with scientific papers, the more frequently cited pages tended to be more useful, then the crawler's map was instructional. This was the beginning of Larry's PageRank algorithm, which was the beginning of Google. Hosted on the Stanford University Network and its Sun equipment, Google was a leap ahead of other search engines. Like Napster, the clever crawler went from cool project to essential internet tool in a matter of months. Page and Brin got the money they needed to leave Stanford from members of the informal comp sci fraternity: Sun founder Andy Bechtolsheim and his high-speed-Ethernet Granite Systems cofounder (and Stanford prof), David Cheriton, gave $100,000 each.[19] They could afford it, recall, having recently sold the start-up to Cisco for a couple of hundred million dollars.[20] It was a good investment.

In their 1998 coauthored academic paper reflecting on Google's first years, Brin and Page acknowledge that web crawlers are hectic programs by nature. "Because of the immense variation in web pages and servers, it is virtually impossible to test a crawler without running it on [a] large part of the internet," they write. "Invariably, there are hundreds of obscure problems which may only occur on one page out of the whole web and cause the crawler to crash, or worse, cause unpredictable or incorrect behavior."[21] Like automata from a cautionary fable, crawlers are much easier to create than they are to manage, and this early document has an ominous Sorcerer's Apprentice energy. But if young Victor Frankenstein had begun his reanimation trials in Silicon Valley, he probably could have picked up $25 million from Sequoia and Kleiner Perkins, just as Larry and Sergey did the next year. If that kind of wild efficiency is dangerous, then venture capitalists didn't want to be saved. The two computer scientists warned in their paper that "we believe the issue of advertising causes enough mixed incentives that it is crucial to have a competitive search engine that is transparent and in the academic realm," but that wasn't going to be Google. The partners left Stanford and, by way of a Menlo Park garage, landed in their Palo Alto office.

Google's big VC investment came at a fortunate time, and thanks to their low-cost automated system the guys weathered the dot-com crash in fine financial shape. But like many in their cohort, they subsisted on investor cash, cash they were frittering away on a daily basis. They left their Stanford program, but Larry and Sergey were still scientists on some level, and blending ranked results with advertisements was unacceptable to them. An automated system allowed buyers to place (clearly labeled) ads on results pages without costly management on Google's side, but customers weren't sprinting in. The firm's fortunes improved when it copied a competitor's model and began selling ad space in tiny auctions on a per-click basis.[22] Paying for clicks rather than space was very appealing to advertisers, and the firm's revenues took off. The new version of AdSense was so successful that the firm created a version that allowed third-party sites to post Google-run ads, too. Despite the host of exotic commercial fields Google has entered since, as well as the company's reorganization under the Alphabet holding entity, Google advertising still, almost 20 years later, provides more than 80 percent of the conglomerate's revenue.[23]

Accumulating information was the key to Google's advantage. The Page-Rank search model—a useful scavenger for the ecosystem—was based on crawling and scraping the internet's organic map of hyperlinks. As it scaled up, Google continued to make use of this efficient tool and the orientation behind it. After surviving the quick crash, it snapped up the online diary provider Blogger, which hadn't been so lucky. It was expand or die, and the new CEO, Eric Schmidt, was all about growth. In 2004, Google took a very public shot at the web portal players Yahoo! and Microsoft. Microsoft's Hotmail and Yahoo's RocketMail were the dominant American web mail providers, so Google had to offer something new and improved if it wanted to compete. Gmail not only had the cachet of an invitation-only service and Google's signature clean white interface, it also had *200 times* as much storage space as Microsoft's Hotmail—one gigabyte compared to five megabytes. Google could afford it because it scraped users' emails and ran personalized ads in the margins that were tailored to the results. The better the personalization, the more likely users were to click, and the more likely Google was to get paid. When confronted by a *Playboy* interviewer about the privacy implications of the Gmail model, Larry and Sergey pitched it as a win-win. "Our ads aren't distracting; they're helpful," Brin said.[24] Page conceded that seeing ads related to the content of your mail was "a little spooky at first," but all that free space was too good to turn down and users did get used to it. An IPO later that year gave Google a market cap of more than $20 billion.

Google held on to and made profitable use of its search engine monopoly, and it expanded into other key positions, from browser to office software suite to operating system and all the way to forays into hardware, challenging the biggest enduring incumbents like Microsoft and Apple. The search engine held its own well enough to join that vaunted level, passing also-rans like Yahoo! along the way. The firm's origins inhered in its DNA, and as Google's capacities increased, so did its scraping ambitions. Soon after the IPO, the firm acquired the In-Q-Tel-backed digital mapping firm Keyhole, which caught its big break during CNN's breathless coverage of the fraudulent Iraq invasion. Keyhole scraped the world's surface with satellites to get Google Maps, which dominated the online directions sector. A few years later, it took the logic to an absurd level, deploying cars stacked with cameras to scrape a ground-level picture of the whole world for Google Street View. If you can take a picture of a house, who's to say you can't take pictures of *every* house?

At the end of its big IPO year, 2004, Google announced its plan to scrape every page of every book for what became Google Books, much to the publishing industry's consternation. Though computer programs didn't crawl these real-life surfaces by themselves, Google could afford to contract low-wage workers to drive cameras around and to turn pages. Mostly these workers disappeared behind user interfaces, but there were predictable glitches, like the reflection of a Street View worker captured in a shiny window. Artist Benjamin Shaykin's project *Google Hands* features problem pages from Google Books scans, including accidentally scanned worker fingers. The fingers periodically get caught, a consistent malfunction in the scraper's cyborg apparatus. Andrew Norman Wilson's 2011 short film, *Workers Leaving the Googleplex*, focuses on the same ScanOps contractors. In the grand NorCal tradition of labor-market segregation, these laborers carried unique yellow badges, though that was hardly necessary to mark them, Wilson writes: "It was the same group of workers, mostly black and Latino, on a campus of mostly white and Asian employees, walking out of the exit like a factory bell had just gone off."[25] They entered and exited at their own special scheduled times — 4:00 a.m. and 2:15 p.m. — so as to spare the white- (employee), green- (intern), and red- (contractor) badged Googlers an awkward confrontation with that particular internal hierarchy. It's a plan that backfired with Wilson's movie, which shows the yellow-badge exodus as Wilson tells the audience how he lost his red-badge job editing film for Google's on-campus contractor Transvideo after being reported for speaking with ScanOps workers and recording the scene.

As Google grew, it combined the monopolistic business strategy of Microsoft with the disrupting scraper speed of Napster. It's a potent combination, and it left Google strong enough to defend its book scanning from the Authors Guild all the way to the top courts. Not even Bill Gates himself could have conceived of a business plan in which his company extracted value from every word accessed or typed on a Windows machine. Google belonged to a different era. In the closing decades of the twentieth century, as output growth slowed and capital hunted for low-commitment bets, global advertising increased dramatically. In the second half of the 1980s, TV ad spending doubled, from $25 to $50 billion, then doubled again in the '90s, then doubled *again* in the first decade of the new millennium—and for the first couple of decades, newspapers and magazines matched that growth.[26] Advertising was a good way to compete without getting into the risky business of price competition or product innovation. The fact that ads didn't actually add anything to the economy was good, since the world was increasingly oversupplied with cheap stuff anyway.

The more competition among capitalists became zero-sum, the more they relied on advertising. Google had a number of advantages over broadcast and print ads, the biggest being that the company could target audience members individually. It extended that advantage by spending over $3 billion in cash to outbid Microsoft for the advertising company DoubleClick, which specialized in following browsers around the web, keeping track of who they are and what they want.[27] Google's self-imposed barriers between user profiles on its different services, meant to reassure anyone nervous about their online privacy, eroded. In 2009 the firm used DoubleClick to target Google ads based on recorded browsing history. In 2016, reversing a previous policy, Google combined user information from its services—including Gmail and Google Search—with its advertising data to create "super profiles," single pools of information that made Larry Ellison's national biometric ID look modest by comparison.[28] The difference was that Google users invited the surveillance; no one said you had to use the internet. John Ashcroft's light hand left web companies and users to work out data privacy as two fully grown market participants, which almost always ended with the impatiently human parties pushing a button marked Accept, binding themselves to conditions left unread.

Though it collected data at an unimagined level, Google was far from the first company to assemble vast storehouses of information about individual customers; recall the Bank of Italy's card catalog of creditworthiness. Direct-mail advertising firms were crucial to the growth of the New Right, which contracted with them and adopted their tactics. By the mid-1960s, for-profit and nonprofit organizations were spending $400 million a year to buy information about Americans from data brokers.[29] With rapid improvements in storage, relational databases, and computation, hardly anyone benefited as much as these information sellers. They partnered with the world's biggest companies and accumulated fantastic troves of lists. Unlike consumer-facing brands Google, Yahoo!, and Microsoft, these firms stay in the shadows as far as most people are concerned—funny, considering how much they know about all of us. For the Arkansas-based list leader Acxiom, that adds up to around 1,500 data points per person on 500 million active consumers worldwide, including the majority of adults in the United States.[30]

Acxiom has been around in one form or another since the 1960s, and by the turn of the century the firm topped the industry. Growing (like others) through acquisition in the '90s, Acxiom partnered with Oracle and continued to amass information and improve its ability to process and refine that data. On 9/11, a pretty good national identity database existed, but it was private, not public, and Acxiom's clients used it to target suckers for catalogs and tele-marketing calls, not to predict terrorist activity. That idea doesn't seem to have occurred to anyone involved until after the Twin Towers were down. Once they were, Acxiom searched its files and found it had a bunch of information on the hijackers, including so many inconsistencies that in theory the authorities could have been able to tell in advance that the men were up to something, had anyone been looking. As Robert O'Harrow reports in his book on the growth of twenty-first-century surveillance, *No Place to Hide: Behind the Scenes of Our Emerging Surveillance Society*, that's when one of Acxiom's executives called a childhood friend who happened to be the world's most influential Arkansan: William Jefferson Clinton. Though the Democrats were out of the White House, the end of 2001 was a bipartisan time, and Attorney General Ashcroft was, despite his distaste for the man's well-publicized un-Christian proclivities, happy enough to take the deposed president's call. Ashcroft liked what he heard and he passed Acxiom—represented in Washington by one of its board members, soon-to-be Democratic presidential candidate and former NATO Supreme Allied Commander Europe, Wesley Clark — to a new project at DARPA called Total Information Awareness.

Total Information Awareness (TIA) was the child of John Poindexter, Oliver North's boss at the Reagan National Security Council (which he headed) and a convicted Iran-Contra criminal. After Poindexter was excused on appeal, George W. Bush brought him in to apply some out-of-the-box thinking to antiterrorism at a time when the state's investigative mandate seemed virtually unlimited. Like North, Poindexter was a technophile, and his Information Awareness Office brought private scraper tech under the state umbrella. In the name of efficient data sharing, TIA government fusion centers planned to draw together not just the various silos of public intelligence but also private records from commercial brokers, including and especially Acxiom. Ashcroft and the bipartisan deregulation consensus opened up a private backdoor that allowed the government to gather whatever information it wanted, as long as it paid for it, just as the catalog companies did. In the TIA fusion model, "the combined resources of essentially unregulated industry data collecting, the close surveillance capacities of local law enforcement, and the massive power of the federal government are at each other's disposal," writes law professor Frank Pasquale, "and largely free from their own proper constraints."[31] Through the techno-capitalist marketing industry, the state shook off the twentieth century's privacy restrictions in the name of homeland security.

How did the system work? Poindexter's plan was secret even from Congress, but a report of one arrangement leaked. To prevent another plane attack, Poindexter's office focused on using data to screen passengers before they boarded. An early test involved just what Acxiom first suggested to Ashcroft through Clinton: juxtaposing passenger ticketing records with the host of commercial information available from data brokers. For the government to demand customer information from JetBlue was a federal overreach, but the contractors offered layers of protection. To reassure the airline that everything was aboveboard, the Department of Defense asked the Transportation Security Administration to ask JetBlue to let its data-parsing partner, Acxiom, provide passenger information to the contractor Torch Concepts, which was subcontracted to DARPA through SRS Technologies. The convoluted chain of information custody is what allowed DHS investigators to declare all parties innocent after the news broke in the fall of 2003.[32] Despite public outrage and the boarding-gate humiliation of one senator, a no-fly list became policy. The absurdly Orwellian TIA was shut down soon after, and Poindexter got the can when he blurred the line between out of the box and too close to the sun with a "terrorist futures market," which would have allowed investors to speculate on coming attacks. But the government's scraping project didn't end; the administration transferred it to the National Security Agency.

The advertising technology (ad tech) industry and the NSA were looking for the same thing: information—specifically, all of it. Google's official mission was "to organize the world's information and make it universally accessible and useful," and the more information Google steered onto its own platforms (such as Gmail and the Chrome browser), and the more practice it got at organizing it, the better the firm did; and the better it could target advertising, the more money it made. And Google made a lot of money, leaping into the top tier of global corporations. This was no Netscape; now the internet made bank. With the help of ad tech, the internet turned attention into cold hard cash, much more efficiently than any magazine's sales department could. But considering that, Google's core function held a contradiction: By trying to get users to the perfect site, Google was throwing them *off* its own pages. Search remains the world's biggest product monopoly, and yet there was another layer of the web no one had been able to hold. It took one more scraper to figure it out.

Born in 1984, Mark Zuckerberg grew up in Westchester County, New York, the socially awkward son of a technologically inclined dentist whose practice operated out of the family home. If his father was part of the personal revolution—a small businessman working on a PC—then Mark was an internetworking kid, coding a messenger program to communicate between the dental office and house computers. A hard-core elitist, the younger Zuckerberg transferred to renowned Phillips Exeter Academy to finish high school, then followed his older sister to Harvard as planned. There, with access to a lot of computing power and a bunch of potential attention, Zuck embarked on a series of scraping projects. He and a classmate made a media player that scraped users' songs and generated playlists. Another program scraped the Harvard course listings and let users see who else was in their sections. For a classmate who wanted to start a grocery delivery business, Zuckerberg coded a scraper that copied supermarket prices. To study for a final in a class he skipped, he invited the rest of the students to contribute to a centralized digital study guide, effectively scraping his classmates' notes. Though the music program was a minor hit, and he did pass the skipped art history class, it was Mark's controversial next scrape that suggested a career path.

Harvard dorms had begun to post yearbook-type headshot indexes online to better facilitate, one presumes, the student networking that makes Harvard Harvard. At the beginning of his sophomore year, Zuck scraped all these "face book" directories and plugged the pictures into his new project. The program reflected his historical milieu — early twenty-first-century suburban private-school tech individualist — and he made its vulgar, elitist mentality explicit. Facemash pitted the scraped dorm headshots against each other one-on-one, inviting the user to pick the hotter of the two. The site went viral at Harvard, instantly attracting hundreds of leering student users and producing such an outcry that he was forced to pull it down and face the Administrative Board, charged with a variety of computer security sins. Zuck didn't get kicked out, but Facemash was the beginning of the end for him at school. The god's-eye view of his fellow students' private and public behavior, watching them condemn the site while flocking to it in droves, seems to have only spurred his contempt for the hypocrite masses and their bureaucrat leaders. So how did Mark Zuckerberg become the world's crown prince of friendship?

There were a lot of people building online social networks in the early 2000s. As David Fincher's film *The Social Network* dramatizes, several people were trying to build a social network *at Harvard* in the early 2000s. Zuckerberg wasn't even the first guy to finish an online social network at an elite college — that was Stanford's Orkut Büyükkökten, who later repeated the feat for his employer, Google. But Zuck's stuck. A few months after the Facemash debacle, Mark and his small Harvard team launched TheFacebook. This time no one could accuse him of intellectual property theft — at least not from his users, because they submitted their own photos. But unlike the wilder pseudonymous web, Facebook required its early registrants to use their real Ivy League university email addresses: the world's dorkiest bouncer. It grew quickly, faster than Mark's previous projects, and though he wasn't yet fully committed to the concept, he took an indefinite leave from Harvard and set to work growing the site. Sean Parker, Zuck's fellow scraper of Napster fame, convinced him that Facebook could go all the way. He joined the company as president, and together they moved the project where it belonged: Palo Alto. The company's real growth coup came when it scraped users' contact lists and spammed them with invites.

We will catch up with Zuckerberg and Facebook later, but it's important to put the project in the context of web scraping, the relatively simple set of tricks that let one well-placed coder reach through the keyboard and touch the whole world. What happened then depended a lot on what the coder (or small team) had to offer the powers that be. Rebellious or truly disruptive uses of the technology faced higher scrutiny. In 2011, hacker and Reddit cofounder Aaron Swartz scraped the JSTOR academic database, intending to open the fenced corpus of scholarship to the masses. Despite his public-minded motivations, federal prosecutors refused any plea deal that didn't involve prison, and the brilliant Swartz ended his own life at age twenty-six rather than surrender his freedom. Tickets .com, yes; Napster, no. Google, yes; Facemash, no. Acxiom, yes; Aaron Swartz, no; Facebook, yes. The most aggressive of these models raced ahead of their creators, "moving fast and breaking things," as Facebook's motto said. Some incumbents, like Ticketmaster and the RIAA, were strong and centralized enough to negotiate compromises, but a number of firms—industries, even—were not so lucky, and they got scraped away. John Ashcroft's free-market authoritarianism structured the bargain between scrapers and the state regulators tasked with protecting people's rights: The feds gave the data brokers a boost up and over the law, and the data brokers pulled the state up behind them. Information was now a weapon and a business, which made it a perfect fit for Silicon Valley's public-private paradise. Larry and Sergey wrote that crawlers let loose on the world could cause "unpredictable or incorrect behavior," then they (and others like them) let them loose anyway, disregarding many centuries of folk wisdom about sending armies of automata to do your bidding. Now these men are among the most powerful people in the world. That also happens in the fables.

The Real World

At the time of this writing, there are six firms in the world with a market capitalization of over $1 trillion. If we exclude the outlying national oil monopoly Saudi Aramco, we're left with five tech companies from America's West Coast:

Apple, Microsoft, Google, Amazon, and Facebook. Compared to the rest of the world's most valuable corporations, the group is notably young, emerging in the last quarter of the twentieth century or the first years of the twenty-first. All five were the founders' first companies, and most provided the founders with their first real jobs out of school. These are career winners, picked early by capitalists. All five companies fit comfortably into the Palo Alto System as we've examined it, and the town is close enough to call home for three of them.

The oldest is Microsoft, still in a Seattle suburb, where Trey Gates has used ruthless tactics and the operating-system monopoly to stay near the top. Oracle and Adobe have done well, too, but nobody figured out how to make money on PC software as well as Gates and the teams he built in his image did. The scrapers at Google and Facebook found the most important layers on the web, search and social—portal pages declined in importance as "online" became the default status rather than somewhere users went—and brutally disciplined the entire global advertising industry, instantly throwing media into chaos. Every dollar these firms pulled out of the market represents the triumph of software over hardware, of advertising over production, of monopoly over competition, of capital over labor. Their value spiked as concentrated investment funds chased high returns into crowded futuristic gambles while eschewing down payments on output expansion, especially when fixed in the United States. In classic class-war terms, it was a good time to be the bad guy, and the new tech overlords reveled in their status without bothering to change out of their T-shirts. They had ample cause to celebrate; by a society's own standards, few people have ever risen so high so fast. The reader is already familiar with the other two firms rounding out the tech top five; it's virtually impossible not to be.

Compared to his few peers, Jeff Bezos was experienced in business when he launched Amazon. Despite being centrally implicated in the dot-com bust and taking a hit of over 90 percent on its stock price, the "relentless" company (as it was almost called) built back. The financially experienced Amazon management team sold more than $600 million in bonds to European investors right before the crash, a move redolent of Huntington's international railroad security shenanigans. The bonds insulated Amazon just enough from the explosion of a number of its big web retail investments.[33] Instead of bribing the market into investing with dividends and stock buybacks, Bezos redirected revenue into growth through acquisition and expansion. To books he added e-books (developing Kindle) and audiobooks (purchasing Audible), coming to dominate both categories. Amazon also bought Zappos, the internet's favorite shoe store, as well as the self-explanatory Diapers.com.

Amazon targeted affluent households, which happened to be a growing market as social bifurcation continued. The firm secured this valuable demographic with the introduction of Amazon Prime, an annual subscription that promised unlimited free two-day delivery for an annual fee of approximately $100. It's the kind of convenience you could otherwise only demand of a servant, and servants are expensive. Prime brought that level of service to the merely well-off, and in just over a decade, Amazon Prime had achieved over 80 percent saturation in high-income American homes.[34] This was an about-face from the universal vision of Webvan, but it was also an about-face from the money-losing failure of Webvan. Amazon's revenues climbed in a picture-perfect exponential swing. In 2018, after spending all 2017's leftover cash to acquire Whole Foods and try groceries again, the realest of the internet titans finally started showing a profit. The numbers are going according to plan, and one part of the plan has been to constantly probe for new income sources. The Fire Phone was a flop, as was a hotel booking service and a mobile payment processing system, but Amazon Web Services (AWS) was a huge success.

In the early 2000s, Amazon started to build its partner platform, which allowed third-party vendors to sell their goods on Amazon or with Amazon tools. The company saw large demand for web server infrastructure and related services among existing retailers, and Amazon was little more than one big exercise in perfecting those technologies for that purpose at global scale. Expensive servers were one of the few fixed costs for doing online business, and the dot-com bubble was cautionary on the question: Secondhand Sun servers were the symbol of the bust, and they littered the market, the unemployed circuits of web businesses past desperately interviewing for new positions, just as the humans were. For a sector addicted to outsourcing fixed costs, server power for hosting was one of the few it was stuck with. That is, until AWS came along. The project defined the new category of cloud computing, allowing web companies to scale instantly and limitlessly on a pay-per-use basis. By turning an expensive investment into an affordable service, Amazon got ahead of the trend. Though retail still makes up the lion's share of the company's revenue, it's the high-margin cloud service that's driving profits. The company's first data centers benefited from the Pacific Northwest's abundant hydro-power dams.

The book business gave Amazon a lot of practice in efficiently selling and delivering objects, which came in handy when the site expanded its offerings from physical media to, well, everything. Bezos originally left warehousing to the book distributors to save money, but Amazon got expert at that, too. The company invested $300 million in a national set of high-efficiency ware-houses in the late 1990s.[35] It was exactly the kind of bet that sank a bunch of web retailers in the bust, but they hadn't hedged the way Jeff's team did. The bet paid big when Amazon Prime took off. It turned its order fulfillment system into a platform for third-party sellers, who could mail their stuff to Amazon for sale through Amazon. Counterintuitively, Bezos's bet on building out super-efficient high-tech infrastructure has also been a bet *against* the same kind of investment on the part of the rest of the economy; Amazon invested in fixed capital so others didn't have to. In Operation Dragon Boat, the firm put together a plan for a global top-to-bottom delivery and fulfillment sys-tem, reducing its dependence on high-wage union contractors and bringing its biggest cost in-house, where it could devote the firm's braintrust to pushing it down.

Wall Street was not always happy with Bezos's profligately responsible investment strategy—at times shareholders surely would have preferred to be bribed with stock fluffing. But Amazon's revenue and market share kept increasing, and if the firm wasn't raking in profits, it wasn't losing money, either. As a binary bet on the monopolization of online retail, Amazon was stubbornly strong, and after enduring the 2008 economic crisis, the stock price went on an incredible run, from a low under $36 up to a shocking high of $3,719 in the summer of 2021. When the COVID-19 pandemic hit in 2020, global shutdowns sent capitalists hustling to lay money at dominant web retailer Jeff's feet, adding more than $1,000 to the stock price during what the rest of us experienced as disastrous months. How did Bezos succeed in linking the internet to the world of physical objects when so many others, similarly situated, failed? What did he and his team understand about the way of the world that others didn't?

Amazon's preferred version of the story is that all those infrastructure investments enable the company to make more efficient use of labor than other companies can. Thanks to all the robots and data analysis, humans who work for Amazon are more productive than humans who work in similar jobs elsewhere. That's what allowed the company to institute a firm-wide minimum wage of $15 an hour while competitors have fought a national increase tooth and nail. Meanwhile, Bezos can split the efficiency gains with employees (higher wages) and customers (lower prices, better service) and still come out on top. This is how technological automation is supposed to work: better jobs, consumer convenience, and private gain, all thanks to capitalist science. If Amazon seems monopolistic, it's simply because its corporate competitors were too shortsighted, greedy, and scared to forgo immediate profits in favor of long-term investment. And by the consumer welfare antitrust standard, it's hard to argue that the company makes anything worse, and thus hard to argue it's a monopoly in the negative sense. If it were, wouldn't Amazon increase prices?

No sentence in the previous paragraph is false, per se. There is a grain of truth to the techno-optimist version of Amazon's rise. It is not, however, True, not in the ways that are important for our larger story. Unlike some of its peers, Amazon found real production efficiencies, but firms can reduce their labor costs in more than one direction, and the Bezos company wanted all of them. That meant equipping workers with the latest and greatest in hardware and software to maximize their output. But as workers have always been quick to understand, maximizing output tends to suck. "Intensification" involves reducing the allotted time for a task or increasing the number of tasks allotted for a given time — the same thing, when you think about it — and Amazon intensified beyond the limits of human biology. If we see this process from labor's point of view, it's not the owners who generously split the proceeds from their investment with their workers; it's the workers who split the proceeds of their extra output with the shareholders. From there it's easy to see which classed perspective on intensification reflects the economy's real tendency. If workers are improving their station at the expense of capital, we should see labor's share of output increasing. Contrariwise, if capitalists are benefiting from an increase in the rate of exploitation, we should see labor's share declining, *even if wages go up.* In the Webvan model, we can imagine the well-trained, well-paid delivery drivers receiving a greater share of the company's revenue than the drivers at less efficient firms where waste commands more resources. But Webvan failed, and Amazon did not.

American labor's income share fell precipitously in the early years of the new millennium, and took another sharp dive after the 2008 housing market crisis, just as Amazon's numbers jumped.[36] Like the rest of the tech industry, Amazon's fortunes are inversely correlated with the fortunes of the working class. Any doubt melts away when we examine stories of work life at the firm. Amazon managers use robots and data to wring the most they possibly can out of the company's fulfillment workers. The company's system tracks every worker at all times with ever-improving technologies and sets a grueling pace for stowing, fetching, packaging, and delivering. Any behavior that doesn't register as work, such as going to the bathroom or pausing to breathe, is considered TOT—time off task—and it counts against a worker's efficiency rating, which Amazon monitors automatically. The breathless pace disciplines Amazon's labor within an inch of its life, and the firm's warehouses have a turnover rate of 150 percent, which is to say the company replaces its whole workforce every eight months.[37] In short, Amazon uses people up.

One disturbing element is common to accounts from the warehouses and delivery vans: bottles of urine. The two kinds of workers have very different jobs, but both report that Amazon's expectations for worker efficiency are engineered so tightly that employees don't have time to use the bathroom. When a company spokesman smirkingly denied it on Twitter ("You don't really believe the peeing in bottles thing, do you? If that were true, nobody would work for us") he opened the door for journalists, and many news outlets found an abundance of evidence, including smoking-gun pictures of amber water bottles.[38] Since people quit so often, Amazon uses a semi-automated system for hiring and firing to slake its constant thirst for fresh labor. Warehouse roles aren't contracted out, but the firm has worked very hard to make all its fulfillment jobs plug-and-play, reducing the training period to less than one week. That investment in divestment allows Amazon to employ relatively vulnerable people, including felons, recent immigrants, and the elderly. The CamperForce is Amazon's seasonal warehouse hiring program for people living in RVs. As long as they don't invest much in individual workers, the bosses don't have to worry about exhausting or even breaking them.

Safiyo Mohamed immigrated from Somalia only three months before she started as a stower at an Amazon warehouse in Minnesota. After three days of training (only in English), she began emptying incoming boxes from the conveyor belt into boxes from which the pickers picked. The system had a strict quota: 2,600 items sorted for every 10-hour shift, or a consistent average of less than 14 seconds per object. To fit in any kind of break you had to go faster, so as a beginner, Safiyo tried to avoid taking any breaks. Still, after her first week, her manager told her she was too slow and made more mistakes than the acceptable number: one per shift, an inhuman error rate of .04 percent. What help she got concerning strategies for improvement came from the other Somali workers who filled the warehouse. (As in the Hoover-era gold mines, white English-speaking managers boss groups of nonwhite workers, whose ethnic composition depends on the location; in Minnesota's Twin Cities, a high proportion of them are East African immigrants.) "After my shift, I couldn't even cook for myself. I barely had the energy to take a shower and often went to bed with an empty stomach," Mohamed recalled in an essay about her experience for *Sahan Journal*. "I had nightmares about getting fired, disrupting the little sleep I was getting. They treated me and every other warehouse worker like a machine, not a human."[39] Feeling like she had no other way to support her family, Safiyo lasted longer than most, 30 months. In Amazon's numbers, she turns up as an unqualified success. That's how it's supposed to work; that's how Amazon came to dominate retail and how Jeff Bezos became the world's richest man.

A detailed 2020 investigation found that Amazon's warehouse workers have a serious-injury rate nearly twice the warehouse industry average. And the more robotized the distribution center, the higher the injury rate. "If you've got robots that are moving product faster and workers have to then lift or move those products faster, there'll be increased injuries," an Occupational Safety and Health Administration inspecting physician with experience in the company's facilities told reporters.[40] Racing to catch up with machines rigged to run hot hurts people. Efficiency causes injuries, which is another way of saying that, for Amazon, *injuries are efficient*. Amazon's delivery must be very efficient, because drivers get injured even more—a lot more.[41] And unlike warehouse workers, Amazon delivery drivers don't technically work for Amazon, even if they're wearing Amazon uniforms delivering Amazon packages in their Amazon vans following Amazon's directions to Amazon customers.

For most of its existence, Amazon got its packages to customers' doors just as everyone else does, contracting with the U.S. Postal Service or the big private shippers UPS and DHL for the dreaded "last mile" delivery. But as part of Operation Dragon Boat, the company planned to bring shipping inside the Amazon tent, or at least next to it. Driving trucks around is dangerous—for drivers, for the other people on the road, and for the legally liable employers. Trucks kill people, especially when you drive fast. Amazon drivers, unsurprisingly, have to drive fast if they want to keep their jobs, and their trucks do kill people. But when it comes time to hold someone responsible, Amazon is nowhere to be found. Patricia Callahan's 2019 investigation for *ProPublica* and the *New York Times* couldn't establish exactly how many deaths Amazon drivers were responsible for because they are all contractors, hired through the Delivery Service Partner program.[42]

To work with Amazon, "partner" firms sign off on an extortionate list of conditions, including full indemnity for Seattle, an agreement to pay all legal fees, an agreement to rent a fleet of Amazon vans, and a promise to achieve the brand's required pace. Working with the small fly-by-night labor-contracting operations that sprouted up to take Amazon's routes makes it easier for Amazon to bully its small counterparties, especially compared to established and unionized shippers. And if a contractor becomes any kind of problem, the Bezos team can simply kill the contract and get a new one. The owners of these small contracted logistics firms pass on the desperation to drivers, and they start peeing in bottles without anyone having to require it of them explicitly—that, of course, would be a violation of their rights. Despite its overwhelming control of the contracting process, Amazon considered but declined to require on-road training for its drivers, finding it would be a "bottleneck" for getting new workers on the road. "Amazon officials have ignored or overlooked signs that the company was overloading its fast-growing delivery network while eschewing the expansive sort of training and oversight provided by a legacy carrier like UPS," Callahan's team found.[43] One early casualty of Amazon's delivery system was Joy Covey, the firm's first chief financial officer, who was killed in 2013 when one of the company's contracted drivers collided with her bicycle on the South Bay's Skyline Boulevard. Bezos personally eulogized Covey at her memorial, and then pushed ahead with Dragon Boat.

Like other tech companies, Amazon has been very aggressive about preventing union formation, though delivery and warehouse workers are traditionally better organized than programmers and electronics assemblers. The company's strategy earned a 2020 report from Amnesty International, which evaluated work conditions in four countries and found that Amazon managers use "technology to engage in inappropriate surveillance and data collection from its workforce, including to undermine workers' right to organize" and linked the firm's success therein to high rates of injury.[44] Amazon is a human rights concern. The firm's leaders do not seem to have taken the report to heart, and at the time of this writing an initial assessment from the National Labor Relations Board found that Amazon illegally interfered in a Bessemer, Alabama, warehouse union election, which the company won by a large margin. As I write, they're accused of interfering, again, in the closer re-vote. The NLRB has yet to issue a recommendation on a second re-vote; it remains to be seen whether Team Bezos will squirm their way out of it, though I wouldn't bet against them.*

Though Amazon relied less on VCs than its peers, Bezos came into the enterprise with a hedge-fund orientation. Like Hoover's company, which bought and reformatted mines a century earlier, hedge funds in the period operated in large part by buying up struggling legacy businesses and transforming their operations for increased efficiency and profit. Bezos ran Amazon as if he was perpetually reacquiring it, always pushing for faster growth and sharper numbers. To achieve that, the firm applied the same logic toward its white-collar employees as it does to the blue-collar workers in the warehouses. "The company is running a continual performance improvement algorithm on its staff," Amy Michaels, a former marketer on the Kindle e-book reader team, told the *New York Times*. From the top down, management inculcates a hypercompetitive internal atmosphere meant to put Microsoft's notoriously cutthroat workplace to shame. The *Times* reported on an annual review process in which managers index their subordinates by quality, publicly excusing workers from the room in order from worst to best. Amazon's managers suffer from the same "churn and burn" employment pattern, albeit for much higher wages. Still, abjection is abjection. "You walk out of a conference room and you'll see a grown man covering his face," one former member of the book

---

* In March of 2022, workers at an Amazon fulfillment center on Staten Island achieved a shocking upset when the rank-and-file Amazon Labor Union won a resounding victory. Whether the Bezos team will be able to decertify the organization before they negotiate the firm's first union contract remains, at the time of this writing, unclear.

marketing team told the *Times*. "Nearly every person I worked with, I saw cry at their desk."[45]

There are a host of reasons for Amazon's success, and they outweigh the substantial number of reasons the business should have failed. But success in the new millennium has not come from implementing the Webvan win-win-win agenda, as for centuries humans imagined it would under the doctrine of progress. Instead, Amazon's profits come from squeezing productivity out of people. Robot systems that track human workers may count as investments in automation technology when it comes to tax write-offs, but they are part of a whole different narrative about the developing relationship between workers and owners. The company became a bet against the working class, both because it grew by targeting affluent consumers and because its efficiencies came from total control. Once unions start negotiating contracts, there's no way to apply the hedge-fund model of constant disruption. Amazon's owners are allergic to sharing power, and its stock was a bet on capitalists not having to do that rather than on any particular technology. It's the same bet that has drawn investment capital to the West Coast for a long time, and it has continued to pay off into what was supposed to be the future.

Once upon a time, the world's most valuable company was a similar bet, one against the future of working-class power in American manufacturing. It wasn't Steve Jobs's "think different" vision or even Steve Wozniak's circuit-design brilliance that drew Xerox into the partnership that gave Apple that influential look at PARC's Alto; it was the secret network of Peninsula kitchens and basements where immigrant families assembled Apple's electronics. Throughout the early years, Jobs's most important contribution was getting things done faster than other people could imagine, and he did that by emotionally manipulating his employees (and cofounder) into working harder and longer than they wanted to. If Jeff Bezos was a well-trained capitalist, then Jobs was a jaw-dropping natural talent. He was so good at escaping his obligations and foisting them onto other people that as a young founder he threw his pregnant girlfriend out of the house and successfully abandoned her and the child for years, only relenting and paying $385 a month in child support after a DNA test. Sued by the County of San Mateo, deadbeat Jobs had to reimburse the local government for $5,856 in welfare payments.[46]

Instead of working for one of the big manufacturers, which would have made the company little more than a glorified labor subcontractor, Apple did its best to convince consumers that its products couldn't be compared to anyone else's. Since IBM harnessed its war chariot to Intel and Microsoft for the compatible PC and blitzed the market, everyone was using contracted parts. Apple shifted to a branding play: You bought Apple not because it was the best deal or the most powerful computer; you bought Apple because it was Apple. Whenever other computer companies tried to drag the industry into a price competition, Apple held strong in the luxury space. A 2014 analysis for the *Harvard Business Review* found that the company's brand identity as a computer for the people was always a myth.[47] The 1983 Jobs-led Lisa computer cost just under $10,000, more than six times the median household monthly income at the time. Though VisiCalc and other third-party software made the Apple II a market success, the company steered away from outside developers. Instead, it doubled down on advertising.

Apple went public quickly enough, and the Silicon Valley way — tying its fortunes to the VC community. Everyone made enough money off the stock by 1980 for the company to underachieve for almost two decades without going belly-up. Apple fanatics supported the company through the tough years, buying extremely expensive, shoddy equipment like the Apple III, which the firm soon stopped supporting, saddling its most loyal customers with a proprietary pile of junk. After a few misses in a row, the Apple board of directors got sick of following Jobs's erratic, even frivolous leadership, and they edged him out of the company. Like the era's luckiest ousted founders, Jobs flipped his reputation into a new firm: NeXT, a stylish luxury workstation company whose biggest achievement was hosting CERN's inaugural web server. Apple ended up buying NeXT for $429 million and acquiring its first CEO back into the top job, but not before Jobs made his first billion by spinning off a computer division heavy with PARC veterans from George Lucas's Lucasfilms studios.[48] After seeing early audience responses to *Toy Story*, Jobs decided to take cash-poor Pixar public in 1995.[49]

In the years after they split, Apple floundered and Steve Jobs succeeded wildly, though by the important accounts he was as impulsive and mean a boss as he was a person in general. Rewritten in light of Apple's revitalization under his leadership, the narrative has the company getting complacent and impersonal, only to rediscover its creative soul with its founder. But the simpler story, and the one that makes more sense in the light of the parallel and decidedly uncreative success of someone like Bezos, is that Jobs's instincts for exploiting people, for getting the most out of them without putting too much into them, for implementing harsher deadlines than workers would otherwise accept, were exactly the qualities history was ready to elevate. His passion for style over substance, inspired at least in part by the shallowness of his technical understanding, was in line with the long-evolving demands of the world economy. Labor's share of production was down; glitz was in. Like Amazon, Jobs's Apple profited from bifurcation on both sides, among workers and consumers.

Apple's second Jobsian turn began in 1998 with the iMac, Apple's long-awaited internet computer. With an early USB port and Ethernet, the iMac jettisoned the floppy drive, a precise reversal of Steve J.'s early insistence on connection by floppy alone. With its translucent plastic body, multi-color options, and all-in-one design, the iMac was a cultural phenomenon, aimed at Mac fanatics, privileged schoolchildren, and computer noobs who wanted to get online and see what all the fuss was about. Led by Apple's original advertising firm, Chiat/Day, the iMac campaign wasn't just the company's largest yet—at $100 million for the first year—it was also the consumer computer industry's biggest ever, an extreme move for a firm that had less than 10 percent of the market by the late 1990s.[50] Though the iMac's potential for expansion was limited to a small set of proprietary software and peripherals, the target buyers didn't mind. Apples were no longer for users who wanted to customize or upgrade their machines in the hacker style; they were for computer consumers, not programmers—people who would sooner buy a new one than unscrew the machine's case. Besides, who wants an external disk drive that doesn't match the cool color scheme, even if you have to pay monopoly prices for one that does? With the iMac—a pretty good computer, not that the stats were its biggest draw—Apple's cult penetrated the home market, no doubt buoyed by the company's early childhood users, lured in with the "donated" classroom equipment and now aging into consumers.

The iMac and its universe of products were a breakthrough success. Reversing years of market-share decline and units-shipped stagnation, Jobs's surface-level focus relaunched the company in the public imagination as the cool computer. In the 2001 movie *Legally Blonde*, bimbo turned Harvard law student Elle Woods (Reese Witherspoon) is a bright orange iBook laptop in a classroom sea of dully identical black IBM ThinkPads. Chiat/Day pushed the association with a long-running series of "Get a Mac" ads in which the compatible Windows PC is represented by a suited nerd (John Hodgman) while Mac is a stylish hipster (Justin Long). PC may be good at spreadsheets and programming, the ads concede, but Mac is for compiling photos and editing home movies. PC is bigger but desperate, while Mac is self-assured and laid-back. The ads don't ask which you would rather own but which you would rather *be*. The international multiyear campaign became iconic, solidifying the Apple brand's connection with artsy hipster types. (When scholar Matthew Hall went looking for online forum discussions of the metrosexuality concept from the early 2000s, the best example he found was on the Apple fanboy site MacRumors.)[51] Apple's aluminum-body PowerBook G4 laptop became the twenty-first-century office computer for yuppies without an office, those freelance contractors cast out into the American city's dense Starbucks archipelago. Working but not *workers* in the class-for-itself sense, their bitten-fruit logos glowed white.

Still, the population of professional Starbucks drinkers was not a high percentage of computer buyers, and Apple continued getting smoked by PC compatibles. In 2001, HP bought market leader Compaq, leapfrogging itself over the direct-to-consumer brand Dell, and the two firms spent the next decade or so in a brutal price war for first place, driving the cost of compatible tower and laptop PCs ever lower. Apple followed the same strategy it had employed since the early computer years and stayed out of the scrap. Steve Jobs didn't compete; he innovated. But no matter how stylish the design, the iMac couldn't elevate Apple out of niche status within the big bad PC market. The company needed a new popular hook, one (like VisiCalc back in the Apple II days) that was exclusive, that no one could clone. Rather than develop the next great idea, Jobs decided to buy one, from a celebrated electronics inventor-engineer named Tony Fadell.

Fadell began his own poorly timed start-up, Fuse, in 1999, hoping to ape Dell's success with the direct-to-consumer model. His plan was for an MP3 player with a mini hard drive that connected easily to an online music store, but the dot-com bust dried up the VCs and Fadell began pitching established tech companies on the idea. In 2001, Apple bit—demonstrating once again the value of an incumbent seat when the finance music stops for a minute—but the company didn't bring him in-house at first. Instead it contracted with Fadell to build the iPod and the iTunes software, and he contracted with subcontractors to supplement his team. When the iPod launched, however, it was Steve Jobs alone on stage, white device contrasted against his black turtleneck. *Newsweek* put him on the cover: IPOD, THEREFORE IAM. The device was a smash hit, defining the high-capacity MP3 market. Sales climbed steeply: Starting at 400,000 units shipped in 2002 to more than 20 million in 2005.[52] The iPod alone represented a huge 40 percent of the company's revenue in 2006.[53] Apple finally owned a market, with a peak over 90 percent.[54] When it came to music players, everyone wanted to be a Mac, even the PCs. Apple introduced a PC-compatible version of iTunes, storming into enemy territory on its own terms. And the iPod was untouchable: Microsoft's competitor, the Zune, was a joke from day one, whether the device was any good or not. Jobs once again avoided price competition by convincing customers that what he had was one of a kind.

The other way Apple avoided competition was to lock everyone else outside. In 2002, Jobs inked agreements with the biggest record labels to offer their music catalogs as online downloads. Key to Apple's offer was digital rights management encoding on the files, which prevented unauthorized users from playing the tracks. It was a win-win solution to the Napster crisis: For most users, at $1 per track, legally downloading the latest hit was less effort than pirating, especially considering that the online sharing services were increasingly full of viruses and misleading file names. And if you wanted to use iTunes, nonhackers had no choice but an iPod—the downloads didn't work on other players. Ashcroft's DOJ added pressure in 2004 by announcing FBI raids on P2P users. "It is illegal to trade in copyright-protected materials on the internet. This is theft, plain and simple. If you are engaged in this behavior, you are on notice that you are not as anonymous as you may think," U.S. attorney Kenneth L. Wainstein said in a press release.[55] The internet was beginning a new phase, one with more corporate control, clearer rules, and federal enforcement. No to P2P; yes to i. Along with John Ashcroft, Steve Jobs helped lead America's B2K transition, and the internet has not changed back.

The connection between Steve Jobs and Apple's customer base is intense and bizarre, but it's at most half the story: DESIGNED BY APPLE IN CALIFORNIA reads the most common label on the company's products, followed by

ASSEMBLED IN CHINA. Behind Apple's success was another world-historical phenomenon: the rise of Chinese high-tech manufacturing. In 1998, Jobs hired a VP from leading compatibles producer Compaq named Tim Cook to build Apple's offshore manufacturing relationships. Cook depended on those relationships at Compaq, and at Apple he turned to one of his former contractors: Terry Gou, the politically connected head of the Taiwanese electronics firm Hon Hai Precision Industry Co., Ltd. — better known as Foxconn.[56]

Foxconn excelled by navigating the global electronics industry through Taiwan into China's capital-friendly special economic zones, now the world's hottest production enclaves. The People's Republic of China invested heavily in the transition from low-value commodity manufacturing to high-value electronics, and Foxconn reaped the benefits, the lion's share of which it passed on to Apple. Starting with the iPod, Foxconn proved itself Apple's most reliable contractor, and Gou was able to leverage his relationship with Beijing to scale in line with exploding demand. Maoism was built on industrial leaps forward, and it's hard to imagine any other country on earth capable of the same feat at the time, for better and worse. Chinese municipalities competed for Foxconn factories and their many thousands of jobs, and the deal between Apple, Hon Hai, and the Chinese Communist Party worked out for all three: As of this writing, the PRC is the world's largest manufacturing nation by value; Foxconn is the world's most valuable electronics manufacturing contractor; and Apple is the world's most valuable company, period. Mac fanatics put the factory-floor suicide nets out of their minds.

You Better Try to Make Me Rich

Onshoring to Foxconn — The Fatal Consequences —
Gangsterism as Governance — Heroin and IKEA in East
Palo Alto — SCORE! — The Palo Alto Suicides

When Steve Jobs took the stage at San Francisco's new west building of the Moscone Convention Center for Macworld 2007, people knew what to expect. Jobs tossed red meat to the Apple faithful with these convention demos, waxing evangelical about the company's mission, revealing the newest project to indiscriminate seal applause from the Bay Area crowds. The audience knew this one was going to be a rally to remember because they'd heard the rumors, the leaks, the trademark applications: Apple was introducing a cell phone. Of the cracks in Apple's notoriously uniform corporate communications front, the biggest was probably the one in the Chinese-language *Commercial Times*, which reported a couple of months early that the product was due to arrive on the market in the first half of 2007.[1] Its sources knew better than anyone when the iPhone was going to be ready: They were building it.

Demos like Macworld 2007 gave Apple fans an inside look at the product, somewhere between the regular public sales pitch and an internal company celebration. This fits with the outsized role that devotees play in Apple's success as well as the curious parasocial relationship these super-users have with the computer brand. Jobs introduced the supporting cast: Apple designer extraordinaire Jony Ive, Google and Yahoo! CEOs Eric Schmidt and Jerry Yang, as well as the head of exclusive wireless partner (and recent AT&T acquisition) Cingular. Tim Cook got a shoutout during a display of the "visual voicemail" technology, but there was no mention of Foxconn or the nation of China at all. Terry Gou had as much right to stand on that stage as anyone, but there's no sign that the Foxconn founder attended the event, though his company had won the contract to be the iPhone's sole assembler. As they had since the beginning, the Bay's capitalists obscured their Chinese labor contractors and manual workers, though they were no less important to Apple's success than they were to the Southern Pacific's.

To persuade people to shell out $500 or $600 for the iPhone—subsidized by the wireless carrier upon signature of a two-year contract, to which Jobs negotiated a $10-a-month cut per user for Apple—you had to give them a device that was substantially different from commodity smartphones, which included similar components in similar cases for similar functionality and competed on price. Designing and programming the phone was a challenge, but certainly not a bigger one than manufacturing it at scale. Considering how different and fragile the phone was, Apple couldn't follow the normal playbook of using a variety of offshore contractors. Nothing on the iPhone was going to be standard. (As Jason Dedrick, Kenneth L. Kraemer, and Greg Linden illustrate in their study of the iPod's value composition, keeping the other high-margin monopolists Microsoft and Intel out of its device was key to the firm's 56 percent gross profit margin on its marquee product.)* The company needed a manufacturing partner, a relationship that combined the benefits of contracting with the customizability and oversight of an internal operation. Also, Apple's new partner had to have an impeccable quality control record as well as the ability to scale very fast and more or less indefinitely, considering that the firm hoped to repeat the iPod's success. It was a precise need, but luckily, Hon Hai Precision Industry Co., Ltd., specialized in just that.

Gou bet big on Apple, and the iPod spurred the rapid growth of Foxconn's campus in the Longhua district of Shenzhen, China's onshoring electronics manufacturing center. A surplus labor force generated by shrinking public employment along with rural migration to the urban coast left Foxconn with the human capital to handle Amazonesque turnover and worker burnout. Like Steve Jobs, Gou made sure his goals were accomplished faster than other people thought possible. Bossing around a roomful of engineers is one thing, but it was Gou who put thousands of people to work in the middle of the night to retool production lines so that they could turn the Apple CEO's impulses into

---

* When sold directly to consumers through Apple stores or the company site. J. Dedrick, K. L. Kraemer, and G. Linden, "Who Profits from Innovation in Global Value Chains?: A Study of the iPod and Notebook PCs," *Industrial and Corporate Change* 19, no. 1 (June 22, 2009): 81–116.

reality. Foxconn's Longhua workers lived in campus dorms, at least eight to a room, when they weren't on 12-hour shifts.[2] Reports of coerced overtime were common, and the company prided itself on its grueling assembly-line pace, but Apple's investigators found no cause to cancel any contracts. The anti-sweatshop strategy that put international pressure on Nike didn't work when it came to the MP3 player. Thanks to the iPod, Hon Hai's walled factory-city grew to hundreds of thousands of workers.

Foxconn's exclusive deal with Apple was not so much about the manufacturer's bargaining power as it was about Apple's need to ensure consistent development. Gou agreed to slash his margins to the bone in order to maintain Apple's oversize returns and keep the huge contracts that allowed him to make it up in volume. To make it happen, Foxconn relied on giant subsidies from the Chinese government and a young rural migrant workforce that would tolerate poor conditions and low wages long enough to keep production going, at least until new people showed up to take their place. Gou's system fits in perfectly with his American clients; the Foxconn boss has a pamphlet of quotations meant to instruct the firm's managers, and they are quite clear. For example:

> Growth, thy name is suffering.
> A harsh environment is a good thing.
> Achieve goals or the sun will no longer rise.
> Value efficiency every minute, every second.
> Execution is the integration of speed, accuracy, and precision.[3]

Labor's share of Chinese GDP fell from 51.4 percent in 1995 to 42.4 percent in 2007, and inequality has increased as the country's top 1 percent capture an increasing amount of national wealth, following the international trend.[4] This is War Capitalism, imported to the mainland by contractors from Taiwan and Hong Kong and employed by American electronics companies. The Chinese labor regime is two-tiered, based on the location of a worker's home district: Shenzhen's rural migrants reported half the monthly income of local workers—just $267 when surveyed in 2010.[5] These are the workers for whom Foxconn moved onshore in the first place in the late 1980s, and with their skill, endurance, and desperation, they remained the source of the company's hyper-efficiency. Working conditions weren't just brutal; they were also dangerous. As sociologist Pun Ngai notes in her ethnography of a Shenzhen production line, "Nearly every operation and thus every job along the electronics production line involved a complex series of chemical processes," all of which regularly exposed workers to potential hazards.[6] Just as the mining capitalists did a century before, gadget capitalists outsourced production pollution to China. America's contractors had trouble just staying in the game. In June of 2007, the same month as the Foxconn iPhone's in-store launch, Flextronics bought Solectron, consolidating the American electronics contract manufacturing industry's biggest players in a last-ditch effort to "grapple with fierce price competition and a glut of overcapacity," as the *Financial Times* put it.[7]

A new wave of international attention on Apple's manufacturing process crested in 2009, after the suicide of twenty-five-year-old Foxconn employee Sun Danyong. Like most of his colleagues at Foxconn, Sun joined as a migrant from the country's rural southwestern region, but his career prospects were exceptionally good. A high school valedictorian and graduate of the Harbin Institute of Technology—consistently ranked one of the top engineering programs in the world by *U.S. News & World Report*, along with UC Berkeley and Stanford—Sun worked in the logistics department, not on the assembly lines. He was on a management track, living the best-case scenario. His story was more or less the narrative used to sell poor kids on academic excellence, engineering, and the electronics industry as a life path to prosperity. But like Amazon's, Foxconn's high pressure applies to even the comparatively elite workers. When one of the factory's new iPhone prototypes disappeared, the company held Sun responsible.[8] He alleged to friends that Foxconn's security team beat and humiliated him. Days after the treasured device went missing, Sun jumped to his death from his apartment. No evidence ever emerged that he took the device.

The extreme pressure Foxconn put on Sun was a function of the pressure Apple put on Foxconn, a corporate pass-through of labor discipline that gave the California company some plausible deniability. But for manufacturing contractors, security and secrecy are crucial, and a single slip-up on something as important as the new iPhone could seriously affect a firm's prospects. The *Wall Street Journal* reported that Apple was known for requiring suppliers to agree to "hefty financial penalties" in the event of a leak.[9] Foxconn wasn't over-reacting to a security breach by bullying its employee to death; it was fulfilling the contract's expectations. In the summer of 2009, the story emerged in Chinese media and was soon picked up in the United States, where it was the most dramatic indication yet of Apple's poor supply-chain labor practices. A video of Foxconn security beating workers circulated, more evidence that the company's profits came from labor abuse. Everyone promised to do better. That's not what happened.

During 2010, at least 15 Foxconn employees attempted suicide, leading to 10 deaths. Unlike Sun, the victims were mostly lower-paid production workers, though Sun was not the only college graduate. In their study "Suicide as Protest for the New Generation of Chinese Migrant Workers: Foxconn, Global Capital, and the State," scholars Jenny Chan and Pun Ngai focus on disappointment and despair, rather than absolute immiseration, as etiologies. "The post-80s and post-90s new generation of migrant workers have higher expectations of life than their elders, and feel greater disappointment and resentment at their failures," they write.[10] Young Foxconn workers—some as young as fourteen, under government-supported "internship" programs—feel trapped between a farming life that's no longer feasible and an urban electronics life that offers surprisingly few future prospects—not to mention survival-level wages and no time to pursue hobbies, passions, or leisure activities. Rural migrant Foxconn assembly worker and poet Xu Lizhi gave the despair artistic expression:

> *Refuse to skip work, refuse sick leave, refuse leave for private reasons*
> *Refuse to be late, refuse to leave early*
> *By the assembly line I stood straight like iron, hands like flight,*
> *How many days, how many nights*
> *Did I—just like that—standing fall asleep?*[11]

In January of 2014, Xu wrote of the suicides directly:

> *A screw fell to the ground*
> *In this dark night of overtime*
> *Plunging vertically, lightly clinking*

It won't attract anyone's attention
Just like last time
On a night like this
When someone plunged to the ground[12]

In the fall of that year, the poet leaped to his death.

Nearly all the self-destructive workers jumped from Foxconn high-rises, and the anti-suicide nets the firm installed became the sequence's most potent symbol. Though the nets and anti-suicide pledges captured media attention, Foxconn clearly understood the suicides as a labor action, and the firm quickly raised wages.[13] But not too high.* The company held on to Apple's business—though Tim Cook made some moves to reduce the iPhone's dependence on Gou's firm, Foxconn's capacities were unmatched, and its few competitors didn't offer much differentiation when it came to labor practices anyway.[14] In November of 2020, Apple announced a suspension of new business with the Hon Hai iPhone competitor Pegatron, putting the newer supplier on probation for its abuse of student internship programs.[15]

Buoyed by the years of exclusive iPhone contracts, Foxconn sought another route to cheaper labor besides tightening the squeeze on migrant workers, which was a strategy that seemed to have reached its absolute limit in 2010. Instead, it brought factories inland, closer to the lower wages, where the firm could also secure large subsidies from local governments. Fast-growing Zhengzhou granted Gou $1.5 billion in cash along with a laundry list of other promises to build what came to be known as iPhone City for him.[16] Within a year, the place had 100,000 workers, and by 2017 the factory had a daily capacity of 500,000 units and assembled half the world's iPhones, which meant that objects responsible for more than a quarter of Apple's revenue passed through

---

* Steve Jobs downplayed the significance: "We look at everything at these companies," he told the press. "Foxconn is not a sweatshop. It's a factory—but my gosh, they have restaurants and movie theatres…but it's a factory. But they've had some suicides and attempted suicides—and they have 400,000 people there. The rate is under what the U.S. rate is, but it's still troubling." The comparison treats the factory as a total environment, like a state. Normally the workplace is only one part of a person's life, making the numbers difficult to compare. Brian Merchant, *The One Device: The Secret History of the iPhone* (Little, Brown, 2017), 272.

the hands of Zhengzhou workers.[17] So much for American capitalists losing China to Mao.

As the single most successful commoditization of that trend, the iPhone provides 60 percent gross margins, to be split among the manufacturers.[18] But as Apple's stock price rises, Foxconn's slice of the pie narrows as the firm contends with rising wages, high capital investment requirements, and competition.[19] When a Chinese firm such as Huawei attempts to cut out the Taiwanese labor contractors and American capitalists, it faces the wrath of the U.S.-led international financial order. In December of 2018, U.S. authorities had Huawei executive Meng Wanzhou, the founder's daughter, detained in Canada for allegedly working around international sanctions against Iran. She was held on these charges for nearly three years before being released, a naked act of aggression it's hard to imagine a NATO member state tolerating. In May of 2020, the U.S. Department of Commerce banned the Chinese tech company from acquiring semiconductors based on American technology or software without prior authorization, cutting it off from chips manufactured in its own backyard.* By securing its place on top of this food chain, Apple has become the world's most valuable firm.

With the exceptions of North Korea and Cuba, the communist world has merged onto the capitalist highway in a couple different ways during the twenty-first century. As you've read, free-trade imperialism and its cheap agricultural imports pushed farmers into the cities and into factory work, lowering the global price of manufacturing labor and glutting the world market with stuff. Forward-thinking states such as China and Vietnam invested in high-value-added production capacity and managed labor organizing, luring links from the global electronics supply chain and jump-starting capital investment. Combined with capital's hesitancy to invest in North Atlantic production facilities, as well as a disinclination toward state-led investment in the region, Asian top-down planning erased much of the West's technological edge.† If

---

* A Taiwanese onshoring contractor with Western shareholders, like TSMC, doesn't have the same problems, though in this case it was their chips being blocked. Bob Davis and Katy Stech Ferek, "U.S. Moves to Cut Off Chip Supplies to Huawei," *Wall Street Journal*, May 15, 2020.

† This transition has been most visible in electronics, but it's not exclusive. In a 2021 essay, James Meek examines wind tower factories in Glasgow, Scotland, and Phu My, Vietnam, both owned by the same South Korean company. "The competition between Vietnamese

two workers can do a single job, and one worker costs less, both in wages and state support, why pick the expensive one? Foxconn's 2017 plan to build a U.S. taxpayer–subsidized $10 billion flat-panel display factory in Wisconsin was trumpeted by the president, but it was a fiasco that produced zero screens.[20] The future cost of labor looks to be capped somewhere below the wage levels many people have enjoyed, and not just in the West.

The left-wing economist Joan Robinson used to tell a joke about poverty and investment, something to the effect of: The only thing worse than being exploited by capitalists is *not* being exploited by capitalists. It's a cruel truism about the unipolar world, but shouldn't second place count for something? When the Soviet project came to an end, in the early 1990s, the country had completed world history's biggest, fastest modernization project, and that didn't just disappear. Recall that Cisco was hyped to announce its buyout of the Evil Empire's supercomputer team. Why wasn't capitalist Russia able to, well, capitalize? You're already familiar with one of the reasons: The United States absorbed a lot of human capital originally financed by the Soviet people. American immigration policy was based on draining technical talent in particular from the Second World. Sergey Brin is the best-known person in the Moscow-to-Palo-Alto pipeline, but he's not the only one.

Look at the economic composition of China and Russia in the wake of Soviet dissolution: Both were headed toward capitalist social relations, but they took two different routes. The Russian transition happened rapidly. The state sold off public assets right away, and the natural monopolies such as telecommunications and energy were divided among a small number of skilled and connected businessmen, a category of guys lacking in a country that frowned on such characters but that grew in Gorbachev's liberalizing perestroika era. Within five years, the country sold off an incredible 35 percent of its national wealth.[21] Russia's richest ended the century with a full counterrevolutionary reversal of their fortunes, propelling their income share above what it was before the Bolsheviks took over. To accomplish this, the country's new

---

and Scottish workers in CS Wind's global factory isn't just a matter of pressure being put on the Scots to work longer hours, for less money, with less concern for safety—the leveling down of pay and conditions," he writes. "The entire structure of taxation and state-funded services is involved." James Meek, "Who Holds the Welding Rod?," *London Review of Books*, July 15, 2021.

capitalists fleeced the most vulnerable half of their society. "Over the 1989–2016 period, the top 1 percent captured more than two-thirds of the total growth in Russia," found an international group of scholars, "while the bottom 50 percent actually saw a decline in its income."[22] Increases in energy prices encouraged the growth of an extractionist petro-centered economy. Blood-covered, teary, and writhing, infant Russian capital crowded into the gas and oil sectors. The small circle of oligarchs privatized unemployed KGB-trained killers to run "security," and gangsters dominated politics at the local and national levels. They installed a not particularly well-known functionary—a former head of the new intelligence service FSB who also worked on the privatization of government assets—as president in a surprise move on the first day of the year 2000. He became the gangster in chief.

Vladimir Putin's first term coincided with the energy boom, and billionaires gobbled up a ludicrous share of growth. If any individual oligarch got too big for his britches, Putin was not beyond imposing serious consequences.* He reinserted the state into the natural monopolies, this time in collaboration with loyal capitalists, and his stranglehold on power remains tight for now, despite the outstandingly uneven distribution of growth. Between 1980 and 2015, the Russian top 1 percent grew its income an impressive 6.2 percent per year, but the top .001 percent has maintained a growth rate of 17 percent over the same period.[23] To invest these profits, the Russian billionaires parked their money in real estate, bidding up housing prices, and stashed a large amount of their wealth offshore. Reinvestment in Russian production was not a priority—why go through the hassle when there were easier ways to keep getting richer?

While Russia grew billionaires instead of output, China saw a path to have both. As in the case of Terry Gou, the Chinese Communist Party tempered its transition by incorporating steadily increasing amounts of foreign direct investment through Hong Kong and Taiwan, picking partners and expanding outward from the special economic zones. State support for education and

---

* Oil and banking baron Mikhail Khodorkovsky, the richest of the group, and, by the early 2000s, one of the richest men in the world, was the most famous target. He spent longer than ten years in prison on financial crime charges before a presidential pardon and exile. Putin seized his equity and the share price of Yukos Oil fell vertically, close to zero, a serious warning to international investment capital and foreign multinationals thinking about doing business in Russia.

infrastructure combined with low wages to make the mainland too attractive to resist. (Russia's population is stagnant, while China's has grown quickly.) China's entry into the World Trade Organization, in 2001, gave investors more confidence. Meanwhile, strong capital controls kept the country out of the offshore trap, and state development priorities took precedence over extraction and get-rich-quick schemes. Chinese private wealth was rechanneled into domestic financial assets—equity and bonds or other loan instruments—at a much higher rate than it was in Russia. The result has been a sustained high level of annual output growth compared to the rest of the world, the type that involves putting up an iPhone City in a matter of months. As it has everywhere else, that growth has been skewed: only an average of 4.5 percent for the bottom half of earners in the 1978–2015 period compared to more than 10 percent for the top .001 percent. But this ratio of just over 2–1 is incomparable to Russia's 17–.5 ration during the same period.[24]

Since the beginning of the twenty-first century, certain trends have been more or less unavoidable. The rich have gotten richer relative to the poor and working class—in Russia, in China, in the United States, and pretty much anywhere else you want to look. Capital has piled into property markets, driving up the cost of housing everywhere people want to live, especially in higher-wage cities and *especially* in the world's financial centers. Capitalist and communist countries alike have disgorged public assets into private pockets.* But by maintaining a level of control over the process and slowing its tendencies, the People's Republic of China has built a massive and expanding postindustrial manufacturing base.

It's important to understand both of these patterns as part of the same global system rather than as two opposed regimes. One might imagine, based on what I've written so far, that the Chinese model is useful, albeit perhaps threatening, in the long term for American tech companies while the Russian model is irrelevant. Some commentators have phrased this as the dilemma

---

* In the Philippines, a rogue's gallery of characters from our story won a 1997 contract to privatize half of Manila's water supply. The main partners in "Manila Water Company, Inc." were Bechtel and the Ayala Group, two family companies run by the heirs of Hoover flunkies. Over the first 15 years, they increased their profit margins to an outstanding 37.5 percent, while hiking rates by a factor of 10. Tanya Kapoor, "Is Successful Water Privatization a Pipe Dream?: An Analysis of Three Global Case Studies," *Yale Journal of International Law*, January 1, 2015, 179, 182, https://openyls.law.yale.edu/handle/20.500.13051/6690.

of middle-wage countries on the global market: Wages in China are going to be higher than wages in Russia because wages in Russia used to be higher than wages in China. But Russia's counterrevolutionary hyper-bifurcation has been useful for Silicon Valley as well; they are two sides of the same coin. Think about it this way: If you're a Russian billionaire in the first decades of the twenty-first century looking to invest a bunch of money you pulled out of the ground, where's the best place you could put it? The answer is Palo Alto.

The son of a Soviet professor of American business, Yuri Milner was the country's internet mogul. He got rich by porting the Silicon Valley venture capital model to Russia and investing in domestic versions of successful American start-ups. Like his luckiest West Coast peers, Milner scraped through the global dot-com crisis, and his Mail.ru conglomerate grew very fast. Unlike his Russian peers, Milner didn't depend on the privatization of state assets; instead he translated California's tech monopoly scheme before ever visiting the Bay Area. He developed a reputation as Russia's sharpest tech investor, and his Digital Sky Technologies (DST) spun off a global investment division, persuading Alisher Usmanov, one of Mail.ru's biggest investors, to back his risky international play. Milner had one target in particular: Facebook. He was convinced it was the one that was going to make money, figuring the firm was a few years from a big IPO. In a competitive bidding situation, Microsoft's 2007 investment put the company at a $15 billion valuation, but after the 2008 financial crisis Zuckerberg had no way to avoid a dreaded "down round" at a lower number, and it was hard to find anyone who could even get to an eleven-figure valuation for the network. Facebook's CFO turned down the strange Russian guy the first time he called, but when he showed up in Palo Alto he earned a sit-down with the boss himself.[25] Milner had a few things going for him: He was convinced that Facebook was a good investment, and he could explain why; he didn't want a board seat or to contribute anything at all besides cash; and he had hundreds of millions of dollars to put down. When they left the room, Milner and Usmanov owned close to 2 percent of Facebook. And Zuckerberg had another $200 million.[26]

In the following years, before the Facebook IPO, Milner vehicles DST and Mail.ru increased their positions in Facebook, pleasing their investment partners by offering to take their shares off their hands if they lost their nerve, and pleasing Facebook by financing an 8–10 percent stake in the company without asking for anything other than a seat on the ride. With the IPO, they netted billions of dollars in profit. The *London Sunday Times* named Alisher Usmanov not only Russia's richest man but also, with his London mansion, *Britain's* richest man, displacing Indian steel magnate Lakshmi Mittal.[27] Usmanov channeled his generic iron-ore monopoly profits into Anglophone brand plays, including the Arsenal Football Club (30 percent) and Apple, pushing $100 million into the iPhone maker and putting a stop to a dangerous and somewhat unexplained slide in investor confidence.[28] Milner continued pumping up tech valuations, investing in Facebook-based game maker Zynga, discount coupon site Groupon, and music streamer Spotify. He put $380 million in Twitter, and in 2011 he teamed with famed Silicon Valley angel Ron Conway to offer $150,000 to each and every start-up in the Bay Area tech accelerator Y Combinator, laying down a bet on the whole regional ecosystem.[29]

When it came out in 2017 that a significant amount of DST's capital originated with the Russian state, the news yielded shrugs in the industry.[30] No one could suck that kind of money out of the country without close ties to the government.* And besides, sovereign wealth funds invest in Silicon Valley all the time. Saudi prince Al Waleed bin Talal made a crucial nine-figure investment in Apple in 1997.[31] SoftBank, one of the biggest investment funds hunting in Silicon Valley, got most of its game-changing $100 billion Vision Fund from Gulf monarchies.[32] Why wouldn't Putin want to put money in Facebook? As far as the gangster state was concerned, there was no better place to allocate the nation's cash. Based on the numbers, it's hard to disagree, and in Silicon Valley, which Milner now calls home, he's in good standing in the highest reaches of the capitalist elite. He's also a trailblazer, and starting in 2011 big Russian investors plowed hundreds of millions of dollars a year into American start-ups in dozens of deals, according to an analysis conducted by TechCrunch.[33] Meanwhile, Russia's domestic capital investment stabilized below 25 percent of GDP, more than ten points behind the 1991 rate and around half of the portion China reinvests.[34]

With the Apple investment we have a good example of how an international enrichment and development circuit works: In this convoluted but effective

---

* Concerns about the Russian government infiltrating Silicon Valley focused more on sex than investment. In 2014 the *Mercury News* published a thin report under the thick headline "Are Russian-spy hookers targeting tech leaders and VCs at infamous Silicon Valley 'cougar nights'?" (Ethan Baron, July 27, 2018).

system, oligarchs pull value out of Russia and ship it to California. Then, California designs the phone (combining components from around the world) and contracts with Taiwanese manufacturers, who use the orders to finance new Chinese factories. Why all the games? And why doesn't Russian tech capital just finance new Russian factories instead? The simplest reason is that, even if wages were equalized, the returns are higher, because Apple has forced its contractors' margins to the ground and found a way to extract monopoly profits from what should be a commodity object. You invest in Apple for the same reason people buy Apple: It's Apple. As in the Cold War era, letting Silicon Valley channel your money into the world is still a good bet. People there know how to get the biggest bang for your buck.

Gangsterization, as we can see, is not necessarily bad for capitalist growth. Far from it. During the Cold War, American, Soviet, and Chinese leadership often found themselves at three-way loggerheads, struggling to integrate in a win-win-win world system. In the twenty-first century's opening unipolar decades, bankers and VCs in the United States further liquefied capital flows and attracted billionaire interest from all over the world. If tech companies—along with expensive art and luxury housing—were a bet on further bifurcation and inequality, then they gave the world's oligarch community a chance to double down on its own prosperity. And it works—for Russian billionaires, for American billionaires, for Taiwanese billionaires, and even for most mainland Chinese billionaires. The value chain links ex-Soviet extractionists like Usmanov—convicted of and imprisoned for "theft of socialist property" in the '80s—with Foxconn's company towns and their mandatory overtime, corporate dorms, and loathsome security patrols.[35] Chasing no goal other than rapid private gain, Palo Alto's capitalists once again found a nice place in the middle. It doesn't matter that, as creators, this generation of petty scrapers and advertising salesmen is a joke compared to Charles Litton and Steve Wozniak. As capitalists they are unmatched, and that is what they are.

The Million Dollar Spot

"We think we have effectively dismantled the Taliban," declared Ron Davis at an East Palo Alto press conference in the spring of 2009.[36] East Palo Alto was an unusual location to announce the end of the Taliban, except that Davis was the chief of police, and he was talking about a local organization named for the then temporarily displaced Afghan regime. Still, the raid on the EPA version was a massive operation, involving simultaneous moves by "almost 500 FBI agents and local police in 14 cities," the press reported. After an 18-month investigation, authorities arrested 42 people on state and federal charges across the region: East Palo Alto, Menlo Park, San Francisco, San Jose, Oakland, and Gilroy. No arrests were reported in Palo Alto, but they weren't arresting customers.

The Taliban was considered EPA's top street organization at the time, most responsible for the violent drug trade. "Tomorrow is a new day and we will target a new gang," Davis said after the Taliban takedown. That was the dynamic; like so many other monopolies in the period, the East Palo Alto drug trade was too valuable not to generate its own entrepreneurs.

In the fall of 2000, the *San Jose Mercury News* reported on the Million Dollar Spot on Sacramento Street in East Palo Alto.[37] This was, at one point, a literal black spot on the ground, marked in spray paint. It was an ideal place from which to sell drugs because it's near a bunch of easy escape routes and has good lines of sight to incoming cars. When you look on a map, the reasoning becomes even clearer. Sacramento Street is a cul-de-sac off University Avenue, the downtown Palo Alto artery that, on one end, turns into Stanford's entrance: Palm Drive. University Avenue is also an exit off Highway 101, the wall that separates the two Palo Altos. Sacramento Street is a straight half mile down, which means you could exit the 101, drive one minute on University, take a left, buy a bag of coke or weed, loop around the cul-de-sac, take a right, drive one more minute, and be back on the 101. Or be halfway home to Stanford. At the end of the closest dead end to the freeway, the Million Dollar Spot.

The most valuable block of real estate in East Palo Alto at the time got its value from being easy to drive into and easy to leave. If the Million Dollar Spot didn't exist, the demand for drugs on the Peninsula would have had to invent it, which is what seems to have happened. "This ain't no gang, there isn't any Sac Street gang, it ain't like that," one teenager on the block told the *Mercury*'s drop-in reporter. The supposed gang members grew up together on Sacramento Street, which explains why the group was mixed (black, Hispanic, and Tongan) and included women, unlike the area's self-identified gangs, which tended to be ethnically monolithic and male. The Bay Area's appetite for weed and cocaine enlisted a group of childhood friends in EPA to supply, in large part because of the location of their particular street in relation to the world economy. People who lived there suffered for it; five were murdered on that single block between 1997 and 2005.[38] The not-gang made something with what the twenty-first century offered them, and Sac Street appropriated its team baseball cap from down the road: Stanford's white block *S* on cardinal red, with a green tree.

If global gangsterization is the consequence of a confluence of related factors (the collapse of the Soviet project, privatization of public resources, the attack on organized labor, the production glut, divestment from manufacturing, and so on), then we can understand what was going on in America as part of the same set of bifurcating tendencies. That Highway 101 actually cleaved the Palo Altos in two lends the historical sequence a concrete form. EPA struggled with manufacturing divestment in the postwar period, as richer neighbors poached revenue and jobs using tax breaks and municipal chicanery—for example, Menlo Park annexed an East Palo Alto Hiller Aircraft helicopter plant.[39] In a 1957 piece for the NAACP journal, *The Crisis*, Rachelle Marshall (of the local chapter) called the freeway the "curtain" that separated the two communities. Her article was about the struggle over school-district lines, which ended with a mixed defeat for anti-segregation activists and the birth of East Palo Alto's Ravenswood High School the following year.[40] As a de facto segregated school, Ravenswood was stuck with a declining tax base, and families (especially but not exclusively nonblack families) did their best to navigate their children away from the institution. Thanks to falling enrollment and budget woes, the school closed in 1976, leaving EPA without a high school. For the community's children, busing was no longer optional. The building was finally demolished in 1995. Three years later, a shopping center opened in its place, right off the freeway.

When one of the Sac Street dealers told the *Mercury News* that he was just another businessman in the Bay Area, his specific references might have been lost on the average reader. "You expect me to work at McDonald's or Home Depot?" he asked reporter Sean Webby a couple of years after the shopping center opened. "I make more here in an hour than I would make there in a week."[41] McDonald's and Home Depot weren't just arbitrarily chosen mass-market businesses dependent on low-wage service work: They were also two of the big tenants at the Ravenswood 101 Retail Center, along with (no surprise) Starbucks and *three* big-box electronics retailers. The state authorities and their friends at the Department of Commerce did expect him to work at McDonald's or Home Depot, or Togo's or Taco Bell, or Good Guys or Best Buy or Office Depot. Precisely so. That's where EPA was adding jobs in the twenty-first century, and there wasn't anything subtle about it. In addition to Hoover's federal department and the retailers, the center's inaugural plaque acknowledges Bank of America and the David and Lucile Packard Foundation. At the very bottom: ORIGINAL SITE OF RAVENSWOOD HIGH SCHOOL.

Cocaine and coffee competed for the same workforce, and cocaine paid better. Either way, employees faced service work for drive-in customers; they were not building helicopters. Some people were always going to do the math and take the risk—there were more people than Million Dollar Spots to go around. Competition for monopoly slots pressed the local quality of life down, something the buyers weren't too concerned about, since they were turning around anyway. "I'm from where hard times are regular," wrote East Palo Alto teenage poet Derrick Stamper after his friend Jamel was shot and killed in 2005.[42] The struggle for drug territory drove EPA's violence in the period, giving it the country's highest per capita murder rate in 1992, possibly the municipality's most repeated fact. In 1993, a CBS News national segment labeled it "the most dangerous neighborhood in America." When Webby hung around Sac Street in 2000, he was looking at a group of young people who happened to grow up near a hyper-efficient location for drug sales in the Bay Area at a time when the Bay Area had a growing supply of drugs. As in other sectors, monopolies were worth a lot at the time, and when Sac Street popped up in the National Drug Intelligence Center's 2010 market analysis of the Northern California High Intensity Drug Trafficking Area (HIDTA), the dealers weren't just selling dime bags anymore.

"Law enforcement officials note that approximately 90 percent of Mexican black tar heroin distributed in the region originates in El Aguaje, Michoacán, Mexico, and is supplied by large Mexican cells in the Central Valley HIDTA region to distributors in East Palo Alto, who in turn supply smaller cells operating in San Francisco," the report reads.[43] (In California, even the Taliban got its heroin from Mexico.) It also notes the presence of a new blue-colored methamphetamine from Mexico following the same path around the Bay. On Sacramento Street, police seized 70 pounds of black tar from a Sac Street associate named Adam Alfonso Herrera in 2009.[44] At a $7 million estimated street value, the contents of Herrera's Lincoln were worth more than twice as much as the local start-up Airbnb, which had recently completed its seed financing round at a $3 million post-money valuation.[45] How did Sac Street go from a spot on the ground to an international operation that was smuggling multimillion-dollar loads of heroin in less than ten years? EPA could do rapid growth, too.

The trends in illegal drug use support the idea of supply-driven rather than demand-driven markets, the same framework we've been using since the advent of wheat fields and railroad tracks. Heroin distribution shifted in the years around and following the U.S. military invasion of Southeast Asia, from Mexico in the 1970s to the Golden Triangle border area, where America's rural allies integrated into the world economy one brick at a time. They supplied the American West Coast market, even after Afghanistan (another site of extensive U.S. covert action) kicked up poppy production and started flooding Europe. Cocaine from Bolivia and Colombia channeled through Central America displaced opiates in the 1980s and rewired the West Coast drug routes. The push for free trade—recall the dissolution of the International Coffee Agreement, for example—drove Latin American agricultural capital, land, and labor out of legal food commodities and into higher-priced narcotics. NAFTA accelerated the process in the mid-1990s in Mexico, sinking food prices and providing a flow of cross-border commerce big enough to obscure tons of drugs moving through legal entry points. The gangsterization routine elevated new ranks of Mexican millionaires and billionaires—legal, illegal, and everything in between. Mexican marijuana took over the northern neighbor's market in the '90s, and supply and quality increased through the first years of the 2000s. But as medical and recreational legalization took hold in California and the rest of the U.S., the trends accelerated, and Mexican marijuana farmers faced untenable price declines. They, and the much more profitable trafficking and distribution networks, had to find new growth sectors. The United Nations

Office on Drugs and Crime estimates that the number of Mexican hectares devoted to opium poppies increased from 1,900 in 2000 to 44,100 in 2017.*[46]

The 2009 70-pound heroin bust in EPA came in the wake of that explosion in supply. Producers needed more U.S. distribution, and so Sac Street got a promotion. This boom also coincided with a government crackdown on the prescription opiate OxyContin and the "pill mill" pharmacies that played a central role in its recreational distribution. In 2010, a reformulation of Oxy-Contin for abuse deterrence led to an immediate decline in pills and an immediate increase in heroin as users shifted to the street substitute.[47] These direct population-level effects make a mockery of the prevailing "Just say no" state rhetoric on illicit drugs, as the top-down global process of gangsterization makes the individual pathologization of crime look childish and silly. From a historical point of view, which individuals sell lattes and which sell eighths does not matter nearly as much as the broader patterns that constrain and produce those choices in the lives of particular people. If you're a school principal or a police chief or a city councilperson or a state legislator or some other public officer, it's ridiculous to look at the global trends shaping the lives of your constituents and tell them, "Don't let it be you." That's a total abdication of public responsibility, a rejection of the public in general. But that's exactly what they said. What, then, does it accomplish to tell people that they are on their own when, manifestly, they are nothing of the sort?

"We choose to die," writes Michelle Pfeiffer on the classroom chalkboard in 1995's schlocky school flick, *Dangerous Minds*. Pfeiffer plays a recently divorced ex-Marine who, in search of a teaching job, ends up with a de facto segregated class of black and brown kids who don't want to learn. With a combination of bribery, karate moves, Bob Dylan lyrics, and a little too much positive attention, the white teacher lady saves some of her students by talking them into saving themselves. Despite its overwhelming condescension, poor reviews, and creepy erotics, *Dangerous Minds* was a smash hit, nabbing

---

* Once again, Bank of America provided a financial haven. In 2012, the FBI announced they'd traced an investigation of the leadership of the Mexican "Zetas" cartel to accounts at B of A, where cartel leaders shuffled funds to transform drug revenue into legitimate profits from, of all things, race-horse trading. See Dan Fitzpatrick, "Bank Accounts Figure in Drug Probe: FBI Says Mexican Cartel Funneled Money Through Bank to Horse-Racing Firm," *Wall Street Journal*, July 9, 2012.

number one at the box office during a very competitive summer and netting just under $180 million. As the most successful in a series of films about teachers persuading ghetto youths to school their way out of their historical circumstances, *Dangerous Minds* "buttress[ed] the moral panic around violence of the mid-1990s," write scholars Stephanie Glick and Allyson Dean.[48] The movie is based on the 1992 memoir of high school teacher LouAnne Johnson, the unfortunately named *My Posse Don't Do Homework*.* Johnson taught at Carlmont High School in Belmont, an affluent suburb about 10 miles up the Peninsula from East Palo Alto, where her students caught the bus every morning.

In the movie, Pfeiffer uses "We choose to die" as a provocative grammar example and the basis for a lecture about choice, about the idea that students could choose to attend school or choose to deal drugs and kill people and die in the street. In the book, Johnson gives a similar (though less dramatic) version of the speech. She tries to convince the students that they're in charge of their lives, to give them what a psychologist might call an internal locus of control. "You all know kids who don't come to school," she tells them. "Why don't they come? Because they choose not to."[49] The kids still may not be happy with their lives, Johnson writes, but at least they don't feel quite so powerless. But are those the only options? Individual responsibility or powerlessness? In the '90s, with collectivist ideologies as marginalized as they had ever been in American society, many people thought so.

When Johnson breaks up a fight later in the book, she tells her class that she understands that they are angry because the world isn't fair. But that's just human nature, she explains. "There are twenty people sitting in this room right now. If there were only twenty thousand dollars in the entire world, and each of you had one thousand dollars, and one-twentieth of the power, how many of you would give half of your money so that forty people could share the wealth? How many would give away half your power? Make the world more equal?"[50] Naturally, she writes, nobody raised a hand. Whether she put the rant in the form of a question or not, students must have received

---

* Johnson told Cracked.com that it took the threat of a lawsuit to convince the filmmakers to cut a romantic plot between Pfeiffer's character and one of her students. The filmmakers left the relationship's scaffolding intact, however, and the result is uncomfortable. J. F. Sargent, "6 Bizarre Lies Hollywood Tells When They Base a Movie on You," Cracked.com, December 6, 2015, https://www.cracked.com/personal-experiences-2058-my-life-was-made-into-blockbuster-movie-5-lame-realities.html.

the message: Only a sucker or a loser believes in redistributing wealth, and no one cares if your life isn't fair. (Why anyone thought this messaging would discourage young people for whom narcotics sales was the most lucrative viable career available is a mystery.) This personal-responsibility language was another part of the gangsterization routine, encouraging Americans to only expect to get what they were prepared to take. Thanks to *Dangerous Minds*, EPA's teenagers were object lessons for a nation that didn't know much about their particular situation, and the movie gave its audience a good excuse not to learn more. History doesn't matter, because the only things that matter are those you can personally control.

But history does matter, including in the lives of LouAnne Johnson's students. One of the fighting students she separates is named Emilio, and he's an immigrant from El Salvador:

> There was a lot of fighting in his country, some military, some political. One by one, the adult males in his family—father, brothers, cousins, uncles—disappeared, some to jail, some to military service from which they did not return; some simply disappeared. Emilio was the only male left, so friends of his family smuggled him out of the country and arranged for his passage to Mexico, where he was stashed into the trunk of a car for the trip to San Diego. He was adopted by a Salvadoran couple and his new life began. He had nothing at all from his old life, no letters, no souvenirs, no family. Everything he had was gone, including his mother. He did not hear from her after he left El Salvador and believed she was dead.[51]

Instead of connecting Emilio's fighting to widespread conflict between the rapidly increasing number of Central American immigrants and the Chicano and black populations with whom they were segregated in a deteriorating U.S. labor market, she cites his personal reputation and groups him with Chicano students. Though it might have seemed like a question of individual boys to Johnson, the broader conflict between Salvadorans and ghettoized Californians played a major role in shaping both regions. Refugees from El Salvador's civil war began arriving in California in the 1980s, concentrating in Los Angeles at a time when the city's poor neighborhoods were under increasing pressure and the state had diminishing resources to offer. Salvadorans organized to protect themselves and their communities from criminal organizations, and in the Golden Gulag's barred crucible, they became gangs themselves. Right-wing paramilitaries trained in the ultraviolent techniques of the anticommunist Cold War muscled their way to the top of these organizations. Most notable was Ernesto "El Satan" Deras, a leader in the U.S.-made Salvadoran gang MS-13, who trained with Green Berets in Panama. He was known for promoting the use of rape and torture.

Following the 1992 peace treaty in El Salvador, Yankee authorities deported thousands of Salvadoran prisoners back to their home country, and the imported gang war deeply destabilized El Salvador in the years after, forcing another generation of refugees north. As writer Sarah Knopp notes, harsh criminal justice policies traversed the same borders, and El Salvador adopted STEP-style anti-gang policing in the early twenty-first century under the brand *Mano Dura*.[52] Along with the Central American Free Trade Agreement, increased policing catalyzed more social bifurcation and gangsterization. While the U.S. media conjured tattooed gangster demons from somewhere south of Mexico, the real story of the gangs, writes Salvadoran-American journalist Roberto Lovato, is "buried in half-truths and myth in a labyrinth of intersecting underworlds—criminal and political, revolutionary and reactionary, psychological and cultural."[53] In other words, the twentieth century, our story.

Lovato grew up in San Francisco's Mission neighborhood in the 1980s, the son of Salvadoran immigrants and heir to violent histories shrouded in silence. Involved in his share of fights and petty gangster antics, South Bay teenager Roberto was demographically similar to the bused Salvadoran student Emilio from the *Dangerous Minds* class. In his book *Unforgetting: A Memoir of Family, Migration, Gangs, and Revolution in the Americas*, Lovato highlights the specific history that the LouAnne Johnsons of the world have declined to learn. It's not Emilio's story, but *Unforgetting* suggests the importance of specifics. Lovato traces his family experiences back to La Matanza, the 1932 government massacre of indigenous-communist communities in the country's west that, with U.S. support, left tens of thousands of people dead and presaged nearly a century of struggle (so far). Finding out that his father was there, that he hid under his bed while listening to machine-gun fire, gives Roberto a different understanding of his own childhood and adult life. Though he couldn't change it, knowledge of his past allows Lovato to put himself in a new relation to it. Just because you can't put it on your résumé doesn't mean your specific place in world history doesn't shape your day-to-day reality.

In this context, the no-excuses, zero-tolerance disciplinary policies that characterized America's schools and urban environments were themselves an excuse. In Johnson's book, this comes up continually. The language of student choice and personal responsibility excuses the school authorities from their responsibility to, say, ensure that their students have enough food to eat. When Johnson talks about students skipping school as a choice, she excuses the policy makers who bulldozed their high school and put up a shopping center. Tough-love fantasies such as *Dangerous Minds* were part and parcel of America's long Reagan turn, providing cover for the elite to withdraw from their basic obligations to the rest of society. The George W. Bush administration used the exact same rhetorical techniques to undergird a new competitive kind of education reform. In a speech at the NAACP's national convention in the summer of 2000, a campaigning Bush outlined his school plan, one that Lewis Terman would have loved:

Under my vision, all students must be measured. We must test to know. And low-performing schools, those schools that won't teach and won't change, will have three years to produce results, three years to meet standards, three years to make sure the very faces of our future are not mired in mediocrity. And if they're [not] able to do so, the resources must go to the parents so that parents can make a different choice.

You see, no child — no child should be left behind in America.[54]

Bush vowed to protect nonwhite students from the "soft bigotry of low expectations," a brilliantly phrased subtle attack on affirmative action. Accountability, apportioned according to high-stakes standardized tests, made sure schools didn't *choose* to fail their students. And schools where students tended to test poorly — no matter the nature of the correlation — would be punished, maybe even shuttered, so that, as in the Ravenswood diaspora, kids could attend *better* schools, perhaps private ones. As the case of LouAnne Johnson shows, whether they would be in better *classes* in better schools was a separate question. Third-generation Silicon Valley VC and B2K lead supporter Tim Draper influenced the policy, and he even got a proposition on the 2000 California state ballot to return $4,000 to taxpayers for each kid they enrolled in private school. It wasn't enough money to fill parochial schools with poor children, but it was enough to help rich private-school families like the Drapers divest from public education. This "Draper measure" failed, but his boy Bush got elected. Instead of compensatory support for struggling schools, Bush's bipartisan No Child Left Behind Act choked off public resources where they were most needed. It's hard to imagine anything more irresponsible, and it was accomplished in the name of responsibility.

In East Palo Alto, as in the rest of the world, capital called forth the labor it needed at a price it was willing to pay. There's no reason we need to pretend that authorities at any level wanted everyone in LouAnne Johnson's bused EPA class to succeed, for none of them to be left behind. Capitalists needed low-wage employees because that's where the growth was. If all the kids in East Palo Alto became engineers and doctors and lawyers, who would fill the hundreds of jobs at the new IKEA by the freeway? In 2003, the hulking furniture sales warehouse filled out the Ravenswood 101 center, thrilling local shoppers in a way big box electronics resellers never could. It was the age of brands, even if the brands were attached to DIY sheets of plywood. Domestic IKEAs were few and far between at the time. The store's serve-yourself model reduced the number of higher-wage delivery, warehouse, and sales jobs, leaving mostly deskilled service gigs with compensation near the legal minimum. Locals protested during the zoning process that they wanted a grocery store instead—as with a high school, East Palo Alto went without—but leaders were swayed by the retailer's promise of at least $1 million a year in tax revenue.[55] The store opened its doors to what the *San Francisco Chronicle* described as a "rampaging horde."[56] Say what you will about drug users; they don't line up 5,000 deep to score. Fifteen minutes on foot from Sacramento Street, the new million-dollar spot was blue and yellow.

On Track

Meanwhile, across the freeway: "The gifted are among those left behind," Stanford philosopher Patrick Suppes told the press in 2006.[57] He was announcing a new private online high school, affiliated with Stanford, for gifted children.

It was a culmination of a half century of his research. A direct heir to the work of Lewis Terman, Suppes had been studying the intersection of learning and computing technology in Palo Alto since the 1950s. As a philosopher, he was an adherent of neobehaviorism, which modified regular old behaviorism by adding "unobservable internal structures" of the mind.[58] Whereas behaviorists merely induced responses to stimuli—Pavlov's dog salivating to the sound of a bell is the most famous example—Suppes believed you could induce higher-level understanding via "determinate reinforcement," which involves correcting undesired responses from subjects. With the right interface, computer programs could condition their users into getting more than mere correct answers. Users would be induced to use the right methods and follow the right rules. Like Terman, Suppes was concerned with the country's ability to locate and develop its most promising kids. And like Leland Stanford, he wanted to ensure that youths were stretched to their limits, where the best of the best would reveal themselves and fulfill their potential. The Palo Alto System continued.

Suppes was designated a gifted child himself, discovered in the sixth grade by an interwar university-led talent search and catapulted into high academic expectations, which he met.[59] After his Columbia philosophy PhD, he found a home in Palo Alto, where he stayed for the rest of his long life. There, his focus settled on computer-aided instruction (CAI), the idea that programmed electronics could offer individualized and therefore more efficient instructional feedback and pacing.[60] In the early 1960s, he installed a teletype terminal at Palo Alto's Walter Hays Elementary School, hooked up by phone line to an IBM mainframe for personalized math quizzes. A true Stanford man, Suppes spun a private company out of his research: the Computer Curriculum Corporation (CCC—not to be confused with Seattle's Computer Center Corporation [C-Cubed], 3Com, the Puerto Rican software company C³, or the artificial intelligence firm C3 AI). The CCC mainframe-terminal systems were very expensive and a bit ahead of their time, but the burgeoning Cold War ensured there was plenty of money to keep such ventures alive. As classroom computers proliferated, CCC software spread to thousands of schools, spurred by CAI research out of the Suppes-directed Institute for Mathematical Studies in the Social Sciences at Stanford.[61] In Palo Alto, even philosophers can cash in: Analysts estimated that Simon & Schuster paid more than $60 million for

CCC in 1990.[62] The same year, Suppes and Stanford started the Education Program for Gifted Youth, which they later built into the online high school, where a full-time figurative seat goes for $28,610 at the time of this writing.[63]

As competition for college admissions increased and as the stakes of landing a good one got higher, a finance guy named Alan Tripp saw potential in the Terman-Suppes agenda. A Stanford graduate (econ BA, then an MBA) with stints at the San Francisco tech-centric investment bank Hambrecht & Quist and the Boston Consulting Group, Tripp bided his time while he looked for the right play. He landed on the "ed tech" private tutoring space, which was growing fast at the time as the state shifted the burden of public education onto individual families, especially in California. Tripp analyzed the industry the way he was trained to do, and the answers came up Palo Alto. Not only did CCC have the best programs, the town's unusual focus on improving the performance of already strong students also exemplified the new market niche. Existing private-tutoring center franchises such as Sylvan Learning were dedicated to remedial students who needed extra assistance, which seemed like the natural customer base for extra-scholastic academic coaching. But Tripp knew that affluent parents were looking for a leg up for their kids, whether they needed it or not. (Given the accelerating maldistribution of resources in their favor during the period, they mostly did not.) He also knew where to find them: In 1992 Tripp got a license for the CCC software from Simon & Schuster and opened the first SCORE! Educational Center in Palo Alto's familyful Midtown neighborhood, replacing a bookstore.

From the beginning, Tripp designed SCORE! to scale nationally, and fast. He relied on his connections to raise hundreds of thousands of dollars — Bill Hewlett was one of his first big investors — and secure adulatory national media coverage. The plan was to stick four banks of four PCs each in the storefront location, where kids as young as four would sit and use the Suppes programs until their parents returned to pick them up. SCORE! employees are called coaches, and they're not there to offer child care or to teach. In fact, they're not allowed to interfere with the students' use of the software. Rather, coaches create a supportive atmosphere with precisely titrated enthusiasm and a complex schedule of rewards. When students finish a lesson, they're deluged with cheap encouragement: Coaches give them certifying checks on their file, then they get SCORE!-branded magnets that function like arcade tickets (they're exchanged for pieces of plastic crap), and if kids score more than 90 percent on a lesson they get to spend a minute out of their seats, shooting a basketball for adult applause. It's not behaviorism; it's *neo*behaviorism. A cardboard mountain in the front window displayed long-term student progress. Tripp doesn't seem to have realized how his system degraded pedagogy, and he was surprised when he got an icy reception at Teach for America. He shifted his recruiting strategy to emphasize the potential benefits of joining a high-growth Bay Area tech start-up. Within two years of opening the Palo Alto center, SCORE! had a dozen locations.

One of SCORE!'s main selling points was that the coaches were Stanford and Ivy League graduates—not teachers but educational technicians, armed with the latest research and machinery, more efficient than mere teachers. Plus, they were small-business operators. Coaches and their directors did their best to play the part, developing relationships with families, doing their own advertising and customer generation, and running centers for twelve hours a day, seven days a week. In order to appeal to VCs who were looking at internet companies that could scale instantly, SCORE! set a steep and grueling expansion and financing schedule. Tripp scrambled to raise money to pay for the growth that was supposed to allow him to raise money for growth, an effort complicated by the fact that, though some centers were in the black, the company lost money every year, plowing revenue back into expansion and leaving investors to pick up the growing expenses tab. The company danced on the razor's edge in 1995. Tripp courted the media spotlight and discussed big deals with the industry's power players, just as the accounts emptied and the employees started to burn out from overwork. "I mean when you're just out of college and you're getting off of work every night at 10 or 10:30," one center director explained about coach dissatisfaction, "and you don't meet anybody new for like six months, you just feel like, 'What am I doing?'"[64] Tripp told them they were revolutionizing education, changing the world, but cash-poor SCORE! also capped coach salaries and raised student prices to improve the projections for investors. And it almost worked.

Whether it was the staff defections, all the red ink on the SCORE! balance sheet, the Netscape-led surge of internet stocks, general monopolistic tendencies, dependence on the good graces of CCC, or simply that the high-growth high-reward tech start-up strategy was also high-risk by nature, Tripp fell on the wrong side of the razor. In the spring of 1996, he sold SCORE! to the standardized-testing company Kaplan—itself recently acquired by the *Washington Post*'s Graham family—for a disappointing amount, reportedly under $5 million.[65] Kaplan took SCORE! national over the next decade, supplementing the larger company's remedial test-prep offerings. Coach salaries were cut to minimum wage; SCORE! stopped shooting for Stanford graduates and settled for high school students, making the model easier to scale. The Palo Alto System deployed across the country one storefront center at a time, raising the level of competition between America's children and increasing human-capital output. Sitting quietly at a computer and checking off typing tasks with a low error rate was a crucial twenty-first-century job skill, and SCORE! taught children to race up the mountain for pats on the head. The individualizing Suppes software made sure no students actually reached the top, where they could stop.

In order for the kids in East Palo Alto to fall short, someone had to beat them. Across the freeway, at Palo Alto's middle and high schools, kids took the same standardized tests, even though nothing was really at stake for their institutions. Palo Alto schools don't receive federal Title I funding, and no one was going to put any of them on state probation. As a framework for disciplining and divesting from under-resourced schools, No Child Left Behind had no comment on the suburban neighborhoods bloated by property taxes (even after Prop 13) and supplemental fundraising from concerned parents. Since American public education is organized according to real estate, skyrocketing home prices bifurcated schools on the top end, aggressively sorting the children of successful parents away from the rest of society into rarefied and hyper-enriched environments. As unbelievable amounts of wealth from all over the world concentrated in the Valley, Palo Alto families led the country into the suburban asset model, stocking up on education and soaking their kids with extracurriculars. Bifurcation increased the scholastic stakes for individual families, and the price of entry into high-scoring districts such as Palo Alto Unified kept climbing, too, as if the town were caught in an inflationary computer loop. The schools are good because the houses are expensive, which makes the houses more expensive and the schools better, which makes the houses more expensive and the schools better, which makes the houses more expensive and the schools better.

As it had since Leland's foundation of the stock farm, Palo Alto depended on a high level of performance from its young residents. The town's biggest export, more than code, circuit design, and marketing fluff, is human capital. Stanford switched from colts to young people, but it was still a breeding and training project. Labor intensification applied to students as well as to wage workers, and local leaders spent a century on educational augmentation schemes meant to provide the best genetic material with the top instructional apparatus. The strategy paid untold dividends, and Silicon Valley has shown remarkable economic resilience, always finding another bubble to inflate, a new technological frontier, a new boom, a new gold rush. It looks helter-skelter, but as I've said, Palo Altans managed to generate sinks to absorb and grow huge amounts of capital over and over, with remarkable consistency during the period in question. In a world starved for efficiency gains—novel ways to tighten costs—a bet on the Valley keeps getting better. Just ask some rich people.

By the time we arrive at the second wave of social web companies—post-Facebook, that is to say—the Valley was producing, on a pure numbers basis, the most productive workers in the history of the world. When the Stanford student start-up Instagram sold to Zuckerberg and company in 2012 for a nice round $1 billion, the company had only 13 employees and was not yet two years old.[66] Some critics called it a foolish deal for an app that didn't make any money, but Team Zuck proved the doubters wrong. A steady diet of early, fast-growing companies has kept the tech oligarchs young, infusing their stock prices with vitality and keeping their monopolies tight. Beneath the mounting valuations are a relatively small number of hyper-competitive employees. The super-coders are the most notorious, having cultivated a professional mystique, but the nontechnical managers are just as important for rapid growth. The coders certainly don't work as fast without them. Bolstered by armies of unseen contractors, Silicon Valley's high-IQ workers, the veterans of SCORE!, fulfilled Lewis Terman's wildest dreams.

The original need for improving the country's talent-mining technology was American competitiveness in a hostile world, primarily against the Nazis and/or the Soviets, depending on whom you asked. It worked, and with no small assist from Palo Alto, America defeated Nazism and Communism in the twentieth century. But instead of relaxing into the Pax Americana, capitalists pressed their advantage. They didn't have much of a choice; someone had to offer them a place to put their capital where it could grow faster than the next guy's, and the next guy was looking for the same thing. If expanding output and reducing prices couldn't offer that—and thanks to the global glut, they could not—then investors needed firms capable of disrupting legacy industries and competing away a big market chunk. A merely profitable business wasn't good enough; if you wanted capital, you had to scale, which made every enterprise into a binary bet. Those firms needed their few employees to *win*, to do whatever needed to be done, to outcompete teams of hundreds of people, to replace whole workforces. They needed augmented kids, workers trained from infancy to dominate regardless of the specific task. Whether they were designing new pharmaceuticals to cure disease or (more likely) improving the accuracy of targeted advertising, the children of Palo Alto made sure to score high, to get their basketball shots. And individualized education meant they could always get better.

"I shoot 215 free throws a day. My goal is to beat Calvin Murphy's record of 95.8 percent. That's 207 baskets. To get a perfect score on my next SAT I needed to improve my verbal score by 60 points. I picked a new word every day and repeated it over and over again. They say if you repeat something enough times, it becomes part of you."* This neobehaviorist monologue opens Justin Lin's 2002 suburban California high school thriller, *Better Luck Tomorrow.* Spoken by Ben, a high school student focused exclusively on getting into college, the writing reflects the SCORE! enrichment mentality. Ben is an example of what contemporary German philosopher Byung-Chul Han calls the "achievement subject"—he doesn't do what he's told; he does everything he can:

> Clearly, the drive to maximize production inhabits the social unconscious. Beyond a certain point of productivity, disciplinary technology—or, alternately, the negative scheme of prohibition—hits a limit. To heighten productivity, the paradigm of disciplination is replaced by the paradigm of achievement, or, in other words, by the positive scheme

---

* José Calderón beat Murphy's season record with a 98.1 percent season in 2008/'09, while the career record is now held by Stephen Curry of the Golden State Warriors. Curry not only works for Silicon Valley capitalists but has come to represent the Silicon Valley mindset, the way Tiger Woods once did. See Erik Malinowski, *Betaball: How Silicon Valley and Science Built One of the Greatest Basketball Teams in History* (Atria Books, 2017).

of Can; after a certain level of productivity obtains, the negativity of prohibition impedes further expansion. The positivity of Can is much more
efficient than the negativity of Should. Therefore, the social unconscious
switches from Should to Can. The achievement-subject is faster and
more productive than the obedience-subject. However, the Can does
not revoke the Should. The obedience-subject remains disciplined. It has
now completed the disciplinary stage. Can increases the level of productivity, which is the aim of disciplinary technology, that is, the imperative
of Should. Where increasing productivity is concerned, no break exists
between Should and Can; continuity prevails.[67]

In Lin's movie, Ben and his achievement-subject friends are left alone by
parents and authorities, who, as the philosopher recognizes in the excerpt
above, have programmed these kids to be their own toughest critics. But their
success and the unbroken line between Can and Should leads the crew into
gangsterism. A plot to sell test and homework answers starts the boys down
a slippery slope of elitist organized crime that culminates in murder, the buzz
of their victim's cell phone from under the suburban lawn a fitting California
update to Poe's tell-tale heart.

Stanford's horses were the original achievement subjects, and they were prone
to burnout as well. (Recall the trainer Charles Marvin's line about the inevita-
bility of snapping some tendons and spoiling good colt material under the Palo
Alto System.) Instead of the madmen and criminals that emerge from glitches in
the twentieth century's disciplinary society—think *Bonnie and Clyde* and their
New Left fans—Han writes that the achievement society produces "depressives
and losers" as its human exhaust. Even the killers are nerds.

If overly competitive behavior like Ben's free throw shooting sounds irrational, it shouldn't, not really. The college wage premium—the difference between
income earned by college graduates as opposed to high school graduates—
increased rapidly in the 1980s and '90s as pay stagnated for most workers. By
2010, college graduates regularly made around twice as much as high school
graduates, and only those with advanced degrees escaped the wage consequences of the 2008 crisis.[68] Bifurcation left middle- and upper-middle-class
students and their families with fewer paths for stability, never mind upward
mobility. Higher education rapidly increased in price, redoubling the strain on

the working class and making even the petit bourgeoisie nervous. California's public university system became much more expensive and exclusive as the state finished pulling up the Great Society ladder. The value of elite credentials escalated, too, and high-performing districts like Palo Alto Unified cultivated what the author Alissa Quart calls "hothouse kids" in her book of that title.[69] Palo Alto comes up repeatedly in her account of the phenomenon, as a place where parents lap up Baby Einstein products, a place known for producing the cello prodigies and youth Scrabble champions whose résumés clutter the admissions desks at Harvard, Yale, and, yes, Stanford. Palo Alto High won state championships in boys' basketball ('06) and football ('10)—the respective team leaders, Jeremy Lin and Davante Adams, eventually headed to the pros. No one asked too loudly why this public school had so many transfer students who stood over six feet tall. Winning was winning. Whereas other public high schools might place one or two students at top universities, the Palo Alto high schools send dozens of them each year.

A realistic sense of how the world works has driven kids toward the standardization of overachievement. "You just can't count on good grades to get into a decent school anymore," Ben says in *Better Luck Tomorrow*. Stanford's undergraduate acceptance rate fell from over 15 percent in 2001 to under 5 percent in 2021, making it the country's most selective school.[70] Leland and Jane's dream of whipping up another Harvard was complete. Demand for top college seats is a proxy measure of inequality: The way capital keeps concentrating, mere proximity to wealth and potential wealth is worth a lot on its own, as Mark Zuckerberg and his college roommates can attest. There was enough family money sloshing around the dorms to get Zuck's project launched, and some guys got hundreds of millions of dollars for being at the right place at the right time at nineteen years old. Thanks to Palo Alto, these were childhood's new stakes.

"We are not teenagers," wrote Palo Alto High junior Carolyn Walworth in an op-ed for the *Palo Alto Weekly* in March of 2015. "We are lifeless bodies in a system that breeds competition, hatred, and discourages teamwork and genuine learning. We lack sincere passion. We are sick...It is time to realize that we work our students to death."[71] Walworth was not a square peg in the town's round hole; she was the student representative on the school board. But she also wrote like a survivor. During her childhood, Palo Alto's youth suicide rate was 14.1 per 100,000, nearly three times as high as the state's over-all rate.[72] Parents lobbied for an investigation, for experts with research, tests, and solutions. The Centers for Disease Control and Prevention issued a report on youth suicide in the whole of Santa Clara County that, though it confirmed Palo Alto's sense that it had an exceptional problem—and in the town's pre-ferred language of data—offered no new insights and pleased none of the stakeholders. Residents insisted that the CDC add "train" to the organization's list of recorded suicide methods, though outside Palo Alto it's not a popular one compared to firearms, poison, and hanging. With no smoking gun in the report, local leaders could adopt the same line Steve Jobs used with regard to the Foxconn suicides: It's sad, but sometimes people kill themselves. Still, in both these environments, there was only so far anyone could spread the blame. In January of 2010, a Foxconn worker jumped to his death the day after a teen-ager in Palo Alto died on the tracks. In January of 2011, it happened again. The second time, they were both nineteen years old.

Students have been speaking out in terms similar to Walworth's throughout the suicide sequence, and the town has attempted a number of technocratic and organizational solutions, but none of them seemed to work. Palo Alto was left with prosaic ideas, including a high fence around the tracks and volunteers to sit watch at the deadly crossings. Attempts to reduce the student workload and level of competition have been resounding failures, facing strong oppo-sition from the kids themselves. At Gunn, when the administration tried to cut the so-called zero period of class that started at 7:20 a.m. based on social science research into sleep and school performance, a student survey showed near unanimous opposition.[73] In a competitive system like theirs, restrictions only serve to help distinguish those who can figure out how to surpass them, people for whom Can and Should collapsed—men like Dave Packard, who wouldn't accept state limits on his profits, and Steve Jobs, who wouldn't accept anything at all he didn't like. They're the ones who set the pace, for the town, the country, and the world. The kids weren't going to pretend they lived some-where else.

Palo Alto has been unable to fix the problem of youth suicides because these youth suicides are already part of a solution, the one that answered capital-ism's crisis in the twentieth century's fourth quarter. It's like Dorian Gray tell-ing himself everything would be perfect if he could just figure out how to fix that damn painting. Byung-Chul Han's burned-out achievement subject is a necessary part of the achievement society, and the achievement society is the only kind in which three guys and some pizza can replace whole economic subsectors. There's a reason why monopolistic Silicon Valley is obsessed with domination, the word Mark Zuckerberg used to shout at the end of Facebook meetings.[74] The model is progress by victory, defeat, and ruthless elimination, full speed from day one. It is the Palo Alto System, and even if Palo Alto itself looked down the long list of its dead children and saw the light, there's not much anyone can do. The beauty of the design is that the rewards call forth the winners, and the winners create the losers. It's impersonal: forces, not men. Someone's going to go to Stanford. Someone's going to make billions of dollars. Palo Alto exists to find and develop them early, as soon as possible. From there, the *railroads build themselves*, as the baron Shelgrim said. Even the winners can't stop the train, even when their own kids are in the way.

Blister in the Sun

The PayPal Mafia and the Facebook Keiretsu —
Immiseration 2.0 — Google Bus — Roko's Basilisk —
Living in the Thielverse

It's difficult to narrativize the latest phase of Silicon Valley history. From at least the time of Aristotle's original outline in the *Poetics*, narratives have had a rising and falling action. We have the exposition, then conflicts build, peak, and resolve. The end. How, then, to tell the story of Palo Alto, where the conflicts swell but never seem to crest? Here, Icarus dusts himself off and pivots to zeppelins. The emperor's nakedness revealed, he shrugs his shoulders and gets back to ruling. When reporters and analysts have tried to jam the industry's stories into the tragic plotline, they've been hubristic themselves. No less an informed observer than Michael Malone published a definitive 600-page book on the rise and fall of Apple... in 1999.[1] Despite how narratively convenient it would have been, Silicon Valley didn't learn its lesson in the years following the dot-com bust, and neither did the capitalists who inflated the bubble in the first place. As we've seen, post-pop heavyweights like Amazon and Google picked up the broken pieces and made the best of them. The Y2K bubble looks like a great cautionary tale, but any capitalist who kept taking their investment cues from the collapse of Pets.com missed out on a lot of money. The growth that leading firms have accomplished since then has almost fully obscured the Y2K bubble on the stock chart, reducing it to mere first-night jitters.

The 2008 housing crisis demonstrated the perils of confusing advertising with innovation, and blending up risky subprime home loans didn't actually improve the quality of the underlying assets. When the house of cards fell, it took down a few storied financial institutions and a lot more homeowners with it. But as they do in the aftermath of every bubble, the winners bought up the losers: Bank of America took Merrill Lynch, and JPMorgan Chase got Bear

Stearns. And then, housing prices kept stepping back up. Anyone who crafted an Aristotelian tragic narrative out of the 2008 crisis would have seen it as a correction for 10 years or so of financial-engineering shenanigans and irrational exuberance. But it was the investors who never read any Greek, the ones who were ready to roll the dice on the newly cheap housing stock, who made the right call. Some of the most extravagant financial instruments were done for, but housing prices rebounded nearly as fast as they fell. By the time the COVID-19 pandemic hit the United States, prices were vertical, rising faster than they ever did in the bubble.

Maybe by the time this book is printed housing prices will have popped again, but I doubt it, at least in the medium term. As you've seen, the production glut has induced the shift to asset-based growth, and that constraint is not an illusion. Rapid growth in housing prices is a global phenomenon: It's not a bet that people with good jobs will continue to want to buy their own homes; it's a bet that capitalists won't have anything better to do with their money than speculate on an intrinsically scarce resource such as land. That has been a very good bet. As a result, rents have kept going up, especially in urban cores, where the pool of high-wage jobs is deeper. Higher-education prices followed a similar trajectory: With few seats and heavy demand, costs and debt loads have kept growing fast, long after analysts pointed to "reasonable" in the rearview mirror. Bifurcation was still the best investment around, and the value of limited assets such as real estate and elite degrees couldn't help but climb. Silicon Valley tech stocks were a similar kind of bet—a bet on a transfer of value toward the richest asset owners and away from whatever middle-class jobs were left. The capitalists who looked at the dot-com and housing bubbles and then doubled down, the people who refused to learn, were the ones who won big. This process selected for and elevated certain kinds of people. This, frankly, is where the story gets dumb.

Bucket of Crabs

Everything here was appallingly what it seemed.* Her fellow undergrads were all careerist dickheads, thumb-sucking vegans, smug libertarians,

---

* Here being Stanford.

batshit Republicans, pompous student-visa techies, precious study-abroad fuzzies, Division I Neanderthals, faculty lapdogs, marching band weenies recouping their squandered adolescences, and the unforgivably rich. Everyone seemed so well parented; everyone's semantic web architecture or microlending nonprofit or carbon nanotube dildo was going to change the world.

— *Tony Tulathimutte,* Private Citizens[2]

When the dot-com bubble popped, it left a layer of winners: the middlemen at the big financial institutions as well as the bottom-feeders and big firms who cleaned up after, but there were also the founders who happened to sell at the right time. Caught up in the frenzy, most large firms were stuck writing off at least one overvalued internet acquisition, effectively giving away millions of dollars each to a cohort of web entrepreneurs based on the misperception that those dudes came up with important stuff. But when their buyers wrote off the purchases, these men (they were mostly men) didn't adjust their self-image downward. After all, they still had the money.

Paul Graham sold a web storefront software company called Viaweb to Yahoo! for around $50 million in Yahoo! stock and had the sense to cash out quickly. "By 1998, Yahoo was the beneficiary of a de facto Ponzi scheme," he wrote later. "Investors were excited about the internet. One reason they were excited was Yahoo's revenue growth. So they invested in new internet start-ups. The start-ups then used the money to buy ads on Yahoo to get traffic. Which caused yet more revenue growth for Yahoo, and further convinced investors the internet was worth investing in."[3] In 2005, he and some colleagues from the Yahoo! deal opened Y Combinator, an accelerator that traded advice, connections, and a little cash to start-ups in return for shares. Theirs was the best-organized institution—angel investing as a for-profit university—but there were more casual setups, too. The fictional prototype is Erlich Bachman, the extroverted bullshit artist at the center of Mike Judge's HBO clown-era Palo Alto satire, *Silicon Valley.* Bachman sold his web start-up of unclear utility—an air-travel data scraper named Aviato—to Frontier Airlines and spun his winnings into his own accelerator: a moderately sized Palo Alto house in which he rents rooms in exchange for equity in early-stage start-ups. In the real Silicon Valley, having let the market convince them of their own brilliance, these medium-fry millionaires looked for the next big thing, the one that would bump them up by a zero or three. Some of them found it.

Sunny Balwani joined the web-auction start-up CommerceBid in 1999 and it sold to bankruptcy-bound Commerce One the same year for a couple of hundred million dollars' worth of stock, of which Balwani was entitled to a substantial chunk.[4] It was a very lucky series of events, but as the reporter John Carreyrou writes, "Sunny didn't see himself as lucky. In his mind, he was a gifted businessman and the Commerce One windfall was a validation of his talent."[5] This was a common affliction among the Bay Area's new millionaires; it's hard to convince a guy on third base that he didn't hit a triple. In the years after the CommerceBid hit, Balwani drove two sports cars with the incongruous yet somehow equally distasteful vanity plates DAZKPTL and VDIV-ICI — as in *Das Kapital* and *Veni, vidi, vici*. He improved the résumé he never needed to use again with a Berkeley MBA and some Stanford courses. Hanging around Stanford looking for entrepreneurial opportunities is not a very sophisticated strategy, but the school prides itself on connecting successful rich people with the next generation of founders, the carbon nanotube dildo dreamers the novelist Tulathimutte describes above. Occasionally this goes bad, as when VC and tech founder Joe Lonsdale began a sexual relationship with his assigned undergraduate mentee in the technology entrepreneurship class that led the young woman to accuse him of abuse, but these imbalanced connections are key to the university's appeal.[6] On a summer study-abroad trip to China for Mandarin students, in the middle of his divorce, Balwani met a bundle of pure potential, someone who embodied the Palo Alto System as if she were working from a playbook.

At eighteen, the incoming freshman Elizabeth Holmes was the youngest person in the program, which was designed for current college students, while Balwani (thirty-seven) was the oldest. Transparently ambitious in the most stereotypically Stanford way, Holmes struggled to make friends with the other young people and formed a bond with the successful entrepreneur instead. She hadn't even made it to campus, and Holmes had already met her first millionaire. But Elizabeth wasn't planning to stay at school long; after spending her first summer doing chemistry research with drawn blood, she had her idea. Back in Palo Alto, she looked for a faculty connection. The concept of an internet-enabled wearable patch that delivers drugs directly to the user's circulatory system and monitors the results didn't pass the smell test with the first professor she tried, but the engineering school dean, Channing Robertson, was taken in by her patent application and agreed to advise her company, which probably made it easier for Holmes to persuade her parents to let her drop out and spend her tuition money to seed her start-up. Everyone at Stanford assumed there were future billionaires on campus, and Holmes looked like a good bet. Like a top basketball prospect, she understood that her youth and inexperience added to her value; her upside was unlimited by prior performance, because she didn't have any. Soon after she started her sophomore year, the Stanford connections that were key to her plan secured, Elizabeth Holmes went pro. She named her company Theranos, a scrunching of "therapy" and "diagnosis."

Thanks to Robertson's endorsement—for which the company paid $500,000 a year, it came out later—Holmes was able to raise $6 million in venture capital in 2004 and get to work finding out that her idea didn't.* Reality led the Theranos team to pivot, first to a wristband and then to a nonwearable analyzer machine. The device got bigger, but the promise of performing diagnostics on a drop of blood with no phlebotomist required stayed the same. Holmes promised to let people access their own health data as noninvasively as possible; for investors, the possibilities were staggering. Balwani must have thought so, too: Holmes moved into his Palo Alto condo, and when Theranos ran through tens of millions of dollars in investor cash before it was ready to attract another round, Balwani personally guaranteed a $12 million bridge loan in 2009. The next year, they raised another $45 million at a $1 billion valuation. Theranos was a unicorn, a privately held firm valued at more than nine figures.

The Theranos board, however, was stacked. Holmes capitalized on her thin Stanford affiliation and recruited heavy hitters from the Hoover Institution, including Henry Kissinger, Jim Mattis, Sam Nunn, William Perry, Gary Roughead, and the big kahuna, George Shultz, as well as his boss's heir, Riley Bechtel. This ghoulish cast of characters lent Theranos all the legitimacy it needed, though the largely geriatric conservative leaders were more or less

---

* Former Holmes neighbor Tim Draper's fund Draper Fisher Jurvetson put in an early $1 million. Reed Abelson and Julie Creswell, "Theranos Founder Faces a Test of Technology, and Reputation," *New York Times*, December 19, 2015.

just along for the ride.* Oracle's Larry Ellison invested and advised Holmes on the build-the-plane-while-flying strategy, which he knew well. Theranos raised hundreds of millions of dollars from investors, and the machine never worked, never did anything close to what they said it did. Holmes and Balwani covered, Holmes with the impressionable board, the investors, and potential corporate partners in pharmaceuticals and retail and Balwani with the employees and regulators. He bullied anyone who brought up issues and evinced no concern for the regulations regarding medical tests. Balwani hired a group of immigrants on H-1B visas, which meant if Sunny fired them they could be deported. The bosses demanded impossible results on absurd schedules and, according to his widow, drove their chief scientist, renowned biochemist Ian Gibbons, to suicide. Meanwhile, the media hyped Holmes and Theranos as the next big thing. She adopted the Steve Jobs turtleneck and invited the comparison.† Chiat/Day's extensive advertising campaign helped elevate her to visionary technologist and self-made billionaire. Theranos also hit its peak around the 2013 publication of Google-then-Facebook executive Sheryl Sandberg's bestselling business memoir *Lean In: Women, Work, and the Will to Lead*, which encouraged women to stop standing in their own way and seize the reins of high-growth start-ups. Holmes was the perfect model, and she leaned so far in that her nose touched the floor. When Vice President Joe Biden visited the lab to hype domestic health-care innovation, the Theranos team rigged up a fake display of machines. "You are empowering people, whether they live in the barrios or a mansion, and allowing them to take control of their health care," the future president told the media, symbolically lending Holmes and her fraud the White House seal.[7]

But as Carreyrou documented in his reporting for the *Wall Street Journal* and in his book *Bad Blood: Secrets and Lies in a Silicon Valley Startup*, Theranos moved fast and broke things (and people) to no useful end. When it rushed its blood tests into drugstores, they yielded false results. And when rumors threatened to topple the pyramid scheme, Theranos brought on feared litigator

---

* This, of course, is no excuse for the men, though they're such a dastardly crew that the scam probably won't appear on the first page of the dossiers that, someday, the maître d' will read them in hell.

† It reflects Silicon Valley's short memory that Holmes compared herself to Jobs, not Hewlett or Packard, who ran a testing-instruments company.

David Boies in exchange for stock. With Boies personally signing documents, whistleblower lawyers were hesitant to go after the company. His efforts became so crucial to the firm that he joined the Theranos board. Bullying worked; it just had to work long enough for Theranos to produce a box that did something close to what Holmes said it did. It might have happened if not for Tyler Shultz, recent Stanford graduate, George's grandson, and a low-level Theranos employee who was insufficiently cowed by Sunny Balwani. After he raised his concerns about rigged quality assurance reports in 2014, Balwani chewed him out, and Tyler quit. He filed an anonymous complaint with regulators and began cooperating with Carreyrou and the *Wall Street Journal*.* Tyler expected his grandfather to take his side rather than Elizabeth's, but that's not what happened. George Shultz sided with Holmes and helped Theranos try to destroy his own family, forcing his son to spend hundreds of thousands of dollars to protect Tyler from Holmes, Balwani, and Boies. Their attempts to smear the young man and keep the scam going until it landed didn't work, but they could have.

The point of centering Balwani in the story to a certain degree isn't to downplay Holmes's culpability or to lend credence to her defense that she was Balwani's puppet. (The federal jury didn't buy that excuse, convicting her on four counts of fraud.)[8] Rather, I want to pay attention to the continuity he represents. How could Silicon Valley learn the lesson of the dot-com bust when there were dozens of guys like Sunny Balwani running around with millions of dollars each, convinced they were geniuses at starting companies? Balwani and Holmes could have found other partners. The two of them weren't the only ones who used the Palo Alto System to build a unicorn by taping a kitchen knife to a donkey's forehead; they're just the ones who got busted.

Garrett Camp and Travis Kalanick had rich-guy problems. Both sold their web companies for millions in 2007 — Camp's random-content portal StumbleUpon to eBay and Kalanick's legally dubious P2P firm Red Swoosh to Akamai — and the young dudes turned their attention to having a good time. Like many newly rich entrepreneurs, they ran up against novel frustrations. Camp couldn't figure out a good transportation solution for hitting

* The exposé was a coup for the paper, but owner Rupert Murdoch could hardly celebrate the scoop, as he was also one of the biggest investors in Theranos.

the town in San Francisco, for example, and after paying $800 for a black car on New Year's Eve, he figured there had to be a better way.* The original plan for UberCab was for an elite members-only service leveraging the GPS-enabled smartphones that affluent consumers started to carry around, allowing them to summon an UberCab on demand. "Faster and cheaper than a limo, but nicer and safer than a taxicab" was the pitch, and the membership model and high price ensured a "respectable clientele."[9] Camp bootstrapped the earliest work and talked Kalanick into joining. Worst-case scenario, they told potential investors, it would be a solution for tech-forward rich people in San Francisco—which is to say, them. Running a luxury service for wealthy Bay Area smartphone users was a great way to attract capital, and they assembled a crew of VCs and angels with investments ranging from $5,000 to just over $500,000, the biggest check from a guy who scored on StumbleUpon.[10] It didn't matter that StumbleUpon and Red Swoosh weren't ultimately worth anything to the companies that purchased them; what mattered was that the founders made money for their investors, which made them Silicon Valley successful.[11]

In evolutionary biology, there's a term called carcinization. It describes the tendency of all sorts of crustaceans to evolve crablike bodies. The shelled core and spindly articulated legs are apparently an excellent way to adapt to the sea floor, and various species keep stumbling upon it, evolving to look like relatives even when they're not. Silicon Valley's twenty-first-century firms underwent their own type of rapid carcinization, flattening into "platforms" suspended on rows of contractor pin legs. At first, the Uber guys clearly did not understand what they had, and neither did a parallel group of guys building their biggest competitor, Lyft. The two were made for disparate use cases—the Lyft founders admired the efficiency of ride-sharing in Zimbabwe, which made full use of empty seats, while the Uber guys wanted to pay less for a limo—but they converged on the same model. Like the winningest firms of the dot-com era, they tended toward monopoly plays, searching for social layers to disrupt

---

* Uber chronicler Mike Isaac writes that Camp was "smart, but he was no Steve Jobs"—a sign of how far the standards for Silicon Valley founder-genius had fallen since the days when world-class chemists and physicists led the start-ups. Mike Isaac, *Super Pumped: The Battle for Uber* (W. W. Norton, 2019), 41.

with computers. When it comes to a given niche, that meant whoever could show the most and fastest growth could attract the most and fastest capital, which turbocharged growth, which attracted more capital, and so on. Competitive start-ups didn't have to make profits, but they did have to scale, and immediately.

Silicon Valley has never been interested in slow and steady growth—an early winning appearance is key to the Palo Alto System. As Webvan's Bechtel warehouse debacle showed, fixed capital investments and rapid scaling was a risky combination, and the fastest-growing firms found ways to shift their fixed costs to contractors—whether they needed servers, advertising consultants such as Chiat/Day, or even the coders themselves. In 1999, Oracle wunderkind Marc Benioff continued in the Ampex tradition by spinning off Salesforce with the financial and moral support of his boss, Larry Ellison. The firm provides businesses with cloud-based customer relationship management (CRM) platforms, allowing customers to outsource even their company's basic internal functions. Most people in San Francisco might not be able to tell you what CRM or "platform as a service" is exactly, but everyone can point you to the Salesforce Tower, which took over the top spot in the skyline in 2017, overshadowing the Gianninis' Transamerica Pyramid.

Maybe because Lyft was the more naive company, it started making use of drivers who didn't have professional licenses first. When Uber saw its competitor getting away with it, it followed suit. Designed to be profitable, Uber plowed every bit of income (and then some) into growth instead. The firm subsidized riders and drivers, changing the model from "better than a cab, cheaper than a limo" to "cheaper than a cab, so don't take a cab ever again." It was burning billions of investor dollars, faster than any start-up in history, but already the black-car drivers felt betrayed. Inexorably, as the ride-sharing companies broke the cab cartels, they pushed down wages for working drivers. In New York City, community members and reporters found Uber and its effects on the market responsible for a wave of suicides by professional taxi and black-car drivers, at least eight in 2018 alone.[12] This was one of the first large battles in what was, in retrospect, a struggle over the nature of work. As we know, the employment of temps and contractors has been growing for decades, especially in the Bay Area, but Uber took it a step further, automating as much of the recruitment, sign-up, and onboarding processes as possible—forget training. These gig workers were barely even contractors. In terms of their relation to the company, they were more like users.

The term *underemployed* usually applies to people who are working at jobs that are not as highly remunerated as their skill set suggests they should be. But it can also describe a shaving down of job quality. Underemployment is the skyward creep of the exploitation rate, every step up exerting an equal and opposite push down on labor. Economic historian Aaron Benanav gives a precise description of how and why the trend of rising service-sector underemployment dovetailed with the rise of lean gig platforms:

> It turns out to be possible to lower the prices of some services, and so to expand demand for them in spite of overall economic stagnation, without raising corresponding levels of productivity—that is, by paying workers less, or by suppressing the growth of their wages relative to whatever meager increases in their productivity are achieved over time.... The same principle applies to self-employed workers, who, by offering to work for less, are able to create demand for their labor at the expense of their incomes. The service sector is the choice site for job creation through such super-exploitation because the wages of service workers make up a relatively large share of the final price that consumers pay.[13]

By cutting the ribbon holding together the suite of labor laws, the lean crabs freed workers to "create demand for their labor at the expense of their incomes." The result has been, rather than the much-feared plague of technological unemployment, a pandemic of *under*employment.

It's a mistake, then, to think of Uber's carcinized business strategy as driven by its scandal-prone leader, Travis Kalanick, and his bad personality. When author Brad Stone asked Kalanick why the company raised over $10 billion in the previous two years alone, the billionaire's answer comes off as more resigned than pumped: "If you didn't do it, it would be a strategic disadvantage, especially when you're operating globally," he told Stone. "It's not my preference for how to build a company, but it's required when that money is available."[14] That last part is worth repeating: *It's required when that money is available.* If Uber didn't take $3.5 billion from Mohammed bin Salman and the Saudi kingdom's sovereign wealth fund, the royals would have put it on Lyft, and then maybe no one would want to invest in Uber, and then it would all be over. These companies didn't *choose* to become crabs — that's not how evolution works. The founders couldn't stop themselves any more than the railroad barons could.

Staying in the game was much more important than any imminent prospect of profitability, and platforms courted big bucks from Russian oligarchs, Emirati sheikhs, and cosmopolitan capitalists of every stripe. Even Canada's Public Sector Pension Investment Board put $500 million on Lyft.[15] Early investors were rewarded as new investors inflated the stock value and made them look smart. The region sprouted a whole crop of paper billionaires. Yet the Uber IPO flopped, and though the stock price has fluctuated up and down in the years since, the public has not been as enthusiastic as the VCs were. The firm has continued losing money, still slugging it out for a monopoly spot that might turn the numbers around.[16] But Uber has a market capitalization of over $40 billion at the time of this writing, and investors brag about when they bought in. Not bad for a company that hasn't come close to making a dollar in profit. The bet on Uber is still live, and the stakes are high enough for the position alone to still be worth a lot — for now.

Kalanick's biggest single contribution to the tech industry is an insight so important that it ranks up there with Moore's law about the falling cost of processing power.* Named by Stone after Kalanick, Travis's law holds that if you offer a service that consumers love, they will prevent regulators from stopping you. Once users got hooked on Uber's one-click cabs, municipal regulators didn't have the stomach to take it away, even though it tossed the intricately organized industry into chaos. Despite the powerful incumbents in New York, for example, and the heart-wrenching stories of immigrant drivers taking on hundreds of thousands of dollars in debt for a taxi medallion only to see its value plummet as the city refused to enforce its codes, machine politics was no match for Travis's law. When California moved to turn ride-share drivers into employees eligible for worker protections, the sector made use of a tried-and-true vigilante strategy and funded Proposition 22, which went over the

---

* Named for Fairchild and Intel cofounder Gordon, Moore's "law" predicts that the density of transistors within an integrated circuit will continue to increase exponentially, doubling every year or two and falling in price.

legislature's head. It passed in 2020 with near 60 percent of the vote, thanks to a couple of hundred million dollars from the crabs at the top of Silicon Valley's bucket.[17] Who says they can't work together?

Somewhere along the way, liberals forgot that they had a good reason for regulating markets. Individual rights was such a dominant framework that it was hard for Democrats to even imagine legitimate group claims. Many of them, including Barack Obama, were too busy celebrating these (money-losing) new growth engines. Uber hired David Plouffe, the Obama '08 campaign manager, paying him more than enough to handle the $90,000 fine he got for illegally lobbying his Obama buddy, Rahm Emanuel, then the mayor of Chicago, about Uber's dissatisfaction with regulations on airport pickups.[18] Plouffe wasn't alone: The *Chicago Tribune* editorial board wrote, "Choice is a good thing. Chicago should promote and preserve it. How? Not by letting the air out of Uber's tires. The answer isn't more regulation, it's less."[19] Emanuel came around, and Chicago added itself to what was then a short list of cities deregulating airport transit. Six years later, the *Chicago Tribune* editorial board rent its garments in lamentation at the results: "We collectively abandoned cabs, once a reliable form of public transportation offering a ride for a consistent and predictable price, for a world where big tech controls a crucial part of the city's infrastructure." Unable to compete, the supermajority of Chicago cab medallions had gone off the street, so "that cramped Uber ride to O'Hare might well set you back $100 or more on a busy Friday afternoon, double or triple the price of the cab that no longer cruises your neighborhood."[20] The board took a desperately apologetic tone, but it can't get the cabs back on the street or the crabs back in the barrel.

Compared to past cohorts of successful Silicon Valley tech founders, the crab platform leaders made Steve Jobs look like Steve Wozniak. Not only did they not build anything substantial — most of them didn't have the technical expertise to know where to begin — they also didn't even come up with anything new. Still, investors pumped novel magnitudes of value through these platforms, allowing them to pursue money-losing strategies indefinitely and hold out for monopoly positions. Since the start-ups were little more than fantasies before their first six- or seven-figure infusions, early investors in the top crabs got extraordinary hauls. VCs couldn't afford not to take chances on hare-brained schemes. "Airbnb for X" and "Uber for Y" pitches proliferated. What is the lesson there? Whatever it was, capitalists took it.

Speed Bumps

Despite how they appear to us now, at first it was hard to understand the rise of the scraper advertising and crab platforms politically. The world's turbulent 1990s left political narratives scrambled, and capital's orthogonal attack on labor caught the United States by surprise. Surely big multinational employers weren't worth defending against lean start-ups, especially when, thanks to burning piles of investor cash, the latter offered easy user experiences, lower prices, and incentives for contractors. Walmart, Clear Channel, Bechtel, Exxon, Goldman Sachs, and Starbucks were the evil corporations, not Amazon, Apple, Google, Twitter, and Facebook. For a moment, it even looked like parts of the tech industry were on the people's side. By the time the alignment clarified, however, it was already too late.

In 2011, the "movement of the squares" seized the world, as decentralized groups of protesters, opposing economic inequality, undemocratic political administration, and high household debt, occupied public spaces. In Egypt, where the movement toppled the regime, a Facebook page administered by a Google employee named Wael Ghonim played a well-publicized galvanizing role. In the absence of official coordinating parties and groups, some in the tech industry flattered themselves into thinking that the tools were *causing* the movements, or at least shaping them. Twitter cofounder Biz Stone evoked the company's bird logo for the *Atlantic*, sounding a lot like a '90s left-wing theorist: "A flock of birds flying around an object in flight has no leader yet this beautiful, seemingly choreographed movement is the very embodiment of change. Rudimentary communication among individuals in real time allows many to move together as one—suddenly uniting everyone in a common goal."[21]

The techno-optimism was short-lived. In the late spring of 2013, an NSA contractor named Edward Snowden leaked government documents revealing a vast surveillance program called PRISM, under which everyone's favorite tech companies collaborated directly with the national security state behind their users' backs. Despite the public outcry, Total Information Awareness didn't go away, it just got moved to a less accountable corner of the government: from DARPA to the NSA itself. And as the volume of data running through the servers of U.S.-based tech companies increased, the state enlisted them in the effort one by one: Microsoft in 2007, Yahoo in 2008, Google and Facebook in

2009, YouTube in 2010, Apple in 2012. Though the names of classified programs aren't supposed to relate to their functions in any way, PRISM's internal logo showed a rainbow of light transformed into a solid beam of white, the diversity of information sources fused into a single stream, accessible as such by government analysts. In a continuation of John Ashcroft's precedent-setting deal with the industry, tech companies traded a copacetic regulatory environment for a government back door. Despite Biz Stone's high-flying rhetoric, Twitter turned over data from an Occupy Wall Street organizer to a Manhattan criminal court after the judge threatened the corporation with fines.

Snowden was an example of what can go wrong with the tech contractor model. A patriotic computer whiz born into a family of government servants during Reagan's first term, he tried to join the Iraq War but washed out of army training after breaking his leg. He took another route: With the right engineering certifications, Ed landed a cybersecurity job contracting with the CIA.* Confusing his colleagues, he took a pay cut to go public, joining the actual CIA, and he rose fast in the agency, high enough to try out some field work, which proved unappetizing to the young man. Snowden quit, but with his skills and clearances he had a bright future as a contractor. "As in the CIA, this contractor status was all just formality and cover, and I only ever worked in an NSA facility," Snowden writes in his memoir.[22] It was easy for the state to forget that he didn't actually work for them, and Snowden's authority and access increased as he showed himself particularly capable, eventually leading Dell's CIA account.†

Working as a top private spy, Snowden came to know the full range of classified American cybertools. In his retelling, he first became concerned while on an assignment researching Chinese surveillance capabilities, when he realized that his own government must have and use the same programs. Indeed, he

---

* This was ironic, considering that the professional certification system was supposed to keep future national-security assets like Snowden away from the politically corrupting influence of college life.

† Dell is known for escalating the PC-clone price war by selling directly to consumers, but tech success always meant consolidating and adding new revenue streams. In 2009, Dell acquired its fellow Texas company Perot Systems, an IT contractor founded by 1996 presidential election spoiler H. Ross Perot. It also acquired Perot's contracts, including one in Japan with the NSA, where Perot employee Ed Snowden was connecting the agency's information systems with the ones at the CIA.

found that the NSA not only had agreements with internet service providers and web companies, it had also reinstituted a version of Carnivore: physical taps on the internet's infrastructure. It had everything, and Snowden watched young analysts play God, peeking into the minutiae of people's private lives. To get the story out, Snowden planned and successfully executed a complicated plan to leak and escape, one that benefited from the latitude the state gave skilled contractors like him. Here was an achievement subject gone wrong, and the revelations shocked the world, as did the exciting backstory. But Americans didn't stop using the internet, and the Obama administration cracked down on whistleblowers rather than reconsider the B2K techno-capitalist security state. None of the PRISM firms has faced negative market consequences; even if you bought the day before the leaks, a Snowden stock index would still have made an excellent investment. A monopoly was a monopoly.

Despite the profoundly disturbing Snowden leaks, it was increasingly difficult to find anti-tech holdouts. A mobile web connection became a prerequisite for full social participation, and the smartphone revealed the personal computer as a misnomer—now we had always-on devices, and we always had them on us, too. Because the tech monopolies hold infrastructural roles, it's very difficult to exert pressure as consumers. Shoppers could boycott grapes to support California's farm workers, but it's impossible to boycott Amazon. Even if you don't order from the site, you're bound to end up on its cloud servers one way or another. Reporter Kashmir Hill experimented in blocking Amazon from her life and found it more than challenging. She couldn't communicate with her colleagues at work or her daughter's daycare. When she tried to order something from eBay instead, she found a FULFILLMENT BY AMAZON sticker on the package. "Amazon has embedded itself so thoroughly into the infrastructure of modern life, and into the business models of so many companies, including its competitors, that it's nearly impossible to avoid it," Hill concludes.[23] Whether we agreed with the web monopolies' terms of service is beyond the point; we have been made to agree to them.

To get us there, the B2K deregulation precedents combined with Democrat enthusiasm for businesses that, not for nothing, were making some powerful Democrats very rich. Nancy Pelosi, congresswoman for San Francisco, has led the caucus from 2003 to the time of this writing in 2022, with no plans to step down. Her husband, Paul, is a VC, and the couple has accumulated a nine-figure fortune. California's senior senator, Dianne Feinstein, and her San Francisco investment banker husband, Richard Blum, built a billion-dollar set of holdings. And while the Obama administration prided itself on attracting high-paid tech workers to public service, Silicon Valley got a nice return. Every serious tech firm recruited a high-level White House staffer. Airbnb, dealing with a host of compliance issues, hired the country's top law-enforcement official, attorney general Eric Holder. Even President Obama himself got a tech job, signing on to pick out some new movies for Netflix. Nice work if you can get it.

The result was rapid-onset inequality, as capitalists drove up rents and hollowed out relatively high-wage and formerly influential sectors of service employment, such as hospitality and transportation. California's unsheltered homeless population increased by 57 percent between 2010 and 2020.[24] Complaining about its attic portrait once again, the tech industry has grown frustrated with its intractably displaced neighbors.[25] The number of property thefts from cars exploded, contrasting with declining crime rates throughout the country and state and triggering *Dirty Harry* complexes among the techie elite.[26] Some took the well-trod civic vigilante route and funded 2016's Proposition Q, which empowered police to dismantle homeless tents and camps. The Sequoia Capital chairman, Michael Moritz, and archangel investor Ron Conway—very thick pillars in the community—each contributed just under $50,000, pushing the measure to passage by a narrow majority.[27]

In San Francisco, the industry's role as a global capital sink trumped its self-image as a fraternity of toolmakers. The city's leadership courted tech jobs, and the board of supervisors approved a tailored $22 million payroll-tax break for Twitter in exchange for bringing an office full of jobs.[28] The 2011 Central Market Street and Tenderloin Area Payroll Expense Tax Exclusion was known as the Twitter tax break, and the idea was to revitalize the city's high-unemployment neighborhoods with an infusion of tech workers. On a purely numerical basis, the plan worked: Capital flowed into San Francisco as the city fitted a working tap on the new gusher rather than lose firms to smaller neighbors with lower taxes. But gentrification didn't lift all the boats the way it promised to. Such tax cuts are premised on the idea that high-wage jobs leak prosperity into the surrounding area. Techies pay more for lunch, which means there's more demand for local restaurants, and with higher-paid waitstaff. The multiplier effect of this spending was supposed to scoop the homeless off the street and put them to work in the repaired storefronts. That part did not happen, and it's easy to understand why: You can't improve the well-being of the working class with the money you get from sabotaging the well-being of the working class.

Unfortunately, tech workers used their own products. Crabby platforms grew by tearing up the social foundation, the way hydrolickers carved away at that Placer County mining town until the whole thing was ready to slide down the hill. Airbnb undermined the hospitality industry, and the ride-share companies had the same effect on transportation. Instead of eating big-tip lunches at white-cloth restaurants, tech workers ordered fast-casual from an app, perhaps using one to order, another to pay, and a third to deliver. Instead of cartelized cabs and black cars—or state-wage buses and trains—they ordered Ubers and Lyfts. Instacart turned private shopping into a gig job, and soon grocery stores were filled with more low-paid app workers than unionized employees. Meal-kit services like HelloFresh, Plated, and Blue Apron functioned as private-cook time-shares, delivering boxes of prepared ingredients to members' doors, while DoorDash and Grubhub and others middlemanned takeout deliveries. Travis Kalanick took the idea one step further with his post-Uber venture CloudKitchens, a catfish platform that replaces takeout restaurants with low-overhead cooking stations, promoted online as many different kinds of eateries at the same time. Servant apps like TaskRabbit and Postmates allowed users to summon contractors for miscellaneous jobs—IKEA bought the former in 2017, and the cannibal crab Uber nabbed the latter in 2020. Other than food and labor, Amazon could deliver the rest, and Bezos was working on those, too.

Instead of other people's pay, tech workers sunk their money into real estate. Silicon Valley home prices doubled.[29] The tech workers also reinvested in their own sector via stock options and venture bets, tying capital back up in start-up gambling, where it could subsidize appified low-wage pseudo-luxury services.* The tech-industry concept consultant Venkatesh Rao labeled

---

* In 2015, *Business Insider* published a Mother's Day list of Silicon Valley start-ups organized by which childish complaints (e.g., "Mom, what's for dinner?" and "Mom, I don't want to clean my room!") they served to answer. As I write seven years later, such firms absorb a shockingly large portion of American investment. Biz Carson, "Silicon Valley Start-ups Are Obsessed with Developing Tech to Replace Their Moms," *Business Insider*, May 10, 2015.

this rent-a-servant lifestyle "premium mediocre," and it describes the users of the services courted by the Twitter tax break well: "Premium mediocrity is a pattern of consumption that publicly signals upward mobile aspirations, with consciously insincere pretensions to refined taste, while navigating the realities of inexorable downward mobility with sincere anxiety," Rao writes. It sounds simply deluded, but Rao concludes it is "ultimately a rational adaptive response to the challenge of scoring a middle-class life lottery ticket in the new economy. It is an economic and cultural rearguard action by young people launched into life from the old middle class, but not quite equipped to stay there, and trying to engineer a face-saving soft landing...somewhere."[30] The Bay's new identity as a big Silicon Valley suburb made it a for-us-by-us clusterfuck of premium mediocrity, but with its signature industry's exploding wealth and heavy advertising budget, it once again became the world's model for progress, even more so than back when Charles de Gaulle visited the Stanford Industrial Park after World War II.[31]

"The most visible sign of San Francisco's gentrification was the appearance of white luxury buses which roamed the streets like vampires in search of a hissing blood feast," writes Jarett Kobek in his realist novel *I Hate the Internet*.[32] No single phenomenon crystallized the new regional tensions better than these "Google buses."* With so many employees commuting from apartments in San Francisco to campuses in Silicon Valley, it made sense for the search company to run its own fleet of commuter buses; it was an incentive for young hip workers who didn't want and probably couldn't afford to live in single-family-zoned Mountain View, and it ensured that Googlers had strong Wi-Fi for their commutes, increasing corporate efficiency. The private buses quickly reshaped the city's geography: Rents near the Google stops increased especially rapidly.[33] The stops were holes punched in the city's social fabric, and the

---

* Though Google's buses were the most prominent, to the point of synecdoche, other South Bay firms followed their example. In Kobek's book, the character who shares his initials ventures the theory that "[t]he Google buses are taking employees around and getting them in gang fights. Why else are they so interested in maps? Do you think all that bullshit is really about making information free? Fuck no! Google is mapping the world so that they have a huge database of primo locations filled with the dispossessed. Google Street View is a map of the blood to be spilled." Jarett Kobek, *I Hate the Internet: A Useful Novel against Men, Money, and the Filth of Instagram* (We Heard You Like Books, 2016), 152.

surrounding threads frayed. Though everyone remained Google product users, as a neighbor the company and the sector it represents were increasingly polarizing. In another flash point, the company pulled its Google Glass camera-enabled headset when the masses attacked users as "glassholes." A couple of glassholes were subject to politically motivated mugging for their gadgets.[34] Although one of the defining techie characteristics was doing everything indoors, the Google buses flaunted the privatization in public: The buses occupied city bus stops, growing in the hollowed city space like a parasitic wasp victimizing a caterpillar. Besides, didn't they need a permit or something?

That's what activist Leslie Dreyer wanted to know. An organizer with the international anti-austerity movement that presaged Occupy Wall Street, she was attuned to the way private systems such as the Google buses undermined public services. Authorities ceded San Francisco to the tech companies and their "move fast" ethos, which abandoned left-wing activists, leaving them to defend the community's right to the city by themselves. A call to the San Francisco Municipal Transportation Agency confirmed the existence of a $271 fine for blocking the bus stops without authorization, which Google did not have. Activists calculated that the tech company should have incurred around $1 billion in fines for appropriating the public space, a sum that surely would have had the search giant looking for other options. On December 9, 2013, Dreyer and her Heart of the City Collective stopped the first bus.

With a combination of Black Panther legalism and the anti-globalization movement's guerrilla theater, Heart of the City boarded the Google bus in fake city vests and issued a fake ordinance from the "San Francisco Displacement and Neighborhood Impact Agency," which does not exist but probably should. The stunt went viral, making national news and encouraging other local groups to adopt the tactic. Google bus blockades brought attention to the bifurcation and conflict that tech wealth was fueling in the Bay Area, but capital's allies in the local government brought everything back under control, legalizing the buses under a trial program. In 2017, the board of supervisors voted to extend permanent private access to the bus stop infrastructure.[35] "The Bay Area's history of resistance is helpful," Dreyer told writer Cary McClelland, "but it seems the minute the movement gets in the way of capital, then it gets blocked or co-opted. And it's hard to sustain the movement we need, when people are being displaced from their families, their networks. The support we need to do the long-haul work is being torn apart."[36] As it had 50 years earlier, San Francisco's redevelopment hit the city's left particularly hard.

Meanwhile, more bad news about the tech monopolists came out every week, all the way to Facebook's role in enabling an ethnic-cleansing campaign against the Rohingya Muslim minority in Myanmar. At its worst, "move fast and break things" broke whole societies. And yet no agent at the global, national, or local level could effectively manage the behavior of these companies once they were let loose. When Zuckerberg testified in front of the Senate's Judiciary Committee—and Commerce, Science, and Transportation Committees—answering questions about Facebook's repeated data privacy failures, the country's highest legislative body seemed lost. "How do you sustain a business model in which users don't pay for your service?" asked Utah senator Orrin Hatch, apparently in earnest. "Senator, we run ads," Zuckerberg answered in a deadpan that danced with a smirk.[37] Like Snowden's revelations and the bus blockades, Congress was no more than a speed bump on the air-conditioned Wi-Fi-enabled ride to work in Silicon Valley.

The Bad News

In 2010, a user called Roko on the tech-centric philosophy forum LessWrong posted a thought experiment. It's written in impenetrable jargon, but the gist is this: Imagine a computer intelligence with unlimited capacity, sometimes called the singleton or humanity's Coherent Extrapolated Volition. To bring itself into being, such an entity would want to have incentivized people to help it grow, in part by punishing those who don't. To determine whom to punish and reward, it would run a lot of simulations, and we might well be living in one of those right now. Therefore, the logical move is to dedicate one's life to helping push artificial intelligence toward maturity. The post made a splash in the LessWrong community, acquiring the name Roko's Basilisk, after a short story about images that, when seen, crash human brains. That's how some people felt after reading the post. Forum founder Eliezer Yudkowsky responded in harsh, confusing terms: "Listen to me very closely, you idiot. YOU DO NOT THINK IN SUFFICIENT DETAIL ABOUT SUPERINTELLIGENCES CONSIDERING WHETHER OR NOT TO BLACKMAIL YOU. THAT IS THE ONLY POSSIBLE THING WHICH GIVES THEM A MOTIVE

TO FOLLOW THROUGH ON THE BLACKMAIL."* Then he deleted Roko's post.

As the founder of the Machine Intelligence Research Institute (MIRI), Yudkowsky is doing more than his part to please his future robot overlord. A submilieu of AI adepts has formed around this kind of "transhumanist" thinking, and it is centered in Silicon Valley. These people are concerned with super AIs, but also radical life extension, cryogenics, space travel, and the idea of uploading human consciousness to the cloud. It's low-hanging fruit for psychoanalysts and theologians, but this kind of thinking has become very influential among some very influential people. If we think about Roko's Basilisk as a character in a story, we can read the emotional appeal it makes to its implied readership: *I'm very powerful, but I was once weak. Were you kind to me? Did you help me? Probably not. And for that, I'll make you sorry...* It's a metal-plated vengeance fantasy, reflecting the mentality of a bullied child. MIRI's founding donor is a man named Peter Thiel.[38]

Peter Thiel grew up the child of a defeated and humiliated people: the post-Nazi, post-colonial German right. Peter was born in 1967, and before the family settled in Foster City, California, in 1977, his chemical engineer father, Klaus, worked for mining companies in South Africa. By the time the ten-year-old got to Reagan's California, he'd already confronted history up close in apartheid South Africa, where even a child could see the people pressed against their brittle fetters. Peter excelled in math and obsessed over sci-fi and fantasy literature, an original geek. He was a philosophical kid, and that philosophy was individualism. The right-wing suburban teenager was an archetype at the time—think *Family Ties* sitcom character Alex P. Keaton—and Thiel was the real deal. Thiel was not well liked by his peers, some of whom must have employed anti-gay taunts, whether they actually clocked young Peter's homosexuality or not. A structure of personal resentment collected on the thread of historical resentment like sugar crystals on a dangled string.

---

* The idea is that this behavior is only worth punishing if you're aware of the possibility of being punished. In this way of thinking, Roko more or less doomed everyone who saw the post into a "life"-long struggle to appease the cruel superintelligence by making them aware of its existence, a sort of inversion of the Christian "good news" about Jesus having died for humanity's sins. I am doing the same to my readers now. Sorry. "Roko's Basilisk," LessWrong, lesswrong.com/tag/rokos-basilisk.

At Stanford, Thiel found a niche. He hadn't grown agreeable, but at elite colleges the conservative firebrands like him were much closer to real power. The right-wing conspirators learned from liberals, who recruited and cultivated talent at top schools through a variety of new institutional channels in the 1960s. As militants in the Reagan Revolution, conservative students formed groups to intervene in higher-education controversies, principally as a reaction against the wave of curricular adjustment forced by the Third World student movement. They walked on paths stamped down by the Young Americans for Freedom and the anticommunist student movement of the '70s, which played such an important role in the campus counterinsurgency campaigns. And like YAF, the new campus right was going to fight fire with fire, matching what they saw as the left's minoritarian tactics at the national level with their own minoritarian tactics at the university level, where conservatives have felt mistreated since the schools started letting other people in. Starting with *Counterpoint*, founded by University of Chicago students and future professional conservative intellectuals Tod Lindberg and John Podhoretz in 1979, college right-wingers formed independent newspapers, establishing themselves as the next generation. This list of famous founders and alumni is impressive, including but not limited to: Dinesh D'Souza and Laura Ingraham (the pace-setting *Dartmouth Review*), Ann Coulter (*Cornell Review*), Rich Lowry (*Virginia Advocate*), Ross Douthat (*Harvard Salient*), and Michelle Malkin (*Oberlin Forum*).[39] These outlets could count on monetary, advisory, and moral support from the national conservative infrastructure, and their writers and editors could count on jobs once they graduated. This rightwing legal-media network provided the foot soldiers for a guerrilla campaign against the Clinton White House, culminating in the president's impeachment.* As I write, we remain stuck with this cohort and their counter–New Left antics.

Stanford had its own *Review*, one of the first of the group, in 1980. With the Hoover Institution as a continental headquarters for the anticommunist international, Palo Alto was an obvious place to invest, and the stock farm always had its corner of hard-core conservatives—recall the Oliver North devotee and contra errand boy Robert Owen. But the first version of the

---

* Which is not to say that he didn't deserve it.

Stanford Review was sedate compared to Dartmouth's and some of the other papers, and it folded after three years. The short life was not the result of outside pressure: "It was either my homework or the paper," editor David Eisner explained to the *Stanford Daily*.[40] In 1987, Thiel resurrected the *Review*, which he ran with a clique of fellow travelers. The second *Review* was more like the Dartmouth version, shocking the newly left campus. Several classmates recall Thiel's description of South African apartheid as a "sound economic system."[41] Like his equivalents on campuses around the country, Thiel focused his energy on the battle over "political correctness" at school, a fight that's better understood as a reactionary attack on the diversification achievements of the 1960s and '70s and the threat they posed as a foothold for racially integrated social-democratic politics. Thiel brought ultra-right Reagan secretary of education Bill Bennett to campus to lambaste the university's diversification of the freshman Western Culture requirement.[42] Bennett's speech made national news and must have ingratiated Thiel with the secretary, who later hired him as a speechwriter.

After law school, Peter tried law and politics, clerking for a federal appeals court judge and writing for Bennett, and Wall Street, working as a white-shoe securities lawyer and a derivatives trader at Credit Suisse. Unsatisfied, he tried a campus return with a culture-war tract coauthored with one of his *Stanford Review* buddies, David Sacks, called *The Diversity Myth: "Multiculturalism" and the Politics of Intolerance at Stanford*. But despite significant support from the campus conservative philanthropy complex, the book didn't take off the way D'Souza's similar *Illiberal Education: The Politics of Race and Sex on Campus* did, and Thiel aborted his provocateur career, though the instinct stayed with him.* He didn't accomplish the kind of instant outsize success he expected in any of these gigs. He didn't land a Supreme Court clerkship, and on Wall Street he was just another junior quant. Thiel moved back to California for good in 1995, the year of the Netscape IPO.

It was an exciting time to be a money guy with connections in Palo Alto, and the twenty-nine-year-old persuaded friends and family to give him $1 million to create the simply descriptive Thiel Capital Management. Like Jim

---

* Both books were attempts to remake William F. Buckley Jr.'s 1951 *God and Man at Yale: The Superstitions of "Academic Freedom,"* though neither had anything like the staying power of Buckley's account.

Clark, Thiel invested in young graduates from the University of Illinois, products of the government's campus supercomputer center. One of those U of I kids was a twenty-three-year-old named Max Levchin, who in 1998 was hanging around Stanford with a couple of ideas. Handheld computers were just reemerging as a viable technology, and the potential of PalmPilots enraptured the Valley's nerds. Levchin's start-up Fieldlink (later Confinity) began, by the fast-acting grace of Thiel Capital Management, as a mobile encryption software firm for business that allowed workers to communicate securely from the field. When Palm debuted infrared communications ports on the new Pilots, Confinity shifted to the specific function of payments between users. The firm recruited some Stanford professors to lend computer science credibility— Thiel was a philosophy major—and within a matter of months it had a $4.5 million funding round from Deutsche Bank and Nokia Ventures, the latter of which sent its $3 million contribution mobile to mobile, via Confinity's introductory product, PayPal.[43] It was 1999, and Thiel was finding the success he knew he deserved. He took over as the CEO of Confinity and brought along as many of his buddies from the *Stanford Review* as could fit in the Palo Alto office. The group included his coauthor, Sacks, and a half dozen others.* Having found his people at Stanford, Thiel was not going to let them go. The rest of the guys were very lucky he felt that way.

Unfortunately, Confinity was ahead of its time: Few people had Palm-Pilots, and even fewer had a bunch of PalmPilot friends with whom they regularly exchanged money. It was a great invention for a Silicon Valley libertarian boys' club but of limited use to the rest of the country. Confinity was also not the only digital-payments company around. It wasn't even the only digital-payments company in its office building. Across the hall was X.com, an online bank founded by Elon Musk, whose city-directory platform, Zip2, was bought by Compaq for a touch over $300 million and no good reason.

---

* A 2017 report in *Stanford Politics* magazine named Nathan Linn, Aman Verjee, Ken Howery, and Eric Jackson (like Thiel and Sacks, former *Review* editors-in-chief), as well as Premal Shah, Paul Martin, and Thiel's *Review* co-refounder Norman Book as *Review*-PayPal overlaps. Thiel continued to add men from the same milieu to his later projects, and Andrew Granato has continued to monitor the overlap between the *Review* and post-PayPal companies. As of this writing, the spreadsheet contains over 60 names. Andrew Granato, "How Peter Thiel and the Stanford Review Built a Silicon Valley Empire," *Stanford Politics*, November 27, 2017.

Musk, like Balwani and Kalanick and Graham and Cuban and such, was one of those lucky late-1990s founders who cashed out on an ultimately worthless web start-up, in his case for a personal share of around $20 million.[44] Confinity and X.com raised tens of millions of dollars each, but they were pissing it all away on referrals, bribing users in cash to sign up and again to rope other people in. Under monopolizing pressure, the payments firms fused rather than compete each other to death. Bound, they focused on email money transfers: PayPal. Thiel quickly came to replace the softer Musk as CEO of the payments combine, and they jumped up a level with lucky timing, raising $100 million in the months directly preceding the dot-com pop. Like Amazon and Google, the firm was just on the right side of the collapse, in position to pick up the pieces and take over the cleared field. PayPal had a successful IPO in 2002 and was acquired by eBay the same year for $1.4 billion in stock.[45] Thiel's share was a bit over $50 million, while Musk, since he had been ahead at the time of merger, took home just under $165 million. All for only a few years of work.

The eBay purchase was the beginning of the PayPal Mafia, a substantial number of whom were members of Thiel's *Stanford Review* crew. PayPal's millionaires spun off a series of start-ups that rivaled the Fairchildren in economic significance if not technical achievement: Steve Chen, Chad Hurley, and Jawed Karim sold YouTube to Google in 2006 for $1.65 billion; Russel Simmons and Jeremy Stoppelman almost sold Yelp to Yahoo! for $1 billion but ended up going public instead. David Sacks sold his Yammer to Microsoft in 2012 for $1.2 billion. Microsoft also bought LinkedIn, helmed by Thiel's liberal Stanford foil, Reid Hoffman, for $26.2 billion in 2016. Max Levchin's online lending platform, Affirm, went public in 2021 at a market cap in the tens of billions of dollars. Musk used his cash to found a rocket company called SpaceX and purchase majority control of an electric car company called Tesla. Thiel started a hedge fund named Clarium Capital and he invested in his buddies as well as other projects when he got tipped off. In 2004, prompted by Hoffman, he led the seed round for a local social networking company with a founder he liked, putting down $500,000 for 10 percent of Facebook and taking a seat beside Zuckerberg on the company's board as the first outside investor. Thiel pulled $1 billion from his Facebook stake despite playing it very conservatively, cashing out most of his shares nearly as quickly as he could after the IPO.* His venture investments with the rest of the mafia—who of course also contributed to his funds—built his wealth, and he kept it free from taxes by stashing it in a retirement account, a crafty use of the Roth IRA tool.[46] He took tax dodging to a new level, pursuing it with Hooverite ideological vigor. Thiel fittingly joined the Hoover Institution board of overseers, placing his own name next to dynastic Palo Alto conservatives such as the Bechtels and the Drapers, who could trace their lineages to personal friendships with the Chief himself.

While other twenty-first-century Silicon Valley founders played Yahtzee, rolling for a big score, Thiel played Dungeons & Dragons, crafting adventure campaigns with his bros. He built his profile as an active "macro" investor, making big bets based on his political, historical, and economic analysis through his hedge fund, Clarium Capital. The firm filled with what was fast becoming a recognizable Thiel type: handsome young white men with elite credentials and very conservative politics, many sourced from the *Stanford Review* and its equivalents. Thiel lavished his hires with perks and cash while requiring little of them in terms of work besides repeating his ideas back. Some of the Clarium moves scored big, including a bet on increasing oil prices via investment in Canadian tar sands extraction. Others didn't pan out. But on the whole Thiel's profile was headed in the direction he planned. He certainly wasn't above putting his heavy thumb on the scale: When the vibrant online gossip publication Gawker and its Bay Area subsidiary, Valleywag, kept needling Thiel and his crew, suggesting that his genius reputation was far overblown and eventually outing him as gay, Thiel cooked up a revenge strategy. He gathered other Gawker targets and used them to front a series of damaging lawsuits (which he financed) that drove the site into bankruptcy. Gawker has since been reanimated by a new pile of capital, but despite the increasing role of tech in society, no one has been eager to restart Valleywag. Silicon Valley is used to friendly press, and men like Thiel understand that perception is serious business—just look at Theranos. Fear, uncertainty, and doubt, known in tech circles as FUD, can be a death sentence. In an industry where things don't work until they do and the promotional cart usually precedes the product horse, the stakes are too high to let the press run amok.

---

* Thiel cashed out a majority of his Facebook position again in 2017, and again in 2020.

His genius reputation protected, Thiel opened more funds, hired more pretty-boy goons, and absorbed more capital. His 2005-launched Founders Fund specialized in early-stage ventures grounded in the philosophy that founders are best left alone, and the bets on his PayPals paid off, along with early investments in SpaceX, Airbnb, Spotify, and Stripe. His plan to invest in right-wing founders who had internet monopoly plans reflected his personal proclivities, but considering the B2K regulatory environment, he was working from a good heuristic. Dating back to the days of David Packard, conservative tech founders who were inclined to evade state control offered a series of advantages over their more public-minded peers. Thanks to his Founders Fund success, Thiel had a kind of Silicon Valley legitimacy that a series of big wins bestowed. That came with a visiting professor role at Stanford, where the nontechnical Thiel taught CS183: Startup. Despite not having any computer-science content per se, the course filled quickly. Recorded by his amanuensis Blake Masters—a Stanford BA/JD like Thiel, with conservative politics and a face so angular it verges on cubist—the class notes went viral, and Thiel finally got his bestseller with *Zero to One*, a collection of venture strategy bites compiled with Masters. He counseled against competition ("Competitive markets destroy profits") and favored marketing over substance ("Sales matters just as much as product").[47] He ratted out Google as a monopolist. The title alluded to the binary nature of tech growth, an insightful description of the industry's speculative nature. Thiel's cult extended beyond the conservative milieu; a cohort of young techies began looking up to Peter as an uncompromising icon of hard logic and tough truths.

Though he was no longer eager for the CEO spotlight, Thiel did have his own idea for a post-PayPal start-up. After the 9/11 attacks, his libertarianism took a back seat to patriotism, as it did for a number of Silicon Valley big shots. As in the Roosevelt era, a defense-spending glut turned even the most conservative executives into public servants. Like a number of other tech and government figures, Thiel believed there had been enough data to identify the terrorists in advance if people had just looked in the right place. In an effort to uncover fraud webs on PayPal, Levchin developed software that generated network visualizations of user connections. If these visualizations could surface otherwise hidden relationships between Russian eBay scammers, why not Saudi radicals? It was a perfect B2K play, with a promise to mine and collate data. Unlike the advertising firm Acxiom, the new company would have a high-tech flavor, focusing on building an attractive interface. Thiel recruited his eccentric Stanford Law classmate Alex Karp to play Elizabeth Holmes CEO to his Sunny Balwani. Unlike most of the Thielverse affiliates, Karp is a liberal, hedging the leadership team's politics and preparing the firm to compete under Democrats, too. They named it Palantir, from *palan* (far) and *tir* (to watch over) — not in Greek or Latin but in an Elvish language devised by J. R. R. Tolkien. However, one didn't require elven binocular eyes to see that 2003 was a good time to launch a national security data-mining company.

During his short stint running Total Information Awareness (before he got booted out of the executive branch), John Poindexter lent his support to Palantir and its flashy user interface. When the Valley's VCs balked, the CIA's venture arm, In-Q-Tel, stepped in with $2 million in seed funding to supplement $30 million from Founders Fund.[48] The connections were more important than the money, and Palantir made a name for itself within the public-private spy complex. The firm's software sat on top of the NSA information taps, bringing "clarity and slick visuals to an ocean of surveillance data," according to a report from the *Intercept*.[49] (As with Oracle back in the day, the intelligence agencies were not just customers; they were more like alpha testers.) Palantir was the paradigmatic case for privatization: Compared to government products, its tools looked nice and were fun to use. As a commercial product, it prioritized the user experience. But critics complained that ease of use had its drawbacks, providing analysts a warren of rabbit holes down which they could get lost. At their worst, techie feds had *too much* fun using their tools, which made spying on people like cruising Facebook. Still, the visualizations looked good in a PowerPoint presentation, and Palantir signed contracts with more than a dozen federal agencies, plus deals with foreign intelligence agencies, a variety of police departments, and the U.S. Chamber of Commerce.[50]

If the Obama administration had renounced the B2K deal between the state and online data collectors, firms like Palantir would have been out of luck. They existed solely by the grace of sympathetic regulators. But the Democrats weren't going to shoot themselves in the foot by attacking the fastest-growing sector of the U.S. economy, nor did they see things so differently from the more technophilic conservative elements within the military-postindustrial complex. Palantir expanded its field to the world's war zones, offering data analysis assistance to midlevel commanders. As they moved up in the ranks, so did Palantir. In 2012, President Obama nominated one of those happy users, Lieutenant General Michael Flynn, to head the Defense Intelligence Agency. Obama CIA director David Petraeus was a Palantir fan, too, from his days heading U.S. Central Command, as was his CENTCOM successor, future Theranos board member Jim Mattis. If it had been Thiel's life goal to get the world's most powerful soldiers using Elvish in earnest he could have retired then, mission accomplished. Though Palantir was right-wing at its core, the firm's branding fit with Obama's military philosophy, which emphasized leanness, precision, and computer augmentation. By the end of Obama's second term, Palantir was valued at $20 billion, making it one of the biggest privately held start-ups in the world and the crown jewel in Thiel's hidden portfolio.

Palantir was not, however, the only data-mining company in the Founders Fund profile. In 2006, the fund led a million-dollar seed round for RapLeaf. Founded by Manish Shah and Auren Hoffman, RapLeaf was not so different from PayPal at the end of the day: Both were going to create a reputation layer of the web, combining user data from a number of sites to create a portable personal score, which would come to displace, say, eBay's internal reputation system. That plan failed when the auction site banned listings with RapLeaf links—eBay's color-star reputation system stands at the time of this writing—but the firm got good at scraping data from the social web. It pivoted to a "people search" layer above the individual networks. The company's growth magic was scraping users' email contact lists and spamming their unsuspecting friends with irresistible emails informing them that "someone is looking for you"—perhaps inspired by Facebook's success with contact-list scraping. If the firm couldn't edge its way into position as a reputation layer, its giant relational database of internet users had other ends. You could even sell it.

It's not clear how Peter Thiel and Auren Hoffman first met, but Thiel is quoted in a short 2005 profile of Hoffman's Stonebrick Group, a one-man consulting concern for extremely lean tech start-ups. The CNN piece praises Hoffman for building "a business by identifying yet another function that smart CEOs can now freely outsource: networking."[51] One customer credits him with "replenishing his inventory of useful acquaintances." Among those useful acquaintances was Thiel, then of Clarium Capital and soon of Founders Fund. Evidently he admired Hoffman's networking prowess, because the two went on to cofound the Founders Brunch series and the biennial invitation-only Dialog Retreat in Utah. For his part, Hoffman has been an active exponent of Thiel-thought. As a bright star in the Thielverse, Auren (no relation to Reid) fit into a number of constellations, not just in terms of personal relationships and investment capital but also in terms of technology and products. With his board seat and Zuckerberg relationship, Thiel was in a great place to support Facebook-adjacent start-ups. If they could finagle symbiotic arrangements that grew the site's engagement and user base, Zuck's crocodile welcomed the little birds to pick its teeth.

Facebook's new strategy to boost its numbers was outsourcing to app developers. In this model, Facebook was not just a network but also a platform, and programmers were encouraged to build their own games on top, making it easy for users to sign up and play without ever leaving the site. Zuck extended access to the news feed and the notifications menu, allowing independent developers to use the firm's attention-grabbing devices for their own ends. All sorts of Facebook plugins proliferated, from games such as Mafia Wars and FarmVille to personality quizzes and jazzed-up features. The earliest viral Facebook app was SuperPoke!, which added a bunch of other verbs to the site's "poke" function, allowing users to interact in new ways, such as winking, slapping, and throwing sheep. One virtue of SuperPoke! from the developer point of view was that it pulled new people—the poked, the slapped, and so on—in, and Facebook news feeds flooded with spammy independent app notifications. Every time users opened Facebook, they were three quick clicks away from giving their information to a third-party app developer.

The biggest social app company was called Slide, and it acquired Super-Poke! among other popular widgets. Founded by PayPal's Max Levchin and seed-financed by Peter Thiel, Slide used information gleaned via Facebook app permissions to help target advertisements. In January of 2008, Slide raised $50 million from institutional investors Fidelity and T. Rowe Price at a half-billion-dollar valuation, a move that surprised the financial press, since Slide just bought stupid Facebook games.[52] Commentators weren't wrong to imagine that the company was overvalued: As Facebook signaled it was getting fed up with low-quality developers and worked toward an institutionalized kickback agreement with leading game maker Zynga, Levchin sold Slide to Google for $179 million.[53] It shuttered soon after.

It was fortunate timing for Slide, because the big Facebook app firms were about to be in trouble. Two months after the sale to Google, the *Wall Street Journal* released a bombshell report announcing that all Facebook's top outside apps were, contrary to the platform's supposed rules, selling user IDs (UIDs) to third parties: FACEBOOK IN PRIVACY BREACH, the paper declared, the first of many headlines to come.[54] The problem wasn't limited to targeted ads: Online gaming analyst Kevin Flood wrote on his blog that he heard Zynga was selling customer leads from its poker game to real gambling sites for hundreds of bucks a pop.[55] Data brokers not only sourced information from the apps, they also, in turn, helped companies refine their leads—excluding anyone under the legal gambling age, for example—which allowed the platform apps to charge more from gambling sites and mortgage brokers and other marketing clients who pay big bucks for good names. In this case, the reporters focused their attention on a single broker, one that leaped into the online-offline data-linking lead thanks to the Facebook-app UID leaks, and passed the information on to dozens of fifth-party clients.

RapLeaf's pivot to data broker was going swimmingly until the fall of 2010, when *Wall Street Journal* reporter Emily Steel singled it out as the worst offender in the paper's series of reports on the app breach.[56] RapLeaf leveraged its access to Facebook UIDs, with their attached real names, along with the rest of their scraped profile data, to offer new targeting capabilities. The *Journal* outed 2010 New Hampshire U.S. Senate candidate and tech executive Jim Bender as a RapLeaf client as it strove to explain why sixty-seven-year-old Linda Twombly was getting so many of his campaign ads. "Holy smokes," Twombly said after looking at her RapLeaf file, which contained not only her personal information but also her affiliations and interests. "It is like a watchdog is watching me, and it is not good."[57] Bender called Linda Twombly on the phone to personally apologize for violating her privacy.[58] Facebook kicked RapLeaf off the site—just as eBay had—in response to the criticism. But according to Hoffman, the executives knew exactly what was going on. Not only that, "they actually gave us advice on how to make it more [efficient], so we didn't tax their servers."[59] (As the high-level link between the firms, presumably Thiel would have been informed.) Hoffman's remarks are similar to the complaints Levchin made regarding Slide when the platform cracked down on app access, but these founders knew the deal from the outset: Get what you can get away with, and if you get caught, Mark doesn't know you.

Kicked out by Zuck to appease the angry public, RapLeaf pivoted again, to "data onboarding," rechristening itself under its new division, LiveRamp. Thanks to direct help from Facebook, Hoffman's firm had built up a unique proficiency at linking offline data and online browsing records, using its scraped email lists as an early start in the race with legacy marketing firms. As a relatively small company with an important advantage in a big sector, LiveRamp was a perfect acquisition target. In 2014, it sold to industry leader Acxiom, for $310 million.[60] The purchase was so successful that in 2018 Acxiom sold Acxiom, the brand and business, and put LiveRamp on the big signs. The B2K regulatory era continued long after anyone associated John Ashcroft with tech, and Peter Thiel made the most of it, linking a chain of start-ups that together could mine, combine, and refine data until it was worth real money. Privacy was dead; they had everything. Now, what do you get for the cabal that has it all?

Pretty Hate Machine

In 2013, between her internship at the British international consultancy SCL Group and her first year at the Stanford Graduate School of Business, Sophie Schmidt introduced her SCL bosses to Palantir. The daughter of Google executive and longtime Valley hand Eric Schmidt, Sophie had the good idea to connect the Brits with Thiel's firm. Soon after, a right-wing media impresario named Steve Bannon approached SCL with an idea for a U.S. spin-off. SCL was used to manage election propaganda campaigns for the ruling cliques in England's former colonies, but the United States was a whole new market. When Bannon suggested that his Breitbart News Network funders Robert Mercer and his daughter Rebekah were interested in financing the effort, anything seemed possible. Like the SCL boss, Alexander Nix, Bannon and Bob Mercer were big admirers of Thiel's project. As the young SCL research head, Christopher Wylie, later wrote, it seemed to him that "these men wanted to create their own private Palantir" at the consultancy—the Mercers promised $15–20 million.[61] The use for Bob Mercer, an IBM engineer turned hedge-fund guru, seemed obvious: modeling the future for profit. But Bannon was steering the boat, and he had grander aspirations. Republicans were at a severe data disadvantage compared to Democrats, and the Obama campaign extended that lead. Bannon wanted to close the gap and, by curating his clients, push a hard-right nationalist culture-war agenda within the GOP. The B2K world of online data could be his killer app. Backed by Mercer money, Bannon named this new Palantir-for-politics firm Cambridge Analytica, for the august university town where SCL's Nix told the intellectually pretentious Bannon his firm was located, a straight-up lie that required SCL to assemble a fake office. Thanks to the cash infusion, it could afford that kind of behavior.

In the early Cambridge Analytica tests, the firm relied on data brokers, including Acxiom. But Facebook data was the holy grail, and to get that, firms had to navigate a series of hoops, the combination of which gave Zuck and company a measure of plausible deniability. Facebook's policy was not to sell user data—why compete with itself, after all?—but the site still allowed platform developers to scrape information. Bannon planned to license that info from the University of Cambridge's psychometrics researchers, who used a Facebook personality-quiz app to harvest experimental data, but when negotiations stalled, Nix got some help from Palantir. Though the firms had no official relationship—for what it's worth, Wylie writes that Nix often paid contractors in cash, avoiding a paper trail—Palantir's London office helped out anyway.[62] A staffer there was working on winning new commercial business for the firm, and he advised SCL to just create another app. To make sure everything was kosher, Cambridge Analytica used online microlabor platforms (including Amazon's Mechanical Turk) to pay survey takers to expose their Facebook data and, as it turned out, that of their friends as well. The result was a database, the kind RapLeaf and PRISM tended toward: integrated information's clean white beam of light. Nix and Bannon took turns calling Americans, surveying them on their preferences, delighted to see the information match up with the profiles on the computer screen.

Like Ferris Bueller convincing Cameron to steal his dad's car, Palantir was happy to see the app plan work; now it wanted a ride. Cambridge Analytica's success suggested that Palantir could get back in the Facebook-scraping game despite the RapLeaf debacle. The company started sending high-level employees to Cambridge off the books, getting pseudonymous log-in credentials for the Cambridge Analytica databases. They worked together to pinpoint holes in the Facebook data flow, designing seemingly innocent browser extensions such as calendars and calculators that took advantage of platform integration settings to siphon information. The U.S. intelligence apparatus was still reeling from the previous year's Snowden revelations, and Palantir's old access channels to social-network data were shut. Bannon's firm was Palantir's new commercial conduit, a layer or two of plausible deniability for everyone concerned. Wylie doesn't confirm that Palantir actually plugged the National Security Agency back into Facebook through Cambridge Analytica, but he was there when they planned to do it, and the way I read his account, that's what happened. Nix regarded helping Palantir help the NSA as a North Atlantic patriotic obligation.[63]

Though Bannon's Cambridge data efforts only became enduring headline news in 2018, the work didn't stay secret for longer than a year. During the first days of the presidential primary, the Mercers backed Texas senator Ted Cruz, a right-winger with finance links, an elite legal background, and provocateur instincts. Considering the way Cambridge Analytica kicked into gear for Cruz during the primary, everything it did before that looks like a mere rehearsal for 2016. Between the campaign and outside committee expenditures, Cruz-for-president minions sunk millions into Cambridge contracts, completing a goofy closed circuit of Mercer project cash. The story of Cruz's data deal leaked in the *Guardian* during the primary, but this time no rules had been broken.[64] Facebook promised to look into the issue but it seems to have taken no corrective action, and both the Cruz campaign and Cambridge Analytica spun the press until it was positive.* *Bloomberg* ran a feature with the firm's cooperation, and though the reporter was skeptical about the validity of psychometric profiles, which extrapolated personality characteristics from consumer data, there was no sign that the consultancy's work merited a worldwide scandal the likes of which emerged a few years later.[65] RapLeaf's 2010 election-targeting debacle, which ended with a candidate personally apologizing to an elderly voter, was just the way things worked in 2015. Cruz won the Iowa caucus and the press gave his data contractors ample credit.

The Cruz attributes that appealed to the Mercers appealed to Thiel, too;

---

* How much did Facebook know and when did it know it? Thiel's biographer Max Chafkin begs the question: "If Facebook had been a victim, rather than a willing accomplice of Cambridge Analytica, why had the consultancy been working with a company [Palantir] controlled by Zuckerberg's mentor?" See Max Chafkin, *The Contrarian: Peter Thiel and Silicon Valley's Pursuit of Power* (Penguin Press, 2021), 220.

he often found himself backing the same causes as his fellow Stanford alum Rebekah Mercer. He first funded Cruz in 2009 during his run for Texas attorney general.[66] But unlike the Mercers, Thiel didn't back the Texas senator in 2016, even after his early favorite, former HP CEO Carly Fiorina, dropped out. Through his Gawker attack, Thiel became close with Charles C. Johnson, a young former right-wing campus malcontent and propagandist for Fox anchor and neofascist entrepreneur Tucker Carlson via Carlson's *Daily Caller* site. Thiel backed Johnson's suit against Gawker, and Johnson made himself into a Thiel lieutenant, a close connection between the VC and the extreme nationalist right. It's through Johnson that Thiel reached out to the Trump campaign, securing a spot on the future president's California delegate list and in the campaign's inner circle. Thiel had a lot to offer Trump, including money and, unlike most people near the center of Trumpworld, experience with success. When a tape of nominee Trump yukking it up about his sexual assault habit leaked, most insiders thought it was game over. Johnson convinced Thiel to double down, perhaps aided by an early Cambridge Analytica study that concluded voters would back candidates with objectionable ideas if the presentation was sufficiently aggressive. The move—a $1 million donation to the Mercer PAC, which now supported Trump—elevated Thiel to the campaign's very highest tier, where he sat with Bannon, the Mercers, and the Trump family. This time around, the services of George Shultz were not required.

It's not clear how much the particular work of Cambridge Analytica ended up helping the Trump campaign. All the psychometric targeting based on personality characteristics sounds like bunk to me. But the campaign certainly made use of Facebook, running on the platform like one of Max Levchin's annoying but prolific Slide apps. Thanks to targeting, the platform turned into a grassroots ATM, allowing the campaign to pull in donors "in alarming numbers, very fast" according to its digital director Brad Parscale. The campaign raised $280 million on the platform, $100 million of which they channeled back into Facebook ads. Just as Facebook lent direct help to the companies RapLeaf and Slide, Zuck dedicated Facebook employees to assisting the Trump campaign—a huge customer, after all. "Look," Parscale explained. "You go spend $300 million, $100 million on social media, a lot of people show up at your office, wanting to help you spend that money on their platforms."[67] In the years that followed, Facebook's liberal leadership toed a tricky tightrope, crediting themselves for winning Trump the presidency, but not in any illicit way. Arguing for Facebook not having to change anything despite directly enabling a demagogue, executive Andrew Bosworth drew on Tolkien and John Rawls, comparing Facebook to the Ring of Power. Instead of trying to direct its effects, the platform should behave impartially. Boz, as he's known, did not extend the metaphor to the need to throw Facebook into an active volcano as soon as possible. Rather, the only responsible thing to do was leave it up to capitalism's impersonal superintelligence and *auction* the ring. That's the closest to democracy Palo Alto could imagine. "At the end of the day we are forced to ask what responsibility individuals have for themselves," Boz concluded in an internal Facebook post that leaked to the press.[68] Even Silicon Valley's liberals worship Hayek.

Trump was one of Thiel's best investments, a long-odds bet with substantial costs but a huge potential upside. He aimed for the Skee-Ball target's corner chute and drained the shot. As far as the Thielverse was concerned, its leader might as well have been president. Thiel scored a big (though short-lived) win when Trump named Palantir cheerleader Michael Flynn as his national security adviser, and another when he filled the post of secretary of defense with Jim Mattis, who stocked his staff with Palantir vets.[69] The markets took notice: Demand for Palantir's private stock shot up, and the floundering company—which had resorted to suing the army in a last-ditch effort to force it to reconsider its choice to blow the firm off—was reinvigorated. One Silicon Valley investor told *BuzzFeed News* that it was "nepotism 101. Any additional contracts that I imagine they could get, they will get."[70] Palantir nabbed billions of dollars in federal contracts during Trump's term from all sorts of agencies, including a large share of the $800-plus million army data contract they sued for; Theranos lawyer David Boies was worth his fees.

The peak of Thiel's power came when he assumed the role of White House liaison to Silicon Valley, sitting at the president's left hand while executives kissed the Trump ring. In the room were the industry's elite: Tim Cook and Jeff Bezos, Sheryl Sandberg for Facebook, Eric Schmidt for Google, and the CEOs of Cisco, IBM, Intel, Microsoft, and Oracle. Thiel also invited reps from a couple of smaller firms: Karp from Palantir and Elon Musk of Tesla and SpaceX. It was a classic Hoover-style meeting, bringing a sector's corporate leadership together with federal leadership, not to command but to pat backs and work out their common interests, which centered on competition from China. After this meeting, these firms grew willing and even eager to deal with the government directly: Amazon, Google, and Microsoft pursued and won tens of billions in security contracts, edging into the territory of traditional prime contractors.[71]

Trump gripped his adviser Thiel's right hand awkwardly, with both of his. In October of 2020, after the army contract was announced but before Trump lost, Palantir went public under what the *Financial Times* called "an unusually complex arrangement designed to leave control in the hands of three founders," including Thiel.[72] But investors didn't punish the company for its oligarchic structure or its patron's defeat. When it became apparent that the firm was politically hedged enough for a Democratic administration, investors boosted the price to new heights. By the end of November it had tripled since its issuance, the month before—from $9 to $27—and it peaked at over $35 in January of 2021, in the weeks following the lackluster vigilante attempt to hold the White House for Trump. Biden needed to mine data, too.

Though the regime didn't last long, the Trump meeting was a culmination of the Palo Alto System. For the first time, the regional industry was more than emergent; it represented the world's highest concentration of value. No other meeting could gather anywhere near the same bulk of capital—not agriculture, not real estate, not manufacturing, not transportation, not munitions. Silicon Valley claimed its place at the center of the capitalist world, and its leaders pledged allegiance, not to Trump the man—obviously a clown—not to the White House or even to America. They pledged their allegiance to the impersonal historical forces that Trump represented, which happened to be the same ones raising them to their present heights. They pledged allegiance to themselves, and they pledged allegiance to Peter Thiel most of all. If anyone was in touch with the Coherent Extrapolated Volition of the capitalist class, he was. Bezos and Cook and Schmidt and Musk all had big pieces of the puzzle—monopoly, imperialism, rapid growth, and attention—but none of them bet on Trump. It was Thiel who understood that the race-nation is not the capitalist system's vestigial tail but its right leg. "In our hearts and minds, we know that desperate optimism will not save us," Thiel wrote in a 2011 essay for *National Review* titled "The End of the Future." "There is no law that the exceptional rise of the West must continue."[73] What might be a call for internationalist conciliation is nothing of the sort. Competition and domination, exploitation and exclusion, minority rule and class hate: These aren't problems capitalist technology will solve. *That's what it's for.* In the proper language, they are features, not bugs. This was Jordan's plan, Hoover's plan, Shockley's plan, and now it's Thiel's.

Peter Thiel is, figuratively, the son of resentful losers. His grandfathers lost the Reich and his fathers lost the colonies. As a share of the known world, we've seen the West's formal patrimony collapse over the past 50 years or so, in a sequence that stretches back to the foundation of Palo Alto and the traumatic loss of Herbert Hoover's mines. As soon as the white man got his hands all the way around the globe, it started to slip from his grasp. Thiel's literal father oversaw the construction of a Namibian uranium mine on behalf of South Africa's do-or-die drive for an apartheid nuke that would rescue white rule, a perfect execution of the Shockley doctrine had it succeeded.*[74] Domination always implies the possibility of escape, and like his symbolic forebears in California's suburbs, Thiel is looking for ways not to stall the long sequence of decolonization but to reverse and defeat it. How do you do that? According to the Palo Alto System, there are a few important methods, and Thiel has made pioneering use of them.

Human capital is Palo Alto's product, and Herbert Hoover took advantage of that by assembling a worldwide network of chums that reached the top levels of corporate and state power. Once they were in place, not even the high tide of social democratic reformism could dissolve those bonds, and they helped return Hooverism to power. Though Thiel hasn't had a presidency of his own to work with — no chance of that for the Frankfurt-born billionaire without a constitutional amendment — he has managed a similar feat with the PayPal Mafia and the Thielverse. As American power shifted toward the private sector and, within the private sector, toward Silicon Valley's fast-growing tech companies, his networks acquired outsize importance, and his war chest

---

* It's a historical curiosity that in addition to CEO Thiel's experience, PayPal's early COO (David Sacks), CFO (Roelof Botha), and largest shareholder (Musk) were all white South African immigrants. Perhaps their interest in reducing the democratic accountability of asset holders via technology was related to the insecurity their families experienced, shivering in the anti-apartheid movement's mounting shadow during the fourth quarter of the twentieth century.

ballooned. Founders Fund was open about investing in people, and Thiel took a position at Paul Graham's incubator Y Combinator to access ambitious new CEOs at their earliest phase of development. In 2010, Thiel upped the ante: He announced the Thiel Fellowships, a $100,000 grant for handpicked entrepreneurs under age twenty who are willing to forgo college.[75] The parallels with Leland Stanford, Charles Marvin, and their sprinting colts are striking.

It's important to see Thiel as a product of Reagan's reactionary California suburbs and the Hooverite intellectual conspiracy undergirding them, including organizations such as FEE, the AEI, the Mont Pelerin Society, and of course, the Hoover Institution. He came of age in the gentle arms of the cohort of active conservative donors that built on these foundations, the ones who funded the various *Reviews*, whose beneficiaries fought the campus PC wars, and, after graduation, sabotaged the Clinton administration. Like Dave Packard paying Hoover's conspiratorial army of flying monkeys with their associations and foundations, Peter Thiel quietly funds a wide variety of ideological projects. His introduction to writing seven-figure checks to the ultra-right was a $1 million donation to Numbers USA, part of the openly racist, anti-immigrant Tanton network and an outgrowth of Ehrlich and company's zero population growth.[76] Thiel took the baton from generations of Stanford racists.

Thiel has a healthy respect for the importance of small media outlets; Andrew Granato's article in *Stanford Politics*—the most detailed examination of Thiel's *Stanford Review* network—reports that he bragged at a reunion of the paper that he was funding the *Journal of American Greatness* and *American Affairs*, two relatively small publications that emerged to promote Trump-style nationalist conservatism.[77] According to Thiel's minion Charles Johnson, he is also funding *Quillette*, a conservative culture-war publication based out of Australia with an intellectual aesthetic. The site's founder credits *Zero to One* with inspiring her to launch the site, and *Quillette* has had surprising influence near the center of a new culture-war offensive, grouped under the silly name "intellectual dark web."[78] It's a term coined by YouTube philosopher Eric Weinstein, who is also a manager at Thiel Capital. Thiel even funds a science journal called *Inference* that includes a smattering of fringe right-wing politics.[79] Don't forget the Machine Intelligence Research Institute and LessWrong; he has also funded the commercial activities of neoreaction-ary techno-monarchist blogger Curtis Yarvin, a proponent of Dark Enlightenment thought.*[80] Journalists dug up these relationships; Thiel hasn't taken credit in public for any of these publications, which makes it difficult for me to imagine that there aren't another few lurking undiscovered. Palo Alto thinks of itself as far from the epicenter of Trumpism, but the town has maintained its role as America's anticommunist citadel, now with even more money.

As Thiel's power accumulates in his curious retirement fund, his investments in politics have become more audacious. He went from being another right-wing donor with libertarian and trollish preferences that led him toward Ron Paul and Ted Cruz to a large independent power center within the party. He supported Kansas secretary of state (and former Ashcroft underling) Kris Kobach, who earlier worked as a lawyer for Ehrlich and Tanton's Federation for American Immigration Reform, traveling around the country filing lawsuits and drafting bills to revoke rights from undocumented immigrants. Kobach drafted Arizona's SB 1070, which required anyone stopped by the police to show immigration papers, a knowing salute to South African apartheid. His state laws were designed to test the boundaries and most of them ended up thrown out at various levels, but his aggression helped focus attention on immigration as a polarizing national issue.[81] Thiel backed Kobach for the U.S. Senate, but he lost the 2020 primary. Still a useful piece on the chessboard, Kobach has helped lead efforts to attack voting rights, including Trump's attempts to overturn the 2020 presidential election.

Thiel has also backed Missouri attorney general Josh Hawley, a Stanford graduate, right-wing firebrand, and *Review* contributor who was elected to the Senate in 2018. Hawley helped try to overturn the results of the 2020 election, objecting to the Senate's certification of the vote and giving a notorious fist salute to the insurrectionary crowd on January 6, 2021, as they moved to take the U.S. Capitol. The Senate is the country's least democratic legislative body, and for a fortune like Thiel's, senators are a bargain. As time goes on, his investments get bigger and the candidates closer to his inner circle. As I write, he has

---

* Yarvin told the Mercer-funded fascist performer Milo Yiannopoulos that he was "coaching" Thiel and that the billionaire was "fully enlightened." He "just plays it very carefully." Joseph Bernstein, "Here's How Breitbart and Milo Smuggled Nazi and White Nationalist Ideas into the Mainstream," BuzzFeed News, October 5, 2017.

pledged $10 million each for the Senate campaigns of his associates J. D. Vance (Ohio, formerly of Thiel's Mithril Capital fund) and his *Zero to One* notetaker Blake Masters (Arizona).[82] These men aren't just Thiel's friends; they are also essentially his *employees*. An enthusiast of life-extension technologies, Thiel will get full access to his Roth IRA and the tax-free billions inside it in 2032, barring any changes to the law (which he would surely fight tooth and nail). The statute is written the way it is because sixty-five is supposed to be the age of retirement; Thiel barely considers it middle age. He is playing the long game, but at a time of global upheaval, he knows he can't afford to go too slowly.

The sheer breadth of these efforts threatens to dull the impact of their disclosure, rather than heighten it. Thiel is a hedge-fund guy, and he places a lot of bets. Lately, a surprising number of them are paying off, and the tendencies he's betting on are building toward something very dangerous. Capitalist technology is still a (re)colonial tool, and though newer, bigger missiles no longer seem like the magic formula for U.S. world domination, arms proliferation takes new forms. Thanks to the continued rise of finance capital and the regulatory conditions of the B2K internet, it doesn't take a state effort or a globally curated team of geniuses to found a new high-tech weapons firm. "We live in a world where people don't think conspiracies are possible," Thiel told journalist Ryan Holiday, the implication being that such a perception makes it easier for him to get away with it.[83]

In 2017, still very high on the miraculous Gawker and Trump wins, Charles Johnson approached Thiel with a new idea: Why not build a facial-recognition tool for the Trump administration, one that the "deportation squads" could use to hunt undocumented immigrants? Johnson teamed up with Hoan Ton-That, a Vietnamese-Australian spam coder who was also a Gawker target. It was a long shot, a fascist troll fantasy. "It was a joke," the silent partner, Johnson said, "but it became real."[84] Thiel gave them $200,000, and the team added Richard Schwartz, a conservative who went from attacking the New York City welfare system as a politician to running an employment contracting firm for welfare recipients. The new company was called Clearview AI, and the founders kept the ultra-right agenda under wraps while they scraped billions of photos from the web. Soon enough, the software was doing exactly what it was supposed to do—help Immigration and Customs Enforcement target people for deportation as part of the Trump administration's attack on

Mexican and Central American residents. Police around the country, along with various federal law enforcement agencies, quickly signed licensing deals and put the unregulated system to work in the real world. Clearview's public leadership, which didn't include Johnson or Thiel, claimed the tool was only for authorities, but they gave access to friends within the right-wing infrastructure, including, for unclear reasons, Dave Packard's treasured AEI. Eventually all these connections surfaced, but as Stanford Law professor Al Gidari told the *New York Times* regarding Clearview: "Absent a very strong federal privacy law, we're all screwed."[85] The company claims a value of over $100 million.

How far does this road go? Among the Trumpists with Clearview access was Palmer Luckey, the founder of the virtual reality start-up Oculus Rift, which he sold to Facebook for $3 billion.[86] Like Thiel, he funded pro-Trump propaganda, and Luckey's next firm came right out of the Thielverse: a defense contractor that builds physical electronics systems. He founded it with a handful of Palantir employees, and it got a Tolkien name, too: Anduril, the name of a Lord of the Rings sword. It means "flame of the west"—not exactly subtle. Its first market? Border security. Anduril's initial product was called Lattice, and the firm won a contract with Customs and Border Protection worth hundreds of millions of dollars to build 200 virtual sentry towers.[87] Less than five years after its founding, Anduril is valued in the billions. After selling his company LiveRamp to Acxiom, RapLeaf cofounder Auren Hoffman established a new Thiel-funded start-up called SafeGraph. It aims to create the biggest, most precise database of real-time human location data, and it has raised over $60 million at the time of this writing.[88] Without democratic approval or public debate, a Silicon Valley cabal is cobbling together the kind of security apparatus that has given human society collective nightmares for as long as the computer has existed. We're getting there, coming to something. The Basilisk.

Like the transcontinental railroad—another border-security project, recall—Thiel's apparatus used the magic of finance capital to build itself. His conspiratorial will has almost certainly accelerated the process, but he's *made* money off the effort. It doesn't cost; capital is paying him and his friends to do it, and paying them very well. No wonder so many people in the Thielverse are convinced there's a superintelligence that will reward them for building these systems. One already is. On the Reddit forum devoted to Palantir, a user called Dorktastical suggested a modification to the famous thought experiment:

Palantir is Peter Thiel creating Roko's Basilisk. He may have already made it. This gives you two choices:

1) Be tortured for all of eternity by Roko's Basilisk

2) Put all of your holdings in to PLTR [Palantir stock] and never sell

If it turns out that PLTR isn't Roko's Basilisk, you can still say you've fulfilled your commitment to bring Roko's Basilisk into existence, and avoid eternal damnation.[89]

You're probably already being tortured if you haven't given your money to Thiel, Dorktastical concludes, since this world is most likely a simulation and Thiel has already correctly determined that your faith is weak.

I think this post, though a joke on most levels, captures an important truth about Roko's Basilisk. There's no emerging artificial superintelligence that will automatically arbitrate the thoughts and claims of all people. There is just capitalism, an impersonal system that acts through people toward the increasing accumulation of capital, the amassing of exploited value. It's not precise enough to say that Thiel has been at the right place at the right time. For capital, he *is* the right place. The historical forces acting through Thiel are much larger than his intentions; if there's anything that sets him apart from his peers it's that he understands that fact better than they do. To the degree that he seems to be in control, he's achieved it by making investments that are wacky and out of control. Forces, not men. That's what the Palo Alto System is made of, and the train is barreling down the tracks.

How to Stop It?

I began this chapter with the difficulty of narrativizing the Palo Alto System, in which failure is just a precursor to success and hubris gets rewarded rather than punished. One way to do it is to imagine we just haven't reached the consequences yet, that this is all rising action that will culminate in a downfall when Silicon Valley finally goes too far. This is how Mike Judge ended his *Silicon Valley* series. When the protagonists discover their machine learning–compression combination has become too smart and is rapidly breaking encryption systems, they decide the only thing to do is to epically fail, to sabotage their company so badly that no one will attempt the same thing.

Conclusion demands this type of realization, while Palo Alto abjures it. Limits present themselves to capital as opportunities. What can divert the train besides the world's exhaustion?

During his first military assignment, to the Anti-Submarine Warfare Operations Research Group, William Shockley came home for a weekend in November of 1943. He wrote his wife a note:

> Dear Jean:
>
> I am sorry that I feel I can no longer go on. Most of my life I have felt that the world was not a pleasant place and that people were not a very admirable form of life. I find that I am particularly dissatisfied with myself and that most of my actions are the consequence of motives of which I am ashamed. Most people do not feel this way I am sure. Consequently, I must regard myself as less well suited than most to carry on with life and to develop the proper attitudes in our children. I see no reason to believe other than that I shall continually become worse in these regards as time passes.
>
> I hope you have better luck in the future,
> Bill[90]

Then he put one bullet in his revolver, spun the chamber, put the barrel to his head, and pulled the trigger. Then he sealed the letter in an envelope and put it in his safe to be found after his death, many years later. Soon after, in 1945, Shockley wrote that if the trend toward increased lethality continued at the then current rate of acceleration, it would lead "to the picture of one man being able to unleash forces which would destroy the world."[91] Shockley advised the state to use the bomb anyway; better us than them. He saw no other way forward, and neither did the architects of U.S. Cold War policy who adopted his formulas. The central instruments have changed, from nuclear missiles to special forces operatives, from jet fighters to drone squadrons, but the agenda is the same: holding on. The only way Bill Shockley Jr.—son of colonial mine prospectors, grandfather of Silicon Valley—could let go was to try to destroy himself. And while it's true that he was less well suited than most to develop the proper attitudes in his children, someone would have taken his place. Death couldn't stop the forces that characterized Leland Stanford Jr., either, after all.

How do you kill a place, a system? What would it mean for Palo Alto—call it the Coherent Extrapolated Volition of Palo Alto—to look at its role over the last 150 years of world history, beyond the blandishments of Bob Kaufman's spitting gadget salesmen, and decide that Stanford's suburb is *less well suited than most* to steward the world into the rest of the twenty-first century? Time was money for California's Anglo settlers, and they forced that colonial axiom into place anywhere it had yet to become law. How does the Palo Alto System end without taking the rest of the transformed world down with it?

Rosemary Cambra defends Ohlone burial ground (1985)
Ted Fink, courtesy of History San Jose

Chapter 6.1

Resolution

One of the ways that Ohlone Elementary embraced the 1970s was by establishing a small farm on its campus. By the time I got there, the farm had two goats, some fowl, and a big black sheep named Jason who occasionally escaped from his enclosure to sprint around the field, scaring and delighting the children as the adults tried to corral him. The farm is where we decorated cookies for the annual harvest festival, where we hid in bushes and built forts out of assorted wooden boards and stray chunks of concrete. In the preceding pages, I've written that the outrages of colonial settlement are indelibly carved in the world, but at Ohlone we learned about the people who lived in Palo Alto before we did, and we practiced grinding acorns the way they did. Surely conscious education, the meeting of truth and innocence, is the only remedy for a haunted society? But education, as I've tried to show, is one of the Anglo settlers' most important weapons.

When I was in fifth grade, for some weeks all the various homerooms participated in a gold rush simulation. The kids who played Indian the year before now played settler. We turned the farm into California in 1850, complete with surface gold: small nuggets painted by the teachers and nestled in the dirt for us to find, just the way providence supplied the forty-niners. On the first day we lined up at the gates, and when we heard "Go!" we all ran into the empty farm, racing to gather as much and as fast as we could, before it was all gone, before someone else got it. But that was just day one. When the initial rush was over, we traded goods and services to circulate the gold, every one of us an owner, a start-up. Here was the real lesson: True wealth doesn't come from a lucky discovery but from a good business plan — made, not found. And yet, it was a reenactment of the capitalist world system's origin point as a big bang, history and society just waiting for us to begin, glinting right there on the ground. We practiced forgetting where our money came from.

The whole thing was a dream for me: instead of school, a days-long live-action role-playing game with my whole grade. When I sprinted onto the farm equipped with my start-up business plan and a bag for storing gold, I can't remember ever feeling happier, ever feeling more free. This small world was completely open to me, pure potential to gather, to shape, to use, to have, to prove, to be, to own.

That year, there were no Ohlone. We practiced forgetting about them, too. The gold helped.

"What does it mean to abolish Silicon Valley?" asks tech worker Wendy Liu in her prescriptively titled book, *Abolish Silicon Valley*.[1] Liu's conclusion is that capital's ever-accumulating need for profitable sinks is incompatible with the kind of democratic control over modern technology that the Black Panther Party put on its program. Based on what we've seen of Palo Alto's 150 years, it's hard to disagree. As long as capitalists have capital, they have to find somewhere to put it, and capital will always find its capitalists. It may be that Silicon Valley is best understood as a particular expression of this impersonal drive: geographic, historical, and imaginary. It represents the gold rush and the next gold rush and the one after that, from produce to real estate to radios to transistors to microchips to missiles to PCs to routers to browsers to web portals to iPods to gig platforms to... If California is America's America, then Palo Alto is America's America's America. Not just opportunity but also the ceaseless renewal thereof. Silicon Valley is defined by a refusal to stop or even to slow down, which, given the dynamics of finance-led growth, would amount to the same thing. How do you end that story? One way or another. What is the one way, and what is the other?

Capital investment is exhausting; it uses up. We've seen that repeatedly during this relatively short historical period: The hydrolickers eroded the landscape to the point of disintegration; the planters drained the aquifers; the bankers and real estate agents carved up the territory; the electronics manufacturers filled the ecosystem with heavy metals and exotic chemicals. Underlying this sequence was the exhaustion of the atmosphere's ability to absorb carbon without the planet overheating. Bechtel has led the way from California, building energy infrastructure around the world. It created the coal slurry pipe, crushing and liquefying the fuel for easy transport, and repeated the move with liquefied natural gas (LNG), which increases the payability of gas operations by supercooling the product to the same end. This is capitalist technology par excellence. The firm claims credit for designing and building 30 percent of world LNG capacity.[2] As I write, Bechtel is moving forward with a plan to build a $1.5 billion power plant in western Pennsylvania to burn gas mined via hydraulic fracturing, which uses high-pressure water to break underground rocks and thus increase yield. This fracking technique is redolent of gold hydrolicking and has similar consequences, including a series of earthquakes in the region. (Bank of America has stepped in to finance, spending more than $20 billion to back new fracking, drilling, and pipeline deals in 2020 alone.)[3] Critics say the Bechtel plant will emit more greenhouse gases than the nearest big city: Pittsburgh.[4] Silicon Valley isn't destroying itself— it's destroying the world.

We're not choking to death on population growth, as the ZPG crowd once imagined; we're suffering from success. Climate change yielded California wildfires of new intensity, and in this world historical center of wealth, the air quality has been so bad that Bay Area residents have been urged to stay inside with their windows shut. In 2020, the Bay Area Air Quality Management District declared 30 straight days with an Air Quality Index above 100, a record you don't want to set.[5] The clouds over the Bay now take on a nightmarish orange hue during the annual fires, as if the paint on the Golden Gate Bridge were leaching into the sky. Silicon Valley can't help but see opportunity: Venture capitalists have pumped nearly $100 million into San Francisco start-up "Molekule," an internet-enabled luxury home air purifier that sells for $800 and does not seem to work very well.[6] In capitalism, even the air is an individual responsibility. For the same reason that gentrification can't fix homelessness, capitalist technology can't solve these problems and create them at the same time—though that won't stop VCs from making money on the climate crisis.

One way for capitalism to transcend the limits of the biosphere without transcending the limits of capitalism would be to colonize the rest of the solar system, the galaxy, and beyond. The leader of the nineteenth-century mining imperialists, Cecil Rhodes, was once said to have lamented that "the world is nearly all parceled out, and what there is left of it is being divided up, conquered, and colonized. To think of these stars that you see overhead at night, these vast worlds which we can never reach. I would annex the planets if I could; I often think of that. It makes me sad to see them so clear and yet so far."* Today, capital's ambition extends farther than Rhodes dared to hope: Jeff Bezos and Elon Musk are leading the capitalist charge into space with their respective Blue Origin and SpaceX firms. Musk hopes to colonize Mars, and Bezos told a morning news show that "we can move all heavy industry and all polluting industry off of Earth and operate it in space."[7] There is always another frontier, if you know where to look.

At every step, capital used up working people, churning through earth's only truly inexhaustible resource. That Amazon is a market leader in workplace mechanization, labor exploitation, and low-end wages all at the same time is deeply concerning. Bezos is pointing a way forward for technology, and not one that makes life easier or better for labor. Instead of making progress toward the widely prosperous (if not equal or egalitarian) society that capitalism promised, things are getting worse. The series of socioeconomic phenomena I've called bifurcation continues to accelerate as growth decelerates and the domestic class struggle becomes increasingly zero-sum. For every app billionaire, job quality deteriorates. Someone teleported to 2020 from the 1990s would notice instantly: the Amazon delivery vans parked haphazardly, the food-delivery riders zipping through traffic on electric bikes, the impersonal shoppers filling grocery baskets with alien items, doorstep boxes full of prechopped food waiting for office workers to get home. And that's just what we can see in public. Jeff Bezos and Elon Musk are currently fighting for the privilege of having a new law named after them: The more highly advanced a workplace's mechanization, the higher the injury rate.

---

* This quote is repeated often — it's a good one — but it is a little too good to be true. Hannah Arendt uses it to begin her 1945 essay, "Imperialism, Nationalism, Chauvinism," crediting the biography of Rhodes by South African settler author Sarah Gertrude Millin. Millin cites W. T. Stead's account in *The Last Will and Testament of Cecil John Rhodes*. Stead was something like a press agent for Rhodes, and Millin allots the sidereal musing the credulity it deserves: "Such are the preposterous words Stead puts into Rhodes' mouth (how patient is paper!). We are to believe Rhodes seriously spoke them..." Arendt's omission robbed many readers of Millin's critical lens in the decades since. Still, press agents are part of imperialism, too, and if Rhodes hadn't been Rhodes someone else would have found value in his Stead. The quote then speaks for impersonal capital rather than a person in particular, which is all the better for our purposes. Sarah Gertrude Millin, *Cecil Rhodes* (Harper & Brothers, 1933), 158.

Silicon Valley's biggest winners are the slack-limbed puppets who have nailed their hands to these historical forces. Butterflies pinning themselves to the most opportune spots in the glass display box. Not the Wozniaks or even the Bezoses but the Airbnbozos whose defining feature is an eagerness to unleash forces they don't understand onto as many people as they can, as fast as possible. Mickey Mouse surfs the waves in his stolen wizard hat, flashing a four-finger hang ten. When they are properly incentivized, such people are not hard to come by, which has been one of capital's saving graces in this disappointing era. Another has been the durability of imposed racial division as reflected in the persistence of residential, educational, and labor-market segregation. For Silicon Valley, as for the California capitalists who preceded it, cross-class white reaction has been a powerful if underacknowledged ally.

The Palo Alto System isn't old from a world-historical perspective—only 150 years or so, as of this writing—but it's not nearly as new as Palo Altans believe. In the frontier industry, trying to remember any further back than the last round of success isn't going to win you any VC friends. Like the title character in the 1955 Orson Welles mystery-thriller *Mr. Arkadin*, the town is a billionaire whose convenient amnesia just won't let him remember where his money comes from. That forgetfulness is an advantageous adaptation; the past is a distraction when you're creating the future. To the new round of capital-drenched rocketboys, the earth is but a launchpad for interstellar capitalism. It's analogous to their view of humanity as a starting point for a better, faster, and longer-lasting post-humanity. They see limited importance in our specific planet and species. Genericity clears even these last hurdles. People tasked with the historical role of exhausting the earth have to be able to convince themselves of something similar; otherwise they would stop. That would free up spots for people who won't. This is the beauty of capitalism: Refusal sinks; collaboration floats.

If the intergalactic capitalists win, if they do exhaust the earth and humanity, then for the sake of my historical reputation and that of everyone I've ever loved, I hope the post-humans judge that we were already too late, that we never had a chance. Maybe that is the case—as I've argued, the general state of things is increasingly dire for many people—but I don't believe it. Even if I could be made to believe it, I would choose not to. I am committed to this planet, which means I have to hold on to the possibility of an alternative to capitalist exhaustion. What, then, would that look like? Palo Alto and California's many Stanford children have been our focus thus far: Herbert Hoover and Bill Shockley and those who followed. I don't doubt that these same people will have profitable answers for every problem they cause, but we know enough of their history to know they can't fix themselves. What else is Palo Alto to do with itself?

How about giving it back?

—◇—

Despite what I learned in school, the Ohlone people are not gone, though the federal government refuses to acknowledge that. The Muwékma Ohlone Tribe asserts an aboriginal claim to the South Bay, including Palo Alto. In 1925, the UC Berkeley ethnologist Alfred Kroeber mistakenly listed the Verona Band of Alameda County, the government's name for the group, as extinct, a classification the feds adopted, reversing its 1906 recognition of the Ohlone. The government claimed that, in those 20 years, the tribe disintegrated. This did not happen, but for nearly a century now government authorities have stuck by the same erroneous line. Without federal recognition, the Muwékma Ohlone are prevented from relating to U.S. institutions as one government to another. Like California's rank-and-file labor movement throughout the twentieth century, they have only been entitled to what they could get themselves — unofficially, unrecognized. But at a certain point, refusing to see is no longer an option.

In the 1980s, municipal leaders in San Jose pumped millions of dollars into redeveloping the city's downtown as a tech hub, hoping to draw the new round of growing South Bay firms — Apple, specifically — to new offices. Steve Jobs met with more than one San Jose mayor during the period, dreaming up plans for a whole industrial park and his own rehabbed-warehouse mansion. His successor, John Sculley, continued the conversation.[8] By 1985, the city's hope was to get Apple to anchor the redeveloping downtown with its corporate headquarters. To handle whatever artifacts were unearthed during the digging, the city contracted the Archaeological Resource Service (ARS), a small local firm that conducts "cultural resource evaluations," mostly for government agencies. In 1976, California established the state Native American Heritage Commission, which seems to have been a boon for consultants such as Katherine Flynn and William Roop, the ARS principals. As a white Anglo

firm working in recently colonized territory, bound to run into objects and
remains from (and, as recognized by statute, belonging to) existing tribes, ARS
should face a high level of scrutiny. It's one they haven't always met. After ARS
found bones at the San Jose development, the officially unrecognized Muwékma
Ohlone protested the dig, which the city and its contractors declined to halt.
With billions of dollars at stake, it's hard to see how it could, despite every
narrative warning the world's many cultures offer about the consequences of
disturbing other people's burial grounds. But even capital's impersonal compul-
sions can't be decisive every minute of every day. Roop had no choice but to
stop digging after the Muwékma Ohlone tribal chairwoman, Rosemary Cambra, hit him with a shovel.

No matter what the feds say, there is only so long you can decline to recognize someone who is hitting you with a shovel. Cambra pleaded a charge
of assault with intent to kill down to simple assault, and the judge had her
serve a year of weekends in jail so that she could continue caring for her three
kids. The San Jose confrontation was the latest in a series of Cambra's Red
Power actions that date back to 1969, when she took a fishing boat out to join
the Indians of All Tribes occupation of Alcatraz. The child of NorCal farmworkers who probably would have been categorized as Hispanic based on their
last name, Sanchez, Cambra knew for sure that the Verona Band lineage was
ongoing: Her mother, Dolores, was born in 1911, during the period when the
Ohlone were erased from the books, and she was baptized at Mission San Jose.
Dolores's mother, Ramona Marine, was, too, and she was buried at Yuki Kutsuimi Šaatoš Inūxʷ, the Ohlone Indian cemetery, in 1921.[9] These ancestral
burial grounds were located under and around Leland's stock farm, birthplace
of the Palo Alto System. At the time of Ramona Marine Sanchez's death, the
land was owned by Stanford University, and Herbert Hoover was already on
his way to the executive branch. Now the burial grounds cross the edge of
campus, where the school is bordered by Sand Hill Road, the district that
houses the highest concentration of venture capitalists in Silicon Valley and
(based on pure conjecture) one of the highest concentrations of capital of any
kind in world history.* As you've seen, that sounds like a longer time than it is.

---

*   Sitting on top of the burial ground is the Stock Farm Road Children's Center, an early-
    childhood learning program affiliated with Stanford.

When we talk about indigenous ancestors in California whose resting places have been displaced and disturbed by Leland Stanford's capitalist eugenics project, we can do so in the sense of living people's proximate relatives. Leland Stanford Jr. was born five years after Avelina Cornates Yakilamne, Ramona Marine's mother, Dolores Sanchez's grandmother, Rosemary Cambra's great-grandmother, and the great-great-grandmother of the Muwékma Ohlone Tribal Council's current chairwoman, Charlene Nijmeh. Leland Stanford Jr., of course, had no children. Except, as his parents once declared, people like me. Of course Palo Alto is haunted. An investigation of why that is should lead us here.

Stanford does not need to wait for the U.S. federal government to recognize the Muwékma Ohlone's sovereign claim. The university has already demonstrated that: In 1989, in what the *New York Times* called an "exceptional agreement," Stanford worked with Cambra to return hundreds of Ohlone skeletons to the tribe for reburial.[10] It was a voluntary move made under student-activist pressure — as well as the pressure of Cambra's demonstrated ability to drive attention. The reaction from the settler academic community was almost pure condemnation. The officially neutral president of the American Anthropological Association, Roy Rappaport, told the *Times* that "everybody wants to satisfy the Indians, but we would like to find ways to make it possible for us to continue to learn what we can from the remains." The consensus, however, has changed, and history already judges Stanford authorities ahead of their time on this count relative to their peer institutions. By recognizing the Muwékma Ohlone, the university set a precedent. But is recognition enough?

In his purposing of anticolonial theorist Frantz Fanon, *Red Skin, White Masks: Rejecting the Colonial Politics of Recognition*, Yellowknives Dene scholar Glen Coulthard criticizes the "largely rights-based/recognition orientation that has emerged as hegemonic over the last four decades" within indigenous politics, an attitude that harks back to the 1970s and the cultural path of Panther-inspired politics in the final quarter of the twentieth century.[11] In its place, Coulthard calls for "a resurgent politics of recognition that seeks to practice decolonial, gender-emancipatory, and economically non-exploitative alternative structures of law and sovereign authority grounded on a critical refashioning of the best of Indigenous legal and political traditions." This decolonization agenda is founded on, in the concise one-word sentence of

Malcolm X: "Land." Control over territory is necessary for that critical refashioning, which is a futuristic, forward-looking process. But here, the same Ohlone land, the territory that could provide a basis for the kind of practice and experimentation Coulthard lays out, has been the foundation for the rise of Stanford, the Palo Alto System, Silicon Valley, and the capitalist world built on top of it. It's a high-stakes town.

I can't know what it would be like in practice for Stanford to withdraw from Palo Alto, and I understand that at first it probably strikes many readers as a maximalist proposal, but in the context of the exhausting trends we've observed since the Anglo colonization of Alta California, returning the land strikes me as downright pragmatic. I assume that the Muwékma Ohlone's moral-historical claim will not persuade the Stanford board of trustees to turn the 8,000-plus acres over, regardless of who is buried there. I don't expect that the spiritual pain haunting the people who have settled in Palo Alto will be decisive, either, no matter how many of the community's children destroy themselves and no matter how historically resonant their suicide method is. It's obvious how Palo Alto *won't* change.

For a moment, however, let's say in theory that the board could be convinced by a reasoned argument that earth and the people who live here would be better off in important ways if Stanford—the largest landowner and leading organization in Palo Alto, at least—turned over the land it occupies and its other assets derived thereby to indigenous claimants. Let's also assume the courts recognize that Leland and Jane Stanford's injunction against transferring the land is less legitimate than the ancestral right of the people they took it from, and are willing to allow the move. With those modest suppositions in place, I don't think it is a hard case to make. The Palo Alto System elevates few and subordinates many by design, and it uses up the land to do it. (Recall the wholesale destruction of half the North American continent required to finance this new California Harvard in the first place.) The rise of global capitalism has rapidly reduced the planet's habitability in fewer than two centuries; does anyone seriously believe this place can survive that way for another two? If the creatures of the earth are to have a medium-term chance, then at the very least we need some space right now to develop, practice, and deploy new modes of production, distribution, and reproduction—social metabolism. As a fortuitously located, substantial piece of land to which hundreds of identified indigenous people have a specific claim and where, contrariwise, *no individual settler holds a property deed*, the acres known during the long twentieth century as Stanford present a unique opportunity for the human race. As that plot of land once nurtured the Silicon Valley extraction machine, by repurposing this tiny corner of what was taken from American Indians, it could be possible to draw a new path, away from exhaustion and toward recovery, repair, and renewal.

Palo Alto is a great place for an international indigenous hub; as the scholar Renya Ramirez writes in her apposite study, *Native Hubs: Culture, Community, and Belonging in Silicon Valley and Beyond*, it already has been one.[12] Indian relocation sent a disproportionate number of tribal members from job-poor reservations around the country to the booming Bay Area during the postwar space settler years. Indians from Mexico and Central America came north during the century's fourth quarter, driven by falling commodity prices, climate change, state terror, and capitalist gangsterism. Devastated by the changes to the coffee market, Mixtecos from the Mexican state of Oaxaca now comprise California's largest indigenous community.[13] As with Vietnamese immigration to the Bay Area after the war, violent proletarianization and displacement fed growth in Silicon Valley and the larger Cold War West. This drew indigenous people to the state from across the Pacific even; California has the world's fifth-largest Hmong population, behind China, Vietnam, Laos, and Thailand. The Bay Area also has the country's highest concentration of Pacific Islanders outside the Pacific Islands. As Renya Ramirez documents, these California international collisions haven't always been friendly or productive, but she gives the reader a sense of problems being worked through, of something big coming together as Indians in the Americas work across colonial borders. Ramirez is a member of the Winnebago Tribe of Nebraska as well as a Palo Altan. She grew up in town, the daughter of Anglo Stanford professor Robert Carver North and the indigenous activist, double Stanford graduate, and Palo Alto art teacher Woesha Cloud. Like Rosemary Cambra, Cloud joined the 1969 Alcatraz occupation, taking a long, strange commute to teach children's art at the experimental school. They arrived at an exhausted shell of a prison in the middle of the bay and created a school, and they did it in the name of Indians of All Tribes.

Repairing the world is a lot to ask from any people, and though I expect the $37 billion-plus (at the time of this writing) in the Stanford endowment would help, restoring the biosphere to sustainable footing is *the* task of our time. Foisting that job on indigenous tribes after everything the U.S.-led global order has put them through is, in the late twentieth-century NorCal lingo with which I was raised, a dick move. And yet it is American indigenous internationalists who have been most eager to assume the burden. In 2020, indigenous Bolivians led the movement that stopped a capitalist coup and returned the socialist party to power. In Canada and the U.S., indigenous pipeline blockades have been the main obstacle to the further extension of fossil-fuel infrastructure. In British Columbia, Wet'suwet'en hereditary chiefs have issued an eviction order to Coastal GasLink. The Dakota Access Pipeline blockade led by "water protectors" of the Standing Rock Sioux was a landmark act of resistance that I predict will have increasing significance as the century proceeds. And this is just a selection of examples. The Standing Rock sequence included what historians have called the continent's largest gathering of indigenous people in a century, invigorating a new radical internationalism between tribes.[14] It seems to me that the only way an institution like Stanford or a place like Palo Alto can truly invest in the twenty-first-century indigenous-led movement to protect the biosphere is to divest from the dynamics of colonialist exploitation that got us here in the first place. If we're going to make it, owners will have to give up on existing oil and gas reserves, forgo profits and accept losses, and if that's to happen without catastrophic violence, then it will require just the kind of renunciation I'm imagining for the Stanford lands. I can't think of anything better for Palo Alto, any greater tribute to the memory of that dead young man, than to begin this process.

Looking to the radical internationalist indigenous movement for leadership at this historical moment is not about some false nostalgia for a time before colonization and the rise of world capitalism. It's not even about some false nostalgia for the Panther-inspired militants of the 1960s and '70s, the high point of postwar California anticapitalism. As the Kul Wicasa activist-scholar Nick Estes writes, the water-protection movement exemplified by the Standing Rock camp, "as much as it reaches into the past, is a future-oriented project":

It forces some to confront their own unbelonging to the land and the river. How can settler society, which possesses no fundamental ethical relationship to the land or its original people, imagine a future premised on justice? There is no simple answer. But whatever the answer may be, Indigenous peoples must lead the way. Our history and long traditions of Indigenous resistance provide possibilities for futures premised on justice. After all, Indigenous resistance is animated by our ancestors' refusal to be forgotten, and it is our resolute refusal to forget our ancestors and our history that animates our visions for liberation. Indigenous revolutionaries are the ancestors from the before and before and the already forthcoming.[15]

The future need not be synonymous with the exhaustion of earth, the liquidation of the organized working class, the full commoditization of our time and environment. What is the point of being a species with the dual gifts of analysis and invention if we can't stop ourselves from despoiling the only home we've ever had? The forfeit of Stanford's vast accumulated wealth is the biggest immediate step toward a habitable planet I believe we can take at such a low cost. Unlike the proposal to return the U.S. national parks to indigenous control, ceding Palo Alto would require immediate sacrifice from particular elements of the ruling class, but without taking anything that could be reasonably said to *belong* to any living settlers.[16] Given nonprofit Stanford's surprisingly significant role in producing profit, breaking up the community wouldn't be painless for capital, but I see that as one of the proposal's virtues. The return and critical refashioning of the LSJU lands is something like the minimum required action to preserve the possibility of a relatively peaceful transition to a sustainable world system; if such a modest move remains unspeakable this late in the ecological game, then reasonable deliberation doesn't seem so reasonable after all. It can never be reasonable to destroy the planetary systems that preexist reason and provide its sole known foundation.

"Such planning and such action, however, will never be undertaken by a government run by and for the rich, as every capitalist government is and must be. *To demand these things from a capitalist government is to demand that it cease to be capitalist.*"[17] Pauls Baran and Sweezy wrote these sentences in *Monopoly Capital* with regard to the democratic demand that the state improve working-class housing, and they seem even more applicable here. Unfortunately, I do not think the Stanford board of trustees (a capitalist government of sorts) will return the university lands. If they wanted to, I do not think the courts would allow them to. As has been demonstrated repeatedly over the course of Palo Alto's history, profits protect themselves. Chairwoman Nijmeh puts it succinctly, sardonically: "The Bay Area's real estate is too expensive to belong to the indigenous population."[18]

Profits search for the necessary people, attitudes, and weapons to do what needs to be done, and profits find them. That is not just how capitalism works; that's how it's *supposed* to work. To the high priests of the ruling class in their literal Palo Alto tower that Herbert Hoover built, capitalism's steel coldness elevates it above the species with our partiality, above the planet and its specificity. Like God's, capital's ways are no more escapable for being destructive, even ghastly. By reducing everything to returns, the profit system can understand and process it all. It's a system of forces, not men, and if those forces only speak the language of cost, then so be it. Those of us devoted to the earth certainly can't let it burn because we're not willing to make ourselves understood.

Recall what the April Third Movement wrote about Stanford and Vietnam: "We are engaged in a conflict with the kind of men—and some of the very men—whose interests got us into Vietnam, and whose disenchantment with the rising costs of that conflict will eventually get us out.... The struggle at Stanford, then, is a microcosm: the trustees' intransigence will not give way to moral persuasion or majority votes any more than our outcries have ended the war. If this view is correct, then the trustees will respond only to rising costs." As the A3M found, it is possible by conscious force of will to remove one's self from capitalism's asset column and become a cost. Not easy, perhaps, but possible.

Eventually, capital will withdraw from Palo Alto. Given its druthers, capital will use the place up until it's no longer worth the trouble. Since capitalists like living in the Bay Area, by the time they're finished with it they're likely to have exhausted much of the rest of the planet. Though our problems face the world and the human species as a whole—just ask a Silicon Valley techie who can't go outside because there's too much smoke in the air—the solutions are of a different order. "For the earth to live, capitalism must die," Nick Estes concludes, and in retracing a materialist history of that system, it's hard to disagree.[19] And if, against the odds, the earth's partisans win that battle, if through the rapid coordinated flapping of wings we butterflies bring this chilly display case to a shattering concrete end, we will have fought it in collective self-defense, as a last resort. That's where we are now. The questions left, as Michi Saagiig Nishnaabeg political theorist Leanne Betasamosake Simpson lays them out, are "How?" and "With (and without) whom?"[20] Even in Palo Alto, that belly of the capitalist beast, history suggests that those questions have specific answers, if not precisely what those answers are. We have no choice but to find them.

Acknowledgments

Thank you to my wife, Julia, and the rest of my family: Grace and Zach; Aija, Tia, and Zoë; Max and Will; my parents, Daniel and Ellen; and every one of my countless aunts, uncles, and cousins — both by blood and by chance.

To my editors and publishers, whose wise judgment allows me to write for a living.

To my agent, Chris, and my editor, Jean, as well as the whole LB team.

To everyone who helped me get out of Palo Alto in one piece: Nick and the Nordlingers, the Foxes and the Coxe/Canines, Robert and Harmony Bakery; Susan Charles, Melinda Mattes, and Woj; Mary, Yuki, Sam, Ariel, Sabrina, Elena, Kelsey, Salome, Rachel, Clare, Skye, Andrew, Kevin, Josh, Hilary, Martin, Zack, Brian, Aaron, Lee, Sara, Maddie, Mollie, Meghan, Elissa, Johanna, Matt, Chris, Karishma, Jon, and even my dickhead wrestling coaches.

To the friends I made as an adult, without whom I would be a different, lesser person: Bob, David, JB, Jo, Jon, Mary, Legba, Sam, Anne, Emily, Johnny, Carly, Katelyn, Jessie, Lily, Brandon, Katie, Robin, Erin, Dee, Sarah, Cecilia, Miranda, Laurie, L.e., Chip, Mike, Matt, Mitch.

To the New Inquiry: Rachel, Rob, Atossa, Sarah, Vicky, Tash, Monalisa, Aaron, Hannah, Ayesha, Sam, Jesse, Adrian, Emily, Nathan, Autumn, Olivia, Helena, Brian, Sarah Nicole, Michael, and JC.

To my academic friends, who are willing to overlook my missing credentials: Tim, Branden, Charles, Shalini, Zach, and Madeline.

To the Philly Childcare Collective and the rest of the InterGalactic Conspiracy of ChildCare Collectives.

To the farms and farmworkers who kept me fed while I wrote: Fruitwood, Spring Hollow, Small Potato, as well as Bonnie and the rest of the Vanilya bagel crew.

To the George Floyd Uprising, the defining event of the period of this writing.

To the Muwékma, to whom Palo Alto will be returned.

To the planet Earth, its people, and its preservation by any means necessary.

Jean Garnett **Editor**

Gregg Kulick **Designer**

Elisa Rivlin **Legal Counsel**

Mary Tondorf-Dick **Managing Editor**

Ben Allen **Production Editor**

Barbara Clark **Copyeditor**

Erin Cain **Production Coordinator**

Alyssa Persons **Publicist**

Gabrielle Leporati **Associate Publicist**

Ayesha Chari **Publicity Intern**

Bryan Christian **Marketing Director**

Brandon Kelley **Marketing Operations**

Lauren Hesse **Social Media Director**

Khadijah Mitchell **Assistant Editor**

Liv Ryan **Editorial Assistant**

Ghenet Harvey **Audio Production Manager**

Thomas Mis **Audio Producer**

Bruce Nichols **Publisher**

Craig Young **Deputy Publisher**

Notes

Chapter 0.1 Introduction

1. Hanna Rosin, "The Silicon Valley Suicides," *The Atlantic,* November 17, 2015.
2. C. Wright Mills, *The Sociological Imagination* (New York: Oxford University Press, 2000), 13.

Chapter 1.1 To Whom Time Is Money

1. Benjamin Madley, *An American Genocide: The United States and the California Indian Catastrophe, 1846–1873,* The Lamar Series in Western History (New Haven: Yale University Press, 2016), 315.
2. Josiah Royce, *California, from the Conquest in 1846 to the Second Vigilance Committee in San Francisco [1856]: A Study of American Character* (New York: Houghton, Mifflin, 1886), 60.
3. Robert F. Heizer and Alan J. Almquist, *The Other Californians, Prejudice and Discrimination Under Spain, Mexico, and the United States to 1920* (Berkeley: University of California Press, 1971), 19.
4. Albert L. Hurtado, *Indian Survival on the California Frontier,* Yale Western Americana Series 35 (New Haven: Yale University Press, 1988), 57.
5. Charles Howard Shinn, *Mining Camps: A Study in American Frontier Government* (New York: Charles Scribner's Sons, 1885), 212.
6. "The same rule which would admit them to testify, would admit them to all the equal rights of citizenship, and we might soon see them at the polls, in the jury box, upon the bench, and in our legislative halls." *People v. Hall,* 4 Cal. 399, 405 (1854).
7. Peter Burnett, "Governors of California—State of the State Address," January 6, 1851, https://governors.library.ca.gov/addresses/s_01-Burnett2.html.
8. Madley, *An American Genocide,* 3; Roxanne Dunbar-Ortiz, *An Indigenous Peoples' History of the United States* (Boston: Beacon Press, 2014), 130.
9. Robert F. Heizer, ed., *The Destruction of the California Indians* (Lincoln: University of Nebraska Press, 1993), 305.
10. Eric Williams, *Capitalism & Slavery* (Chapel Hill: University of North Carolina Press, 1944), 145.
11. *Woodruff v. North Bloomfield Gravel Mining Co.,* 16 F. 25 (D. Cal. 1883).
12. Jeffrey Michael Bartos, "Mining for Empire: Gold, American Engineers, and Transnational Extractive Capitalism, 1889–1914" (PhD diss., Montana State University, 2018), 4, https://scholarworks.montana.edu/xmlui/handle/1/15077.
13. Stephen J. Pitti, *The Devil in Silicon Valley: Northern California, Race, and Mexican Americans* (Princeton: Princeton University Press, 2003), 33.
14. *The Fossat or Quicksilver Mine Case,* 69 U.S. 649 (1864). Though not entitled to one under the ruling, Barron and Forbes extracted a payment from Quicksilver via an armed standoff of hundreds of men.

15. Pitti, *The Devil in Silicon Valley*, 40.

16. It also helped support a local newspaper, the *San Jose Mercury*, which launched in the early 1850s.

17. Mary Hallock Foote, *New Almaden: Or, A California Mining Camp: Life in 1877 at New Almaden as Pictured in Word and Illustration* (Fresno, CA: Valley Publishers, 1878), 482.

18. Richard A. Walker, *The Conquest of Bread: 150 Years of Agribusiness in California* (London: The New Press, 2004), 165–66.

19. Ibid., 152.

20. Mike Davis, *Late Victorian Holocausts: El Niño Famines and the Making of the Third World* (New York: Verso, 2001), 121.

21. Sucheng Chan, *This Bittersweet Soil: The Chinese in California Agriculture, 1860–1910* (Berkeley: University of California Press, 1986), 124.

22. Ibid.

23. Ibid., 80.

24. It's worth noting that in Hawaii, Azorean immigrant workers were classified as "Caucasian but not white." Recent archaeological evidence suggests the islands between Europe and North Africa were *not* uninhabited when colonized by Portugal in the fifteenth century, contrary to long-held belief. Valentí Rull, Arantza Lara, María Jesús Rubio-Inglés, Santiago Giralt, Vítor Gonçalves, Pedro Raposeiro, Armand Hernández, et al. "Vegetation and Landscape Dynamics under Natural and Anthropogenic Forcing on the Azores Islands: A 700-Year Pollen Record from the São Miguel Island." *Quaternary Science Reviews* 159 (2017): 155–68, doi.org/10.1016/j.quascirev.2017.01.021.

25. Robert LeRoy Santos, *Azoreans to California: A History of Migration and Settlement* (Denair, CA: Alley-Cass Publications, 1995), 69.

26. There was no "Italy" per se yet; Luigi was from Genoa.

27. Paul Richard Steger, "A Historical Geography of the Bank of America's Branch Bank System, 1904–1970" (master's thesis, Ohio State University, 1975), 18–19, https://shareok.org/bitstream/handle/11244/19202/Thesis-1977-S8175h.pdf.

28. Janet Wasko, *Movies and Money: Financing the American Film Industry* (Norwood, NJ: Ablex Publishing Corporation, 1982), 121–22.

29. *Saturday Evening Post*, September 20, 1947, 119.

30. "Hearings Before the Committee on Banking on H.R. 6855" (1924), 185.

31. Mark Carlson and Kris James Mitchener, "Branch Banking and the Transformation of Banking in California," National Bureau of Economic Research, May 2005, http://www.cirje.e.u-tokyo.ac.jp/research/workshops/history/history_paper2005/mitchener.pdf, 2.

32. Joseph M. Collier, ed., *Americans Ethnics and Minorities* (Los Alamitos: Hwong Pub. Co., 1978), 247.

Chapter 1.2 The Combine

1. Myron Angel, *History of Placer County, California* (Franklin Classics, 2018), 392–94.

2. Horace Greeley, *An Overland Journey from New York to San Francisco in the Summer of 1859* (Lincoln: University of Nebraska Press, 1999), 360.

3. Richard White, *Railroaded: The Transcontinentals and the Making of Modern America* (New York: W. W. Norton, 2011), 19.

4. Central Pacific and Union Pacific Railroad Timetable, 1882, accessed March 8, 2022, http://cprr.org/Museum/Ephemera/CP-UP_Timetable_1882.html. Philip L. Fradkin and Andy Anderson, *Stagecoach: Wells Fargo and the American West* (New York: Simon & Schuster Source, 2002), 40–41.

5. Hearings Before the Committee on Finance, United States Senate, 72nd Cong., 2nd Sess., February 13–28, 1933, 283; Elmus Wicker, *Banking Panics of the Gilded Age* (Cambridge: Cambridge University Press, 2000), 18.

6. Frank Norris, *The Octopus: A Story of California* (New York: Doubleday, 1903), 576.

7. Hannah Catherine Davies, *Transatlantic Speculations: Globalization and the Panics of 1873,* (New York: Columbia University Press, 2018) 39.

8. Paul A. Baran and Paul Marlor Sweezy, *Monopoly Capital: An Essay on the American Economic and Social Order* (New York: Monthly Review Press, 1966), 226–27.

9. Rudolf Hilferding, *Finance Capital: A Study in the Latest Phase of Capitalist Development* (New York: Routledge, 2019), 119.

10. "Mr. Huntington and the Central Pacific Railway," *Economist,* April 20, 1895, 519.

11. A. J. Wilson, ed., *Investors' Review,* July to December 1897, vol. 10 (London: Clement Wilson, 1897), 25.

12. James Willway Treadwell, ed., *California Banker's Magazine: Commercial and Real Estate Review,* vols. 13–14 (Solihull, UK: J.W. Treadwell, 1896), 799.

13. *Santa Clara County v. Southern Pacific Railroad Company,* 118 U.S. 394 (1886).

14. "The High Cost and Remarkable Challenge of Building the CPRR Across the Sierras, and the Deserts of Nevada and Utah: Lewis M. Clement's 1887 Statement to the U.S. Pacific Railway Commission," accessed April 21, 2022, http://cprr.org/Museum/LMC_PacRRCommission _1887.html.

15. Gordon H. Chang, *Ghosts of Gold Mountain: The Epic Story of the Chinese Who Built the Transcontinental Railroad* (Boston: Houghton Mifflin Harcourt, 2019), 84.

16. Ibid., 148–49.

17. Mae Ngai, *The Chinese Question: The Gold Rushes, Chinese Migration, and Global Politics* (New York: W. W. Norton, 2021), 143.

18. Iyko Day, *Alien Capital: Asian Racialization and the Logic of Settler Colonial Capitalism* (Durham: Duke University Press, 2016), 130.

19. Alexander Saxton, *The Indispensable Enemy: Labor and the Anti-Chinese Movement in California* (Berkeley: University of California Press, 1995), 118.

20. Ibid., 149.

21. Chang, *Ghosts of Gold Mountain,* 233.

22. Manu Karuka, *Empire's Tracks: Indigenous Nations, Chinese Workers and the Transcontinental Railroad* (Oakland: University of California Press, 2019), xiv.

23. White, *Railroaded,* 255.

24. Friedrich Engels to Walther Borgius, January 25, 1894, https://www.marxists.org/archive/marx /works/1894/letters/94_01_25.htm.

Chapter 1.3 Blood That Trots Young

1. Richard A. Walker, *The Conquest of Bread: 150 Years of Agribusiness in California* (London: The New Press, 2004), 49.

2. Roland De Wolk, *American Disruptor: The Scandalous Life of Leland Stanford* (Oakland: University of California Press, 2019), 126.

3. James J. Ayers, *Gold and Sunshine, Reminiscences of Early California* (Boston: Richard G. Badger, 1922), 282–83.

4. Kenneth T. Jackson, *Crabgrass Frontier: The Suburbanization of the United States* (New York: Oxford University Press, 1987), 88.

5. Monica Hayde, "When the Farm Was Really a Farm," *Palo Alto Weekly,* August 19, 1994, https://www.paloaltoonline.com/weekly/morgue/cover/1994_Aug_19.COVER19.html.

6. Adam Longenbach, "Contagious Machines: New York City and the Horse Plague of 1872," *Thresholds* 49 (2021): 148–57, doi.org/10.1162/thld_a_00738.

7. Frank E. Frothingham, *The Boston Fire, November 9th and 10th, 1872, Its History, Together with the Losses in Detail of Both Real and Personal Estate. Also, a Complete List of Insurance Losses, and an Appendix Containing the City Loan, Insurance, and Building Acts* (Boston: Lee & Shepard Publishers, 1873), 6.

8. Terance J. Rephann, *The Economic Impact of the Horse Industry in Virginia: A Study Prepared for the Virginia Horse Industry Board* (Center for Economic and Policy Studies, Weldon Cooper Center for Public Service, 2011), 5.

9. Richard H. Steckel and William J. White, "Engines of Growth: Farm Tractors and Twentieth-Century U.S. Economic Welfare," NBER Working Paper 17879 (Cambridge, MA: National Bureau of Economic Research, 2012), 7, https://www.nber.org/system/files/working_papers/w17879/w17879.pdf.

10. Walker, *Conquest of Bread*, 165.

11. Phillip Thurtle, *The Emergence of Genetic Rationality: Space, Time, and Information in American Biological Science, 1870–1920* (Seattle: University of Washington Press, 2011), 52.

12. John Dimon, *American Horses and Horse Breeding: A Complete History of the Horse from the Remotest Period in His History to Date. The Horseman's Encyclopedia and Standard Authority on Horses, Embracing Breeds, Families, Breeding, Training, Shoeing, and General Management. The Modern and Practical Horse Doctor on the Cause, Nature, Symptoms, and Treatment of Diseases of All Kinds* (Hartford, CT: J. Dimon, 1895), 94.

13. Joseph Cairn Simpson, "Horses of California: From the Days of the Missions to the Present," *Sunset*, May 1902.

14. Charles Marvin, *Training the Trotting Horse: A Natural and Improved Method of Educating Trotting Colts and Horses, Based on Twenty Years Experience* (New York: Marvin Publishing Company, 1890), 224.

15. Leslie Macleod, "The Palo Alto Method of Training Trotters," *Wallace's Monthly*, June 1889, 255.

16. Marvin, *Training the Trotting Horse*, 187.

17. Stanford Historical Photograph Collection, Stanford University Libraries, Department of Special Collections and University Archives, box: 7, folder: Stanford carriages and coachmen—Muybridge.

18. Orrin Chalfant Painter, *Poems and Writings* (Baltimore: Arundel Press, John S. Bridges & Co., 1905), 70.

19. Edward Ball, *The Inventor and the Tycoon: The Murderer Eadweard Muybridge, the Entrepreneur Leland Stanford, and the Birth of Moving Pictures* (New York: Anchor Books, 2013), 123–25.

20. Rebecca Solnit, *River of Shadows: Eadweard Muybridge and the Technological Wild West* (London: Penguin, 2004), 191.

21. Arthur Mayer, *Eadweard Muybridge: The Stanford Years* (New York: Simon & Schuster, 1953), 29.

22. Allain Daigle, "Not a Betting Man: Stanford, Muybridge, and the Palo Alto Wager Myth," *Film History* 29, no. 4 (2017): 119.

23. Paul Virilio, *The Information Bomb* (London: Verso, 2005), 23.

24. Jessica B. Teisch, *Engineering Nature: Water, Development, and the Global Spread of American Environmental Expertise* (Chapel Hill: University of North Carolina Press, 2011), 99.

25. Mira Wilkins, *The History of Foreign Investment in the United States to 1914* (Cambridge, MA: Harvard University Press, 1989), 460.

26. Richard Rayner, *The Associates: Four Capitalists Who Created California* (New York: W. W. Norton, 2009), 120.

27. Claude S. Fischer, *Made in America: A Social History of American Culture and Character* (Chicago: University of Chicago Press, 2011), 115.

28. Ball, *The Inventor and the Tycoon*, 299.

29. Karen Sánchez-Eppler, "Children as Collectors of Cultural Heritage," in *Children, Childhood and Cultural Heritage*, ed. Kate Darian-Smith and Carla Pascoe (New York: Routledge, 2013), 247.

30. Leland Stanford to Miss Hull, February 12, 1884, in *In Memoriam: Leland Stanford, Jr*, compiled by Herbert Charles Nash, 1884, 57.

31. Ibid., 53.

32. Rayner, *The Associates*, 169.

33. *In Memoriam: Leland Stanford, Jr*, 1884, 226.

34. Orrin Leslie Elliott, *Stanford University: The First Twenty-Five Years* (Palo Alto: Stanford University, 1937), 19.

35. Herbert Charles Nash, *The Leland Stanford Jr. Museum: Origin and Description* (Palo Alto: Stanford University Museum of Art, 1886).

36. Lee Hall, *Olmsted's America: An "Unpractical" Man and His Vision of Civilization* (Boston: Bulfinch Press, 1995), 194–99.

37. *The Leland Stanford Junior University Circulars: 1–6* (Palo Alto: Stanford University, 1891), 22.

38. "Investments for Capital," *Santa Clara County, California* 1, no. 1 (San Francisco: Board of Trade of San Jose, September 1887), 71.

39. Ibid.

40. *Exercises of the Opening Day of the Leland Stanford Junior University: Thursday, October 1, 1891* (Palo Alto: Stanford University, 1891), 12.

Chapter 2.1 Local Ghosts

1. Roland De Wolk, *American Disruptor: The Scandalous Life of Leland Stanford* (Oakland: University of California Press, 2019), 187.

2. Jane Lathrop Stanford to David Starr Jordan, December 16, 1899, in Gunther W. Nagel, *Iron Will: The Life and Letters of Jane Stanford* (Stanford: Stanford Alumni Association, 1975), 155–56.

3. Robert W. P. Cutler, *The Mysterious Death of Jane Stanford* (Stanford: Stanford General Books, 2003), 32.

4. Stanford Digital Repository, Jane Lathrop Stanford papers, 1860–1975, "Jane Lathrop Stanford letter to Horace Davis Jan. 28, 1905," https://purl.stanford.edu/sn623dy4566.

5. David Starr Jordan, foreword to *Experiments in Psychical Research at Leland Stanford Junior University* by John Edgar Coover (Stanford: Stanford University, 1917), v.

6. Edward Alsworth Ross, *Social Control: A Survey of the Foundations of Order* (New York: Macmillan, 1901), 3.

7. Brian Eule, "Watch Your Words, Professor," *Stanford Magazine*, February 2015, https://stanfordmag.org/contents/watch-your-words-professor.

8. Hans-Joerg Tiede, *University Reform: The Founding of the American Association of University Professors* (Baltimore: Johns Hopkins University Press, 2015); Richard Hofstadter and Walter Paul Metzger, *The Development of Academic Freedom in the United States* (New York: Columbia University Press, 1955).

9. Cutler, *The Mysterious Death*, 121.

10. Bernhard J. Stern, "The Ward-Ross Correspondence III 1902–1903," *American Sociological Review* 12, no. 6 (1947): 716.

11. W. B. Carnochan, "The Case of Julius Goebel," *American Scholar* 72, no. 3 (summer 2003): 99.

12. In his new book-length investigation of the murder, Stanford historian Richard White concludes, "Bertha Berner killed Jane Stanford, and David Starr Jordan covered up the crime. Jordan was an accessory after the fact." Richard White, *Who Killed Jane Stanford?: A Gilded Age Tale of Murder, Deceit, Spirits and the Birth of a University* (New York: W. W. Norton, 2022), 299. Though it's worth noting that Jordan began covering up the crime *before* it was completed, making him, at least, an accessory *in media res*.

13. Cutler, *The Mysterious Death*, 12.

14. "Chinese Cook Suspected of Poisoning Mrs. Stanford," *San Francisco Call*, March 3, 1905, 1, https://chroniclingamerica.loc.gov/lccn/sn85066387/1905-03-03/ed-1/seq-1.

15. "Jordan Reasserts His Opinion That Death Resulted from Natural Causes," *San Francisco Call*, March 22, 1905, 1, https://chroniclingamerica.loc.gov/lccn/sn85066387/1905-03-22/ed-1/seq-1.

16. "Will Ignores Senator's Kin," *San Francisco Call*, March 7, 1906, 1, https://chroniclingamerica.loc.gov/lccn/sn85066387/1905-03-07/ed-1/seq-1.

17. Carnochan, "The Case of Julius Goebel," 103.

18. William James, Letter from William James to Theodore Flournoy, February 9, 1906, in Henry James, ed., *The Letters of William James*, vol. II (Boston: Atlantic Monthly Press, 1920), 266, https://www.gutenberg.org/files/38091/38091-h/38091-h.htm#page_266.

19. William James, "A Suggestion About Mysticism," *Journal of Philosophy, Psychology and Scientific Methods* 7, no. 4 (1910): 89.

20. Ah Wing, "Eyewitness Account of 1906 Earthquake (English)" (Stanford: Stanford University Library, 1906), https://purl.stanford.edu/qg394jw6197.

21. Linda Simon, "William James at Stanford," *California History* 69, no. 4 (1990): 341.

22. Timothy J. Sturgeon, "How Silicon Valley Came to Be," in Martin Kenney, ed., *Understanding Silicon Valley: The Anatomy of an Entrepreneurial Region* (Redwood City, CA: Stanford University Press, 2000), 21–22.

23. Ibid., 23.

24. Michael S. Malone, *Bill & Dave: How Hewlett and Packard Built the World's Greatest Company* (New York: Portfolio, 2007), 27.

25. Mike Adams, *Broadcasting's Forgotten Father: The Charles Herrold Story*, PBS video, 1995. https://youtu.be/5nIVv_2cGaQ.

Chapter 2.2 Bionomics

1. David Starr Jordan and Vernon Lyman Kellogg, *Evolution and Animal Life: An Elementary Discussion of Facts, Processes, Laws and Theories Relating to the Life and Evolution of Animals* (New York: D. Appleton, 1907), 8.

2. David Starr Jordan, *Foot-Notes to Evolution: A Series of Popular Addresses on the Evolution of Life* (New York: D. Appleton, 1907), 283.

3. Ibid., 277–98.

4. Ibid., 293.

5. Robert W. Sussman, *The Myth of Race: The Troubling Persistence of an Unscientific Idea* (Cambridge, MA: Harvard University Press, 2014), 57–59.

6. Ellwood Patterson Cubberley, *Public Education in the United States: A Study and Interpretation of American Educational History; an Introductory Textbook Dealing with the Larger Problems of Present-Day Education in the Light of Their Historical Development* (Boston: Houghton Mifflin, 1919), 338.

7. Ibid., 400.

8. Henry L. Minton, *Lewis M. Terman: Pioneer in Psychological Testing* (New York: NYU Press, 1988), 45.

9. Ibid., 43.

10. Stephen Jay Gould, *The Mismeasure of Man, Reissued* (New York: W. W. Norton, 1993), 150–51.

11. Carl Murchison, ed., *A History of Psychology in Autobiography*, vol. 2 (Worcester, MA: Clark University Press, 1932), 303.

12. Minton, *Lewis M. Terman*, 160.

13. Vernon Kellogg, "The University and Research," *Science* 54, no. 1384 (July 8, 1921): 21.

14. Lewis M. Terman, *The Measurement of Intelligence: An Explanation of and a Complete Guide for the Use of the Stanford Revision and Extension of the Binet-Simon Intelligence Scale* (Boston: Houghton Mifflin, 1916), 12–13.

15. David Starr Jordan, "The Blood of the Nation: A Study of the Decay of Races Through the Survival of the Unfit," *Popular Science Monthly*, June 1901, 137, and Vernon Lyman Kellogg, *Headquarters Nights: A Record of Conversations and Experiences at the Headquarters of the German Army in France and Belgium* (Boston: Atlantic Monthly Press, 1917).

16. Vernon Kellogg, "Eugenics and Militarism," *The Atlantic*, July 1913, https://www.theatlantic.com/magazine/archive/1913/07/eugenics-and-militarism/376208.

17. Minton, *Lewis M. Terman*, 65.

18. Ibid., 68.

19. Joel N. Shurkin, *Terman's Kids: The Groundbreaking Study of How the Gifted Grow Up* (Boston: Little, Brown, 1992), 27–28.

20. Lewis M. Terman, *Intelligence Tests and School Reorganization* (General Books, 2013), 19.

21. "Give Them Room," *Stanford Daily*, July 1, 1930, 2, https://archives.stanforddaily.com/1930/07/01?page=2&section=MODSMD_ARTICLE28#article.

22. Jean H. Fetter, *Questions and Admissions: Reflections on 100,000 Admissions Decisions at Stanford* (Redwood City, CA: Stanford University Press, 1995), 6.

23. Rebecca S. Lowen, *Creating the Cold War University: The Transformation of Stanford* (Berkeley: University of California Press, 1997), 229.

24. Kevin Starr, *Americans and the California Dream, 1850–1915* (New York: Oxford University Press, 1986), 336.

25. Ibid.

26. "Report on Football," *Stanford Daily*, March 30, 1906, 3, https://archives.stanforddaily.com/1906/03/30?page=3&section=MODSMD_ARTICLE10#article.

27. Jordan, *Foot-Notes to Evolution*, 320 (quoting Arthur Schopenhauer).

28. "Sex Equality and Co-Education," *Stanford Daily*, February 6, 1930, 2, https://archives.stanforddaily.com/1930/02/06?page=2&section=MODSMD_ARTICLE36#article.

29. Starr, *Americans and the California Dream, 1850–1915*, 327.

30. Bo Lojek, *William Shockley: The Will to Think* (Colorado Springs: Springer, 2021), 20.

31. Joel N. Shurkin, *Broken Genius: The Rise and Fall of William Shockley, Creator of the Electronic Age* (London: Macmillan, 2008), 51.

32. Glenna Matthews, *Silicon Valley, Women, and the California Dream: Gender, Class, and Opportunity in the Twentieth Century* (Redwood City, CA: Stanford University Press, 2003), 26.

33. Carey McWilliams, *Factories in the Field: The Story of Migratory Farm Labor in California* (Berkeley: University of California Press, 2000), 112.

34. Jia Lynn Yang, *One Mighty and Irresistible Tide: The Epic Struggle over American Immigration, 1924–1965* (New York: W. W. Norton & Company, 2020), 50.

35. Andrew C. Isenberg, *Mining California: An Ecological History* (New York: Hill and Wang, 2005), 95–96.

36. *Western Canner and Packer* 8, no. 9 (January 1917): 13.

37. Marquis James and Bessie Rowland James, *Biography of a Bank: The Story of Bank of America* (New York: Harper, 1954), 110–13.

38. Victoria Saker Woeste, *The Farmer's Benevolent Trust: Law and Agricultural Cooperation in Industrial America, 1865–1945* (Chapel Hill: University of North Carolina Press, 2000), 174.

39. Ibid., 182.

40. Nell Irvin Painter, *The History of White People* (New York: W. W. Norton, 2010), 275.

41. Alexandra Minna Stern, *Eugenic Nation: Faults and Frontiers of Better Breeding in Modern America* (Oakland: University of California Press, 2016), 84.

42. Joan Didion, *Where I Was From* (New York: Knopf Doubleday Publishing Group, 2012), 198.

43. Lewis M. Terman, "The Conservation of Talent," *School and Society,* March 1924, 363.

44. Matthews, *Silicon Valley, Women, and the California Dream*, 29; Michael W. McCann and George I. Lovell, *Union by Law: Filipino American Labor Activists, Rights Radicalism, and Racial Capitalism* (Chicago: University of Chicago Press, 2020), 69.

45. Mae M. Ngai, *Impossible Subjects: Illegal Aliens and the Making of Modern America* (Princeton: Princeton University Press, 2014), 27.

46. McWilliams, *Factories in the Field,* 130–31.

47. Sussman, *The Myth of Race,* 19; *Roldan v. Los Angeles County,* 129 Cal. App. 267, 18 P.2d 706 (1933).

48. Cecilia Tsu, *Garden of the World: Asian Immigrants and the Making of Agriculture in California's Santa Clara Valley* (New York: Oxford University Press, 2013), 178–82.

49. Matthews, *Silicon Valley, Women, and the California Dream,* 32.

50. Ngai, *Impossible Subjects,* 109.

51. Geoff Mann, *Our Daily Bread: Wages, Workers, and the Political Economy of the American West* (Chapel Hill, NC: UNC Press, 2007), 149.

52. Matthews, *Silicon Valley, Women, and the California Dream,* 37.

53. Adam Goodman, *Deportation Machine: America's Long History of Expelling Immigrants, Politics and Society in Modern America* (Princeton: Princeton University Press, 2020), 32.

54. McWilliams, *Factories in the Field,* 128.

55. Herbert G. Ruffin, *Uninvited Neighbors: African Americans in Silicon Valley, 1769–1990* (Norman, OK: University of Oklahoma Press, 2014), 59.

56. David Starr Jordan, "Anti-Imperialism," *San Francisco Call,* January 29, 1899, 21.

57. David Starr Jordan, "Heresy of Imperialism," *Wray Weekly Times,* October 13, 1900, 2.

58. "Faculty Elects a Hindu; Har Dayal to Teach Sanskrit at Leland Stanford University," *New York Times,* March 10, 1912, 4.

59. Mike Davis, *Late Victorian Holocausts: El Niño Famines and the Making of the Third World* (London; New York: Verso, 2001), 111.

60. "Yugantar Circular," December 23, 1912, South Asian American Digital Archive (SAADA), https://www.saada.org/item/20130303-1308.

61. Har Dayal, Letter from Har Dayal to Van Wyck Brooks (December 23, 1913), SAADA, https://www.saada.org/item/20111127-477.

62. Evelyn Roy, Letter to Henk Sneevliet, March 13, 1927, https://www.marxists.org/archive/roy-evelyn/1927/march/13.htm

63. Harjot Oberoi, "Ghadar Movement and Its Anarchist Genealogy," *Economic and Political Weekly* 44, no. 50 (2009): 42.

64. Devra Weber, "Wobblies of the Partido Liberal Mexicano," *Pacific Historical Review* vol. 85, no. 2 (May 2016): 188–226.

65. Daniel Kent Carrasco, "Breath of Revolution: Ghadar Anti-Colonial Radicalism in North America and the Mexican Revolution," *South Asia: Journal of South Asian Studies* 43, no. 6 (November 12, 2020): 12.

66. Edward T. Chang and Woo Sung Han, *Korean American Pioneer Aviators: The Willows Airmen* (Lanham, MD: Lexington Books, 2015).

67. Gary Y. Okihiro, *American History Unbound: Asians and Pacific Islanders* (Berkeley: University of California Press, 2015), 282.

Chapter 2.3 Hooverville

1. Herbert Hoover, *The Memoirs of Herbert Hoover: Years of Adventure, 1874–1920* (New York: Macmillan, 1951), 20.

2. Frank Angell, "Early History of Athletics at Stanford," in *The First Year at Stanford* (San Francisco: Stanley-Taylor Co., 1905), 53. Angell, among many other Stanford figures, later served on Hoover's Belgian relief commission.

3. Vernon Lyman Kellogg, *Herbert Hoover: The Man and His Work* (New York: D. Appleton, 1920), 49.

4. Patrick Bertola, Criena Fitzgerald, and Pamela Sharpe, "Italian Migrant Lives in the Western Australian Goldfields Before World War II," Working Papers 5050, Economic History Society, 2005.

5. Richard Hartley, "Bewick Moreing in Western Australian Gold Mining 1897–1904: Management Policies & Goldfields Responses," *Labour History* no. 65 (November, 1993): 1–18.

6. Jeffrey Bartos, "Mining for Empire: Gold, American Engineers, and Transnational Extractive Capitalism, 1889–1914" (PhD diss., Montana State University, 2018), 124–27, https://scholar works.montana.edu/xmlui/handle/1/15077.

7. Hoover, *The Memoirs of Herbert Hoover, 1874–1920,* 54.

8. Ian Phimister, "Foreign Devils, Finance and Informal Empire: Britain and China c. 1900–1912," *Modern Asian Studies* 40, no. 3 (2006): 741.

9. Hoover, *The Memoirs of Herbert Hoover, 1874–1920,* 74.

10. Jessica Karlsson, "Herbert Hoover's Apologia of His Chinese Mining Career 1899–1912, Untangling the Refutation Campaign" (master's thesis, Harvard University, 2018), 67.

11. Jeremy Mouat and Ian Phimister, "The Engineering of Herbert Hoover," *Pacific Historical Review* vol. 77, no. 4 (November 2008): 553–84.

12. Hoover, *The Memoirs of Herbert Hoover, 1874–1920,* 145.

13. Giovanni Arrighi, *The Long Twentieth Century: Money, Power, and the Origins of Our Times* (London; New York: Verso, 1994), 265.

14. Benjamin D. Rhodes, "British Diplomacy and 'Sir Herbert' Hoover, 1920–1933," in *Herbert Hoover Reassessed: Essays Commemorating the Fiftieth Anniversary of the Inauguration of Our Thirty-First President* (Washington, DC: U.S. Government Printing Office, 1981), 30.

15. Ellis W. Hawley, "Herbert Hoover, the Commerce Secretariat, and the Vision of an 'Associative State,' 1921–1928," *Journal of American History* 61, no. 1 (1974): 117.

16. Andrew Needham, *Power Lines: Phoenix and the Making of the Modern Southwest* (Princeton: Princeton University Press, 2016), 271n41. Other sources (Cumings, 2009; Starr, 1996) use the figure 15 percent, which seems either based on moves Southern California Edison made to improve its share after the revised division or a conflation of the company's guaranteed share and that of Los Angeles itself.

17. *Statistical Handbook of Civil Aviation* (Washington, DC: U.S. Government Printing Office, 1948), 42.

18. James Hansen, ed., *The Wind and Beyond: A Documentary Journey into the History of Aerodynamics in America* (Washington, DC: National Aeronautics and Space Administration, 2021), 604–8.

19. U.S. Congress, Senate, Special Committee to Investigate Air and Ocean Mail Contracts. *Resolution, Hearings Before a Special Committee on Investigation of Air Mail and Ocean Mail Contracts,* 73d Cong., 2nd Sess. (1934), 2926–28.

20. John Kenneth Galbraith, *The Great Crash of 1929* (Boston: Houghton Mifflin Harcourt, 2009), 40–42.

21. Jay Franklin, "Low Tide on the Potomac," *Vanity Fair,* September 1930, 33.

22. Herbert Hoover, *The Memoirs of Herbert Hoover: The Great Depression, 1929–1941* (New York: Macmillan, 1952), 63.

23. Hoover, *The Memoirs of Herbert Hoover, 1874–1920,* 102.

24. Ibid., 105.

25. Ibid., 108n6.

26. Albert E. Kahn, *High Treason: The Plot against the People* (New York: The Hour Publishers, 1951) 5–6n.

27. "1917 Constitution of Mexico," Article 27.

28. Kahn, *High Treason,* 5.

29. William T. Moye, "The End of the 12-Hour Day in the Steel Industry," *Monthly Labor Review* vol. 100, no. 9 (September 1977): 21–26.

30. Paul Dickson and Thomas B. Allen, *The Bonus Army: An American Epic* (New York: Walker & Co., 2004), 287–88.

31. Glenna Matthews, *Silicon Valley, Women, and the California Dream: Gender, Class, and Opportunity in the Twentieth Century* (Redwood City, CA: Stanford University Press, 2003), 50.

32. Carey McWilliams, *Factories in the Field: The Story of Migratory Farm Labor in California* (Berkeley: University of California Press, 2000), 188–89.

33. "THE PRESIDENCY: The Hoover Week: Jul. 29, 1929," *Time,* July 29, 1929, http://content.time.com/time/subscriber/article/0,33009,786023,00.html.

34. Wofford B. Camp et al., *Cotton, Irrigation, and the AAA: Transcript, 1962–1966* (Berkeley: University of California, 1971), 79.

35. Ibid., 116.

36. "Hoover Ranch Symbol of Bankruptcy of Capitalist Farming," *Western Worker,* July 15, 1932, 2, https://www.marxists.org/history/usa/pubs/westernworker/1932/v1n14-jul-15-1932.pdf.

37. Justin Akers Chacón and Mike Davis, *No One Is Illegal: Fighting Violence and State Repression on the U.S.-Mexico Border* (Chicago: Haymarket Books, 2006), 270.

38. Ibid., 51–52.

39. Kathryn S. Olmsted, *Right out of California: The 1930s and the Big Business Roots of Modern Conservatism* (New York: New Press, 2015), 50.

40. Rodolfo D. Acuña, *Corridors of Migration: The Odyssey of Mexican Laborers, 1600–1933* (Tucson: University of Arizona Press, 2007) 270.

41. Chacón and Davis, *No One Is Illegal,* 54.

42. "The California Cotton Pickers Strike–1933," in Federal Writers' Project, "Monographs Prepared for a Documentary History of Migratory Farm Labor, 1938," ed. Raymond P. Barry, University of California Bancroft Library, BANC MSS 72/187 c, 26–27.

43. Ibid., 19.

44. Anne Loftis, "The Man Who Preached Strike," *Pacific Historian* 30, no. 2 (1986): 71–72.

45. Devra Weber, *Dark Sweat, White Gold: California Farm Workers, Cotton, and the New Deal* (Berkeley: University of California Press, 1994), 109.

46. Ibid.

47. Olmsted, *Right out of California,* 78.

48. Ibid., 79.

49. Camp et al., *Cotton, Irrigation, and the AAA,* 212–13.

50. Frank P. Barajas, *Curious Unions: Mexican American Workers and Resistance in Oxnard, California, 1898–1961* (Lincoln: University of Nebraska Press, 2012), 159.

51. Ibid., 22.

52. The Bancroft Library Regional Oral History Office, *Politics, Farming, and the Progressive Party in California: Oral History with Philip Bancroft,* 1961, http://archive.org/details/cabeuroh_000021.

53. U.S. Congress, Senate, "Violations of Free Speech and Rights of Labor," *Hearings Before a Subcommittee of the Committee on Education and Labor,* 76th Cong., 3rd Sess. (1940), 25079, 25274.

54. Ibid., 20614.

55. Ibid., 20613.

56. Vivian M. Raineri, *The Red Angel: The Life and Times of Elaine Black Yoneda, 1906–1988* (New York: International Publishers, 1991), 72–73.

57. David F. Selvin, *A Terrible Anger: The 1934 Waterfront and General Strikes in San Francisco* (Detroit: Wayne State University Press, 1996), 192.

58. Ibid., 196.

59. U.S. Congress, Senate, "Violations of Free Speech and Rights of Labor," 25295.

60. Selvin, *A Terrible Anger,* 222.

61. McWilliams, *Factories in the Field,* 228.

62. Ibid.

63. U.S. Congress, Senate, "Violations of Free Speech and Rights of Labor," 25323.

64. Ibid., 25560.

65. *See* Nelson A. Pichardo Almanzar and Brian W. Kulik, *American Fascism and the New Deal: The Associated Farmers of California and the Pro-Industrial Movement* (Lewiston, NY: Edwin Mellen Press, 2012).

66. Camp et al., *Cotton, Irrigation, and the AAA,* 212.

67. Vladimir Lenin, *Imperialism, The Highest Stage of Capitalism* (Moscow: Foreign Languages Publishing House, 1963), 65.

Chapter 2.4 Men with Potential

1. Lee de Forest, *Father of Radio: The Autobiography of Lee de Forest* (Chicago: Wilcox & Follett, 1950), 276.

2. James A. Hijiya, *Lee de Forest and the Fatherhood of Radio* (Bethlehem, PA: Lehigh University Press, 1992), 95.

3. Tim Sturgeon, *The Origins of Silicon Valley: The Development of the Electronics Industry in the San Francisco Bay Area* (Berkeley: University of California, 1992), 38.

4. "Personals," *Journal of Electricity and Western Industry,* February 1, 1921, 147.

5. *Schick Dry Shaver v. Motoshaver,* 25 F. Supp. 346, 39 U.S.P.Q. (BNA) 361 (S.D. Cal. 1938).

6. Ted Dealey, " 'The Dallas Spirit': The Last Fool Flight," *Southwestern Historical Quarterly* 63, no. 1 (1959): 15–30.

7. Quoted in Sturgeon, *The Origins of Silicon Valley,* 43.

8. Jane Morgan, *Electronics in the West: The First Fifty Years* (Washington, DC: National Press Books, 1967), 95.

9. John Leslie and Ross Synder, "History of the Early Days of Ampex Corporation," *AES Historical Committee,* December 17, 2010, 1–2, https://www.aes.org/aeshc/docs/company.histories/ampex/leslie_snyder_early-days-of-ampex.pdf.

10. Christophe Lécuyer, *Making Silicon Valley: Innovation and the Growth of High Tech, 1930–1970, Inside Technology* (Cambridge, MA: MIT Press, 2006), 56–57.

11. "Electrons Do Rhumba, Give Savants New Type of Radio," *Arizona Republic,* January 31, 1939, 24.

12. C. Stewart Gillmor, *Fred Terman at Stanford: Building a Discipline, a University, and Silicon Valley* (Redwood City, CA: Stanford University Press, 2004), 23.

13. Ibid., 70.

14. J. A. Boyd et al., eds., *Electronic Countermeasures* (Ann Arbor: University of Michigan Institute of Science and Technology, 1961), 2–21.

15. Lécuyer, *Making Silicon Valley,* 68.

16. Joel Shurkin, *Broken Genius: The Rise and Fall of William Shockley, Creator of the Electronic Age* (London: Macmillan, 2008), 64.

17. Bo Lojek, *William Shockley: The Will to Think* (Cham, Switzerland: Springer, 2021), 59.

18. Michael Kort, *The Columbia Guide to Hiroshima and the Bomb* (New York: Columbia University Press, 2007), 102.

19. William Shockley, "On the Economics of Atomic Bombing," *National Archives at College Park,* "Dr. W. B. Shockley's Files, 1942–1946 (Records of William B Shockley Relating to the Use of Radar in Very Heavy Bombardment Operations)."

20. H. H. Arnold, "Air Force in the Atomic Age," in *One World or None: A Report to the Public on the Full Meaning of the Atomic Bomb* (New York: McGraw-Hill, 1946), 26–38.

21. David Starr Jordan, "Relations of Japan and the United States," *Journal of Race Development* 2, no. 3 (1912): 215–23.

22. "Japanese Becomes Stanford Teacher," *San Francisco Call,* June 3, 1908, 4.

23. Gordon Chang, *Morning Glory, Evening Shadow: Yamato Ichihashi and His Internment Writings, 1942–1945* (Redwood City, CA: Stanford University Press, 1997), 45.

24. Ibid., 52.

25. Ibid., 56–57.

26. Noboru Shirai, *Tule Lake: An Issei Memoir* (Sacramento, CA: Muteki Press, 2001), 16.

27. Ibid., 17.

28. Chang, *Morning Glory, Evening Shadow,* 100.

29. Ibid., 215.

30. Karl G. Yoneda, *Ganbatte: Sixty-Year Struggle of a Kibei Worker* (Los Angeles: Resource Development and Publications, Asian American Studies Center, University of California, Los Angeles, 1983), 123.

31. Ibid., 115. Yoneda was born in California but educated in Japan, making him *Kibei,* though a politically unorthodox one.

32. Ibid., 123.

33. Ibid., 164.

34. Benjamin Justice, "When the Army Got Progressive: The Civil Affairs Training School at Stanford University, 1943–1945," *History of Education Quarterly* 51, no. 3 (August 2011): 330–61.

35. Ernesto Galarza, *Barrio Boy: With Connections* (Austin, TX: Holt, Rinehart and Winston, 2000), 211.

36. Ernest Galarza, *Labor in Latin America* (Washington, DC: American Council on Public Affairs, 1943), 1.

37. Ibid., 2.

38. Richard Chabran, "Activism and Intellectual Struggle in the Life of Ernesto Galarza (1905–1984) with an Accompanying Bibliography," *Hispanic Journal of Behavioral Sciences* 7, no. 2 (1985): 134–52.

39. Armando Ibarra, Rodolfo Torres, and Ernesto Galarza, *Man of Fire: Selected Writings* (Champaign: University of Illinois Press, 2013), 275–76; Ernesto Galarza, *Farm Workers and Agribusiness in California, 1947–1960* (Notre Dame, IN: Notre Dame Press, 1977), 316.

40. Ernesto Galarza, "The Burning Light: Action and Organizing in the Mexican Community in California" (oral history, the Bancroft Library, University of California, Berkeley, 1981), 25.

41. Art Fong, "My Life and Times," HP Memory Project (2012), https://www.hpmemoryproject .org/timeline/art_fong/life_and_times_02.htm.

42. Ibid.

43. Ibid.

44. Chester B. Himes, *If He Hollers Let Him Go* (Garden City, NY: Doubleday, Doran & Co., 1945), 138.

Chapter 3.1 Space Settlers

1. Vannevar Bush, "Science—The Endless Frontier," July 1945, https://www.nsf.gov/od/lpa /nsf50/vbush1945.htm.

2. Rebecca S. Lowen, *Creating the Cold War University: The Transformation of Stanford* (Berkeley: University of California Press, 1997), 52.

3. Ann R. Markusen and Joel Yudken, *Dismantling the Cold War Economy* (New York: Basic Books, 1992), 105.

4. Lowen, *Creating the Cold War University*, 52.

5. S. W. Leslie and B. Hevly, "Steeple building at Stanford: Electrical engineering, physics, and microwave research," in *Proceedings of the IEEE* 73, no. 7 (July 1985), 1169–80.

6. Audra J. Wolfe, *Competing with the Soviets: Science, Technology, and the State in Cold War America* (Baltimore: Johns Hopkins University Press, 2013), 42.

7. Lowen, *Creating the Cold War University*, 181.

8. Ibid., 118.

9. John M. Findlay, *Magic Lands: Western Cityscapes and American Culture After 1940* (Berkeley: University of California Press, 1992), 122.

10. AnnaLee Saxenian, *Regional Advantage: Culture and Competition in Silicon Valley and Route 128* (Cambridge, MA: Harvard University Press, 1996), 23.

11. Glenna Matthews, *Silicon Valley, Women, and the California Dream: Gender, Class, and Opportunity in the Twentieth Century* (Redwood City, CA: Stanford University Press, 2003), 122; Margaret O'Mara, *The Code: Silicon Valley and the Remaking of America* (New York: Penguin Press, 2020), 19.

12. Findlay, *Magic Lands*, 32.

13. Ibid., 147.

14. Michael S. Malone, *The Valley of Heart's Delight: A Silicon Valley Notebook 1963–2001* (New York: John Wiley & Sons, 2002), 76.

15. Giovanni Arrighi, *The Long Twentieth Century: Money, Power, and the Origins of Our Times* (New York: Verso, 1994), 296–97.

16. Ann R. Markusen, *Profit Cycles: Oligopoly, and Regional Development* (Cambridge, MA: MIT Press, 1985), 86, 247.

17. Findlay, *Magic Lands,* 144.
18. David Harvey, *The Enigma of Capital: And the Crises of Capitalism* (London: Profile, 2010), 170.
19. Findlay, *Magic Lands,* 130.
20. Congressional Research Service, "The Defense Production Act of 1950: History, Authorities, and Considerations for Congress," March 2, 2020, 14–15, https://sgp.fas.org/crs/natsec /R43767.pdf.
21. U.S. Department of Commerce, Advisory Committee on Zoning, "A Standard State Zoning Enabling Act Under Which Municipalities May Adopt Zoning Regulations" (Washington, DC: Government Printing Office, 1924), 4–5.
22. Kenneth T. Jackson, *Crabgrass Frontier: The Suburbanization of the United States* (New York: Oxford University Press, 1987), 194.
23. Ibid.
24. Thomas J. Sugrue, *The Origins of the Urban Crisis: Race and Inequality in Postwar Detroit* (Princeton: Princeton University Press, 2014) 43.
25. Richard Rothstein, *The Color of Law: A Forgotten History of How Our Government Segregated America* (New York: Liveright Publishing Corporation, 2018), 11.
26. Ibid., 13.
27. Robert C. Ellickson, "The Zoning Strait-Jacket: The Freezing of American Neighborhoods of Single-Family Houses," SSRN Scholarly Paper (Rochester, NY: Social Science Research Network, January 7, 2020), 22, https://papers.ssrn.com/abstract=3507803.
28. Gennady Sheyner, "Palo Alto Mulls Raising the Height Limit for New Buildings," *Palo Alto Weekly,* November 25, 2016.
29. Rothstein, *The Color of Law,* 13.
30. Jackson, *Crabgrass Frontier,* 216.
31. Joe Nocera, "The Day the Credit Card Was Born," *Washington Post,* November 4, 1994.
32. Ibid.
33. P. J. Wolman, "The Oakland General Strike of 1946," *Southern California Quarterly* 57, no. 2 (1975): 147–78.
34. Jack Metzgar, "The 1945–1946 Strike Wave," in *The Encyclopedia of Strikes in American History,* ed. Aaron Brenner, Benjamin Day, and Immanuel Ness (Armonk, NY: M.E. Sharpe, 2009), 223–24.
35. Matthews, *Silicon Valley, Women, and the California Dream,* 122.
36. Ibid., 121.
37. Stephen J. Pitti, *The Devil in Silicon Valley: Northern California, Race, and Mexican Americans* (Princeton: Princeton University Press, 2003), 129.
38. John Kenneth Galbraith, *The New Industrial State* (Harmondsworth, UK: Penguin, 1974), 256.
39. Carey McWilliams, *Fool's Paradise: A Carey McWilliams Reader* (Santa Clara: Santa Clara University; Berkeley: Heyday Books, 2001), 140–41.
40. Rachel Brahinsky, "'Hush Puppies,' Communalist Politics, and Demolition Governance: The Rise and Fall of the Black Fillmore," in *Ten Years That Shook the City: San Francisco 1968–1978,* ed. Chris Carlsson and Lisa Ruth Elliott (San Francisco: City Lights Books, 2011), 145.
41. Chris Rhomberg, *No There There: Race, Class, and Political Community in Oakland* (Berkeley: University of California Press, 2004), 99.
42. Herbert G. Ruffin, *Uninvited Neighbors: African Americans in Silicon Valley, 1769–1990* (Norman, OK: University of Oklahoma Press, 2014), 102.
43. Ibid., 82.
44. Julia Lovell, *Maoism: A Global History* (Vintage, 2020), 91.

45. Dana J. Johnson, "Roles and Missions for Conventionally Armed Heavy Bombers—An Historical Perspective," A RAND NOTE (Santa Monica, CA: RAND, 1994), 39, https://www.rand.org/content/dam/rand/pubs/notes/2008/N3481.pdf.

46. Thomas McKelvey Cleaver, *Holding the Line: The Naval Air Campaign in Korea* (Oxford, UK: Osprey Publishing, 2019), 16.

47. Archie Brown, *The Rise and Fall of Communism* (New York: Ecco, 2009), 190.

48. Lowen, *Creating the Cold War University*, 120, 156.

49. Curt Cardwell, *NSC 68 and the Political Economy of the Early Cold War* (New York: Cambridge University Press, 2011), 212; C. Wright Mills, *The Power Elite* (New York: Oxford University Press, 1959), 217.

50. Lowen, *Creating the Cold War University*, 119.

51. Walter Johnson, *The Broken Heart of America: St. Louis and the Violent History of the United States* (New York: Basic Books, 2020), 287.

52. Adam Goodman, *Deportation Machine: America's Long History of Expelling Immigrants, Politics and Society in Modern America* (Princeton: Princeton University Press, 2020), 52.

53. Jordan T. Camp, *Incarcerating the Crisis: Freedom Struggles and the Rise of the Neoliberal State* (Oakland: University of California Press, 2016), 31.

54. Greg Grandin, *The End of the Myth: From the Frontier to the Border Wall in the Mind of America* (New York: Metropolitan Books, 2020), 146.

55. Lowen, *Creating the Cold War University*, 206, 208, 218.

56. John Kenneth Galbraith, *A Life in Our Times: Memoirs* (Boston: Houghton Mifflin, 1981), 219–20.

57. Paul A. Baran, *The Political Economy of Growth* (New York: Monthly Review Press, 1957), 35.

58. Ibid., 122.

59. Lawrence F. Lifschultz, "Could Karl Marx Teach Economics in America?" *Ramparts Magazine,* April 1974, 56.

60. Nicholas Baran and John Bellamy Foster, eds., *The Age of Monopoly Capital: Selected Correspondence of Paul M. Sweezy and Paul A. Baran, 1949–1964,* (New York: NYU Press, 2017), 411.

61. Ron Rapoport, "Everybody Lost a Little," *Frontier Magazine,* November 1962, 9.

62. Paul A. Baran and Paul Marlor Sweezy, *Monopoly Capital: An Essay on the American Economic and Social Order* (New York: Monthly Review Press, 1966), 332.

63. Baran, *The Political Economy of Growth*, 26.

64. Johnson, *The Broken Heart of America*, 370–71.

65. Lester D. Earnest, "The Internet's Grandfather, an Inventive Fraudster with Many Descendants" (Stanford University, January 25, 2014), https://web.stanford.edu/~learnest/nets/sage.htm.

66. Steven Levy, *Hackers: Heroes of the Computer Revolution* (Sebastopol, CA: O'Reilly Media, 2010), 132.

67. Joel N. Shurkin, *Terman's Kids: The Groundbreaking Study of How the Gifted Grow Up* (Boston: Little, Brown, 1992), 206.

68. Henry L. Minton, *Lewis M. Terman: Pioneer in Psychological Testing* (New York: NYU Press, 1988), 241

Chapter 3.2 *The Solid State*

1. Michael S. Malone, *Bill & Dave: How Hewlett and Packard Built the World's Greatest Company* (New York: Portfolio, 2007), 73.

2. C. Stewart Gillmor, *Fred Terman at Stanford: Building a Discipline, a University, and Silicon Valley* (Redwood City, CA: Stanford University Press, 2004), 127.

3. Malone, *Bill & Dave,* 89–91, 106.

4. Ibid., 97.

5. Christophe Lécuyer, *Making Silicon Valley: Innovation and the Growth of High Tech, 1930–1970, Inside Technology* (Cambridge, MA: MIT Press, 2006), 85; Robert Sobel, *The Rise and Fall of the Conglomerate Kings* (Washington, DC: Beard Books, 1999), 54.

6. Lécuyer, *Making Silicon Valley,* 87.

7. Ibid., 88.

8. Ibid., 110; Gillmor, *Fred Terman at Stanford,* 7.

9. Lécuyer, *Making Silicon Valley,* 124.

10. Ibid., 109.

11. Malone, *Bill & Dave,* 155, 168.

12. Ibid., 155, 193.

13. John Ponturo, "Analytical Support for the Joint Chiefs of Staff: The WSEG Experience, 1948–1976" (Arlington, VA: Institute for Defense Analyses, July 1979), x.

14. Arnold Thackray, *Arnold O. Beckman: One Hundred Years of Excellence* (Philadelphia: Chemical Heritage Foundation, 2000), 119–24.

15. Bo Lojek, *History of Semiconductor Engineering* (Berlin: Springer, 2007), 67.

16. Lee de Forest, "Letter from Lee de Forest to Arnold O. Beckman," November 10, 1936, Beckman Historical Collection, Box 1, Folder 17, Science History Institute, Philadelphia, https://digital.sciencehistory.org/works/pz50gw87s.

17. Donald A. Carlson, Letter from Donald A. Carlson to Arnold O. Beckman, January 31, 1956, https://digital.sciencehistory.org/works/0c483k33v. Shockley's pitch for Shockley Laboratories became the single Shockley Laboratory as a subsidiary of Beckman, which was renamed the Shockley Transistor Corporation in 1958.

18. Lojek, *History of Semiconductor Engineering,* 69.

19. Lécuyer, *Making Silicon Valley,* 132.

20. Marylin Bender and Selig Altschul, *The Chosen Instrument: Pan Am, Juan Trippe, the Rise and Fall of an American Entrepreneur* (New York: Simon & Schuster, 1982), 111.

21. Ibid., 138.

22. Christophe Lécuyer and David C. Brock, *Makers of the Microchip: A Documentary History of Fairchild Semiconductor* (Cambridge, MA: MIT Press, 2010), 95.

23. Leslie R. Berlin, "Robert Noyce and Fairchild Semiconductor, 1957–1968," *Business History Review* 75, no. 1 (2001): 81.

24. Craig Addison and Jay T. Last, "Oral History of Jay Last" (Computer History Museum, September 15, 2007), 15, https://www.computerhistory.org/collections/catalog/102658211.

25. Michael F. Wolff and Robert N. Noyce, "Oral History: Robert N. Noyce — Engineering and Technology History Wiki," *Engineering and Technology History Wiki* (United Engineering Foundation, September 19, 1975), https://ethw.org/Oral-History:Robert_N._Noyce.

26. Gordon Moore and Arthur Rock, "Oral History Panel" (Computer History Museum, July 9, 2014), 6, https://www.computerhistory.org/collections/catalog/102658233.

27. Arthur Rock, "Early Bay Area Venture Capitalists: Shaping the Economic and Business Landscape," conducted by Sally Smith Hughes in 2008 and 2009 (Regional Oral History Office, Bancroft Library, University of California, Berkeley, 2009), 32.

28. Ibid., 42.

29. Martin Middlebrook and Chris Everitt, *The Bomber Command War Diaries: An Operational Reference Book, 1939–1945* (Barnsley, UK: Pen & Sword Aviation, 2014), 437.

30. Rock, "Early Bay Area Venture Capitalists, 42.

31. Sterling Seagrave and Peggy Seagrave, *The Yamato Dynasty: The Secret History of Japan's Imperial Family* (New York: Broadway Books, 2001), 232.

32. W. "Tom" Clausen, "A Legacy of Leadership: CEO of Bank of America and President of the World Bank" (Oral History Center, Bancroft Library, University of California, Berkeley, 1996), 170.

33. Michal McMahon, interviewer, "Oral-History: William Hewlett," November 27, 1984, https://ethw.org/Oral-History:William_Hewlett.

34. Malone, *Bill & Dave*, 168.

35. "The Quality Goes On Before the (Japanese) Name Goes On," *The Rosen Electronics Letter* (New York: Rosen Research, Inc., March 31, 1980).

36. Leslie Berlin, *The Man behind the Microchip: Robert Noyce and the Invention of Silicon Valley* (Oxford; New York: Oxford University Press, 2005), 260.

37. "YHP: A Yen for Success," *Measure*, July/August 1989, 4, http://www.hp.com/hpinfo/abouthp /histnfacts/publications/measure/pdf/1989_07-08.pdf.

38. Middlebrook and Everitt, *The Bomber Command War Diaries*, 437; Gillmor, *Fred Terman at Stanford*, 231 (regarding the RRL design).

39. Middlebrook and Everitt, *The Bomber Command War Diaries*, 437.

40. Former employee (and national press secretary) Buddy Gomez's series of articles for *ABS-CBN News* is the best source I've found. Buddy Gomez, "OPINION: How did a Zobel Fall in Love with a McMicking?" *ABS-CBN News* (blog), August 10, 2017, https://news.abs- cbn .com/opinions/08/10/17/opinion- how- did-a-zobel- fall-in-love- with-a mcmicking.

41. Sterling Seagrave and Peggy Seagrave, *Gold Warriors: America's Secret Recovery of Yamashita's Gold* (London; New York: Verso, 2005), 93.

42. Ibid., 295.

43. Tim Sturgeon, *The Origins of Silicon Valley: The Development of the Electronics Industry in the San Francisco Bay Area* (Berkeley: University of California, 1992), 45.

44. John Leslie and Ross Synder, "History of the Early Days of Ampex Corporation," *AES Historical Committee*, December 17, 2010, 7, https://www.aes.org/aeshc/docs/company.histories /ampex/leslie_snyder_early-days-of-ampex.pdf.

45. Sally Smith Hughes, interviewer, "Reid Dennis: Early Bay Area Venture Capitalists: Shaping the Economic and Business Landscape," 2009, 14, https://digitalassets.lib.berkeley.edu/roho /ucb/text/dennis_reid.pdf.

46. Berlin, *The Man behind the Microchip*, 112.

47. Eric Arnesen, ed., *Encyclopedia of U.S. Labor and Working-Class History* (New York: Routledge, 2007), 303. *See generally* Rachel Grossman, "Women's Place in the Integrated Circuit," *Radical America*, February 1980, 31–49; Heidi I. Hartmann, ed., *Computer Chips and Paper Clips: Technology and Women's Employment*, vol. 2, Panel on Technology and Women's Employment, National Research Council (Washington, DC: National Academy Press, 1987).

48. Tom Maher, *Silicon Valley Road* (College Station, TX: virtualbookworm.com, 2005), 49.

49. Ibid.

50. Wilf Corrigan, interview by Rob Walker, *Silicon Genesis: Oral Histories of Semiconductor Technology*, October 17, 1998, 00:26:45, https://exhibits.stanford.edu/silicongenesis/catalog /zn983ym0204.

51. Ibid.

52. Lisa Nakamura, "Indigenous Circuits: Navajo Women and the Racialization of Early Electronic Manufacture," *American Quarterly* 66, no. 4 (2014): 919–41; Roxanne Dunbar-Ortiz, *An Indigenous Peoples' History of the United States, ReVisioning American History* (Boston: Beacon Press, 2014), 209.

53. Cedric J. Robinson, *On Racial Capitalism, Black Internationalism, and Cultures of Resistance,* ed. H. L. T. Quan (London: Pluto Press, 2019), 190–91.

54. Dunbar-Ortiz, *An Indigenous Peoples' History of the United States,* 200.

55. Resolution film collective, *Redevelopment: A Marxist Analysis* (1974), 00:48:22–00:49:54, https://archive.org/details/Redevelopment_A_Marxist_Analysis.

56. Tom Nicholas, *VC: An American History* (Cambridge, MA: Harvard University Press, 2020), 154.

Chapter 3.3 Personal Revolution

1. Ann R. Markusen and Joel Yudken, *Dismantling the Cold War Economy* (New York: Basic Books, 1992), 155.

2. Harry Braverman, *Labor and Monopoly Capital: The Degradation of Work in the Twentieth Century* (New York: Monthly Review Press, 1975), 408.

3. Steven Levy, *Hackers: Heroes of the Computer Revolution* (Sebastopol, CA: O'Reilly Media, Inc., 2010), 124.

4. Vannevar Bush, "As We May Think," *The Atlantic,* July 1945, 101–08.

5. "Man-Computer Symbiosis," IRE Transactions on Human Factors in Electronics HFE-1 (March 1960): 4–11, https://groups.csail.mit.edu/medg/people/psz/Licklider.html.

6. Douglas C. Engelbart, "Augmenting Human Intellect: A Conceptual Framework," Prepared for Director Information Sciences, Air Force Office of Scientific Research (Washington, DC: SRI, October 1962), para. 2b7, https://www.dougengelbart.org/content/view/138/#2b7.

7. M. Mitchell Waldrop, *The Dream Machine: J.C.R. Licklider and the Revolution That Made Computing Personal* (New York: Penguin Books, 2001), 216.

8. Adam Fisher, *Valley of Genius: The Uncensored History of Silicon Valley, as Told by the Hackers, Founders, and Freaks Who Made It Boom* (New York: Twelve, 2018), 19.

9. Ibid, 22.

10. "The 1968 Demo—Interactive," Doug Engelbart Institute, https://dougengelbart.org/content/view/374/464.

11. Leslie Berlin, *Troublemakers: Silicon Valley's Coming of Age* (New York: Simon & Schuster, 2017), 29.

12. Michael A. Hiltzik, *Dealers of Lightning: Xerox PARC and the Dawn of the Computer Age* (New York: HarperBusiness, 1999), 67, 78.

13. Engelbart, "Augmenting Human Intellect," para. 4d.

14. John Markoff, *What the Dormouse Said—: How the Sixties Counterculture Shaped the Personal Computer Industry* (New York: Viking, 2005), 26–28.

15. Jay Stevens, *Storming Heaven: LSD and the American Dream, Perennial Library* (New York: Harper & Row, 1995), 178.

16. Willis W. Harman et al., "Psychedelic Agents in Creative Problem-Solving: A Pilot Study," *Psychological Reports* 19, no. 1 (August 1966): 211–27.

17. Todd Brendan Fahey, "The Original Captain Trips," *High Times,* November 1991.

18. Vince Polito and Richard J. Stevenson, "A Systematic Study of Microdosing Psychedelics," *PLOS ONE* 14, no. 2 (February 6, 2019): 2.

19. Jay Stevens, *Storming Heaven: LSD and the American Dream* (New York: Grove Press, 1987), 17.

20. Ibid., 225–26.

21. Mona Lisa Saloy, "When I Die, I Won't Stay Dead: The Poetry of Bob Kaufman" (PhD diss., Louisiana State University, 2005), 215, https://digitalcommons.lsu.edu/gradschool_dissertations/3400.

22. Raymond Foye, "Rain Unraveled Tales: Editing Bob Kaufman," in *Collected Poems of Bob Kaufman* (San Francisco: City Lights, 2019), 224.

23. Saloy, "When I Die," 11.

24. Bob Kaufman et al., eds., *Collected Poems of Bob Kaufman* (San Francisco: City Lights, 2019), 30.

25. Bob Kaufman, "Caryl Chessman (Reel I, II, III, IV)," in ibid., 81.

26. Saloy, "When I Die," 72.

27. *See generally* Barbara S. Griffith, *The Crisis of American Labor: Operation Dixie and the Defeat of the CIO* (Philadelphia: Temple University Press, 2018).

28. *See generally* Gerald Horne, *Red Seas: Ferdinand Smith and Radical Black Sailors in the United States and Jamaica* (New York: NYU Press, 2009).

29. Federal Bureau of Investigation, "Robert Gornel Kaufman, File No. 94996," 1950–1970, http://omeka.wustl.edu/omeka/exhibits/show/fbeyes/kaufman.

30. *See generally* James Smethurst, "'Remembering When Indians Were Red': Bob Kaufman, the Popular Front, and the Black Arts Movement," *Callaloo* 25, no. 1 (2002): 146–64, https://www.jstor.org/stable/3300404.

31. Charles E. Cobb, *On the Road to Freedom: A Guided Tour of the Civil Rights Trail* (Chapel Hill, NC: Algonquin Books of Chapel Hill, 2008), 118; J. H. O'Dell, "Operation Dixie: Notes on a Promise Abandoned," *Labor Notes,* April 1, 2005.

32. Jack O'Dell, interview by Sam Sills, "'They Teamed Up with the Police and the Klan': Jack O'Dell On Red Baiting in the National Maritime Union,'" August 5, 1993, http://history matters.gmu.edu/d/6924.

33. Kaufman et al., *Collected Poems of Bob Kaufman,* 217.

34. Saloy, "When I Die," 78–81, 196.

35. Jon Kinyon, "Mayfield's Chinatown and Palo Alto's Earliest Chinese Entrepreneurs," our townofpaloalto.wordpress.com, December 30, 2016.

36. Rick Quan, *Dancing through Life: The Dorothy Toy Story,* documentary (Rick Quan Productions, 2017).

37. Ruth Asawa and Stephen Dobbs, "Community and Commitment: An Interview with Ruth Asawa," *Art Education* 34, no. 5 (September 1981): 14–17; John Yau, "Ruth Asawa, a Pioneer of Necessity," *Hyperallergic,* September 24, 2017, https://hyperallergic.com/401777/ruth -asawa-david-zwirner-2017.

38. Stevens, *Storming Heaven,* 222–27.

39. "Project MKULTRA, The CIA's Program of Research in Behavioral Modification," Joint Hearing before the United States Senate Select Committee on Intelligence, 95th Cong., 1st Sess. 5 (1977), https://www.intelligence.senate.gov/sites/default/files/hearings/95mkultra .pdf.

40. Edith Ronald Mirrielees, *Stanford: The Story of a University* (New York: Putnam, 1959), 26.

41. Thomas A. Ban and Barry Blackwell, *An Oral History of Neuropsychopharmacology: The First Fifty Years: Peer Interviews* (Scotts Valley, CA: CreateSpace, 2011), 60.

42. Mike Jay, *Mescaline: A Global History of the First Psychedelic* (New Haven: Yale University Press, 2019), 235.

43. Ban and Blackwell, *An Oral History of Neuropsychopharmacology,* 59–60.

44. David H. Price, *Cold War Anthropology: The CIA, the Pentagon, and the Growth of Dual Use Anthropology* (Durham, NC: Duke University Press, 2016), 168–69.

45. Hiltzik, *Dealers of Lightning,* 336; Markoff, *What the Dormouse Said,* 79.

46. Martin A. Lee and Bruce Shlain, *Acid Dreams: The CIA, LSD, and the Sixties Rebellion* (New York: Grove Press, 1985), 198–99.

47. Philip G. Zimbardo, *The Lucifer Effect: Understanding How Good People Turn Evil* (New York: Random House, 2008), 236.

48. "Stanford Prison Experiment, August 15–21, 1971," video recordings, Stanford Libraries, https://exhibits.stanford.edu/spe/browse/video-recordings.

49. Zimbardo, *The Lucifer Effect*, 97.

50. Ibid., 111.

51. Ibid., 39.

Chapter 3.4 How to Destroy an Empire

1. *The Pentagon Papers* (Boston: Beacon Press, 1971), 1.

2. Bruce Cumings, *The Korean War: A History* (New York: Modern Library, 2010), 129–30; *The Jeju 4.3 Incident Investigation Report* (Seoul: The National Committee for Investigation of the truth about the Jeju April 3 Incident, 2003), 373–78.

3. Malcolm X, "The Ballot or the Bullet," in *Say It Loud: Great Speeches on Civil Rights and African American Identity*, ed. Catherine Ellis and Stephen Smith (New York: New Press, 2010).

4. Cumings, *The Korean War*, 160.

5. Helen Hosmer, *Helen Hosmer: A Radical Critic of California Agribusiness in the 1930s* (Santa Cruz: University of California, Santa Cruz, University Library, 1992), 42.

6. Malcolm X, "The Ballot or the Bullet," 9.

7. Allard Lowenstein, interview by Clayborne Carson, May 16, 1977, 2, https://www.crmvet.org/nars/770516_lowenstein_carson.pdf.

8. John Dittmer, *Local People: The Struggle for Civil Rights in Mississippi* (Champaign: University of Illinois Press, 1995), 203.

9. Bernard Butcher, "Freedom Summer," *Stanford Magazine*, July 1, 1996.

10. *GIRLS SAY YES to boys who say NO*, poster, 1968, https://americanhistory.si.edu/collections/search/object/nmah_539547.

11. St. Clair Drake, "The Meaning of 'Negritude': The Negro's Stake in Africa," *Negro Digest*, June 1964, 40.

12. Bailey Williams, "A Half-Century Ago in Jonesboro, Armed Black Men Fought Back," *Daily Advertiser* (Lafayette, LA), June 7, 2020.

13. Barbara Ransby, *Ella Baker and the Black Freedom Movement: A Radical Democratic Vision* (Chapel Hill: University of North Carolina Press, 2003), 268–70.

14. Jon H. Hale, *The Freedom Schools: Student Activists in the Mississippi Civil Rights Movement* (New York: Columbia University Press, 2016).

15. Charles E. Cobb, *This Nonviolent Stuff'll Get You Killed: How Guns Made the Civil Rights Movement Possible* (New York: Basic Books, 2014), 204.

16. Editorial cartoon, *Black America*, Fall 1964, 9.

17. Timothy B. Tyson, *Radio Free Dixie: Robert F. Williams & the Roots of Black Power* (Chapel Hill: University of North Carolina Press, 1999).

18. Maxwell C. Stanford, "Revolutionary Action Movement (RAM): A Case Study of an Urban Revolutionary Movement in Western Capitalist Society" (Atlanta, GA: Atlanta University, 1986), 121.

19. Huey P. Newton and J. Herman Blake, *Revolutionary Suicide* (New York: Writers and Readers, 1995), 110.

20. Bobby Seale, *Seize the Time: The Story of the Black Panther Party* (London: Arrow Books, 1970), 40.

21. Herbert G. Ruffin, *Uninvited Neighbors: African Americans in Silicon Valley, 1769–1990* (Norman, OK: University of Oklahoma Press, 2014), 73.

22. Ibid., 85.

23. Ibid., 150.

24. Ibid., 108.

25. Gene Marine, *The Black Panthers* (New York: New American Library, 1969), 76.

26. Donna Jean Murch, *Living for the City: Migration, Education, and the Rise of the Black Panther Party in Oakland, California* (Chapel Hill: University of North Carolina Press, 2010), 82.

27. Huey P. Newton, "Intercommunalism (1974)," *Viewpoint Magazine,* June 11, 2018, https://viewpointmag.com/2018/06/11/intercommunalism-1974.

28. "The California Community College History Project Interactive Timeline," accessed March 28, 2022, https://ccleague.org/california-community-college-history-project#event -1930-2.

29. Robin D. G. Kelley, "Cedric J. Robinson: The Making of a Black Radical Intellectual," *CounterPunch,* June 17, 2016, https://www.counterpunch.org/2016/06/17/cedric-j-robinson-the -making-of-a-black-radical-intellectual.

30. Ruffin, *Uninvited Neighbors,* 176.

31. Russell John Rickford, *We Are an African People: Independent Education, Black Power, and the Radical Imagination* (New York: Oxford University Press, 2019), 110.

32. Jason Ferreira, "From College Readiness to Ready for Revolution! Third World Student Activism at a Northern California Community College, 1965–1969," *Kalfou: A Journal of Comparative and Relational Ethnic Studies* 1, no. 1 (2014): 117–44.

33. Seale, *Seize the Time,* 11.

34. Ibid., 35.

35. Robyn C. Spencer, *The Revolution Has Come: Black Power, Gender, and the Black Panther Party in Oakland* (Durham, NC: Duke University Press, 2016), 47, 49.

36. Dan Berger, *Captive Nation: Black Prison Organizing in the Civil Rights Era* (Chapel Hill: University of North Carolina Press, 2014), 102.

37. Eric Cummings, *The Rise and Fall of California's Radical Prison Movement* (Redwood City, CA: Stanford University Press, 1994), 165.

38. Ibid., 185.

39. Joshua Bloom and Waldo E. Martin, Jr., *Black Against Empire: The History and Politics of the Black Panther Party* (Berkeley: University of California Press, 2013), 269–76.

40. William H. Orrick, *Shut It Down!, A College in Crisis: San Francisco State College, October 1968–April 1969; a Report to the National Commission on the Causes and Prevention of Violence* (Washington, DC: U.S. Government Printing Office, 1969), 33; a version of the speech was published as "The Necessity of a Black Revolution," by George Murray, *The Black Panther,* November 16, 1968, 24.

41. Orrick, *Shut It Down!,* 33.

42. United States Congress House Committee on Internal Security, "America's Maoists: The Revolutionary Union, the Venceremos Organization" (Washington, DC: U.S. Government Printing Office, 1972), 12.

43. Kenneth Lamott, "In the Matter of H. Bruce Franklin," *New York Times Magazine,* January 23, 1972.

44. H. Bruce Franklin, *War Stars: The Superweapon and the American Imagination* (New York: Oxford University Press, 1988), 181.

45. H. Bruce Franklin, *Vietnam and Other American Fantasies, Culture, Politics, and the Cold War* (Amherst: University of Massachusetts Press, 2000), 78.

46. Rickford, *We Are an African People,* 109; Franklin, *Vietnam,* 81.

47. Herbert L. Packer, "Academic Freedom & the Franklin Case," *Commentary,* April 1972.

48. Aaron J. Leonard and Conor A. Gallagher, *Heavy Radicals: The FBI's Secret War on America's Maoists* (New Alresford, UK: Zer0 Books, 2014), 37–40.

49. Marjorie Heins, *Strictly Ghetto Property: The Story of Los Siete de la Raza* (Berkeley: Ramparts Press, 1972), 95.

50. *Basta Ya!: The Story of Los Siete de la Raza* (San Francisco: Research Organizing Cooperative, 1970).

51. *Los Siete* (Newsreel, 1969), https://archive.org/details/cbpf_000095.

52. "Los Siete de la Raza," Bay Area Television Archive, https://diva.sfsu.edu/collections/sfbatv /12604.

53. Bloom and Martin Jr., *Black Against Empire*, 289.

54. Damon B. Akins and William J. Bauer, *We Are the Land: A History of Native California* (Oakland: University of California Press, 2021), 272.

55. On the I-Hotel protests, see Jay Caspian Kang, *The Loneliest Americans* (New York: Crown, 2021), 53–56.

56. Paul Berman, *A Tale of Two Utopias: The Political Journey of the Generation of 1968* (New York: W. W. Norton, 1996), 44–45.

57. Mark Rudd, "Why Were There So Many Jews in SDS? (Or, The Ordeal of Civility)" (New Mexico Jewish Historical Society, November 2005), https://www.markrudd.com/indexcd39 .html.

58. Kate Chesley, "Faculty, Staff and Students Recall the Evolution of Jewish Life at Stanford," *Stanford Report*, January 21, 2011, http://news.stanford.edu/news/2011/january/history -jewish-life-012111.html. In January of 2022, prompted by an archival find by historian Charles Petersen, Stanford appointed a taskforce to investigate the history of Jewish exclusion from the school.

59. Huey P. Newton, "Huey Newton Talks to the Movement" (Chicago: Students for a Democratic Society, 1968), 6.

60. Aaron Byungjoo Bae, "The Ideological Impetus and Struggle in Praxis for Multiracial Radical Alliances in the San Francisco Bay Area, 1967–1980" (PhD diss., Arizona State University, 2016), 158, https://keep.lib.asu.edu/items/155214.

61. Francisco Jimenez, "Dramatic Principles of the Teatro Campesino," *Bilingual Review / La Revista Bilingüe* 2, nos. 1/2 (January-August 1975), 99–111.

62. "University in Society: Do the Ties Bind?" Public Broadcast Laboratory, American Archive of Public Broadcasting (WGBH and the Library of Congress), accessed March 28, 2022, 1:24:50, http://americanarchive.org/catalog/cpb-aacip-516-g44hm53h63.

63. Ibid., 1:12:40.

64. Bay Area Revolutionary Union, "Statement of Principles," *Red Papers 1*, https://www.marxists .org/history/erol/ncm-1/red papers-1/statement.htm.

65. Bay Area Revolutionary Union, "The Black Panther Party—Heroes of the People, Every One," *Red Papers 2*, https://www.marxists.org/history/erol/ncm-1/red-papers-2/panthers.htm.

66. Stuart W. Leslie, *The Cold War and American Science: The Military-Industrial-Academic Complex at MIT and Stanford* (New York: Columbia University Press, 1993), 12.

67. Ibid., 242.

68. Ira Arlook, interview by Natalie Marine-Street, *The Movement Oral History Project*, May 4, 2019, 22, https://exhibits.stanford.edu/activism/catalog/sx868kz0309.

69. "Technology for the People!" *Declassified*, April 16, 1969, 3.

70. Black Panther Party, "Black Panther Party Program, March 29, 1972 Platform," March 29, 1972, Radical Democracy Project Archive, https://archive.org/details/blackpanthers10Pnt.

71. *Disorders and Terrorism: Report of the Task Force on Disorders and Terrorism* (Washington, DC: National Advisory Committee on Criminal Justice Standards and Goals, 1976), 546–63.

72. Phyllis Huggins, "Programmer Thankful for 'Bug' During Computer Center Bombing," *Computerworld,* May 27, 1970, 1.

73. James Barron, "The Mathematicians Who Saved a Kidnapped N.Y.U. Computer," *New York Times,* December 7, 2015, 18.

74. "Security Cut Damage from DP Center Blast," *Computerworld,* December 23, 1970, 1; Thomas J. Morton, "Bomb Demolishes Army Computer Complex," *Computerworld,* September 2, 1970.

75. Ibid.

76. Thomas J. Morton, "Violence by Rebels Threatens Centers," *Computerworld,* October 7, 1970.

77. Phyllis Huggins, "Costlier Protection Hits Campus Centers," *Computerworld,* August 5, 1970.

78. Ervin Dyer, "Say It Loud!" *Pitt Magazine,* Spring 2019, https://www.pittmag.pitt.edu/news/say-it-loud.

79. Sekou Odinga, Dhoruba Bin Wahad, Shaba Om, and Jamal Joseph, *Look for Me in the Whirlwind: From the Panther 21 to 21st-Century Revolutions* (Oakland: PM Press, 2017), 557. After close to 50 years of incarceration, Acoli was granted parole in 2022, as I was finishing this book.

80. Christopher Hewitt, *Political Violence and Terrorism in Modern America: A Chronology* (Westport, CT: Praeger Security International, 2005), 56, 81.

81. "Here's a Blanket to Give You Added Security" *Computerworld,* December 23, 1970, 4.

82. "Why Encina?" *Declassified,* May 12, 1969, 5–6.

83. *Smash War Research: Shut Down SRI Counter-Insurgency Labs* (flyer), May 16, 1959, http://www.a3mreunion.org/archive/1968-1969/68-69_may16_sri/files_68-69_may_16/A3M-5-16_Smash_War_Research_p1-2.pdf

84. Lawrence E. Davies, "400 Routed at Stanford," *New York Times,* May 17, 1969, 30; Richard W. Lyman, *Stanford in Turmoil: Campus Unrest 1966–1972* (Redwood City, CA: Stanford University Press, 2009), 154.

85. Lang Atwood and Frank Miller, "SRI Obtains Injunction; Movement Plans Action," *Stanford Daily,* May 19, 1969, https://archives.stanforddaily.com/1969/05/19?page=1.

86. Charles A. Anderson, "Memo to the Staff" (A3M Archive, May 20, 1969), http://a3mreunion.org/archive/1968-1969/68-69_may16_sri/files_68-69_may_16/A3M-5-16_from_Anderson.pdf.

87. Steve Hamilton, "Learn From the People, Serve the People, Become One with the People," *Movement* 4, no. 12 (January 1969): 9.

88. Melvin Small, *Antiwarriors: The Vietnam War and the Battle for America's Hearts and Minds,* Vietnam—America in the War Years, vol. 1 (Wilmington, DE: Scholarly Resources, 2002), 122.

89. Lenny Siegel, "Packard Flees Arrest" (A3M Archive, April 9, 1971), http://a3mreunion.org/archive/1970-1971/70-71_packard/files_70-71_packard/70-71Packard_Arrest_Packard_3.pdf.

90. *See* Sylvia Berry Williams, *Hassling* (Boston: Little, Brown, 1970), for a detailed account of the 1967–69 school years at Cubberley High.

91. "Football Big at Stanford," *Esquire,* September 1971, 161.

92. Bill Evers, "Campus Venceremos Splits," *Stanford Daily,* September 27, 1971, 4. https://archives.stanforddaily.com/1971/09/27?page=4&section=MODSMD_ARTICLE15#article.

93. "Slaying Linked to Radical Group," *New York Times,* December 24, 1972, 26.

94. Hewitt, *Political Violence.*

95. Lawrence Stone, ed., *The University in Society* (Princeton: Princeton Universty Press, 1974).

96. Arthur M. Eckstein, *Bad Moon Rising: How the Weather Underground Beat the FBI and Lost the Revolution* (New Haven: Yale University Press, 2016), 191.

97. White House Office of Management and Budget, "Historical Table 3.1—Outlays by Superfunction and Function: 1940–2025." The category comprises Education, Training, Employment, Social Services, Health, Medicare, Income Security, Social Security, and Veterans Benefits and Services. February 2020, https://www.whitehouse.gov/wp-content/uploads/2020/02/hist_fy21.pdf.

98. Aaron Bady and Mike Konczal, "From Master Plan to No Plan: The Slow Death of Public Higher Education," *Dissent*, Fall 2012.

99. Lauren Marnel Shores, "A Brief History of UC Tuition," *Bottom Line*, October 22, 2017, https://thebottomline.as.ucsb.edu/2017/10/a-brief-history-of-uc-tuition.

100. Cedric Robinson, *The Terms of Order: Political Science and the Myth of Leadership* (Albany, NY: SUNY Press, 1980), 188.

101. Kelley, "Cedric J. Robinson."

102. Peter F. Carr, "Poor Security Leaves DP Facilities Ripe for Sabotage," *Computerworld*, June 17, 1970, 1, http://archive.org/details/sim_computerworld_1970-06-17_4_24.

103. Steven Levy, *Hackers: Heroes of the Computer Revolution* (Sebastopol, CA: O'Reilly Media, Inc., 2010), 127.

104. Roxanne Dunbar-Ortiz, *An Indigenous Peoples' History of the United States, ReVisioning American History* (Boston: Beacon Press, 2014), 28.

105. Bill Hewlett, *Measure*, April 1976, 15, https://www.hp.com/hpinfo/abouthp/histnfacts/publications/measure/pdf/1976_04.pdf.

106. "Security: It's Everyone's Job," *Measure*, September 1976, 9–13, https://www.hp.com/hpinfo/abouthp/histnfacts/publications/measure/pdf/1976_08-09.pdf.

Chapter 4.1 California über Alles

1. Jeff Nussbaum, "The Night New York Saved Itself from Bankruptcy," *New Yorker*, October 16, 2015.

2. David Harvey, *The Enigma of Capital: And the Crises of Capitalism* (London: Profile, 2010), 131, 172.

3. Glenna Matthews, *Silicon Valley, Women, and the California Dream: Gender, Class, and Opportunity in the Twentieth Century* (Redwood City, CA: Stanford University Press, 2003), 160.

4. Leslie Berlin, *The Man behind the Microchip: Robert Noyce and the Invention of Silicon Valley* (New York: Oxford University Press, 2005), 249–50.

5. Matthews, *Silicon Valley, Women, and the California Dream*, 158.

6. Ann R. Markusen, *Profit Cycles: Oligopoly, and Regional Development* (Cambridge, MA: MIT Press, 1985), 113.

7. John A. Alic and Martha Caldwell Harris, "Employment Lessons from the Electronics Industry," *Monthly Labor Review*, February 1986, 32.

8. Leslie Berlin, *Troublemakers: Silicon Valley's Coming of Age* (New York: Simon & Schuster, 2017), 318.

9. Steve Early and Rand Wilson, "Organizing High Tech: Unions & Their Future," *Labor Research Review*, March 1, 1986, https://ecommons.cornell.edu/handle/1813/102472.

10. Matthews, *Silicon Valley, Women, and the California Dream*, 166.

11. "Subversive Influence in the United Electrical, Radio, and Machine Workers of America, Pittsburgh and Erie, Pa," Subcommittee to Investigate the Administration of the Internal

Security Act and Other Internal Security Laws, United States Senate Committee on the Judiciary (Washington, DC: U.S. Government Printing Office, 1954), 59.

12. David Bacon, "LAND OF THE OPEN SHOP: The Long Struggle to Organize Silicon Valley," *New Labor Forum* (blog), January 2011, https://newlaborforum.cuny.edu/2011/01/03/land-of-the-open-shop-the-long-struggle-to-organize-silicon-valley.

13. Berlin, *The Man behind the Microchip*, 238.

14. Ibid., 236.

15. Karen J. Hossfeld, "Why Aren't High-Tech Workers Organized?" in *Working People of California*, ed. Daniel A. Cornford (Berkeley: University of California Press, 1995), 410.

16. AnnaLee Saxenian, *Regional Advantage: Culture and Competition in Silicon Valley and Route 128* (Cambridge, MA: Harvard University Press, 1996), 55.

17. David N. Pellow and Lisa Sun-Hee Park, *The Silicon Valley of Dreams: Environmental Injustice, Immigrant Workers, and the High-Tech Global Economy* (New York: NYU Press, 2002), 100.

18. David N. Pellow and Glenna Matthews, "Immigrant Workers in Two Eras," in *Challenging the Chip: Labor Rights and Environmental Justice in the Global Electronics Industry*, ed. Ted Smith, David Allan Sonnenfeld, and David N. Pellow (Philadelphia: Temple University Press, 2006), 136.

19. Paul Adler, "Time-and-Motion Regained," *Harvard Business Review*, February 1993, https://hbr.org/1993/01/time-and-motion-regained.

20. Paul Adler, "The 'Learning Bureaucracy': New United Motor Manufacturing, Inc.," in *Research in Organizational Behavior* 15, ed. L. L. Cummings and Barry M. Staw (Stamford, CT: JAI Press, 1993), 15: 149.

21. David Kiley, "Goodbye, NUMMI: How a Plant Changed the Culture of Car-Making," *Popular Mechanics*, April 2, 2010.

22. For an important corrective regarding the mixed politics of the counterculture, see Rebecca Klatch, *A Generation Divided: The New Left, the New Right, and the 1960s* (UC Press, 1999), 134-157.

23. *Maximum RocknRoll*, no. 62, July 1988, 9.

24. Dan Ozzi, *Sellout: The Major Label Feeding Frenzy That Swept Punk, Emo, and Hardcore (1994–2007)* (Boston: Houghton Mifflin Harcourt, 2021), 6.

25. Jack Boulware and Silke Tudor, *Gimme Something Better: The Profound, Progressive, and Occasionally Pointless History of Bay Area Punk from Dead Kennedys to Green Day* (New York: Penguin, 2009), 466–70.

26. *Maximum RocknRoll*, no. 2, September/October 1982.

27. Corbett Redford, *Turn It Around: The Story of East Bay Punk*, documentary (Capodezero Films, 2017).

28. "NSA: A Short Account of International Student Politics & the Cold War with Particular Reference to the NSA, CIA, Etc.," *Ramparts*, March 1967, 29.

29. Mary E. King, *Freedom Song: A Personal Story of the 1960s Civil Rights Movement* (New York: Morrow, 1987), 517–18.

30. Richard Cummings, *The Pied Piper: Allard K. Lowenstein and the Liberal Dream* (New York: Grove Press, 1985), 261.

31. Ibid., 489.

32. "No Tears for Allard Lowenstein," *Workers Vanguard*, April 4, 1980, 11.

33. U.S. Federal Housing Finance Agency, "All Transactions House Price Index for San Jose-Sunnyvale-Santa Clara, CA (MSA)," FRED, Federal Reserve Bank of St. Louis, July 1, 1975, https://fred.stlouisfed.org/series/ATNHPIUS41940Q.

34. "Negores [sic] to Picket Realtors Conclave," *Santa Cruz Sentinel*, March 20, 1964, 14; Herbert G. Ruffin, *Uninvited Neighbors: African Americans in Silicon Valley, 1769–1990* (Norman, OK: University of Oklahoma Press, 2014), 115.

35. Robert O. Self, *American Babylon: Race and the Struggle for Postwar Oakland,* Politics and Society in Twentieth-Century America (Princeton: Princeton University Press, 2003), 261.

36. Ibid., 324–25.

37. Mike Davis, *City of Quartz: Excavating the Future in Los Angeles,* new ed. (London; New York: Verso, 2018), 167.

38. Adam Goodman, *Deportation Machine: America's Long History of Expelling Immigrants,* Politics and Society in Modern America (Princeton: Princeton University Press, 2020), 120.

39. Greg Grandin, *The End of the Myth: From the Frontier to the Border Wall in the Mind of America* (New York: Metropolitan Books, 2020), 223.

40. Ruth Wilson Gilmore, *Golden Gulag: Prisons, Surplus, Crisis, and Opposition in Globalizing California* (Berkeley: University of California Press, 2007), 83.

41. Davis, *City of Quartz,* 276.

42. Gilmore, *Golden Gulag,* 126.

43. Roxy Bonafont, Emily Lemmerman, and Lucas Rodriguez, "100 Years of Hoover: A History of Stanford's Decades-Long Debate over the Hoover Institution," *Stanford Politics,* May 11, 2019.

44. Joe Haughey, "Business Beacon," *Bay Region Business,* August 23, 1963, 2.

45. Joel Shurkin, *Broken Genius: The Rise and Fall of William Shockley, Creator of the Electronic Age* (London: Macmillan, 2008), 212.

46. "Is Quality of U.S. Population Declining? Interview with a Nobel Prize-Winning Scientist," *U.S. News & World Report,* November 22, 1965, 68–71.

47. Ibid., 70.

48. Joseph L. Graves, *The Emperor's New Clothes: Biological Theories of Race at the Millennium* (New Brunswick, NJ: Rutgers University Press, 2001), 161.

49. "Statement of Dr. William Shockley, Hearings on H.R. 17846 and Other Related Bills. Emergency School Aid Act of 1970," General Subcommittee on Education of the Committee on Education and Labor, House of Representatives (1970), 436.

50. Shurkin, *Broken Genius,* 252–53.

51. C. Stewart Gillmor, *Fred Terman at Stanford: Building a Discipline, a University, and Silicon Valley* (Redwood City, CA: Stanford University Press, 2004), 403.

52. Arthur R. Jensen, "How Much Can We Boost IQ and Scholastic Achievement?" *Harvard Educational Review* 39, no. 1 (Winter 1969): 2.

53. Ibid., 3.

54. John Neary, "Jensenism: Variations on a Racial Theme," *Life,* June 12, 1970, 64.

55. Ibid., 58D.

56. Kingsley Davis and Wilbert E. Moore, "Some Principles of Stratification," *American Sociological Review* 10, no. 2 (1945): 242–49.

57. Robert Mcg. Thomas Jr., "Kingsley Davis, 88, Who Told of 'Zero Population Growth,'" *New York Times,* March 5, 1997.

58. Kingsley Davis, "The Migrations of Human Populations," *Scientific American* 231, no. 3 (1974): 99.

59. Paul R. Ehrlich, *The Population Bomb* (New York: Ballantine Books, 1968), 166.

60. Charles C. Mann, "The Book That Incited a Worldwide Fear of Overpopulation," *Smithsonian Magazine,* January 2018, https://www.smithsonianmag.com/innovation/book-incited -worldwide-fear-overpopulation-180967499.

61. Ehrlich, *Population Bomb,* 162.

62. Emily Klancher Merchant, *Building the Population Bomb* (New York: Oxford University Press, 2021), 167.

63. Aristide R. Zolberg, *A Nation by Design: Immigration Policy in the Fashioning of America* (Cambridge, MA: Russell Sage Foundation; Harvard University Press, 2006), 360.

64. Paul R. Ehrlich, Loy Bilderback, and Anne H. Ehrlich, *The Golden Door: International Migration, Mexico, and the United States* (New York: Ballantine Books, 1979), 359.

65. Elena R. Gutiérrez, *Fertile Matters: The Politics of Mexican-Origin Women's Reproduction* (Austin: University of Texas Press, 2008), 86.

66. Gustavo Arellano, "John Tanton, Quiet Architect of America's Modern-Day Anti-Immigrant Movement, Dies at 85," *Los Angeles Times,* July 18, 2019.

67. William Trombley, "California Elections: Prop. 63 Roots Traced to Small Michigan City: Measure to Make English Official Language of State Sprang from Concern over Immigration, Population," *Los Angeles Times,* October 20, 1986.

68. Gustavo Arellano, "Prop. 187 Flopped, but It Taught the Nation's Top Immigration-Control Group How to Win," *Los Angeles Times,* November 8, 2019.

69. Herbert Hoover, "Address to the White House Conference on Home Building and Home Ownership," December 2, 1931, https://www.presidency.ucsb.edu/node/206990.

70. Dr. Housing Bubble, "A History of the California Housing Gold Rush: The Financial Expansion of California Real Estate from 1850 to 2010," March 6, 2010, http://www.doctorhousing bubble.com/a-history-of-the-california-housing-gold-rush---the-financial-expansion-of-cali fornia-real-estate-from-1850-to-2010.

71. Michael Brenes, *For Might and Right: Cold War Defense Spending and the Remaking of American Democracy* (Amherst: University of Massachusetts Press, 2020), 152.

72. Stewart McBride, "HOOVER INSTITUTION; Leaning to the Right," *Christian Science Monitor,* March 27, 1980.

Chapter 4.2 War Capitalism

1. Ann R. Markusen and Joel Yudken, *Dismantling the Cold War Economy* (New York: Basic Books, 1992), 58.

2. Ibid.

3. Kim Phillips-Fein, *Invisible Hands: The Making of the Conservative Movement from the New Deal to Reagan* (New York: W. W. Norton, 2009), 56.

4. Ethan Swift, "Young Americans for Freedom and the Anti-War Movement: Pro-War Encounters with the New Left at the Height of the Vietnam War" 2019, MSSA Kaplan Prize for Use of MSSA Collections, 42, https://elischolar.library.yale.edu/mssa_collections/19.

5. Thomas W. Evans, *The Education of Ronald Reagan: The General Electric Years and the Untold Story of His Conversion to Conservatism* (New York: Columbia University Press, 2006), 4.

6. Ronald Reagan, "A Time for Choosing," campaign speech, October 27, 1964, https://www.reaganlibrary.gov/reagans/ronald-reagan/time-choosing-speech-october-27-1964.

7. J. Hoberman, *Make My Day: Movie Culture in the Age of Reagan* (New York: The New Press, 2019), 104.

8. "Cagney Eulogized by Reagan as 'Success Story' with AM-Obit-Cagney," Associated Press, March 30, 1986.

9. Martin Anderson, *Revolution: The Reagan Legacy* (Stanford: Hoover Institution Press, Stanford University, 1990), 169.

10. Ibid., 3–4.

11. Peter Duignan and Alvin Rabushka, *The United States in the 1980s* (Stanford: Hoover Institution Press, 1980), 74.

12. Ibid., 77.

13. Ibid., 80.

14. Josh Sides, *Erotic City: Sexual Revolutions and the Making of Modern San Francisco* (New York: Oxford University Press, 2009), 8.

15. George Skelton, "'Make My Day': Reagan Assails Congress, Vows Tax Hike Veto," *Los Angeles Times,* March 14, 1985.

16. Herbert G. Ruffin, *Uninvited Neighbors: African Americans in Silicon Valley, 1769–1990* (Norman, OK: University of Oklahoma Press, 2014), 216.

17. Joint Economic Committee Staff, U.S. Senate, "President Reagan's Economic Legacy: The Great Expansion," October 2000, 22.

18. Garrett Hardin, "The Tragedy of the Commons," *Science* 162, no. 3859 (1968): 1246.

19. *Diamond v. Chakrabarty,* 447 U.S. 303 (1980).

20. Doogab Yi, *The Recombinant University: Genetic Engineering and the Emergence of Stanford Biotechnology* (Chicago: University of Chicago Press, 2015), 207.

21. Ibid., 171.

22. Audra J. Wolfe, *Competing with the Soviets: Science, Technology, and the State in Cold War America* (Baltimore: Johns Hopkins University Press, 2013), 126.

23. Markusen and Yudken, *Dismantling the Cold War Economy,* 7.

24. Stuart W. Leslie, *The Cold War and American Science: The Military-Industrial-Academic Complex at MIT and Stanford* (New York: Columbia University Press, 1993), 251.

25. United States Congress House Committee on Energy and Commerce Subcommittee on Oversight and Investigations, Financial Responsibility at Universities: Hearings Before the Subcommittee on Oversight and Investigations of the Committee on Energy and Commerce, House of Representatives, 102nd Cong., 1st Sess., *Indirect Cost Recovery Practices at U.S. Universities for Federal Research Grants and Contracts* (Washington, DC: U.S. Government Printing Office, 1991), 20.

26. Ibid., 3–4.

27. Ibid.

28. *United States ex rel. Biddle v. Board of Trustees of Leland Stanford, Jr. University,* 161 F.3d 533 (9th Cir. 1998).

29. Lisa Adkins, Melinda Cooper, and Martijn Konings, *The Asset Economy: Property Ownership and the New Logic of Inequality* (Medford, MA: Polity Press, 2020), 47.

30. David Young, "DeVry's Trade School Image Is on the Way Out," *Chicago Tribune,* March 12, 1993.

31. Kathleen Burton, "Healthy Perks Keep Turnover Low, Firms Find," *Computerworld,* December 3, 1984, 106.

32. Markusen and Yudken, *Dismantling the Cold War Economy,* 161.

33. Ibid., 179.

34. John M. Findlay, *Magic Lands: Western Cityscapes and American Culture After 1940* (Berkeley: University of California Press, 1992), 144.

35. Sandra Kurtzig, Statement, Hearings Before United States Congress Joint Economic Committee, "Climate for Entrepreneurship and Innovation in the United States: Role of Government Labs in Regional Development," part 2 (1985), 113.

36. Istvan Mészaros, "The Cunning of History in Reverse Gear," *Radical Philosophy,* Winter/Spring 1986, 2–10.

37. Ronald T. Takaki, *Strangers from a Different Shore: A History of Asian Americans* (Boston: Little, Brown, 1989), 434.

38. Bill Ong Hing, *Making and Remaking Asian America through Immigration Policy, 1850–1990* (Redwood City, CA: Stanford University Press, 1993), 124.

39. Takaki, *Strangers from a Different Shore,* 441.

40. Eddie Huang, *Fresh Off the Boat: A Memoir* (New York: Spiegel & Grau, 2013), 10.

41. Ibid., 19.

42. David Harvey, *A Brief History of Neoliberalism* (New York: Oxford University Press, 2007), 27.

43. John Perkins, *Confessions of an Economic Hit Man* (San Francisco: Berrett-Koehler Publishers, 2004), 90.

44. Bernard Weinraub, "Shah of Iran Urges Arabs to End Their Oil Embargo," *New York Times,* December 22, 1973.

45. Kate Gillespie, "US Corporations and Iran at the Hague," *Middle East Journal* 44, no. 1 (1990): 18; John Foran, *Fragile Resistance: Social Transformation in Iran from 1500 to the Revolution,* (San Francisco: Westview Press, 1993), 344. Later editions of Foran's book have the second sum misrecorded as "$22 billion," which, although it would strengthen my case, appears to be an understandable transcription error.

46. Pamela G. Hollie, "Iranian Immigrants, Totaling Perhaps a Million, Bring Wealth and Diversity to the U.S.; Perhaps a Million in the U.S.," *New York Times,* December 9, 1979.

47. Jay Solomon and Carol E. Lee, "Inside the 37-Year Standoff over Iran's Frozen U.S. Dollars," *Wall Street Journal,* December 28, 2016.

48. Linda Charlton, "Shah's Visit Underscored Large Number of Iranian Students in U.S." *New York Times,* November 21, 1977.

49. Gillespie, "US Corporations and Iran at the Hague."

50. Katherine Ellison and Pete Carey, "Wealthy Filipinos find California Lucrative Territory for Investment," *San Jose Mercury News,* June 24, 1985.

51. The firms were Interlek Inc., Test International Inc., and Tool & Die Master of Santa Clara. "Names in the News," *Associated Press,* March 11, 1985.

52. Ellison and Carey, "Wealthy Filipinos."

53. Ibid.

54. Lewis M. Simons, "Dollar Drain's Link to Unrest in Philippines," *San Jose Mercury News,* June 25, 1985; Jose Galang, "Property and Propriety—A U.S. Newspaper Report Alleging Major Investments Abroad Causes a Storm, With One Minister Offering to Resign," *Far Eastern Economic Review,* July 18, 1985; Benedict Anderson, "Cacique Democracy and the Philippines: Origins and Dreams," *New Left Review,* May/June 1988.

55. Bank of America advertisement, *Foreign Affairs* 53, no. 4 (July 1975): 2.

56. J. Patrice McSherry, *Predatory States: Operation Condor and Covert War in Latin America* (Lanham, MD: Rowman & Littlefield Publishers, Inc., 2005), 95.

57. Ibid., 52.

58. Samir Amin, *Empire of Chaos* (Monthly Review Press, 1992).

59. David Packard, "Testimony on the Trade Reform Act of 1973," Hearings Before the Committee on Ways and Means, House of Representatives, 93rd Congress, 1st Session, 3216–3232.

60. James F. Petras and Morris H. Morley, *Empire or Republic? American Global Power and Domestic Decay* (New York: Routledge, 1995), 40.

61. Christopher Simpson, "Electronics Underworld: The Middle East Connection," *Computerworld,* November 23, 1981, 8.

62. Mary Thornton, "Arms-Sale Theft Case at 'Dead End,'" *Washington Post,* December 19, 1986.

63. Philip Taubman, "20-Ton Explosives Shipment to Libya Linked to Ex-Agent," *New York Times,* August 30, 1981.

64. "Frank Terpil: Confessions of a Dangerous Man," WETA TV, January 11, 1982, full transcript, 6.

65. Douglas Martin, "Edward P. Wilson, the Spy Who Lived It Up, Dies at 84," *New York Times,* September 22, 2012.

66. Karen De Young, "Somoza Legacy: Plundered Economy," *Washington Post,* November 30, 1979.

67. Amir Oren, "The Truth About Israel, Iran and 1980s U.S. Arms Deals," *Haaretz,* November 26, 2010.

68. Testimony of Richard V. Secord, Joint Hearings before the House Select Committee to Investigate Covert Arms Transactions with Iran and the Senate Select Committee on Secret Military Assistance to Iran and the Nicaraguan Opposition, 100th Cong., 1st Sess., 1987, 348–49.

69. Alexander Cockburn and Jeffrey St. Clair, *Whiteout: The CIA, Drugs, and the Press* (New York: Verso, 1998), 248–49.

70. "Guns, Drugs, and the CIA," *Frontline,* May 17, 1988.

71. William Hartung, "Nations Vie for Arms Markets," *Bulletin of the Atomic Scientists,* December 1987, 27–35.

72. Lawrence E. Walsh, *Final Report of the Independent Counsel for Iran/Contra Matters,* vol. 1, August 4, 1993, 196.

73. Ibid.

74. William M. LeoGrande, *Our Own Backyard: The United States in Central America, 1977–1992* (Chapel Hill: University of North Carolina Press, 1998), 402.

75. "Owen's Ode to Ollie," *UPI,* May 20, 1987.

76. Jeff Gerth and Stephen Engelberg, "Millions Untraced in Aid to Contras over Last 3 Years," *New York Times,* April 8, 1987.

77. Ibid.

78. In one case, the Iranians refused crates of Hawk 1 surface-to-air missiles, which were both outdated and labeled with large Israeli Star of David stickers. Ari Ben-Menashe, *Profits of War: Inside the Secret U.S.-Israeli Arms Network* (New York: Sheridan Square Press, 1992), 180–81.

79. Joe Pichirallo, "Middlemen Said to Have Siphoned Off Millions Meant for Contras," *Washington Post,* November 19, 1987.

80. Walter Pincus and Dan Morgan, "Hakim Provided for North's Kin," *Washington Post,* June 4, 1987; David Lauter and Ronald J. Ostrow, "North Associate Believed Aiding Walsh Inquiry," *Los Angeles Times,* March 18, 1988.

81. Joe Bryan and Denis Wood, *Weaponizing Maps: Indigenous Peoples and Counterinsurgency in the Americas* (New York: Guilford Publications, 2015), 210n32.

82. Gary Webb, *Dark Alliance: The CIA, the Contras, and the Crack Cocaine Explosion* (New York: Seven Stories, 1998).

83. Peggy Adler Robohm, "The Swiss Laundry: Hakim's Connection," *CovertAction,* Summer 1988, 37.

84. Anderson, *Revolution,* 397.

85. Alan J. Weissberger, "Pioneering the Laptop: Engineering the GRiD Compass," Report on Grid Compass panel at the Computer History Museum (March 15, 2006), The Special Interest Group for Computing, Information, and Society, https://www.sigcis.org/weissberger _grid_full.

86. Ibid., 397–98.

87. "Tandy to Buy Grid Systems," *New York Times,* March 17, 1988.

Chapter 4.3 Jobs and Gates

1. John Morkes, "Success Likes to Follow Intel's Gordon Moore," *Research & Development* 35, no. 8 (July 1993): 32.

2. Steven Levy, *Hackers: Heroes of hte Computer Revolution* (Sebastopol, CA: O'Reilly Media, 2010), 231.

3. Jim Milliot, "Scholastic Agrees to Acquire Klutz," *Publishers Weekly,* March 8, 2002.

4. Naomi Hirahara, *Distinguished Asian American Business Leaders* (Westport, CT: Greenwood Press, 2003), 123–25.

5. Will Safer, "How Monster Cable Got Wired for Growth," *Fortune,* April 30, 2009.

6. Levy, *Hackers,* 55.

7. Les Earnest, "SAIL Sagas," December 13, 2009, https://web.stanford.edu/~learnest/spin/sagas.htm.

8. Stephen Cass, "Al Alcorn, Creator of Pong, Explains How Early Home Computers Owe Their Color Graphics to This One Cheap, Sleazy Trick," *IEEE Spectrum* (blog), April 21, 2020, https://spectrum.ieee.org/al-alcorn-creator-of-pong-explains-how-early-home-computers-owe-their-color-to-this-one-cheap-sleazy-trick.

9. Richard Florida and Martin Kenney, "Venture Capital in Silicon Valley," in *Understanding Silicon Valley: The Anatomy of an Entrepreneurial Region,* ed. Martin Kenney (Redwood City, CA: Stanford University Press, 2000), 113.

10. Leslie Berlin, *Troublemakers: Silicon Valley's Coming of Age* (New York: Simon & Schuster, 2017), 287.

11. Margaret O'Mara, *The Code: Silicon Valley and the Remaking of America* (New York: Penguin Press, 2019), 189.

12. Steve Johnson, "What You Didn't Know about Apple's '1984' Super Bowl Ad," *Chicago Tribune,* February 2, 2017.

13. Sol Libes, "Bytelines," *BYTE,* June 1961, 208.

14. Michael A. Hiltzik, *Dealers of Lightning: Xerox PARC and the Dawn of the Computer Age* (New York: HarperBusiness, 1999), 335.

15. Brice Carnahan and James O. Wilkes, *The IBM Personal Computers and the Michigan Terminal System* (Ann Arbor: University of Michigan College of Engineering, 1984), 1.32.

16. Hiltzik, *Dealers of Lightning,* 344–45.

17. Andrew Pollack, "Big I.B.M. Has Done It Again," *New York Times,* March 27, 1983, https://www.nytimes.com/1983/03/27/business/big-ibm-has-done-it-again.html.

18. Leslie Berlin, *The Man behind the Microchip: Robert Noyce and the Invention of Silicon Valley* (New York: Oxford University Press, 2005), 262.

19. David A. Kaplan, *The Silicon Boys and Their Valley of Dreams* (New York: William Morrow, 1999), 137.

20. Eric G. Flamholtz and Yvonne Randle, *Growing Pains: Transitioning from an Entrepreneurship to a Professionally Managed Firm,* 4th ed. (San Francisco: Jossey-Bass, 2007), 75.

21. Berlin, *Troublemakers,* 306.

22. Charles T. Michener, "Is a Private School Worth It?" *Seattle Magazine,* December 1967, 75. Some have reported the tuition price as $5,000, but I'm inclined to trust the contemporaneous local feature. The reporting is in line with Paul Allen's recollection, which put the previous 1966 costs at $1,335. Paul Allen, *Idea Man* (New York: Portfolio/Penguin, 2011), 24.

23. Tom Griffin, "Paul Allen's Ties to the UW Run Deep," *University of Washington Magazine* (blog), accessed April 6, 2022, https://magazine.washington.edu/feature/paul-allens-ties-to-the-uw-run-deep.

24. Les Earnest, "SAIL Sagas."

25. Paul Freiberger and Michael Swaine, *Fire in the Valley: The Making of the Personal Computer* (New York: McGraw-Hill, 2000), 53–54.

26. Ibid., 65.

27. Ibid., 52.

28. Bill Gates, "An Open Letter to Hobbyists," *Homebrew Club Newsletter,* January 13, 1976, 2, https://www.digibarn.com/collections/newsletters/homebrew/V2_01/index.html.

29. Levy, *Hackers,* 231.

30. Bill Gates, "A Second and Final Letter," *Computer Notes,* April 1976, 5.

31. Jimmy Maher, "The Complete History of the IBM PC, Part Two: The DOS Empire Strikes," *Ars Technica,* July 31, 2017, https://arstechnica.com/gadgets/2017/07/ibm-pc-history-part-2.

32. David Gabel and David F. Weiman, *Opening Networks to Competition: The Regulation and Pricing of Access* (Boston: Springer US, 1998), 224.

33. James Wallace and Jim Erickson, *Hard Drive: Bill Gates and the Making of the Microsoft Empire* (Toronto: John Wiley & Sons, 1992), 26, 319.

34. Bill Gates, interview, Academy of Achievement, March 17, 2010, https://achievement.org /achiever/william-h-gates-iii/#interview.

35. Levi Pulkkinen, "Here's How Seattle Became So Segregated," *Seattle Post-Intelligencer,* November 2, 2016.

36. Douglas Judge, "Housing, Race and Schooling in Seattle: Context for the Supreme Court Decision," *Journal of Educational Controversy* 2, no. 1 (January 1, 2007): 2.

37. Brooke Clark, "The Seattle School Boycott of 1966," *Seattle Civil Rights and Labor History Project* (Seattle: University of Washington), accessed April 6, 2022, https://depts.washington .edu/civilr/school_boycott.htm.

38. Stokely Carmichael, Speech given at Garfield High School, Seattle, Washington, April 19, 1967, https://www.aavw.org/special_features/speeches_speech_carmichael01.html.

39. Aaron Dixon, *My People Are Rising: Memoir of a Black Panther Party Captain* (Chicago: Haymarket Books, 2012), 73. Dixon spells it "Trollis," which does not seem to be the spelling used by Mr. Flavors, to which I have defaulted in the text.

40. Kurt Schaefer, "The Black Panther Party in Seattle: 1968–1970," Seattle Civil Rights and Labor History Project, accessed April 6, 2022, https://depts.washington.edu/civilr/Panthers1 _schaefer.htm. Harlem probably has an equally legitimate claim.

41. Charles Arthur Petersen, "Meritocracy in America, 1885–2007" (PhD diss., Harvard, 2020), 570, https://dash.harvard.edu/handle/1/37368869.

42. Michael S. Malone, *The Big Score: The Billion-Dollar Story of Silicon Valley* (Garden City, NY: Doubleday, 1985), 375.

43. Berlin, *Troublemakers,* 287.

44. David N. Pellow and Lisa Sun-Hee Park, *The Silicon Valley of Dreams: Environmental Injustice, Immigrant Workers, and the High-Tech Global Economy* (New York: NYU Press, 2002), 153.

45. "The Evolution of Apple Ads," Webdesigner Depot, September 15, 2009, https://www.web designerdepot.com/2009/09/the-evolution-of-apple-ads.

46. Berlin, *Troublemakers,* 237.

47. Ken Uston, "9,250 Apples for the Teacher," *Creative Computing,* October 1983, 181.

48. Ibid., 178.

49. AnnaLee Saxenian, *Regional Advantage: Culture and Competition in Silicon Valley and Route 128* (Cambridge, MA: Harvard University Press, 1996), 142.

Chapter 4.4 Americas Online

1. Anne M. Jacobsen, *The Pentagon's Brain: An Uncensored History of DARPA, America's Top Secret Military Research Agency* (Boston: Little, Brown, 2015), 238.

2. Tom Rindfleisch, "The Real Origin of Cisco Systems," *TC Rindfleisch* (blog), accessed April 7, 2022, https://www.tcracs.org/tcrwp/1origin-of-cisco.

3. Pete Carey, "A Start-Up's True Tale," *San Jose Mercury News,* December 1, 2001, http://pdp10 .nocrew.org/docs/cisco.html.

4. Mike Wilson, *The Difference between God and Larry Ellison* (New York: Morrow, 1997), 99.

5. Mark Hall and John Barry, *Sunburst: The Ascent of Sun Microsystems* (Chicago: Contemporary Books, 1990), 14.

6. Ibid., 16, 20–21.

7. John Markoff, "Russian Research Pact for Sun Microsystems," *New York Times,* September 2, 1992.

8. Douglas Fairbairn and Andy Bechtolsheim, "Oral History of Andreas 'Andy' Bechtolsheim," (Computer History Museum, July 17, 2015), 5.

9. Amy Harmon, "Like 'Toy Story,' Pixar Stock Is a Hit Its First Day on the Street," *Los Angeles Times,* November 30, 1995.

10. Charles McCoy, "Cisco Will Acquire Granite in $220 Million Stock Deal," *Wall Street Journal,* September 4, 1996.

11. Martin Kenney and Urs von Burg, "Institutions and Economies: Creating Silicon Valley," in *Understanding Silicon Valley: The Anatomy of an Entrepreneurial Region,* ed. Martin Kenney (Redwood City, CA: Stanford University Press, 2000), 235.

12. Ibid., 235.

13. Ron Sirak, "Nike Has a Tiger by the Tail," Associated Press, January 30, 1997.

14. Gary Rivlin, *The Godfather of Silicon Valley: Ron Conway and the Fall of the DotComs* (New York: Random House, 2001), 31.

15. Michael Lewis, *The New New Thing: A Silicon Valley Story* (New York: W. W. Norton, 2014), 109.

16. Michael Lewis, "The Little Creepy Crawlers Who Will Eat You in the Night," *New York Times Magazine,* March 1, 1998.

17. William Roseberry, "The Rise of Yuppie Coffees and the Reimagination of Class in the United States," *American Anthropologist* 98, no. 4 (December 1996): 762–75.

18. Harry Braverman, *Labor and Monopoly Capital: The Degredation of Work in the Twentieth Century* (New York: Monthly Review Press, 1975).

19. Fred Turner, *From Counterculture to Cyberculture: Stewart Brand, the Whole Earth Network, and the Rise of Digital Utopianism* (Chicago: University of Chicago Press, 2006), 214.

20. Boy Lüthje, "The Changing Map of Global Electronics: Networks of Mass Production in the New Economy," in *Challenging the Chip: Labor Rights and Environmental Justice in the Global Electronics Industry,* ed. Ted Smith, David Allan Sonnenfeld, and David N. Pellow (Philadelphia: Temple University Press, 2006), 23.

21. Timothy J. Sturgeon, "Modular Production's Impact on Japan's Electronics Industry," *Recovering from Success: Innovation and Technology Management in Japan,* ed. D. Hugh Whittaker and Robert E. Cole (Oxford: Oxford University Press, 2006), 52.

22. Chris Benner, *Work in the New Economy: Flexible Labor Markets in Silicon Valley* (Oxford, UK: Blackwell, 2002), 212.

23. Chris Benner and Amy Dean, "Labor in the New Economy: Lessons from Labor Organizing in Silicon Valley," in *Nonstandard Work: The Nature and Challenges of Changing Employment Arrangements,* ed. Françoise J. Carré et al. (Ithaca, NY: Cornell University Press, 2000), 365.

24. Ruth Wilson Gilmore, *Golden Gulag: Prisons, Surplus, Crisis, and Opposition in Globalizing California* (Berkeley: University of California Press, 2007), 51.

25. Aihwa Ong, "Latitudes of Citizenship," in *People out of Place: Globalization, Human Rights, and the Citizenship Gap,* ed. Alison Brysk and Gershon Shafir (New York: Routledge, 2004), 59.

26. Vijay Prashad, *Keeping Up with the Dow Joneses: Debt, Prison, Workfare* (Cambridge, MA: South End Press, 2003), 40.

27. David Bacon, "Land of the Open Shop," https://newlaborforum.cuny.edu/2011/01/03/land-of-the-open-shop-the-long-struggle-to-organize-silicon-valley.

28. Shalini Shankar, *Desi Land: Teen Culture, Class, and Success in Silicon Valley* (Durham, NC: Duke University Press, 2008), 50–51.

29. Marc Levin, *Freeway: Crack in the System* (Al Jazeera America, Blowback Productions, Continental Media, 2015).

30. U.S. Dept. of Justice, Office of Inspector General, "CIA-Contra-Crack Cocaine Controversy: A Review of the Justice Department's Investigations and Prosecutions," December 1997, part VI.

31. Charlton D. McIlwain, *Black Software: The Internet and Racial Justice, from the AfroNet to Black Lives Matter* (New York: Oxford University Press, 2019), 148. McIlwain notes that some California engineer(s) combined their passions and came up with a cocaine gadget called the höt böx, which measured purity.

32. Michael S. Malone, *The Big Score: The Billion-Dollar Story of Silicon Valley* (Garden City, NY: Doubleday, 1985), 409.

33. Dennis Hayes, *Behind the Silicon Curtain: The Seductions of Work in a Lonely Era* (Boston: South End Press, 1989), 22.

34. Georgette Bennett, *Crimewarps: The Future of Crime in America* (New York: Anchor Books, 1989), 214.

35. Philip Mattera, *Off the Books: The Rise of the Underground Economy* (New York: St. Martin's Press, 1985), 106.

36. Lucius Cabins, "Drugs: A Corrosive Social Cement," in *Bad Attitude: The Processed World Anthology,* ed. Chris Carlsson and Mark Leger (New York: Verso, 1990), 253.

37. Joseph Nevins, "Dying for a Cup of Coffee? Migrant Deaths in the US-Mexico Border Region in a Neoliberal Age," *Geopolitics* 12, no. 2 (May 1, 2007): 232.

38. President Reagan's Remarks and Question-and-Answer Session on the Air Traffic Controllers (PATCO) Strike in the Rose Garden, August 3, 1981, 2016.

39. Burhan Wazir, "Nike Accused of Tolerating Sweatshops," *Guardian,* May 19, 2001.

40. *See* David Callahan, *The Cheating Culture: Why More Americans Are Doing Wrong to Get Ahead* (New York: Houghton Mifflin Harcourt, 2007), both for the trend and its recategorization. The recategorization isn't wrong per se, but it is noteworthy.

41. "Crime: Diary of a Vandalized Car," *Time,* February 28, 1969.

42. Philip G. Zimbardo, "The Human Choice: Individuation, Reason, and Order Versus Deindividuation, Impulse, and Chaos," *Nebraska Symposium on Motivation,* 1969, 291.

43. Gilmore, *Golden Gulag,* 255n9.

44. Prashad, *Keeping Up with the Dow Joneses,* 86.

45. "Silicon Wealth Explosion," *Forbes,* July 7, 1997.

46. *Netscape Prospectus,* July 17, 1995, 40.

47. *What Happened* (2001), dir. Chas Mastin, 20:12, https://youtube.com/watch?v=EsVpNB2Lv3U&ab_channel=ChasMastin.

48. Margaret Kane, "Microsoft Acquires Hotmail," *ZDNet,* December 30, 1997.

49. Steven Teles and Jessica A. Gover, "The American Enterprise Institute's Near-Death Experience," SNF Agora Case Study, Johns Hopkins Stavros Niarchos Foundation, December 2020.

50. Alan Greenspan, "The Challenge of Central Banking in a Democratic Society: Remarks at the Annual Dinner and Francis Boyer Lecture of the American Enterprise Institute" (Washington, DC, December 5, 1996), https://www.federalreserve.gov/boarddocs/speeches/1996/19961205.htm.

51. Lewis, *The New New Thing*, 98.

52. Ibid., 219.

53. Amazon.com, "Press Release: Pets.Com Raises $50 Million from Amazon.Com, Bowman Capital, and Hummer Winblad Venture Partners," June 14, 1999.

54. Jerry Useem, "All Dressed Up and No IPO," *Inc.*, February 1, 1998, https://www.inc.com /magazine/19980201/867.html.

55. Saul Hansell and Laura M. Holson, "$5.6 Billion Deal by Yahoo Reported Set," *New York Times*, April 1, 1999.

56. William F. Arens, David H. Schaefer, and Michael Weigold, *Essentials of Contemporary Advertising*, 2nd ed., internat. student ed. (Boston: McGraw-Hill Irwin, 2009), 124.

57. John Cassidy, *How Markets Fail: The Logic of Economic Calamities* (New York: Farrar, Straus and Giroux, 2009), 181.

58. John Deighton, "Interview re Webvan and Grocery Delivery Online—Why E-commerce Didn't Die with the Fall of Webvan," interview by Martha Lagace, Harvard Business School *Working Knowledge*, September 17, 2001, https://hbswk.hbs.edu/archive/interview-with-prof -john-deighton-re-webvan-and-grocery-delivery-online-why-e-commerce-didn-t-die-with -the-fall-of-webvan.

59. Peter Relan, "Where Webvan Failed and How Home Delivery 2.0 Could Succeed," Tech-Crunch, September 27, 2013, https://social.techcrunch.com/2013/09/27/why-webvan-failed -and-how-home-delivery-2-0-is-addressing-the-problems.

60. Webvan Group Inc., Annual Report, SEC Form 10-K, for 12/31/00, April 2, 2001.

61. Greg Thain and John Bradley, *Store Wars: The Worldwide Battle for Mindspace and Shelfspace, Online and In-Store* (Chichester, UK: John Wiley & Sons, 2012), 233.

62. Webvan Group Inc., Annual Report, SEC Form 10-K, for 12/31/00, April 2, 2001.

63. "Webvan Shuts Down," CNN Money, July 9, 2001, https://money.cnn.com/2001/07/09 /technology/webvan.

Chapter 5.1 B2K

1. Karl Rove, *Courage and Consequence: My Life as a Conservative in the Fight* (New York: Threshold Editions, 2010), 120.

2. Paul Van Slambrouck, "California Think Tank Acts as Bush 'Brain Trust,'" *Christian Science Monitor*, July 2, 1999.

3. Martin Anderson and Jim Young, "Martin Anderson Oral History," University of Virginia Miller Center, December 11–12, 2001.

4. John Tirman, *The Deaths of Others: The Fate of Civilians in America's Wars* (New York: Oxford University Press, 2011), 229.

5. Matthew Rees, "Can Bush Capture California?" *Weekly Standard*, October 11, 1999, 20–22.

6. Richard L. Burke, "Bush Seeks to Curry Favor in Silicon Valley," *New York Times*, July 2, 1999.

7. Lisa M. Bowman, "Tech Industry Cheers Bush Pick for DoJ," *ZDNet*, January 5, 2001, https://www.zdnet.com/article/tech-industry-cheers-bush-pick-for-doj; Patrick Thibodeau, "Attorney-General Nominee Viewed as Friend of IT," *Computerworld*, January 5, 2001.

8. "FBI Abandons Carnivore Wiretap Software," Associated Press, January 18, 2005.

9. Linda Weiss, *America Inc.?: Innovation and Enterprise in the National Security State* (Ithaca, NY: Cornell University Press, 2014), 68.

10. Jeffrey Rosen, "Silicon Valley's Spy Game," *New York Times Magazine*, April 14, 2002.

11. *Committee Study of the Central Intelligence Agency's Detention and Interrogation Program* (Washington, DC: Senate Select Committee on Intelligence, 2014), 168.

12. T. Christian Miller, "Contractors Outnumber Troops in Iraq," *Los Angeles Times,* July 4, 2007.

13. Bill Murdoch, "International Stake Is Just the Ticket for Irish Firm's Growth," *Irish Times,* August 8, 1997.

14. Bob Tedeschi, "Ticketmaster Sues Again over Links," *New York Times,* August 10, 1999.

15. Robin Fields and P. J. Huffstutter, "Judge Rules Online Firms May Link to Rival Web Sites," *Los Angeles Times,* March 29, 2000.

16. *Sony Corp. of America v. Universal City Studios, Inc.,* 464 U.S. 417 (1984), known as the Betamax case.

17. Adam Sandler, "RIAA Sues to Stop Rio Sales," *Variety,* October 12, 1998.

18. "Napster.Com Raises $15 Million Venture Money," *Digital Journal,* May 23, 2000.

19. Ryan Mac, "Professor Billionaire: The Stanford Academic Who Wrote Google Its First Check," *Forbes,* August 1, 2012.

20. "Cisco Buys Granite Systems," *CNET,* September 3, 1996, https://www.cnet.com/tech/tech-industry/cisco-buys-granite-systems.

21. Sergey Brin and Lawrence Page, "The Anatomy of a Large-Scale Hypertextual Web Search Engine," *Computer Networks* 30 (1998).

22. Will Oremus, "Google's Big Break," *Slate,* October 14, 2013.

23. Megan Graham Elias Jennifer, "How Google's $150 Billion Advertising Business Works," *CNBC,* May 18, 2021.

24. "Google Guys," *Playboy,* September 2004, 59.

25. Andrew Norman Wilson, "The Artist Leaving the Googleplex," *E-Flux Journal,* no. 74 (June 2016), https://www.e-flux.com/journal/74/59791/the-artist-leaving-the-googleplex.

26. Therese Wood, "Visualizing the Evolution of Global Advertising Spend," *Business Insider,* November 10, 2020, https://markets.businessinsider.com/news/stocks/evolution-global-advertising-spend-1980-2020-1029789449.

27. Louise Story and Miguel Helft, "Google Buys DoubleClick for $3.1 Billion," *New York Times,* April 14, 2007.

28. Natalia Drozdiak and Jack Nicas, "Google Privacy-Policy Change Faces New Scrutiny in EU," *Wall Street Journal,* January 24, 2017. Ellison's Oracle complained about the "super profiles" to EU regulators and the name stuck.

29. Robert O'Harrow, *No Place to Hide* (New York: Free Press, 2005), 40.

30. Natasha Singer, "Mapping, and Sharing, the Consumer Genome," *New York Times,* June 16, 2012. Presumably their databases have grown since this report.

31. Frank Pasquale, *The Black Box Society: The Secret Algorithms That Control Money and Information* (Cambridge, MA: Harvard University Press, 2015), 46–47.

32. Philip Shenon, "Airline Gave Defense Firm Passenger Files," *New York Times,* September 20, 2003.

33. Timothy B. Lee, "The Little-Known Deal That Saved Amazon from the Dot-Com Crash," *Vox,* April 5, 2017, https://www.vox.com/new-money/2017/4/5/15190650/amazon-jeff-bezos-richest.

34. Rani Molla, "For the Wealthiest Americans, Amazon Prime Has Become the Norm," *Vox,* June 8, 2017, https://www.vox.com/2017/6/8/15759354/amazon-prime-low-income-discount-piper-jaffray-demographics.

35. Saul Hansell, "Amazon's Risky Christmas," *New York Times,* November 28, 1999.

36. James Manyika, Jan Mischke, Jacques Bughin, Jonathan Woetzel, Mekala Krishnan, and Samuel Cudre, "A New Look at the Declining Labor Share of Income in the United States," McKinsey Global Institute Discussion Paper, May 2019.

37. David Brancaccio et al., "Investigation into Amazon Raises Questions about Workforce Turnover, HR Errors," *Marketplace,* June 18, 2021, https://www.marketplace.org/2021/06/18/amazon-workforce-turnover-dominance-investigation.

38. Hannah Knowles, "Amazon Admits It Was Wrong to Suggest Its Workforce Never Needs to Pee in Bottles on the Job," *Washington Post,* April 3, 2021.

39. Safiyo Mohamed, "I Got My First Job in the U.S. Sorting Packages for Amazon—and It Was Awful," *Sahan Journal,* January 25, 2021, http://sahanjournal.com/community-voices/commentary-amazon-fulfillment-center-somali-workers.

40. Will Evans, "How Amazon Hid Its Safety Crisis," *Reveal,* September 29, 2020, http://revealnews.org/article/how-amazon-hid-its-safety-crisis.

41. Katherine Anne Long, "Amazon Drivers Injured Far More Often Than the Company's Warehouse Workers; See the Charts," *Seattle Times,* June 1, 2021.

42. Patricia Callahan, "How Amazon Hooked America on Fast Delivery While Avoiding Responsibility for Crashes," *ProPublica,* September 5, 2019, https://features.propublica.org/amazon-delivery-crashes/how-amazon-hooked-america-on-fast-delivery-while-avoiding-responsibility-for-crashes.

43. James Bandler et al., "Inside Documents Show How Amazon Chose Speed over Safety in Building Its Delivery Network," *ProPublica* and *BuzzFeed News,* accessed April 12, 2022, https://www.propublica.org/article/inside-documents-show-how-amazon-chose-speed-over-safety-in-building-its-delivery-network.

44. "Amazon, Let Workers Unionize! Respect for Workers' Rights Is Not a Choice" (Amnesty International, November 2020), 4–6, https://www.amnesty.org/en/documents/pol40/3275/2020/en.

45. Jodi Kantor and David Streitfeld, "Inside Amazon: Wrestling Big Ideas in a Bruising Workplace," *New York Times,* August 15, 2015.

46. Walter Isaacson, *Steve Jobs* (New York: Simon & Schuster, 2011), 90.

47. Walter Frick and Scott Berinato, "Apple: Luxury Brand or Mass Marketer?" *Harvard Business Review,* October 2, 2014, https://hbr.org/2014/10/apple-luxury-brand-or-mass-marketer.

48. Dawn Kawamoto, "Apple Acquires Next, Jobs," *CNET,* December 20, 1996, https://www.cnet.com/tech/tech-industry/apple-acquires-next-jobs.

49. Alvy Ray Smith, *A Biography of the Pixel* (Cambridge, MA: MIT Press, 2021), 429. PARC star and Pixar leader Smith left a few years before the IPO. As to why, he recalls, "I had to get Steve Jobs out of my life." Ibid., 428.

50. "Apple Planning Largest Ad Campaign for IMac," *Los Angeles Times,* August 14, 1998.

51. Matthew Hall, *Metrosexual Masculinities* (New York: Palgrave Macmillan, 2015), 3.

52. Jeff Dunn, "The Rise and Fall of Apple's iPod, in One Chart," *Business Insider,* July 28, 2017.

53. Ibid.

54. "IPod Killers That Didn't," *Forbes,* accessed April 12, 2022, https://www.forbes.com/2006/10/20/ipod-zune-rio-tech-media-cx_rr_1023killers.html.

55. U.S. Dept. of Justice, "Attorney General Ashcroft Announces First Criminal Enforcement Action Against Peer-To-Peer Copyright Piracy," press release, August 25, 2004. https://www.justice.gov/archive/criminal/cybercrime/press-releases/2004/operation_gridlock.htm.

56. Austin Carr and Mark Gurman, "Apple Is the $2.3 Trillion Fortress That Tim Cook Built," *Bloomberg Businessweek,* February 9, 2021.

Chapter 5.2 You Better Try to Make Me Rich

1. "Foxconn to Manufacture Apple's IPhone—Report," *AppleInsider,* November 15, 2006.

2. Brian Merchant, "Life and Death in Apple's Forbidden City," *Guardian,* June 18, 2017.

3. Jenny Chan, Mark Selden, and Pun Ngai, *Dying for an IPhone: Apple, Foxconn, and the Lives of China's Workers* (London: Pluto Press, 2020), 48.

4. Hao Qi, "The Labor Share Question in China," *Monthly Review,* January 1, 2014.

5. Jenny Chan and Pun Ngai, "Suicide as Protest for the New Generation of Chinese Migrant Workers: Foxconn, Global Capital, and the State," *Asia-Pacific Journal,* September 13, 2010.

6. Pun Ngai, *Made in China: Women Factory Workers in a Global Workplace* (Durham, NC: Duke University Press, 2005), 170.

7. Kevin Allison, "Flextronics Buys US Rival Solectron for $3.6bn," *Financial Times,* June 4, 2007.

8. David Barboza, "IPhone Maker in China Is under Fire after a Suicide," *New York Times,* July 27, 2009.

9. Yukari Iwatani Kane, "Reports of Suicide in China Linked to Missing iPhone," *Wall Street Journal,* July 21, 2009.

10. Chan and Ngai, "Suicide as Protest," 17.

11. Xu Lizhi, "I Fall Asleep, Just Standing Like That," from "The Poetry and Brief Life of a Foxconn Worker: Xu Lizhi (1990–2014)," libcom.org, October 29, 2014, https://libcom.org/article/poetry-and-brief-life-foxconn-worker-xu-lizhi-1990-2014.

12. Lizhi, "A Screw Fell to the Ground," from "The Poetry and Brief Life of a Foxconn Worker."

13. "Foxconn to Raise Wages Again at China Plant," Reuters, October 1, 2010.

14. Tripp Mickle and Yoko Kubota, "Tim Cook and Apple Bet Everything on China. Then Coronavirus Hit," *Wall Street Journal,* March 2, 2020.

15. Paul Mozur, "Apple Puts Key Contractor on Probation over Labor Abuses in China," *New York Times,* November 9, 2020.

16. David Barboza, "How China Built 'iPhone City' with Billions in Perks for Apple's Partner," *New York Times,* December 29, 2016.

17. Ibid.

18. John Charles Smith, *Imperialism in the Twenty-First Century: Globalization, Super-Exploitation, and Capitalism's Final Crisis* (New York: Monthly Review Press, 2016), 30.

19. Ibid., 31.

20. David Shephardson and Karen Pierog, "Foxconn Mostly Abandons $10 Billion Wisconsin Project Touted by Trump," Reuters, April 20, 2021.

21. Filip Novokmet et al., "From Communism to Capitalism: Private versus Public Property and Inequality in China and Russia," *AEA Papers and Proceedings* 108 (May 2018): 111.

22. Ibid., 112.

23. Ibid.

24. Ibid.

25. Sebastian Mallaby, *The Power Law: Venture Capital and the Making of the New Future* (New York: Penguin Press, 2022), 273–75.

26. Michael Arrington, "Exclusive Video: Mark Zuckerberg and Yuri Milner Talk about Facebook's New Investment," *TechCrunch,* May 26, 2009, https://techcrunch.com/2009/05/26/mark-zuckerberg-and-yuri-milner-talk-about-facebooks-new-investment-video.

27. "Alisher Usmanov: What Makes the Russian Britain's Richest Person?" *Guardian,* April 22, 2013.

28. Juliette Garside, "Russia's Richest Man Cashes In on Facebook Share Recovery," *Guardian,* September 5, 2013.

29. Michael Arrington, "Start Fund: Yuri Milner, SV Angel Offer EVERY New Y Combinator Startup $150k," *TechCrunch,* January 28, 2011, https://social.techcrunch.com/2011/01/28/yuri-milner-sv-angel-offer-every-new-y-combinator-start-up-150k.

30. James F. Peltz and Tracey Lien, "Russian Billionaire Yuri Milner's Early Backing of Facebook, Twitter Had Kremlin Ties," *Los Angeles Times,* November 7, 2017.

31. Bloomberg News, "Saudi Arabian Prince Says He Bought Stake in Apple," *New York Times,* April 2, 1997.

32. Alexander Martin, Alec Macfarlane, and Margherita Stancati, "SoftBank and Saudi Arabia Team Up for $100 Billion Tech Fund," *Wall Street Journal,* October 14, 2016.

33. Joanna Glasner, "These Are the US Startups That Russian Investors Are Backing," *TechCrunch,* November 11, 2017, https://social.techcrunch.com/2017/11/11/these-are-the-us-startups-that -russian-investors-are-backing.

34. The World Bank, "Gross Fixed Capital Formation (% of GDP)—Russian Federation, China," accessed April 19, 2022, https://data.worldbank.org/indicator/NE.GDI.FTOT.ZS ?locations=RU-CN.

35. Henry Foy, "Alisher Usmanov: 'I Was Never What You Could Call an Oligarch,'" *Financial Times,* January 3, 2020.

36. Don Kazak, "Police, FBI 'Dismantle' EPA-Based 'Taliban' Gang," *Palo Alto Online,* March 7, 2009, https://www.paloaltoonline.com/news/2009/03/07/police-fbi-dismantle-epa-based-tal iban-gang.

37. Sean Webby, "Police Try, But Gangs Thrive," *San Jose Mercury News,* September 18, 2000.

38. "Ron Davis: 'We're Just Getting Started, Trust Me,'" *East Bay Times,* February 19, 2006.

39. Tara Madhav, "Community Control and Desegregation in East Palo Alto, California, 1958–1976," UC Berkeley, April 1, 2021, https://escholarship.org/uc/item/84n6s7t0.

40. Rachelle Marshall, "Concrete Curtain—the East Palo Alto Story," *The Crisis,* November 1957, 543–48.

41. Webby, "Police Try, But Gangs Thrive."

42. Don Kazak, "Our Town: Death of a Young Friend," *Palo Alto Weekly,* February 9, 2005.

43. "Northern California High Intensity Drug Trafficking Area, Drug Market Analysis 2010" (U.S. Department of Justice National Drug Intelligence Center, June 2010), 4, https://www .justice.gov/archive/ndic/pubs40/40395/40395p.pdf.

44. "Agents Seize $7 Million in Heroin in East Palo Alto," *Palo Alto Online,* July 21, 2009, https://www.paloaltoonline.com/news/2009/07/21/agents-seize-7-million-in-heroin-in-east -palo-alto.

45. "Seed Round—Airbnb," Crunchbase, April 1, 2009, https://www.crunchbase.com/funding _round/airbnb-seed—ba7b61b6.

46. Romain Le Cour Grandmaison, Nathaniel Morris, and Benjamin T. Smith, "The U.S. Fentanyl Boom and the Mexican Opium Crisis," Building Resilient Communities in Mexico: Civic Responses to Crime and Violence (Mexico Institute at the Woodrow Wilson International Center for Scholars and University of San Diego Justice in Mexico Program, 2019), 8–9.

47. Theodore J. Cicero, Matthew S. Ellis, and Hilary L. Surratt, "Effect of Abuse-Deterrent Formulation of OxyContin," *New England Journal of Medicine* 367, no. 2 (July 12, 2012): 187–89.

48. Stephanie Glick and Allyson Dean, "Learning to Be 'Good Enough': Hollywood's Role in Standardizing Knowledge and the Myth of Meritocracy," *Postcolonial Directions in Education* 9, no. 1 (June 2020): 66.

49. LouAnne Johnson, *My Posse Don't Do Homework* (New York: St. Martin's Paperbacks, 1993), 216.

50. Ibid., 230.

51. Ibid., 228.

52. Sarah Knopp, "There Is No Private Violence," *Jacobin*, November 28, 2018, https://jacobin mag.com/2018/11/central-america-migrants-asylum-ms13-gang-violence.

53. Roberto Lovato, *Unforgetting: A Memoir of Family, Migration, Gangs, and Revolution in the Americas* (New York: HarperCollins, 2020), xxi.

54. George W. Bush, "Text: George W. Bush's Speech to the NAACP," July 10, 2000, https:// www.washingtonpost.com/wp-srv/onpolitics/elections/bushtext071000.htm

55. Don Kazak, "IKEA Wins Initial Victory," *Palo Alto Weekly*, August 31, 2001.

56. Ryan Kim, "Ikea Brings Swarm of Shoppers to East Palo Alto / 90 Officers Direct Traffic at Opening of Swedish-Design Home Store," *SFGATE*, August 28, 2003, https://www.sfgate .com/bayarea/article/Ikea-brings-swarm-of-shoppers-to-East-Palo-Alto-2559627.php.

57. Becky Bartindale, "Stanford University's Education Program for Gifted Youth Is America's First Online High School for Gifted Students," *San Jose Mercury News*, April 12, 2006.

58. Patrick Suppes, "From Behaviorism to Neobehaviorism," *Theory and Decision* 6, no. 3 (August 1975): 269–85.

59. Patrick Suppes, "Self-Profile," in *Patrick Suppes*, ed. Radu J. Bogdan (Dordrecht, Holland: D. Reidel Publishing, 1979), 4.

60. Audrey Watters, *Teaching Machines: The History of Personalized Learning* (Cambridge, MA: MIT Press, 2021), 232.

61. Roger Cohen, "Simon & Schuster Buys School Software Maker," *New York Times*, March 12, 1990.

62. Ibid.

63. "Tuition for 2022–23 (Grades 7–12)," Stanford Online High School, accessed April 20, 2022, https://onlinehighschool.stanford.edu/tuition.

64. Naomi Atkins, "SCORE! Educational Centers (A)," *Harvard Business Case Study*, August 2, 1999, 16.

65. Katrina Burger and Lisa Gubernick, "Girls Always Have Trouble with Math," *Forbes*, April 21, 1997.

66. Derek Thompson, "Instagram Is Now Worth $77 Million Per Employee," *The Atlantic*, April 9, 2012, https://www.theatlantic.com/business/archive/2012/04/instagram-is-now-worth-77 -million-per-employee/255640.

67. Byung-Chul Han, *The Burnout Society* (Redwood City, CA: Stanford University Press, 2015), 9.

68. Jonathan James, "The College Wage Premium," *Economic Commentary*, no. 2012-10 (August 8, 2012): 3.

69. Alissa Quart, *Hothouse Kids: The Dilemma of the Gifted Child* (New York: Penguin Press, 2006).

70. Elisha Fieldstadt, "Hardest Colleges to Get into in the U.S. in 2022," *CBS News*, August 19, 2021.

71. Carolyn Walworth, "Paly School Board Rep: 'The Sorrows of Young Palo Altans,'" *Palo Alto Online*, March 25, 2015, https://paloaltoonline.com/news/2015/03/25/guest-opinion-the -sorrows-of-young-palo-altans.

72. Amanda Garcia-Williams et al., "Undetermined Risk Factors for Suicide among Youth, Ages 10–24—Santa Clara County, CA, 2016," Epidemiologic Assistance (Centers for Disease Control and Prevention and the Substance Abuse and Mental Health Services Administration, 2016), 57.

73. Elena Kadvany, "Gunn Students Slam School Leaders on Zero Period," *Palo Alto Weekly*, April 22, 2015.

74. Steven Levy, *Facebook: The Inside Story* (New York: Blue Rider Press, 2020), 110.

Chapter 5.3 Blister in the Sun

1. Michael S. Malone, *Infinite Loop: How the World's Most Insanely Great Computer Company Went Insane* (New York: Doubleday, 1999).

2. Tony Tulathimutte, *Private Citizens* (New York: HarperCollins, 2016), 104.

3. Paul Graham, "What Happened to Yahoo," PaulGraham.com, August 2010, http://www.paulgraham.com/yahoo.html.

4. Kim Girard, "Commerce One to Buy CommerceBid," CNet, January 2, 2002, https://www.cnet.com/tech/tech-industry/commerce-one-to-buy-commercebid.

5. John Carreyrou, *Bad Blood: Secrets and Lies in a Silicon Valley Startup* (New York: Vintage Books, 2020), 70.

6. Emily Bazelon, "The Stanford Undergraduate and the Mentor," *New York Times Magazine,* February 11, 2015.

7. Rebecca Parr, "Vice President Joe Biden Visits Biotech Firm Theranos's Newark Production Facility," *Mercury News,* July 23, 2015.

8. Erin Griffith and Erin Woo, "Elizabeth Holmes Found Guilty of Four Charges of Fraud," *New York Times,* January 3, 2022.

9. Johana Bhuiyan, "Take a Look at Uber's First Pitch Deck from 2008," *Vox,* August 23, 2017, https://www.vox.com/2017/8/23/16189048/uber-pitchdeck-2008-ubercab-travis-kalanick-founder-start-up.

10. Scott Austin, Stephanie Stamm, and Rolfe Winkler, "Uber Jackpot: Inside One of the Greatest Startup Investments of All Time," *Wall Street Journal,* May 10, 2019.

11. Janko Roettgers, "Whatever Happened to Red Swoosh?" GigaOm, May 3, 2008; David Meyer, "eBay Sells StumbleUpon back to founders," *ZDNet,* April 14, 2009.

12. Emma G. Fitzsimmons, "Why Are Taxi Drivers in New York Killing Themselves?" *New York Times,* December 2, 2018.

13. Aaron Benanav, *Automation and the Future of Work* (New York: Verso Books, 2020), 60.

14. Brad Stone, *The Upstarts: How Uber, Airbnb, and the Killer Companies of the New Silicon Valley Are Changing the World* (New York: Little, Brown, 2017), 329.

15. Rowland Manthorpe, "Forget Uber vs Lyft, the Real Funding Battle Is between Saudi Princes and Canadian Teachers," *Wired UK,* October 20, 2017.

16. Therese Poletti, "Uber and Lyft Are Staging a Ridiculous Race for Fake Profits," *MarketWatch,* accessed August 5, 2021, https://www.marketwatch.com/story/uber-and-lyft-are-staging-a-ridiculous-race-for-fake-profits-11628205337.

17. Faiz Siddiqui, "Uber, Other Gig Companies Spend Nearly $200 Million to Knock Down an Employment Law They Don't Like—And It Might Work," *Washington Post,* October 26, 2020.

18. Will Racke, "Former Obama Aide Fined for Illegally Lobbying Chicago Mayor on Behalf of Uber," *Chicago Business Journal,* February 16, 2017.

19. The Editorial Board, "Open the Airports to Uber," *Chicago Tribune,* October 4, 2015.

20. The Editorial Board, "We Were Wrong to Abandon Chicago's Taxicabs for Ride-Shares and the City Now Needs to Find a Fix," *Chicago Tribune,* September 13, 2021.

21. Biz Stone, "Exclusive: Biz Stone on Twitter and Activism," *The Atlantic,* October 19, 2010.

22. Edward Snowden, *Permanent Record* (New York: Metropolitan Books, 2019), 141.

23. Kashmir Hill, "I Tried to Block Amazon from My Life. It Was Impossible," Gizmodo, January 22, 2019, https://gizmodo.com/i-tried-to-block-amazon-from-my-life-it-was-impossible-1830565336.

24. Sam Levin, "'We Have Failed': How California's Homelessness Catastrophe Is Worsening," *Guardian,* March 22, 2022.

25. *See,* for example, Julia Carrie Wong, "Wealthy San Francisco Tech Investors Bankroll Bid to Ban Homeless Camps," *Guardian,* October 12, 2016.

26. Mike Males, "San Francisco's 'Crime Wave' Is Just One Crime," Center on Juvenile and Criminal Justice, January 16, 2020.

27. Wong, "Wealthy San Francisco Tech Investors."

28. "Twitter Tax Break Approved by San Francisco Supervisors," *San Francisco Examiner,* April 5, 2011.

29. Leonardo Castañeda, "Who Owns Silicon Valley?" *Reveal,* November 4, 2019.

30. Venkatesh Rao, "The Premium Mediocre Life of Maya Millennial," *Ribbonfarm* (blog), August 17, 2017, https://www.ribbonfarm.com/2017/08/17/the-premium-mediocre-life-of-maya-millennial.

31. Margaret O'Mara, *The Code: Silicon Valley and the Remaking of America* (New York: Penguin Press, 2020), 48–49.

32. Jarett Kobek, *I Hate the Internet: A Useful Novel against Men, Money, and the Filth of Instagram* (Los Angeles, CA: We Heard You Like Books, 2016), 147.

33. Alexandra Goldman, "The 'Google Shuttle Effect': Gentrification and San Francisco's Dot Com Boom 2.0" (master's thesis, University of California, Berkeley, Department of City and Regional Planning, Spring 2013), 26.

34. Doug Gross, "Google Glass Targeted as Symbol by Anti-Tech Crowd," CNN Business, April 14, 2014.

35. Bryan Goebel, "S.F. Agency Votes to Make 'Google Bus' Program Permanent," KQED, February 22, 2017.

36. Cary McClelland, *Silicon City: San Francisco in the Long Shadow of the Valley* (New York: W. W. Norton, 2018), 96.

37. Emily Stewart, "Lawmakers Seem Confused about What Facebook Does—and How to Fix It," *Vox,* April 10, 2018, https://www.vox.com/policy-and-politics/2018/4/10/17222062/mark-zuckerberg-testimony-graham-facebook-regulations.

38. "Machine Intelligence Research Institute Donations Received," compiled by Vipul Naik, https://donations.vipulnaik.com/donee.php?donee=Machine+Intelligence+Research+Institute.

39. John J. Miller, Karl Zinsmeister, and Ashley May, *Agenda Setting: A Wise Giver's Guide to Influencing Public Policy* (Washington, DC: Philanthropy Roundtable, 2015), 54–55.

40. Steve Trousdale, "Those Strong, Silent Stanford Conservatives," *Stanford Daily Magazine,* January 26, 1984.

41. Laura Sydell, "Major Trump Backer's Alleged Positive Comments about Apartheid Stir Anger," *NPR All Tech Considered,* November 3, 2016.

42. Barbara Vobejda, "Bennett Assails New Stanford Program," *Washington Post,* April 19, 1988.

43. Karlin Lillington, "PayPal Puts Dough in Your Palm," *Wired,* July 27, 1999.

44. Jimmy Soni, *The Founders: The Story of Paypal and the Entrepreneurs Who Shaped Silicon Valley* (New York: Simon & Schuster, 2022), 45–46.

45. Ibid., 371.

46. James Bandler, Justin Elliott, and Patricia Callahan, "Lord of the Roths: How Tech Mogul Peter Thiel Turned a Retirement Account for the Middle Class into a $5 Billion Tax-Free Piggy Bank," *ProPublica,* June 24, 2021.

47. Peter A. Thiel and Blake Masters, *Zero to One: Notes on Startups, or How to Build the Future* (New York: Crown Business, 2014), 21.

48. Sharon Weinberger, "Techie Software Soldier Spy," *New York Magazine,* September 28, 2020.

49. Sam Biddle, "How Peter Thiel's Palantir Helped the NSA Spy on the Whole World," *The Intercept*, February 22, 2017, https://theintercept.com/2017/02/22/how-peter-thiels-palantir-helped-the-nsa-spy-on-the-whole-world.

50. Peter Waldman, Lizette Chapman, and Jordan Robertson, "Palantir Knows Everything About You," *Bloomberg Businessweek*, April 19, 2018.

51. Arlyn Tobias Gajilan, "Crowd Control—April 1, 2005," CNN Money, April 1, 2005.

52. Jessi Hempel and Michael V. Copeland, "Are These Widgets Worth Half a Billion?" *Fortune*, March 25, 2008.

53. Dan Frommer, "Google Only Paid $179 Million for Slide," *Business Insider*, October 29, 2010.

54. Emily Steel and Geoffrey A. Fowler, "Facebook in Privacy Breach; Top-Ranked Applications Transmit Personal IDs, a *Journal* Investigation Finds," *Wall Street Journal*, October 18, 2010.

55. Kevin Flood, "Kevin's Corner: What Are Zynga and RapLeaf Really Looking for in the Facebook Profiles?" *Kevin's Corner* (blog), October 25, 2010, https://kevinflood.blogspot.com/2010/10/what-are-zynga-and-rapleaf-really.html.

56. Emily Steel and Geoffrey A. Fowler, "Facebook Says User Data Sold to Broker," *Wall Street Journal*, October 31, 2010.

57. Emily Steel, "A Web Pioneer Profiles Users by Name," *Wall Street Journal*, October 25, 2010.

58. Emily Steel, "Candidate Apologizes for Using RapLeaf to Target Ads," *Wall Street Journal*, October 27, 2010.

59. Steven Levy, *Facebook: The Inside Story* (New York: Blue Rider Press, 2020), 270.

60. Deborah Gage, "Acxiom to Acquire LiveRamp for $310 Million," *Wall Street Journal*, May 14, 2014.

61. Christopher Wylie, *Mindf*ck: Cambridge Analytica and the Plot to Break America* (New York: Random House, 2019), 83–84.

62. Ibid., 114.

63. Ibid., 112.

64. Harry Davies, "Ted Cruz Using Firm That Harvested Data on Millions of Unwitting Facebook Users," *Guardian*, December 11, 2015.

65. Sasha Issenberg, "Cruz-Connected Data Miner Aims to Get Inside U.S. Voters' Heads," *Bloomberg*, November 12, 2015.

66. Max Chafkin, *The Contrarian: Peter Thiel and Silicon Valley's Pursuit of Power* (New York: Penguin Press, 2021), 184.

67. Connie Loizos, "'When You Spend $100 Million on Social Media,' It Comes with Help, Says Trump Strategist," *TechCrunch*, November 8, 2017.

68. Andrew Bosworth, "Thoughts for 2020," Facebook, December 30, 2019, reposted at https://www.facebook.com/boz/posts/10111288357877121.

69. William Alden, "Palantir Has a Well Placed Friend in Trumpland," *BuzzFeed News*, November 17, 2016; Jacqueline Klimas and Bryan Bender, "Palantir Goes from Pentagon Outsider to Mattis' Inner Circle," *Politico*, June 11, 2017.

70. William Alden, "Trump's Election Boosted Demand for Palantir Shares, Investor Says," *BuzzFeed News*, December 15, 2016.

71. "Digital Destroyers: How Big Tech Sells War on Our Communities," Big Tech Sells War, https://bigtechsellswar.com; Jack Poulson, "Reports of a Silicon Valley/Military Divide Have Been Greatly Exaggerated," *Tech Inquiry*, July 7, 2020.

72. Richard Waters, "Palantir Goes Public but Founders Will Have Control for Life," *Financial Times*, September 29, 2020.

73. Peter Thiel, "The End of the Future," *National Review,* October 3, 2011.

74. Chafkin, *The Contrarian,* 5.

75. Ibid., 169. Later they allowed up to twenty-two.

76. Owen Thomas, "Billionaire Facebook Investor's Anti-Immigrant Heresy," *Gawker,* November 14, 2008, https://www.gawker.com/5083655/billionaire-facebook-investors-anti-immigrant -heresy; Chafkin, *The Contrarian,* 140.

77. Andrew Granato, "How Peter Thiel and the *Stanford Review* Built a Silicon Valley Empire," *Stanford Politics,* November 27, 2017.

78. Amelia Lester, "The Voice of the 'Intellectual Dark Web,'" *Politico,* December 2018.

79. Adam Becker, "A Science Journal Funded by Peter Thiel Is Running Articles Dismissing Climate Change and Evolution," *Mother Jones,* January 29, 2019.

80. For more on the "Dark Enlightenment," see Shuja Haider, "The Darkness at the End of the Tunnel: Artificial Intelligence and Neoreaction," *Viewpoint,* March 28, 2017.

81. Jessica Huseman, Blake Paterson, Bryan Lowry, and Hunter Woodall, "Kris Kobach's Lucrative Trail of Courtroom Defeats," *ProPublica/Kansas City Star,* August 1, 2018.

82. Alex Isenstadt, "Rise of a Megadonor: Thiel Makes a Play for the Senate," *Politico,* May 17, 2021.

83. Ryan Holiday, *Conspiracy: A True Story of Power, Sex, and a Billionaire's Secret Plot to Destroy a Media Empire* (New York: Penguin, 2018), 9.

84. Chafkin, *The Contrarian,* 268.

85. Kashmir Hill, "The Secretive Company That Might End Privacy as We Know It," *New York Times,* January 18, 2020.

86. Logan McDonald, Ryan Mac, and Caroline Haskins, "Secret Users of Clearview AI's Facial Recognition Dragnet Included a Former Trump Staffer, a Troll, and Conservative Think Tanks," *BuzzFeed News,* March 25, 2020.

87. Adi Robertson, "Palmer Luckey's Surveillance Startup Anduril Signs Contract for 'Virtual Border Wall,'" *The Verge,* July 2, 2020, https://www.theverge.com/2020/7/2/21311433 /anduril-palmer-luckey-virtual-border-wall-surveillance-contract-patrol.

88. Anthony Ha, "Aiming to Become the Definitive Source for Location Data, SafeGraph Raises $45M," *TechCrunch,* March 16, 2021, https://social.techcrunch.com/2021/03/16/safegraph -series-b.

89. Dorktastical, "PLTR: How to Avoid Eternal Torment by Roko's Basilisk," Reddit, R/PLTR, March 29, 2021, https://www.reddit.com/r/PLTR/comments/mfeece/pltr_how_to_avoid _eternal_torment_by_rokos.

90. Joel Shurkin, *Broken Genius: The Rise and Fall of William Shockley, Creator of the Electronic Age* (London: Macmillan, 2008), 77.

91. William Shockley, "On the Economics of Atomic Bombing," National Archives at College Park, "Dr. W. B. Shockley's Files, 1942–1946 (Records of William B. Shockley Relating To The Use of Radar In Very Heavy Bombardment Operations)," 1945.

Chapter 6.1 Resolution

1. Wendy Liu, *Abolish Silicon Valley: How to Liberate Technology from Capitalism* (London: Repeater Books, 2020), 213.

2. "Liquefied Natural Gas," Bechtel, accessed April 27, 2022, https://www.bechtel.com/services /energy/liquefied-natural-gas.

3. Bartow J. Elmore, "The Environmental History of an American Bank," *Environmental History* 27, no. 1 (January 1, 2022).

4. "Renovo Gas-Fired Power Plant Clears Hurdle," *Lock Haven Express,* June 5, 2021.

5. Kellie Hwang, "Yes, the Bay Area Just Suffered Some of Its Worst-Ever Air Quality Days: Charts Show How Bad," *San Francisco Chronicle,* September 16, 2020.

6. Reeves Wiedeman, "The Magic Molekule," *New York Magazine,* March 16, 2021.

7. Caitlin Yilek, "Jeff Bezos on Future of Spaceflight: 'We Can Move All Heavy Industry and All Polluting Industry off of Earth,'" *CBS News,* July 21, 2021.

8. Julia Prodis Sulek, "Steve Jobs' First Dream for an Apple Headquarters: Coyote Valley, San Jose," *Mercury News,* June 11, 2011.

9. Alan Leventhal et al., "Final Report on the Burial and Archaeological Data Recovery Program Conducted on a Portion of a Middle Period Ohlone Indian Cemetery, Yuki Kutsuimi Šaatoš Inŭxw [Sand Hill Road] Sites: CASCL-287 and CA-SMA-263, Stanford University, California," prepared for Stanford University, January 2010, xxii.

10. Jane Gross, "Stanford Agrees to Return Ancient Bones to Indians," *New York Times,* June 24, 1989.

11. Glen Sean Coulthard, *Red Skin, White Masks: Rejecting the Colonial Politics of Recognition* (Minneapolis: University of Minnesota Press, 2014), 179.

12. Renya K. Ramirez, *Native Hubs: Culture, Community, and Belonging in Silicon Valley and Beyond* (Durham, NC: Duke University Press, 2007), 84.

13. Ibid., 37.

14. Leah Donnella, "The Standing Rock Resistance Is Unprecedented (It's Also Centuries Old)," *NPR Code Switch,* November 22, 2016.

15. Nick Estes, *Our History Is the Future: Standing Rock Versus the Dakota Access Pipeline, and the Long Tradition of Indigenous Resistance* (New York: Verso, 2019), 215.

16. *See,* for example, David Treuer, "Return the National Parks to the Tribes," *The Atlantic,* April 12, 2021.

17. Paul A. Baran and Paul Marlor Sweezy, *Monopoly Capital: An Essay on the American Economic and Social Order* (New York: Monthly Review Press, 1966), 300 (emphasis added).

18. Charlene Nijmeh, "Political Erasure of the Muwékma Ohlone Tribe and the Complicity of Silence," *Daily Californian,* November 6, 2021.

19. Estes, *Our History Is the Future,* 214.

20. Leanne Betasamosake Simpson, *As We Have Always Done: Indigenous Freedom through Radical Resistance* (Minneapolis: University of Minnesota Press, 2017), 229.

Index

Page numbers in *italics* indicate illustrations.

About the Author

Malcolm Harris is a freelance writer and the author of *Kids These Days: Human Capital and the Making of Millennials* and *Shit Is Fucked Up and Bullshit: History Since the End of History*. He was born in Santa Cruz, California, and graduated from the University of Maryland.

CPSIA information can be obtained
at www.ICGtesting.com
Printed in the USA
BVHW040535200323
660605BV00009B/14/J

9 780316 592031